SAP PRESS e-books

Print or e-book, Kindle or iPad, workplace or airplane: Choose where and how to read your SAP PRESS books! You can now get all our titles as e-books, too:

- By download and online access
- For all popular devices
- And, of course, DRM-free

Convinced? Then go to www.sap-press.com and get your e-book today.

Getting Started with SAP® Lumira

SAP PRESS

SAP PRESS is a joint initiative of SAP and Galileo Press. The know-how offered by SAP specialists combined with the expertise of the Galileo Press publishing house offers the reader expert books in the field. SAP PRESS features first-hand information and expert advice, and provides useful skills for professional decision-making.

SAP PRESS offers a variety of books on technical and business-related topics for the SAP user. For further information, please visit our website: *www.sap-press.com*.

Brogden, Sinkwitz, Marks, Orthous
SAP BusinessObjects Web Intelligence (3rd edition)
2014, 691 pp., hardcover
ISBN 978-1-4932-1057-2

Xavier Hacking, Jeroen van der A
Getting Started with SAP BusinessObjects Design Studio
2014, 468 pp., hardcover
ISBN 978-1-59229-895-2

Ah-Soon, Mazoué, Vezzosi
Universe Design with SAP BusinessObjects BI
2014, 729 pp., hardcover
ISBN 978-1-59229-901-0

Greg Myers, Eric Vallo
SAP BusinessObjects BI System Administration (2nd edition)
2015, 503 pp., hardcover
ISBN 978-1-4932-1000-8

Christian Ah-Soon, Peter Snowdon

Getting Started with SAP® Lumira

Galileo Press

Bonn • Boston

Galileo Press is named after the Italian physicist, mathematician, and philosopher Galileo Galilei (1564 – 1642). He is known as one of the founders of modern science and an advocate of our contemporary, heliocentric worldview. His words *Eppur si muove* (And yet it moves) have become legendary. The Galileo Press logo depicts Jupiter orbited by the four Galilean moons, which were discovered by Galileo in 1610.

Editor Sarah Frazier
Acquisitions Editor Kelly Grace Weaver
Copyeditor Melinda Rankin
Cover Design Graham Geary
Photo Credit Shutterstock.com/175620701/© kongsak sumano
Layout Design Vera Brauner
Production Kelly O'Callaghan
Typesetting III-satz, Husby (Germany)
Printed and bound in the United States of America, on paper from sustainable sources

ISBN 978-1-4932-1033-6
© 2015 by Galileo Press Inc., Boston (MA)
1st edition 2015

Library of Congress Cataloging-in-Publication Data
Ah-Soon, Christian.
Getting started with SAP Lumira / Christian Ah-Soon and Peter Snowdon. -- 1st edition.
pages cm
Includes index.
ISBN 978-1-4932-1033-6 (print : alk. paper) -- ISBN 1-4932-1033-5 (print : alk. paper) --
ISBN 978-1-4932-1035-0 (print and ebook : alk. paper) -- ISBN 978-1-4932-1034-3 (ebook)
1. Information visualization--Computer programs. 2. Data mining--Computer programs.
3. SAP Lumira. I. Snowdon, Peter (Computer scientist) II. Title.
QA76.9.I52A39 2014
006.3'12--dc23
                                                              2014035691

All rights reserved. Neither this publication nor any part of it may be copied or reproduced in any form or by any means or translated into another language, without the prior consent of Galileo Press, Rheinwerkallee 4, 53227 Bonn, Germany.

Galileo Press makes no warranties or representations with respect to the content hereof and specifically disclaims any implied warranties of merchantability or fitness for any particular purpose. Galileo Press assumes no responsibility for any errors that may appear in this publication.

"Galileo Press" and the Galileo Press logo are registered trademarks of Galileo Press GmbH, Bonn, Germany, SAP PRESS is an imprint of Galileo Press.

All of the screenshots and graphics reproduced in this book are subject to copyright © SAP SE, Dietmar-Hopp-Allee 16, 69190 Walldorf, Germany.

SAP, the SAP logo, ABAP, BAPI, Duet, mySAP.com, mySAP, SAP ArchiveLink, SAP EarlyWatch, SAP NetWeaver, SAP Business ByDesign, SAP BusinessObjects, SAP BusinessObjects Rapid Mart, SAP BusinessObjects Desktop Intelligence, SAP BusinessObjects Explorer, SAP Rapid Marts, SAP BusinessObjects Watchlist Security, SAP BusinessObjects Web Intelligence, SAP Crystal Reports, SAP GoingLive, SAP HANA, SAP MaxAttention, SAP MaxDB, SAP PartnerEdge, SAP R/2, SAP R/3, SAP R/3 Enterprise, SAP Strategic Enterprise Management (SAP SEM), SAP StreamWork, SAP Sybase Adaptive Server Enterprise (SAP Sybase ASE), SAP Sybase IQ, SAP xApps, SAPPHIRE NOW, and Xcelsius are registered or unregistered trademarks of SAP SE, Walldorf, Germany.

All other products mentioned in this book are registered or unregistered trademarks of their respective companies.

Contents at a Glance

1	Introduction to the SAP Lumira Suite	21
2	Installation and Configuration of SAP Lumira Desktop	35
3	Data Acquisition	79
4	Data Manipulation	149
5	Data Visualization	217
6	Story Composition in SAP Lumira	285
7	Sharing in SAP Lumira	339
8	SAP Lumira Cloud	383
9	SAP Lumira Server	435
10	Integrating SAP Lumira with SAP BusinessObjects BI 4.1	463
11	SAP Lumira Software Development Kits	489
12	Conclusion	527

Dear Reader,

Storytelling is a fundamental part of the human experience. As we become more technologically advanced, the need to effectively communicate more complex ideas becomes even greater. The simple graphs of our yester-years are no longer entirely sufficient in compartmentalizing data into readable compositions. Enter SAP Lumira, SAP's newest self-service visualization software, which is currently breaking all the rules with self-service business intelligence. SAP Lumira provides the tools to go beyond dull data, into interactive and compelling narratives. With this introductory guide to SAP Lumira, you'll learn how to make your data tell its story and discover the hidden insights and trends between the lines.

Written by the incredible Christian Ah-Soon, and data visualization expert and SAP Lumira product team member, Peter Snowdon, this book will familiarize you with the important components and concepts of the SAP Lumira suite. Whether you're working collaboratively in the cloud or through your company's secured server, this guide provides the necessary insights into data acquisition, manipulation, visualization, and composition with SAP Lumira. So, what story does your data tell?

We want to hear from you! What did you think about the first edition of *Getting Started with SAP Lumira*? Your comments and suggestions are the most useful tools to help us make our books the best they can be. We encourage you to visit our website at *www.sap-press.com* and share your feedback.

Thank you for purchasing a book from SAP PRESS!

Sarah Frazier
Editor, SAP PRESS

Galileo Press
Boston, MA

sarah.frazier@galileo-press.com
www.sap-press.com

Contents

Acknowledgments 15
Preface 17

1 Introduction to the SAP Lumira Suite 21

1.1 Changing Requirements and SAP Lumira 22
    1.1.1 Requirements and User Expectations 22
    1.1.2 SAP Lumira and the Data Artisan 24
1.2 Self-Service Business Intelligence with SAP Lumira 24
    1.2.1 From Rapid Acquisition 26
    1.2.2 To Beautiful and Customizable Visualizations 27
    1.2.3 Gathered Into Narrative Stories 28
1.3 SAP Lumira Cloud and SAP Lumira Server 30
1.4 Interoperability with Other SAP Systems 32
1.5 Summary 33

2 Installation and Configuration of SAP Lumira Desktop 35

2.1 License Model 36
    2.1.1 Using the 30-Day Trial 37
    2.1.2 Adding a Keycode 37
2.2 Downloading SAP Lumira Desktop 39
2.3 Installing SAP Lumira Desktop 41
2.4 Uninstallating SAP Lumira Desktop 47
2.5 SAP Lumira Registration 51
2.6 Updating SAP Lumira Desktop 54
    2.6.1 Running Update 54
    2.6.2 Checking for New Updates 57
    2.6.3 Automatically Checking for New Updates 58
2.7 User Interface Presentation 59
    2.7.1 Welcome Page 60
    2.7.2 Rooms 63
    2.7.3 Menu Bar 64
2.8 SAP Lumira File Format 65
    2.8.1 File Extensions and Location 65
    2.8.2 Creating and Opening Documents 66
    2.8.3 Saving and Closing Document 67
2.9 Setting Preferences 69
2.10 Supportability 71

		2.10.1	Online Help	72
		2.10.2	Sending Feedback	72
		2.10.3	Error Messages	74
		2.10.4	Tracing	75
	2.11	Summary		77

3 Data Acquisition ... 79

	3.1	Data Acquisition Overview		79
		3.1.1	Supported Data Sources	80
		3.1.2	Acquisition Offline Mode	80
		3.1.3	Acquisition Online Mode	81
		3.1.4	New Dataset Creation	81
		3.1.5	Active Directory and Single Sign-On	83
		3.1.6	Data Acquisition Parameters for Automatic Detection and Performance	84
	3.2	Text Files		86
	3.3	Windows Clipboard Copy		89
	3.4	Microsoft Excel		91
	3.5	Query with SQL		95
		3.5.1	Standard SQL Drivers	96
		3.5.2	Installing/Uninstalling a Driver	98
		3.5.3	Creating a Dataset from Relational Databases	100
		3.5.4	Creating a Dataset from a Hadoop Database	106
		3.5.5	Creating a Dataset from OData	108
	3.6	SAP HANA		110
		3.6.1	SAP HANA Offline Mode	111
		3.6.2	SAP HANA Online Mode	116
		3.6.3	Answering SAP HANA Variables and Input Parameters	117
	3.7	SAP BusinessObjects BI Universes		121
		3.7.1	Universes Support	122
		3.7.2	Retrieving Data from Universes	123
		3.7.3	Adding Filters	128
		3.7.4	Answering Contexts and Parameters	130
	3.8	SAP BusinessObjects BW		134
		3.8.1	Retrieving Data from SAP BW	134
		3.8.2	Answering SAP BusinessObjects BW Variables	137
	3.9	Dataset Edit and Refresh		142
		3.9.1	Editing Data Sources' Connection Parameters	142
		3.9.2	Editing Dataset Parameters	144
		3.9.3	Refreshing the Dataset	146
	3.10	Summary		147

4 Data Manipulation 149

- 4.1 The Prepare Room 150
  - 4.1.1 Prepare Room Components 150
  - 4.1.2 Menu Bar 151
  - 4.1.3 Grid View 153
  - 4.1.4 Facets View 153
- 4.2 Objects in SAP Lumira 156
  - 4.2.1 Dimensions 156
  - 4.2.2 Measures 157
- 4.3 Hierarchies in SAP Lumira 161
  - 4.3.1 Creating a Time Hierarchy 162
  - 4.3.2 Geographic Hierarchies by Name 165
  - 4.3.3 Geographic Geography by Longitude and Latitude 171
  - 4.3.4 Custom Hierarchies 173
- 4.4 Calculated Objects 174
  - 4.4.1 Calculated Dimension 175
  - 4.4.2 Calculated Measures 176
  - 4.4.3 Formula Syntax 177
  - 4.4.4 Formula Examples 178
  - 4.4.5 Formula Table 180
- 4.5 Object Actions 188
- 4.6 Data Actions 191
  - 4.6.1 Common Actions 191
  - 4.6.2 String Actions 192
  - 4.6.3 Numeric Actions 196
  - 4.6.4 Date Actions 199
  - 4.6.5 Value and Column Actions 199
- 4.7 Filtering and Sorting Data 201
  - 4.7.1 Filtering Data in a Column 202
  - 4.7.2 Displaying Filters in Other Rooms 204
  - 4.7.3 Sorting Data 205
- 4.8 Multiple Datasets 206
  - 4.8.1 Adding a Dataset 206
  - 4.8.2 Merging Dataset 207
  - 4.8.3 Appending Datasets 210
- 4.9 Configuring Auto-Enrichment 212
  - 4.9.1 Enrichment Files 212
  - 4.9.2 Versioning Rule 212
  - 4.9.3 Enrichment File Format 213
  - 4.9.4 File Syntax 214
- 4.10 Summary 216

5 Data Visualization ... 217

- 5.1 Visualize Room Overview ... 218
- 5.2 Building Charts in SAP Lumira ... 220
    - 5.2.1 Aggregation ... 222
    - 5.2.2 Legends ... 224
    - 5.2.3 Trellis ... 225
- 5.3 Charts Types in SAP Lumira ... 227
    - 5.3.1 Column Charts ... 227
    - 5.3.2 Line Charts ... 230
    - 5.3.3 Pie Charts ... 233
    - 5.3.4 Geographic Charts ... 235
    - 5.3.5 Map Charts ... 243
    - 5.3.6 Scatter Charts ... 246
    - 5.3.7 Table Charts ... 248
    - 5.3.8 Point Charts ... 249
    - 5.3.9 Special Charts ... 250
- 5.4 Measures in Charts ... 257
    - 5.4.1 Sorting Charts ... 258
    - 5.4.2 Rank Values ... 260
    - 5.4.3 Add Calculations ... 262
    - 5.4.4 Predictive Calculations ... 267
- 5.5 Chart Customization ... 269
- 5.6 Filters in Charts ... 271
- 5.7 Hierarchies and Navigation in Charts ... 272
- 5.8 Chart Preferences ... 273
- 5.9 Visualization Gallery ... 275
- 5.10 Related Visualizations ... 278
    - 5.10.1 Influencers ... 281
- 5.11 Summary ... 283

6 Story Composition in SAP Lumira ... 285

- 6.1 Compose Room Overview ... 285
- 6.2 Story Anatomy ... 287
- 6.3 Creating a Story ... 288
- 6.4 Compose Room Organization ... 290
- 6.5 Interactive Boards ... 291
    - 6.5.1 Content Layout ... 293
    - 6.5.2 Entity Actions ... 296
    - 6.5.3 Page Settings ... 298

6.6	Infographics		301
	6.6.1	Infographic Layout	302
	6.6.2	Organizing Entities	303
	6.6.3	Resizing and Positioning Entities	304
	6.6.4	Entity Actions	305
	6.6.5	Moving Sections	308
	6.6.6	Page Settings	308
	6.6.7	Refresh Data	309
	6.6.8	Preview	311
6.7	Reports		311
	6.7.1	Report Flow Layout	312
	6.7.2	Using Tables in Reports	314
6.8	Customizing Entities		315
	6.8.1	Visualizations	315
	6.8.2	Infocharts	318
	6.8.3	Text	327
	6.8.4	Images	328
	6.8.5	Pictograms	331
	6.8.6	Shapes	332
	6.8.7	Controls	332
6.9	Summary		337

7 Sharing in SAP Lumira ... 339

7.1	Share Room Overview		340
7.2	Printing Visualizations		343
7.3	Sending Visualizations by Email		345
7.4	Publishing a Dataset or a Story to SAP Lumira Cloud		346
7.5	Republishing and Scheduling with SAP Lumira Agent		351
	7.5.1	Scheduling Documents	351
	7.5.2	Starting SAP Lumira Agent	353
	7.5.3	Scheduling a Document	353
	7.5.4	Managing All Schedules	357
	7.5.5	Running a Schedule	359
7.6	Saving a Document to SAP Lumira Cloud		360
7.7	Publishing a Dataset or a Story to SAP Lumira Server		363
7.8	Publishing Datasets to the File System		366
7.9	Publishing a Dataset to SAP HANA		368
7.10	Publishing a Dataset to SAP Explorer		371
7.11	Publishing Datasets and Visualizations to SAP StreamWork		374
7.12	Publishing Datasets and Stories to SAP BusinessObjects BI		377
7.13	Summary		382

8 SAP Lumira Cloud 383

8.1	SAP Lumira Cloud Access		384
	8.1.1	License Model	384
	8.1.2	Creating Your Account from SAP Lumira Cloud	384
	8.1.3	Creating Your Account from SAP Lumira Desktop	388
	8.1.4	Account Management	389
	8.1.5	Log In to SAP Lumira Cloud	389
	8.1.6	Log Out of SAP Lumira Cloud	389
8.2	Connecting from SAP Lumira Desktop		390
8.3	SAP Lumira Cloud User Interface		392
	8.3.1	General Overview	392
	8.3.2	My Items Tab	393
	8.3.3	Searching for Items	395
	8.3.4	Running Actions	396
	8.3.5	Settings Tab	399
8.4	Importing to SAP Lumira Cloud		402
	8.4.1	Uploading Files or SAP Lumira Documents	402
	8.4.2	Importing Data to Create a Dataset	403
8.5	Visualization and Composition Online		409
	8.5.1	Accessing Online Rooms	409
	8.5.2	Working in the Visualize and Compose Rooms	410
	8.5.3	Saving Your Stories in SAP Lumira Cloud	413
8.6	Sharing Resources in SAP Lumira Cloud		414
	8.6.1	Sharing Methods	414
	8.6.2	Sharing a Resource	414
	8.6.3	Changing Sharing Options	418
	8.6.4	Accessing a Shared Resource	419
8.7	Creating a Team		420
	8.7.1	Members Type	420
	8.7.2	Accessing Team Administration	420
	8.7.3	Inviting and Removing Users	422
	8.7.4	Managing Administrators	423
	8.7.5	Sending Email	424
	8.7.6	Changing the Team Name	424
8.8	Mobile Access		426
	8.8.1	Setting Up SAP Lumira Cloud Connection in SAP BusinessObjects Mobile	426
	8.8.2	Working with SAP BusinessObjects Mobile	428
8.9	Summary		433

9 SAP Lumira Server 435

- 9.1 Downloading SAP Lumira Server 436
- 9.2 Using SAP HANA for SAP Lumira Server 438
  - 9.2.1 SAP HANA Platform Advantages 438
  - 9.2.2 SAP HANA Requirements 439
  - 9.2.3 Installing SAP Lumira Server with SAP HANA Studio 439
  - 9.2.4 SAP Lumira Server Security 442
- 9.3 SAP Lumira Server User Interface 445
  - 9.3.1 Log In to SAP Lumira Server 445
  - 9.3.2 Log Out of SAP Lumira Server 446
  - 9.3.3 General Overview 446
  - 9.3.4 My Items Tab 447
  - 9.3.5 Searching for Items 449
  - 9.3.6 Running Actions 449
  - 9.3.7 Settings 451
  - 9.3.8 Mobile Access 452
- 9.4 Importing to SAP Lumira Server 452
  - 9.4.1 Publishing from SAP Lumira Desktop 452
  - 9.4.2 Importing Data to Create a Dataset 453
  - 9.4.3 Using SAP HANA Dataset 454
- 9.5 Visualization and Composition Online 454
  - 9.5.1 Accessing Online Rooms 454
  - 9.5.2 Working in the Visualize and Compose Rooms 455
  - 9.5.3 Saving Your Story 456
- 9.6 Sharing Resources in SAP Lumira Server 457
  - 9.6.1 Sharing Prerequisites 457
  - 9.6.2 Sharing a Resource 458
  - 9.6.3 Changing Sharing Options 460
  - 9.6.4 Accessing a Shared Resource 461
- 9.7 Summary 462

10 Integrating SAP Lumira with SAP BusinessObjects BI 4.1 463

- 10.1 SAP BusinessObjects BI 4.1 Add-On Overview 464
- 10.2 Installing and Configuring SAP BusinessObjects BI 4.1 Add-On in SAP Lumira 465
  - 10.2.1 Downloading the Add-On for SAP Lumira and the SAP Cryptography Library 466
  - 10.2.2 Installing on a Windows Platform 468
  - 10.2.3 Installing the Cryptography Library and Generating the Assertion Ticket 470

		10.2.4	Configuring SAP HANA with an Assertion Ticket	471
		10.2.5	Creating a User in SAP HANA Dedicated to SAP BusinessObjects BI 4.1	474
		10.2.6	Configuring SAP Lumira Server HTTP	474
		10.2.7	Configuring SAP BusinessObjects BI 4.1 to Communicate with SAP HANA	477
	10.3	Importing SAP Lumira Resources into SAP BusinessObjects BI 4.1		479
		10.3.1	Dataset InfoObject	479
		10.3.2	Story InfoObject	480
	10.4	Viewing SAP Lumira Content in SAP BusinessObjects BI Launch Pad		480
	10.5	Central Management Console		482
		10.5.1	Displaying Stories and Dataset	483
		10.5.2	Managing Datasets in the CMC	483
		10.5.3	Managing Stories in the CMC	484
		10.5.4	Dataset and Story User Security	486
	10.6	Universe Refresh and Scheduling		486
		10.6.1	Refreshing or Scheduling a Dataset	486
	10.7	Summary		488

11 SAP Lumira Software Development Kits ... 489

	11.1	The VizExtensions Software Development Kit		490
		11.1.1	VizExtensions Samples	490
		11.1.2	VizExtensions Custom Charts	494
		11.1.3	VizPacker	494
		11.1.4	Chart Deployment	502
		11.1.5	Debugging	511
		11.1.6	Summary	513
	11.2	The Data Source Software Development Kit		513
		11.2.1	Prerequisites	514
		11.2.2	Talking to SAP Lumira	515
		11.2.3	SAP Lumira Arguments	516
		11.2.4	Task Manager Extension	517
		11.2.5	Creating an EXE	521
		11.2.6	Deployment	523
	11.3	Summary		526

The Authors	529
Index	531

Acknowledgments

I'd like to thank the different people who helped us: Antoine Chabert, Nicolas Mourey, Fabien Aubert, David Mobbs, David Dalley, Sébastien Foucault, Thomas Coan, Jay Xiong, Michael Tsz Hong Sung, Derrick Wan, James Anderson, Kai Chan and the SAP PRESS team: Sarah Frazier, Kelly Grace Weaver, and also Emily Nicholls.

Thank you, Peter, for joining me in this project.

My special thoughts go out to my friends, my family, Claire, Inès, and Elisabeth.

Christian Ah-Soon

To Calvin, Emily, and Muriel, for their patience.

Peter Snowdon

Preface

With SAP Lumira, SAP's ambition is to simplify and modernize business intelligence by putting it into everyone's hands for free through self-service business intelligence.

Instead of multiple individuals working on the various steps—from finding the data in the sources, modeling it, exposing it in business terms, securely providing it to the end users, and creating the reports—SAP Lumira allows you to create analytics easily by yourself. It also proposes some other key advantages:

- Provides fast data access, data mash-up, and data manipulation
- Modernizes analytics by providing beautiful visualizations
- Showcases your data through stories (graphical and navigable narratives that group visualizations, texts, and charts together)
- Enforces your existing SAP systems assets: SAP HANA, SAP BusinessObjects BI, and SAP BW

These are the advantages that SAP Lumira promises; they are described in this book and will be expanded on in greater detail in the chapters ahead.

Book Objectives

The objective of this book is to present how SAP Lumira is breaking business intelligence rules by supporting self-service business intelligence. It explains SAP Lumira's basic functionalities and its powerful, advanced capabilities so that both new and experienced users can fully understand their use and how to benefit from them.

It also presents a complete overview of the SAP Lumira suite—SAP Lumira Desktop, SAP Lumira Cloud, and SAP Lumira Server—and how it integrates with the whole SAP landscape: SAP HANA, SAP BusinessObjects BI, and so on.

In your everyday work, this book can help you to deploy SAP Lumira or use it to analyze your data by providing detailed, complete step-by-step workflows with sample screenshots.

Target Audience

As explained in the next chapters, SAP Lumira's key characteristic is self-service business intelligence. It allows all users—from novices to technical experts—to quickly extract data and create analytics by themselves.

This book, and the information presented within it, can benefit you if any of the following are true:

- You have casual and simple needs. You do not need to grasp all technical details, but need to quickly create dashboards, infographics, and reports. This book contains all of the necessary information to create some beautiful visualizations and stories with SAP Lumira.
- You are a business analyst, data artisan, data scientist, or have a role that requires working with data and extracting business meaning out of it. The book explains how you can use SAP Lumira to retrieve, process, and expose good information from data.
- You manage or work in a business intelligence department or are taking part in a business intelligence project. You can use this book to understand the capabilities of the SAP Lumira suite, how you can integrate it to your roadmap, and the benefits it can bring to your users.
- You are a business intelligence administrator and need to understand how SAP Lumira can integrate and complement your existing SAP BusinessObjects BI and SAP BusinessObjects Mobile framework deployments.

In each case, you can find the information you are looking for in the chapters of this book.

Book Roadmap

This book contains 12 chapters, which are summarized ahead.

Chapter 1 is a description of new business intelligence requirements and how SAP Lumira answers them through the SAP Lumira suite.

Chapter 2 introduces SAP Lumira Desktop installation and configuration, its license model, and a general description of its user interface and framework.

Chapter 3 provides information about data acquisition, the first step when working with SAP Lumira Desktop. It describes all the data sources it can access and how to query them.

Chapter 4 explains how to manipulate the retrieved data to prepare them for the creation of visualizations. It provides deep insights into the possible actions in SAP Lumira and how to create new objects—for example, through its formula language.

Chapter 5 describes how you can create charts to analyze your data and visualizations to be used in stories.

Chapter 6 covers the stories you can use to organize your visualizations and create dashboards, infographics, and reports.

Chapter 7 explains how to export your datasets and stories created in SAP Lumira or share your resources in SAP Lumira Cloud, SAP Lumira Server, SAP HANA, and SAP BusinessObjects BI. It also presents SAP Lumira Agent, used to schedule publications to SAP Lumira Cloud.

Chapter 8 focuses on SAP Lumira Cloud, the SAP Lumira offering on the cloud, including how to register for it, access it, share content on it, and use it to create datasets, visualizations, and stories.

Chapter 9 addresses SAP Lumira Server, the server version of SAP Lumira. Here you will learn how to successfully deploy SAP Lumira Server on your SAP HANA system, how to configure it, and what its capabilities are.

Chapter 10 explains how to integrate SAP Lumira within SAP BusinessObjects BI and how it can take advantage of its framework (security, deployment, etc.).

Chapter 11 covers the two SDKs available to programmatically enhance and extend SAP Lumira data sources and visualizations.

Finally, **Chapter 12** will conclude the book with a brief overview of the content covered and the future SAP Lumira functionalities to look forward to.

Let's begin by looking at new customer requirements in Chapter 1.

The SAP Lumira suite is the new analytics tool proposed by SAP that offers self-service data visualization. This chapter provides an introduction into the SAP Lumira suite and its core component, SAP Lumira Desktop.

1   Introduction to the SAP Lumira Suite

The SAP Lumira suite is self-service data-visualization software that allows for easier manipulation, visualization, and sharing of data on a platform or in the cloud. With it, you can analyze trends and share insights into your data via its versatile components; thanks to SAP Lumira Desktop, SAP Lumira Server, and SAP Lumira Cloud, this suite has you covered. This suite is intended for anyone who needs to analyze and manipulate some data, from the student to the data expert in your company. This suite democratizes business intelligence (BI) by allowing anyone to create their own analytics easily and for free. SAP Lumira is easy to use, but provides powerful analytical capabilities to address the requirements described previously.

In this chapter, we will discuss the suite itself and the core component of the suite: SAP Lumira Desktop.

SAP Lumira Desktop is a standalone desktop application, whereas the SAP Lumira Server is an enterprise solution, and SAP Lumira Cloud offers virtual sharing without physical constraints.

> **SAP Lumira Desktop**
>
> Throughout the remainder of this book, the SAP Lumira Desktop application on-premise is referred to as "SAP Lumira." SAP Lumira Desktop is explicitly used when it could be confused with SAP Lumira suite, SAP Lumira Cloud, or SAP Lumira Server.

Since its first release in 2012, SAP Lumira Desktop has generated a great interest, which can be measured by its high download numbers. It was initially named SAP Visual Intelligence and positioned as an advanced visualization tool.

> **Note**
>
> SAP Lumira does not replace SAP BusinessObjects BI classical products, such as SAP BusinessObjects Web Intelligence, SAP Crystal Reports, SAP Explorer, or SAP Dashboards, but can be used in complement

In this chapter, we'll review how organizations' requirements have evolved and how SAP Lumira suite and SAP Lumira Desktop address these new requirements. We'll show you a standard workflow that uses SAP Lumira and then show how the workflow relates to the SAP Lumira suite that is offered. First, let's address the evolving requirements for today's users and data artisans.

1.1 Changing Requirements and SAP Lumira

In this section, we'll quickly highlight how BI has been changing in recent years before delving deeper into the SAP Lumira suite. Many of the changing BI requirements that organizations have are reflected in the SAP Lumira suite.

1.1.1 Requirements and User Expectations

Deploying a BI solution or optimizing its use remains a priority for many companies, but the shifting world and environments have seen the arrival of new players on the market, changing the way everyone interacts with data and business intelligence. This translates into new requirements and user expectations, including the following:

- **Self-service BI**
  Users no longer accept the classical BI model in which they needed to wait several weeks before IT could modify their reports. BI users want to discover data available to them on their own and generate their own reports immediately.

  As technology and standards evolve, some users cannot wait for IT products to support them, and thus need to be able to extend products themselves.

- **Big data**
  Technical advancements now allow companies to gather and store a very large amount of data. Companies that operate worldwide can generate multiple facts that they need to analyze as a whole. Real-time events can be monitored

through sensors and analyzed in real time or aggregated later on. However, processing such large amounts of data can only be worthwhile if the system performs well.

- **Geo maps**
  In a global world, data may come from different locations, and an easy way to display this data is to use a geo map. Users expect the application to embed geographical maps and to locate and display data on those maps, whether the data is attached to a country, a city, or a more specific location.

- **Predictive**
  Business intelligence has been used to analyze and report past historical data with a powerful engine and to aggregate and drill into it with the objective of improving enterprise governance and planning future actions. Hence, the next step for business intelligence is inferring future trends from past data, which can provide more insight in order to make decisions more quickly and accurately.

From a deployment point of view, the on-premise model is still a common way to use a piece of software, because the user wants to install applications himself on his desktop without IT interaction. Nonetheless, new methods have emerged that are changing the way IT services are provided:

- **Cloud**
  The on-demand model, based on cloud infrastructure, offers very good return on investment, because it reduces administration and deployment costs. Because the services are hosted in the cloud by the service provider, administration, installation, and upgrade are no longer managed by the user. This also avoids heavy infrastructure and hardware management. For this reason, more and more services are now offered on the cloud.

- **Mobile**
  With the emergence of mobile devices, both in our personal and professional lives, our interaction with data has been modified. Mobile devices allow everyone to access his or her data anytime and everywhere using specific interfaces and interactions. It is natural to expect BI mobile services to be available.

A common factor that links all of these requirements is the need for simplification, which is a common demand for SAP products. Simplification can include the following elements:

- Process simplification, with self-service BI
- Data simplification, to turn big data into aggregated indicators
- Maintenance and installation simplification
- Ease of use with mobile devices, the workflows for which must comply with standard mobile usage and thus be easy to learn and self-explanatory

Finally, for all customers who have already invested in other SAP systems, it is mandatory to continue to leverage their previous SAP investments: SAP HANA, SAP BusinessObjects BI, and SAP Business Warehouse (BW).

1.1.2 SAP Lumira and the Data Artisan

SAP Lumira suite's capabilities have constantly been improved to take into consideration customers' new needs and expectations. Today's business intelligence's customers ask for the following:

- Self-service usage and simplicity
- Support for big data
- Predictive analysis, using historical data to predict future data
- Geo mapping, to locate data on maps

It may be that no one is hungrier for these features than company data artisans, better known as those who possess both the technical skills and the business know-how to collect large amounts of data and present that data with unique and compelling clarity. Overall, SAP Lumira is a great option for all those looking to enhance their data.

1.2 Self-Service Business Intelligence with SAP Lumira

Whatever your technical expertise is, you can easily install and use SAP Lumira Desktop. It does not require vast infrastructure, and it can be operational in only a few clicks.

As shown in Figure 1.1, a typical workflow in SAP Lumira Desktop allows the data artisan to retrieve data from the data source and generate a dataset, process it, and create visualizations. From these visualizations, stories can be created and then shared through the other SAP Lumira suite components (SAP Lumira Server and SAP Lumira Cloud) or other SAP systems (SAP HANA, SAP Explorer, SAP StreamWork, SAP BusinessObjects BI 4.1, etc.).

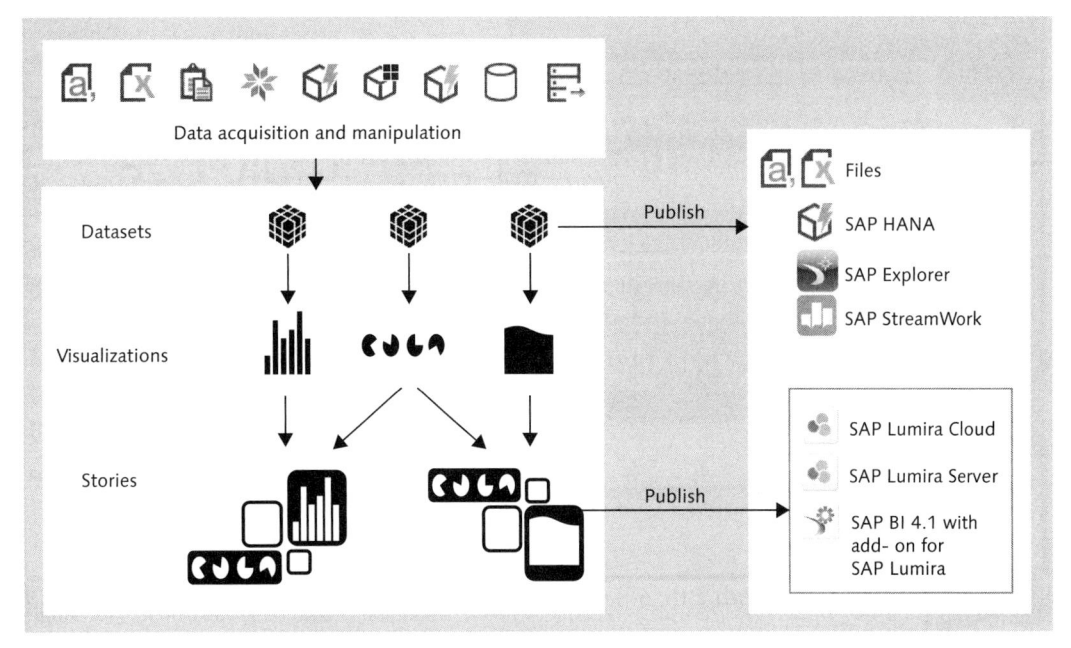

Figure 1.1 Classical Workflow in SAP Lumira

SAP Lumira can be downloaded quickly from the SAP website for free. Once downloaded, you can install it yourself without any external interventions. Because SAP Lumira benefits from a short development cycle, new versions are released on a regular basis; you can update it easily.

Once installed, it is easy to get started and extract your first data from your data sources without external assistance. You can discover and select your data, create your dataset, and generate your visualizations and stories.

On the cloud, you can register yourself and try SAP Lumira Cloud for free. It is also regularly upgraded, allowing you to focus on your functional requirements.

The next sections detail the different steps of the classical workflow for SAP Lumira and how it addresses the requirements previously listed.

1.2.1 From Rapid Acquisition

In the SAP Lumira suite, SAP Lumira Desktop allows you to easily retrieve data from a wide range of data sources, as shown in Figure 1.2. First, it supports some common and popular file formats, such as text or Microsoft Excel files. Access to these files does not require any drivers or middleware installation.

SAP Lumira Desktop can also access relational databases through SQL direct access. In addition to classic relational databases, this SQL direct access can also be used to query a HADOOP data source, often used to store big data, or any data sources that expose an OData interface.

In all cases, the extracted data is saved in a dataset, which can be one of the following:

- Offline: if saved in the SAP Lumira document
- Online: if accessed directly in the data source

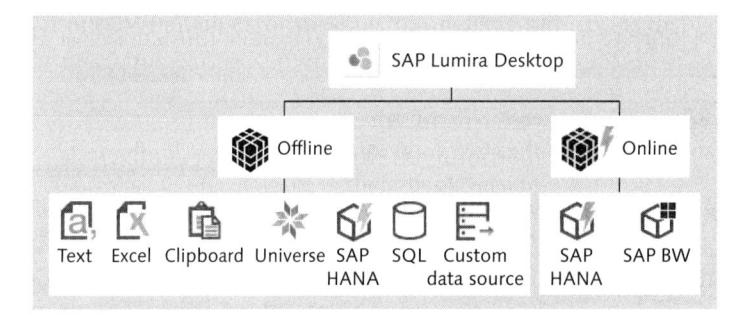

Figure 1.2 Data Source Supported by SAP Lumira Desktop

If you have already deployed an SAP system, you can also use SAP Lumira Desktop to extract data from it, because it natively supports access to the following SAP systems:

- SAP HANA
- SAP BusinessObjects BI universes
- SAP BW

Once data is extracted from data sources, SAP Lumira can process the offline dataset through powerful manipulations and formula engines before using it in visualizations. You may also enrich it by adding additional metadata, such as calculated dimensions, measures, or hierarchies (geography or time). For data sources accessed in online mode, some of these processing options are also available.

1.2.2 To Beautiful and Customizable Visualizations

Once your dataset has been prepared, you create visualizations to graphically display your data. SAP Lumira natively proposes a wide range of charts to cover common situations: column charts, pie charts, line charts, radar charts, tree charts, and so on. For geographical data, SAP Lumira also proposes visualizations with maps from third-party ESRI for their background and countries, regions, and definitions from third-party Nokia/Navteq.

Visualizations can be easily mapped to dataset metadata through simple drag-and-drop actions (see Figure 1.3).

Figure 1.3 Vizualisation in SAP Lumira

For more specific needs, you may create your own custom visualization with the SAP Lumira visualization SDK, connect to the SAP Marketplace to purchase custom visualizations created by SAP partners, or get the ones shared by the SAP Lumira community (see Figure 1.4).

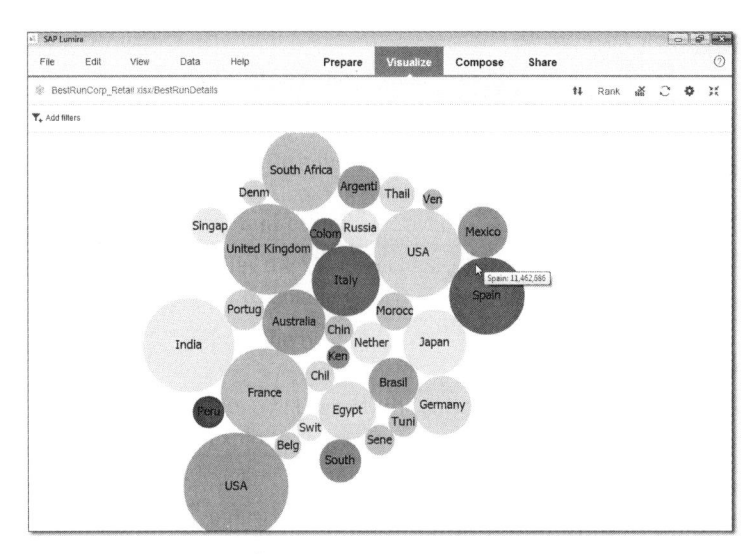

Figure 1.4 Custom Visualization

1.2.3 Gathered Into Narrative Stories

After you have created visualizations, you can use them in *stories*, graphical and navigable narratives used to describe your data by grouping charts together to create a simple presentation.

In stories, the graphical layout organization is important, because it must present and highlight the visualizations. In stories, visualizations can be enhanced by adding text and images.

There are three types of stories:

- **Reports**
  Reports can be compared to the reports you can create with classical business intelligence applications. They can be used to restitute and analyze large amounts of data. To ease analysis, they can be made interactive through section navigation, as shown in Figure 1.5. Reports are based on only one dataset.

- **Interactive boards**
  Interactive boards are used to create cockpits from which you can monitor aggregated data. In interactive boards, graphical representation is more common than textual figures in order to display information that can be easily grasped, as shown in Figure 1.6. Like reports, interactive boards are based on only one dataset. They can be dynamic, thanks to interactive controls.

Self-Service Business Intelligence with SAP Lumira | 1.2

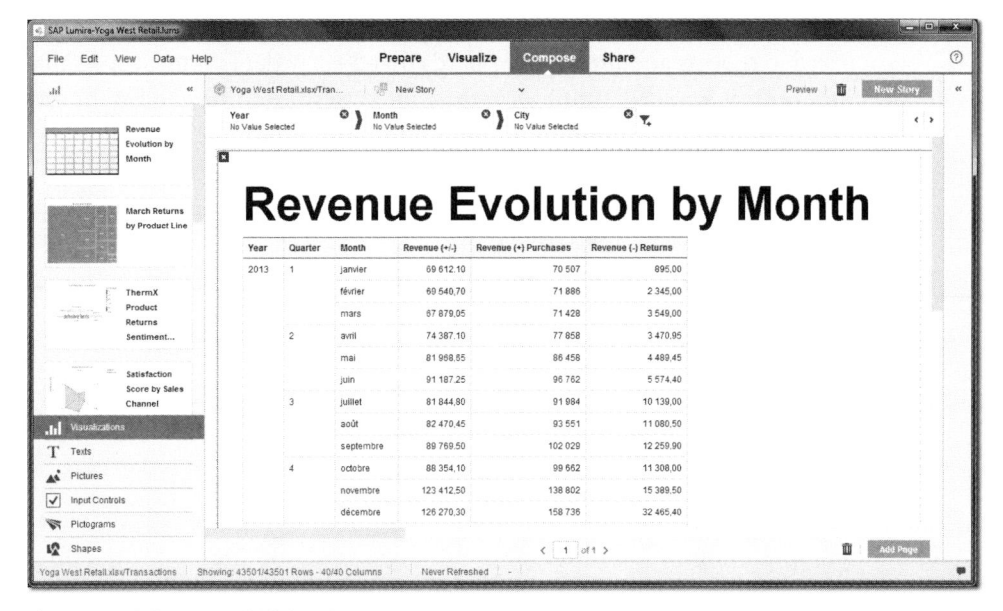

Figure 1.5 A Report in SAP Lumira

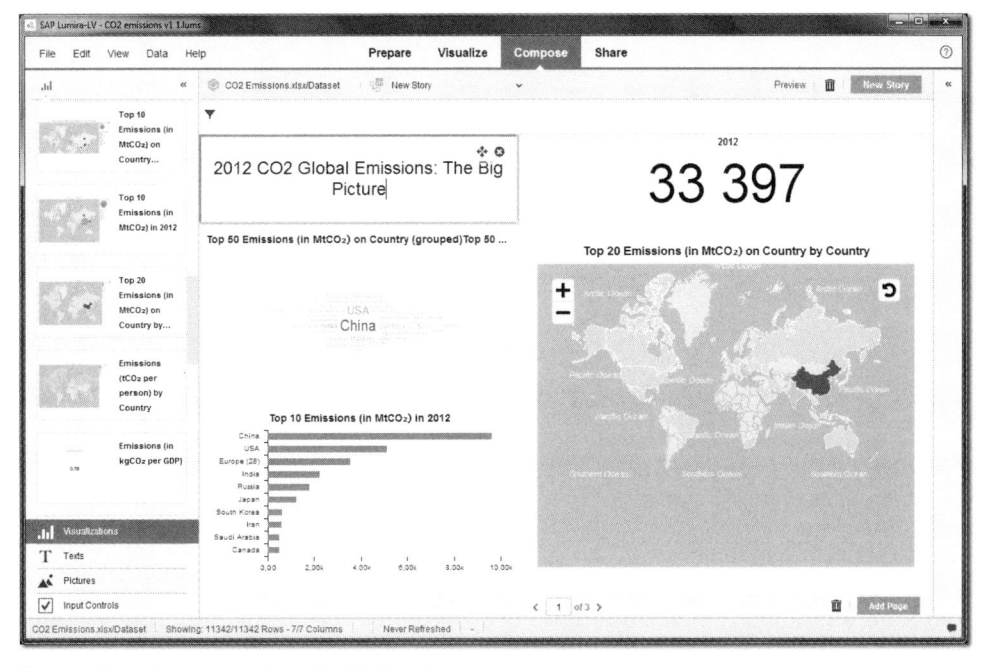

Figure 1.6 An Interactive Board in SAP Lumira

1 | Introduction to the SAP Lumira Suite

▶ **Infographics**
Compared to reports and interactive boards that display data, figures, and numbers in a neutral way, infographics are intended to present simple key figures that highlight a specific message to convey, as seen in Figure 1.7. Infographics are static, but can be based on multiple datasets.

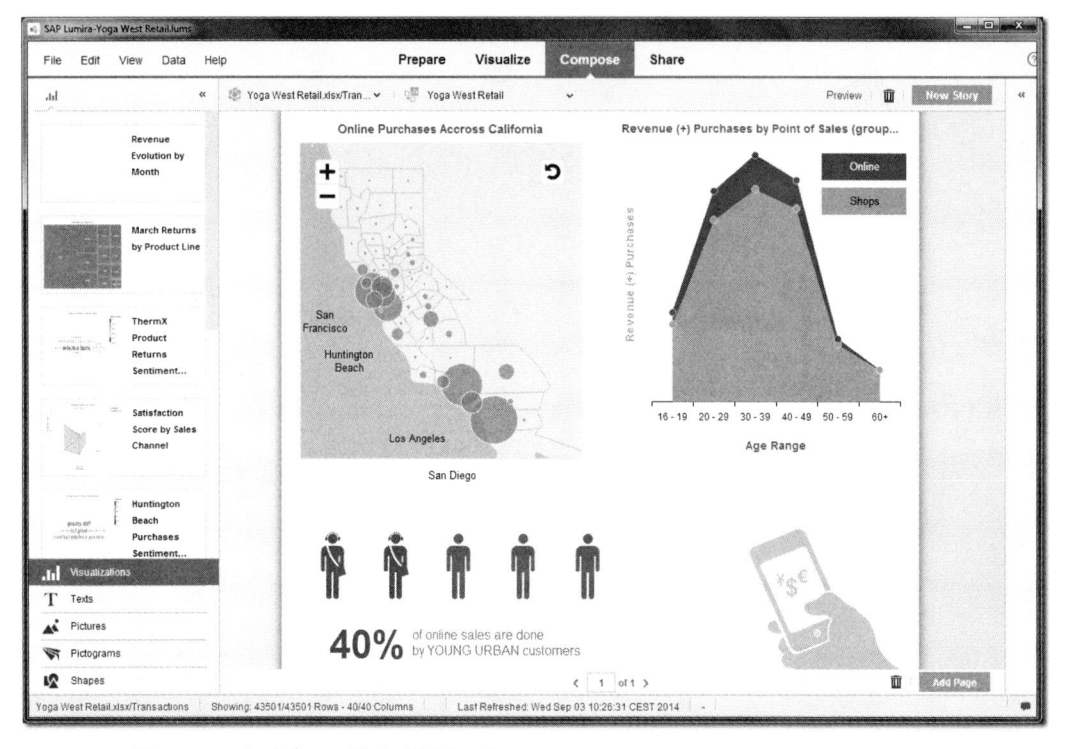

Figure 1.7 An Infographic in SAP Lumira

1.3 SAP Lumira Cloud and SAP Lumira Server

Once you have created your story with SAP Lumira Desktop, you will want to share it, either for further edit by other data artisans or to communicate its data to other people. For this reason, SAP Lumira Desktop integrates into an overall landscape—the SAP Lumira suite—that proposes the following deployment modes (see Figure 1.8):

- **SAP Lumira Cloud**
  SAP Lumira Cloud is the cloud offering dedicated to SAP Lumira.

- **SAP Lumira Server**
  SAP Lumira Server is the server version of SAP Lumira that you can deploy on your own instance of SAP HANA.

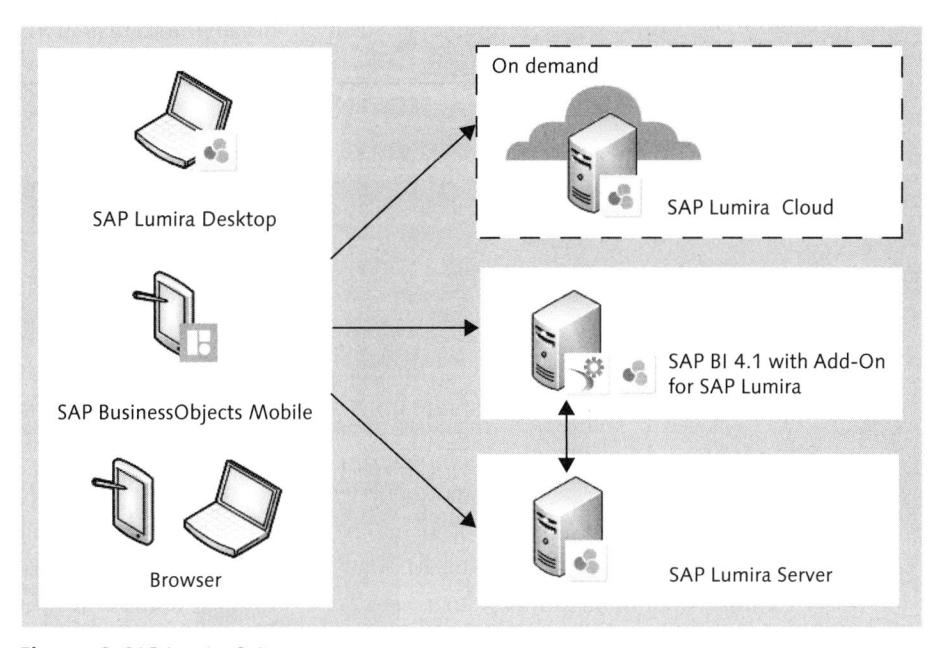

Figure 1.8 SAP Lumira Suite

These two deployment modes propose a centralized location from which you can share your SAP Lumira resources and some common workflows and user interfaces in SAP Lumira Desktop to create datasets, visualizations, and stories.

You can connect to SAP Lumira Cloud or SAP Lumira Server and access your SAP Lumira resources and datasets from any iOS or Android mobile devices, making them available anywhere and anytime so long as you use a browser that supports HTML5, as shown in Figure 1.9. You can also access them through SAP BusinessObjects Mobile.

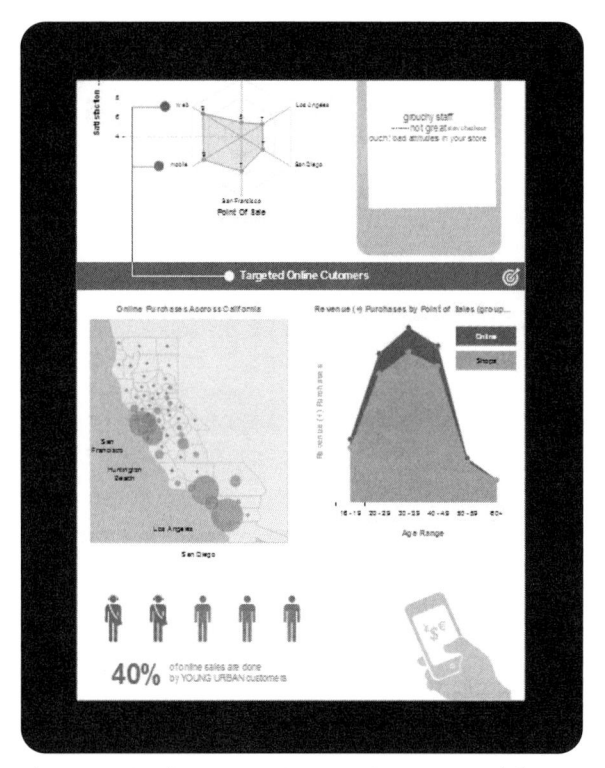

Figure 1.9 Displaying an SAP Lumira Story on a Mobile Device

1.4 Interoperability with Other SAP Systems

In addition to the SAP Lumira suite, SAP Lumira content can also be shared with other SAP systems in order to favor interoperability between SAP products.

For example, if you have deployed SAP BusinessObjects BI 4.1, then you can install its add-on for SAP Lumira. This add-on creates a bridge between your SAP Lumira Server and SAP BusinessObjects BI 4.1. You can use the SAP BusinessObjects BI 4.1 framework to store, display, secure, and manage SAP Lumira content. If you've already set up a security model, then you can inherit from it when integrating SAP Lumira with SAP BusinessObjects BI 4.1.

You can also use SAP Lumira Desktop data acquisition and manipulation engines to extract data from a data source and then publish the generated dataset to other SAP systems:

- SAP HANA; in which the dataset is saved as an analytic view.
- SAP Explorer; in which the dataset is saved as an information space data source.
- SAP StreamWork; in which the dataset is saved as a dataset. You can also save visualizations in SAP StreamWork.

1.5 Summary

The SAP Lumira suite's popularity can be explained easily: it answers several current BI requirements and does so for free.

The SAP Lumira suite consists of a set of products and services available on the desktop, the server, the cloud, and mobile devices. This offering allows you to retrieve data from data sources, turn them into graphical visualizations, and organize them into stories. Such content can be also shared with other SAP products: SAP HANA, SAP Explorer, SAP BusinessObjects BI, and SAP StreamWork.

In the next chapter, we'll discuss the installation and configuration of SAP Lumira Desktop.

Your first steps in SAP Lumira have been simplified in order to ease its adoption. This chapter covers SAP Lumira Desktop's download, installation, and general user interface.

2 Installation and Configuration of SAP Lumira Desktop

One of SAP Lumira's key characteristics is its simplicity. This simplicity is first reflected in the overall process of getting started with SAP Lumira Desktop, which includes the following:

- A simple license model that allows you to use most SAP Lumira features for free
- The capabilities unlocked by this free license that enable you to enjoy SAP Lumira for personal use
- A dedicated website to download SAP Lumira, in addition of the SAP Service Market Place website
- Installation and updates that can be performed with a few clicks

Once installed, SAP Lumira's simple-to-navigate user interface guides you to your different tasks. These topics are described in this chapter before covering important properties of the SAP Lumira framework:

- The file format used to save the documents you create in SAP Lumira
- The SAP Lumira preferences that allow you to fine-tune its behaviors
- Supportability, which gathers all SAP Lumira abilities to help you to solve a problem—from online documents, error messages, and tracing to direct feedback
- A quick description of the samples installed with SAP Lumira

To begin, we will look at the license model available with SAP Lumira.

2.1 License Model

In its desktop version, SAP Lumira supports a very simple license model, which consists of only three options: SAP Lumira Personal Edition, SAP Lumira Standard Edition, and SAP Lumira. Let's look at these in closer detail:

- **SAP Lumira Personal Edition**
  The license for SAP Lumira Personal Edition is free and allows you to discover most SAP Lumira capabilities without time limitations. However, the supported data sources are limited to only text files, Microsoft Excel files, and contractually to SAP HANA One (the version of SAP HANA running on Amazon Web Services). For personal use, these limitations are not critical and do not prevent you from taking advantage of SAP Lumira.

- **SAP Lumira Standard Edition**
  You need to pay a small fee for the standard edition license that unlocks some of the additional capabilities of SAP Lumira. This license allows you to access SAP HANA and relational databases in addition to the SAP Lumira Personal Edition data sources. It also allows you to share datasets in SAP Explorer (contractually with SAP Crystal Server only).

- **SAP Lumira**
  SAP Lumira extends the SAP Lumira Standard Edition by giving access to all data sources supported by SAP Lumira: SAP BusinessObjects BI universes, SAP BW, and so on. This license is intended for enterprise use of SAP Lumira; it unlocks access to systems you are likely to connect with only in a professional environment. You need to contact your SAP account executive for more details and to acquire this license.

> **License Price**
> At the time of writing, the license price for SAP Lumira Standard Edition is $995 and $1,425 for SAP Lumira.

With the SAP Lumira Personal Edition, you can download, install, and try SAP Lumira for free, as described in Section 2.2. SAP Lumira grants you a 30-day trial period in which you can test all its capabilities.

2.1.1 Using the 30-Day Trial

When you have a personal edition license, you may switch to a standard edition for a 30-day testing period. This testing period allows you to test all SAP Lumira capabilities by unlocking them. To do so, click 30 DAYS TRIAL at the bottom of the WELCOME page, as seen in Figure 2.1 ❶.

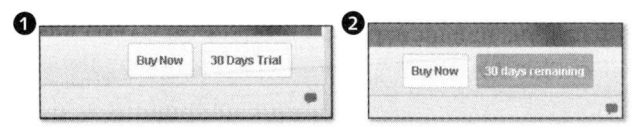

Figure 2.1 30 Days Trial ❶ and Remaining Days Buttons ❷

For 30 days, this button displays the number of remaining days before the end of the trial period, as seen in Figure 2.1 ❷. After 30 days, SAP Lumira returns to the personal edition license, disabling the features that are no longer available. If you are satisfied, to continue using these features, you must acquire an SAP Lumira or SAP Lumira Standard Edition license. Click BUY NOW and follow the SAP Store workflow. Once you have your keycode, you can enter it in SAP Lumira, as described in the next section, in order to permanently enable its features.

2.1.2 Adding a Keycode

After testing SAP Lumira with its free personal edition license, you may unlock all its features by acquiring the standard edition license. To do so, you need to buy this license, retrieve the corresponding keycode, and enter it in SAP Lumira.

There are several ways to acquire a keycode:

- Open your web browser and go to the SAP Lumira website at *http://saplumira.com*. In the top bar, click PRICING to be redirected to the page that displays the SAP Lumira offers. Look for SAP Lumira, and click BUY NOW to open the SAP Online Store website.

- You can, alternately, access the SAP Marketplace website from SAP Lumira Desktop:

  - Click BUY NOW at the bottom of the SAP Lumira WELCOME page (see Section 2.7.1).

  - Or, select the HELP • ENTER KEYCODE command to open the keycode dialog box, and click PURCHASE, as shown in Figure 2.2.

In all of these cases, you will then follow the website workflow to buy and acquire an SAP Lumira keycode.

Once you have received this keycode, start SAP Lumira in order to enter it:

1. In the menu bar, select the command HELP • ENTER KEYCODE to open the keycode dialog box.

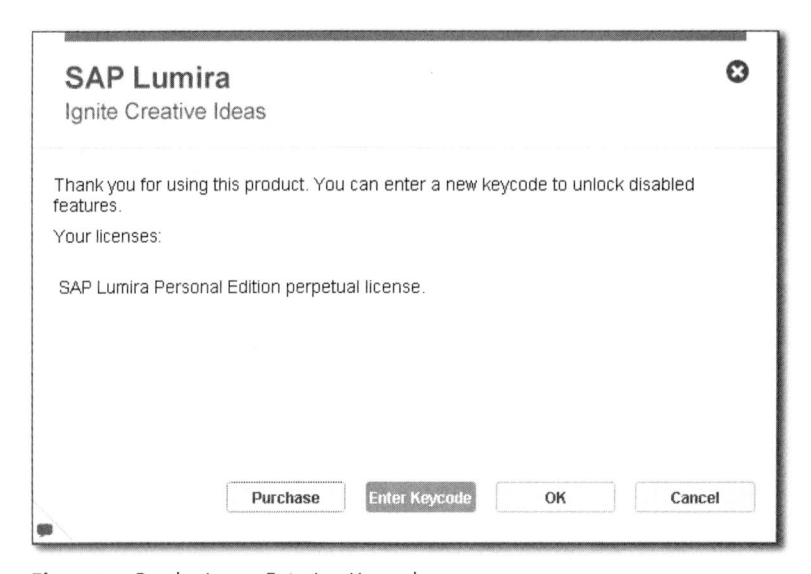

Figure 2.2 Purchasing or Entering Keycode

2. Click ENTER KEYCODE to open a new dialog box, as shown in Figure 2.3.

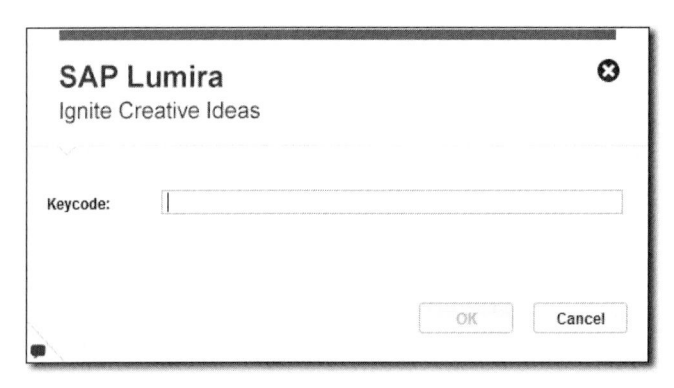

Figure 2.3 Entering Keycode

3. In the KEYCODE text field, enter your keycode.
4. Click OK twice to close the two dialog boxes.

Once your keycode has been saved, you will be given access to all its capabilities for your next sessions with SAP Lumira.

> **Keycode File**
> Keycodes are stored in a properties file created in the *C:/Users/Public/sapvi* folder.

2.2 Downloading SAP Lumira Desktop

Once you have decided which license you want to use and before downloading SAP Lumira Installation Manager, you need to check if the platforms supported by SAP Lumira are consistent with your environment. This list of supported platforms can be found in the Product Availability Matrix, which you can find at this URL: *https://service.sap.com/sap/support/pam*.

Then, you will need to address some of the system requirements imposed by the installer:

- The operating system must be 32-bit if you run the 32-bit version of the Installation Manager or 64-bit if you run its 64-bit version.
- The disk that contains the installation folder must have at least 1 GB of free space.
- The disk that contains your application data folder (for example, on Windows 7, this folder is *C:\Users\<user>\Documents*, where *<user>* is your Windows account) must have at least 2.5 GB of free space.
- The disk that contains your temporary folder (for example, on Windows 7, this folder is *C:\Users\<user>\AppData\Local\Temp*) must have at least 200 MB of free space.
- The HTTP port 6401 must be open, and an HTTP port must be available between 4520 and 4539.

2 | Installation and Configuration of SAP Lumira Desktop

If your machine meets all the system's requirements, then you can download the SAP Lumira Installation Manager, which contains and installs SAP Lumira. Instead of the classical SAP Marketplace, you can download this SAP Lumira Installation Manager for free from the website dedicated to SAP Lumira (*http://saplumira.com*), as seen in Figure 2.4.

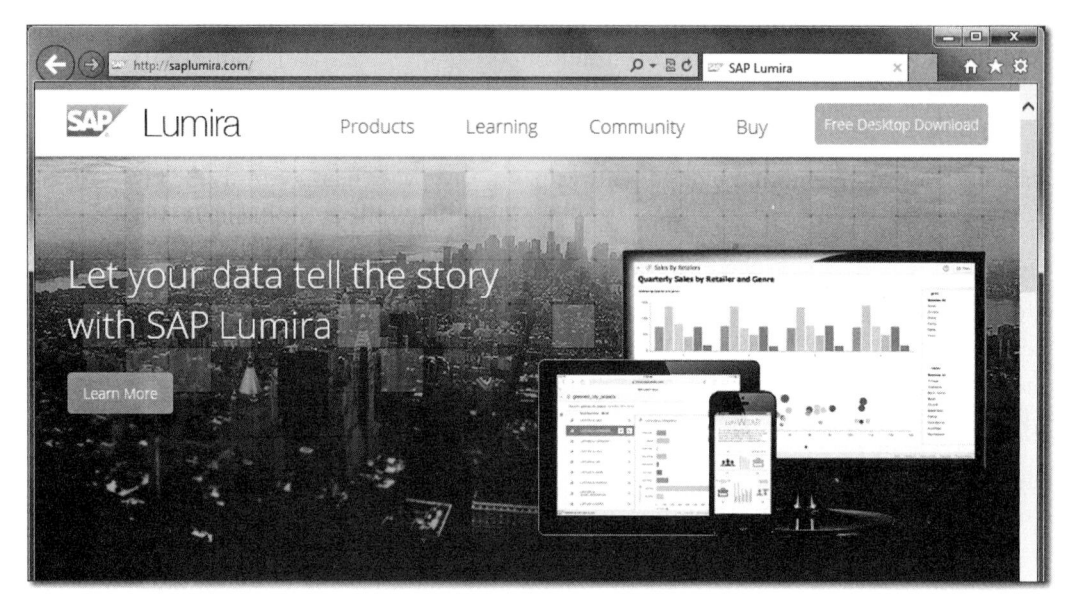

Figure 2.4 SAP Lumira Website

This website contains multiple resources for SAP Lumira: news, videos, and so on. To retrieve the SAP Lumira Installation Manager, follow these steps:

1. In the SAP Lumira website, click FREE DESKTOP DOWNLOAD in the top-right of the home page (make sure to enlarge your web browser width enough so that this button is not hidden).

    You are then redirected to the download page, as seen in Figure 2.5.

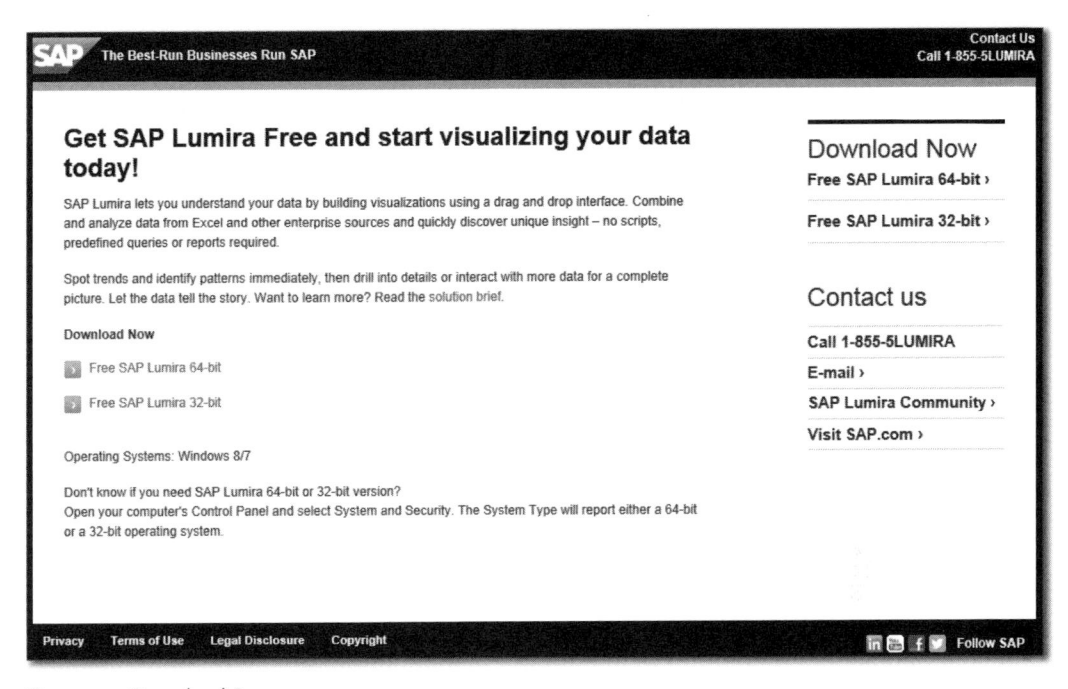

Figure 2.5 Download Page

From this page, you may download the SAP Lumira Installation Manager package and copy it locally on your machine. It is available only for the Windows platform (only Windows 7 and 8 are supported, for both 32-bit or 64-bit operating systems).

2. Click the FREE SAP LUMIRA 64-BIT or FREE SAP LUMIRA 32-BIT link to download the package that corresponds to your operating system.

In order to reduce the download time, the package size has been optimized and remains minimal.

2.3 Installing SAP Lumira Desktop

Once you have downloaded SAP Lumira Installation Manager, it's time to launch it. To do so, follow these steps:

2 | Installation and Configuration of SAP Lumira Desktop

1. The Installation Manager self-extracts its components, and then the SAP LUMIRA SETUP dialog box opens. By default, the installation must go through the five steps that are shown at the top of the dialog box, marking the installation progress.

2. The Installation Manager performs some system requirement checks, as described in Section 2.2. If one of these requirements is not filled, then an error message is displayed in the PREREQUISITES pane, as seen in Figure 2.6. In this case, the install workflow consists of six steps instead of five. The Installation Manager prevents you from moving forward until all requirements are addressed.

You can fix the issues, if any, and then click RETRY (see Figure 2.6).

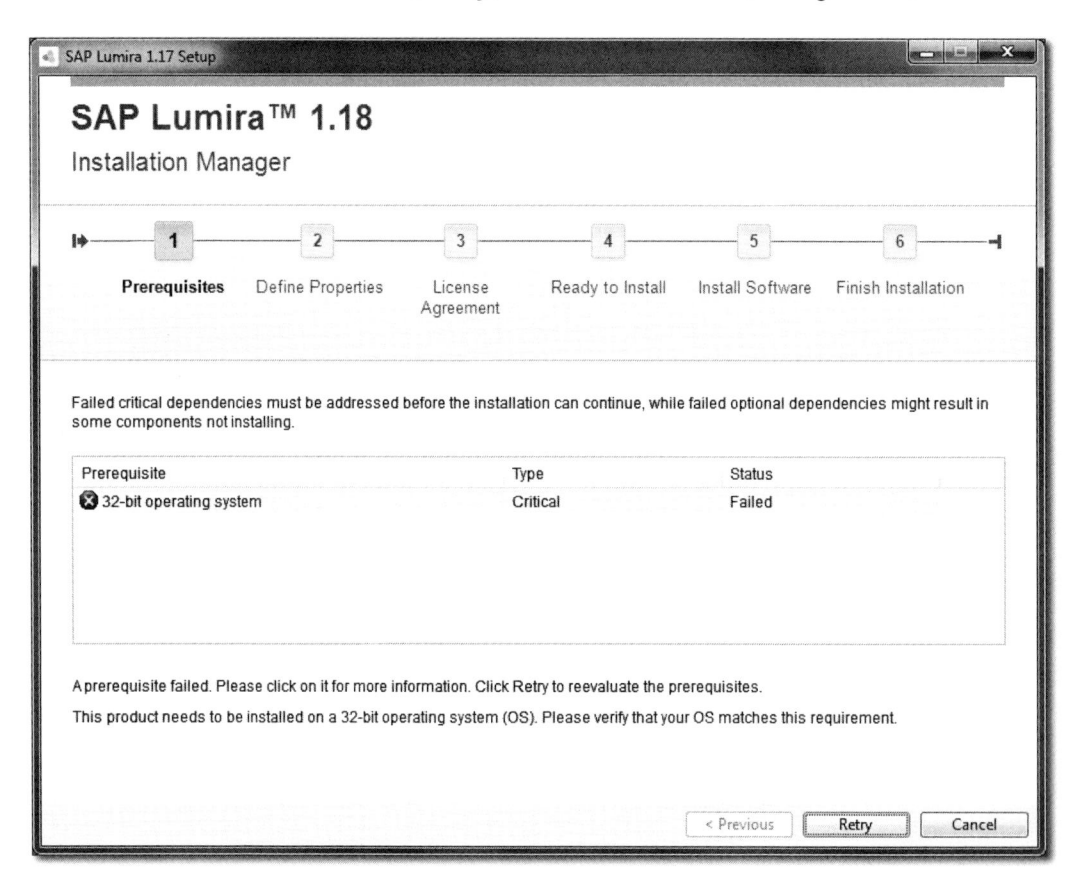

Figure 2.6 SAP Lumira Installation Prerequisites Pane

42

3. If all requirements are met, then in the DEFINE PROPERTIES pane, as shown in Figure 2.7, you may enter the following installation properties:

   ▸ In the SETUP LANGUAGE dropdown menu, select the language for the setup. The available languages are English, French, German, Japanese, Portuguese, Russian, Simplified Chinese, and Spanish.

   ▸ In the ENTER A DESTINATION FOLDER text field, enter the installation folder. By default, this folder is *C:\Program Files\SAP Lumira*. You may click the FOLDER icon to open the BROWSE FOR FOLDER dialog box, navigate in the file system, and select a folder.

4. Click NEXT.

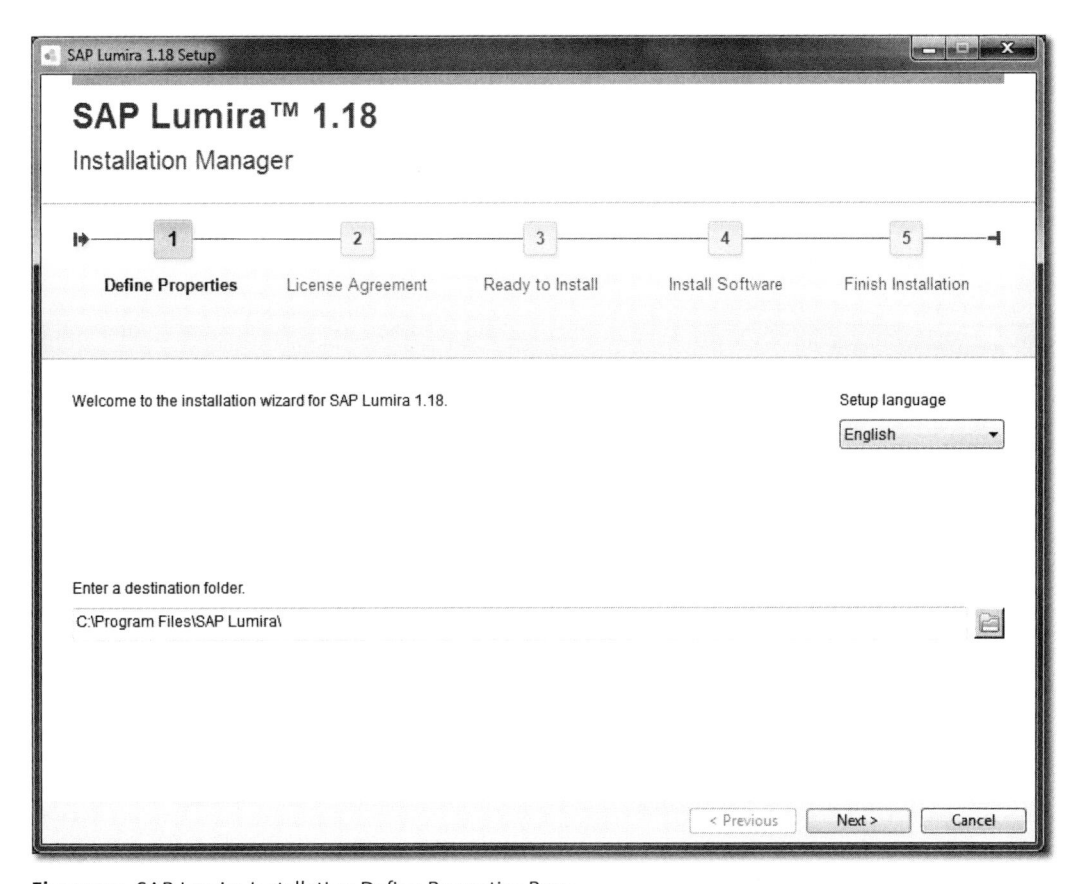

Figure 2.7 SAP Lumira Installation Define Properties Pane

2 | Installation and Configuration of SAP Lumira Desktop

5. In the LICENSE AGREEMENT pane, shown in Figure 2.8, select the I ACCEPT THE LICENSE AGREEMENT checkbox, and then click NEXT.

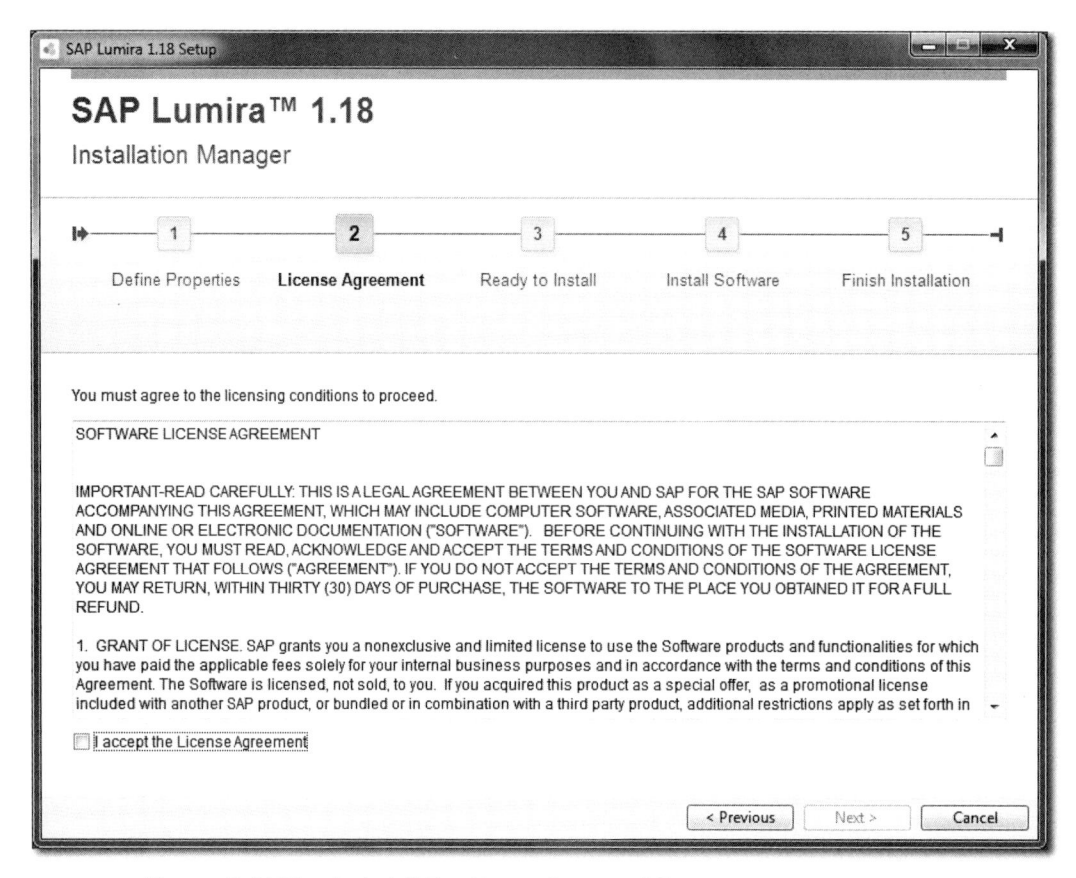

Figure 2.8 SAP Lumira Installation License Agreement Pane

6. In the READY TO INSTALL pane, shown in Figure 2.9, click NEXT to start the installation.

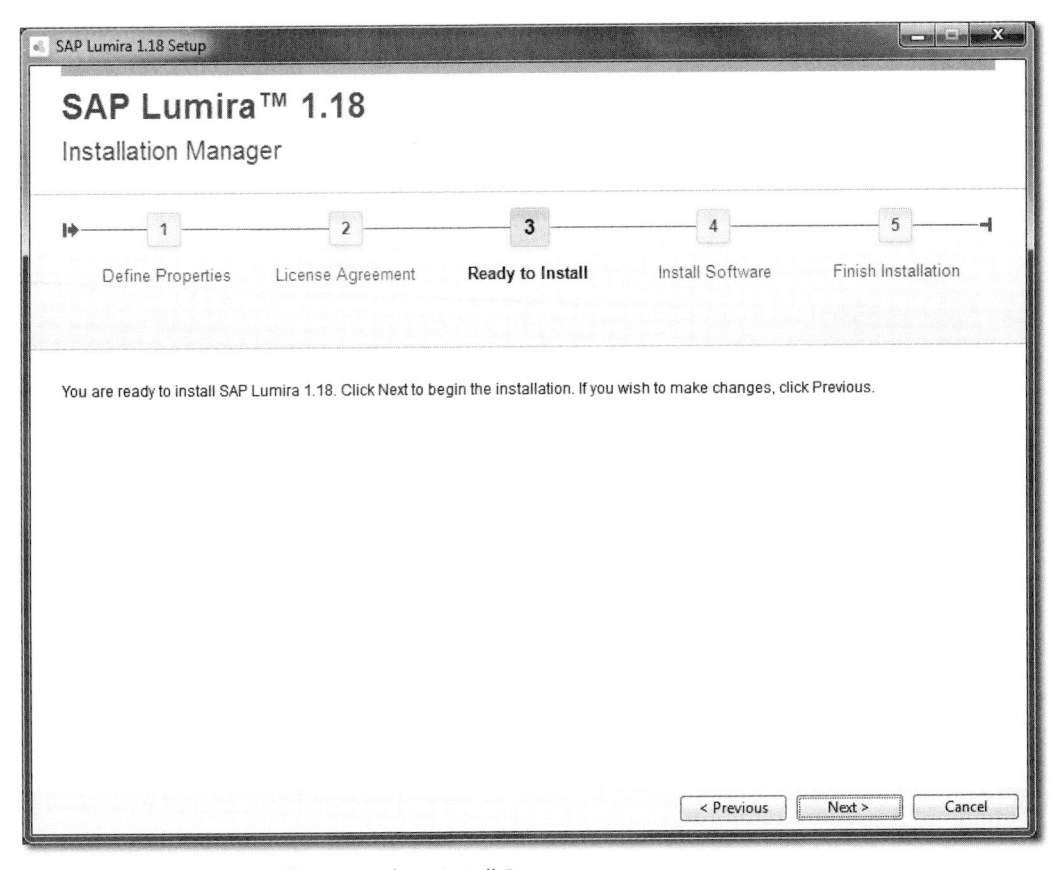

Figure 2.9 SAP Lumira Installation Ready to Install Pane

7. In the INSTALL SOFTWARE pane, a progress bar is displayed while the installation proceeds, as shown in Figure 2.10. The SAP Lumira Installation Manager installs SAP Lumira, which includes the following:

    ▶ Creating the SAP Lumira shortcut on your desktop.
    ▶ Creating the SAP BUSINESS INTELLIGENCE • SAP LUMIRA • SAP LUMIRA command in the START menu.

2   Installation and Configuration of SAP Lumira Desktop

- Creating the SAP LUMIRA DOCUMENTS folder in the MY DOCUMENTS folder. This folder contains the SAMPLES folder, which contains the samples released with SAP Lumira.

- Attaching the .lums extension and icon to the SAP Lumira application and file format (see Section 2.8).

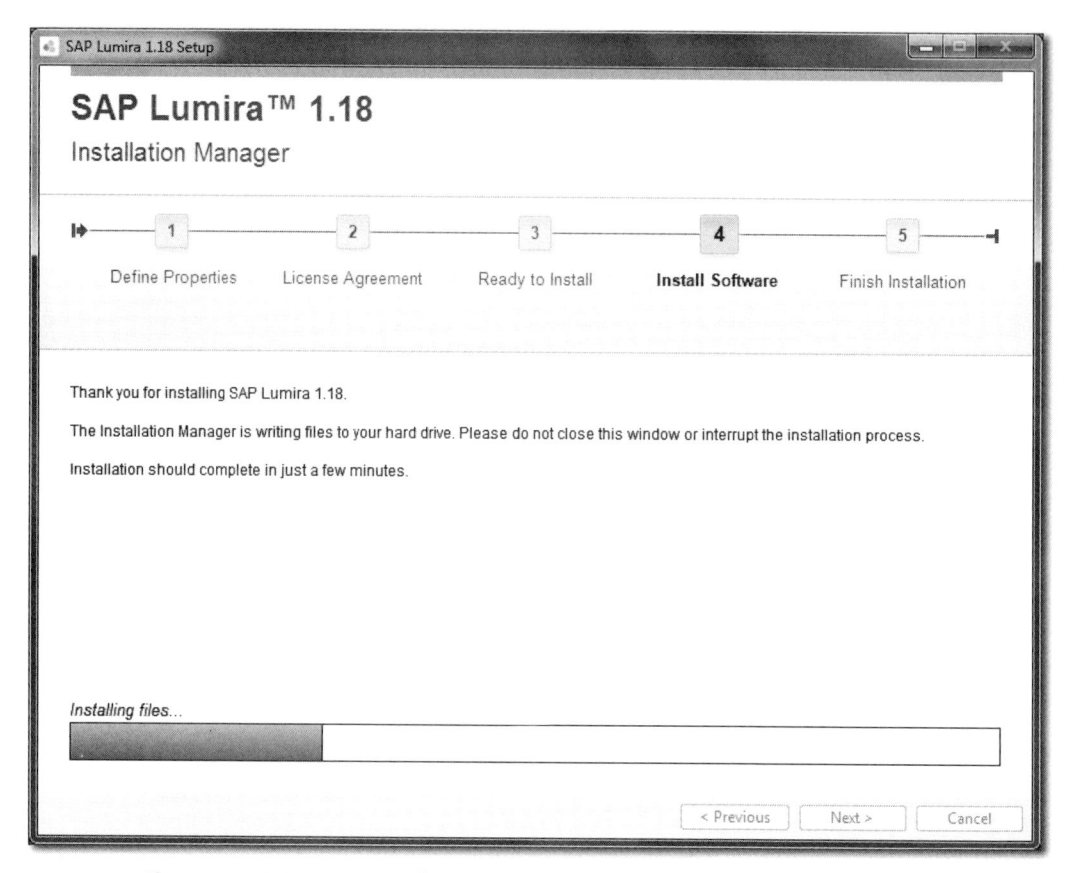

Figure 2.10 SAP Lumira Installation Install Software Pane

8. When the installation is complete, in the FINISH INSTALLATION pane, as shown in Figure 2.11, select the LAUNCH SAP LUMIRA AFTER INSTALLATION COMPLETES checkbox to start SAP Lumira after the Installation Manager closes.

9. Click FINISH to close the Installation Manager.

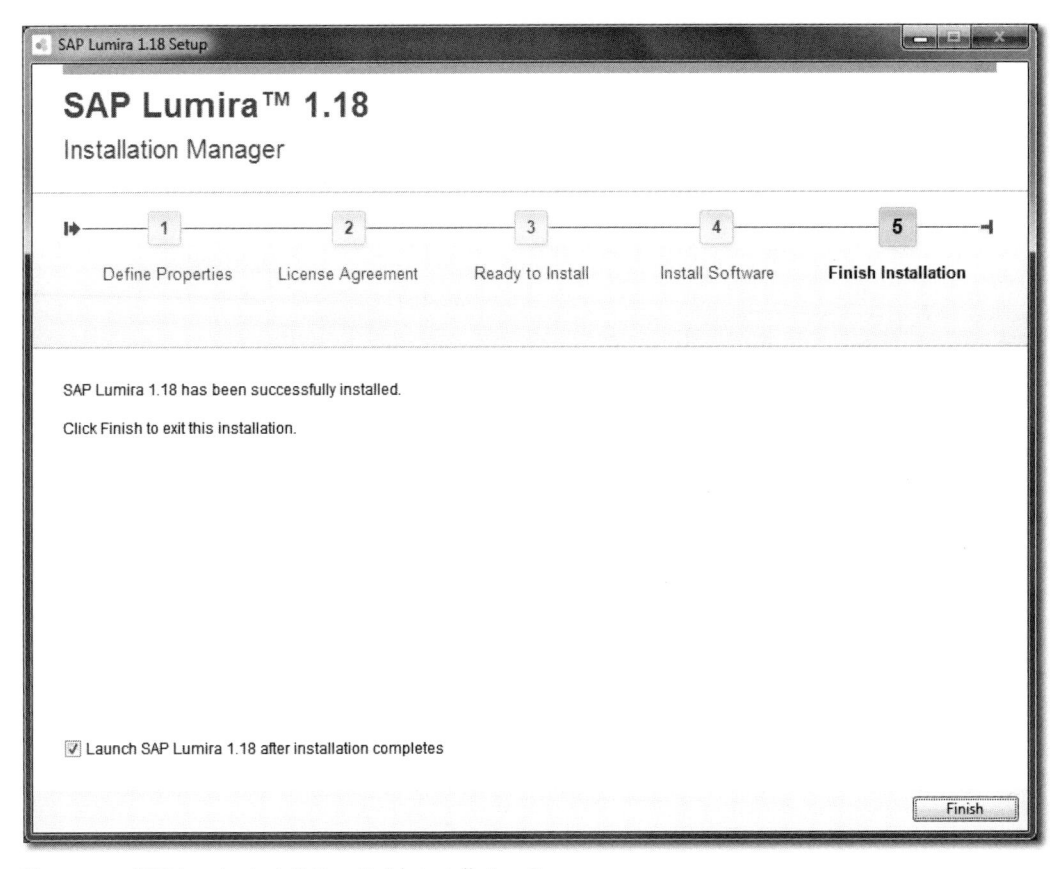

Figure 2.11 SAP Lumira Installation Finish Installation Pane

If you wish to uninstall SAP Lumira, follow the steps in the next section.

2.4 Uninstallating SAP Lumira Desktop

Uninstallation removes SAP Lumira binaries but keeps the SAP Lumira folder that contains documents and the samples.

To uninstall SAP Lumira, follow these steps:

1. If SAP Lumira Desktop or SAP Lumira Agent is running (see Chapter 7, Section 7.5), then close it.
2. Open Windows CONTROL PANEL.
3. In Windows CONTROL PANEL, click UNINSTALL A PROGRAM.
4. In the list of installed programs, select SAP LUMIRA.
5. Click UNINSTALL to open the SAP LUMIRA INSTALLATION MANAGER, as shown in Figure 2.12.

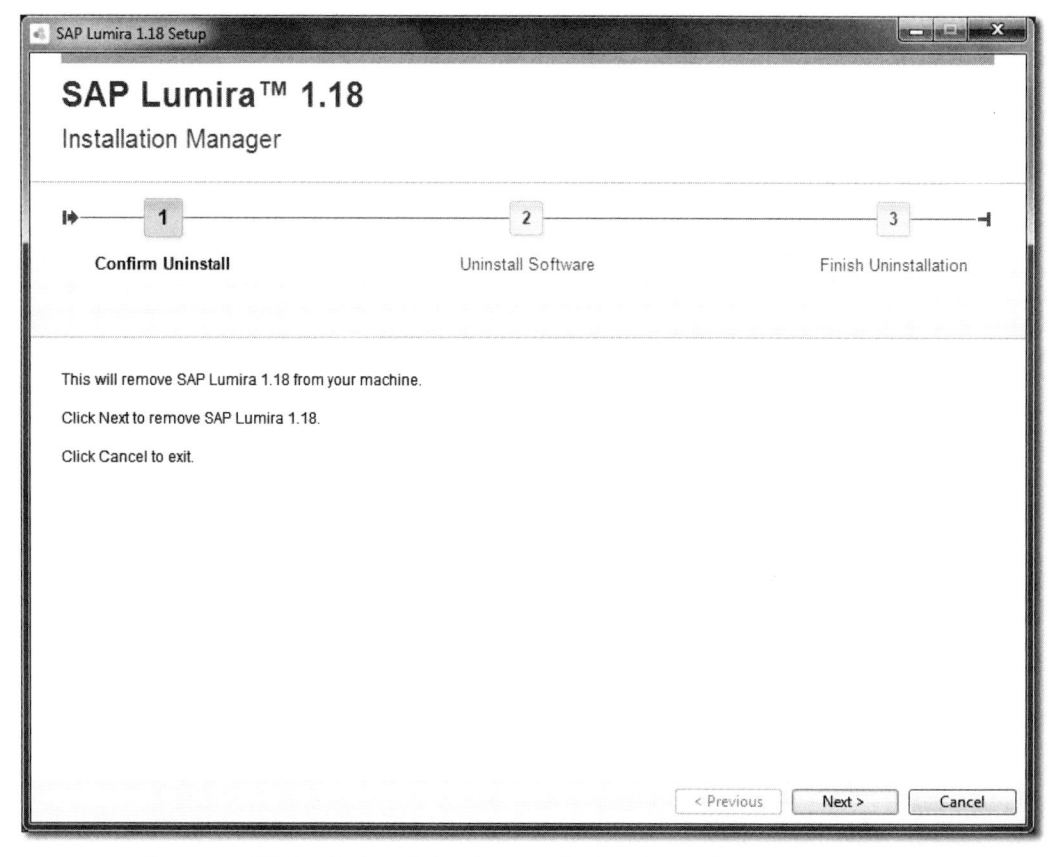

Figure 2.12 SAP Lumira Installation Manager Confirm Uninstall Pane

6. Click NEXT. A progress bar is displayed while the Installation Manager uninstalls SAP Lumira, as shown in Figure 2.13.

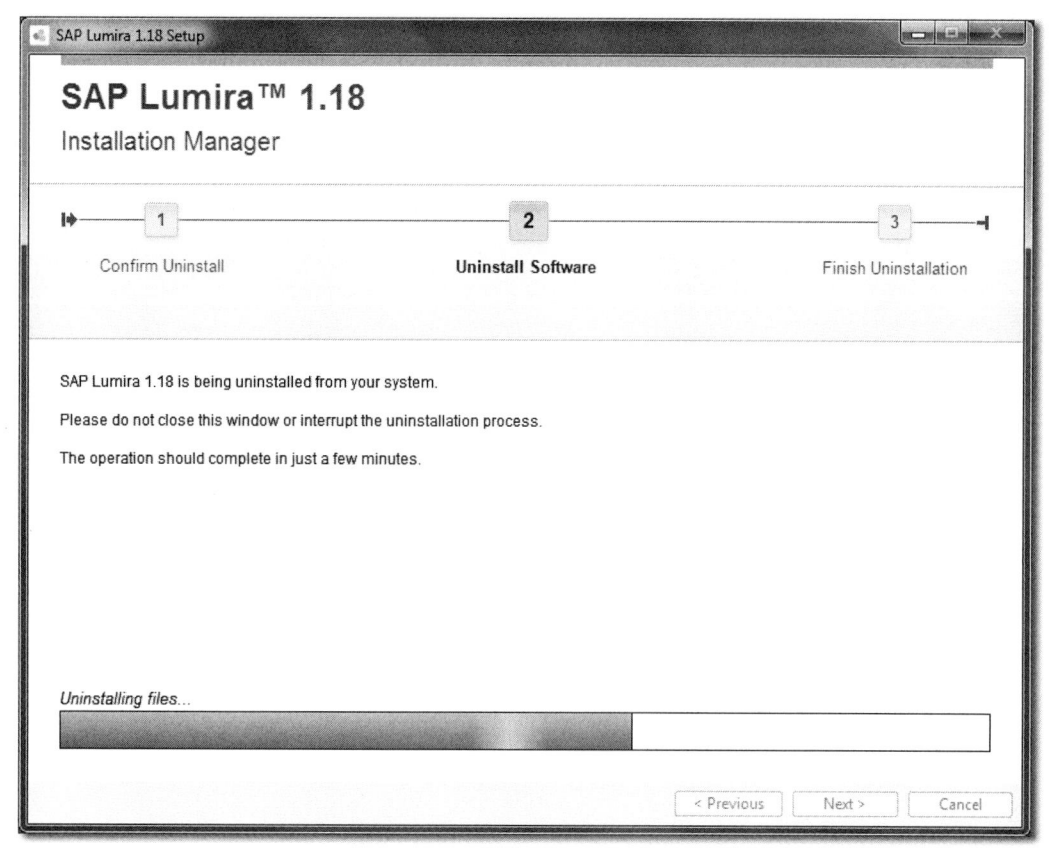

Figure 2.13 SAP Lumira Installation Manager Uninstall Software Pane

7. Once SAP Lumira is uninstalled, click FINISH in the FINISH UNINSTALLATION pane, as shown in Figure 2.14, to close the Installation Manager.

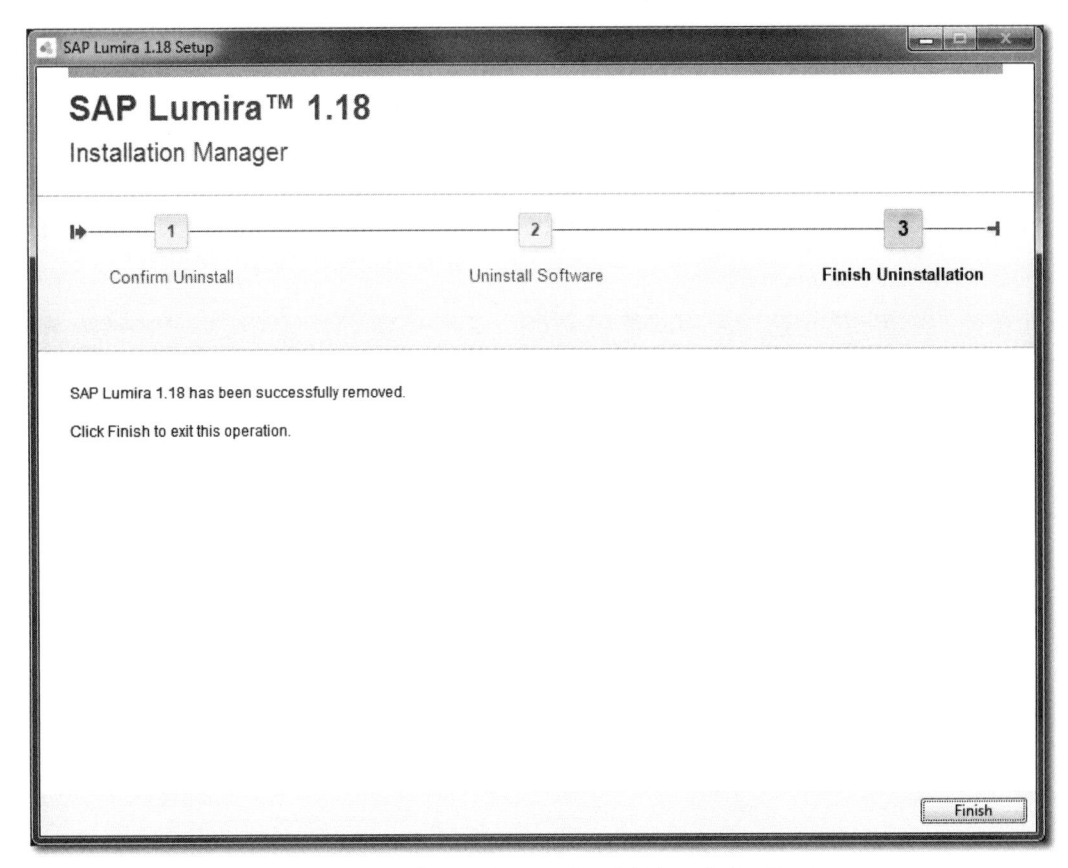

Figure 2.14 SAP Lumira Installation Manager Finish Uninstallation Panel

Assuming that you are looking to install SAP Lumira, the next section discusses the registration process.

2.5   SAP Lumira Registration

When you start SAP Lumira, you must first register it, even if you use the SAP Lumira Personal Edition license.

The first time you start SAP Lumira, the REGISTER YOUR SAP LUMIRA dialog box opens. In this dialog box, click one of the following options in the left pane:

- REGISTER SAP LUMIRA
  Select this option to enter all details for identification and registration. The text fields are displayed in the right pane, as seen in Figure 2.15. The mandatory fields (FIRST NAME, LAST NAME, E-MAIL … and the terms agreement checkbox) are followed by a red asterisk.

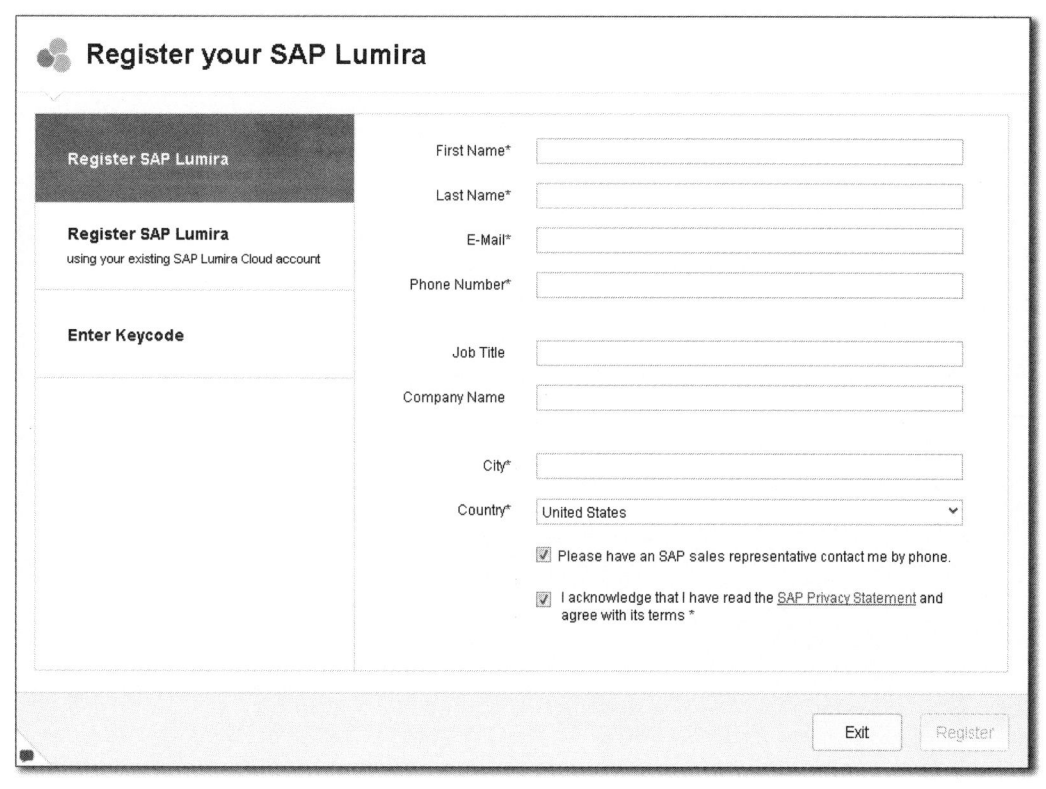

Figure 2.15 Registering SAP Lumira

2 | Installation and Configuration of SAP Lumira Desktop

- ► REGISTER SAP LUMIRA USING YOUR EXISTING SAP LUMIRA CLOUD ACCOUNT
  If you have already created an SAP Lumira Cloud account (see Chapter 8, Section 8.1), you can use it to register SAP Lumira Desktop. Enter your credentials in the E-MAIL ID and PASSWORD text fields, and then click REGISTER, as seen in Figure 2.16.

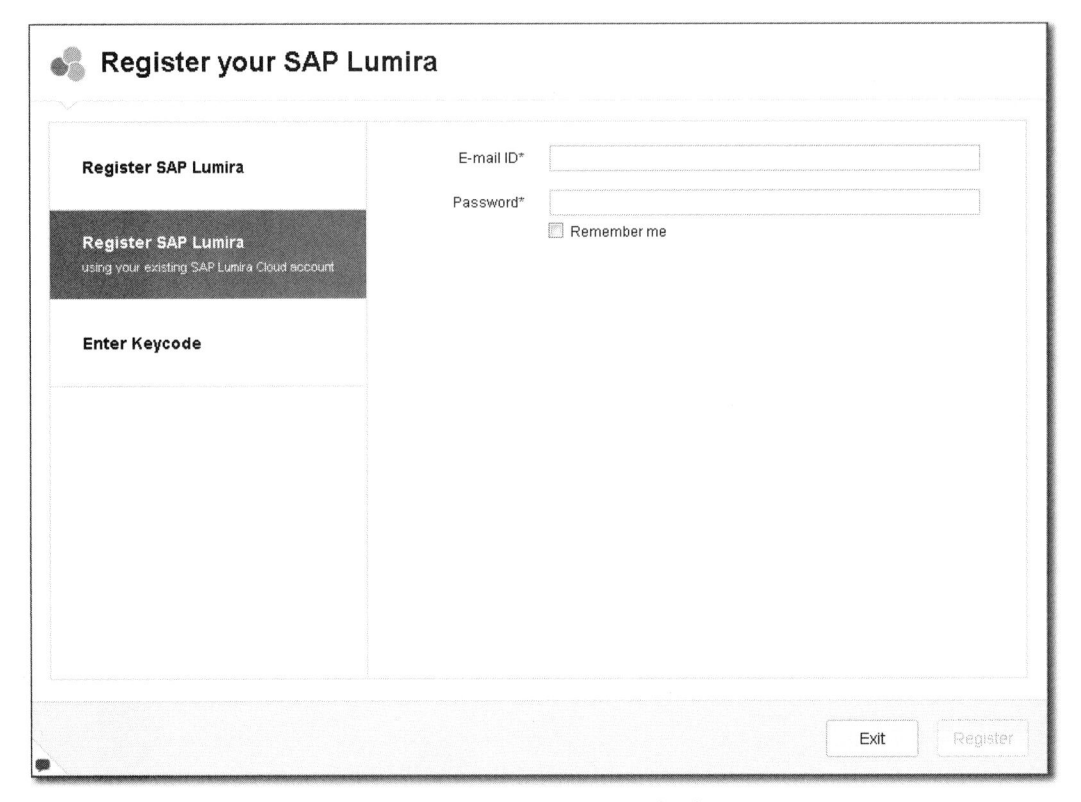

Figure 2.16 Registering SAP Lumira with SAP Lumira Cloud Account

- ► ENTER KEYCODE
  If you have already a keycode, you can use it to register SAP Lumira. Enter this keycode in the KEYCODE text field, as shown in Figure 2.17, and then click REGISTER.

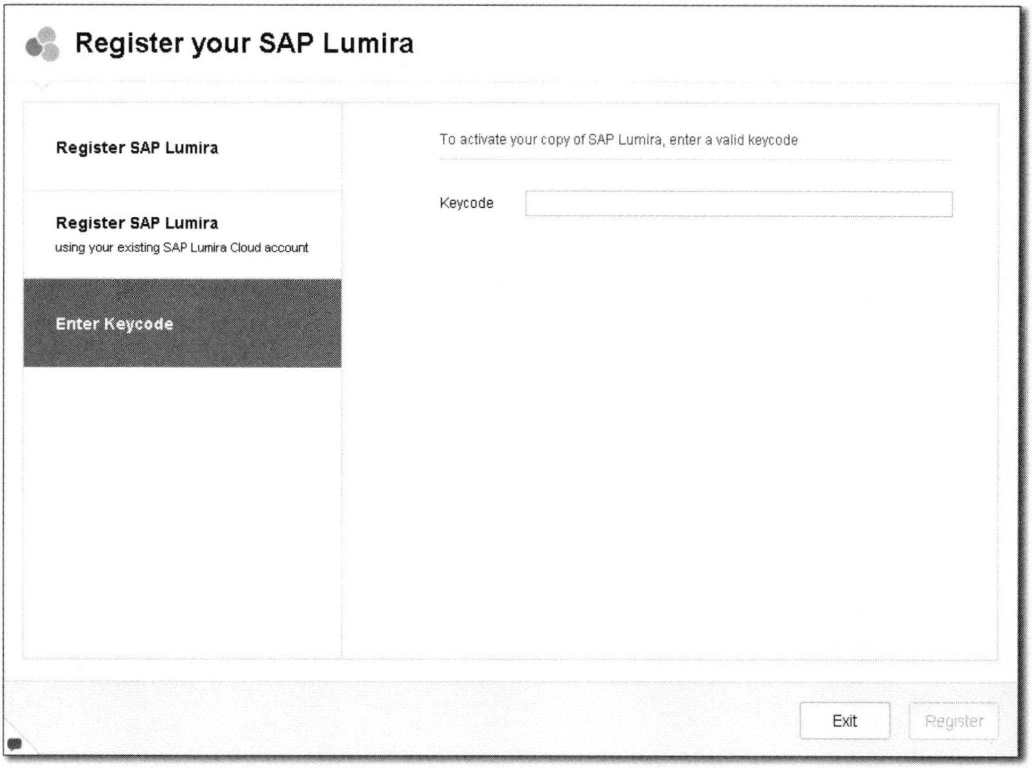

Figure 2.17 Registering SAP Lumira with Keycode

Once you have selected your registration method, click REGISTER to register your installation.

If you select the REGISTER SAP LUMIRA or REGISTER SAP LUMIRA USING YOUR EXISTING SAP LUMIRA CLOUD ACCOUNT option, you need Internet access to register your installation with SAP. If you use a proxy to access the Internet, then SAP Lumira is not able to connect to the SAP server, as shown in Figure 2.18. In this case, click the CLICK HERE FOR PROXY CONFIGURATION link to open the SAP LUMIRA PREFERENCES dialog box, in which you can enter the proxy parameters in the NETWORK section, as described in Section 2.9.

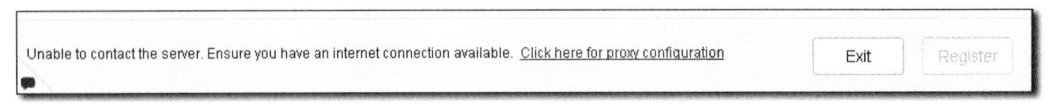

> Unable to contact the server. Ensure you have an internet connection available. Click here for proxy configuration   Exit   Register

Figure 2.18 Proxy Configuration Needed to Register

Next, we will discuss the updating features available for SAP Lumira Desktop.

2.6 Updating SAP Lumira Desktop

SAP Lumira is updated on a regular basis; a new version is released about every two months. It is recommended to always have the latest update to ensure the following benefits:

- Latest supported platforms and defects corrections
- New product enhancements
- Open any version of an SAP Lumira document (it may not be possible to open a document created with a version of SAP Lumira released after your version)

If you have already installed a previous version, you can easily update this version. Furthermore, you can ask SAP Lumira to automatically monitor new updates and warn you when they are available.

In the following sections, we'll explain how to run an update, check for new updates, and how to set up your system to automatically check for updates.

2.6.1 Running Update

When you start an install with the SAP Lumira Installation Manager, if a version of SAP Lumira of a previous release is detected, then the installer asks you to simply update your installation, as seen in Figure 2.19.

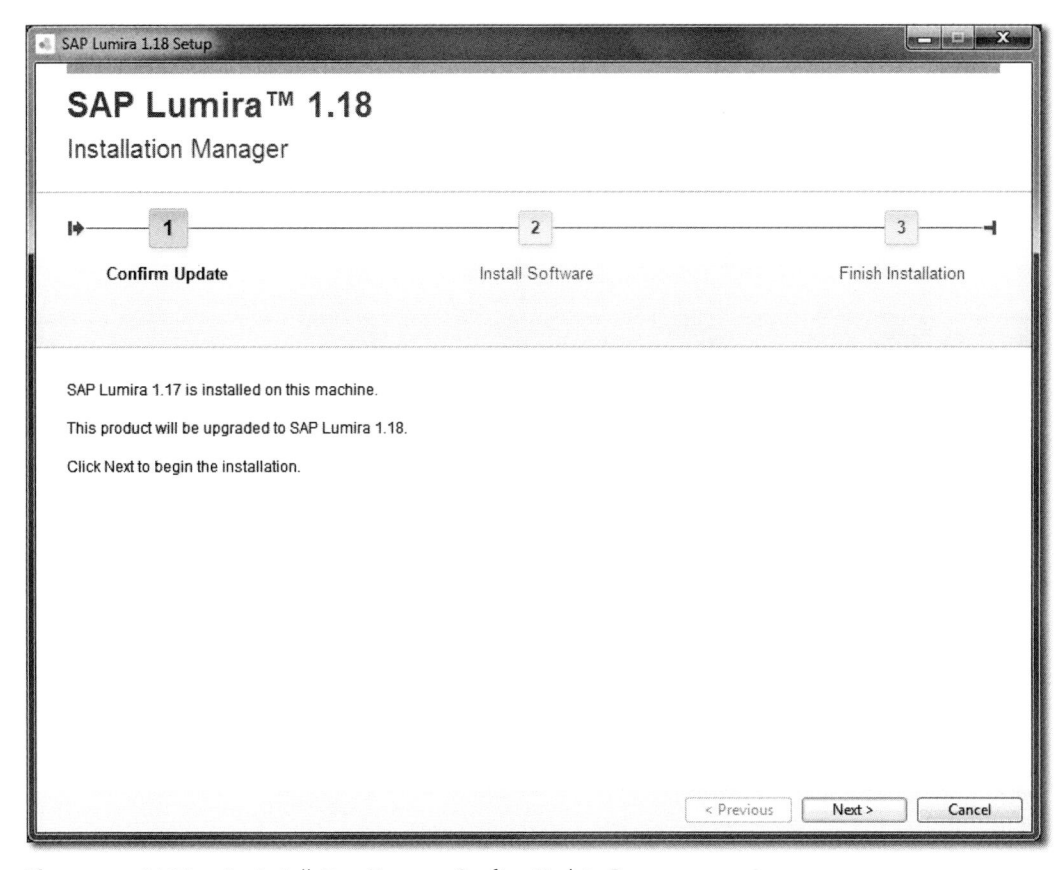

Figure 2.19 SAP Lumira Installation Manager Confirm Update Pane

In this case, simply go through the three panes of the Installation Manager that guide you through this update:

1. Click NEXT to confirm that your version must be updated.
2. Wait while the update progresses, as seen in Figure 2.20. During the update, your installation settings, your keycode, the resources you have created with SAP Lumira, and your preferences are kept.

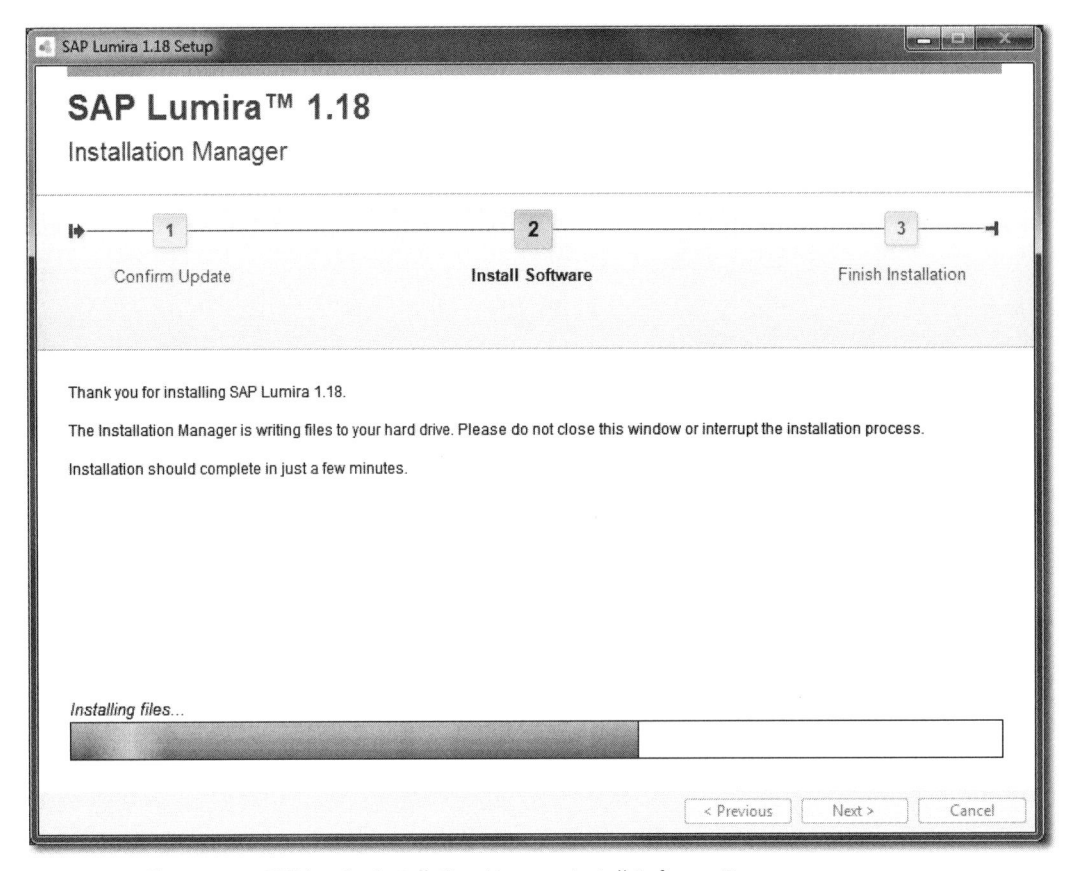

2 | Installation and Configuration of SAP Lumira Desktop

Figure 2.20 SAP Lumira Installation Manager Install Software Pane

3. When the update has completed, in the FINISH INSTALLATION pane shown in Figure 2.21 select the LAUNCH SAP LUMIRA AFTER INSTALLATION COMPLETES checkbox to start SAP Lumira after the Installation Manager closes.

4. Click FINISH to close the Installation Manager.

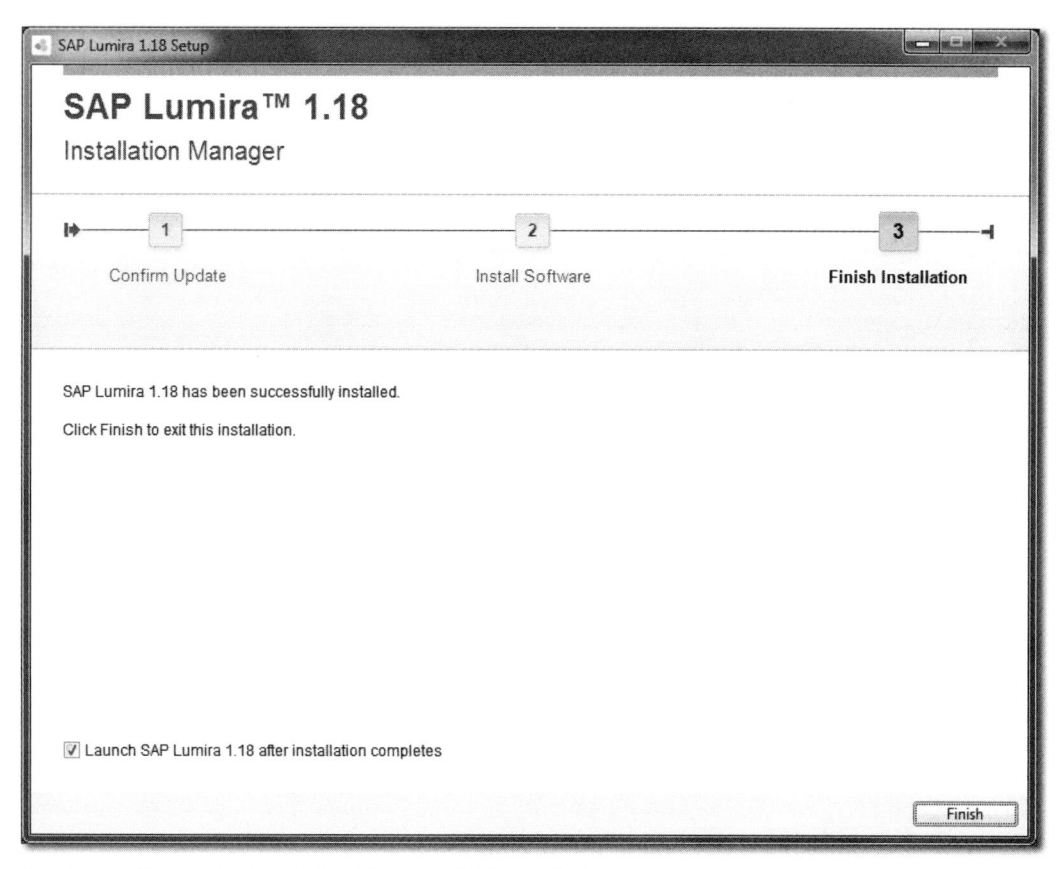

Figure 2.21 SAP Lumira Installation Manager Finish Installation Pane

2.6.2 Checking for New Updates

In SAP Lumira, you can look for new updates by selecting the command HELP •
CHECK FOR NEW UPDATES from the menu bar. If a new update is available, then SAP
Lumira asks if you want to install this new update, as shown in Figure 2.22.

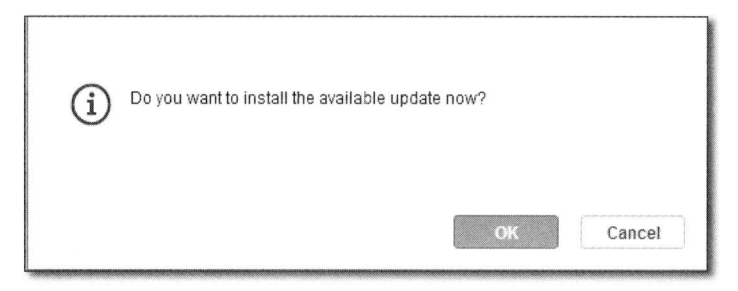

Figure 2.22 Available Update Notification

If you click OK to accept, then the system will take the following actions:

1. SAP Lumira downloads this update and closes.
2. The SAP Lumira Installation Manager self-extracts and is run.
3. SAP Lumira follows the same workflow described in Section 2.6.1 to update SAP Lumira.
4. After the update has completed, you can restart SAP Lumira and benefit from its updates.

2.6.3 Automatically Checking for New Updates

You may also set SAP Lumira's preferences to automatically look for new updates (see Section 2.9). The parameters you can set include the following:

- UPDATES FREQUENCY
  In this dropdown list, select the frequency to check for new updates at startup time (daily, weekly, biweekly, monthly, bimonthly, or none). If you select NONE, then SAP Lumira does not automatically check for updates.
- AUTO UPDATE PROVIDER
  In this dropdown list, you can select the option to check and download SAP Lumira updates from the SAP public website or from the SAP Support website.
- SAP SUPPORT PORTAL USER
  If you select the option to check for updates from the SAP Support website, then enter the account you use to authenticate it.

- SAP Support Portal Password
  If you select the option to check for updates from the SAP Support website, then enter the password associated with the account you use to authenticate it.

At the frequency defined in the Updates Frequency parameter, SAP Lumira checks for new updates at startup time. If a new update is available, then an icon representing a clock is displayed in the status bar, as shown in Figure 2.23, and SAP Lumira asks you to install the new update, as shown in Figure 2.22.

Figure 2.23 Available Update Notification

If you accept, then SAP Lumira closes, and the update process runs, as described in Section 2.6.1. Restart SAP Lumira to take advantage of your update.

If a problem occurs when SAP Lumira checks for available updates, either manually or automatic, then an icon is displayed in the status bar, as shown in Figure 2.24. You may need to check your network connection or the proxy parameters in SAP Lumira preferences (see Section 2.9).

Figure 2.24 Error Notification when Checking for Update

2.7 User Interface Presentation

Once SAP Lumira has been installed, you can start it and discover its innovative interface. The below sections introduce the welcoming page, the "rooms", and the interactive menu bar.

> **Right-click in SAP Lumira**
> SAP Lumira is written in HTML5 to support multiple devices. Typically, right-click on a mouse is generally not supported. To interact with an object or to know if you can interact with an object, look for the little cog icon and click it to open its contextual menu.

2.7.1 Welcome Page

You may launch SAP Lumira from the START menu (SAP BUSINESS INTELLIGENCE • SAP LUMIRA • SAP LUMIRA) or the shortcut created in your desktop during the installation. After the splash screen, SAP Lumira opens with its WELCOME page (see Figure 2.25).

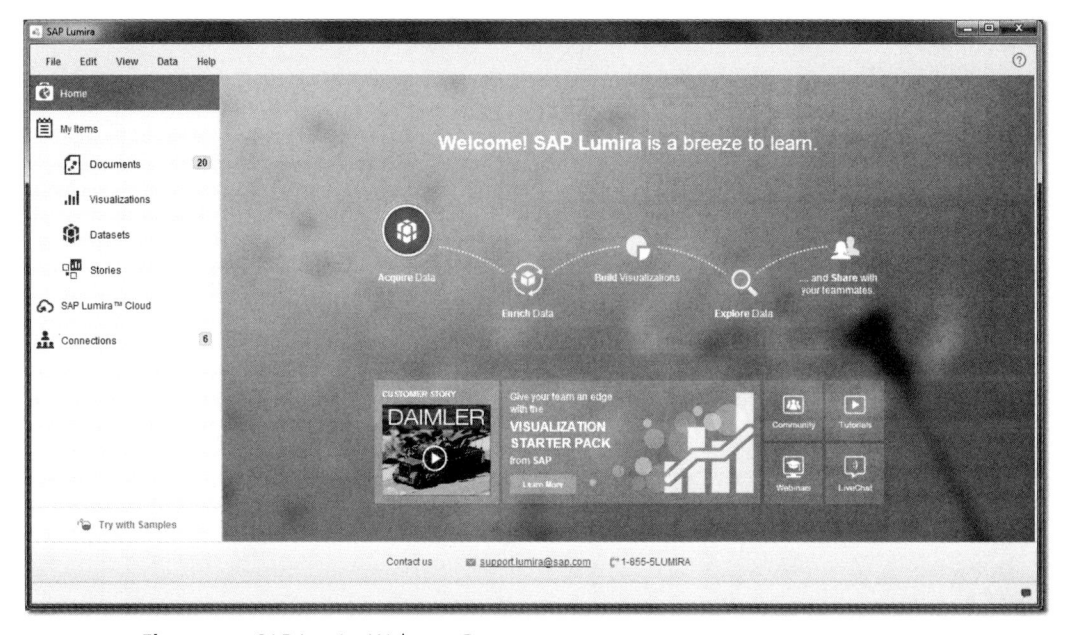

Figure 2.25 SAP Lumira Welcome Page

The WELCOME page's left panel contains different sections that are entry points to several resources. Click them to display the different resources created with SAP Lumira and stored in the SAP Lumira folder. The following are created in your My Documents folder:

- HOME
  As seen in Figure 2.25, this section gives you access via links in the right pane to external webinars and tutorials, the SAP Lumira community on the SAP Developer Network website, and even live chat. You may also click ACQUIRE DATA to create your first dataset (see Chapter 3).

▶ MY ITEMS

Displays the content of the folder used by SAP Lumira to save the resources you have created or need to edit in SAP Lumira Desktop. This SAP Lumira folder is *C:\Users\<Your account>\My Documents\SAP Lumira Documents*. SAP Lumira does not list resources that are saved in this folder's subfolders. Click one of the subsections underneath to filter the resources type to display:

- DOCUMENTS: All SAP Lumira documents stored in this folder, as shown in Figure 2.26.
- VISUALIZATIONS: All visualizations (see Chapter 5) contained in the documents stored in this folder.
- DATASETS: All datasets (see Chapter 3) contained in the documents stored in this folder.
- STORIES: All stories (see Chapter 6) contained in the documents stored in this folder.

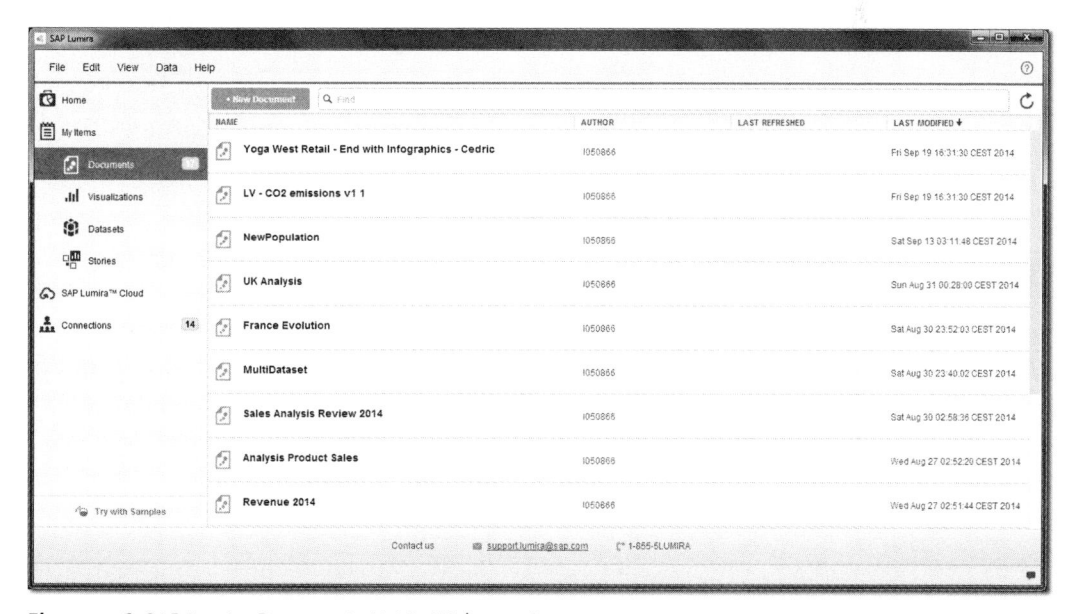

Figure 2.26 SAP Lumira Documents List in Welcome Page

▶ SAP LUMIRA CLOUD

Gives you access to SAP Lumira Cloud (see Chapter 8) and displays the documents saved in this cloud. Accessing the SAP Lumira Cloud requires authentication (see Chapter 8, Section 8.2).

- CONNECTIONS

  Displays all data sources you have used (see Chapter 3). From here, you can modify these data sources' settings and display the documents that use these sources.

- TRY WITH SAMPLES

  Displays the samples installed with the product to demonstrate its capabilities.

The bottom of the WELCOME page contains a link to send an email to SAP Lumira support (technical or sales).

In addition, SAP Lumira comes with several samples you can use to become familiar with the tool and discover its capabilities. These samples are installed in a subfolder of the SAP Lumira documents. For example, on Windows 7, this folder is *C:\Users\<Your account>\My Documents\SAP Lumira Documents\Samples*.

Because these samples are not saved directly in the SAP Lumira document folder, they do not appear in the WELCOME page. To display them, click TRY WITH SAMPLES in the WELCOME page, as shown in Figure 2.27.

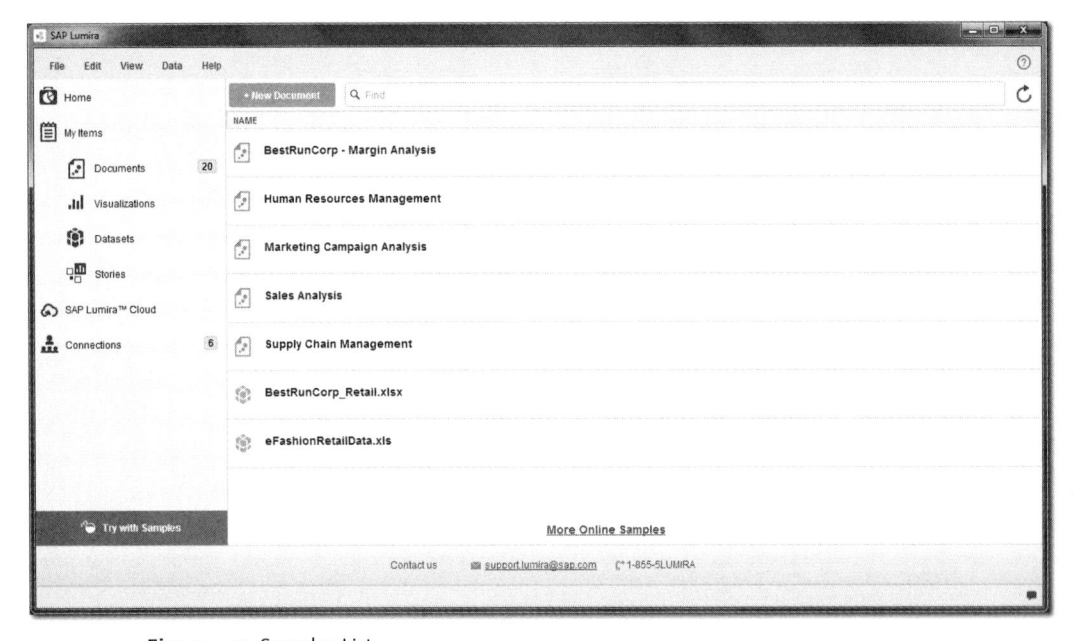

Figure 2.27 Samples List

You can also click MORE ONLINE SAMPLES to connect to the SAP Lumira forum on the SAP Community Network website and access more samples shared by the SAP Lumira community.

2.7.2 Rooms

The SAP Lumira interface contains four workspaces, called rooms, dedicated to a specific set of tasks. Once you have acquired the data to display (see Chapter 3), depending on the task you are doing in the SAP Lumira document you will work in one of these rooms:

- PREPARE
  Edit and manipulate data in the dataset (see Chapter 4)
- VISUALIZE
  Create visualizations from the dataset (see Chapter 5)
- COMPOSE
  Create stories from visualizations (see Chapter 6)
- SHARE
  Share your visualizations and stories with other systems (see Chapter 7)

You can move from one room to another by clicking the corresponding tabs in the menu toolbar, as seen in Figure 2.28. The tab of the current room is highlighted.

Figure 2.28 Rooms Tabs

You can also directly access a room by using the commands in the VIEW menu, as described in next section.

In the SAP Lumira PREFERENCES dialog box, you can select in which room a document you open is displayed by default (see Section 2.9).

> **Predict Room**
> If you install SAP Predictive Analysis, then another room, the PREDICT room, becomes available. The description of this room goes beyond the scope of this book.

2.7.3 Menu Bar

Some commands are available in the SAP Lumira menu bar to perform some common, general actions. The following commands are available:

- In the FILE menu:
    - OPEN: Return to the WELCOME page, where you can open an existing document (see Section 2.8.2).
    - NEW: Open the NEW DATASET dialog box, to create a new dataset (see Chapter 3, Section 3.1.4).
    - IMPORT TO FOLDER: Open an SAP Lumira document from any folder on your file system.
    - SAVE: Save the document. If the document has never been saved, then the SAVE OPTIONS dialog box opens (see Section 2.8.3).
    - SAVE AS: Open the SAVE OPTIONS dialog box, in which you can define where the document must be saved, as described in Section 2.8.3.
    - CLOSE: Close the current document. If you have some unsaved changes in your document, SAP Lumira asks you to save them first.
    - PREFERENCES: Open the SAP LUMIRA PREFERENCES dialog box (see Section 2.9).
    - EXIT: Exit SAP Lumira. If you have some unsaved changes in your document, SAP Lumira asks you to save them first.
- In the EDIT menu, the following commands to undo and redo your changes in the PREPARE room are available:
    - UNDO: This command is available only in the PREPARE room, to undo your previous action.
    - REDO: Reapply an undone action.
- The VIEW menu contains some commands to directly access the PREPARE, VISUALIZE, COMPOSE, or SHARE rooms (see Section 2.7.2).
- In the DATA menu, the following commands to edit the dataset are available:
    - EDIT: Edit the document dataset (see Chapter 3, Section 3.9.2).
    - ADD: Add a new dataset to your document (see Chapter 4, Section 4.8.1).

- COMBINE AS • MERGE: Combine the data from two datasets using the `JOIN` operator (see Chapter 4, Section 4.8.2).
- COMBINE AS • APPEND: Combine the data from two datasets using the `UNION` operator (see Chapter 4, Section 4.8.3).
- CHANGE: Change the document dataset.
- REMOVE: Remove a dataset from a document that contains more than one dataset.
- REFRESH DOCUMENT: Refresh the document dataset (see Chapter 3, Section 3.9.3).

▶ In the HELP menu:
- HELP: Open a browser with SAP Lumira help, available at *http://help.sap.com*.
- CHECK FOR NEW UPDATES: Check if a new update for your SAP Lumira version is available (see Section 2.6.2).
- ENTER KEYCODE: Enter a new keycode (see Section 2.1.2).
- SEND YOUR FEEDBACK: Open a form via which you can directly send your feedback about SAP Lumira to SAP teams (see Section 2.10.2).
- ABOUT SAP LUMIRA: Display copyright and version information.

2.8 SAP Lumira File Format

You can save the resources you create in SAP Lumira in a predefined folder. These documents are saved using a dedicated file format.

2.8.1 File Extensions and Location

SAP Lumira uses the SAP Lumira Documents folder located in your personal folder in the file system as its reference folder to store all SAP Lumira documents. For example, on Windows 7, this folder is *C:\Users\<Your name>\Documents\SAP Lumira Documents*.

Any content created in SAP Lumira can be saved using the SAP Lumira document file format, which can store the following:

- Data source parameters
- Retrieved datasets and the query to retrieve them (a dataset is not saved if you access your data source in online mode; see Chapter 3, Section 3.1.3)
- Enriched metadata
- Visualizations
- Stories (interactive boards, reports, or infographics)

The file extension for an SAP Lumira document is .lums. SAP Lumira is backward compatible; you can open documents created with previous versions of SAP Lumira.

> **SAP Visual Intelligence File Format**
>
> SAP Lumira was previously named Visual Intelligence and supported another file extension, .svid. This file format remains compatible; you can open such files with SAP Lumira. But, if you modify such file and needs to save it, it is saved using the latest SAP Lumira file format.

This file format has no enterprise security capabilities, and therefore no password is required to open it; once on a file system, anyone can open these files with SAP Lumira.

2.8.2 Creating and Opening Documents

To create a new document in SAP Lumira, you need to create a new dataset (this process is described in Chapter 3).

The SAP Lumira Documents folder is the reference folder that contains all SAP Lumira documents. To open a document stored in this folder, go to the WELCOME page and select the document to open, as described in Section 2.7.1.

You may also open an SAP Lumira document that is not saved in this folder, but SAP Lumira has to copy it into this folder first. This is done via the import process described in the following steps:

1. In the menu bar, select FILE IMPORT TO FOLDER to open the OPEN dialog box.
2. Use this dialog box to navigate in the folder tree and select the document to open.
3. Click OPEN to close the dialog box and copy the document into the SAP Lumira Documents folder.
4. In the message box that appears, click YES to confirm and open the document in your default room (see Section 2.7.2).

2.8.3 Saving and Closing Document

You need to save your current document to avoid losing your work. SAP Lumira saves your document in your SAP Lumira Documents folder.

Documents can be saved only in the latest supported file format. If you have opened and modified a document created with a previous version of SAP Lumira that used a deprecated file format, then before saving the document you must confirm its conversion, as shown in Figure 2.29. Once converted, you cannot open the converted file with the version used to create the document.

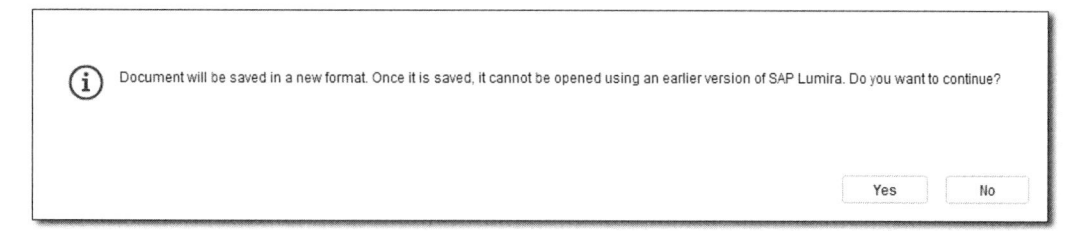

Figure 2.29 File Conversion Confirmation

To save an SAP Lumira document, follow these steps:

1. From the menu bar, select the FILE • SAVE AS command to open the SAVE OPTIONS dialog box, as shown in Figure 2.30.
2. Keep the LOCAL button selected to save your document in your file system in the SAP Lumira Documents folder.

   The SAP LUMIRA CLOUD button is used to save the document in SAP Lumira Cloud, as described in Chapter 7, Section 7.6.

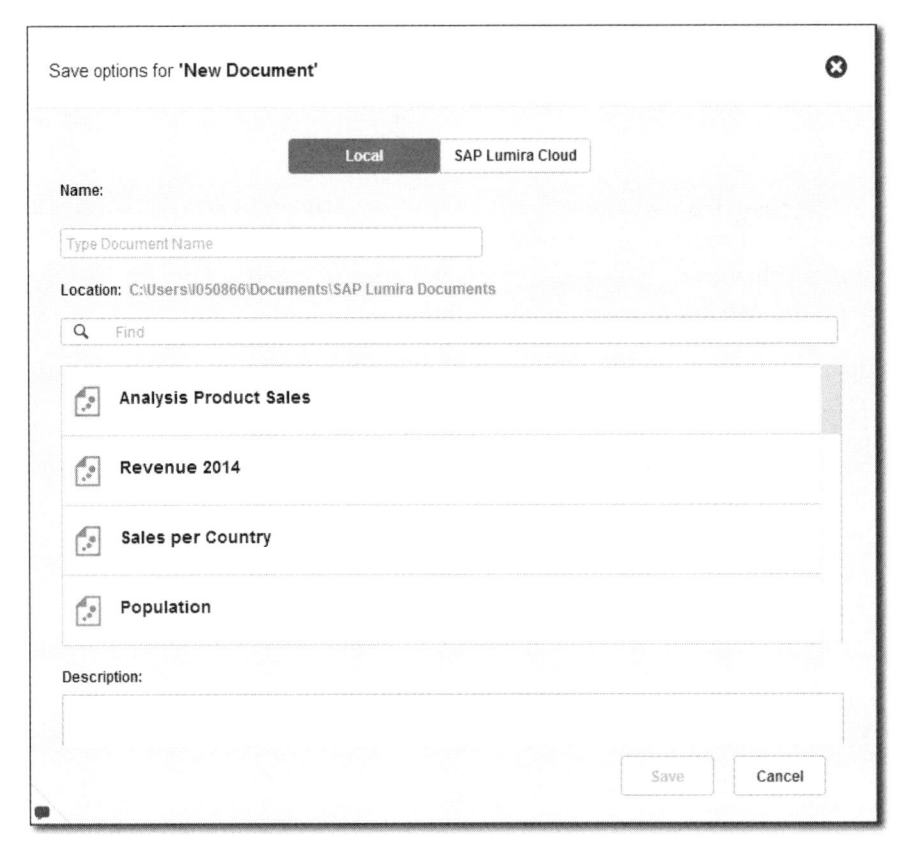

Figure 2.30 Save Dialog Box

3. In the NAME text field, enter the document name. The forbidden characters (*, /, \, ", ?, etc.) are removed as you type them in the document name.

   You may also click a name in the list of recently saved documents to replace the selected document with the document you wish to save. The FIND text field allows you to find a specific document: as you type your text in this field, the list is filtered to display only documents whose name fits this pattern.

4. If required, enter a comment in the DESCRIPTION text field.

If you select the FILE • SAVE command from the menu bar and the document has never been saved, then the SAVE OPTIONS dialog box will appear so that you can save the document as described previously. Otherwise, the document is saved with the name you have already given.

If you select the FILE • CLOSE or FILE • EXIT command from the menu bar to close a document or exit SAP Lumira and some changes have not yet been saved, then SAP Lumira asks you to save your changes first.

2.9   Setting Preferences

SAP Lumira behavior can be modified through some parameters that you can set as preferences. Modify these parameters by following these steps:

1. In the menu bar, select the FILE • PREFERENCES command to open the LUMIRA PREFERENCES dialog box. As shown in Figure 2.31, these parameters are organized by categories listed in the right side of the dialog box.

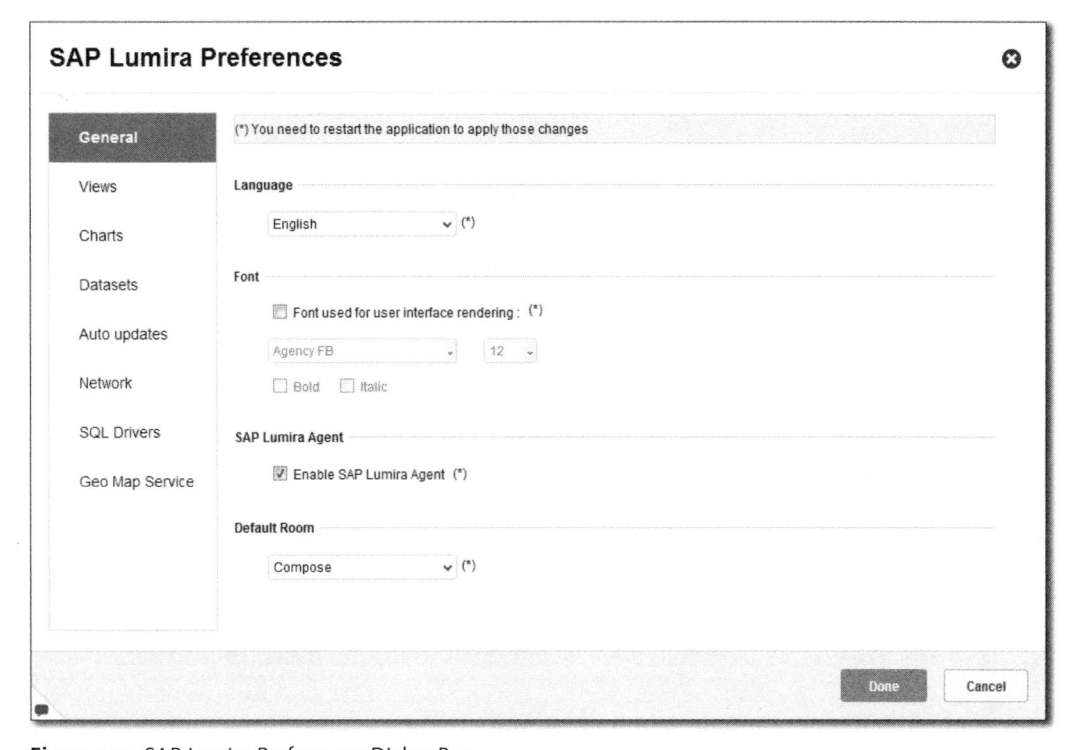

Figure 2.31 SAP Lumira Preferences Dialog Box

2. Select a category to display the corresponding parameters. These categories and their parameters are described in Table 2.1.

3. Modify your parameters.
4. Click DONE to save your changes.

Categories	Parameters
GENERAL	This category contains parameters that apply globally to SAP Lumira: ▸ LANGUAGE: In this dropdown list, select the user interface language. Available languages are English, French, German, Japanese, Portuguese, Russian, Simplified Chinese, and Spanish. ▸ FONT USED FOR UI RENDERING: Select this checkbox to select the font to use in the SAP Lumira interface. If this checkbox is selected, then you can set the font, its size, and typefaces in the FONTS and FONTS SIZE dropdown menus and via the BOLD and ITALIC checkboxes. ▸ ENABLE SAP LUMIRA AGENT: Select this checkbox to start the SAP Lumira Agent the next time you restart SAP Lumira (see Chapter 7, Section 7.5). ▸ DEFAULT ROOM: In this dropdown list, select the room to display by default.
VIEWS	In this category, for each data source type supported by SAP Lumira you can select if the dataset retrieved from such a data source must be displayed as a grid or as facets (see Chapter 4, Section 4.1) by selecting the corresponding option in the dropdown list.
CHARTS	This category gathers the parameters that apply to the VISUALIZE room: ▸ FEEDER PANEL POSITION: use these radio buttons to display the CHART FEEDER on the left or the right. ▸ COLOR PALETTE: in this dropdown list, select the color palette for visualization. The colors of the selected palette are displayed on top of this dropdown list. ▸ TEMPLATE: In this dropdown list, select a look and feel for visualizations. The possible choices include STANDARD for a normal display, FLASHY to use graphical effects, and HIGH CONTRAST to use a black background and use a negative effect. ▸ FONT ZOOM: In this dropdown list, select the zoom ratio to display text in visualizations.
DATASETS	This category contains parameters to enable or disable some time-consuming processing when retrieving datasets from data sources: automatic detection and statistics display (see Chapter 3, Section 3.1.6).

Table 2.1 SAP Lumira Preferences Options

Categories	Parameters
AUTO UPDATES	The parameters in this category define how SAP Lumira checks for new updates (see Section 2.6.2).
NETWORK	This category contains parameters needed to configure an HTTP proxy if you need one for network access, which is required for some SQL drivers based on HTTP or connection to SAP Lumira Cloud, SAP HANA, or SAP StreamWork. Select the CONFIGURE PROXY checkbox to configure an HTTP proxy, and then enter the remaining parameters used to identify it: ▸ HTTP PROXY SERVER: The server hosting the proxy. You must enter a server name ("myserver") and not a URL ("http://myserver"). ▸ HTTP PROXY PORT: The proxy server port. ▸ HTTP PROXY USER and HTTP PROXY PASSWORD: If any, the user and password needed to authenticate the proxy server. This category contains also default values to access SAP systems: ▸ The URLs to connect to SAP Lumira Cloud, SAP Lumira Server, SAP BusinessObjects BI Server, and to send your feedback (see Section 2.10.2) ▸ The URL to connect to SAP StreamWork and the consumer key and consumer secret you must provide to authenticate it.
SQL DRIVERS	This category allows you to manage the drivers to access relational databases. It lists the supported data sources and allows you to install or uninstall their drivers. For more details, see Chapter 3, Section 3.5.2.
GEO MAP SERVICE	This category allows you to enable geo maps from the Esri ArcGIS service if you have a registered account. ▸ ESRI ARCGIS ONLINE: Select this checkbox if you have an Esri ArcGIS account and want to use their geo maps in your visualizations. ▸ USER NAME and PASSWORD: Enter your credentials for the Esri ArcGIS service.

Table 2.1 SAP Lumira Preferences Options (Cont.)

2.10 Supportability

SAP Lumira supportability is intended to ease your everyday work with SAP Lumira, especially if you have a functional or technical problem to resolve. From SAP Lumira, you can easily access its online help or directly send feedback to SAP teams. To ease troubleshooting, SAP Lumira allows you to review its error messages and proposes tracing framework.

> **Support Components**
>
> The components available to escalate incidents to SAP Support consist of the following:
> - BI-LUM-DSK for SAP Lumira Desktop
> - BI-LUM-OD for SAP Lumira Cloud (see Chapter 8)
> - BI-LUM-SRV for SAP Lumira Server (see Chapter 9)

2.10.1 Online Help

In SAP Lumira, you have different options to access the Online Help:

- From the menu bar, select the HELP • HELP command.
- Click the HELP icon, located in the top-right corner of the rooms, as shown in Figure 2.32.

Figure 2.32 Help Icon

In both cases, your default browser opens with the SAP Lumira Online Help on the SAP Help website.

2.10.2 Sending Feedback

From SAP Lumira, you can directly communicate to the SAP teams and send them feedback or technical issues. This can be useful when you encounter an issue you want to remedy. When sending this feedback, SAP Lumira can automatically embed a screenshot of your SAP Lumira screen and your log file.

To send feedback about SAP Lumira, follow these steps:

1. Open the SEND YOUR FEEDBACK dialog box, as shown in Figure 2.33, in one of two ways:
    - In the menu bar, select the HELP • SEND YOUR FEEDBACK command.
    - Click the BALLOON icon located on the right side of the SAP Lumira status bar or in the bottom-left corner of most dialog boxes.

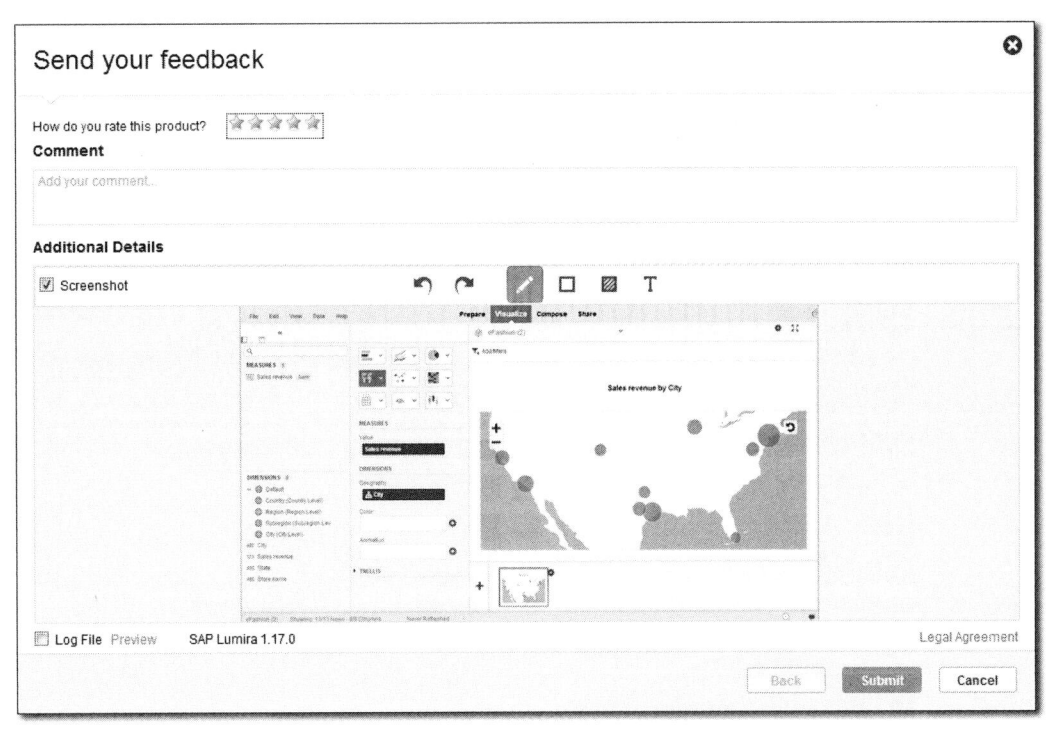

Figure 2.33 Send Your Feedback Dialog Box

2. Once the dialog box is open, you may rate the product by clicking the stars.
3. Type a description of your issue in the COMMENT text field.
4. By default, a screenshot of the application is included in your feedback. Unselect the SCREENSHOT checkbox to not include it.
5. If you include the screenshot, then you can perform some simple edits to it through the buttons located on top of the screenshot. These buttons are described in Table 2.2.
6. Select the LOG FILE checkbox to add the log file to your feedback. You may click the PREVIEW link to display and review this log file content before sending it.
7. Click SUBMIT to close the dialog box and send your feedback.

Button	Description
↶	Undo a previous change in the screenshot editor.
↷	Redo a previously undone change.
✎	Draw on the screenshot.
□	Add a rectangle to the screenshot.
▨	Add a filled rectangle to the screenshot. You can use this to hide a sensitive part of the screenshot.
T	Add some text to the screenshot. Once you have clicked this button, type your text in the text field that appears. With your mouse, select and move this text field around the screenshot, and click on it to add it.

Table 2.2 Screenshot Editor Toolbar Buttons

2.10.3 Error Messages

You can easily review the error messages that may arise when you are using SAP Lumira. When an error message happens, a red icon is displayed in the right side of the status bar, as shown in Figure 2.34.

Figure 2.34 Error Notification in SAP Lumira Status Bar

Click this icon to open the ERRORS dialog box, as shown in Figure 2.35.

This dialog box lists the different error messages raised by SAP Lumira in the current session. In this dialog box, you can:

- click an error message to display more details on it in the DETAILS pane;
- click the CLEAR ALL link to remove all errors from the ERRORS dialog box (these errors are also removed when you exit SAP Lumira);
- click OK to close the ERRORS dialog box.

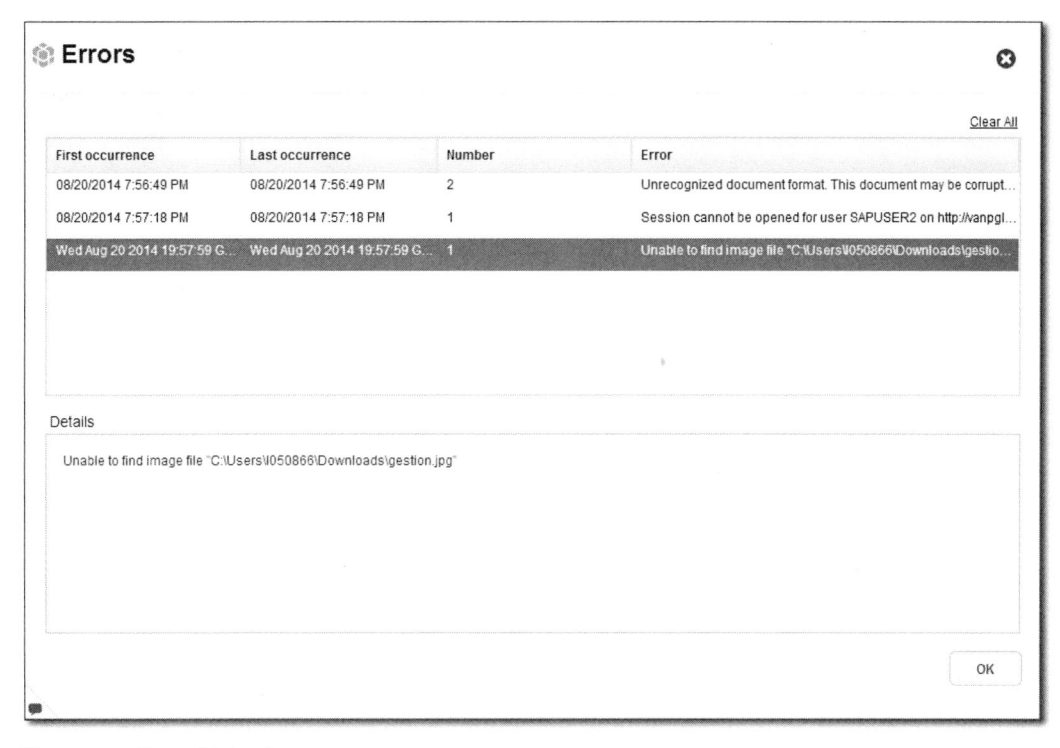

Figure 2.35 Errors Dialog Box

2.10.4 Tracing

SAP Lumira supports the same trace mechanism supported by other SAP BusinessObjects BI products and based on the BO_trace.ini file. This file is located in the *<installation folder>\SAPLumira\Desktop* folder and is used to configure tracing.

To enable the tracing mechanism and set its different parameters, open this file for editing, modify it, and save it. The possible parameters you can set in this file are described in Table 2.3. Any line starting with // or # is seen as a comment and is not taken into consideration.

Parameter	Description
active	Enables the trace mechanism. Possible values are true, to enable it, or false, to disable it.
importance	Defines the importance of the events to be logged. Possible values are shirt-size codes: xs (all possible events are saved), s, m, l, and xl (only the most important events are saved).
alert	Enables the trace mechanism for severe system events. Possible values are true, to enable it, or false, to disable it. Default value is true.
severity	Defines the type of events to be logged. Possible values include the following: ▸ assert: Log only the critical errors. These assert calls can usually only be exploited by SAP support. ▸ error: Log the assert calls and the errors. ▸ warning: Log the assert calls, the errors, and the warnings. ▸ success: Log everything, even the successful events. Default value is error.
size	Maximum number of events saved in the trace file.
keep	Defines if a trace file must be kept once it has reached its maximum size, as defined by the size parameter. Possible values are true, to keep and rename the trace file, or false, to delete it and create a new one.
log_dir	Defines the folder where the trace file is saved; by default, this is the *sapvi/logs* folder in the folder defined by your TMP environment variable. For example, if your TMP is defined by *%USERPROFILE%\AppData\Local\Temp*, then these files are saved in the *C:\Users\<your account>\AppData\Local\Temp\sapvi\logs* folder.
log_ext	Defines the trace file extension; by default, this is .log.

Table 2.3 BO_trace.ini Parameters Description

By default, tracing is enabled and logs those traces with levels of greater than medium importance. Trace files are saved under the name *TraceLog_<**processID**>_<**date**>_<**time**>_trace.<**log_ext**>*—for example, *TraceLog_304_2014_05_04_13_49_21_675_trace.log*.

2.11 Summary

The first steps in SAP Lumira are straightforward, letting you focus on the tool's capabilities. A simple license model provides a free license for personal use and other licenses for enterprise use. Simplified workflows allow you to download, install, update, and uninstall SAP Lumira within a few clicks.

The tool interface is also very simple to learn, with a Welcome page, rooms that clearly identify the actions by areas, supportability features, preferences to fine-tune the tool, and some samples to discover its capabilities.

To save its created resources, SAP Lumira supports its own file format, the extension of which is .lums.

In the next chapter, we will take a look at how to use SAP Lumira for data acquisition.

The first step in creating an SAP Lumira document is data acquisition. This is the process through which you will retrieve data from one of the data sources SAP Lumira supports.

3 Data Acquisition

Retrieving a dataset for display is the first step in creating a document in SAP Lumira. SAP Lumira can query such data from common data sources.

For most data sources, this data acquisition is done offline: the dataset is retrieved from the data source, handled in an internal, in-memory database, and saved in the SAP Lumira document. For SAP HANA and SAP BW, another mode is available, in which the dataset remains in the data source and is only referenced by the SAP Lumira document.

Datasets are created through the NEW DATASET wizard which allows you to select your data source and provide the requested parameters to locate and connect to it. This dialog box adapts to the data source type to query: it can be an SQL query editor for relational databases, a query panel with context, and parameters support for universes.

Once the dataset has been created, you can refresh it to retrieve the latest data from the data source or modify how it is created.

This chapter first describes generalities about how data acquisition is managed in SAP Lumira Desktop. Then, it describes specificities and options for all data sources SAP Lumira can query. To begin, an overview will be provided of what data acquisitions entails in SAP Lumira.

3.1 Data Acquisition Overview

Data acquisition is an important step when creating an SAP Lumira document, and understanding its general workflows can be helpful to optimize this step.

Although SAP Lumira supports different data sources, they all share some common characteristics, which are described in this section.

3.1.1 Supported Data Sources

SAP Lumira can natively access a large range of data sources. Those include:

- Text files saved locally on your file system.
- Microsoft Excel files saved locally on your file system.
- Relational databases, Hadoop databases, and OData data sources through direct Structured Query Language (SQL).
- SAP HANA, the SAP in-memory database and application platform.
- SAP BusinessObjects BI relational universes saved on an SAP BusinessObjects BI 4.1 platform. These universes give SAP Lumira access to the wide range of data sources they support.
- SAP BusinessObjects BW, the SAP analytical, reporting, and data-warehousing application.
- Custom data sources. If your data source is not supported natively by SAP Lumira, then you can write your own connector to it with the Data Source SDK, described in Chapter 11.

In addition to these data sources, you can also directly use the content copied to your clipboard to fill a dataset.

The data sources you are allowed to access depend on your license (see Chapter 2, Section 2.1):

- If you have an SAP Lumira Personal Edition license, you can access only Microsoft Excel files, text files, and SAP HANA One data sources.
- If you have an SAP Lumira Standard Edition license, you can contractually access Microsoft Excel files, text files, SAP HANA data sources, and all relational databases.
- If you have an SAP Lumira license, you can access all supported data sources, including SAP BusinessObjects BI universes and SAP BW.

3.1.2 Acquisition Offline Mode

The default data acquisition mode available for all data sources is the offline mode. Acquiring data for some SAP-specific systems (such as SAP HANA and SAP BW) can also be done in online mode, as described in Section 3.1.3.

In offline mode, SAP Lumira connects to the data source to retrieve data from it and store it as a table. This table can be very large, because it contains all rough, retrieved data. To store this dataset, SAP Lumira embeds its own in-memory database. SAP Lumira allows you to perform complex manipulations on this dataset (see Chapter 4) before turning it into visualizations. These manipulations are performed in the in-memory database. This database is created the first time you start SAP Lumira and is managed by SAP Lumira itself, so you do not need to access it.

The dataset is stored in the document when you save it, and is reloaded in the in-memory database when you reopen it. In this offline mode, there is no connection kept open to the data source unless you explicitly require a data refresh.

This is not the case for online mode, which is described in the next section.

3.1.3 Acquisition Online Mode

As opposed to the offline mode, the online mode is available only for SAP HANA and SAP BW data sources. SAP BW only supports this mode. In this mode, the dataset is not retrieved from the data source and stored in the SAP Lumira document but remains in the SAP HANA or SAP BW system (see Section 3.6.2).

Data is then always updated along with the SAP system content, because SAP Lumira directly connects to it.

The advantages of querying SAP HANA or SAP BW in online mode are as follows:

- You are always working on the last updated data from the data source and you do not need to refresh the dataset.
- When saved, the SAP Lumira document does not store the dataset but only the metadata, visualizations, and stories created in SAP Lumira. This can be useful if you process large datasets.
- For SAP HANA, you benefit from the SAP HANA in-memory capabilities to process computations defined in the SAP HANA view.

However, in this mode the defined dataset cannot be edited, and additional manipulations are not possible in SAP Lumira (see Chapter 4).

3.1.4 New Dataset Creation

You can create a new dataset either from scratch or by reusing a data source you have already used. To do so, follow these steps:

1. Open the New Dataset dialog box, as shown in Figure 3.1, via one of the following options:

   ▶ In the menu bar, select the File • New command.

   ▶ On the Welcome page, click the Acquire Data button.

   ▶ On the Welcome page, click My Items, and then click New Document.

   ▶ In the Prepare room, click New Dataset. In this case, the new dataset is added to the current document.

On the left side of the New Dataset dialog box, the Select a Source list displays the data source types you can access. The data sources that are not granted by your license are disabled in this list.

On the right side of the New Dataset dialog box, the All recently used list displays the data sources you have already used.

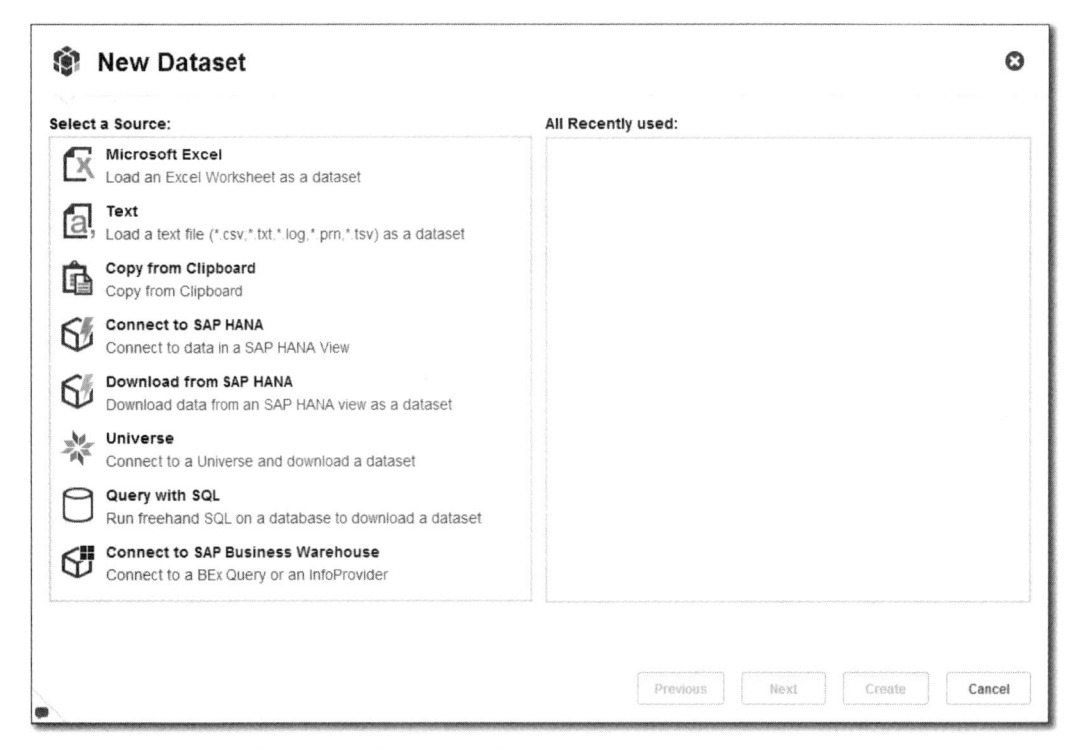

Figure 3.1 New Dataset Source Selection

2. Click the type of data source to create. The list of already used data sources is filtered and displays only the data sources of this type.

3. To add a new data source, click NEXT; to reuse an already used data source, click its name in the list of already used data sources. In both cases, the dialog box displays the appropriate form to connect to the data source. The parameters to enter depend on the data source type you have selected and are described in Section 3.2 to Section 3.8. If you have chosen to reuse an already used data source, then the different fields in the dialog boxes are prefilled with the same values of the data source that you previously used.

4. After you have defined the dataset, SAP Lumira requests a confirmation if the number of cells to retrieve exceeds 15 million cells (if you are running on a 32-bit system) or 30 million cells (for a 64-bit system). This confirmation can warn you before acquiring large datasets from systems such as SAP HANA.

5. Depending on the dataset size to acquire, the acquisition may take a few moments. Once retrieved, SAP Lumira switches to the default room you have set in your preferences (see Chapter 2, Section 2.9). If it is not the Prepare room, you can return to this room to display the dataset content (see Chapter 4).

3.1.5 Active Directory and Single Sign-On

To connect to some systems using Windows Active Directory authentication or through single sign-on, you need to configure Kerberos. This is the case when you access these systems to use them as data sources, such as with SAP HANA (see Section 3.6) or universes in SAP XI 3.x or SAP BusinessObjects BI 4.1 (see Section 3.7), or for resources publication (see Chapter 7).

You need to modify the SAPLumira.ini file, but also the krb5.ini and bscLogin.conf files for Kerberos authentication. You may contact your system administrator for additional help with these changes:

▸ Add the following section to the bscLogin.conf file:

```
com.businessobjects.security.jgss.initiate {
  com.sun.security.auth.module.Krb5LoginModule required;
};
```

▸ Add the following section to the krb5.ini file:

```
[libdefaults]
  default_realm = <Active Directory domain name>
[realms]
```

```
<Active Directory domain name> = {
    kdc = <Hostname of domain controller>
    default_domain = <Active Directory domain name>
}
[domain_realm]
<Domain name/Host name> = <Active Directory domain name>
```

Replace:

- `<Active Directory domain name>` with the Active Directory domain name, entered in fully qualified domain name format and in uppercase—for example, `COMPANY.COM`.
- `<Hostname of domain controller>` with the hostname of the domain controller—for example, `ADSERVER.COMPANY.COM`.
- `<Domain name/Host name>` with a domain name or host name (entered in lowercase) to translate to the Active Directory domain name. You can define several domain or host names.

In our example, the `[domain_realm]` section could be set as follows:

```
[domain_realm]
  .company.com = COMPANY.COM
  company.com = COMPANY.COM
```

- In the SAPLumira.ini file located in *<installation folder>\SAPLumira\Desktop*, add the paths of these two files. For example, if these two files are saved in the *C:\WINNT* folder, append the following two lines:

```
-Djava.security.auth.login.config=C:/WINNT/bscLogin.conf
-Djava.security.krb5.conf=C:/WINNT/krb5.ini
```

3.1.6 Data Acquisition Parameters for Automatic Detection and Performance

When you retrieve data from the data source, SAP Lumira may run some automatic processing to detect and add potential metadata to the dataset:

- Measures are created for columns containing numerical values. By default, they are aggregated with the `Sum` aggregation function.
- Columns containing country, region, subregion, or city names recognized by SAP Lumira are marked as candidates for geographical hierarchies.
- Columns containing data that fit date and time patterns are marked as potential time data.

You can see these additional detected metadata when you display the dataset in the Prepare room (see Chapter 4). It is possible to disable some of these rules, as described in Chapter 4, Section 4.9.

This detection, and other processing on the dataset, can be time-consuming, especially if the dataset is large. You may disable this detection through some parameters available in the SAP LUMIRA PREFERENCES dialog box (see Chapter 2, Section 2.9) in the DATASETS category. These parameters are listed in Table 3.1. Some parameters apply only for online mode (SAP HANA online and SAP BW), whereas others apply only for offline mode.

Online Parameter	Description
Would you like to automatically detect possible enrichments?	Enable or disable dataset enrichments.
Offline Parameter	**Description**
Would you like to automatically detect possible enrichments for all datasets?	Enable or disable dataset enrichments.
Would you like to automatically detect possible enrichments for large datasets (30M cells or more)?	Enable or disable dataset enrichments if the dataset contains more than 30 million cells. This parameter can be selected only if the previous one is selected.
Would you like to see dataset statistics in the status bar?	Enable or disable dataset rows and columns number display in the status bar, as shown in Figure 3.2.
Would you like to display related visualizations and allow influence analysis?	Enable or disable the analysis of the most impacting dimensions in the dataset and the search of the related visualizations based on this analysis (see Chapter 5, Section 5.10).

Table 3.1 Dataset Preferences Parameter

Figure 3.2 Dataset Statistics in Status Bar

The sections ahead describe the different data sources that can be used to create datasets.

3.2　Text Files

A text file is the simplest file format in which to store data. It does not require any specific complex and costly application to generate it; a simple text editor can be used for its creation and manipulation.

In the text file, the different values can be provided in rows as in a vertical table and can be in one of two formats:

- Separated by a character, usually a comma; in this case the file is also called a comma-separated values (CSV) file. SAP Lumira can consider any single character as the separator character. This character must be identical for all rows and columns.
- Saved in columns of fixed width.

SAP Lumira can create a dataset from one or several local text files. If you retrieve data from several files, then the rows from the different files are appended in the same dataset. In the resulting dataset, a new column is added with the name of the source file. You can decide to keep it in the dataset or not. The first file you enter is used as a reference:

- Header is taken from this file if you select to use the first line as the header.
- If another file has fewer columns than this reference file, then it is considered incompatible and is not added to the dataset.
- If another file has more columns than this reference file, then values in the extra columns are not added to the dataset.

To create a new dataset from one or more text files, follow these steps:

1. Open the NEW DATASET dialog box, as described in Section 3.1.4.
2. In the SELECT A SOURCE section, select the TEXT option. The RECENTLY USED section displays the list of text files already used.
3. Click NEXT to enter the parameters to identify a new text file.
4. The OPEN dialog box appears, in which you can select one or several text files to use as data sources.
5. Click OPEN to close the dialog box. The NEW DATASET dialog box is updated with the name of the selected file(s) in the FILE(S) field. A preview of the data

retrieved from the selected text file(s) is displayed in the table, as shown in Figure 3.3. If you have selected several files, then a new column is added that contains the name of the source file of the row.

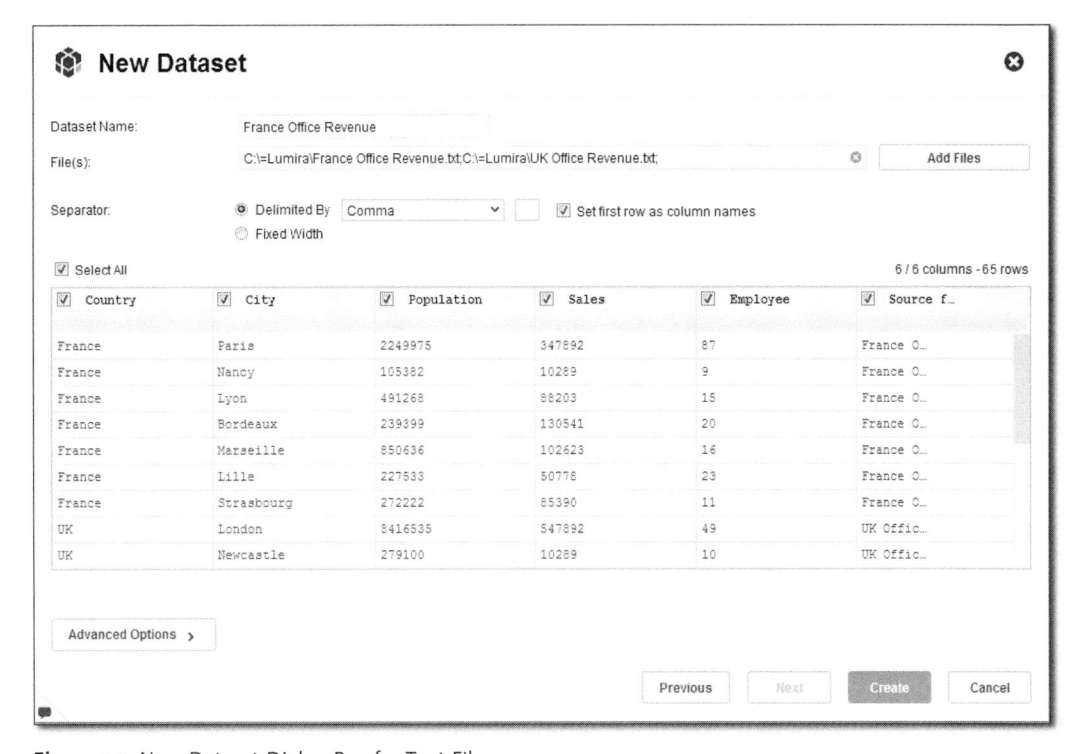

Figure 3.3 New Dataset Dialog Box for Text File

6. To add one or more new files to use as a data source, click ADD FILES to open the OPEN dialog box and select the new files.
7. Enter a name for the dataset in the DATASET NAME text field.
8. In the SEPARATOR section, choose one of the following radio buttons to define how columns are separated in the CSV file:
    ▸ DELIMITED BY: Columns are separated by a fixed character. In the dropdown menu, select this character from among the possible choices: COMMA, TAB, SPACE, SEMICOLON, or OTHER. If you select OTHER, then you can type this character in the text field beside the OTHER label.

▶ FIXED WIDTH: Columns are defined with a fixed width. You may explicitly define these widths in the BREAK COLUMN parameter in the ADVANCED OPTIONS section.

9. Select the SET FIRST ROW AS COLUMN NAMES checkbox to use the first row of the file as the column name. If this option is not enabled, columns name are in the format "column_<n>", where <n> is the column number in the file.

10. In the data preview, select the columns to retrieve in the dataset by clicking the corresponding checkboxes in column header. Select or unselect the SELECT ALL checkbox to select or unselected all columns.

11. Click ADVANCED OPTIONS to display the possible parameters for text file data acquisition, as shown in Figure 3.4:

    ▶ NUMBER FORMAT: Explicitly specify the number format if numbers have not been properly recognized. In the dropdown list, select one number format that describes how numbers are saved in the file.

    ▶ DATE FORMAT: Explicitly specify the date format. In the dropdown list, select one date format that describes how dates are saved in the file. Table 3.2 lists the tokens used in the date format.

    ▶ TRIM VALUES: Select this checkbox to remove space or tab characters before values in the columns.

    ▶ BREAK COLUMN: If you have selected a fixed width for the separator, then enter the width of all columns separated by commas—for example, enter "3, 3, 4, 4, 4" to define two columns of three characters followed by three columns of four characters. Once you have entered the columns' widths, click APPLY to redisplay the dataset in the table with the new column widths.

Figure 3.4 Advanced Options for Text File Acquisition

12. Click CREATE to close the NEW DATASET dialog box and retrieve the data from the text file to create the dataset (see Table 3.2).

Token	Description
d	The day number with no leading zero
dd	The day number forced to two digits with an optional leading zero
EEEE	Full day name (e.g., Monday, Tuesday, etc.)
M	The month number with no leading zero
MM	The month number forced to two digits with an optional leading zero
MMM	The abbreviated name of the month (e.g., Jan, Feb, etc.)
MMMM	The full name of the month (e.g., January, February)
yy	Last two numbers of a year
yyyy	All four numbers of a year

Table 3.2 Token Description in Date Format

3.3 Windows Clipboard Copy

SAP Lumira can also create a dataset from data copied to the Windows clipboard. Text content copied to the clipboard can be edited before being used to create the dataset. Acquisition of this text content is similar to the acquisition of text coming from a text file, as described in Section 3.2.

To create a new dataset from the content copied to the clipboard, follow these steps:

1. Copy some data from any source application to add it to the clipboard.
2. Open the NEW DATASET dialog box, as described in Section 3.1.4.
3. In the SELECT A SOURCE section, select the COPY FROM CLIPBOARD option.
4. Click NEXT. The clipboard content is copied into a text editor, as shown in Figure 3.5. You can manually edit the text in this text editor.

3 | Data Acquisition

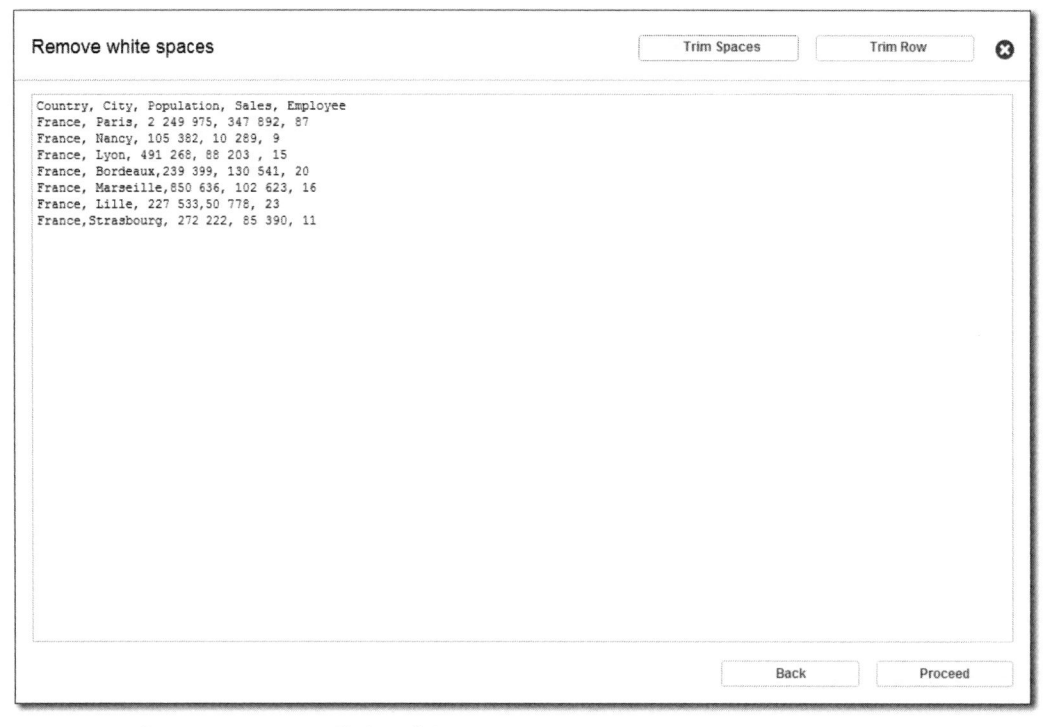

Figure 3.5 Trimming Clipboard Content

5. Click TRIM SPACES to remove spaces and tabs at the beginning and the end of each row.

6. Click TRIM ROW to remove empty rows.

7. Click PROCEED to use the content of the text editor as a source for a dataset. This content is displayed in the NEW DATASET dialog box, as shown in Figure 3.6.

8. Modify the dataset default name in the DATASET NAME text field.

9. Click ADVANCED OPTIONS to display the possible parameters to create a new dataset from the content copied to the clipboard. These parameters are identical to the ones described in Section 3.2 for text file acquisition.

10. Click CREATE to close the NEW DATASET dialog box and create the dataset.

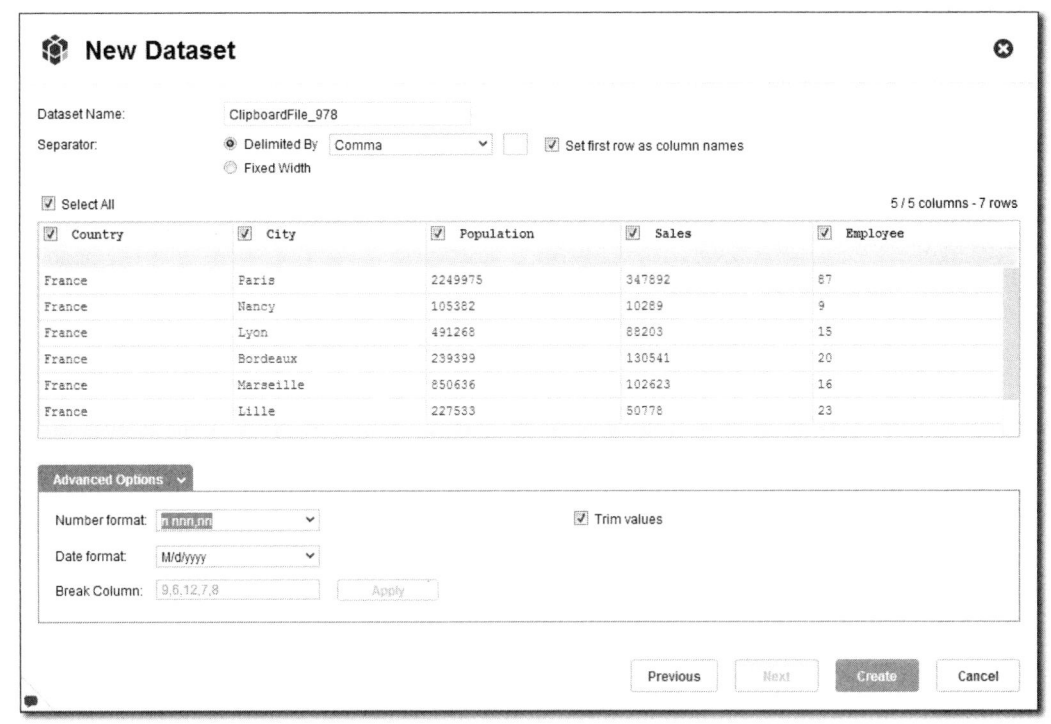

Figure 3.6 New Dataset Dialog Box for Dataset Created From Clipboard

3.4 Microsoft Excel

In many situations, Microsoft Excel spreadsheets can be a simple, convenient way to store, present, and analyze data, because doing so avoids the need to install a database infrastructure. This simplicity allows anyone to create his or her own spreadsheet, but, on the other hand, it facilitates the proliferation of files that do not follow any conventions, that can get lost on the file system, and that are unsecure.

SAP Lumira can create a dataset from one or several local Microsoft Excel files. Supported versions are Microsoft Excel 2007 (.xls file extension), 2010, and 2013 (.xlsx file extension).

If you retrieve data from several files, then the rows from the different files are appended in the same dataset. In the resulting dataset, a new column is added with the name of the source file. You can decide to keep it in the dataset or not. The first file you enter is used as a reference:

- The header is taken from this file if you select to use the first line as the header.
- If another file has fewer columns than this reference file or if the data types in its columns do not fit the ones in the first file, then it is considered incompatible and is not added to the dataset.
- If another file has more columns than this reference file, then values in the extra columns are not added to the dataset.

SAP Lumira can retrieve data from only one sheet or from all sheets of a Microsoft Excel file. You can also define a range of rows and columns to use.

To create a new dataset from one or more Microsoft Excel files, follow these steps:

1. Open the NEW DATASET dialog box, as described in Section 3.1.4.
2. In the SELECT A SOURCE section, select the MICROSOFT EXCEL option.
3. Click NEXT to enter the parameters to identify a new Microsoft Excel file.
4. The OPEN dialog box appears, in which you can select one or several Microsoft Excel files to use as data sources.
5. Click OPEN to close the dialog box. The NEW DATASET dialog box is updated with the name of the selected file(s) in the FILE(S) field. A preview of the data retrieved from the selected Microsoft Excel file(s) is displayed in the table, as shown in Figure 3.7. If you have selected several files, then a new column is added that contains the name of the source file of the row.

   The names of the spreadsheets contained in the first file are listed in the SHEET dropdown list.

Microsoft Excel | 3.4

Figure 3.7 New Dataset Dialog Box for Microsoft Excel Files

6. To add one or more new files to use as data source, click ADD FILES to open the OPEN dialog box and select new files.
7. Enter a name for the dataset in the DATASET NAME text field.
8. In the SHEET dropdown list, select the sheet in the Microsoft Excel file to query. If you retrieve data from several files, then in the other files the selected sheets are the ones in the same position as the selected sheet in the first file. The preview is updated with the selected sheets.
9. Select the following checkboxes to enable these possible options:
    ▸ APPEND ALL SHEETS: Append the rows of all sheets contained in the Microsoft Excel files. A new column named SOURCE SHEET that contains the sheet name the row comes from is also added.

▸ SET FIRST ROW AS COLUMN NAME: Use the first row of the sheet as the column name. If this option is not enabled, columns name are in the format "Column_<n>", where <n> is the column number in the file.

10. In TABLE HEADER TYPE, select how data is organized in the spreadsheet:

    ▸ VERTICAL TABLE: As shown in Figure 3.8 ❶, a vertical table is a table in which values are organized in rows.

    ▸ CROSS TABLE: As shown in Figure 3.8 ❷, a cross table is a two-way table in which values are organized in a matrix, with headers used in both rows and columns.

❶
Year	Country	Sales
2012	France	19231
2013	France	20823
2014	France	21055
2012	US	202401
2013	US	215778
2014	US	230189
2012	China	150230
2013	China	155602
2014	China	167023

❷
	France	US	China
2012	19231	202401	150230
2013	20823	215778	155602
2014	21055	230189	167023

Figure 3.8 Vertical Table ❶ and Cross Table ❷

11. Select the columns to retrieve in the dataset by clicking the corresponding checkboxes in column header.

12. Click ADVANCED OPTIONS to display the possible parameters for Microsoft Excel data acquisition:

    ▸ SHOW HIDDEN COLUMNS: Select this checkbox to display and retrieve data from hidden columns.

    ▸ SHOW HIDDEN ROWS: Select this checkbox to display and retrieve data from hidden rows.

    ▸ DETECT MERGE CELLS: Select this checkbox to fill all cells contained in a merged cell with the merged cell's value. If not selected, then only the first cell of the merged cell is filled with the cell's value and others are left empty.

    If you selected VERTICAL TABLE as the TABLE HEADER TYPE, then advanced parameters also contain the following options, as shown in Figure 3.9:

    ▸ RANGE SELECTION: In this dropdown list, select what data to retrieve from the spreadsheet:

- ALL: Retrieve all data from the spreadsheet.
- CUSTOM RANGE: Retrieve only data contained in a fixed area. In the text field beside CUSTOM RANGE, enter the coordinates of the top-right and bottom-left cells that define the rectangular area that contains the data to retrieve (for example, D3:H300), and then click APPLY.

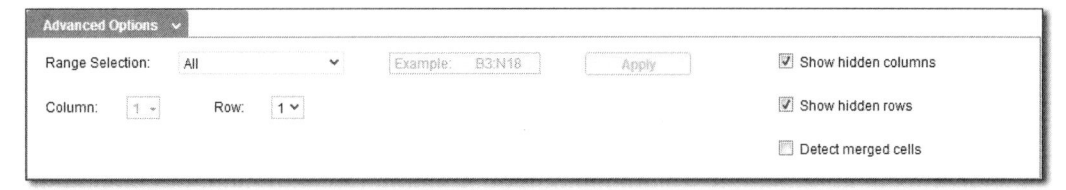

Figure 3.9 Advanced Options for Microsoft Excel File Acquisition: Vertical Table

If you have selected CROSS TABLE as the TABLE HEADER TYPE, then the following parameters also are available, as shown in Figure 3.10:

▶ COLUMN: Defines how many columns in the right side of the spreadsheet must be used as the entry point for the cross table.
▶ ROW: Defines how many rows in the top of the spreadsheet must be used as the entry point for the cross table.

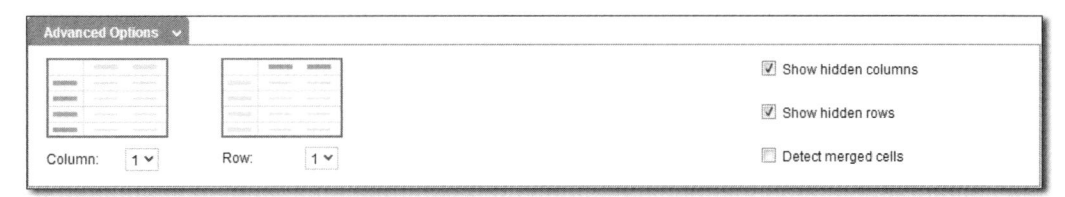

Figure 3.10 Advanced Options for Microsoft Excel File Acquisition: Cross Table

13. Click CREATE to close the NEW DATASET dialog box and create the dataset from data retrieved from the Microsoft Excel file.

3.5 Query with SQL

In your enterprise environment, your data is very likely stored in relational databases, which are the most common systems. Relational databases can be queried by using SQL language.

With SAP Lumira, you can directly query these databases and create a dataset for further use through a SQL sentence to send to the database. The following sections present the SQL drivers supported by SAP Lumira, how you can install or uninstall a driver and create a dataset from a relational database. It also covers access to Hadoop and OData, which are also accessed through SQL, even if they are not relational databases.

3.5.1 Standard SQL Drivers

Through SQL queries, SAP Lumira supports the most common relational databases, listed in Table 3.3.

SAP Lumira uses the Connection Server component used by other SAP BusinessObjects BI tools. For direct SQL access, it is embedded as a library in SAP Lumira. Only a subset of all data sources and middleware supported by the Connection Server are available in SAP Lumira in order to keep its installer small.

To access other vendors and databases not supported by SQL queries, you may use relational universes (see Section 3.5). In this case, SAP Lumira also relies on the Connection Server but indirectly, because it is running server-side.

Provider	Data Access	Driver
Apache	Amazon EMR Hive 0.7	JDBC driver
Apache	Amazon EMR Hive 0.8	JDBC driver
Apache	Apache Hadoop Hive 0.10	JDBC driver
Apache	Derby 10 Embedded	JDBC driver: derby- 10.x.y.z.jar
Generic	Generic JDBC data source	JDBC driver
Generic	Generic OData 2.0	OData Connector embedded in SAP Lumira
GreenPlum	GreenPlum 4	JDBC driver: Postgresql9.1.jar
Hewlett Packard	HP Neoview 2.4	JDBC driver: hpt4jdbc.jar
IBM	DB2 10 for z/OS	JDBC driver: db2jcc4.jar
IBM	DB2 10 for LUW	JDBC driver: db2jcc4.jar
IBM	DB2 v9	JDBC driver: db2jcc.jar
IBM	Informix Dynamic Server 11	JDBC driver: ifxjdbc.jar

Table 3.3 SQL Drivers Supported by SAP Lumira 1.18

Provider	Data Access	Driver
Ingres	Ingres Database 9	JDBC driver: iijdbc-9.x-y.z.a.jar
Microsoft	MS SQL Server 2008	JDBC driver: sqljdbc4.jar
Microsoft	MS SQL Server 2012	JDBC driver: sqljdbc4.jar
Netezza	Netazza Server 4	JDBC driver: nzjdbc.jar
Netezza	Netazza Server 5	JDBC driver: nzjdbc.jar
Netezza	Netazza Server 6	JDBC driver: nzjdbc.jar
Oracle	MySQL 5	JDBC driver: ojdbc6.jar or ojdbc7.jar
Oracle	Oracle 10	JDBC driver: ojdbc14.jar
Oracle	Oracle 11	JDBC driver: ojdbc6.jar
Oracle	Oracle 12	JDBC driver: ojdbc6.jar or ojdbc7.jar
Oracle	Oracle Exadata	JDBC driver: ojdbc6.jar
PostgreSQL	PostgreSQL 8	JDBC driver: postgresql-8.x-yza.jdbc3.jar
PostgreSQL	PostgreSQL 9	JDBC driver: postgresql9.1.jar
Salesforce.com	Salesforce.com	JDBC driver embedded in SAP Lumira
SAP	MaxDB 7.7	JDBC driver embedded in SAP Lumira
SAP	mySAP ERP 2004	SAP Java Connector (SAP JCo)
SAP	SAP ERP 6	SAP Java Connector (SAP JCo)
SAP	SAP HANA database 1.0	JDBC driver embedded in SAP Lumira
SAP	SAP Manufacturing Integration and Intelligence 14.0	JDBC driver embedded in SAP Lumira
SAP	SAP R/3 Release 4	SAP Java Connector (SAP JCo)
Sybase	Sybase Adaptive Server Enterprise 15.5	JDBC driver embedded in SAP Lumira
Sybase	Sybase IQ 15	JDBC driver embedded in SAP Lumira
Sybase	Sybase SQL Anywhere 11	JDBC driver embedded in SAP Lumira
Sybase	Sybase SQL Anywhere 12	JDBC driver embedded in SAP Lumira
Teradata Corporation	Teradata 12	JDBC driver: terajdbc4 and tdgssconfig.jar
Teradata Corporation	Teradata 13	JDBC driver: terajdbc4 and tdgssconfig.jar
Teradata Corporation	Teradata 14	JDBC driver: terajdbc4 and tdgssconfig.jar

Table 3.3 SQL Drivers Supported by SAP Lumira 1.18 (Cont.)

Among the previously supported data sources, two are used to access not relational data but specific databases that are exposed through a relational interface. These data sources are also specific, because they are related to big data on the web:

- Apache Hadoop Hive 0.10 — JDBC driver
- Generic OData 2.0 — OData Connector

For drivers that rely on HTTP protocol (Hadoop, OData, and Salesforce.com), if you access an external network through a proxy you may define proxy parameters in the PREFERENCES dialog box (see Chapter 2, Section 2.9).

> **Alternate Drivers**
>
> The driver for SAP HANA can be used to query SAP HANA using SQL. SAP Lumira also proposes native multidimensional access to SAP HANA views (see Section 3.6).

3.5.2 Installing/Uninstalling a Driver

When a database is released by a vendor, it comes with a set of middleware. This set of components is used by client applications to exchange data with this database. The middleware components have an interface defined in different technologies:

- Standard interfaces: JDBC or OData connector
- Proprietary interfaces: SAP Java Connector (SAP JCo)

SAP can't redistribute the database middleware components, and the components aren't installed with SAP Lumira, except the ones owned by SAP (SAP BW, SAP Sybase, SAP ERP, or SAP HANA) or the ones based on HTTP technology (OData or Salesforce.com). To connect to other databases, you need to install the corresponding middleware provided by the third-party vendor. Refer to the third-party installation procedure to retrieve and install this middleware on your machine.

> **32-bit or 64-bit**
>
> Middleware comes usually in 32-bit and/or 64-bit versions. SAP Lumira is also available in 32-bit and 64-bit versions. You need to install the version of the middleware that matches your SAP Lumira version.

Once this middleware is installed, you must enable and configure an SAP Lumira driver that can use this middleware. This middleware is provided as a Java JAR file, and this configuration step consists of providing this JAR file's path. To do so, follow these steps:

1. In the menu bar, select FILE • PREFERENCES to open the SAP LUMIRA PREFERENCES dialog box.
2. In the left section, click SQL DRIVERS. The list of supported relational databases is displayed in the tree list at the right, as shown in Figure 3.11.

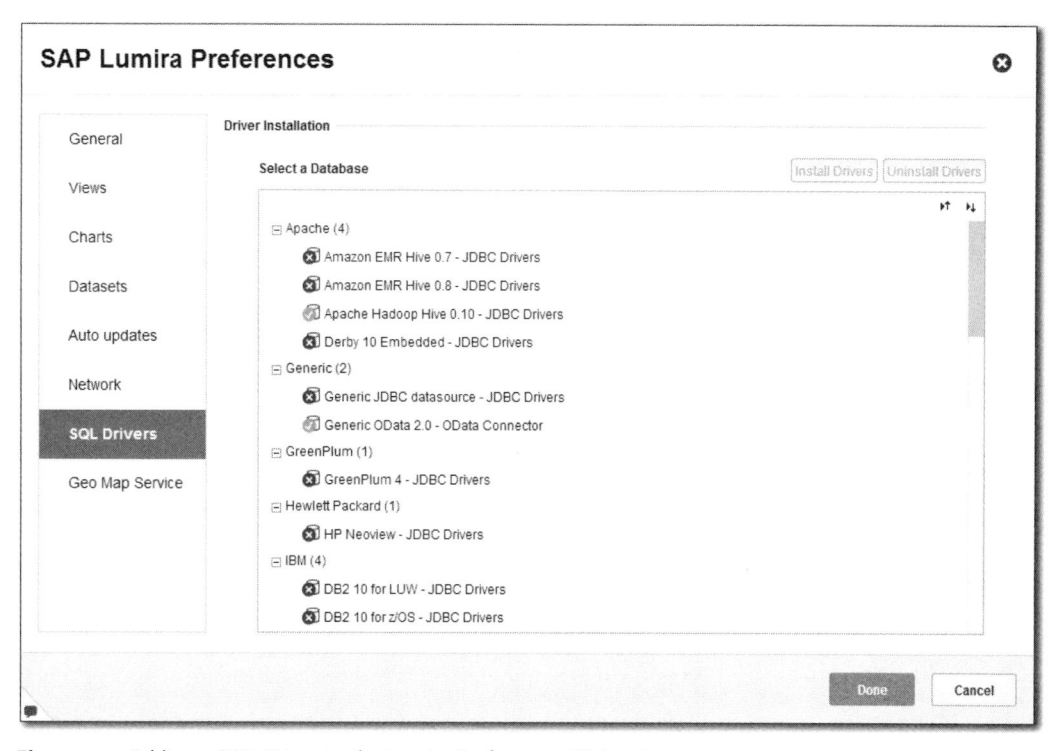

Figure 3.11 Adding a SQL Driver in the Lumira Preferences Dialog Box

3. Navigate in the tree list to find the database to access. If the driver is already configured, a green CHECK icon is displayed before the database name, and you can already acquire data from this database.

4. If the driver is not configured, a red ERROR icon is displayed before the database name. Click this database, and then click INSTALL DRIVERS to open the OPEN dialog box.
5. Navigate in the file system to select the JAR file that contains the third-party middleware you previously installed.
6. Click OPEN. The dialog box closes, and SAP Lumira enables and configures the selected driver.
7. Restart SAP Lumira to take advantage of the new middleware.

In some cases, you may need to disable a driver—for example, to reconfigure it to use a new version of the middleware. To uninstall a driver, follow these steps:

1. In the menu bar, select FILE • PREFERENCES to open the SAP LUMIRA PREFERENCES dialog box.
2. In the left section, click SQL DRIVERS. The list of supported relational databases is displayed in the tree list at the right.
3. In the SELECT A DATABASE list, select an installed driver, and then click UNINSTALL DRIVERS.

3.5.3 Creating a Dataset from Relational Databases

Once the database driver is installed, you can retrieve data from the data source to generate the dataset. To connect to the relational database, you need to provide some credentials. It is recommended to assign an account that has only read access to this database in order to avoid users modifying its content.

To create the dataset, follow these steps:

1. Open the NEW DATASET dialog box, as described in Section 3.1.4.
2. In the SELECT A SOURCE section, select the QUERY WITH SQL option, and click NEXT.
3. By default, the dialog box displays all SQL data sources for which drivers have been installed, as shown in Figure 3.12. Select an installed driver, and click NEXT.

   You may also display the drivers that are not installed by clicking the SHOW ALL checkbox. To install a non-installed driver, select it, and click INSTALL. Follow the steps described in Section 3.5.2 to install a new driver.

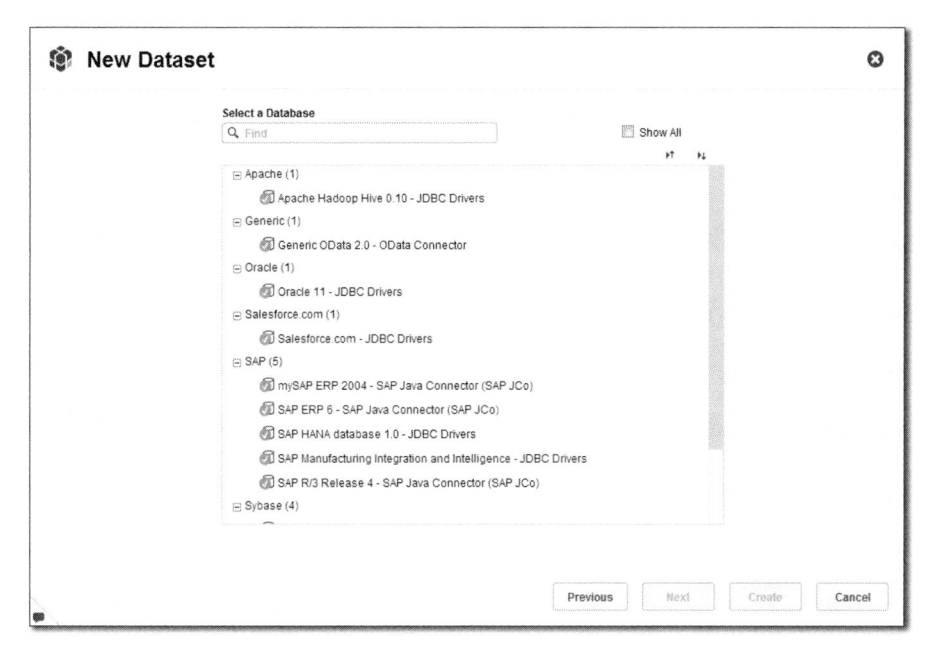

Figure 3.12 Selecting a Database

4. The dialog box displays a list of parameters you need to fill to identify and connect to the relational data source, as shown, for example, in Figure 3.13. This list depends on the data source type. Most data sources require the following parameters:

   ▶ USER NAME and PASSWORD: The credentials to connect to the data source.
   ▶ SERVER: The server name hosting the data source. Depending on the data source, you may need to enter the server port as well.
   ▶ DATABASE: The database's name.

Figure 3.13 Relational Database Connection Parameters

This list is not exhaustive, so refer to your middleware documentation for more details.

5. Click ADVANCED to open the ADVANCED PARAMETERS dialog box, in which you can enter additional parameters to connect to the data source, as shown in Figure 3.14:

    ▸ ARRAY FETCH SIZE: This is the number of rows of data retrieved per slice. When setting this parameter, you must find a balance between performance and memory. A high value reduces the number of calls over the network but has a large memory footprint.

    ▸ LOGIN TIMEOUT: This is the number of seconds SAP Lumira waits for an answer from the database before canceling the request. This parameter is passed to the middleware that manages this timeout.

    ▸ JDBC DRIVER PROPERTIES: This is used to pass JDBC-specific parameters that the middleware supports.

    The other parameters are Connection Server generic parameters that are not used in SAP Lumira: CONNECTION POOL MODE, POOL TIMEOUT, and ARRAY BIND SIZE.

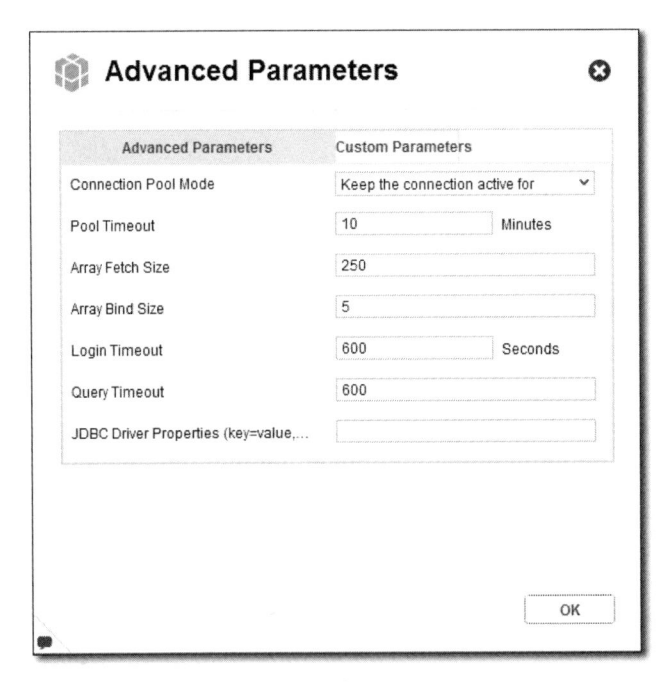

Figure 3.14 Connection Advanced Parameters

6. Some data sources also support custom parameters. To enter such parameters, click the CUSTOM PARAMETERS tab to display the custom parameters list, as shown in Figure 3.15.

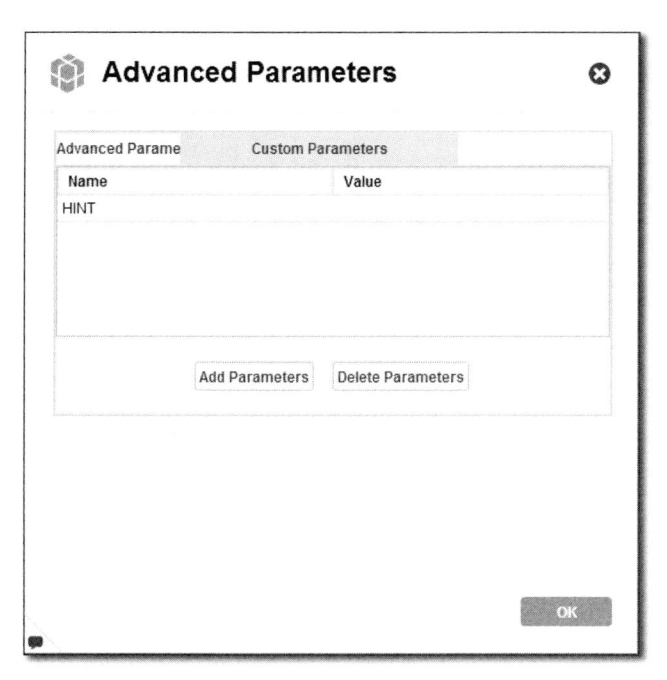

Figure 3.15 Connection Custom Parameters

- Click ADD PARAMETERS to add a new line in the list for a new custom parameter.
- To add or modify a custom parameter name, click its line in the NAME column, and type the parameter name.
- To add or modify a custom parameter value, click its line in the VALUE column, and type the parameter value.
- To delete a custom parameter, click the line containing the custom parameter, and then click DELETE PARAMETERS.

7. Click OK to close the ADVANCED PARAMETERS dialog box.
8. Click CONNECT to connect to the database and display the SQL Editor, in which you can create the query to create the dataset from the database, as shown in Figure 3.16.

3 | Data Acquisition

The left pane of this editor displays the database organization as a tree structure including the list of tables you can access in this database.

In the QUERY text field, you can enter the SQL query to run in order to create the dataset from the database.

Figure 3.16 Relational Database SQL Editor

9. Navigate in the database tree to find the table to query. You may use the FIND text field to filter the tables list.

10. Double-click a table to automatically add the SQL query to retrieve all its columns in the QUERY text field. If a SQL query was already available in this text field, then it is replaced by this new query.

11. You may directly edit the QUERY text field to modify the SQL query to retrieve the dataset.

12. Enter the name of the dataset in the DATASET NAME text field. By default, it is filled with the name of the selected table.
13. Click PREVIEW to display a preview of the result set returned by the query, as shown in Figure 3.17.

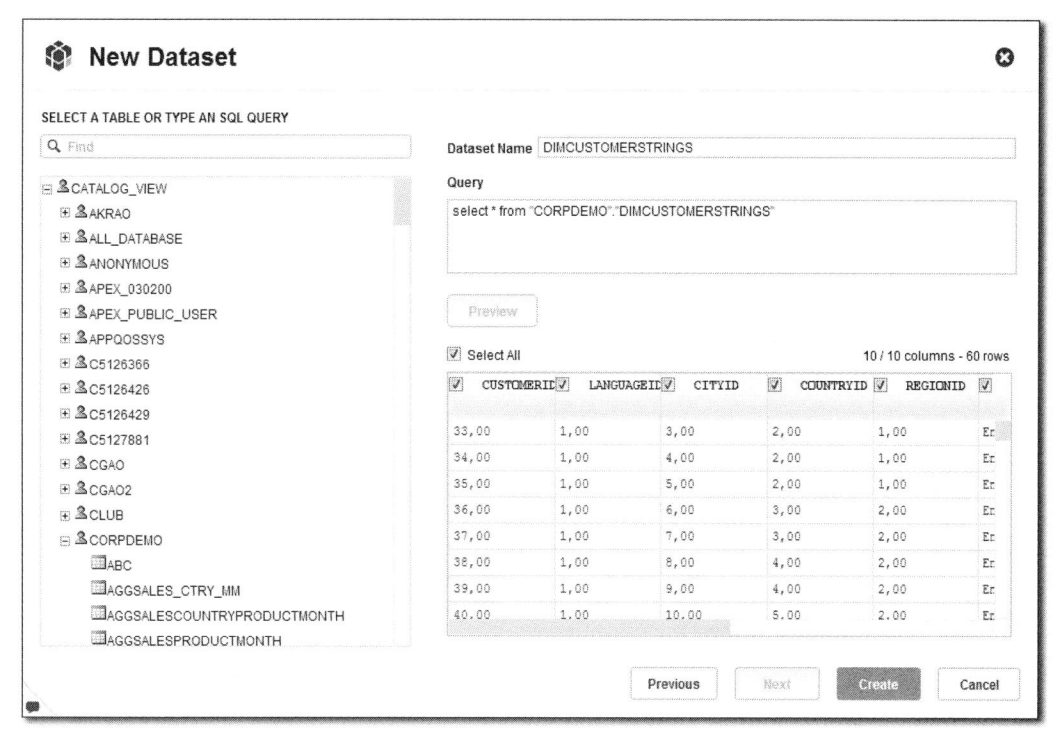

Figure 3.17 Data Preview

14. Review the data displayed in the table preview. Perform the following actions:
    - Click the SELECT ALL checkbox to select/unselect all columns of the table that are to be part of the dataset.
    - You may explicitly add a column in the dataset or remove it by selecting or unselecting the checkbox before the column's name.
    - Click the SHOW RECORD COUNT link to display the number of selected columns and the number of columns and rows returned by the preview.

15. Click CREATE to close the NEW DATASET dialog box and retrieve the data from the relational data source to create the dataset.

3.5.4 Creating a Dataset from a Hadoop Database

Hadoop is a framework intended to handle large-scale data in a distributed infrastructure. Hive is an open source project under the Apache Software Foundation intended to implement a database based on this Hadoop framework.

Hive can be queried using HiveQL, a language similar to SQL. SAP Lumira allows you to create a dataset from a Hive database using an SQL interface that translates SQL queries into HiveQL.

To create a dataset from a Hadoop data source through the SQL interface, follow the same steps described in Section 3.5.3 to create a connection to a relational database; in the list of supported databases, select AMAZON EMR HIVE or APACHE HADOOP HIVE. Then, as shown in Figure 3.18, enter the following parameters: USER NAME, PASSWORD, and SERVER:(PORT)—the server and port hosting the Hadoop server (see Figure 3.18).

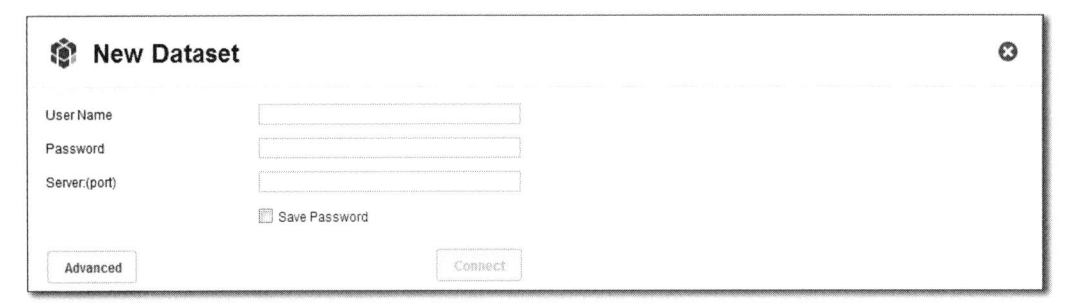

Figure 3.18 Hadoop Parameters

Click ADVANCED to enter additional parameters, as shown in Figure 3.19. Parameters specific to Hadoop data sources are as follows:

▶ FILES TO ADD
The paths to one or more files to add in the list of resources in the Hive distributed cache. Paths must be entered in UNIX format. Several paths can be separated by semicolons—for example:
/usr/hive/script1.py;/usr/hive/script2.py

This parameter is equivalent to the `add FILE <File Path>` command in the Hive interactive shell command.

▶ JAR(S) TO ADD
The paths to one or more JAR files to add to the Java class path. Paths must be entered in UNIX format. Several paths can be separated by semicolons—for example:
/usr/hive/add-on.jar;/usr/hive/ add-on.jar

This parameter is equivalent to the `add JAR <JARPath>` command in the Hive interactive shell command.

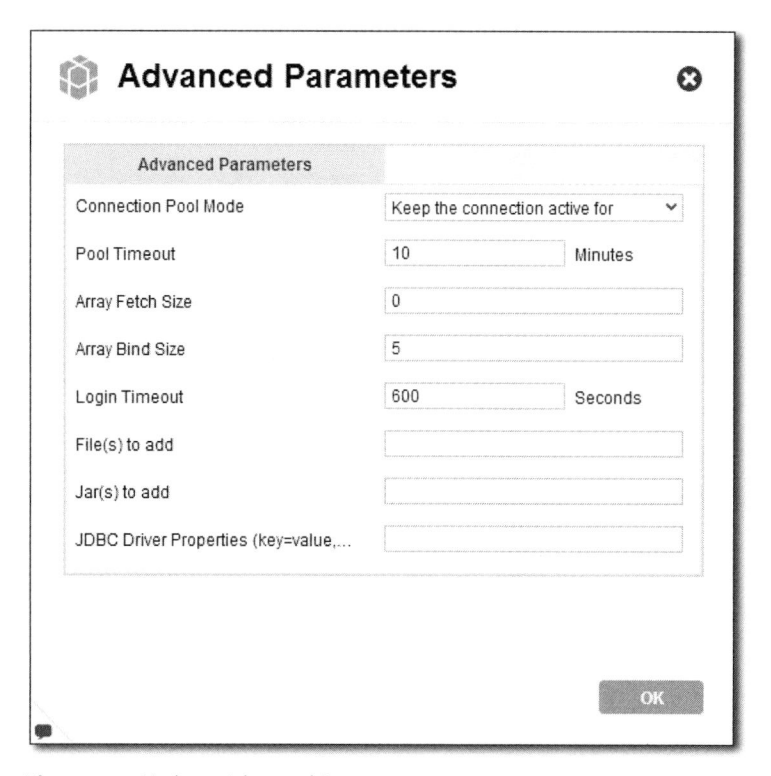

Figure 3.19 Hadoop Advanced Parameters

When your connection to the Hadoop database has been created, you can create your dataset with the same SQL Editor used for classic relational databases (see Section 3.5.3).

3.5.5 Creating a Dataset from OData

OData is a protocol for data access that is used by different companies (Microsoft, IBM, SAP, etc.) for product interoperability in order to exchange data. SAP Lumira supports OData as a data source through an SQL interface it implements.

To create a dataset from an OData data source through the SQL interface, create a connection to a relational database as described in Section 3.5.3. In the list of supported databases, select GENERIC ODATA 2.0. Then, as shown in Figure 3.20, enter the following parameters:

- SERVICE ROOT URI
  As you connect to OData services through HTTP, enter the URI of this data source.

- USER NAME and PASSWORD
  Credentials used to authenticate login to the OData data source.

- PROXY ADDRESS
  The proxy server and port if you need to access the external network through a proxy—for example, *myproxy:80*.

- PROXY USER NAME and PROXY PASSWORD
  Credentials used to authenticate login to the proxy server if you need one to access external network.

- CUSTOM AUTHENTICATION PARAMETERS
  Custom parameters added to the OData URI to authenticate login to the OData data source.

- COLUMN SELECTION
  Select this checkbox to allow the OData data source to execute a SELECT query. If not selected, this operation is filtered by the SAP Lumira driver for OData.

- SUPPORTED FILTER CONDITIONS
  Select this checkbox to allow the OData data source to filter data. If not selected, data is filtered by the SAP Lumira driver for OData.

- SORTING
  Select this checkbox to allow the OData data source to sort data. If not selected, data is sorted by the SAP Lumira driver for OData.

▶ SAVE PASSWORD
Select this checkbox to save the credentials in the connection definition.

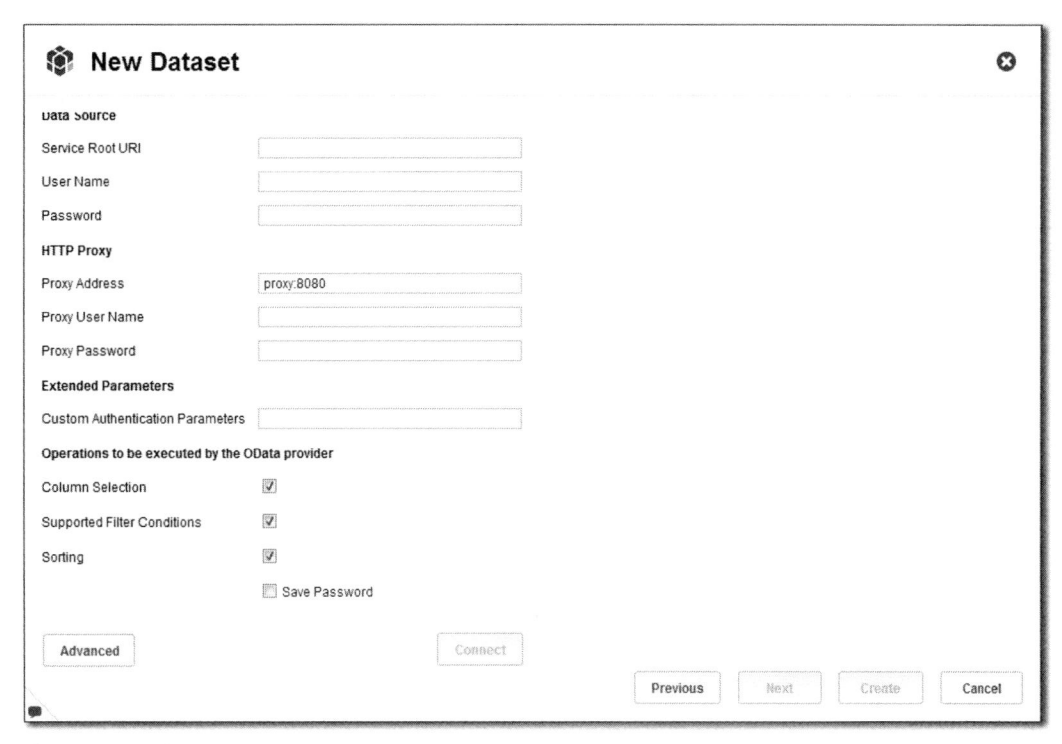

Figure 3.20 OData Connection Parameters

Click ADVANCED to enter additional parameters, as shown in Figure 3.21. Parameters specific to OData are as follows:

▶ CONNECTION TIMEOUT
This parameter defines how many seconds a connection waits for a response from the data source.

▶ CACHE METAMODEL
Select this checkbox to retrieve the metadata model only once instead of retrieving it each time a query is sent to the OData data source.

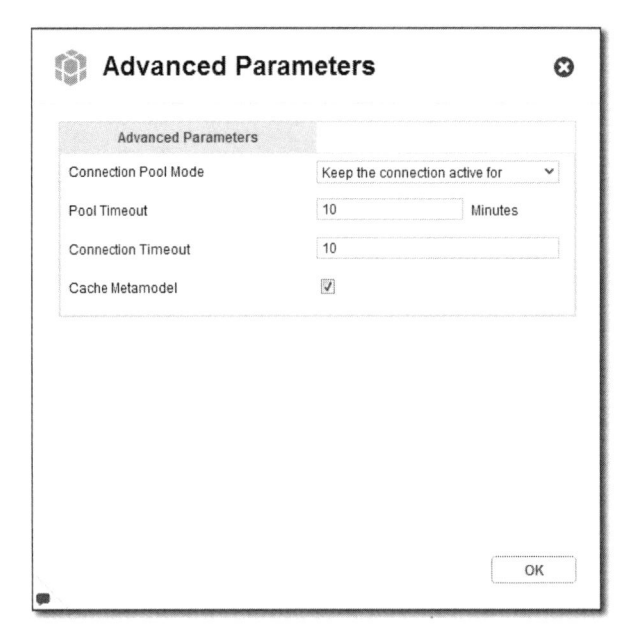

Figure 3.21 OData Connection Advanced Parameters

3.6 SAP HANA

SAP HANA is an in-memory database with row storage and column storage for the tables. SAP HANA is both a relational database and an OLAP engine.

On top of its physical tables, designers can create information models that correspond to specific business requirements. These models, also called SAP HANA views, column views, or SAP HANA cubes, are of three main types:

- **Attribute views**
  Define the dimensions of the model (e.g., product, time, geography).
- **Analytical views**
  Define the measures of the model and their relationships to the dimensions. An analytical view is based on a single fact table.
- **Calculation views**
  Combine several analytic views and other calculation views. Calculation views can contain calculated attributes, calculated measures, and complex calcula-

tions defined with a script language. They are executed when the view is accessed.

SAP Lumira can access SAP HANA through different methods:

- Relational access through direct SQL access (see Section 3.5)
- Access through a relational universe (see Section 3.7)
- Native access to SAP HANA analytical or calculation views

This access to SAP HANA views can occur either in offline mode (see Section 3.1.2), as for other data sources, or online mode (see Section 3.1.3). In online mode, it is not possible to perform any action described in Chapter 4 on the dataset.

The HANA version supported by SAP Lumira 1.18 is SAP HANA 1.0 SP8, Revision 80 or higher.

3.6.1 SAP HANA Offline Mode

To create a dataset from an SAP HANA view in offline mode, follow these steps:

1. Open the NEW DATASET dialog box, as described in Section 3.1.4.
2. In the SELECT A SOURCE section, select the DOWNLOAD FROM SAP HANA option.
3. In the CONNECT TO SAP HANA panel, as shown in Figure 3.22, enter the parameters to connect to the SAP HANA instance:
   - SERVER: SAP HANA server name.
   - INSTANCE/PORT: SAP HANA port number.
   - AUTHENTICATE BY OPERATING SYSTEM (SSO): Select this checkbox to authenticate login to the SAP HANA server using single sign-on (see Section 3.1.5). If you do not use single sign-on, you must provide a user name and password to authenticate.
   - USER and PASSWORD: Credentials used to authenticate login to the SAP HANA system if you do not use single sign-on.
   - SAVE PASSWORD: Select this checkbox to save the password to authenticate login to SAP HANA.

3 | Data Acquisition

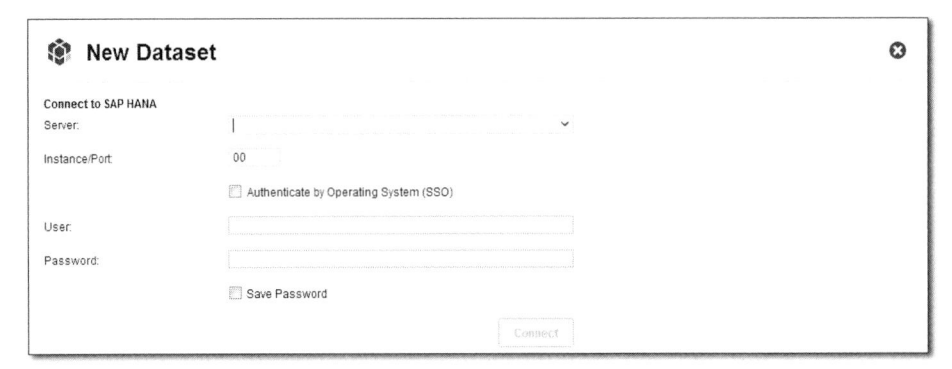

Figure 3.22 SAP HANA Login Page

4. Click CONNECT to connect to the SAP HANA source and display the list of views, as shown in Figure 3.23. Only the views you are allowed to see in the SAP HANA system are displayed.

Figure 3.23 View Selection

5. Select a view. The FIND text field allows you to find a specific view: as you type your text in this field, the view list is filtered to display only those views with names that fit this pattern.

6. In the DATASET NAME field, enter a name for the dataset. By default, it is filled by the name of the selected view.

7. You can either retrieve all data from the view or fine-tune the data to query. Click CREATE to close the dialog box and retrieve all data from the view to create the dataset. If some variables need to be addressed before retrieving data, then see Section 3.6.3, which describes how to do so.

8. Rather than retrieving all data from the view, you can select only a subset of its data by clicking NEXT instead. This displays the list of measures and dimensions, as shown in Figure 3.24:

    ▸ The MEASURES table lists the view's measures and their aggregation function in the view.

    ▸ The DIMENSIONS tables lists the view's dimensions.

    ▸ The FIND text fields allow you to find a specific measure or dimension: as you type your text in this field, the list is filtered to display only measures or dimensions with names that fit this pattern.

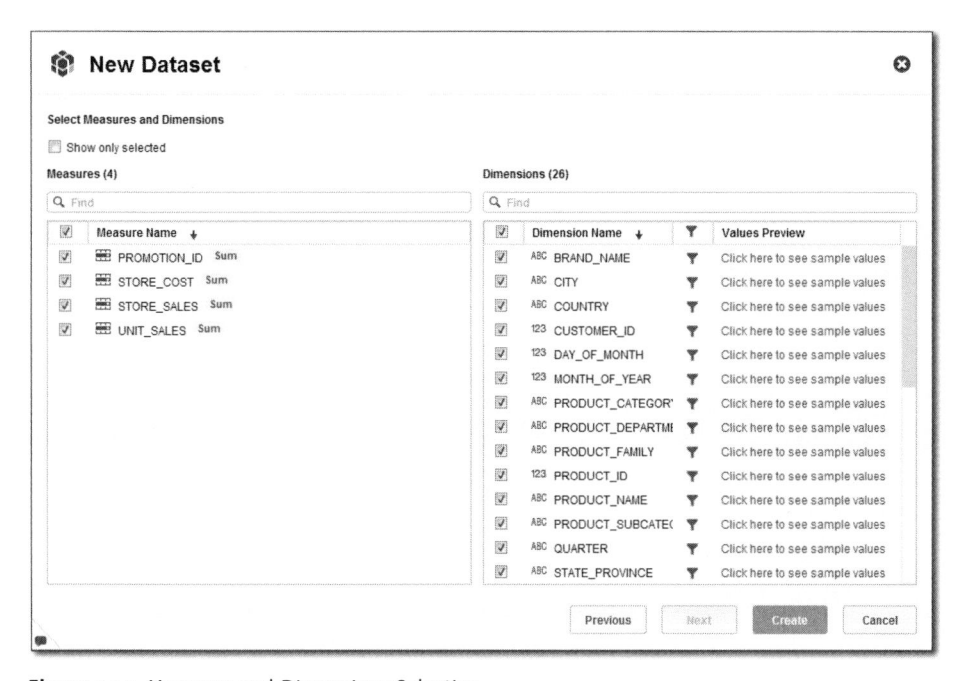

Figure 3.24 Measures and Dimensions Selection

3 | Data Acquisition

9. Select the checkbox before the measures and dimensions' names to select the ones to query to create the dataset. Select the SHOW ONLY SELECTED checkbox to display only the selected measures and dimensions.

10. In the DIMENSIONS table, in the VALUES PREVIEW column, click the CLICK HERE TO SEE SAMPLE VALUES link beside a dimension to preview some values of this dimension and display them in this column, as shown in Figure 3.25 for the COUNTRY dimension.

☑	Dimension Name ↓	▼	Values Preview
☑	ABC BRAND_NAME	▼	Click here to see sample values
☑	ABC CITY	▼	Click here to see sample values
☑	ABC COUNTRY	▼	USA,Mexico,Canada

Figure 3.25 Dimension Values Preview

11. To filter some values of a dimension, click the FILTER icon ▼ next to the dimension name in the DIMENSIONS table. This opens a dialog box that depends on the dimension type.

    If the dimension type is a string, then the dialog box displays the dimension values:

    ▸ Select the values of this object to use as the filter's operands, as shown in Figure 3.26 ❶. The values can be sorted ascending or descending by clicking the arrow on top of the list of values.

    ▸ Select if these values must be kept or removed from the query by selecting the KEEP ONLY or EXCLUDE radio button.

    ▸ Click the VIEW RECORDS link to display the number of occurrences of each value, as shown in Figure 3.26 ❷.

12. If the dimension type is numerical, then you need to define an interval used to filter the numeric values. As shown in Figure 3.27, the dialog box contains the following:

    ▸ Two sliders you can move to set the boundaries of the interval.

    ▸ An EXCLUDE EMPTY VALUES checkbox you can select to filter out empty values.

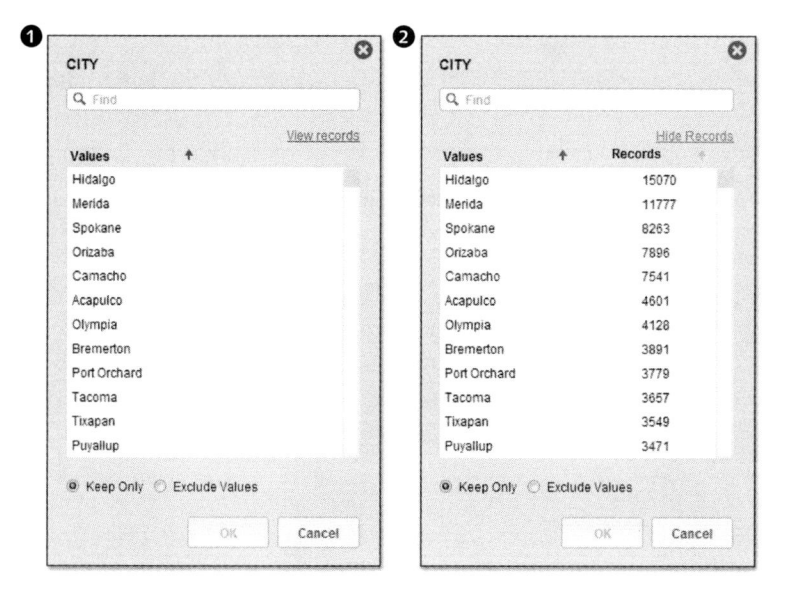

Figure 3.26 Values Selection for Filter

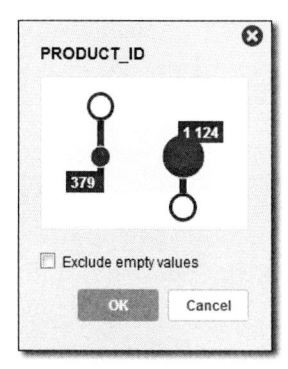

Figure 3.27 Numeric Dimension Filter

13. If the dimension type is a date, then you need to define a date interval used to filter the dates. As shown in Figure 3.28 ❶, the dialog box contains the following:

3 | Data Acquisition

▶ Two sliders you can move to set the boundaries of a date interval.

▶ Two dates fields in which you can enter the boudaries of the date interval. Click the CALENDAR icon 📅 in these fields to open a calendar window in which you can select the date, as shown in Figure 3.28 ❷.

▶ An EXCLUDE EMPTY VALUES checkbox you can select to filter out empty values.

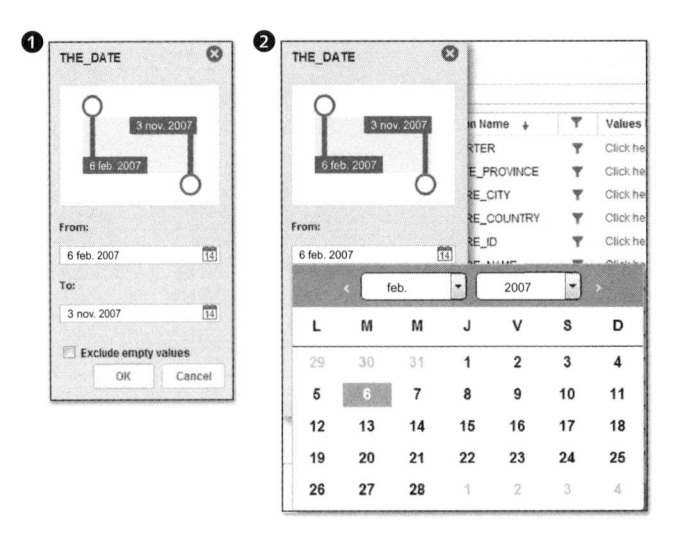

Figure 3.28 Date Dimension Filter

Click OK to close this dialog box. In the DIMENSIONS table, a FILTER icon indicates that you have added a filter for this dimension.

14. Click CREATE to close the NEW DATASET dialog box and retrieve the data for the selected measures and dimensions from the SAP HANA server to create the dataset.

3.6.2 SAP HANA Online Mode

As described in Section 3.1.3, SAP Lumira proposes for SAP HANA a specific access to data that does not require to retrieve the dataset and to keep it in the SAP Lumira document. This online mode takes advantage of the in-memory capabilities of the SAP HANA data source.

This access has some restrictions:

▶ It is not possible to create a measure with a numeric or string dimension.

- It is not possible to create a geographical hierarchy with more than one level.
- It is not possible to publish the retrieved dataset to SAP HANA.
- Some functions are not supported:
  - Methods related to the calendar: `AddMonthToDate`, `AddYearToDate`, `LastDayOfMonth`, `DayOfYear`, `Week`
  - Methods related to string manipulation: `LastWord`, `ExceptLastWord`
- If you access an analytical view that contains an object based on another object of a calculation view, then be aware of the following:
  - When you manipulate data in the Prepare room, the facets show no values when you select a measure, and the GRID view is not available.
  - When you create a visualization in the Visualize room, it is not possible to sort a measure.

The workflow to connect to SAP HANA in online mode is similar to the workflow to retrieve data in offline mode described in the previous section, except that you need to select CONNECT TO SAP HANA in the NEW DATASET dialog box.

After you have clicked CREATE, SAP Lumira connects to SAP HANA and retrieves the dataset. It does not store it in its in-memory database, but relies on SAP HANA to perform any processing.

When you save an SAP Lumira document based on an SAP HANA online dataset, it does not save this dataset in the document, but when you reopen it, you must connect to SAP HANA to get the document's dataset. When defining the SAP HANA data source, if you have not selected the SAVE PASSWORD checkbox to save the password (see Section 3.6.1), then you are prompted for this password. You must enter it before SAP Lumira can open the document and connect to SAP HANA to retrieve the dataset.

3.6.3 Answering SAP HANA Variables and Input Parameters

If variables or input parameters have been defined in the SAP HANA view, you may have to answer them before running the query on top of the view:

- An input parameter is used to define an internal parameterization of the view. A calculated measure or attribute may depend on an input parameter—for example, you may enter a target currency for currency conversion. It is not used to filter data, but rather to define the metadata.

An input parameter can have only one value as its answer. The input parameter value is passed to the engine via the `PLACEHOLDER` clause of the SQL statement.

▸ A variable is used to define a filter on an attribute of the view. A variable can have single value(s), interval(s), or range(s) as its answer. The variable values are passed to the engine via the `WHERE` clause of the SQL statement.

In SAP Lumira, you are prompted for answers in the VARIABLES dialog box that gathers questions for both variables and input parameters requested by the view or the objects you query.

This prompt dialog box is used whether you retrieve data from SAP HANA to create a dataset in offline mode (see Section 3.6.1) or connect to SAP HANA in online mode (see Section 3.6.2).

After you have selected a view, if this view contains a mandatory input parameter or a mandatory variable, then you will be in one the following situations:

▸ If you have selected to choose the objects of the query:
  ▹ Before you can select them, the VARIABLES dialog box opens, in which you must answer the variables and the input parameters.
  ▹ Later, when you select these objects, you can still modify your answers to the variables and the input parameters by clicking EDIT VARIABLES, which opens the VARIABLES dialog box. As shown in Figure 3.29, this button is displayed only if the view contains variables or input parameters.

▸ If you have not selected to choose the objects of the query, then you must answer the variables and the input parameters in the VARIABLES dialog box before running the query.

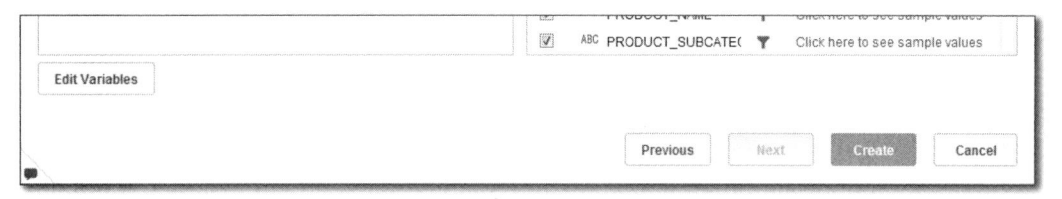

Figure 3.29 Edit Variables Button

If the view contains only optional input parameters or variables:

▸ You can answer prompts in the object selection by clicking EDIT VARIABLES, which opens the VARIABLES dialog box.

▸ You can answer prompts before running the query if you have not selected to choose objects or if you have not yet resolved the prompts.

As shown in Figure 3.30, the VARIABLES dialog box is made of three parts:

▸ On its left side, there is the variables list. This list can contain both variables and input parameters, but it is not possible to differentiate them. A mandatory variable has a red asterisk before its name.
▸ On the top-right side is the list of possible values for the selected variable.
▸ On the bottom-right side are the expressions that define the selected values.

Figure 3.30 Variables Dialog Box

To answer variables, follow these steps:

1. Select a variable in the variables list. If it has a default value, then it is selected in the list of values, and the expression to select it is updated, as seen in Figure 3.31.

3 | Data Acquisition

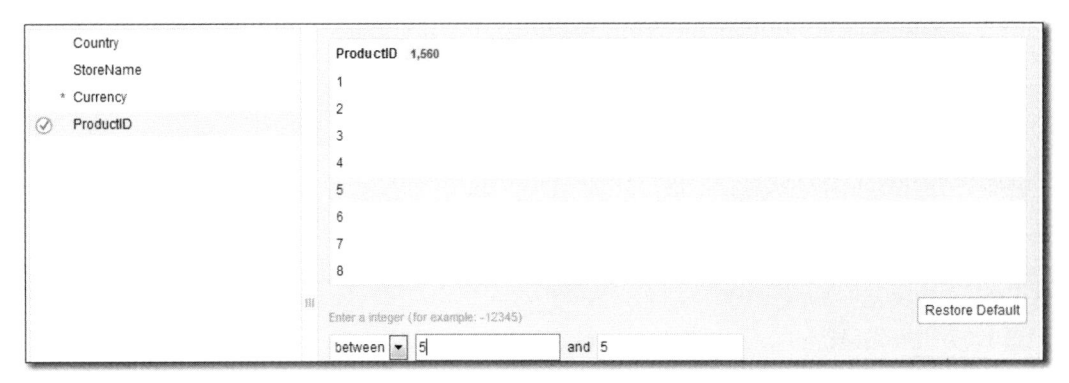

Figure 3.31 Default Values

2. The possible expression depends on the variable type:
    - If it expects a single value, then the expression is based on one or no operands, as shown in Figure 3.32.
    - If it expects an interval, then the expression is based on a lower or an upper limit or both. Hence, it requires one or two operands, as shown in Figure 3.33.
    - If it expects a range, then the expression can be based on a wider set of operators, as shown in Figure 3.34. The expression may require one, two, or no operands.

   Use the dropdown list to select the expression operator. To enter an expression operand, select it, and then type its value or select it in the list of values. When an expression is complete, the values it defines are selected in the list of values.

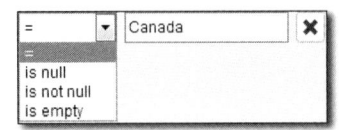

Figure 3.32 Single-Value Expression

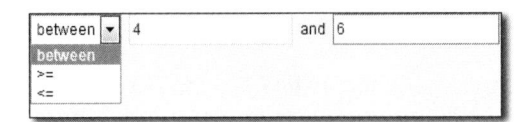

Figure 3.33 Interval Expression

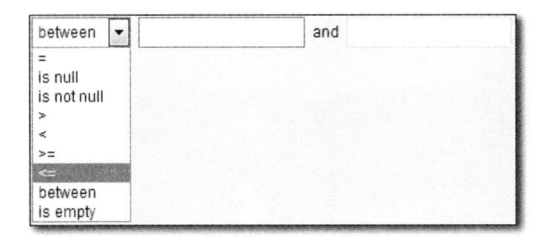

Figure 3.34 Range Expression

3. If the variable accepts several entries, then you can add a new expression by clicking the ADD icon below the expressions, as shown in Figure 3.35. Modify this expression as described previously.

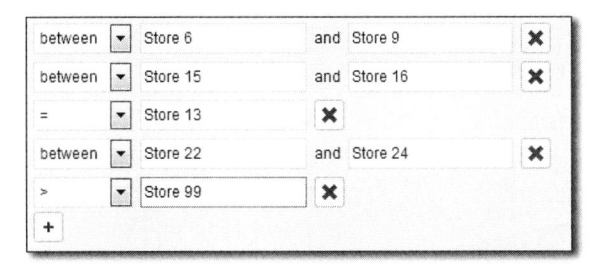

Figure 3.35 Multiple Expressions for a Multiple-Entries Variable

4. To remove an expression, click the DELETE icon beside the expression. Removing an expression unselects the values it defines.
5. To reset the variables' default values, click RESTORE DEFAULT.
6. Repeat these steps until you have answered at least all mandatory variables.
7. Click OK to validate your answers. The VARIABLES dialog box closes, and your answers for variables and input parameters are kept and used when the query is actually run.

3.7 SAP BusinessObjects BI Universes

In SAP BusinessObjects BI landscape, the semantic layer and its universes are a powerful, historical, central component that allows other SAP BusinessObjects BI reporting tools to access a wide range of data sources.

By using universes to retrieve data, you can also benefit from this semantic abstraction in SAP Lumira. Universes also allow you to access your relational data sources by using drivers other than the JDBC drivers installed locally.

> **Additional Reference**
>
> For more details on universes, you can refer to *Universe Design with SAP BusinessObjects BI: The Comprehensive Guide* (SAP PRESS, 2014).

3.7.1 Universes Support

SAP Lumira can benefit from universes' capabilities to query data from a wide range of data sources and create datasets. If you already have an SAP BusinessObjects BI platform with universes you have designed, then you can reuse these universes and have a common semantic layer for all your analytical tools.

SAP Lumira can query the following:

- Relational universes created with the Universe Design Tool. Universes based on an OLAP data source are not supported.
- Relational universes created with the Information Design Tool. Multidimensional universes created with the information design tool are not supported.

SAP Lumira can only query universes if they have been saved in an SAP BusinessObjects BI CMS repository; local universes are not supported. Hence, you need valid credentials to access the CMS repository and the appropriate security rights to query the universe.

The versions supported are as follows:

- For universes created with the Universe Design Tool:
  - SAP XI 3.1 SP6 and SP7
  - SAP BusinessObjects BI 4.0 SP7 to SP9
  - SAP BusinessObjects BI 4.1 to SAP BusinessObjects BI 4.1 SP3.
- For universes created with the Information Design Tool:
  - SAP BusinessObjects BI 4.0 SP7 and higher.
  - SAP BusinessObjects BI 4.1 to SAP BusinessObjects BI 4.1 SP3.

As opposed to the other data sources supported by SAP Lumira for which specific SAP Lumira drivers are used, connections to data sources through universes are processed by components running server-side:

- Connection Server for single-source universes
- Data Federator Query Server for multisource universes
- Information Engine for processing data through universes

3.7.2 Retrieving Data from Universes

To create a dataset from a universe, make sure you have a valid account to connect to the CMS repository with the following security rights granted:

- Universe
    - VIEW OBJECTS
    - CREATE AND EDIT QUERY ON THIS UNIVERSE
    - DATA ACCESS
- Connection
    - VIEW OBJECTS
    - DATA ACCESS
- Folders containing the universe and the connection
    - VIEW OBJECTS

Then, follow these steps to begin creating a dataset from a universe:

1. Open the NEW DATASET dialog box, as described in Section 3.1.4.
2. In the NEW DATASET dialog box that opens, select the UNIVERSE choice in the SELECT A SOURCE list, and click NEXT.
3. In the UNIVERSE CREDENTIALS section, as shown in Figure 3.36, enter the following parameters required to connect to the SAP BusinessObjects BI 4 server:
    - CMS NAME: The name of the SAP BusinessObjects BI 4 server running the SAP server and its port. If you already connected to this server, then you can also enter its cluster name.
    - USER NAME and PASSWORD: Credentials to authenticate login to the SAP BusinessObjects BI 4.1 CMS repository using the previously selected authentication mode.

By default, the password is not saved in order to force password-checking when reconnecting to the CMS repository. To save it for future use, select the SAVE PASSWORD checkbox.

▶ AUTHENTICATION TYPE: Use the dropdown list to select one authentication mode to connect to SAP BusinessObjects BI 4.1 (ENTERPRISE, LDAP, WINDOWS AD, or SAP). To authenticate login with WINDOWS AD, you need to configure Kerberos, as described in Section 3.1.5.

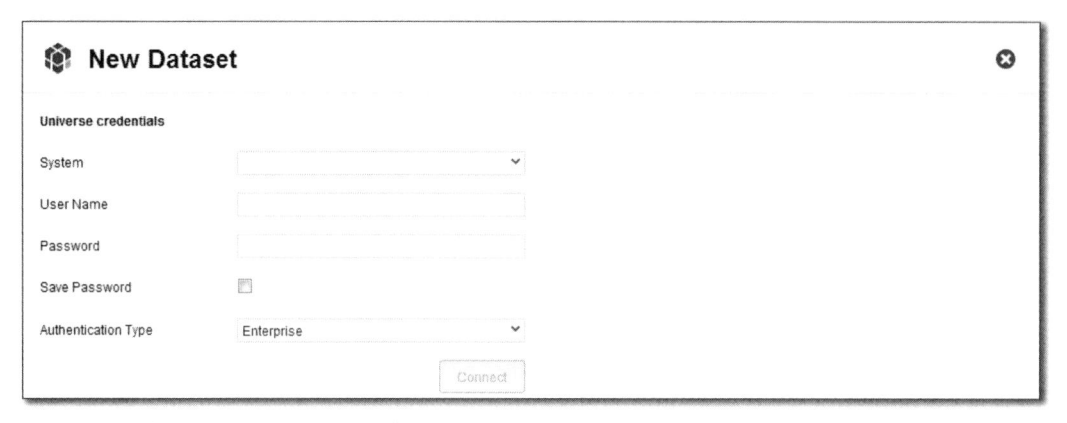

Figure 3.36 SAP BusinessObjects BI CMS Repository Login Page

4. Click CONNECT to connect to the SAP BusinessObjects BI 4 server.
5. Once connected, the SELECT A UNIVERSE section displays the universes published in the *Universes* folder and subfolders in the CMS repository, as shown in Figure 3.37. The icon before the universe name identifies if the universe has been published by the Universe Design Tool or the Information Design Tool.
6. In the DATASET NAME, enter a name for the new dataset.
7. Select a universe from among the ones published in the CMS repository. The universe description is displayed in the DESCRIPTION text field. The FIND text field allows you to find a specific universe: as you type your text in this field, the universe list is filtered to display only universes with names that fit this pattern.

Figure 3.37 Universe Selection

8. Click NEXT. As shown in Figure 3.38, the dialog box displays the universe metadata in the UNIVERSE tree list, on the left: DIMENSIONS, ATTRIBUTES, MEASURES, FOLDERS, and PREDEFINED FILTERS. The FIND text field allows you to find a specific object in the universe: as you type your text in this field, the universe metadata is filtered to display only metadata with names that fit this pattern.

   If the universe master view is denied, then only the first granted view is displayed.

9. In the right side of the panel, two tabs allow you to switch between the list of results objects and the list of filters (see Section 3.7.3).

10. Click the RESULT OBJECTS tab:

    ▶ Double-click an object from the UNIVERSE tree list to add it in the query to run and display it in the tab.

    ▶ Double-click a folder to add all objects (dimensions, measures, and attributes) it contains into the query; predefined filters are not selected.

    Added objects are displayed in the RESULT OBJECTS tab.

3 | Data Acquisition

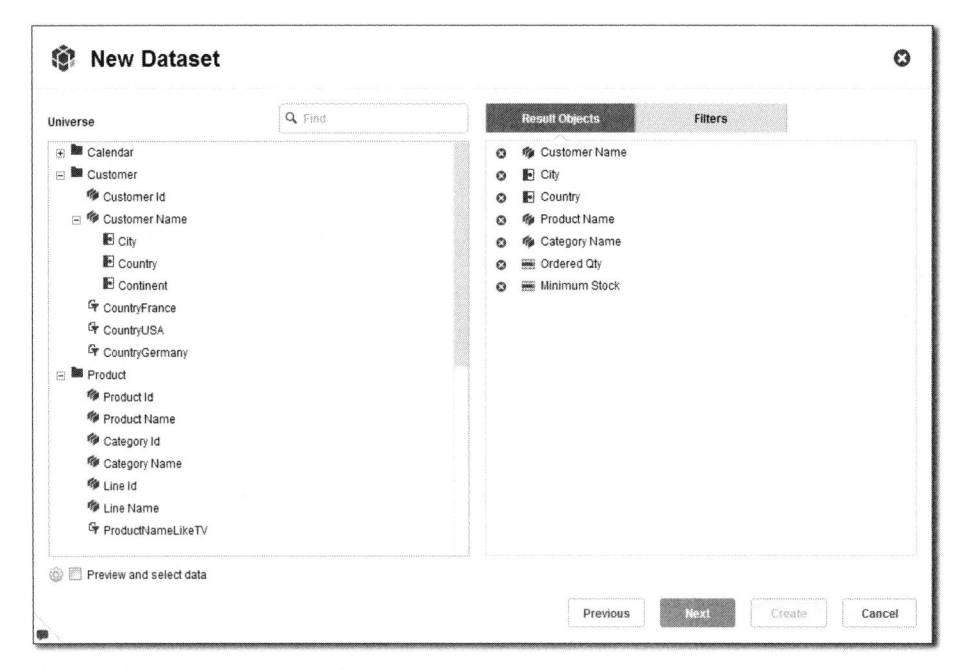

Figure 3.38 Universe Query Panel

11. To remove an object from the query, click the DELETE icon before the object name.

12. Click the QUERY PROPERTIES icon to open the QUERY PROPERTIES dialog box, as shown in Figure 3.39, in which you can modify some query parameters:

    ▶ MAX ROWS RETRIEVED: Select this checkbox, and set a number of rows to limit the number of rows retrieved from the sources. This value overrides the value set in the universe, but you can only provide a lower value than the one defined for the option in the universe.

    ▶ MAX RETRIEVAL TIME: Select this checkbox, and set a number of seconds to limit the time the query can run. This value overrides the value set in the universe, but you can only provide a lower value than the one defined for the option in the universe.

    ▶ RETRIEVE DUPLICATE ROWS: Select this checkbox to retrieve identical rows each time they appear. If this is unchecked, only distinct rows are retrieved.

    Click CLOSE to close the dialog box and save the properties for this query.

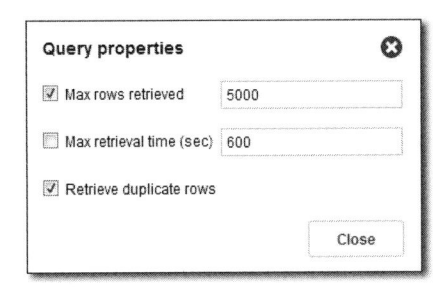

Figure 3.39 Query Properties Dialog Box

13. Select the PREVIEW AND SELECT DATA checkbox to preview the data returned by the query before displaying it in the Prepare room.

14. When your query is ready, click NEXT. Before you run your query, consider the following:

    ▸ If your query contains different filters (predefined filters or filters based on objects), then they are all aggregated using the AND operator (see Section 3.7.3).

    ▸ If the query requires answers to some prompts (contexts or parameters), then they are displayed, and you need to answer them (see Section 3.7.4).

    If you have not selected the PREVIEW AND SELECT DATA checkbox, then the dialog box closes, and the dataset is displayed in the Prepare room.

    Otherwise, if you have selected this checkbox, before actually creating the dataset you can preview a table containing some values returned by the query with columns corresponding to objects in the query, as shown in Figure 3.40. Perform the following actions:

    ▸ Unselect the checkbox before an object name to remove it from the dataset. This does not modify the query definition but indicates only that the object values from the result set must not be used to fill the dataset.

    ▸ Select/unselect the SELECT ALL checkbox to add or remove all objects of the query in the dataset.

    ▸ Click the SHOW RECORD COUNT link to display the number of selected objects and the number of objects and rows returned by the preview.

    ▸ Click CREATE to close the NEW DATASET dialog box, create the dataset from the query result and with the selected columns, and display it in your default room.

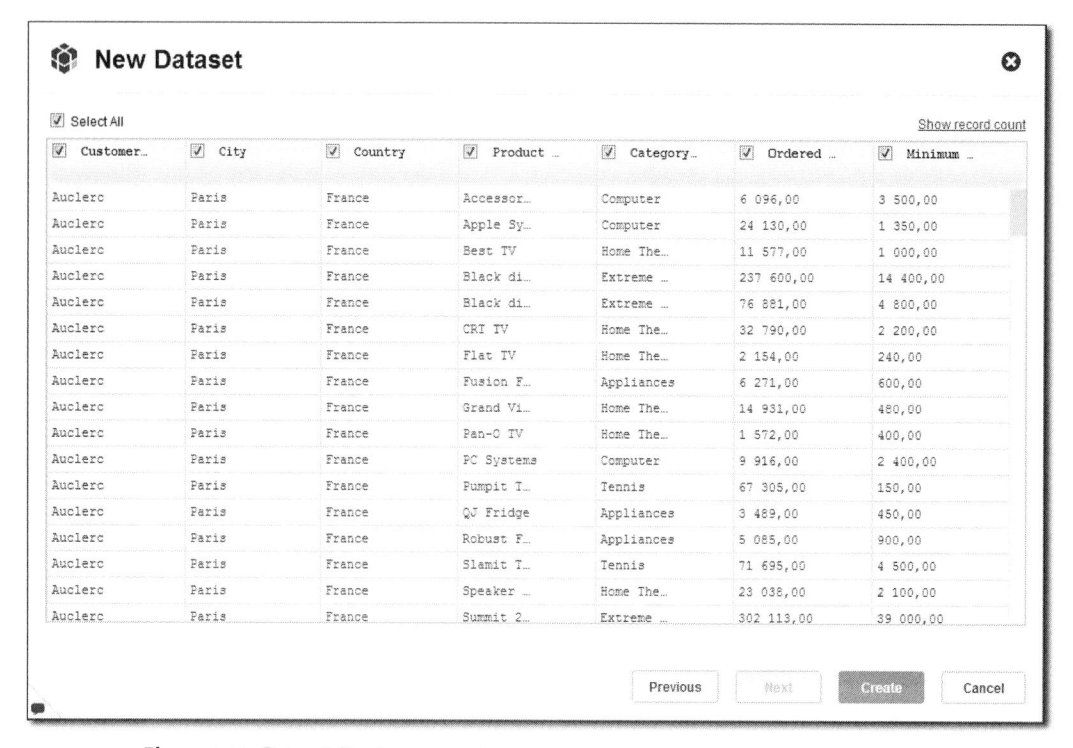

Figure 3.40 Dataset Preview

To customize your query, you can add filters when you create it, as discussed in the next section.

3.7.3 Adding Filters

When creating your query, you can add some filters to narrow the data returned by the query. There are two filter types supported in the SAP Lumira query panel:

- Predefined filters that are defined in the universe.
- Simple filters you can define when creating the query. Complex filters, such as subqueries or ranking, are not supported.

You can add several filters to a query, and they are aggregated using the AND operator. The OR operator is not supported.

To add filters to your query, follow these steps:

1. Create a dataset from a universe, as described in Section 3.7.2.
2. When selecting the universe metadata to add in the query, double-click a predefined filter to add it to the query. This filter is then added in the FILTERS tab, as shown in Figure 3.41. If you have not yet selected it, then the FILTERS tab is automatically selected.

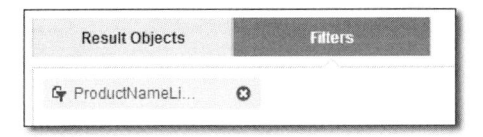

Figure 3.41 Predefined Filter

3. With the FILTERS tab selected, double-click a folder to add all predefined filters it contains to the query.
4. With the FILTERS tab selected, double-click an object to add a new filter based on this object to the query. When the object is added to the FILTERS tab, as shown in Figure 3.42, click the FILTER icon ▼ in the object to open a dialog box to perform the following actions:
   - Select the values of this object to use as the filter's operands, as shown in Figure 3.43. The values can be sorted ascending or descending by clicking the arrow on top of the list of values.
   - Select if these values must be kept or removed from the query by selecting the KEEP ONLY or EXCLUDE radio button.

   Click OK to close this dialog box. The FILTER icon is modified and has a blue background to show that the filter has been completely defined.

Figure 3.42 Filter Based on an Object

Figure 3.43 Values Selection

5. To remove a filter from the query, in the FILTERS tab, click the DELETE icon after the filter or object name.

When your query is ready, click NEXT to run it and retrieve the data, as described in the previous section.

3.7.4 Answering Contexts and Parameters

In SAP XI 3 and SAP BusinessObjects BI 4, universes support contexts, parameters, and lists of values:

▸ Contexts are used to disambiguate paths in the database schema model used by the universe. Before the query is run, you are prompted with the available contexts so that you can select the ones to use for your query.

- Parameters are used to allow you to provide some values that can be used to modify the query definition. The data returned by the data source correspond to the values you have selected. For example, a parameter may allow you to select a country and a year, and the query returns data only for this country and year.
- Lists of values define the possible values you can use to answer a parameter.

In the Information Design Tool, parameters are defined in the universe through the `@prompt` built-in function or parameter objects; in the Universe Design Tool, parameters (also named prompts) can only be defined by using the `@prompt` built-in function.

SAP Lumira supports the following different parameters and lists of values available in the universe:

- **Cascading list of values**
  You are prompted with successive parameters to define the possible list of values—for example, a first parameter asks you to select a country from among a list of countries, and a second parameter asks you to select a city from among a list of cities.
- **Hierarchical list of values**
  Available only for universes created with the Information Design Tool, in which you navigate a hierarchy to select the values—for example, a geographical list of values may allow you to select a value in a hierarchy containing continents, countries, and cities.
- **Multicolumn list of values**
  Available only for universes created with the Information Design Tool, in which the possible values are displayed with additional data—for example, the cities to select can be displayed with their postal codes and population numbers.

If the query requires answering some prompts (contexts or parameters), then these are displayed and you must answer them before you can preview the data or run the query. Perform the following steps to preview the data or run the query:

1. After you have created a query on a universe created with the Information Design Tool or the Universe Design Tool, as described in Section 3.7.2, click NEXT to preview the data or run the query.

2. If the query requires you to select a context, then the possible contexts are displayed, as shown in Figure 3.44. Click the radio button before the name of the context you select, and then click NEXT.

Figure 3.44 Answering Universe Contexts

3. If the query requires you to answer some parameters, then the dialog box is updated to display these parameters, as shown in Figure 3.45:

   ▶ The left side of the dialog box lists the parameters you need to answer. Cascading parameters are displayed using indentations.

   ▶ At the center, you can enter your answer or select it from among the parameter's list of values (if any).

   ▶ The right side of the dialog box displays all of your answers for the parameters.

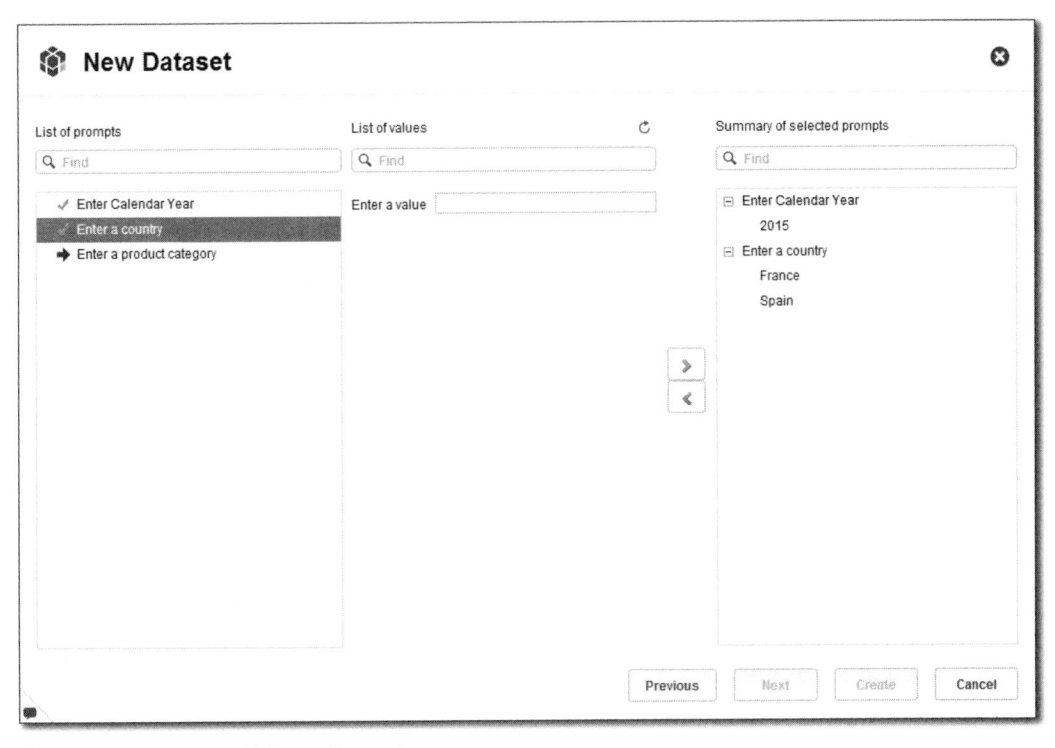

Figure 3.45 Answering Universe Parameters

4. Select the first parameter in the LIST OF PROMPTS list.

   If a list of values is associated with this parameter, then it is displayed in the LIST OF VALUES section. You will then click the ↻ icon to refresh this list of values and use the FIND field to look for a specific value in this list.

   Select a value in the list, then click the RIGHT ARROW button to add it to the selected answers. These answers are displayed in the SUMMARY OF SELECTED PROMPTS panel.

   If the parameter accepts other answers than those in the list, then you may type another answer in the ENTER A VALUE text field and then click the RIGHT ARROW button to add it to the selected answers.

   To remove an answer, select it in the SUMMARY OF SELECTED PROMPTS list, and then click the LEFT ARROW button to remove it from the list.

5. Repeat these steps for all parameters to answer. When all parameters are answered, click NEXT to get a data preview or run the query and create the dataset.

3.8 SAP BusinessObjects BW

SAP Lumira can also query and retrieve data from an SAP BW query (also called a BEx query) or an InfoProvider. The supported versions are as follows:

- SAP BusinessObjects BW 7.0 with Service Pack higher than or equal to 23
- SAP BusinessObjects BW 7.01/7.02 with Service Pack higher than or equal to 08
- SAP BusinessObjects BW 7.30 with Service Pack higher than or equal to 03
- SAP BusinessObjects BW 7.31/7.4

In order to benefit from the libraries it uses to connect to SAP BW system, SAP GUI for Windows must first be installed on the same machine that runs SAP Lumira. You can download it from the SAP Support website (*http://service.sap.com/support*) under the SOFTWARE DOWNLOADS • SAP SOFTWARE DOWNLOAD CENTER tab and then under the G index.

The connection to SAP BusinessObjects BW from SAP Lumira Desktop can only be made in online mode, as for SAP HANA. This means that computations are delegated to the SAP BW system, but this introduces the same limitation as for SAP HANA: it is not possible to perform any action on the dataset (see Chapter 4). In fact, in the current version, data can only be displayed in the Visualize room (see Chapter 5); the Prepare and Compose rooms are not available.

3.8.1 Retrieving Data from SAP BW

To create a dataset from an SAP BW system, follow these steps:

1. Open the NEW DATASET dialog box, as described in Section 3.1.4.

2. In the SELECT A SOURCE section, select the CONNECT TO SAP BUSINESS WAREHOUSE option and click NEXT.

3. In the CONNECT TO SAP BUSINESS WAREHOUSE panel, as shown in Figure 3.46, enter the parameters to connect to the SAP BW system:

   ▶ SERVER: This dropdown list contains the list of SAP BW systems registered in the SAPLogin.ini file stored on your local machine. Select one server in the dropdown list. If your server is not available, then you must create a connection to this server in SAP GUI for Windows and then recreate the connection from SAP Lumira.
   ▶ CLIENT ID: The three numbers that identify the SAP system client.
   ▶ LANGUAGE: The language to access the SAP BW system.
   ▶ USER and PASSWORD: Credentials to connect to the SAP BW system.
   ▶ SAVE PASSWORD: Select this checkbox to save the password to authenticate login to SAP BW.

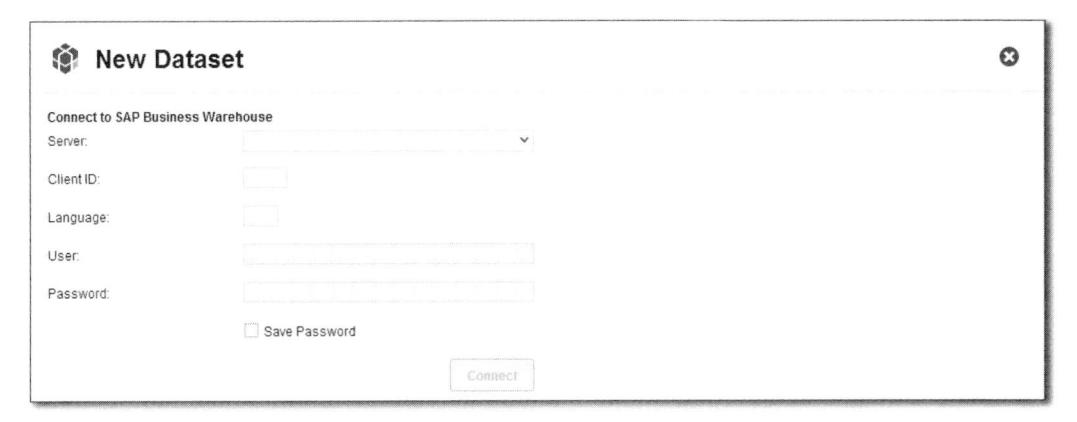

Figure 3.46 SAP BW Login Page

4. Click CONNECT to connect to the SAP BW system.
5. The dialog box is updated to list the InfoProviders and BEx queries from which you can retrieve data.
6. In the VIEW dropdown list, select the ROLES or INFOAREAS option to display InfoProviders and BEx queries by roles or by InfoAreas.
7. Navigate in the tree, and select an InfoProvider or BEx query to use as data source, as shown in Figure 3.47. The folder may take several seconds before it opens and displays its content.

3 | Data Acquisition

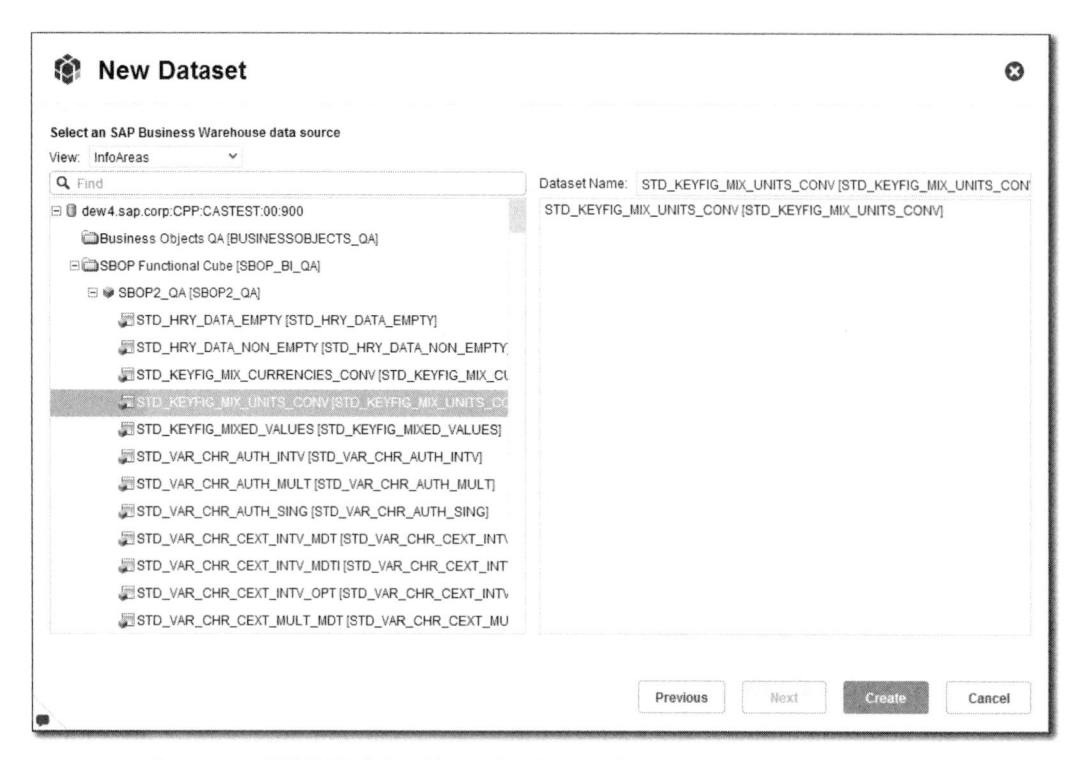

Figure 3.47 SAP BW InfoProvider or BEx Query Selection

8. To find a specific object, type its name in the FIND text field and press Enter.
9. In the DATASET NAME text field, enter a name for the dataset. By default, this dataset is named from the selected InfoProvider or BEx query.
10. Click CREATE to close the NEW DATASET dialog box and query the selected data source.

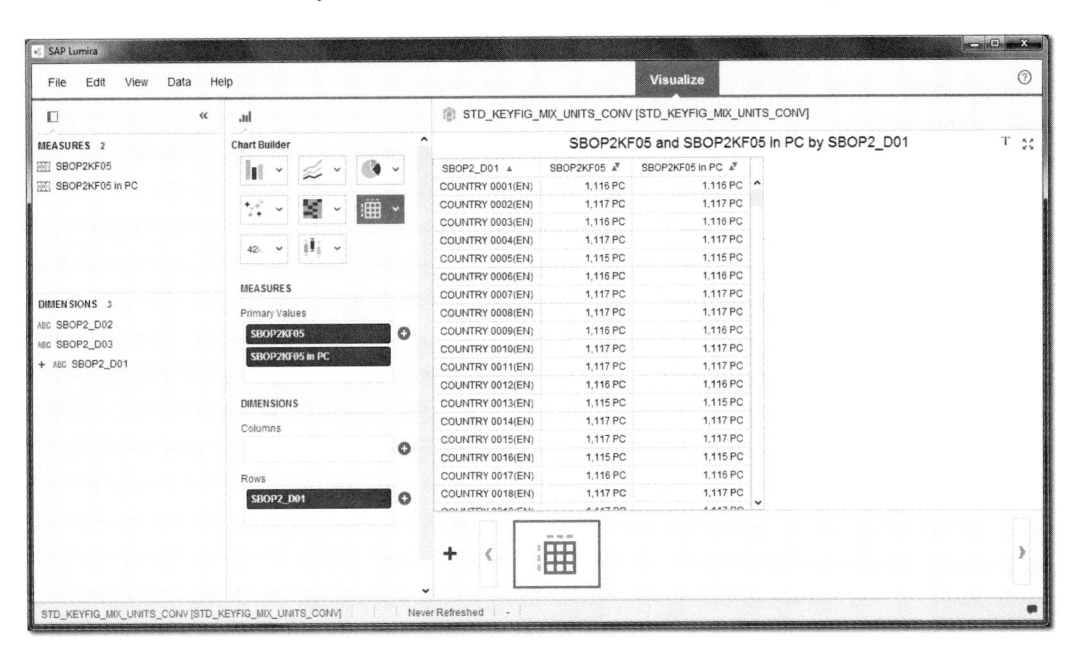

11. The VISUALIZE room opens, with the retrieved data, as shown in Figure 3.48.

Figure 3.48 Data Retrieved from SAP BW and Displayed in a Visualize Room

If the query contains some variables to answer, then they are displayed in a dedicated dialog box, as described in the next section.

3.8.2 Answering SAP BusinessObjects BW Variables

If the query requires some variables to be answered, the PROMPTS dialog box opens in the Visualize room before querying the data source. This dialog box displays the list of variables to answer, as shown in Figure 3.49.

3 | Data Acquisition

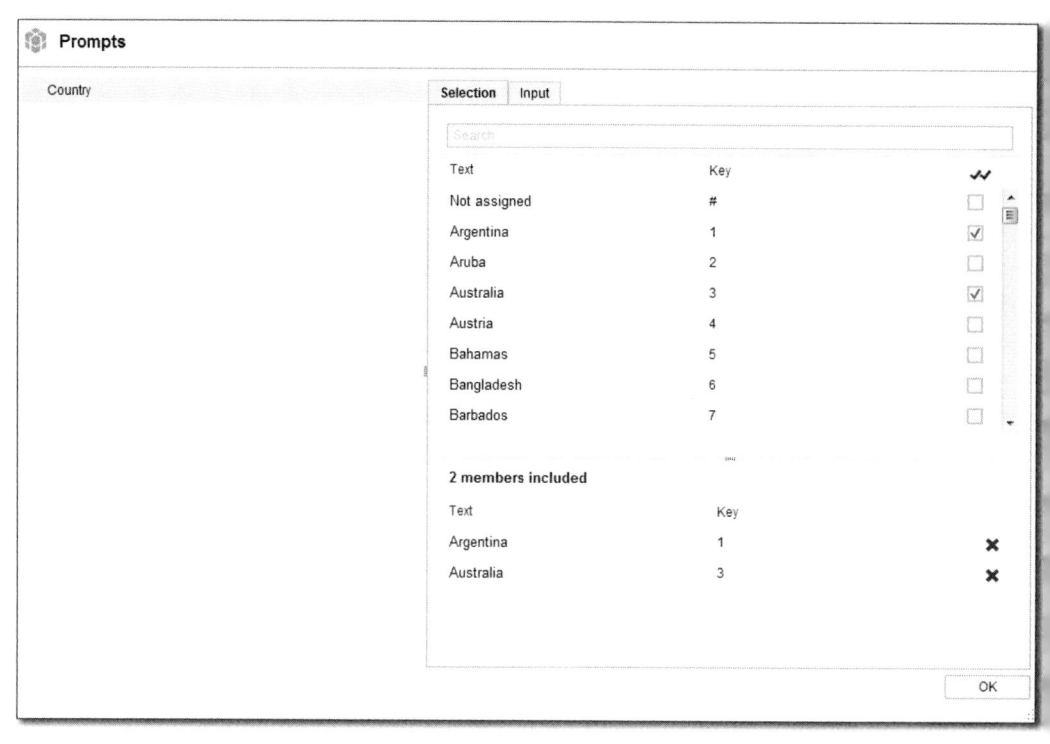

Figure 3.49 Prompts Dialog Box For SAP BusinessObjects BW

If a variable is mandatory, then an asterisk is displayed before its name.

To answer the variables, follow these steps:

1. Select a variable to answer in the left side of the dialog box.
2. The SELECTION tab is updated with the list of possible values, with both their text and key:
   - Click the checkbox beside a value to add it to the list of included members below this values list.
   - Click the DOUBLE-CHECK icon to add all members in the list.

   If there are too many values to display, then no values are displayed, as shown in Figure 3.50.
3. Use the text file to search for a specific value. Type a search string, and then click the SEARCH icon to display the values that fit this search string (see Figure 3.51).

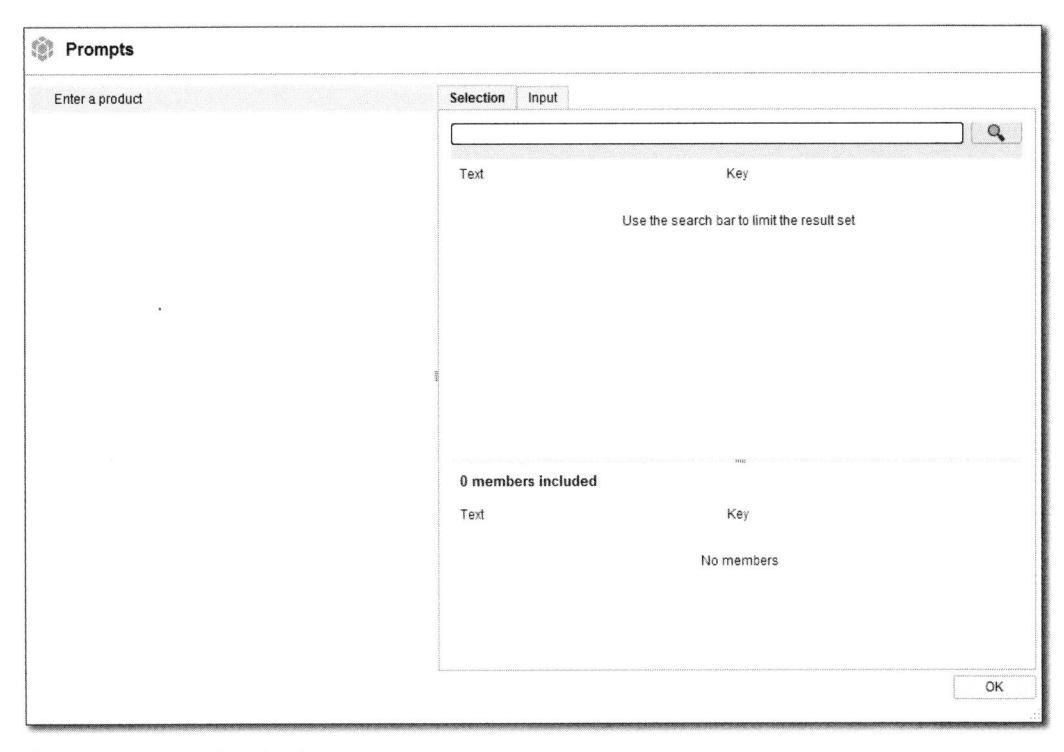

Figure 3.50 No Displayed Values

Figure 3.51 Values Search Results

4. Select values to add them to the list of included members below this values list.
5. Select the EXCLUDE checkbox if the included members define the values that must not be added to the selection.
6. If the variable supports it, click the RANGE tab to make the selection based on a range of values rather than on the individual entries selected (see Figure 3.52).

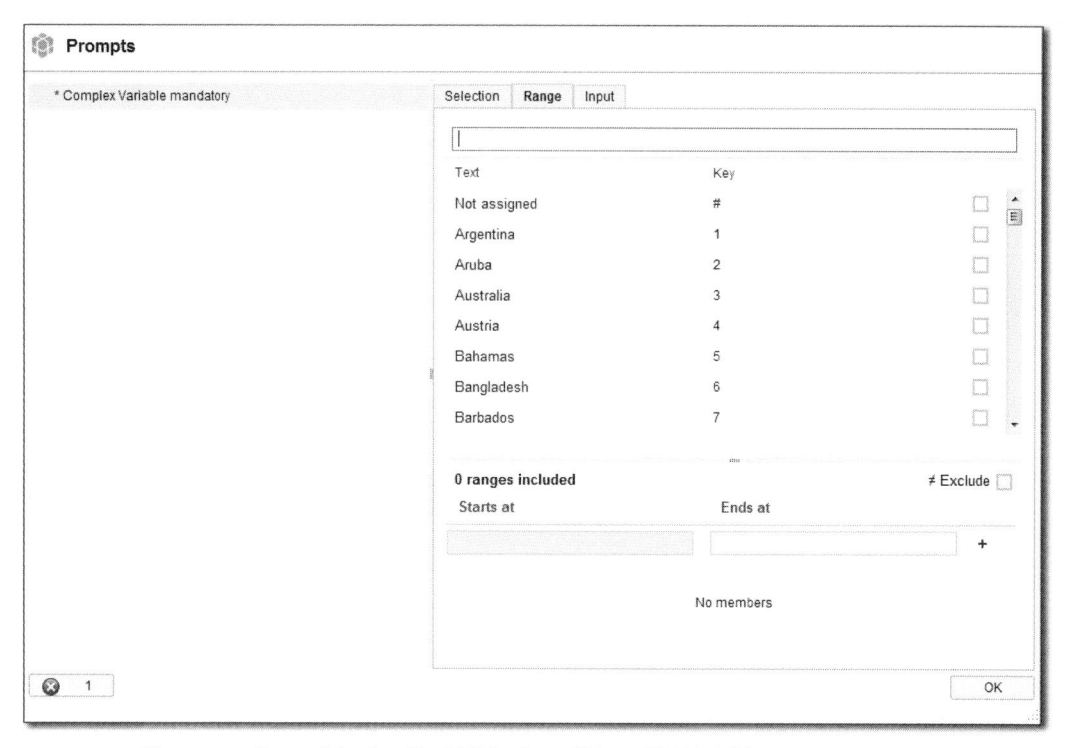

Figure 3.52 Range Selection For SAP BusinessObjects BW Variables

7. Click the STARTS AT text field, and then click a checkbox to select a value in the possible list of values for the lower limit of the range.
8. Repeat the same step for the ENDS AT text field to select an upper limit for the range.

9. If the variable accepts multiple entries, then you may add another range by clicking the ADD icon beside the first range. A new range is added, as shown in Figure 3.53.

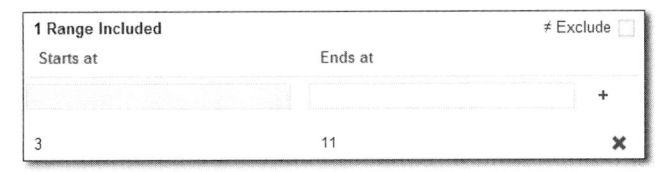

1 Range Included		≠ Exclude
Starts at	Ends at	
		+
3	11	✖

Figure 3.53 Multiple Ranges Selection for SAP BusinessObjects BW Variables

10. To remove a range, click the DELETE icon beside the range.
11. Click the EXCLUDE checkbox if the defined ranges define the values that must not be added to the selection.
12. Rather than selecting your answers in the values proposed by the dialog box or by defining a range, you may manually enter the key of a value:
    ▸ Click the INPUT tab to display a text field, as shown in Figure 3.54.
    ▸ Enter your key in this text field.

    This process can be more convenient if you need to enter only one value that you often use.

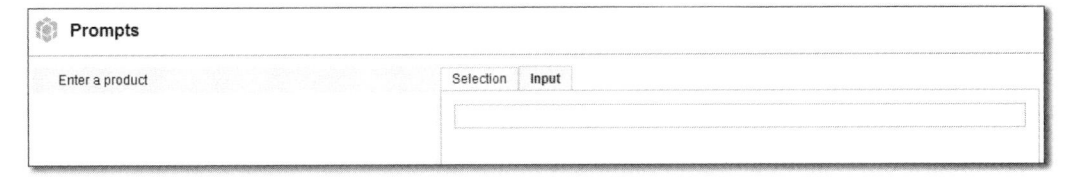

Prompts		
Enter a product	Selection	Input

Figure 3.54 Input Tab for SAP BusinessObjects BW Variables

13. Click OK to run the query with your answers to the variables. If an error in your answers prevents the query from running, then click the ERROR icon to open a dialog box with the error description, as shown in Figure 3.55. Otherwise, if the query is successful, the PROMPTS dialog box closes, and data is displayed in the Visualize room.

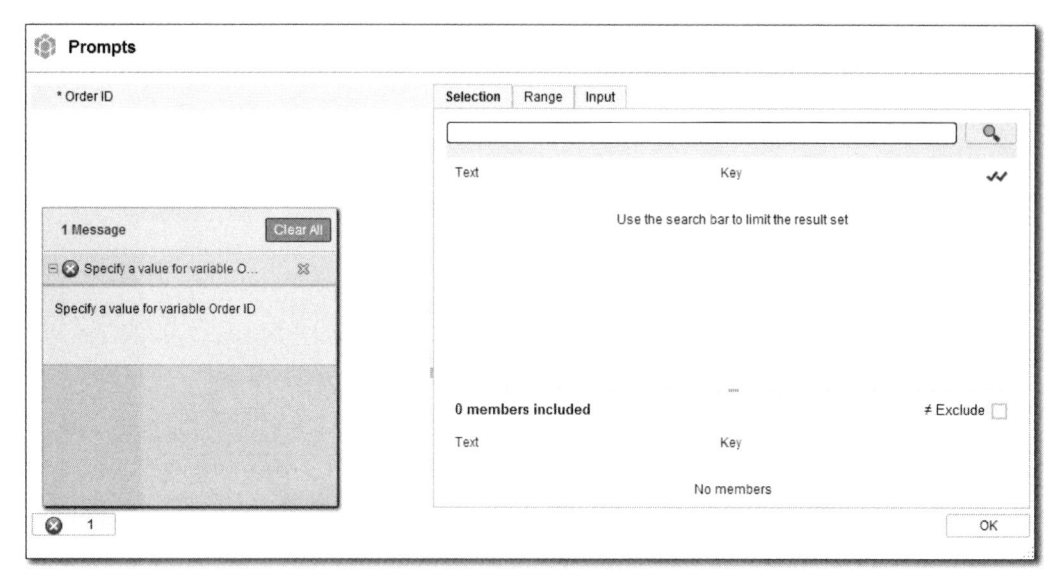

Figure 3.55 Variables Error

3.9 Dataset Edit and Refresh

After you have created your dataset, the data source it came from may have changed: the connections to access it may have changed, and the data it contains may have been updated. On your end, you can modify the data you retrieved from it. In all cases, you need to refresh your dataset.

3.9.1 Editing Data Sources' Connection Parameters

There are different cases in which the connection to the data source used to generate the dataset must be modified:

- You have renamed the text or Microsoft Excel file used as the data source or moved it to another folder.
- The password to the system used as a data source has changed
- The database has been moved to another server.

In such cases, you need to update the connection parameters to reflect these changes. To do so, follow these steps:

1. From the WELCOME page, click the CONNECTIONS tab to list all connections used by your documents.
2. Click a connection to select it, as shown in Figure 3.56:
   ▸ The connection line is expanded to display the parameters saved in the connection.
   ▸ The right pane lists the documents saved in the SAP Lumira Documents folder using the same parameters.

Figure 3.56 Connection Lists

3. Modify the parameters of the connection. These parameters depend on the connection type and have been described in previous sections.
4. In the right pane, select the checkbox beside the document name to select ones that must be updated with the new connection parameters.
5. Click APPLY to modify the connection parameters for the selected documents.

After this change, be aware of the following:

- If the new connection parameters you entered have not yet been used by any document, then a new connection is added to the connection list, and the selected documents are associated with this new connection.
- If a similar connection was already referenced, then the selected documents are removed from the initial connection and listed in the documents using this connection.
- If no more documents reference the initial connection, then it is removed from the CONNECTIONS list.

This change does not modify the metadata used for the dataset, which is done by modifying the dataset parameters.

3.9.2 Editing Dataset Parameters

In some cases, you may need to modify the definition of data you retrieve from the data source. This is typically the case if you want to modify the objects that make your dataset or modify the query sent to an SAP HANA view or an SAP BusinessObjects BI universe.

> **Dataset Based on Clipboard**
>
> Editing the dataset parameters is not possible if the dataset is created from clipboard content.

To edit the dataset parameters, follow these steps:

1. Open your document in the PREPARE or VISUALIZE room.
2. In the menu bar, select the DATA • EDIT command to open the EDIT SOURCE dialog box.
3. This dialog box is similar to the one used to define the data to retrieve from the data source. Hence, it depends on the data source type:
    - For text and Microsoft Excel files, it displays the same dialog box used to create a dataset from these files (see Section 3.2 and Section 3.4). You can add or remove any column(s) from the source file(s) by selecting or unselect-

ing its checkbox(es) in the table preview, but you cannot modify the source files or any other parameters.

▸ For datasets created with a SQL query, it displays the SQL Editor (see Section 3.5.3), but you cannot modify the query or change the data source. You can add or remove any column(s) of this SQL query by selecting or unselecting its checkbox(es) in the table preview.

▸ For SAP HANA, it displays the SELECT THE MEASURES AND DIMENSIONS PANEL used to create the dataset on the view used to create the dataset (see Section 3.6.1). You cannot change this source view, but you can add or remove measures and dimensions of the view and add new filters to dimensions or modify or delete the existing ones.

▸ For SAP BusinessObjects BI universes, it displays the Query Panel on the universe used by the document (see Section 3.7.1 and Section 3.7.2). You cannot change the source universe, but you can completely modify the query used to create the dataset:

– Add or remove new objects to/from the query
– Add or remove filters to/from the query
– Modify the query properties

4. If you unselect an object, a confirmation message is displayed, because removing some columns from a dataset has an impact on the objects based on them (see Figure 3.57).

Figure 3.57 Warning before Removing Columns

Once the data has been edited, a refresh is automatically performed to take into consideration the changes made in the dataset definition.

3.9.3 Refreshing the Dataset

When you create the dataset, you connect to the data source to retrieve the dataset from it. Except for the online mode available for SAP HANA and SAP BW (see Section 3.6.2 and Section 3.8), any further operations are performed in the in-memory database. The next time you open the document, SAP Lumira does not require reconnecting to the database and can work with the dataset it contains.

However, refreshing the dataset is needed when the data in the data source has been updated and the dataset in the SAP Lumira document is no longer synchronized with the data source content.

When you refesh a dataset, any actions you have created on it are kept. The data is retrieved from the data source, and the same actions are replayed to transform your dataset.

If the dataset requires metadata that is no longer available in the data source, then the dataset is not updated, and an error message is displayed. For example, this can be the case if an object used by the query has been removed from a universe or if a column used in the dataset has been removed from a text or Microsoft Excel file.

If the datasource contains more metadata that has been added since the last refresh, then it has no impact on the dataset definition, and the refresh may proceed. The dataset is also automatically refreshed after you have modified its definition (see Section 3.9.2).

You can refresh a dataset if you are displaying a document in the PREPARE, VISUALIZE, or COMPOSE room. To refresh the dataset, follow these steps:

1. In the menu bar, select the DATA • REFRESH DOCUMENT command.
2. If your data source requires authentication and if you did not save the password when creating the dataset, then a dialog box prompts you for this password, as seen in Figure 3.58 for a dataset based on a universe. Enter the password, and then click CONNECT.

Figure 3.58 Password Prompt for Universe Refresh

3. If the query requires some answers to parameters or variables before being run, then the appropriate dialog box is displayed so that you can answer them. This is the case for the following parameters and variables:
    - SAP HANA variables and input parameters, as described in Section 3.6.3
    - SAP BI universe contexts and parameters, as described in Section 3.7.4
    - SAP BW variables, as described in Section 3.8.2
4. The query is run and the document content is updated with the new dataset it has retrieved.

3.10 Summary

To create a document in SAP Lumira, you need a dataset containing the data to display and visualize. Hence, the first step in SAP Lumira is to define this dataset by identifying its source and then defining what data must be retrieved from it and how.

Like all SAP analytical tools, SAP Lumira can natively access a large range of data sources: text and Microsoft Excel files, relational databases, OData data sources, Hadoop databases, SAP HANA, SAP BusinessObjects BI universes, and SAP BW.

Once a dataset is created, it can be refreshed in order to retrieve updated data or edited to modify its definition.

Now that we have acquired our data, it is time for us to manipulate it in the Prepare room.

Data manipulation is at the heart of SAP Lumira, giving you the power you need to turn your raw sources into datasets that can be used to create effective visualizations and stories.

4 Data Manipulation

Once you have acquired your data, the next step is to prepare your data to be able to better use it for analysis, visualization, and presentation. Data manipulation is seen as one of the core activities for self-service business intelligence because it frees users from IT, enabling them to manipulate their data independently.

Among the different actions you can perform are the following:

- Create time, geographic, and custom hierarchies
- Convert values and create data types
- Create semantic objects, such as measures and dimensions
- Find and replace values to clean data
- Merge or append multiple sources into a single dataset

> **SAP HANA**
>
> In the case of SAP HANA online, you are limited in what you can do with your data, because SAP Lumira typically acquires data into its own data engine, allowing it to manipulate and change the structure as required. SAP HANA is different, because it's "live"; you are connected to a remote source rather than working locally. However, you can still create calculations and hierarchies and perform other operations.

In this chapter, we will discuss SAP Lumira's Prepare room, its components, and the available tools that allow users to better manipulate their data. Then, we will move on to how to describe data through objects and the different actions that can be performed to manipulate data.

4 Data Manipulation

4.1 The Prepare Room

The Prepare room is used to display your dataset and manipulate its data. Before describing its capabilities, this section will describe its interface.

4.1.1 Prepare Room Components

The PREPARE room (see Figure 4.1) is split into three core areas:

- OBJECT PICKER
  This is a key component; it contains the list of objects you can use for constructing visualizations, filters, and controls in all of the different rooms. By default, it contains the objects (dimensions, measures, etc.) detected during data acquisition, but you can create new objects that you can use later. The OBJECT PICKER is also used in other rooms to represent your data.

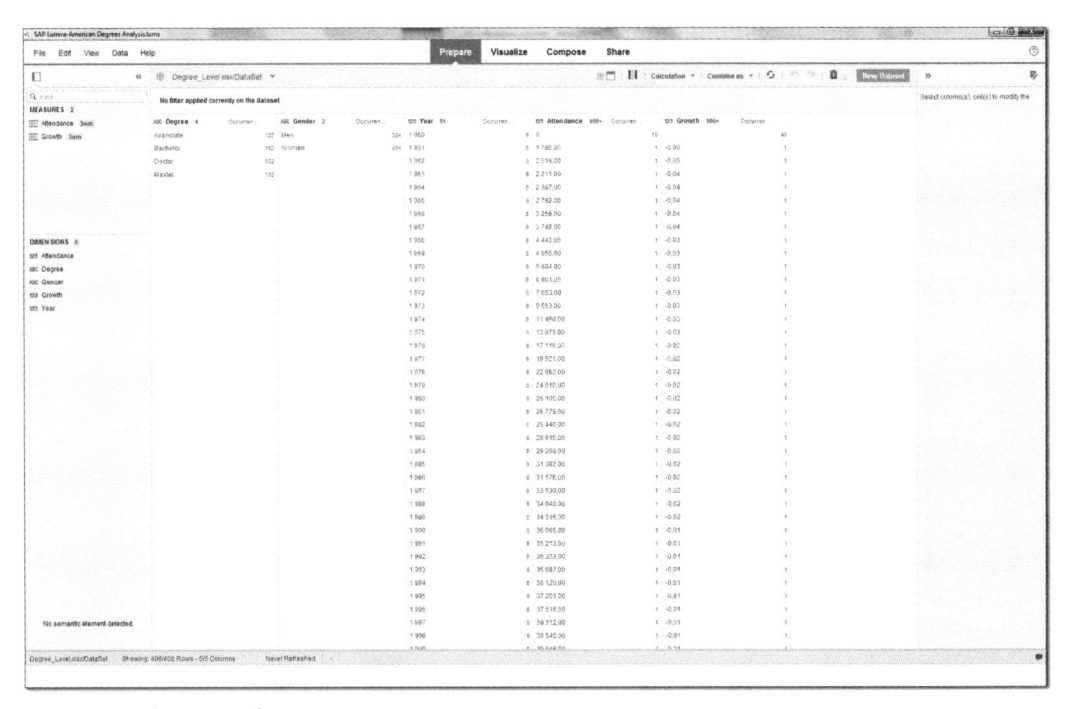

Figure 4.1 The Prepare Room

- DATA GRID DISPLAY
  This is displayed in the center as a view of the underlying data contained in your dataset. This view can display data in either a FACETS VIEW (see Section 4.1.4) or a GRID VIEW (see Section 4.1.3).

- ACTION PANEL
  Here, you edit and manipulate your data. Typically, when you select a cell, column, or object the different actions that are available for that selection appear here. Above the list of actions, a summary panel gives you statistics about your selection (the number of items and an occurrence count).

4.1.2 Menu Bar

Above these three main areas, a menu bar (see Figure 4.2) can be used to run the main actions in the Prepare room. This menu bar appears in every room, but it is contextual, meaning that each room has its own actions.

Figure 4.2 Menu Bar

The Prepare room action bar includes the following:

- DATASET SELECTOR
  In an SAP Lumira document, you can have multiple datasets, but you can only work on one at a time. If your document contains several datasets, use this dropdown list to change the current dataset.

- GRID and FACETS
  Use these buttons to switch between the GRID and FACETS views in the DATA GRID.

- SHOW/HIDE COLUMNS IN GRID AND FACETS VIEW
  Click this button to open the SELECT THE COLUMNS TO BE SHOWN dialog box (see Figure 4.3), in which you can select the columns of the dataset to display in the DATA GRID. By default, all columns of the dataset are shown. With SAP Lumira, you can quickly acquire datasets with a large number of columns, so it can be helpful to simplify your view by hiding unused columns.

4 | Data Manipulation

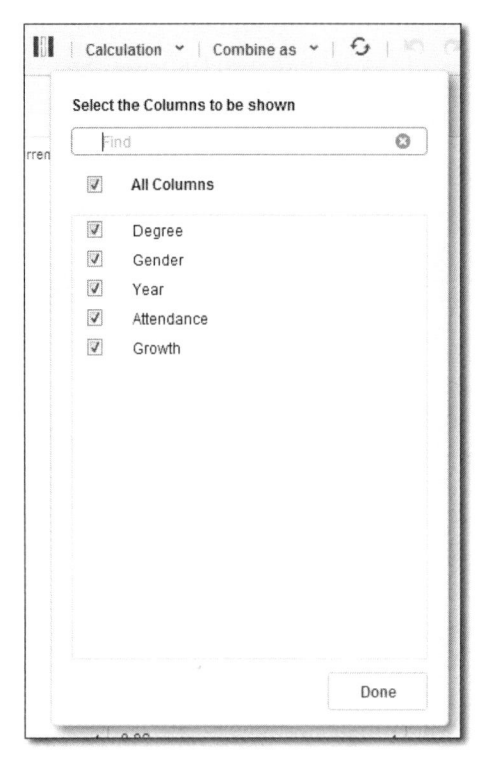

Figure 4.3 Show/Hide Column Menu

- CALCULATION
  This menu allows you to create a calculation dimension or a calculated measure (see Section 4.4).

- COMBINE AS
  This menu allows you to merge or append datasets (see Section 4.8).

- REFRESH
  Click this button to query the data source to refresh your dataset (see Chapter 3, Section 3.9.3).

- DELETE
  This will remove the current dataset if there is more than one in the document (you must have at least one per document). Delete will remove the currently selected dataset (see Section 4.8).

- UNDO and REDO

  Use these buttons to undo/redo your last changes. Currently, only the Prepare room supports undo and redo.

- NEW DATASET

  This will add a new dataset to your current document (see Section 4.8).

The GRID and FACETS buttons allow you to switch between the two different views of the DATA GRID. Let's investigate these views further.

4.1.3 Grid View

The GRID VIEW is a raw view of all your data and is really just one large table. The GRID VIEW is basically a direct view of the table of data that SAP Lumira uses to describe your dataset, similar to a spreadsheet or SQL table. The GRID VIEW does not have much additional functionality compared to the FACETS VIEW, which allows for weighted sorting, for example. However, the GRID VIEW has the strength of showing you all of your data, useful, for example, if you want to visually check the rows of data.

By default, the table rows are not sorted and are displayed as they are returned by the acquisition.

Icons in the columns identify the column types, as follows:

- NUMERIC
- STRING
- DATE
- GEOGRAPHIC HIERARCHY; described in more detail in Section 4.3
- TIME HIERARCHY; described in more detail in Section 4.3

You may resize columns by selecting the right or left header lines. You can also reorganize the columns' order by dragging and dropping them.

4.1.4 Facets View

In SAP Lumira, you can switch from the GRID VIEW to a FACETS VIEW (see Figure 4.4) by click FACETS in the menu bar.

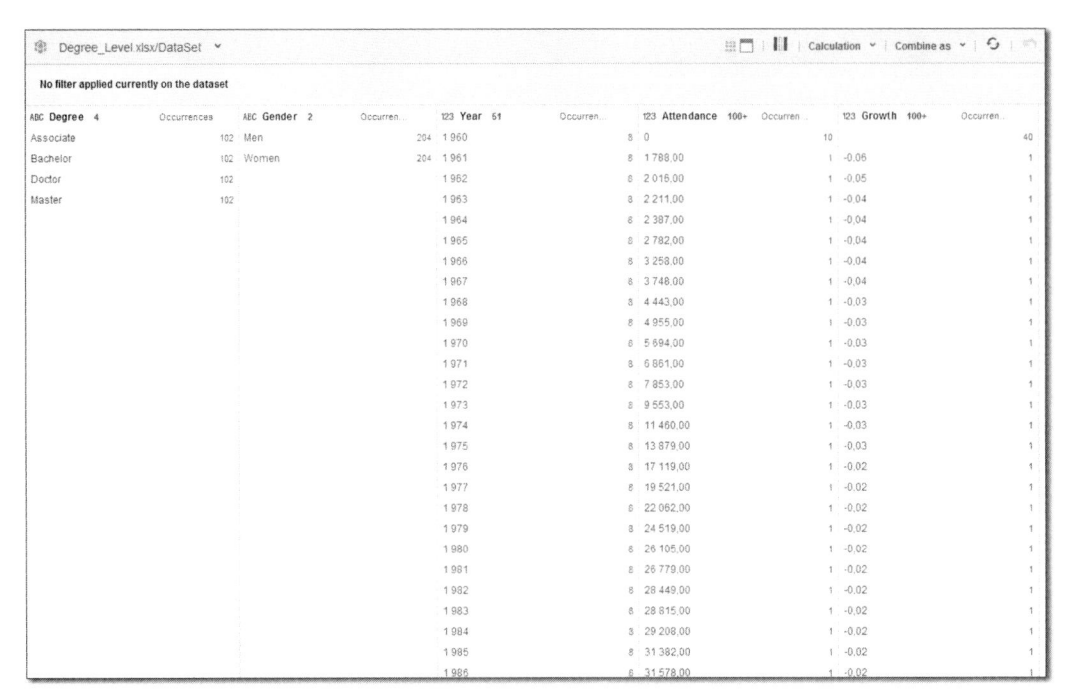

Figure 4.4 Facets View of Data

Facets are lists of distinct values found in a column with a count of the number of occurrences of each value. The header of each column displays an icon describing the data type, the name of the column, and the total number of values. Any column that has more than 100 distinct entries is marked as 100+.

Values in the FACETS VIEW can be sorted by the number of occurrences, but you can change this by using another measure.

To sort by another measure, perform the following steps:

1. In the column, click the OPTIONS icon to open the contextual menu.
2. Select SHOW MEASURES, and then select the measure to use in sorting the data in the column.

For example, a facet displayed with an occurrence count can be changed to another measure by using the menu (see Figure 4.5).

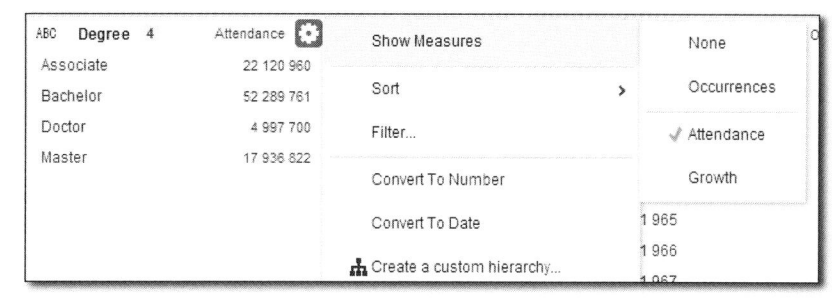

Figure 4.5 Selecting a Measure

The value is changed to ATTENDANCE (the measure that we selected previously) in Figure 4.6.

Figure 4.6 Facet Listed by Measure

Our facet now contains the distinct number of values for the column but also the total ATTENDANCE for each value. These measures can be used to sort values (see Section 4.7.3).

You can also highlight associated values in other facets. To do so, select a value in a column, and click to highlight its associated values in the other columns, as shown in Figure 4.7, in which values associated with the MASTER value for DEGREE are highlighted.

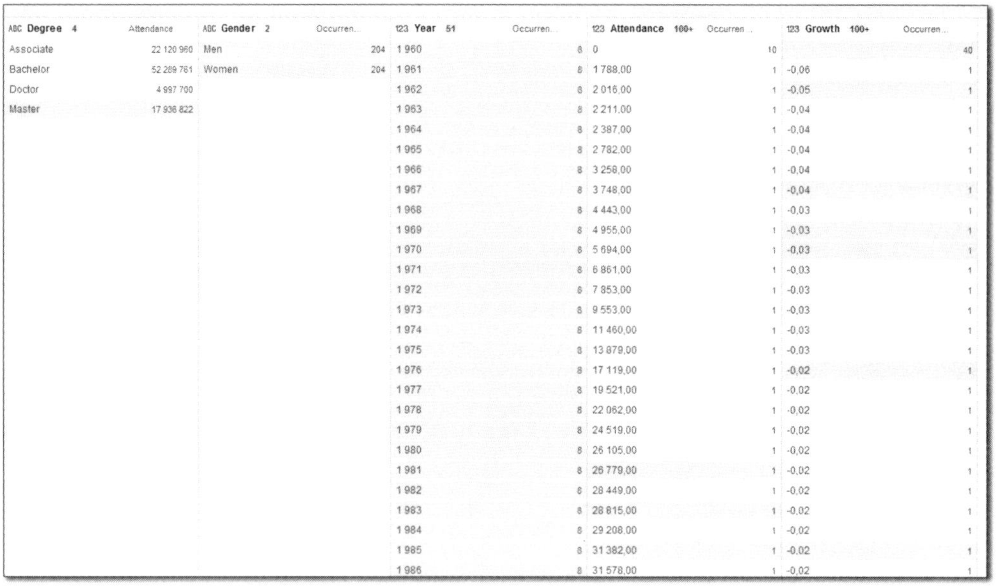

ABC Degree 4	Attendance	ABC Gender 2	Occurren...	123 Year 51	Occurren...	123 Attendance 100+	Occurren...	123 Growth 100+	Occurren...
Associate	22 120 960	Men	204	1 960	8	0	10		40
Bachelor	52 289 761	Women	204	1 961	8	1 788,00	1	-0,06	1
Doctor	4 997 700			1 962	8	2 016,00	1	-0,05	1
Master	17 936 822			1 963	8	2 211,00	1	-0,04	1
				1 964	8	2 387,00	1	-0,04	1
				1 965	8	2 782,00	1	-0,04	1
				1 966	8	3 258,00	1	-0,04	1
				1 967	8	3 748,00	1	-0,04	1
				1 968	8	4 443,00	1	-0,03	1
				1 969	8	4 955,00	1	-0,03	1
				1 970	8	5 694,00	1	-0,03	1
				1 971	8	6 861,00	1	-0,03	1
				1 972	8	7 853,00	1	-0,03	1
				1 973	8	9 553,00	1	-0,03	1
				1 974	8	11 460,00	1	-0,03	1
				1 975	8	13 879,00	1	-0,03	1
				1 976	8	17 119,00	1	-0,02	1
				1 977	8	19 521,00	1	-0,02	1
				1 978	8	22 062,00	1	-0,02	1
				1 979	8	24 519,00	1	-0,02	1
				1 980	8	26 105,00	1	-0,02	1
				1 981	8	26 779,00	1	-0,02	1
				1 982	8	28 449,00	1	-0,02	1
				1 983	8	28 815,00	1	-0,02	1
				1 984	8	29 208,00	1	-0,02	1
				1 985	8	31 382,00	1	-0,02	1
				1 986	8	31 578,00	1	-0,02	1

Figure 4.7 Highlighting Associated Values

The associated values are the values in the other columns that have a connection to this value. You can achieve the same end with a filter, but a filter will remove the other values, whereas highlighting leaves all the values on the screen.

The Prepare room is where you will spend time manipulating your data. Now that we have seen some of these objects in action, we can look in more detail at objects, their semantics, and how to create them in SAP Lumira.

4.2 Objects in SAP Lumira

Objects describe your data and what you want to do with it. There are two key types of object: measures and dimensions. The Object Picker is split into two distinct sections to make this distinction clear. These objects represent the semantics that you create and use in the rest of SAP Lumira. Let's look first at dimensions.

4.2.1 Dimensions

Dimensions are the base objects in SAP Lumira: everything starts from or depends on a dimension. Dimensions are the objects that represent the columns in your dataset. They have different data types, although this can be changed through manipulation.

Data Types

Currently, there are four data types:

- **String**
  Any object can be a string. It is the default for any object that SAP Lumira cannot "enrich," meaning that the real type cannot be determined. For example, imagine we have a source that contains a value: $10 million. It's probable that we would want to use this as a numeric value, but it will be recognized as a string. Section 4.6 describes how to convert these types of values.

- **Numeric**
  The numeric type covers all numbers without discrimination: integers, doubles, currencies, and floats.

- **Date**
  SAP Lumira supports dates, which are required to create time hierarchies.

- **Boolean**
  A true/false data type. One interesting feature in SAP Lumira is that you cannot convert data from the dataset to a Boolean type. To create a Boolean data type, the easiest way is to use an expression that returns only true or false. For example, the expression `{Quantity sold} > 500` can be used to create a Boolean object.

By default, if SAP Lumira does not know what type an object is, then it becomes a string. The preparation tools allow you to create new objects, which can be converted. For example, only numeric dimensions can be converted to measures (except for Count), so you typically convert to a number. A simple example is a Price column in which values are expressed like so: $12.34. By default, SAP Lumira doesn't handle currencies, so you would need to trim the $ and then convert to a number so that you can perform calculations (e.g., find the average price).

4.2.2 Measures

Measures are semantic objects that tell SAP Lumira that you want to aggregate a given value. The difference between measures and dimensions is that dimensions represent the data in your dataset (a column), whereas a measure describes an aggregation or calculation that is calculated for a column. Thus, measures reference columns, but do not represent one. For example, if you delete a dimension, then you will delete the associated column, but deleting a measure will not affect the dataset.

Only numeric dimensions can be used for measures, because these values can be aggregated. You can use other dimensions as measures but only with the aggregation type COUNT or DISTINCT COUNT. Measures are different from dimensions, because they are not columns: dimensions map an object to a column, whereas measures calculate across dimensions. In other words, the column revenue is represented as a dimension and can be referred to by a measure.

Aggregation Types

SAP Lumira exposes the "classic" SQL aggregation types:

- SUM
  Add all the values up.

- AVERAGE
  Calculate the sum and then divide by the number of values.

- MAX
  Return the highest value in a range.

- MIN
  Return the lowest value in a range.

- NONE
  This aggregation means that the value is in fact not aggregated. This aggregation type can appear strange, but it can be useful for expressing a numerical value in a chart without aggregating it. SAP Lumira expects a measure to be used in a chart, but you might have a numerical value to use as just a value. In this case, you create a measure using NONE and place that in your chart.

  The value of NONE may not be clear, but in fact when you create visualizations you are required to add a measure, so if you had an attribute that you wanted to plot but did not want to aggregate you could use the NONE aggregation.

The easiest way to understand the differences between NONE and the other aggregation types is with a very simple example using a table visualization. For example, given the data in Table 4.1, it's quite simple to create a table visualization in SAP Lumira that displays the aggregated values for our dimensions and measures (see Figure 4.8).

City	Value
London	2
London	4
London	6
Paris	2
Paris	4
Paris	5

Table 4.1 Sample Data

sum, min, max and average by City

City	sum	min	max	average
London	12	2	6	4,00
Paris	11	2	5	3,67

Figure 4.8 Visualization of Aggregations

If we add NONE, then we change the table completely, because we are then asking SAP Lumira not to aggregate this value (see Figure 4.9).

sum, min, max, average and none by City

City	sum	min	max	average	none
London	2	2	2	2,00	2
	4	4	4	4,00	4
	6	6	6	6,00	6
Paris	2	2	2	2,00	2
	4	4	4	4,00	4
	5	5	5	5,00	5

Figure 4.9 None Aggregation

This is the equivalent of adding the dimension VALUE to the table with the other measures aggregated accordingly.

Finally, there are two other aggregations that can be used to define a measure:

4 | Data Manipulation

- COUNT
  Return the count of the occurrence of items (see Figure 4.10) in a dimension.
- COUNT DISTINCT
  Count of the number of distinct items in a dimension.

count and count distinct by City		
City	count	count distinct
London	3	1
Paris	3	1

Figure 4.10 Count Measures

You can apply COUNT to any dimension, including date and numeric columns.

Creating Measures

Creating a measure is quite simple: you select the object of interest's cog icon and select CREATE A MEASURE from the menu (see Figure 4.11).

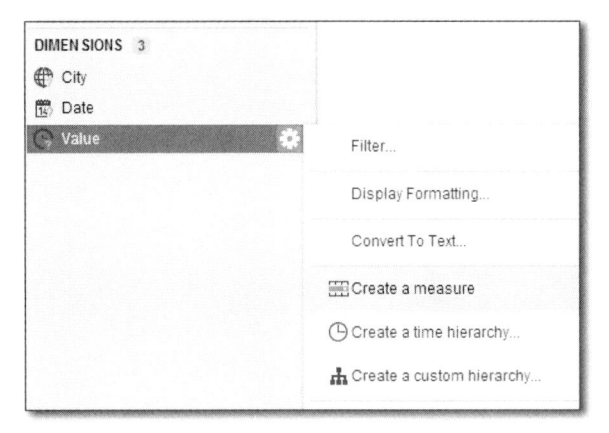

Figure 4.11 Creating a Measure

Selecting this option creates a measure in the list of measures. By default, this new measure is created with the aggregation type SUM. To change the aggregation type, select the menu of the newly created measure object, and select another aggregation type from among the possible ones (see Figure 4.12).

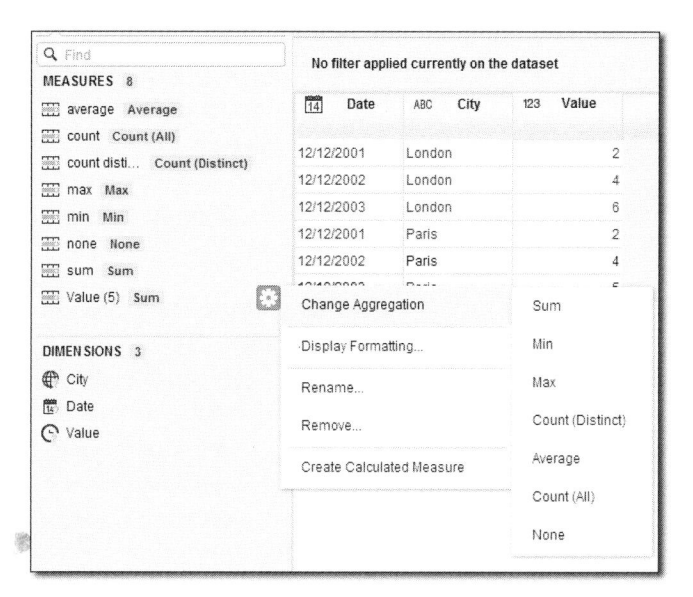

Figure 4.12 Aggregation Menu

Changing the aggregation via this menu changes the current measure only. To get the MAX, MIN, and AVERAGE of a value, you need to create three measures. By default, the measure name uses the attribute name, so you may want to rename the objects for clarity.

In the next section, we will look at how hierarchies create relationships between these dimension objects and their different types and uses in SAP Lumira.

4.3　Hierarchies in SAP Lumira

SAP Lumira supports level-based hierarchies that allow you to create hierarchical structures between dimensions. Level-based hierarchies are strict hierarchies in which there is one parent per child and a single navigation path. For example, countries contain regions, which contain cities. Creating a hierarchy creates a relationship between dimensions: you specify which dimension is a parent level of another dimension—for example, organization is a parent of employee. Hierarchies enable you to determine aggregation levels, because you can roll up values to a parent level—for example, the revenue of all cities in a country. Also, in SAP Lumira you can use hierarchies in specific ways within visualizations: you can use geographic hierarchies to create maps, for example, and also use hierarchies to navigate through data (see Chapter 5, Section 5.3.4 and Section 5.7).

4 | Data Manipulation

You cannot create hierarchies over a single column (as in a parent/child hierarchy). If you have an Employee column and you want to create a manager/employee hierarchy, then you would need to split out the columns. SAP Lumira has two built in types of hierarchy—geographic and time—which are of interest because they are required in some workflows and add additional semantics to your data. It is also possible to create custom hierarchies in which you specify the hierarchical relationship in your data.

In the following sections, we will explain how to create and use these different hierarchies.

4.3.1 Creating a Time Hierarchy

A time hierarchy is a specific type of hierarchy that uses dates to create time periods that can allow you to roll up your data into different levels. For example, if you have a series of dates, then you can use a time hierarchy to roll up aggregations by month or quarter. SAP Lumira will add in the additional levels for you, enabling you to see your data aggregated over different time levels.

Creating a time hierarchy requires a DATE object (see Figure 4.13) or a series of columns that can map to a date. We will look at using a date column first.

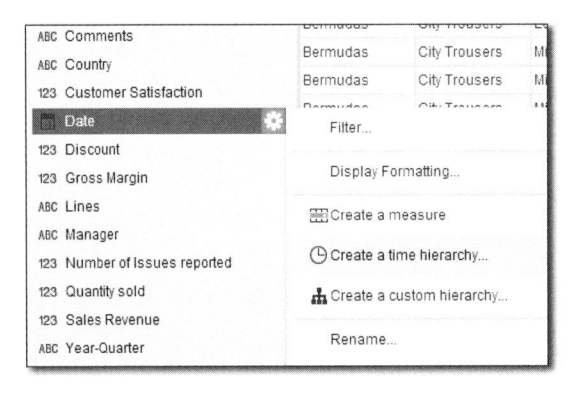

Figure 4.13 Time Hierarchy Menu

Perform the following to create a time hierarchy with the DATE object:

1. In the OBJECT PICKER, select a DATE dimension and click its OPTIONS icon to open its contextual menu.
2. Choose CREATE A TIME HIERARCHY.

162

3. The hierarchy is automatically created with the associated levels, which are YEAR, QUARTER, MONTH, and DAY by default and based on the selected date object. It's not possible to go below the DAY level (no hours or minutes). If your date does not contain all the information, then the levels cannot be generated — for example, you may have day and month but not year.

4. Your hierarchies appear in your list of objects at the top of the dimensions (see Figure 4.14).

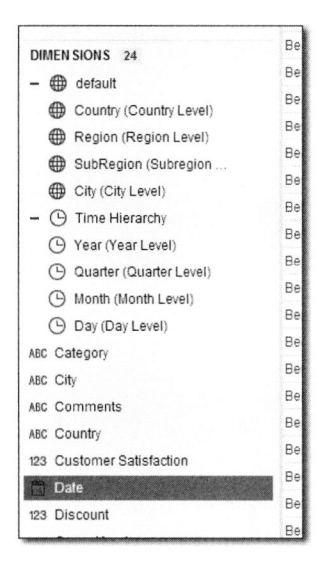

Figure 4.14 Time Hierarchy

A hierarchy is a series of dimensions that are ordered in a hierarchical manner. Each dimension is a level in the hierarchy, but because it is still a dimension SAP Lumira adds additional columns to your dataset.

It is also possible to create a time hierarchy from dimensions that are not initially date columns — for example, if you have a set of columns that represent time periods (see Figure 4.15).

year	month	day
2001	10	1
2001	11	1
2001	12	1
2002	1	1
2002	2	1

Figure 4.15 Year, Month, and Day Columns

You can convert these columns into a time hierarchy by specifying the columns to use for the levels. To do so:

1. Select any numeric attribute and choose CREATE A TIME HIERARCHY in the contextual menu to open the TIME HIERARCHY dialog box (see Figure 4.16).

Figure 4.16 Specifying the Levels for Time Hierarchy

2. In the SHOW dropdown list, select the dimensions that can be mapped with the time hierarchy level:
   - TIME-BASED DIMENSIONS to select all dimensions that have been identified as potential time dimensions. This is based on the dimension values. A dimension containing a value greater than 12 cannot be mapped to a month.
   - ALL DIMENSIONS to select all numerical dimensions.

3. For each possible dimension of the time hierarchy, click its associated down arrow; in the dropdown list that opens, select:
   - A dimension to map it to this level. Time levels that can be mapped to this dimension are displayed in brackets.
   - NONE to skip this level

   If a dimension of the time hierarchy has no possible dimensions, you can select:
   - GENERATE, to automatically generate this dimension
   - DON'T GENERATE, to not generate this dimension

   The YEAR level is mandatory and you can use a dimension for more than one level of the hierarchy.

4. Click OK to close the TIME HIERARCHY dialog box and use the specified dimensions to build a date and create the hierarchy.

In Figure 4.17, we see an additional column, CALCULATEDTIMESTAMP. This is the date that is computed from your columns (YEAR, MONTH, and DAY), and then in turn this date is used to create the hierarchy and its levels. As noted previously, each level is a dimension; therefore each must be a column, and so we can see that the levels are also created: YEAR, QUARTER, MONTH, and DAY.

year	CalculatedTimeStamp_id_56_id_58_id_60	Year	Quarter	Month	Day	month	day
2001	01/10/2001	2001	4	octobre	1	10	1
2001	01/11/2001	2001	4	novembre	1	11	1
2001	01/12/2001	2001	4	décembre	1	12	1
2002	01/01/2002	2002	1	janvier	1	1	1
2002	01/02/2002	2002	1	février	1	2	1

Figure 4.17 Time Hierarchy Table

Note, it is possible to use the date functionality in the formula to create dates if your objects are not recognized.

4.3.2 Geographic Hierarchies by Name

Next we look at geographic hierarchies, which are of particular interest, because in the Visualize room you can use these to place your data on maps. As with any other hierarchy, geographic hierarchies allow you to create the different levels and roll up your aggregations (if you have city data, you can add in country levels to get the totals at a higher level). There are two ways to create geographic hierarchies: BY NAMES and BY LATITUDE/LONGITUDE (see Figure 4.18).

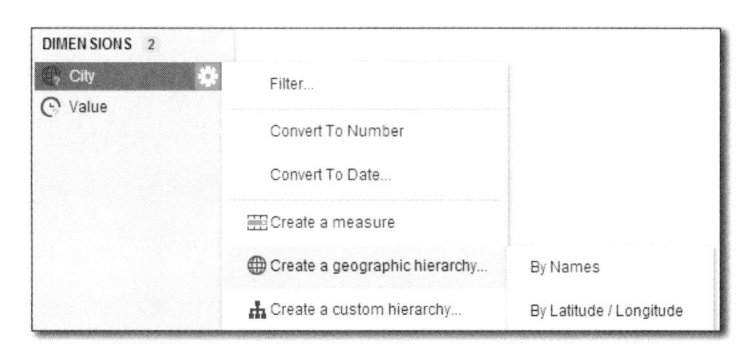

Figure 4.18 Create Geographic Hierarchy

4 | Data Manipulation

The main difference is that the BY LATITUDE/LONGITUDE option enables you to locate more precisely where a place is, but you need to provide the coordinates. BY NAMES uses an internal dictionary of place names to indicate if a name is a known geographic place (e.g., Paris, Yorkshire, and Brazil are all well-known places). We will look first at creating hierarchies by name, because it's the more common option.

First, by default any type of object could be converted to a geographic hierarchy, but typically SAP Lumira will detect the best candidates for promotion and propose these to the user via a small WORLD icon 🌐 , which includes a small question mark to indicate that it is *probable* that it is a geographic entity. It does not mean that it is or should be but that there is a chance.

> **Calculating Geographic Likeliness**
>
> SAP Lumira will sample the values of the column when you acquire data and compare these values to an internal geographic database. If there is a high enough relationship, then it's marked as a candidate. Note, that this sampling is moderately expensive in terms of computation time, so it's possible to switch off this automatic detection in SAP Lumira preferences (see Chapter 2, Section 2.9).

The converse is equally true: we know that STATE is also a geographic object, but it was not detected as such, see Figure 4.19 where only TERRITORY has been detected. SAP Lumira "guesses" at candidates and can make mistakes, but you can always ignore these misses and manually promote any object.

Selecting the action BY NAMES opens the dialog shown in Figure 4.19.

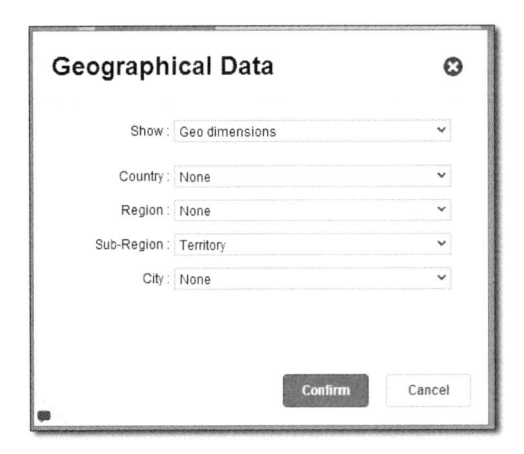

Figure 4.19 By Name Geographical Dialog

The dialog allows you to select whether you want to see only GEO DIMENSIONS or ALL. For example, if your object is not available—for example, TERRITORY—then you need to change the SHOW selection to ALL DIMENSIONS, as seen in Figure 4.20. So, as mentioned, just because an object is not detected as geographical does not mean you cannot enrich it.

You should verify that the correct dimension was chosen for each level (COUNTRY, REGION, SUB-REGION, and CITY). If it was not, you will need to change it by switching to NONE and/or selecting the appropriate dimension.

Clicking CONFIRM will take you to the dialog shown in Figure 4.20.

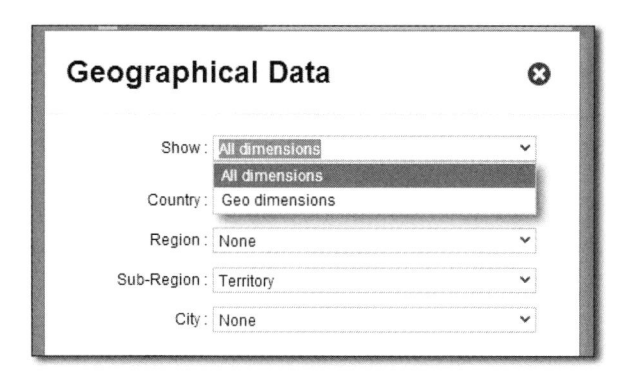

Figure 4.20 Selecting All Dimensions in Geographical Data

SHOW: ALL DIMENSIONS reveals the other objects available for selection in the level construction. If we did not select this, then only columns that were detected as geographic would be available.

The goal is to assign levels to appropriate objects, and as with time hierarchies, SAP Lumira can fill in the missing levels, as we will see ahead. If we continue here with TERRITORY and click CONFIRM, then you will see the dialog box shown in Figure 4.21.

The dialog presents the following information:

- A SUMMARY of the different values:
  - The number of ANALYZED VALUES.
  - The number of SOLVED values; here it is 0. This tells you how many values were located on a map.

4 | Data Manipulation

- The number of UNSOLVED values; here it is 3. What this means is that SAP Lumira has potentially found several possible results for the value. In Figure 4.21, we can see that by selecting from the RECOMMENDATIONS for a value we can determine where the entity is.
- Number of entities NOT FOUND; here it is 0. This means that SAP Lumira has no idea where your entity can be found.

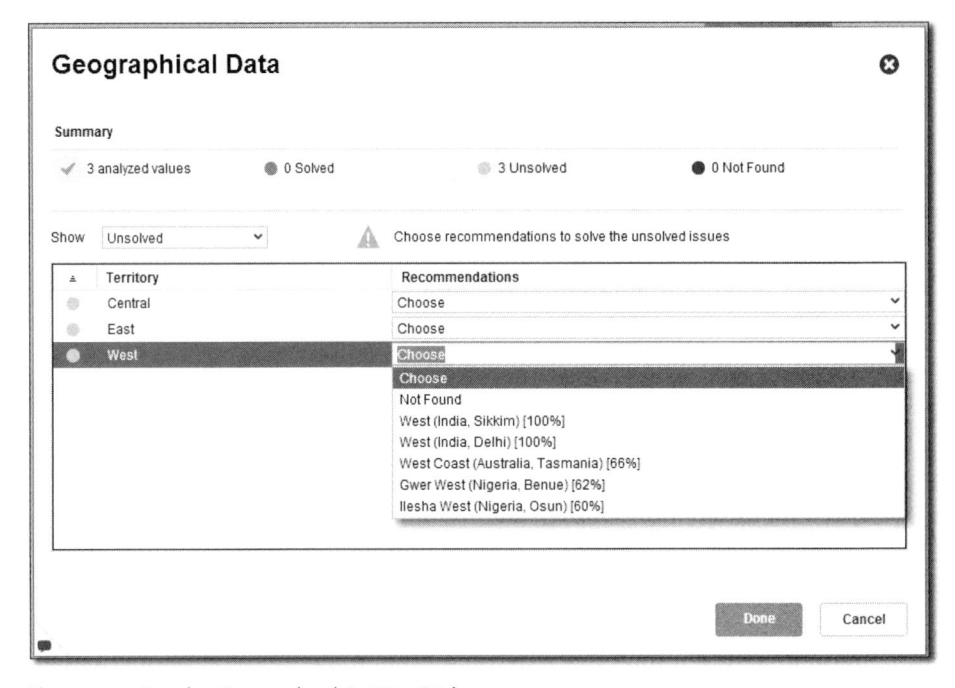

Figure 4.21 Resolve Geographical Entities Dialog

- SHOW allows you to filter the results in the table by category—that is, UNSOLVED, SOLVED, or NOT FOUND.
- The table allows you to see the values that were found or not, or in the case of UNSOLVED you can choose the appropriate value or by selecting NOT FOUND, telling SAP Lumira that it was not located at all.

In this example, TERRITORY was not a good candidate, because it does not correspond to the known list of places in SAP Lumira.

If we try using STATE, although it is not seen by SAP Lumira as a candidate we have a little more success (see Figure 4.22).

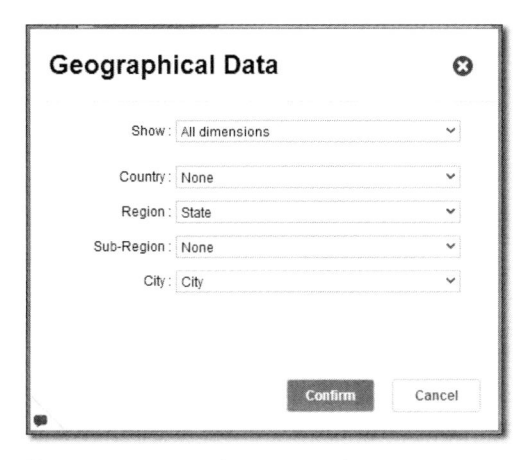

Figure 4.22 State and City as Levels

We selected ALL DIMENSIONS in Figure 4.22 in order to specify STATE as a REGION, and also we are adding CITY at the CITY level. Clicking CONFIRM this time leads to a better result, as seen in Figure 4.23.

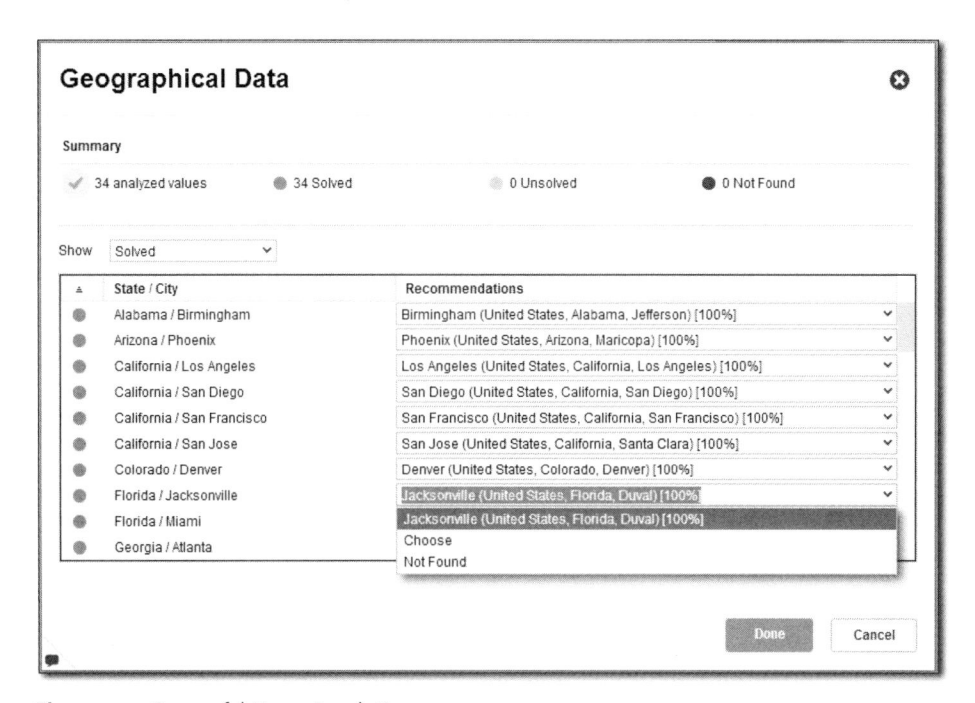

Figure 4.23 Successful Name Resolution

Because all of our values were found correctly, we can now click DONE and create our hierarchy. Note that the other levels, COUNTRY and SUB-REGION, are added in by SAP Lumira.

Editing Names

Your data might not work well, as shown, for example, in Figure 4.24.

We see that England, Scotland, and Wales are not recognized, because SAP Lumira identifies the United Kingdom instead. To resolve these kinds of issues, the only solution is to edit the source values.

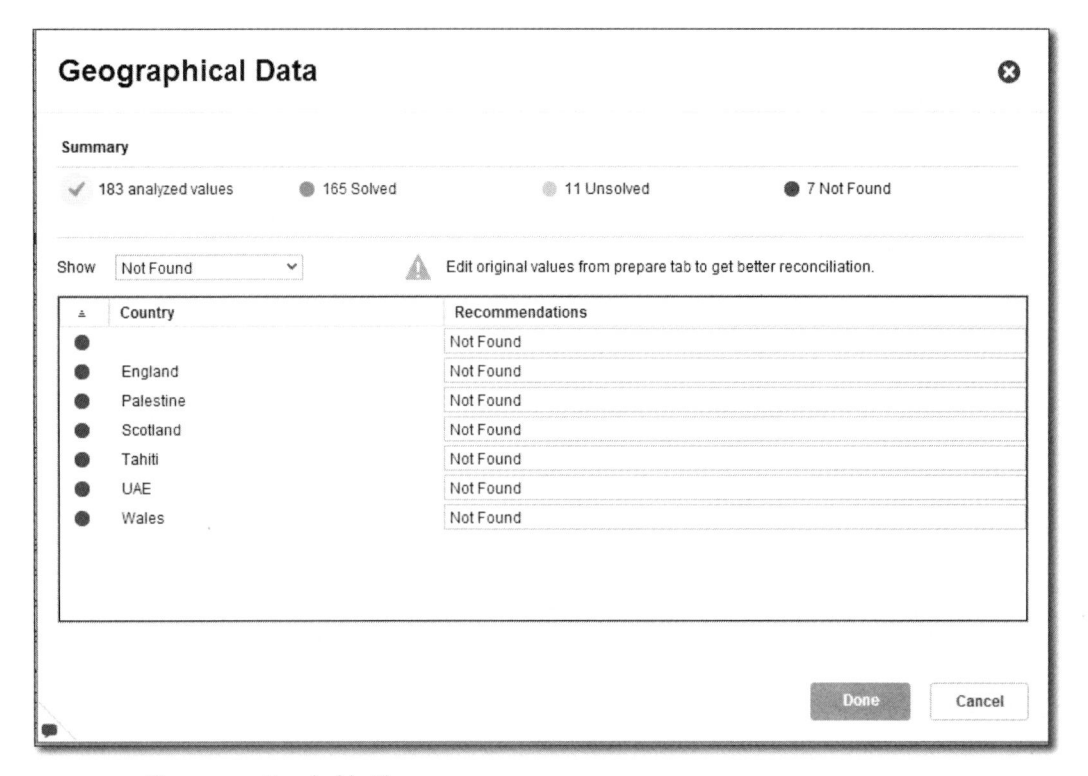

Figure 4.24 Unsolvable Places

For example, by using the FIND AND REPLACE action we can replace ENGLAND with UK, as shown in Figure 4.25.

Figure 4.25 Replacing England with UK

This, in turn, removes ENGLAND from the list of unsolvable places and enters it into the SOLVED list, as shown in Figure 4.26.

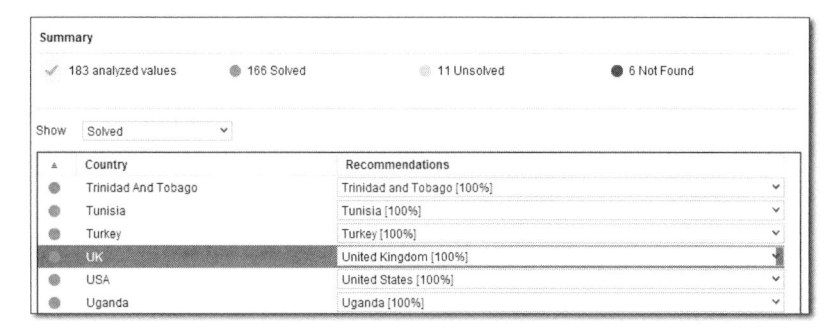

Figure 4.26 UK in Solved List

If you are really struggling with the names approach to creating a hierarchy, the solution might be to locate places exactly via their coordinates.

4.3.3 Geographic Geography by Longitude and Latitude

The alternative to using BY NAMES is to identify exactly where in the world your locations are by using the coordinates (see Figure 4.27). You can access this option under BY LONGITUDE/LATITUDE. To use this option, you must have a dataset that has two columns that contain the coordinates.

In Figure 4.27, you can see that you must select a column as the TARGETED DIMENSION and also two columns that contain the LATITUDE and LONGITUDE values. This means that you must have this data in your dataset, so if necessary you may have to merge in the values from another source.

4 | Data Manipulation

Figure 4.27 Hierarchy using Longitude and Latitude

Note, that in Figure 4.27 you see that there is an option to determine the level that your location represents. If it's not known or not applicable, you can select OTHER. In this case, SAP Lumira will not attempt to complete the levels. The advantage of LONGITUDE and LATITUDE is that you can specify the location precisely, using a level of granularity that is finer even than the CITY level. If you want to generate the levels, then use the dialog box shown in Figure 4.28, which is opened when you select the BY LATITUDE/LONGITUDE option.

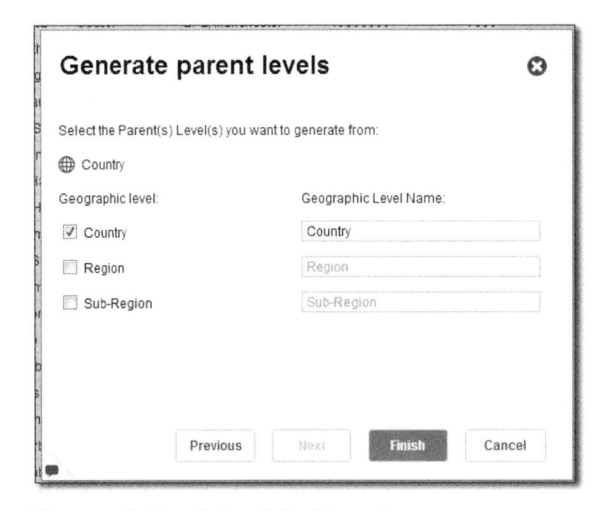

Figure 4.28 Specify Levels for Hierarchy

You can select which parent levels will be generated, although in this case COUNTRY does not have a parent and should be removed.

4.3.4 Custom Hierarchies

In addition to exploiting the semantics of time and geography to create hierarchies, it is also possible to create an arbitrary hierarchy among any set of dimensions. Obviously, the hierarchy will function more effectively if there is a one-to-many relationship among the levels (manager to employee or country to city). To create the hierarchy, you use the ubiquitous cog and select CUSTOM HIERARCHY to open the CREATE HIERARCHY dialog box (see Figure 4.29).

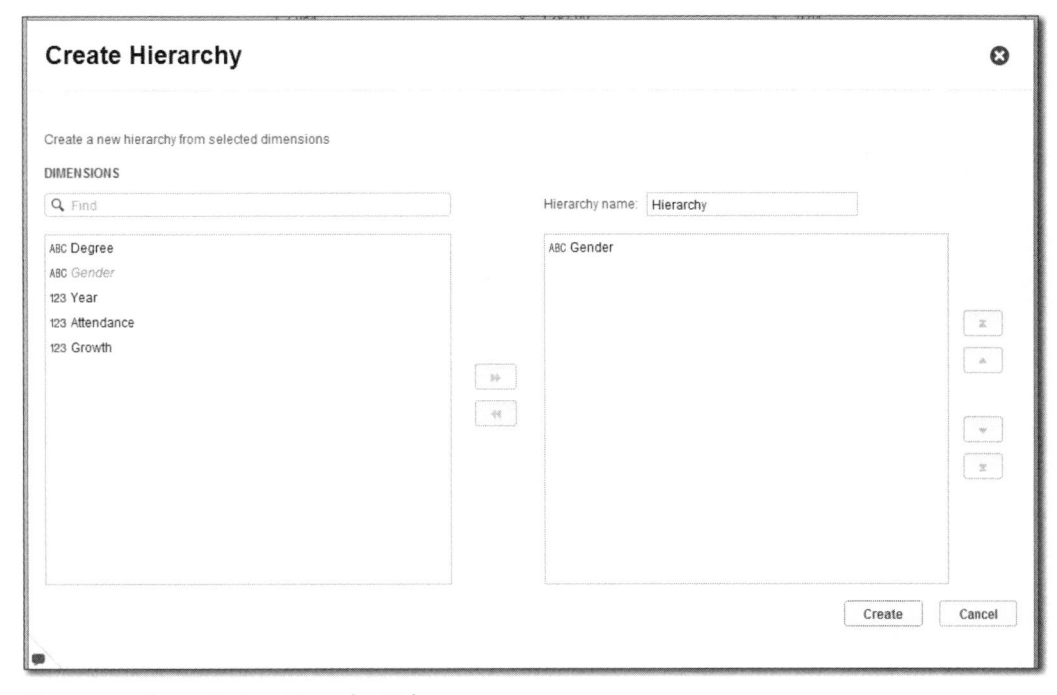

Figure 4.29 Create Custom Hierarchy Dialog

From the dialog box, you can see that on the left-hand side you have a list of the dimensions available and on the right you have the list of dimensions used. Essentially, selecting a dimension adds a level to the hierarchy on the right.

By default, the dimension you used initially is the root level, and subsequent levels are appended under the previous levels. The arrows to the right allow you to move the levels up and down. At the top, you can name the final hierarchy (see Figure 4.30).

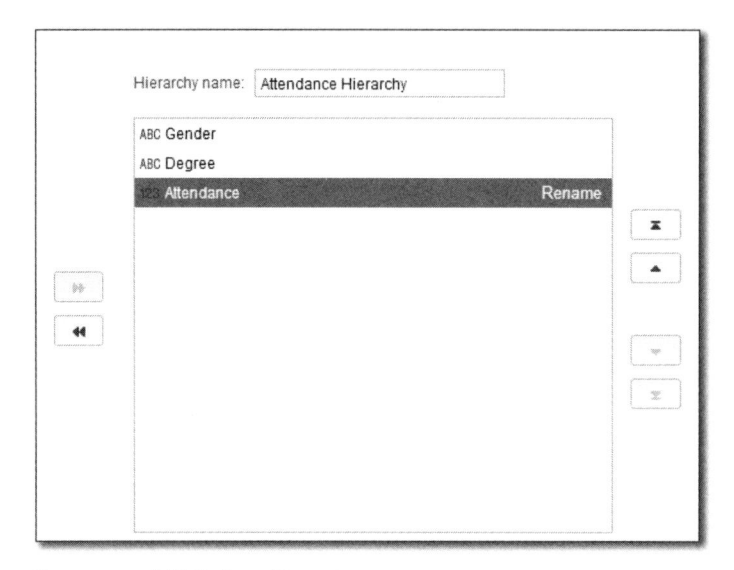

Figure 4.30 Edit Custom Hierarchy

Although custom hierarchies allow you to create relationships among any set of objects, these hierarchies are only exploitable in the Visualize room.

Next, we'll look at calculated dimension and measure objects and the formula language used to create these calculated objects.

4.4 Calculated Objects

SAP Lumira has a formula language, and this can be used to create calculated objects. There are two types of object that you can create: dimensions and measures. Again, calculated dimensions are dimensions that represent and create columns, whereas measures are calculations that reference columns. Creating a calculated dimension will create a new column.

In the sections ahead, we will discuss calculated dimensions and measures, how to create and best utilize them, and the formulas that allow us to create complex calculations, convert data, and perform many other tasks.

4.4.1 Calculated Dimension

A calculated dimension can be created from several locations (select a dimension and use its menu, use the actions panel, or use the menu bar).

Creating a dimension is straightforward, but of course you can create complex expressions, and reference other objects in order to create compound results.

To create a calculated dimension, follow these steps:

1. In the ACTION panel, click CREATE CALCULATED DIMENSION to open the NEW CALCULATED DIMENSION dialog box, as shown in Figure 4.31. You may also select CALCULATION • NEW CALCULATED DIMENSION in the toolbar or select the cog icon and then NEW CALCULATED DIMENSION.

2. Enter the following parameters for your new dimension:

    ▸ DIMENSION NAME: The name of the object and column to create.
    ▸ FORMULA: The text area where you enter your formula text.

    To enter your formula, you may click the items suggested for you in the following sections:

    ▸ DIMENSION: Displays the list of dimensions you can use and has a search field to filter the list.
    ▸ FUNCTIONS: Displays the list of functions and also has a search feature, as can be seen in Figure 4.31, in which CON reduces the list of visible functions to three. When you select a function, its associated help, if any, is displayed in the HELP section.

3. Click OK to close the NEW CALCULATED DIMENSION dialog box. The new dimension appears in the OBJECT PICKER in the DIMENSIONS section.

4. If you need a fixed date, then you can use the DATE PICKER under the list of expressions. You can use the DATE PICKER associated with the CALENDAR icon to enter a specific date into your expression.

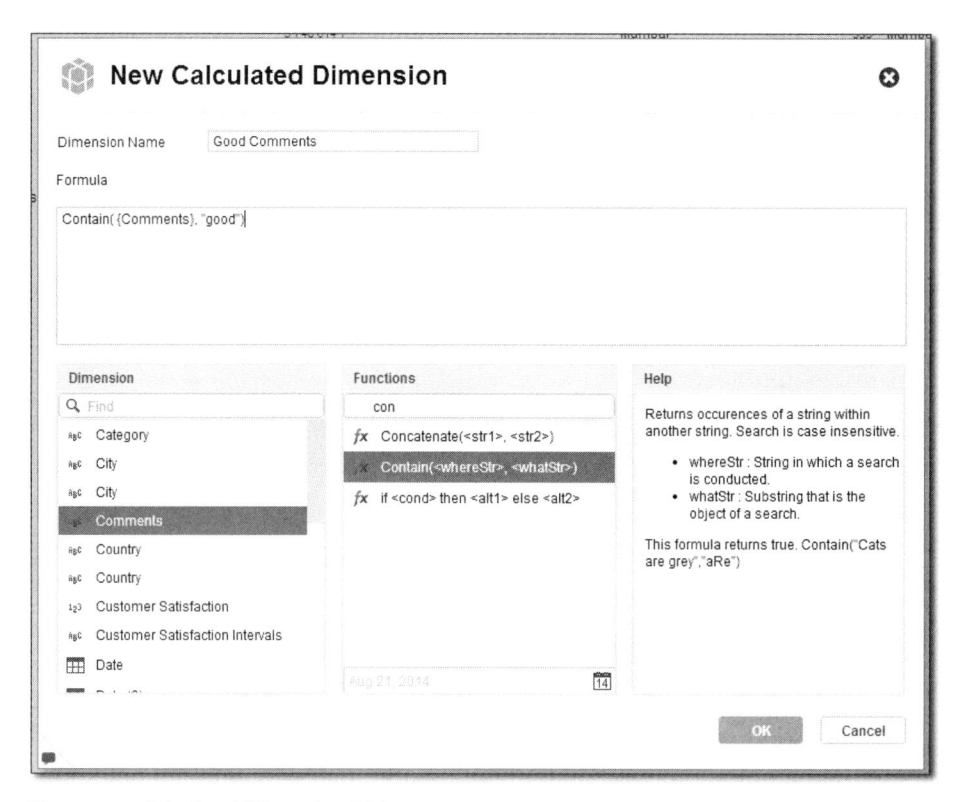

Figure 4.31 Calculated Dimension Dialog

4.4.2 Calculated Measures

SAP Lumira also supports calculated measures, which are created in the same manner as dimensions, but can only return numeric results. Calculated measures are seen as values that can be aggregated, so after you have created your calculation there is still an aggregation type associated with the measure. Because calculated measures are numeric, the dialog only displays measures in the list of objects that can be used (see Figure 4.32).

The rest is the same, except you are expected to return numeric results; if you do not, then SAP Lumira will not know how to aggregate and will thus disable the aggregation selector.

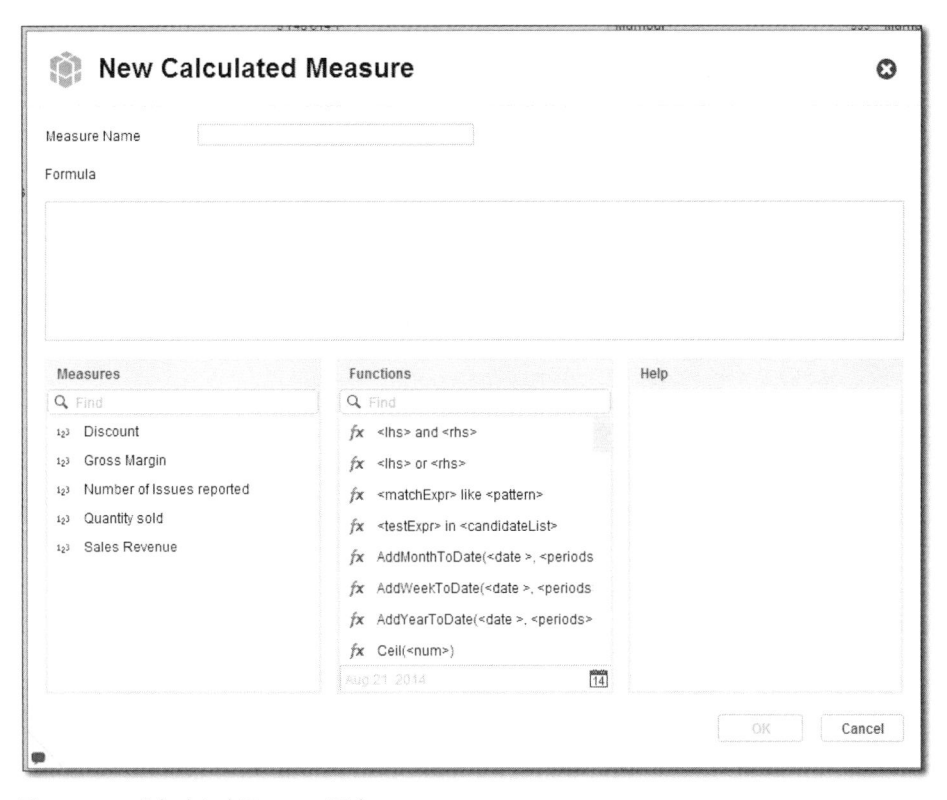

Figure 4.32 Calculated Measure Dialog

4.4.3 Formula Syntax

Formulas are relatively easy to write and must follow these basic rules:

- Objects can be used but must be contained by { and }—for example, {Name} refers to the name object.
- Values can be expressed directly, but strings should be marked by enclosing them with " and "—for example, "strings are possible".
- Numeric values should be expressed as numbers and written directly—for example, 34.2 is OK, but $34.2 is not.
- Booleans are either TRUE or FALSE and could be the result of an expression—for example, IsNull("But I exist") returning false.
- Dates cannot be used directly, but there are several date functions that return dates—for example, MakeDate(2011,11,17) returns 2011-11-17 as a date.

- All functions act on values and return a result. Values can be objects, expressions, or values entered directly. Functions can be chained in order to generate complex expressions.
- Standard operators and logical expressions can be used: `if`, `then`, `else`, `+`, `/`, `*`, and `%`.

Once you have created an expression, any expression that cannot be parsed appears as an error above the expression (see Figure 4.33).

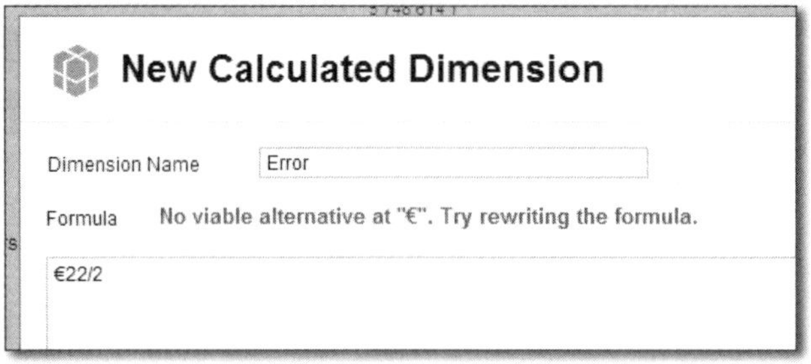

Figure 4.33 Calculation Syntax Error

SAP Lumira will suggest where the problem is, but not a solution. Here, for example, we are trying to perform an arithmetic operation on a value that is a string.

> **Documentation Syntax**
>
> The documentation syntax in SAP Lumira is a little different from the one used here. In SAP Lumira, the parameters are surrounded by ⟨ ⟩ brackets—for example:
>
> `AddMonthToDate (<date>,<periods>)`
>
> The brackets are not part of the expression. They are only part of the documentation to identify the parameters: date and periods. In this chapter, we omit this syntax and will present formulas as follows:
>
> `AddMonthToDate (date,periods)`

4.4.4 Formula Examples

We will now create a simple expression that will create a calculated dimension to tell us if the comments contain the word "bad":

`Contain ({Comments},"bad")`

With this formula, if the `Comments` column contains the word `bad` or `BAD` (`Contain` is case insensitive), then the result returned is `TRUE` or `FALSE`. This expression generates a new column (our calculated dimensions) in which the result is either `TRUE` or `FALSE` depending on the corresponding value in each cell of the `Comments` column.

Let's modify the expression a little and see the result:

```
if(Contain ({Comments},"bad")) then "BAD" else "GOOD"
```

With this formula, if the expression is true, then the result is `BAD`; otherwise it is `GOOD`. We can see this in the Expression Editor shown in Figure 4.34.

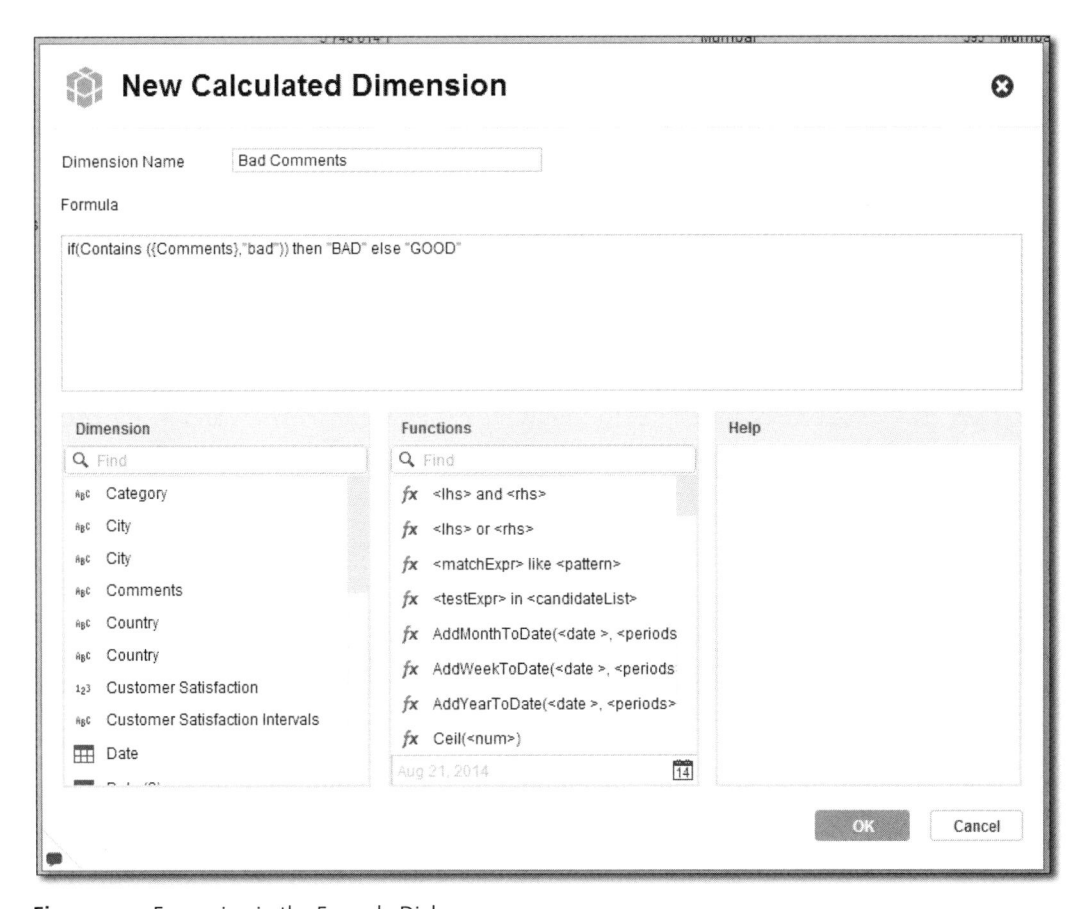

Figure 4.34 Expression in the Formula Dialog

Now, we have a check that tests each value and then uses the result of the evaluation to return GOOD or BAD. This results in a simplified column in which we can quickly see if the product is well-received or not (see Figure 4.35). This is not a replacement for sentiment analysis!

Figure 4.35 Expression Result in Facets View

Expressions can be used to create any type of value and are thus far richer and more powerful than data actions, because you can use more complex expressions. For example, the FIND AND REPLACE data action only matches text, but the `like` and `replace` functions allow you to achieve more exact expressions. Similarly, the NAMED group only allows named values, but you could use a `like` with an `if` expression. For example:

```
if ({Lines} like "city%") then "city clothing" else {Lines}
```

This would check the values for the value `city` (case insensitive and in any order) and create the equivalent of a named group called `city clothing`; otherwise the values would maintain their current name.

The next section lists the different functions that are available in SAP Lumira.

4.4.5 Formula Table

Table 4.2 lists all the formulas available in SAP Lumira. On the left, you will find the function name and the parameters in brackets. On the right, you will find the description of each parameter and a brief example. For legibility, each example uses a constant value, but you will typically replace this with another object—for example, `AddMonthToDate (04/11/2012, 2)` would probably be `AddMonthToDate ({DateColumn}, 2)`.

4.4 Calculated Objects

Function	Definition
AddMonthToDate (date, periods)	Adds a month or months to the specified date. Parameters: ▸ The date to use ▸ The number of periods to add Example: `AddMonthToDate (04/11/2012, 2)` returns 04/01/2013
AddWeekToDate (date, periods)	Adds a week or weeks to the specified date. Parameters: ▸ The date to use ▸ The number of periods to add Example: `AddWeekToDate(04/11/2012, 2)` returns 18/11/2012
AddYearToDate (date, periods)	Adds a year or years to the specified date. Parameters: ▸ The date to use ▸ The number of periods to add Example: `AddYearToDate(04/11/2012, 2)` returns 04/11/2014
Ceil (number)	Returns an integer that is equal or greater than the given number. Parameter: ▸ The number to major Example: `Ceil(23.32)` returns 24
Concatenate (str1, str2)	Returns a single string that is the concatenation of the two strings. Parameters: ▸ String one ▸ String two Example: `concatentate("lets combine", " these")` returns `lets combine these`
Contain (where, what)	Searches to see whether a string contains a string. Parameters: ▸ Where is the string that is searched within ▸ What is the string that is searched for Example: `Container("look for something", "something")` returns `true`.
CurrentDate()	Returns the current date; there are no parameters. Example: `CurrentDate()` returns 01/07/2014

Table 4.2 Formulas Table

Function	Definition
`DateDiffInDays (first, last)`	Returns the difference between two dates in days. Parameters: ▸ Start date or from date ▸ End date or to date Example: `DateDiffInDays(01/07/2014, 01/08/2014)` returns 31
`DateDiffInMonths (first, last)`	Returns the difference between two dates in days. Parameters: ▸ Start date or from date ▸ End date or to date Example: `DateDiffInMonths(01/07/2014, 01/08/2014)` returns 1
`Day(date)`	Returns the day of the month—that is, any number between 1 and 31. Parameter: ▸ The date Example: `Day(01/07/2014)` returns 1
`DayOfWeek(date)`	Returns the day of the week—that is, any number between 1 and 7. Parameter: ▸ The date Example: `DayOfWeek (01/07/2014)` returns 2
`DayOfYear(date)`	Returns the day of the year—that is, any number between 1 and 366. Parameter: ▸ The date Example: `DayOfYear(12/01/2013)` returns 12
`ExceptFirstWord (string, separator)`	Returns a string in which the first word is removed according to a separator. Parameters: ▸ The string to remove the word from ▸ The separator to use Example: `ExceptFirstWord("if you ignore this", " ")` returns you ignore this
`ExceptLastWord (string, separator)`	Returns a string in which the last word is removed according to a separator. Parameters: ▸ The string to remove the word from ▸ The separator to use Example: `ExceptLastWord ("if you ignore this", " ")` returns if you ignore

Table 4.2 Formulas Table (Cont.)

Function	Definition
FirstWord (string, separator)	Returns a string where only the first word is kept in a string. Parameters: ▸ The string to remove the word from ▸ The separator to use Example: `FirstWord("keep me", " ")` returns `keep`
Floor(number)	Returns an integer that is equal or lower than the given number. Parameter: ▸ The number to floor Example: `Floor(234.56)` returns `234`
GroupValues (column, ListOfValues, newValue)	Groups a set of values together into a single named set. Parameters: ▸ The column or object to use ▸ The values to group with [value1, value2] ▸ The name of the group Example: `GroupValues({geo}, ["france", "germany"], "Quarter Final")` returns `Quarter Final` or the original value not in the set.
IsNotNull(object)	Verifies if the value is not null or not. Parameter: ▸ The value to check Example: `IsNotNull("but I'm not")` returns `true`
IsNull(object)	Verifies if the value is null or not. Parameter: ▸ The value to check Example: `IsNull("but I'm not")` returns `false`
LastDayOfMonth (date)	Returns the last day of the given month of a given date. Parameter: ▸ The date to check Example: `LastDayOfMonth(01/07/2014)` returns `31/07/2014`
LastDayOfWeek(date)	Returns the last day of the week for a given date. Parameter: ▸ The date to check Example: `LastDayOfWeek(07/01/2014)` returns `07/06/2014`
LastWord (string, separator)	Returns the last word in a given string. Parameters: ▸ The string to check ▸ Separator Example: `LastWord("keep me", " ")` returns `me`

Table 4.2 Formulas Table (Cont.)

Function	Definition
Length(string)	Returns the length of the string. Parameter: ▸ The string to measure Example: Length("of this") returns 7.
Log(number)	Returns the natural logarithm of a number. Parameter: ▸ The number to log Example: Log(100) returns 4.605.
Log10(number)	Returns the base 10 logarithm of a number. Parameter: ▸ The number to use Example: Log10(100) returns 2.
LowerCase(string)	Returns a string with all characters in lowercase. Parameter: ▸ The string to convert Example: LowerCase("Please Lower THIS") returns please lower this
Lpad(string, length, pad)	Creates a string to the length specified by using a padding character pad the string on the left. Parameters: ▸ The string to pad ▸ The length that is desired ▸ The padding character Example: Lpad("paddle", 10, "%") returns %%%%paddle
MakeDate (year, month, day)	Creates a date from the given year, month, and day values. Parameters: ▸ The year ▸ The month as a number ▸ The day as a number Example: MakeDate(2012, 10,23) returns 23/10/2012
Mod(number, divisor)	Returns the modulus or the remainder of a division. Parameters: ▸ The number to divide ▸ The number to divide by Example: Mod(14, 3) returns 2
Month(date)	Return the month of given date as a number. Parameter: ▸ The date to check Example: Month(03/10/2011) returns 10

Table 4.2 Formulas Table (Cont.)

Function	Definition
Power(number, exponent)	Returns a number to the power of the exponent. Parameters: ▸ The number ▸ The exponent Example: `Power(10,3)` returns `1000`
Quarter(date)	Returns the quarter a date is in—that is, a number from 1 to 4. Parameter: ▸ The date Example: `Quarter(03/10/2011)` returns `4`
Replace(string, target, replacement)	For a given string, the target pattern is replaced by the replacement string. Parameters: ▸ String to modify ▸ The target pattern ▸ The replacement for the target Example: `Replace("something needs to change", "thing", "one")` returns `someone needs to change`
Round(number, digits)	Rounds a number to the number of digits requested. Parameters: ▸ The number to round ▸ The number of places to round to Example: `Round(3.14159265, 2)` returns `3.14`
Rpad(string, length, pad)	Creates a string to the length specified by using a padding character to pad the string on the right. Parameters: ▸ The string to pad ▸ The length that is desired ▸ The padding character Example: `Rpad("paddle", 10, "+")` returns `paddle++++`
Sign(number)	Gives the sign of a number: either negative, zero, or positive (-1, 0, or 1). Parameter: ▸ The number to check Example: `Sign(-25)` returns `-1`

Table 4.2 Formulas Table (Cont.)

Function	Definition
SubString (string, start)	Returns a substring from a given start position. Parameters: ▸ The string to use ▸ The start position Example: `SubString("remove some things", 3)` returns `move some things`.
SubString(string, start, length)	Returns a substring from a given start position and a given length. Parameters: ▸ The string to use ▸ The start position ▸ The length of the string Example: `SubString("remove some things", 3, 18)` returns `move some thing`
ToDate (string, dateFormat)	For a given string, a date is returned using the date format string. This format follows a pattern in which day, month, and year are specified in order with a delineator—for example, dd/mm/yy. You can use d,dd, EEEE, M, MM, MMM, MMMM, yy, yyyy and slash ("/"), minus ("-"), or dot (".") for the delineator. Parameters: ▸ The string to format ▸ The date format to use Example: `ToDate("12-JAN-2001", "dd-MMM-yyyy")` returns `12/01/2001`
ToNumber(object)	Converts or attempts to convert the given value to a number. Parameter: ▸ The object to convert Example: `ToNumber("42")` returns `42`
ToText(object)	Converts the given object or value to a string. Parameter: ▸ The object to convert Example: `ToText(not false)` returns `true`
ToText (number, digits)	Converts the given number to a string rounding to the desired number of places. Parameters: ▸ The number to convert ▸ The number of places Example: `ToText(34.567, 2)` returns `34.57`

Table 4.2 Formulas Table (Cont.)

Function	Definition
`Trim(string, trim)`	Trim a given string by removing the leading and trailing instances of a character. Parameters: ▸ The string to trim ▸ The trim character Example: `Trim(" need to trim ", " ")` returns `need to trim`
`TrimLeft (string, trim)`	Trim a given string by removing the leading instance of a character. Parameters: ▸ The string to trim ▸ The trim character Example: `TrimLeft(" need to trim ", " ")` returns `"need to trim "`
`TrimRight (string, trim)`	Trim a given string by removing the trailing instance of a character. Parameters: ▸ The string to trim ▸ The trim character Example: `TrimRight(" need to trim ", " ")` returns `" need to trim"`
`Truncate (number, digits)`	Truncates a given number to the number of places. Parameters: ▸ The number to truncate ▸ The number of places Example: `Truncate(34.567, 2)` returns `34.56`
`UpperCase(string)`	Converts a string to uppercase. Parameter: ▸ The string to convert Example: `UpperCase("lets up")` return `LETS UP`
`Week(date)`	Returns the week of the year—that is, any number between 1 and 52. Parameter: ▸ The date Example: `Week(01/01/2000)` returns `1`
`Year(date)`	Returns the year of a given date. Parameter: ▸ The date Example: `Year(01/01/2000)` returns `2000`

Table 4.2 Formulas Table (Cont.)

Formulas allow you to expand your data and create more complex calculations. In the next section, we will discuss object actions and their available menu features.

4.5 Object Actions

In SAP Lumira, each object in the Object Picker has a number of associated actions. The menu for these actions is available from the cog icon associated with every object. The list of possible actions for a dimension are as follows:

- FILTER
  For information on filters, see Section 4.7.
- DISPLAY FORMATTING
  This is only applicable for numeric values and dates. Selecting this formatting option will open one of two possible dialog boxes, numbers or dates:
  - Number formatting: Allows you to define how the values will be rendered using SCIENTIFIC NUMBER FORMAT, 1000 SEPARATOR, or NONE. This means that 1963.50 will be rendered as is (none), as 1 963.50 with 1000 separator, or as 1.96E+3 in scientific format using two decimal places (see Figure 4.36). The number separator used will depend on the local settings of your machine.
  - Date formatting: Dates can also be formatted, rendered based on the chosen arrangement (see Figure 4.37).
- SAP Lumira then displays your dates in the selected format.

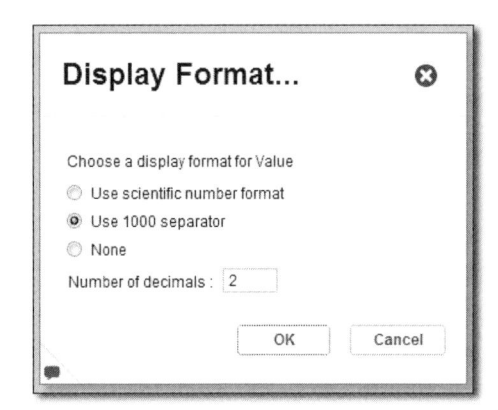

Figure 4.36 Number Formatting Dialog

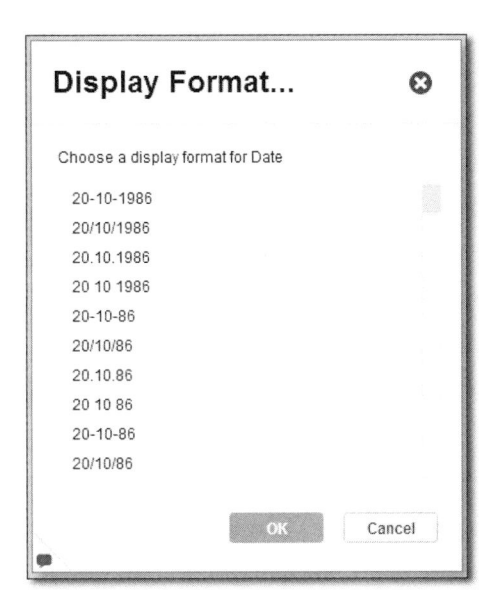

Figure 4.37 Date Formatting Dialog Box

The other actions that are available are as follows:

- CONVERT TO TEXT/NUMERIC/DATE
  Depending on the source type of an object, you can convert it to another format. If it's a string, then you can convert to a number or date, a number can become a string, and a date can become a string. Conversion to number is automatic, and there is no user input; however, for dates you need to select the format (see CONVERT TO DATE).

- CREATE A MEASURE
  Numeric types can be directly converted to any type of measure. All other types can have measures of type COUNT. Measures are discussed in Section 4.2.2.

- CREATE A TIME HIERARCHY
  Time hierarchies are discussed in Section 4.3.

- RENAME
  Allows you to rename any object. If it's a dimension object, then the associated column's name is changed.

- DUPLICATE
  Creates a copy of the object. Its associated column is also duplicated in the dataset.

▶ REMOVE
Removes the object and its associated column. If there are derived objects—for example, a measure—then you are warned that the associated objects will also be removed. Because objects can be referenced by other objects or other elements (for example, you will use dimensions and measures to create visualizations), an impact analysis is performed. If there are impacted objects, then you will be warned (see Figure 4.38).

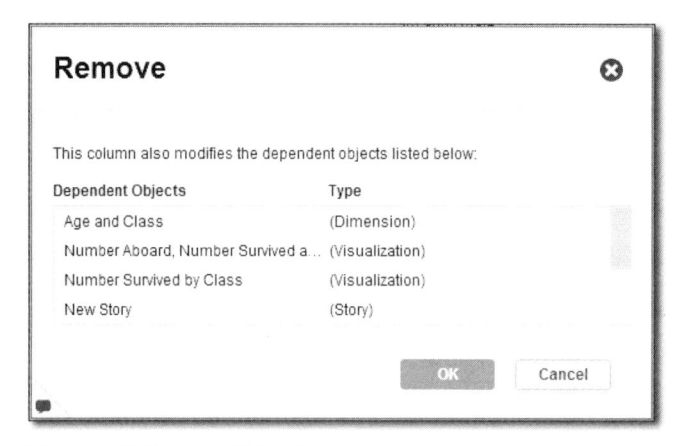

Figure 4.38 Remove Dialog Box

The impact of the action depends on the type of element:

- Objects like dimensions and measures are deleted.
- Visualizations will have the object removed from the chart.
- Stories maybe impacted, but the direct impact is less clear.
- Objects used as filter controls will be removed

▶ MERGE THIS COLUMN
This is a shortcut to the merge dialog that is discussed in Section 4.8.2.

▶ HIDE FROM THE DATA SET PANEL
This is a shortcut for the customize view discussed previously. It hides the object and its associated data from the grid but does not delete the data from the dataset.

▶ CREATE CALCULATED DIMENSION
This is a shortcut for creating a calculated dimension; see Section 4.4 for more details.

Measures have a different set of options:

- CHANGE AGGREGATION
  Enables you to change the AGGREGATION FUNCTION of a measure e.g. SUM to AVERAGE.
- DISPLAY FORMATTING
  You can change the formatting, which is always a number format.
- RENAME
  As for a dimension, it renames the measure.
- REMOVE
  As for a dimension, it deletes the measure.
- CREATE CALCULATED MEASURE
  This is a shortcut for creating a calculated measure; see Section 4.4.2 for more details.

Now that we have discussed object actions, let's move on to data actions, which are central to editing your data.

4.6   Data Actions

Data actions are central to the Prepare room, as they allow you to edit and simplify your data. As we have seen already with geographic hierarchies, we might need to change value names in order for them to be usable. REPLACE is just one of the actions available to you; there are others that allow you to rename objects or even create complex groups.

Most of the actions are quite straightforward, so we will provide some simple examples and highlight the most useful, such as converting types. Actions differ by data type, although there are a number of common actions, which we will look at first. In the following sections, we will discuss the different action types for our data.

4.6.1   Common Actions

The common actions for all objects are as listed in the OBJECT PICKER context menu:

4 | Data Manipulation

- DUPLICATE
  Creates an exact copy of the column with an associated object.
- RENAME
  Allows you to rename an object or column. You simply enter the required name and click APPLY (see Figure 4.39).
- REMOVE
  Deletes an object or column.

Figure 4.39 Rename Dialog

One other action available to all columns is the GROUPING function, as described in Section 4.8.2.

4.6.2 String Actions

There are different actions for each type; we will start with strings, then look at numeric types, and then data objects. Here is a list of actions for strings:

- SPLIT
  Splits a column of data into multiple columns based on a separator that you choose: space, comma, semicolon, or enter any character (see Figure 4.40).

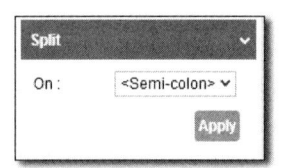

Figure 4.40 Split Dialog

- CONVERT CASE
  Changes a column's text to all uppercase or lowercase. This can be useful if, for example, you have two datasets that you want to merge and the join column does not contain the same case (see Figure 4.41).

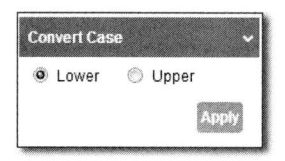

Figure 4.41 Convert Case Dialog

- FILL
  Pads your values either to the left or right with a character for a given total value. The value you enter is the expected length of the string—that is, your value will be padded so that the string has a total length of 30, for example (see Figure 4.42). The results look like the example in Figure 4.43.

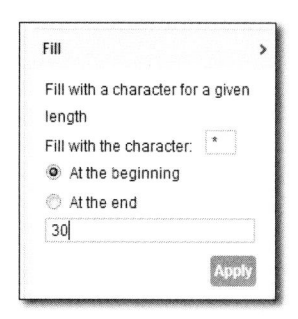

Figure 4.42 Fill Dialog

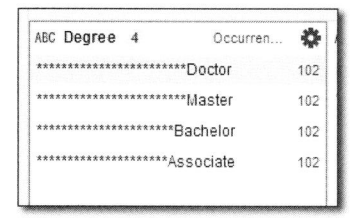

Figure 4.43 Left Padding

- CONVERT TO NUMBER
  Converting text to numbers can be useful, because you can then aggregate/create measures. Be careful how you use the function, because you run the risk of creating dirty data.

- CONVERT TO DATE
  This lets you create dates using a pattern that is selectable from the list. It's

quite straightforward, but it will assume that your cells are correctly formatted. Note the following conventions:

- dd, day
- MM, month
- yyyy, full year
- d, single digit days below 10
- M, single digit months below 10
- yy, the last two digits of a year—for example, 98

Dates can be separated by different tokens: slash ("/"), minus ("-"), or space (" "). In order to convert 12-11-2012 (that is, the 12th of November, 2012) you would choose dd-MM-yyyy (see Figure 4.44).

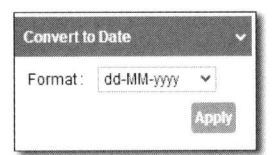

Figure 4.44 Convert to Date

Currently, you cannot set your own date format. If you have dates that don't match any of the patterns, you could use any of the other manipulation tools to format the date string into something that can be parsed.

- TRIM
  Removes any white space found at the beginning or the end of a value. This can be useful to ensure that two values are treated as exactly the same in a comparison (see Figure 4.45).

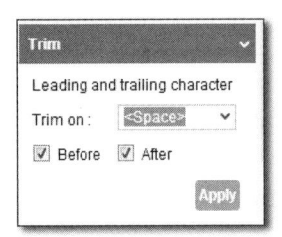

Figure 4.45 Trim Dialog

▶ GROUP BY SELECTION
This allows you to create named groups, enabling you to create something like a hierarchy. Groups are basically collections of values that SAP Lumira will use to group and aggregate.

Once you have selected NAMED GROUP, you will see a dialog box, as shown in Figure 4.46, which allows you to create a series of named buckets that you can add and remove values to and from.

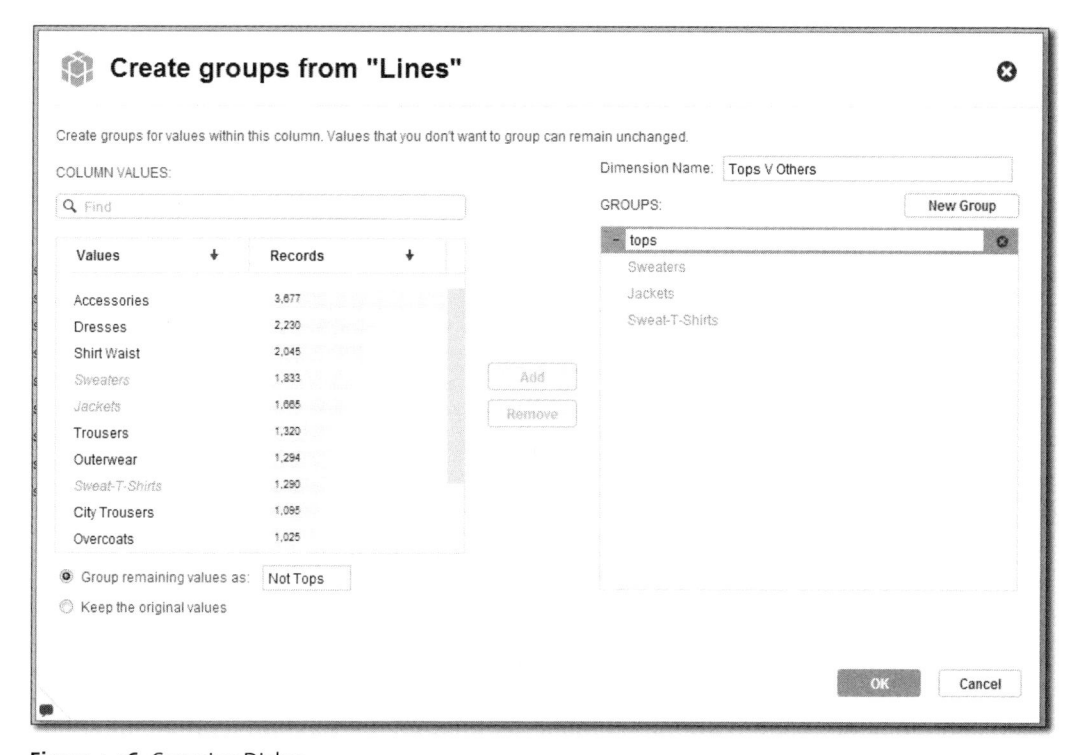

Figure 4.46 Grouping Dialog

If there are items that you cannot group, you can choose one of the following actions:

- ▶ GROUP RENAMING VALUES AS into a single bucket called OTHERS by default, but you can change this name.
- ▶ If you select KEEP THE ORIGINAL VALUES, then there will be no group for values not already placed. In other words, the other values will remain as they are and will not be grouped together.

4 | Data Manipulation

In Figure 4.47, you can see the value of creating groups, because they allow you to quickly create a chart that aggregates the named groups and lets you see how tops compare to other clothing.

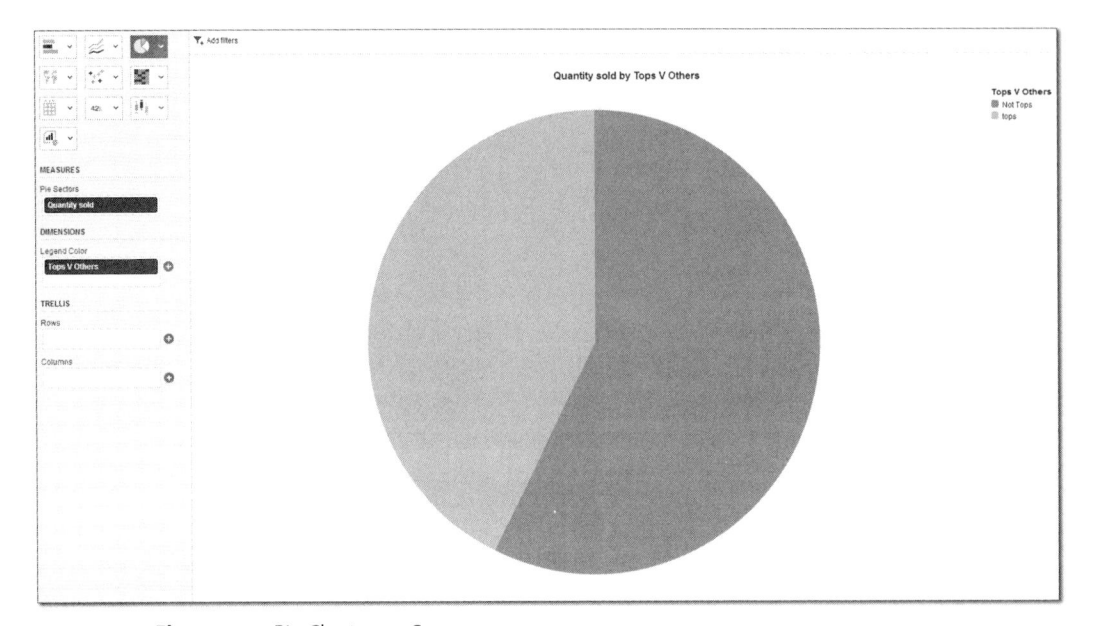

Figure 4.47 Pie Chart on a Group

4.6.3 Numeric Actions

Numeric columns have the same actions as strings:

- DUPLICATE
- RENAME
- REMOVE
- NAMED GROUP
- CREATE CALCULATED DIMENSION

However, there are also two additional actions:

- CONVERT TO TEXT
  Converts your number into a string. The number of digits to keep indicates that numbers can be rounded but also the inverse; a whole number will gain digits, for example, if set to keep two digits (see Figure 4.48).

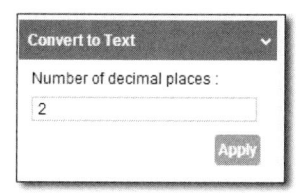

Figure 4.48 Convert to Text

- 23.456 will become 23.45 (numbers are not rounded but cut)
- 23 will become 23.00

This might create some "noise" in your data if you convert to and from text, because you can gain characters and lose values.

- GROUP BY RANGE

  In addition to creating named groups with numeric values, you can create groups by range. If you have selected a numeric object/column, then you can select the option CREATE GROUP BY RANGE (see Figure 4.49).

Figure 4.49 Group by Range Dialog Box

To create a GROUP BY RANGE numeric action, perform the following steps (as seen in Figure 4.49):

1. In the NEW DIMENSION NAME field, enter the desired name. In our example, we used "Customer Satisfaction Intervals".
2. In the CREATE field, enter a number of intervals, which are used to divide your values into groups. In our example, we used 7.
3. In the FROM field, specify the starting value, which by default is the lowest value. Our example is 0.51.
4. In the TO field, specify the value (by default the highest value). Our example is 0.95.
5. In the GROUP REMAINING VALUES AS field, you can specify the name to group the rest of your values. Our example in Figure 4.49 uses "Others".
6. You can specify the format for this range and per number formatting by clicking the DISPLAY FORMATTING... button, which opens the DISPLAY FORMAT dialog box, described in Section 4.5.

Click OK to close the dialog box. The result of a numeric range will be seen as a new column, as shown in Figure 4.50.

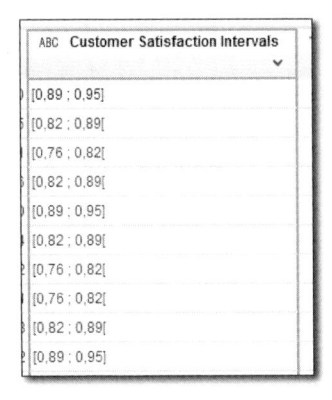

Figure 4.50 Output of Group by Range

The ranges in this new column are described by:

▸ [<startRange>; <endRange>[for the first created ranges; since <startRange> is included in the range, but not <endRange>

▸ [<startRange> ; <endRange>] for the last created range, both <startRange>; <endRange> being included in the range.

4.6.4 Date Actions

Dates have no actions to add to the common actions already described:

- DUPLICATE
- RENAME
- REMOVE
- NAMED GROUP
- CREATE CALCULATED DIMENSION

4.6.5 Value and Column Actions

In addition to manipulating objects or columns, you can also act on string values. In order to do this, you just have to select a value in the grid or facet. Date and numeric values don't support any action, but strings allow you to apply the common string actions:

- CONVERT CASE
- REPLACE
- FILL
- TRIM

The difference to note is that you can now choose to apply your actions to all cells or only to cells of the same value; see Figure 4.51.

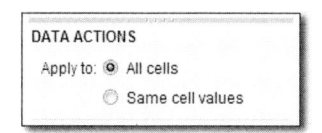

Figure 4.51 Apply to All Cells

This means you could convert the case for specific values but leave the others as they are, for example.

There is one additional new action, INSERT AT CARET POSITION, as can be seen in Figure 4.52.

4 | Data Manipulation

Figure 4.52 Insert at Caret Position

In order to activate this action, you must select a cell and then double-click it. You can then place your "caret" (the TEXT icon) at any position (see Figure 4.53), enter any text in the text field, and it will be inserted at that position.

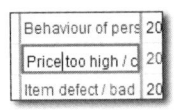

Figure 4.53 Sample Caret Selection

If, as seen in Figure 4.54, we enter "FOO" after "price" and select APPLY FOR ALL VALUES, then FOO is entered at the caret position.

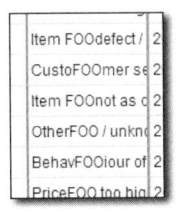

Figure 4.54 FOO Inserted

Note, that it's not the character but the position that counts. If you choose SAME CELL VALUES, then only PRICE TOO HIGH will be changed.

It is also possible to CONCATENATE COLUMNS into a single column by selecting multiple columns. Note, that the order you select effects the concatenate order. In Figure 4.55, selecting CATEGORY before CITY or vice versa is important.

Once you have selected several columns, the CONCATENATE action will appear in the DATA ACTIONS list. Click CONCATENATE to display the concatenate options (see Figure 4.56).

200

Figure 4.55 Concatenate Columns

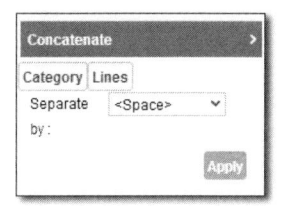

Figure 4.56 Concatenate Action

The order for the columns is displayed in this section. In the SEPARATE BY field, click the down arrow and in the dropdown list, select a character to separate the merged values: space, comma, colon, or semi-colon. You can type any string in this field.

Click APPLY to generate a new column containing the merged values from the selected columns.

Now that we have looked at the actions available for your data, let's see how to create subsets of your data through filtering and sorting.

4.7 Filtering and Sorting Data

Filters allow you to see a subset of your data. For example, you may want to see only values for the United States or a particular manager. To create a filter, you select a dimension and from that dimension's list of values select the values you want to use as a filter. A filter does not remove values; it only hides them. Removing a filter reveals your data again.

4 | Data Manipulation

Filters created in the Prepare room are slightly special and are called *global filters*, because they are applied to all other rooms and also published data. This is explained ahead. It is not possible, currently, to use a measure as a filter in SAP Lumira (you can use a numeric dimension).

4.7.1 Filtering Data in a Column

Create a filter by selecting the dimension in the OBJECT PICKER or the column. Selection opens the filter option, as shown in Figure 4.57.

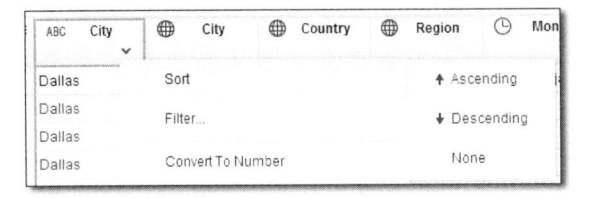

Figure 4.57 Filter Menu Option

Once you have chosen the FILTER ... option, a dialog box appears that allows you to choose values, as seen in Figure 4.58.

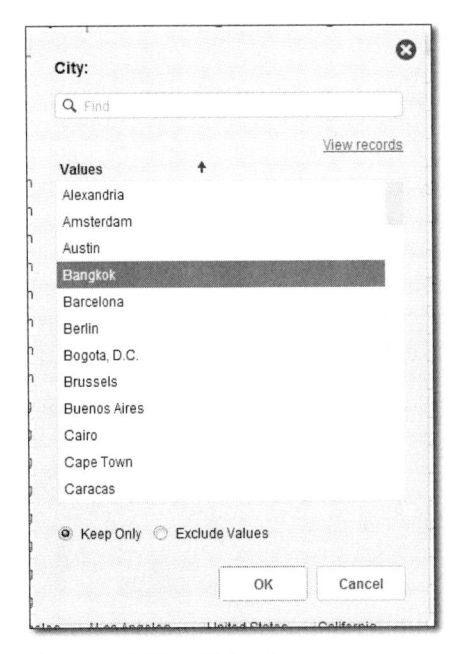

Figure 4.58 Filter Dialog Box

You can then choose the values and tone that you want of the following options:

- KEEP ONLY
  These values are kept.
- EXCLUDE VALUES
  These values are excluded.

Once a filter has been generated, it appears in the FILTER BAR above the dataset panel (see Figure 4.59).

Figure 4.59 Filter Crumb

Your data will be immediately filtered. If you want to combine filters from the same column, then you can select the breadcrumb above and reopen the dialog. Excluded values are indicated by strikethrough text (see Figure 4.60).

Figure 4.60 Exclude Filter

> **Note**
> The FILTER BAR is sometimes referred to as the breadcrumb as it's like a trail of crumbs telling you where you are.

The breadcrumb also indicates the number of values in a filter. You can remove a filter by clicking the DELETE icon. You cannot mix keep and exclude in a single column, and there are no filters on measures.

Combining Filters

You can combine filters from different columns by repeating the process over multiple dimensions: select one, create your filter, and then select another. Of course, the values for the subsequent filters will already be filtered by the previous values; if you selected Germany, then you will only be able to filter by German cities. Each filter will appear as a series of crumbs (see Figure 4.61) in the FILTER BAR.

4 | Data Manipulation

Figure 4.61 Combining Filters

Note, that each crumb tells you the number of values selected in that filter. The strikethrough tells you that the values are excluded, not included, in the filter. You can delete a filter by clicking the DELETE icon.

4.7.2 Displaying Filters in Other Rooms

The effect of the filter in the Prepare room has an impact on all the other rooms in the desktop and affects the published content. Global filters appear in each of the other rooms as a dark grey crumb (see Figure 4.62, top left).

The FILTER BAR does not have a consistent look and feel throughout the different rooms, but the same principles always apply (filter crumbs are rendered as dimensions with the values underneath in the Visualize and Compose rooms).

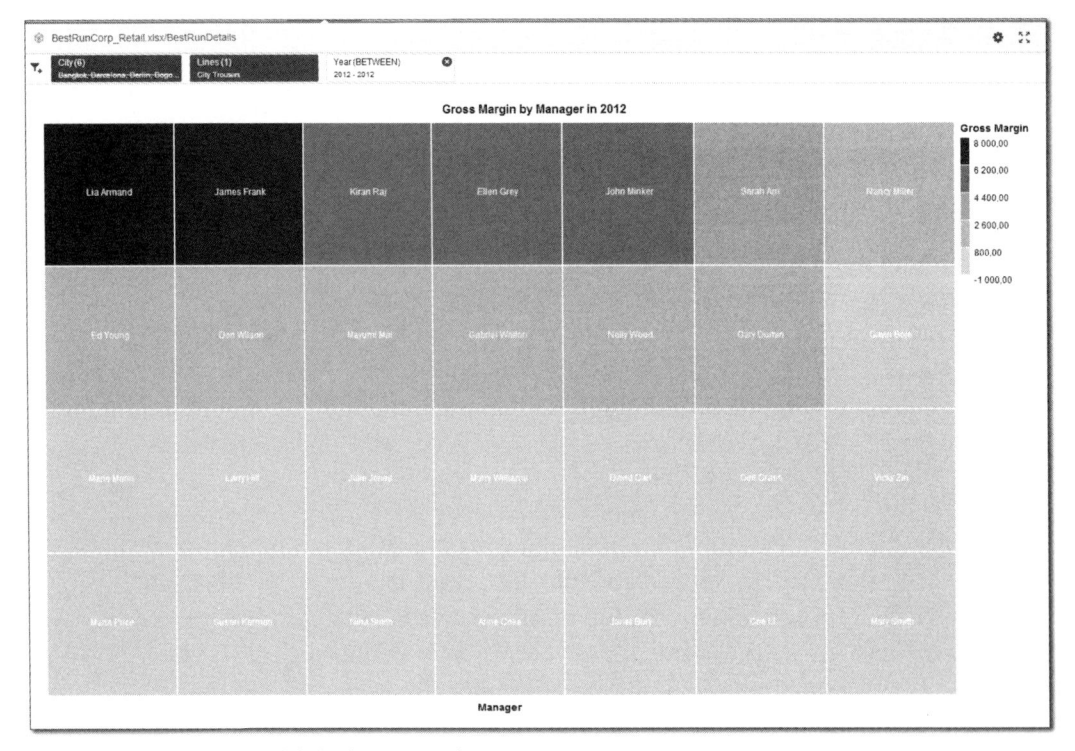

Figure 4.62 Global Filter in Visualize Room

These filters cannot be removed or edited from either visualizations or stories. If you publish a story to the server or cloud, then the filter in the story is persisted and present in the story that is consumed on the cloud or server.

4.7.3 Sorting Data

Sorts can be applied to any column and will use the data type to determine the correct order. Strings are treated alphabetically, numeric data by value, and dates by precedence. Sorts can be either ascending or descending; simply select the sort order you prefer from the options shown in Figure 4.57.

In FACETS mode, there is an additional option to filter the values by the associated measure and not the value directly (see Section 4.1.4). The FACETS VIEW only displays distinct values rather than all values, and therefore there is an implicit associated count (occurrences) for the value—for example, trousers appears 1,000 times in the column and thus has an occurrence of 1,000. By using a measure to sort, you replace the occurrence count for the aggregation of the measure selected, such as trousers by quantity sold. Each value in the facet is calculated as well. This can only be applied in FACETS mode, because in GRID VIEW you see all the values and not the distinct set; thus the occurrence is always 1, and there is nothing to aggregate by.

First, select the measure, as shown in Figure 4.63, then follow these steps:

1. In the OBJECT PICKER, select an object.
2. Click the cog icon, and in the contextual menu select the SORT submenu.
3. Depending on the desired sort criteria, select one of the following options:
    - SORT DIMENSION ASCENDING
      Sort alphanumerically from A to Z or 1 to *n* or, for dates, in chronological order (low to high).
    - SORT DIMENSION DESCENDING
      Sort alphanumerically in the opposite direction (high to low).
    - SORT MEASURE ASCENDING
      Sort by using the aggregated measure value for each value in the dimension from lowest to highest. This is only available in FACETS mode.
    - SORT MEASURE DESCENDING
      Same as SORT MEASURE ASCENDING but from highest to lowest.

You will then have the option in the SORT menu to sort by the dimension or the selected measure (see Figure 4.63).

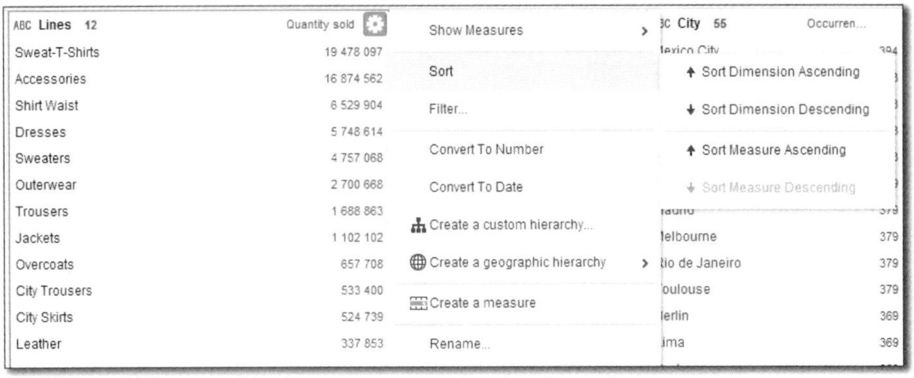

Figure 4.63 Sort by Measure

So far we have looked at the different actions and manipulations that you can perform on your dataset. However, the Prepare room has another role as it also allows you to work with multiple datasets and enables you to merge these datasets together into a single model.

4.8 Multiple Datasets

SAP Lumira allows you to have multiple datasets in a single document. There are two ways to work with these datasets: independently, switching between separate sets, or by combining datasets into a single data model. The main reason to combine datasets is that you cannot use multiple datasets in a single visualization. If, for example, you had multiple Microsoft Excel files covering different time periods, then you could append them in order to aggregate them in a single chart.

Currently, you cannot use multiple online datasets in SAP Lumira, so the following actions only apply to acquired data.

4.8.1 Adding a Dataset

Adding a dataset is almost exactly the same as creating a new document, but rather than using NEW you select NEW DATASET in the top-right menu of an existing document (see Figure 4.64). Note, that you cannot reuse a dataset from an existing document; you need to import the source. Because the workflow is exactly the same as for acquisition, please refer to Chapter 3 for details.

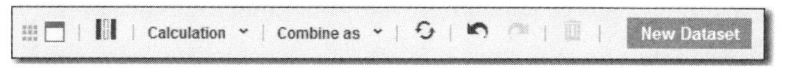

Figure 4.64 New Dataset Menu

If you have more than one dataset in your document, then you can switch between them at any point by using the DATASET SELECTOR. It's also possible to add datasets when you merge or append datasets, as we will see ahead.

4.8.2 Merging Dataset

Merging datasets is performed via the COMBINE AS option on the Prepare room menu bar. In order to merge, you need two datasets, so if you do not have a second you can either add it as discussed previously, or add it via the MERGE DATA dialog box (see Figure 4.65).

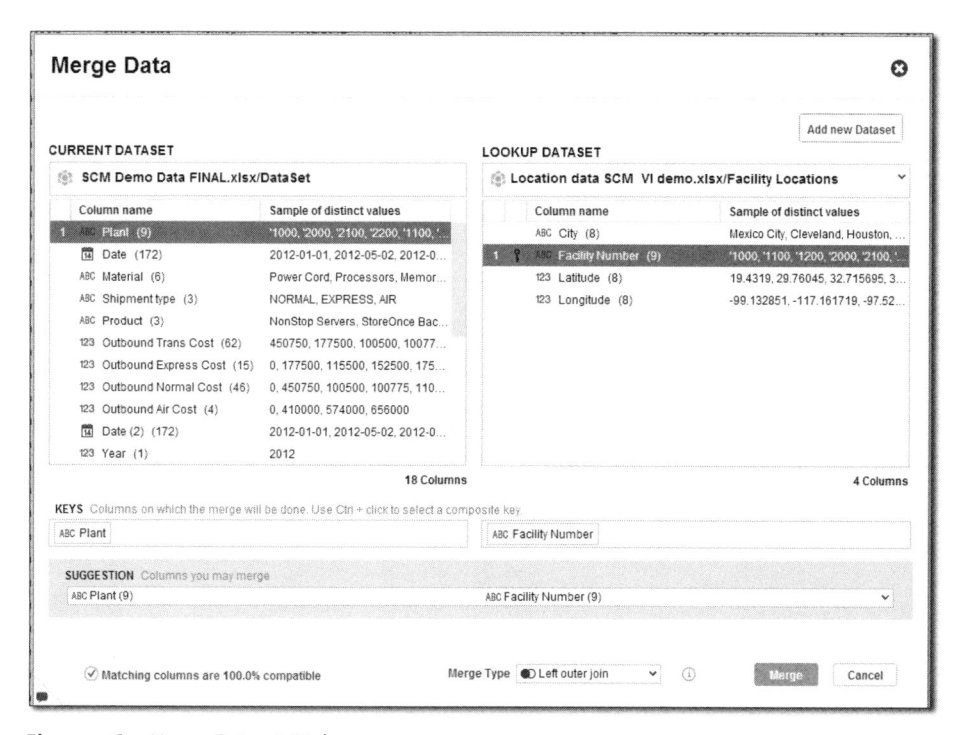

Figure 4.65 Merge Dataset Dialog

We can see that the PLANT and FACILITY NUMBER columns are detected as a match. To merge the data, follow these steps:

1. In the MERGE DATA dialog box, you have to select the columns to merge.
2. You can select one or more columns to create composite keys. The objects selected can be seen in the KEYS section.
3. Select the MERGE button from the bottom of the dialog box. You can choose from LEFT OUTER JOIN or INNER JOIN.
4. If there is a possible match, then you will see the matching columns and percent compatibility.
5. MERGE will then merge the data from the LOOKUP DATASET section into the CURRENT DATASET section.

These are the basic steps, but there are some additional points to consider:

- Data is merged from right to left. In other words, the LOOKUP DATASET is pushed into the CURRENT DATASET. If you want to change the order, then you need to leave the dialog and switch datasets in the Prepare room, because the current dataset in the Prepare room is the one used as the CURRENT DATASET in the merge operation.
- Data is merged by choosing the key columns that SAP Lumira uses to join the data together. You can select any pair of columns, but SAP Lumira expects columns that contain unique values (somewhat like a KEY column in a database). This means that you can only merge datasets that contain the same unique column. It does not mean that you have to have a 100% union between the datasets. In the preceding example, you can see that SAP Lumira will determine the match between two columns; in this case, it's 50%.
- Union type defines the result of the join. You can either have a left outer join in which all data is kept or an inner ioin in which only the common data is kept. Columns are always added.

Let's briefly look at the differences between the join types via a practical example.

Join Types

One of the useful features of joining data in SAP Lumira is that you can merge coordinates for places: one table contains your data, and you enrich it with the longitude and latitude of locations. Although this operation is quite straightforward, it's important to see the difference in the joins.

Start with a simple source dataset that contains our data—for example, see Figure 4.66, in which we display some simple revenue figures.

country	city	temperature
USA	Paris	45
France	Paris	26
China	Shanghai	33

Figure 4.66 Source Dataset

We would like to locate these revenues on a map using location coordinates, which we have available for two of the locations (see Figure 4.67).

country	city	revenue
USA	Paris	420
France	Paris	170

Figure 4.67 Target Dataset

First, we must merge these two datasets together using the left outer join (see Figure 4.68) and using COUNTRY and CITY.

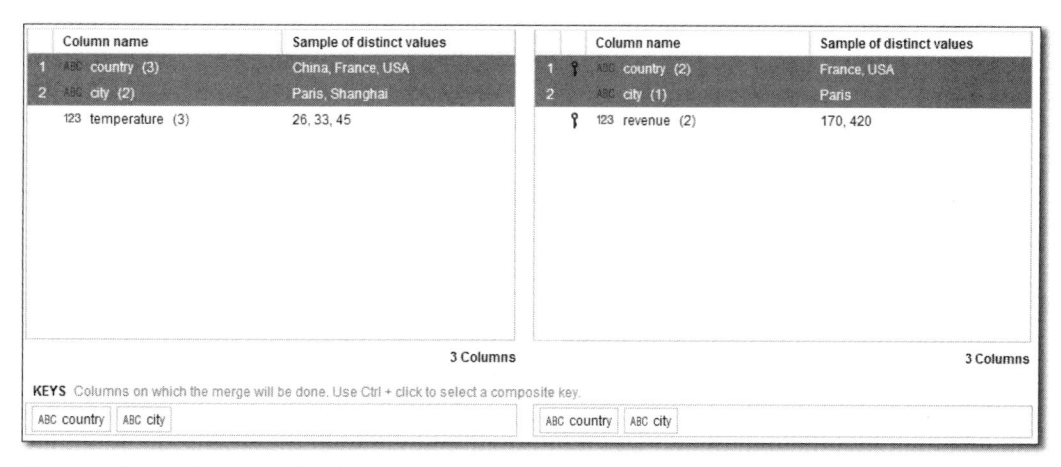

Figure 4.68 Left Outer Join Merging

The results of the merge are shown in Figure 4.69.

ABC country	ABC city	123 revenue	123 temperatur
USA	Paris	420	45
France	Paris	170	26
China	Shanghai		33

Figure 4.69 Left Outer Join Table

Using the left outer join, we see that all of the data is joined: we have added our new column and kept all of the rows. The results if we use the inner join instead are shown in Figure 4.70.

ABC country	ABC city	123 revenue	123 temperatur
USA	Paris	420	45
France	Paris	170	26

Figure 4.70 Inner Join

The inner join will only return matched data. Because the China row was not matched, it is excluded.

Finally, you can merge multiple datasets, but you can only merge two at a time. If you want to merge three (or more), then be careful to plan the merge as an *n*-step process; first source 1 into current, then source 2 into the merged current model.

4.8.3 Appending Datasets

It is also possible to append datasets, which can be useful if you have a periodic dataset, such as a spreadsheet that you receive every month. With the APPEND feature, you can add the data to your existing dataset. The data is not merged but is appended to the end of the current data; the preceding example would not work in this case, because there is no attempt to reconcile the data (see Figure 4.71).

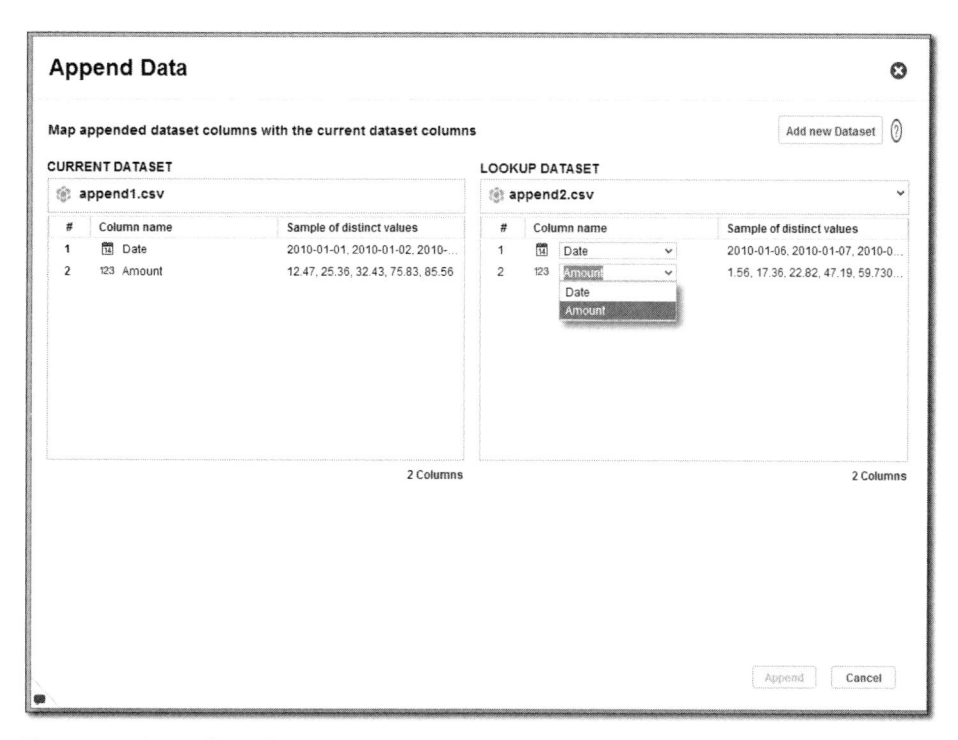

Figure 4.71 Appending a Dataset

To do this, perform the following steps:

1. The LOOKUP DATASET section will be appended to the CURRENT DATASET section. You can select an existing dataset or add a new one.

2. Columns are mapped in order from 1 to n, and by selecting the column name you can change the column for each position. This means that your lookup does not have to be in the same order; you only have to check the ordering and that the data types are the same.

3. Merge will now append the lookup to the current dataset, adding all additional rows to the end of the current dataset.

We have now looked at all of the enrichment and data features in the Prepare room. Before we move on, however, there is one optimization for the Prepare room that can be used to change the way in which auto-enrichments are handled.

4.9 Configuring Auto-Enrichment

One of the issues that you might find with auto-enrichment is that it creates too many objects or unwanted objects. Imagine that you have a date or time split over three columns: year, month, and day. These three values will be detected first as numeric values and second as probable date values. Because they are numeric, associated measures that you probably don't want will be created. This could become annoying if it recurs frequently, because you will have to manually update your data or live with several unwanted objects. For this reason, SAP Lumira exposes a kind of rules system that allows you to change the behavior on acquisition in order to prevent these enhancements.

Note that these rules discussed ahead are only applied to your data if you have selected automatic enrichments in the preferences for datasets.

4.9.1 Enrichment Files

The files that hold the rules are stored in the .sapvi folder inder your Windows personal folder, for example:

C:\users\<user>\.sapvi, where <user> is your Windows account.

This folder contains some example files already created with a file name of the following form:

enrichment_suggestions.<versionnumber>.txt

For example, *enrichment_suggestions.1.18.0.txt*.

The file is versioned so that you know the current version of file you are using. This file is parsed and used to determine whether an object should be converted to a measure, a time, or a geographic hierarchy.

4.9.2 Versioning Rule

Whenever a new version of SAP Lumira is installed, a new associated rules file will be created rather than replacing the existing file. However, your current rules will not be automatically migrated over, so you will need to migrate your rules manually.

4.9.3 Enrichment File Format

The rules essentially define what should *not* happen—for example, column year should not become a measure (see Listing 4.1).

```
{
       "objectName":"(?i).*year.*|.*month.*|.*quarter.*|.*week|.*day|
          .*semester.*|.*hour|.*minute|.*second",
       "dataTypes":["integer", "biginteger", "double"],
       "enrichment":"MEASURE",
       "rule":"hide"
}
```
Listing 4.1 Enrichment Syntax

The rule in Listing 4.1 is available by default and basically states in what manner any object that matches the name `year` should be treated. The dataType is noted as numeric, and the enrichment MEASURE should be hidden. This is the default behavior, if you have the following values in your data source:

```
YEAR,VALUE
2001,12
2010,22
```

You will acquire what is shown in Figure 4.72 as a new dataset.

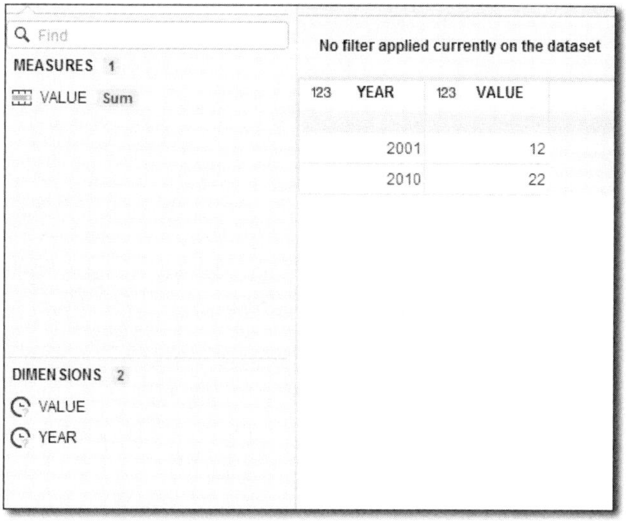

Figure 4.72 Year Ignored as Measure

In Figure 4.72, the value is still converted to a measure, but the year correctly has been ignored. It is still considered a potential time hierarchy, but we can of course add another rule to ignore this. For example, let's exclude value as a potential time hierarchy (see Listing 4.2).

```
{
        "objectName":"(?i).*value.*",
        "dataTypes":["integer", "biginteger", "double"],
        "enrichment":"TIME",
        "rule":"hide"
}
```

Listing 4.2 Excluding Time Enrichment.

Now, we should see the results displayed in Figure 4.73.

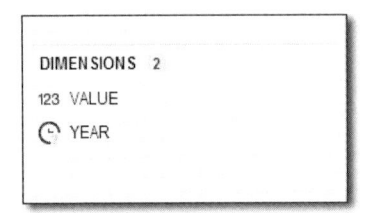

Figure 4.73 Numeric Value Ignored

In Figure 4.73, value is no longer given the time treatment. There are different rules that you can configure; we will now look at these rules in the file format.

4.9.4 File Syntax

The enrichment file rules are written in JSON (JSON or JavaScript Object Notation, is a readable data language used primarily in web applications and can be compared to XML). As it is JSON, you can verify that you have correctly generated the file by using an online syntax checker or JSON editor. The rules are defined in Table 4.3.

Attribute	Description
objectName	The name of a regular expression that can be matched to the name of the object. The object name is always the column header as it's acquired.
dataType	The data type or types that are associated with the column. You might apply the rule for a numeric value but not a string, for example. Possible types include the following: ▸ INTEGER ▸ BIGINTEGER ▸ STRING ▸ DATE ▸ BOOLEAN You can specify NONE or all types. If NONE is specified, then all types are considered.
enrichment	This specifies the type of enrichment to consider. You can specify the following: ▸ MEASURE ▸ TIME ▸ GEO Selecting one of these means that you are excluding the object from enrichment. Measure will exclude an object from being turned into a measure when you acquire data. Time will prevent an object from being treated as a candidate for a time hierarchy and similarly Geo will mean your object will not be treated as a geographical candidate.
Rule	The only supported value is HIDE, meaning that the enrichment will not be applied.

Table 4.3 Auto-configuration Rules

Auto-configuration may not be something that you will need to use very often. However, if there are some common datasets that you are using for which you do not want to have to manually remove the default enrichments, then it can be of value.

4.10 Summary

The Prepare room in SAP Lumira frees the end user: you can clean, merge, add calculations, and enrich your datasets without calling the IT department. As we have seen, it's possible to clean data with actions, create calculations, and enrich hierarchies.

In the next chapters, we will see how you can use this enriched data to create visualizations and, later, stories.

Data visualization helps you to present your data clearly and coherently. In SAP Lumira, the Visualize room is where you can visually analyze your data and prepare charts to share with your colleagues.

5 Data Visualization

In SAP Lumira, the VISUALIZE room is where you create visualizations in order to analyze and present your data. There are a large number of visualizations to choose from: standard bar, pie, and line charts, more complex box plots, waterfalls, maps, and many others (see Figure 5.1).

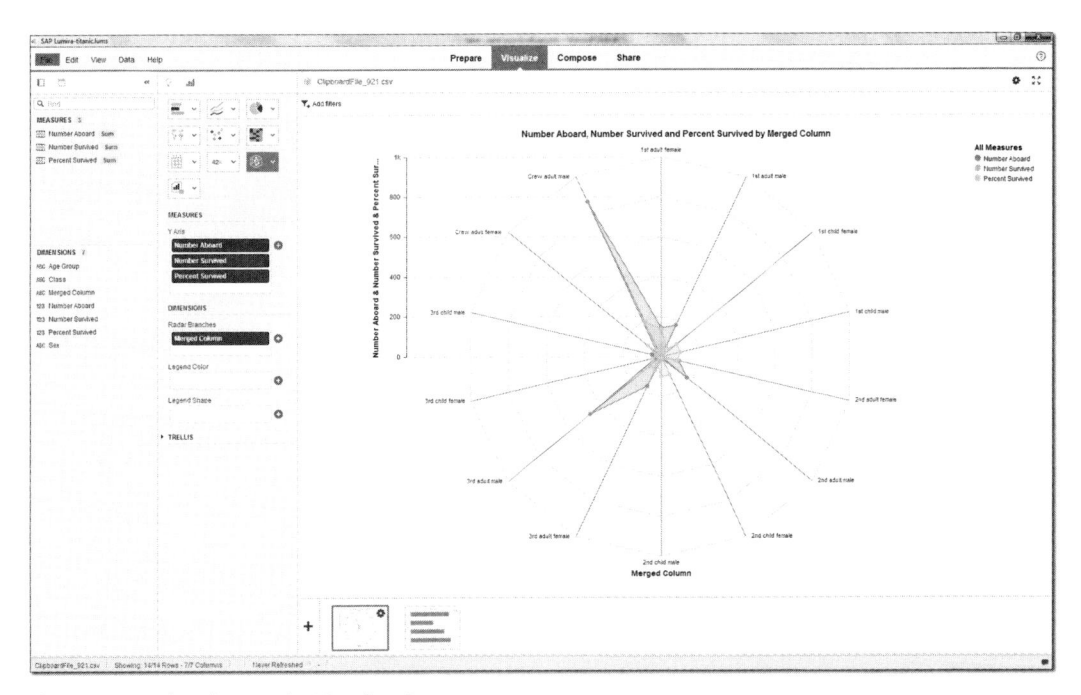

Figure 5.1 Radar Chart in the Visualize Room

5 | Data Visualization

> **Charts and Visualizations**
>
> Often we will use the term "chart" when speaking about visualizations, and it can be hard to understand the difference between the two: what is a chart and what is a visualization? The distinction is that we *use* charts to *visualize* data. You could see this as a chart is the noun and visualize is the verb: you use one to do the other.

Visualizations make use of the metadata defined in the Prepare room in order to determine what to display in the Visualize room, principally by using measures to aggregate your data, but also you can navigate through hierarchies or take advantage of time and geographical enrichments. Through geographic hierarchies, it's possible to use the built-in geographical charts and third-party charts and maps from Esri (see Section 5.3.4).

First, we will look at the structure of the Visualize room itself and how it provides the tools needed to create dynamic data presentations. Then, in the sections that follow, we will explore how to build our charts in SAP Lumira and some of the chart types and functionalities available.

> **Color Images**
>
> Please note that, though the print book shows the application images in grayscale, full color versions are viewable in the e-book version.

5.1 Visualize Room Overview

The VISUALIZE room is organized in a similar fashion as the Prepare room (see Figure 5.2).

From left to right, the following panels are shown:

- The OBJECT PICKER is as in the Prepare room. The OBJECT PICKER is used to create charts; you will use the objects listed here to feed your charts by dragging them onto the FEEDING panel or directly onto the CHART AREA. Some manipulation actions are available from the picker, but for the complete set of actions you need to move back to the Prepare room. This chapter does not cover any of the data manipulation actions.

- The FEEDING panel, to the right, has two roles: it is where you select the type of chart that you wish to use, and in turn this choice affects the feeding elements below. The feeding elements are where you place measures and dimensions to define what your chart will display. You will also see a lightbulb icon above that enables another view called the RELATED VISUALIZATIONS. SAP Lumira can propose and suggest visualizations based on your data.
- Again, to the right is the CHART DISPLAY area or chart canvas. The charts are always rendered here, allowing direct interaction when constructing and analyzing your charts.
- Underneath the canvas is the GALLERY that lists the visualizations that you have constructed. Each visualization will have a thumbnail that is a view of the current state of the chart to simplify selection. There are also some actions available from here for the management of visualizations.

Figure 5.2 Visualize Room

Before looking in detail at the different charts and options available in the Visualize room, we will explain how charts are built and structured in SAP Lumira.

5.2　Building Charts in SAP Lumira

Because all charts are built the same way, we will look at a simple example before entering into the details of each individual chart and possible customizations. First, you need to select the type of chart you wish to use from the GALLERY (see Figure 5.3).

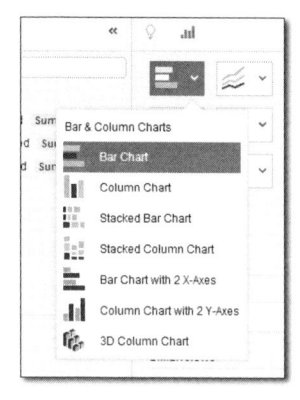

Figure 5.3　Selecting a Chart Type

The chart you select will immediately impact the interface, because it will modify the feeding options. In Figure 5.4, we have selected a column chart.

Figure 5.4　The Chart Feeding Panel

The FEEDING panel is where you place the dimensions and measures that you wish to use. Each chart will have different configurations that bind your data to the structure of the chart. For example, in Figure 5.5, we have selected a bar chart so that we can place a measure on the y-axis and a dimension on the x-axis.

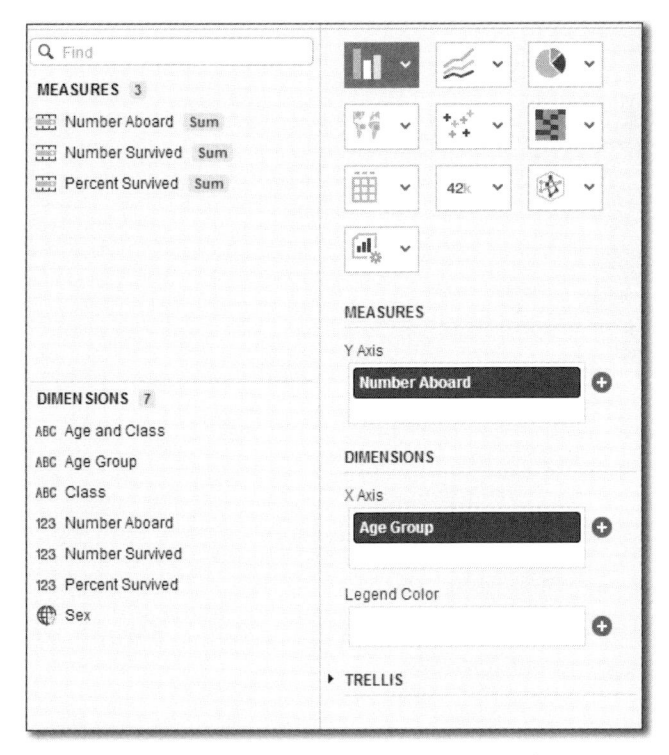

Figure 5.5 Measures and Dimensions in Feeding Panel

Selecting these objects will produce the chart seen in Figure 5.6.

Charts use the metadata in your objects that you created to determine what to render. In other words, what we are seeing is the SUM of passengers aggregated by AGE GROUP.

You can drag and drop objects directly onto the FEEDING panel in order to create the chart. For example, we can add AGE GROUP and NUMBER ABOARD. (It is also possible to add objects by double-clicking them, dropping them onto the canvas directly, or using the small PLUS icon located next to each feed element.)

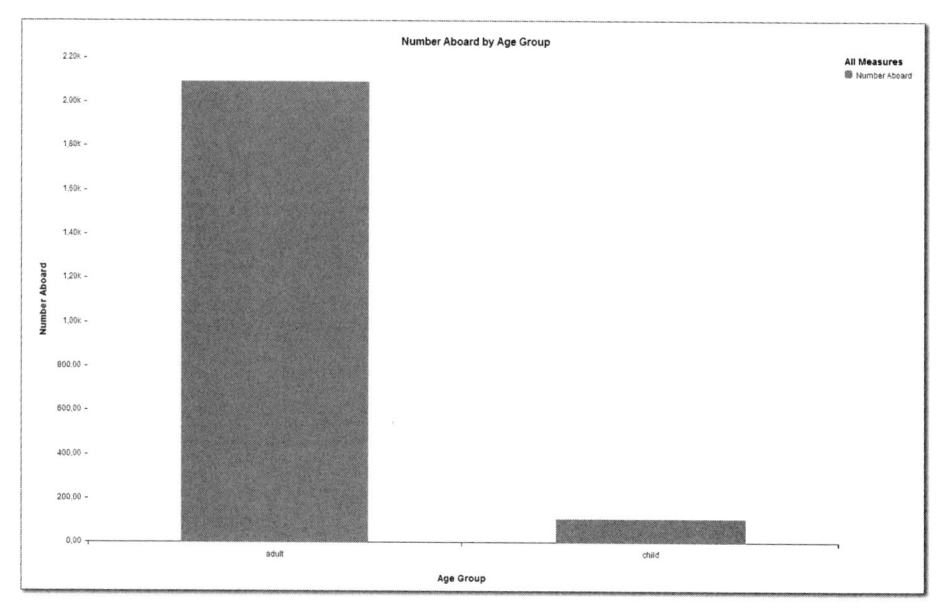

Figure 5.6 Colmun/Bar Chart

In summary, to create a chart, take the following actions:

- Choose the type of chart that you wish to use.
- The FEEDING panel will define how your objects can be used and on which axis you can place your dimensions and measures.
- Place the objects that you wish to visualize.

> **Public Data**
>
> SAP Lumira is available to anyone and can use any data, so here we will use some examples built from datasets found on the web. The charts ahead were built using data about the survivors of the Titanic shipwreck. We will use some other datasets in this chapter as well, including stock data and data from the 2012 Summer Olympics and survivors of the Titanic.

5.2.1 Aggregation

Visualizations are tied to the objects used and in turn to the data; a change in the measure or the aggregation of a measure will immediately be seen in the chart (see Figure 5.7).

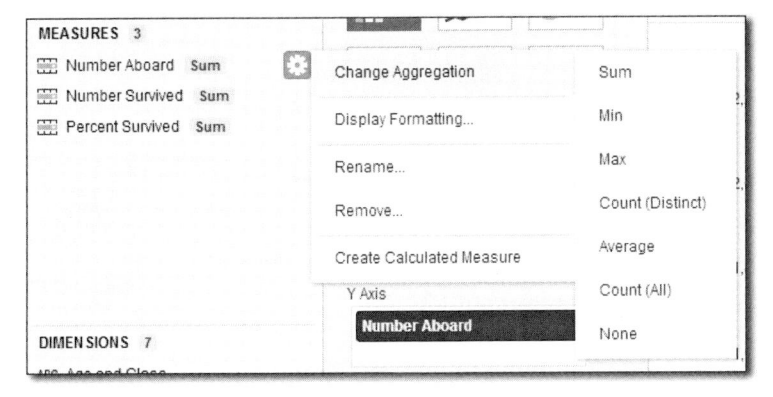

Figure 5.7 Change from Sum to Average

If you change the aggregation from SUM to AVERAGE, then this will be immediately visible in your chart (see Figure 5.8).

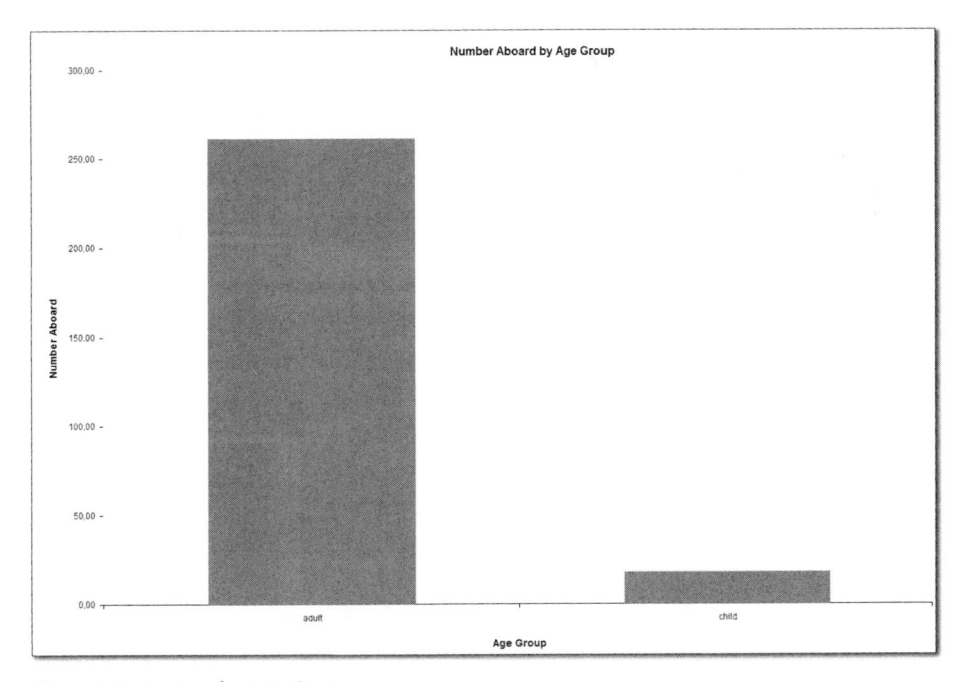

Figure 5.8 Average by Age Group

Dimensions are aggregated according to the aggregation function of the measure—for example, the sum of the number of passengers by AGE GROUP.

> **Using a Measure in Multiple Charts**
>
> If you use a measure in multiple charts, then you may need to create multiple measures to ensure that you are aggregating what you want; if you want to plot AVERAGE revenue and TOTAL revenue you should create two measures.

Now that we have explored the aggregation types and functions available, let's express the information in our charts further using legends.

5.2.2 Legends

Charts can have *legends* that can help you understand what you are seeing and also enrich your chart. By default, a legend is a map of the values in your chart to associated colors, which aids legibility. A chart that supports a legend will display this as a legend feed in the FEEDING panel. You can add a dimension to the legend just as you would a measure or dimension to an axis. You can add the same dimension that you used for the previous example (see Figure 5.9).

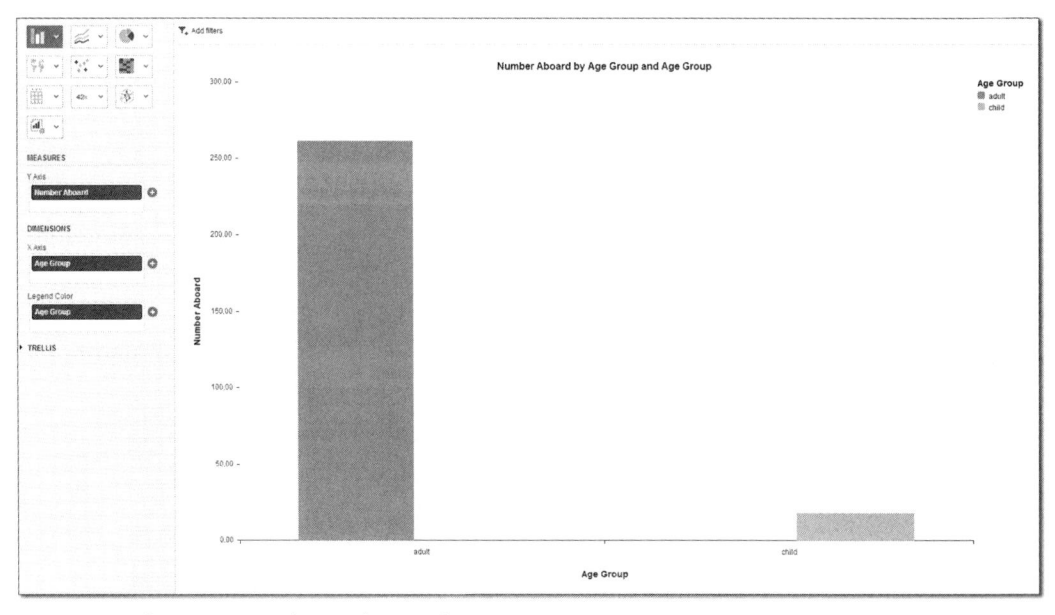

Figure 5.9 Bar Chart with Legend

This creates a legend with a color code for the columns.

You are not always required to use the same dimension for the legend that you are using for an axis. Adding an additional dimension to the legend will add an additional dimension to the axis, creating an aggregation for the legend grouped by the axis dimension.

For example, we can add a CLASS. Notice the legend added to the top-right corner of the chart (see Figure 5.10).

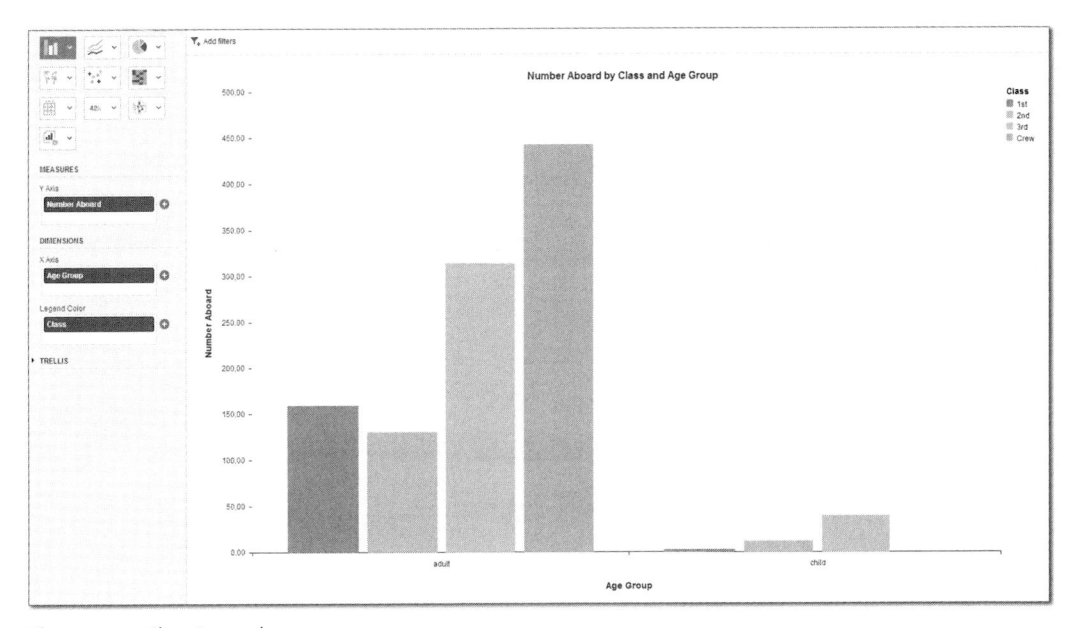

Figure 5.10 Class Legend

This has the effect of adding an additional dimension to the chart grouped by the axis dimension. The legend colors are mapped to the column labels. Note, that the columns are grouped by our two categories.

If you want to express patterns in your data, a useful tool might be a trellis.

5.2.3 Trellis

A trellis is useful for finding the patterns in complex data. It allows you to create a series of similar charts over a given dimension or dimensions and even measures. To create a trellis, add a dimension to either the ROWS or COLUMNS field of the TRELLIS section. Your chart will be split vertically or horizontally according to your choice (see Figure 5.11).

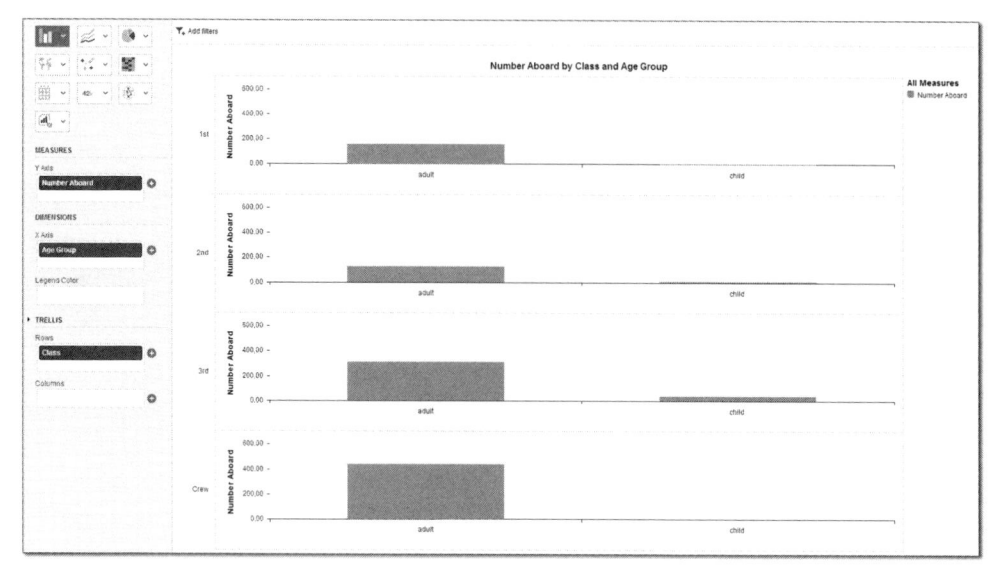

Figure 5.11 Trellis on Class

A trellis allows you to separate out data points into clusters that are still comparable, because they share a common aggregation. It is also possible to create a trellis on both rows and columns to create a matrix (see Figure 5.12).

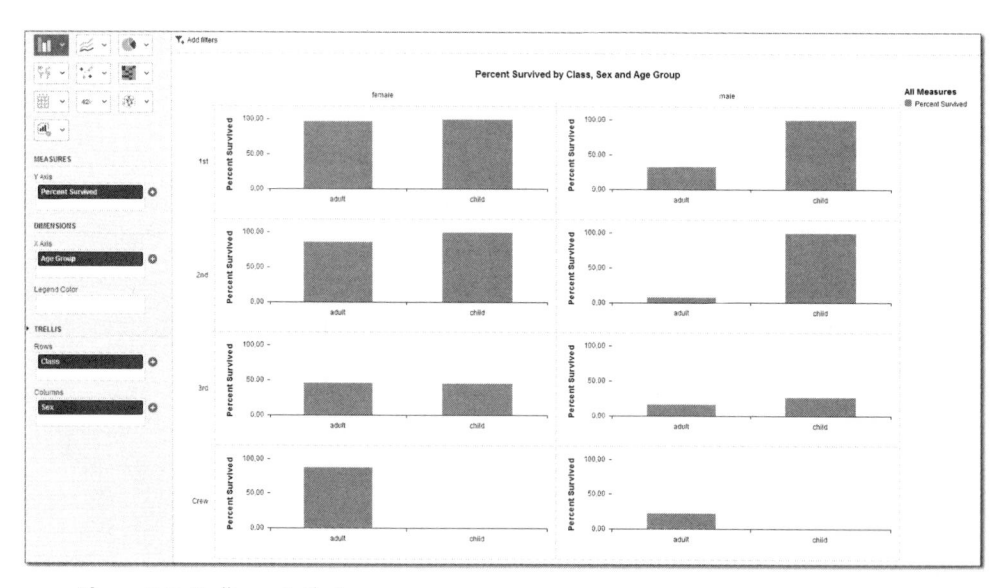

Figure 5.12 Trellis on Both Axes

This kind of trellis can help you identify patterns or anomalies. In this case, we can see a clear decline in survival rates by class and sex for survivors of the Titanic.

In summary, you use measures and dimensions to build charts with dimensions that drive the aggregations. We will now look at the different charts that are available in SAP Lumira before looking at some of the other features of the Visualize room.

5.3 Charts Types in SAP Lumira

There are many different chart types available in SAP Lumira, and, as you can see in Figure 5.3, charts are grouped by families, columns, areas, and so on. This section is thus split into the different families. In the next section, we will change the dataset to the 2012 Summer Olympics.

5.3.1 Column Charts

Column or bar charts use proportional rectangular bars that are bound to a value to allow quick visual comparisons. Column charts can be displayed either horizontally (bar) or vertically (column). Previously, we looked at a column chart, and in Figure 5.13 we can see a bar chart that has multiple measures on the x-axis.

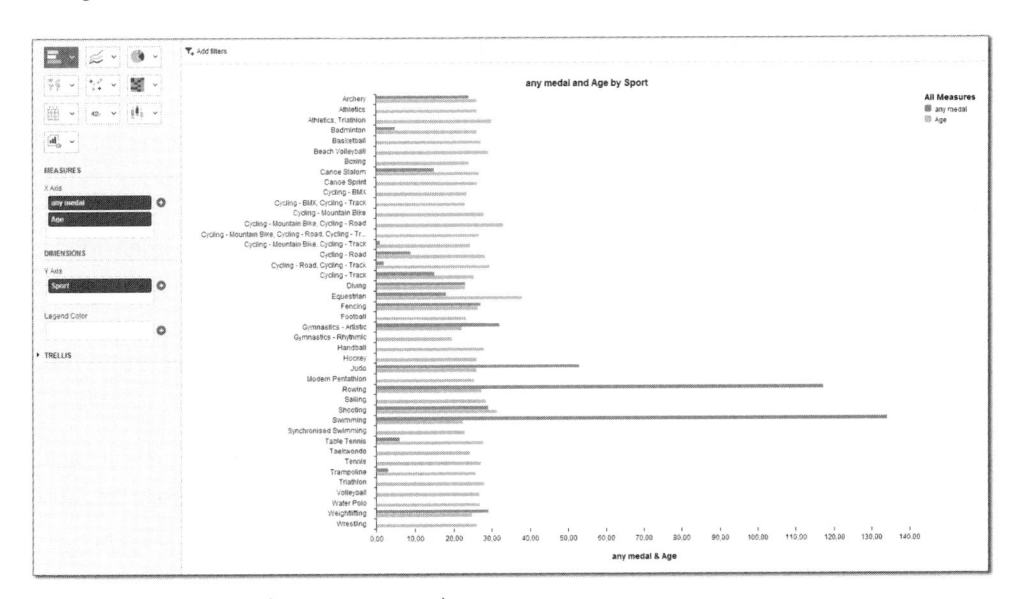

Figure 5.13 Bar Chart with Dimensions on the Y Axis

5 | Data Visualization

Bar and columns charts support multiple measures and render each dimension as a separate bar for each value.

You can also place multiple dimensions on the x-axis (or y-axis if in COLUMN mode), and SAP Lumira will render the values in the order that they are added and create a grouping (see Figure 5.14) by the first dimension. This is a kind of hierarchy in which values are grouped in the order that they are placed.

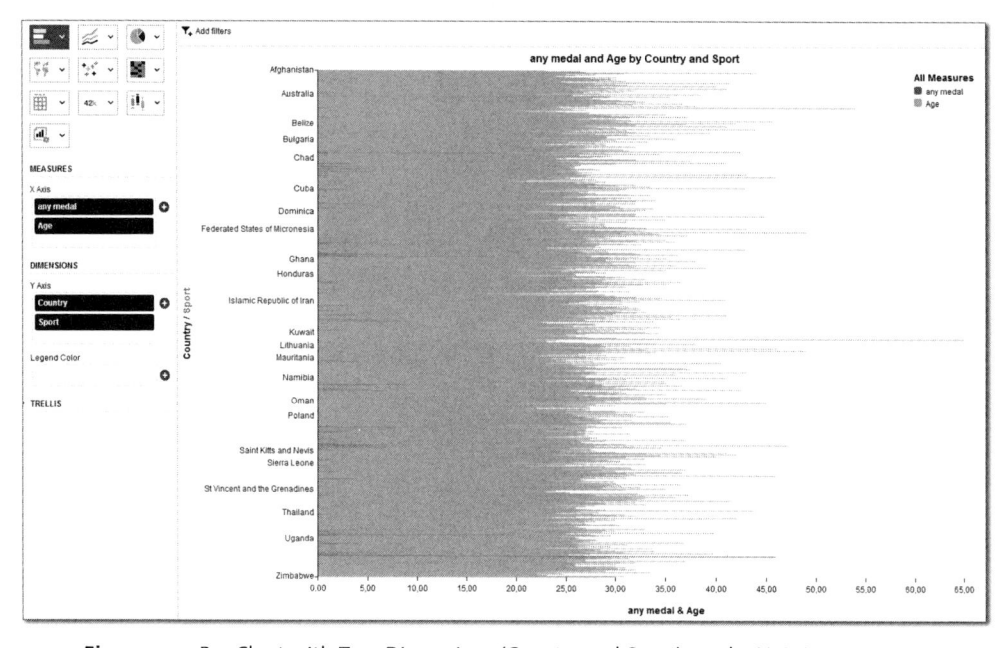

Figure 5.14 Bar Chart with Two Dimensions (Country and Sport) on the Y-Axis

As you can see, although it's possible to add multiple measures and dimensions to your chart they can be illegible due to the high number of values being rendered. For this reason, there are variations that you can consider.

Stack Charts

With a stack bar, you place a second dimension on the legend. The values are then rendered according to the dimensions on the x- or y-axis. The values are also split within the bar according to the secondary value (see Figure 5.15).

The legend explains the stack bars' colors. Stack bars allow you to add an additional dimension without adding additional bars or columns.

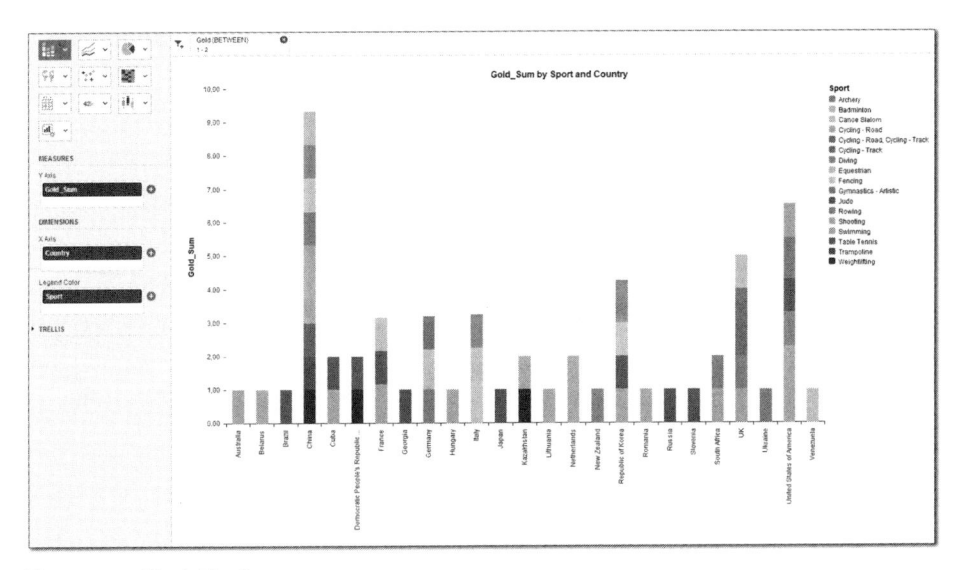

Figure 5.15 Stack Chart

Dual Axes

One problem with multiple measures in bar charts is that the scales might be quite different, making values harder to visualize. Dual axes render a second measure with a separate scale (see Figure 5.16).

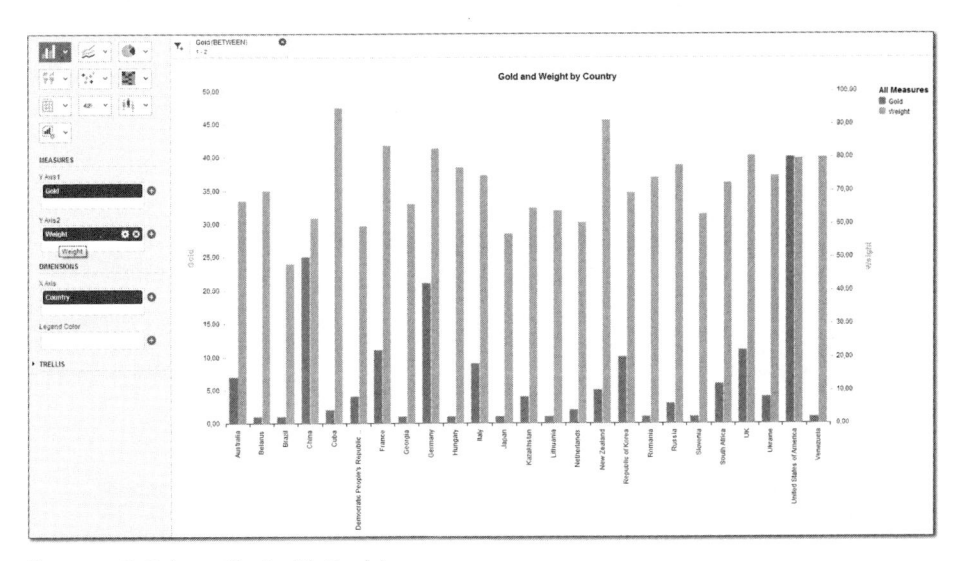

Figure 5.16 Column Chart with Dual Axes

5 | Data Visualization

A dual axis chart is rendered with two scales, with the legend describing which bar is associated with which axis.

3-D Column Charts

A 3-D column chart is rendered in three dimensions, with measures rendered on the z-axis (see Figure 5.17). You can place as many measures as you like, and they are rendered in order. If your measures are not of a similar scale, then SAP Lumira will use the largest range of values; this can mean that your lower values lose visual distinction (which is why we place WEIGHT last here, as it would hide the smaller values).

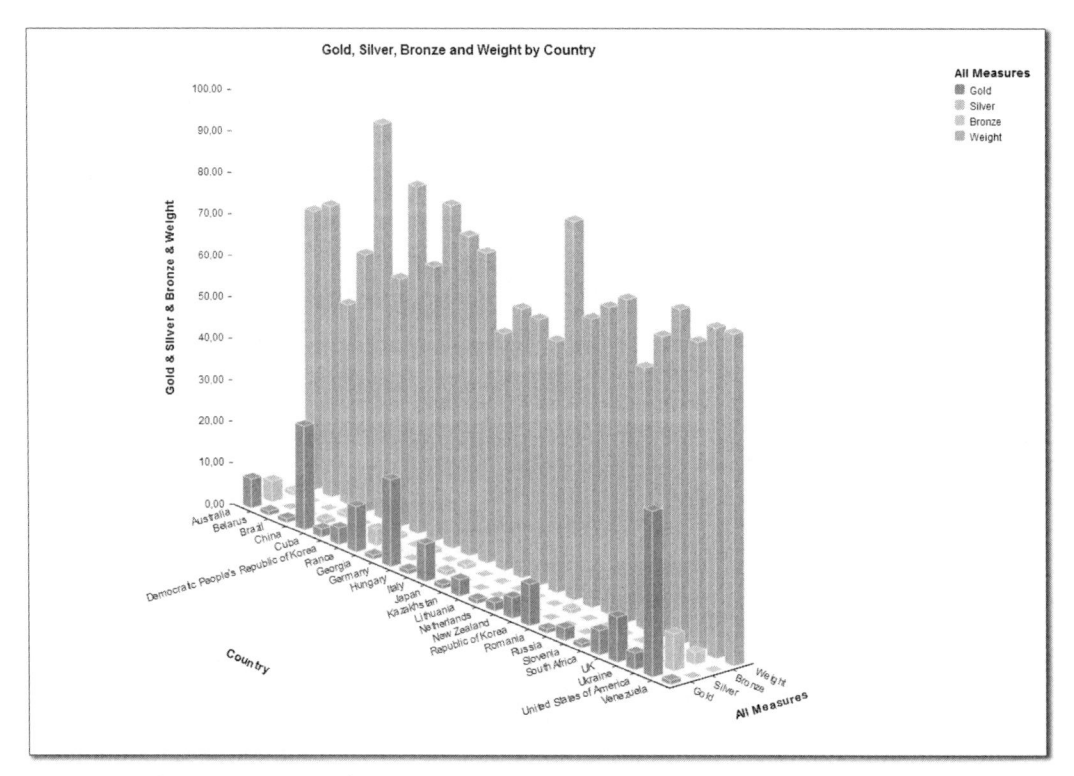

Figure 5.17 3-D Bar chart

5.3.2 Line Charts

Line charts are rendered using data points and are linked with a continuous line. The value of these charts is that you can see trends and directions, making them perfect for time-based data. Note, in Figure 5.18, we see the share price for SAP over time. Line charts are best used with time based data so we change from the Olympics which is a single event to series of events over time; a time series.

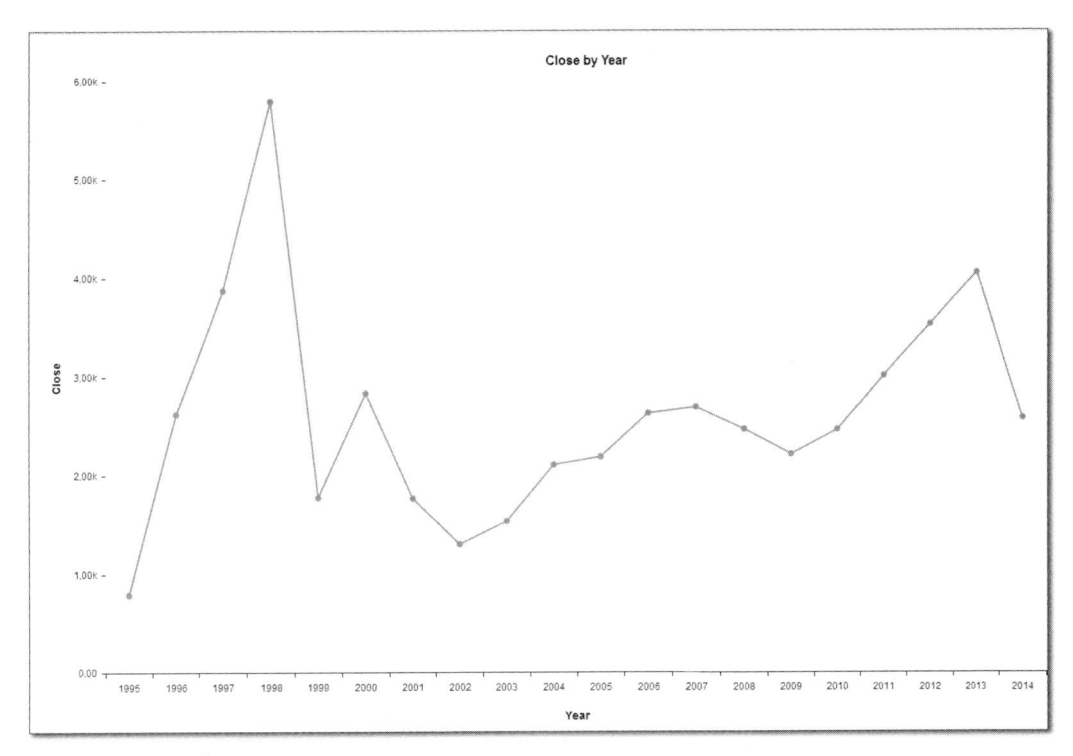

Figure 5.18 Line Chart

Line charts are constructed exactly like bar charts. You are not limited to using time, but there are some additional features that are only available within line charts that use time as the axis dimension (see Section 5.4.4). As with bar charts, you can add multiple measures and use multiple measures on the y-axis. The difference is that you will render additional lines as a series rather than additional bars, which can result in more detail in some cases.

Line and Column Charts

Line and column charts allow you to combine both lines and columns into a single chart (see Figure 5.19). The second measure placed will be plotted as columns rather than as lines.

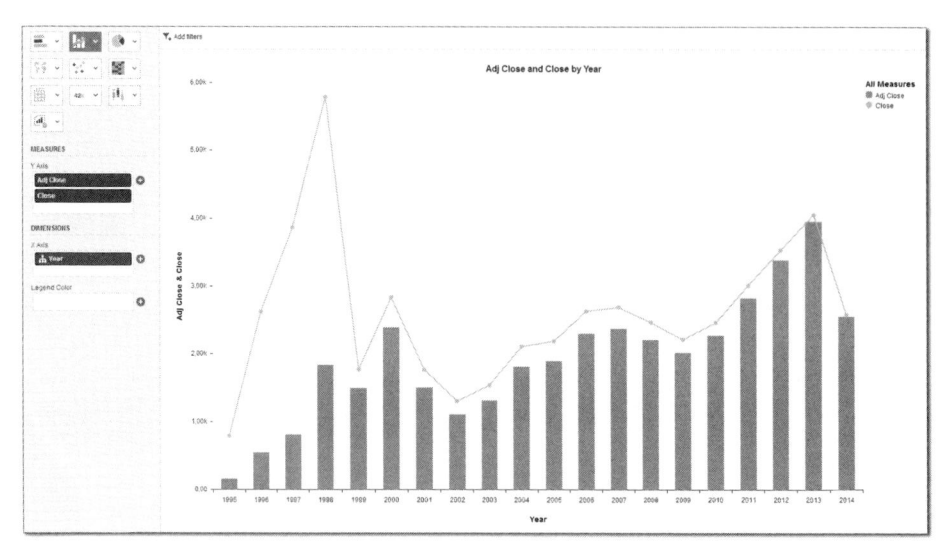

Figure 5.19 Line and Column Chart Combined

Area Charts

Area charts are a type of line chart, but they fill in the space between lines in order to be able to visually compare the relative weight or difference (see Figure 5.20).

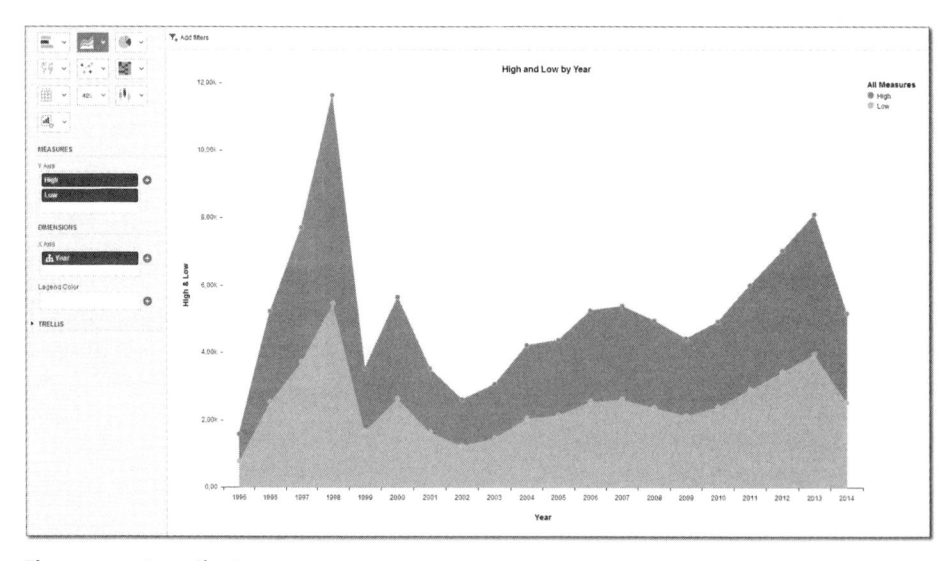

Figure 5.20 Area Chart

There is no difference between this and a line chart, but the shading in an area chart can be a visual aid.

Line Chart with Two Axes

As with bar charts, it's possible to use two axes for measures (see Figure 5.21).

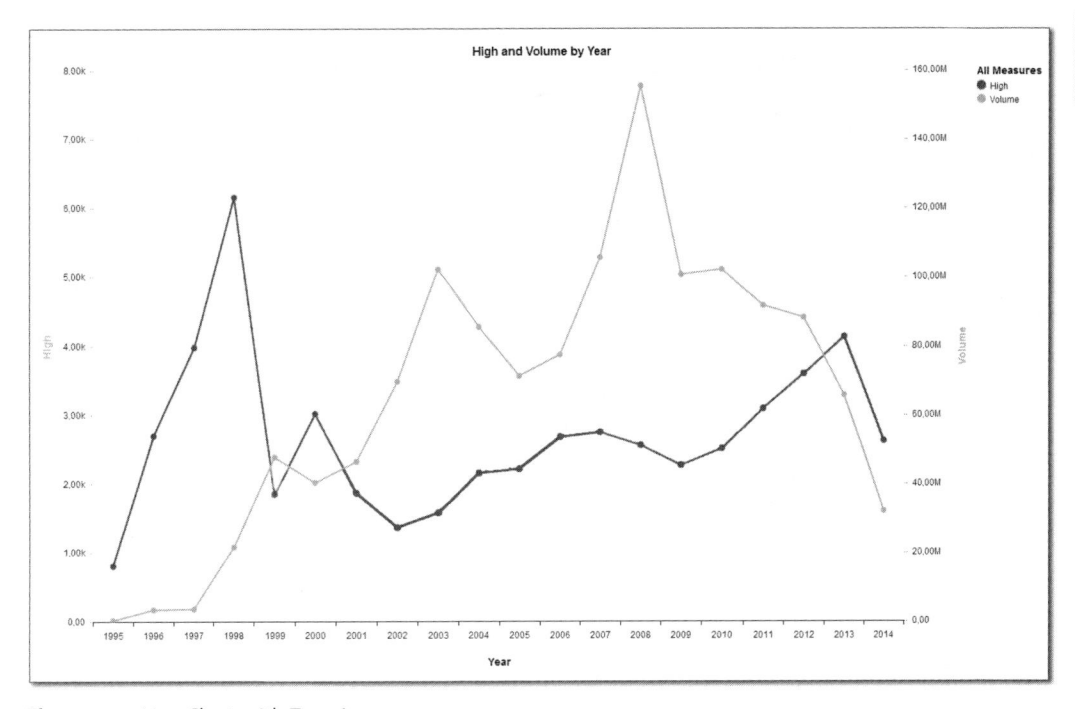

Figure 5.21 Line Chart with Two Axes

These are constructed in the same manner as bar charts, with the second measure plotted on the opposite axis.

5.3.3 Pie Charts

Pie charts divide a circle into areas that are a ratio of the total values to be plotted. The arc or sector sizes thus allow you to compare differences in values (see Figure 5.22).

Pie charts do not support multiple measures or dimensions nor can you add additional dimensions to the legend. You can use a trellis, however.

5 | Data Visualization

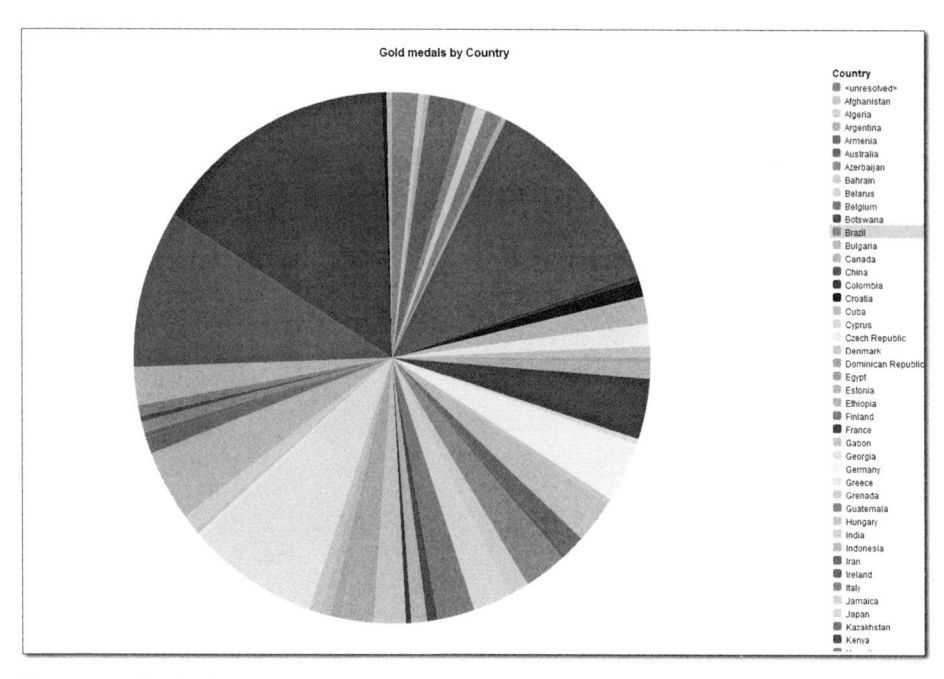

Figure 5.22 Pie Chart

Donut Charts

Donut charts are the same as pie charts, but they provide a space in the center (see Figure 5.23).

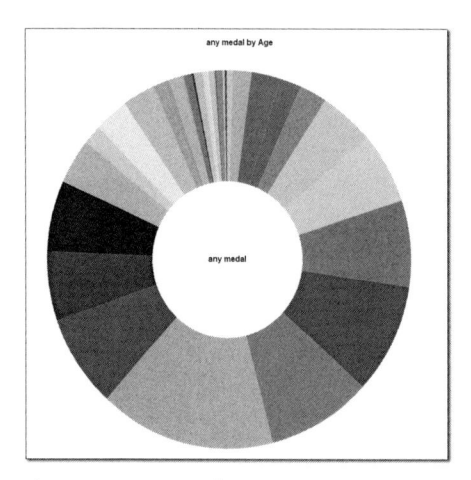

Figure 5.23 Donut Chart

Other than the space in the center that gives the donut its name, there is no difference between pie and donut charts.

3-D Pie Chart with Depth

Depth pie charts allow you to add a second measure that is used to scale a depth to the pie sector (see Figure 5.24).

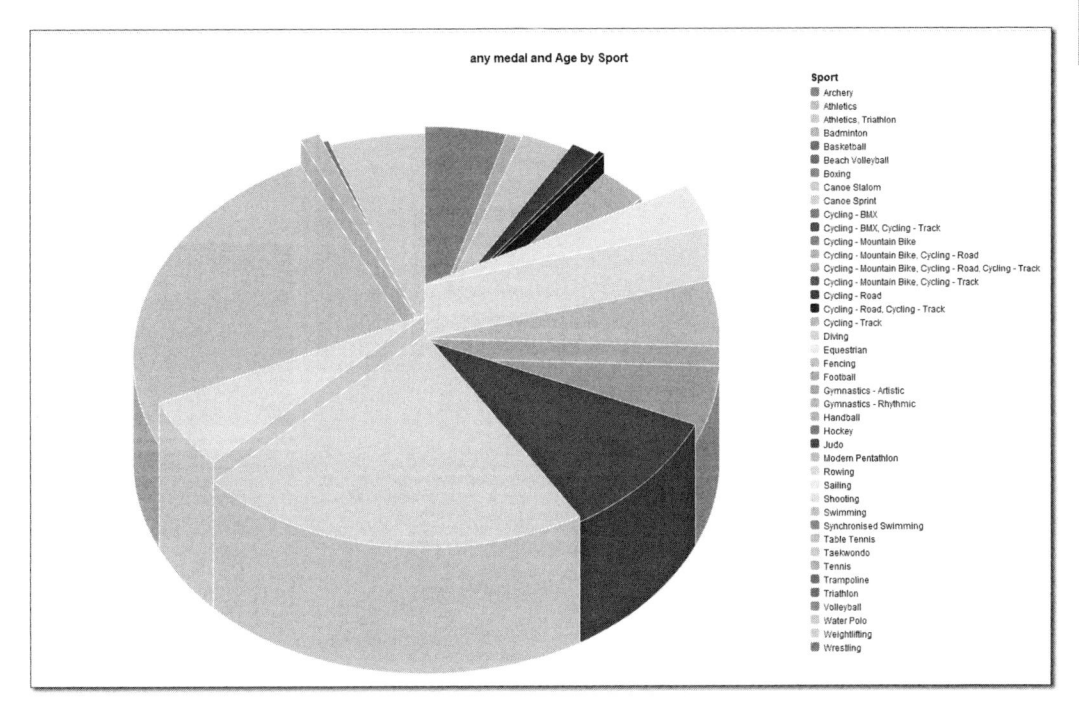

Figure 5.24 3-D Pie Chart

The additional dimension is used to render the pie sectors vertically, creating a 3-D effect.

5.3.4 Geographic Charts

Geographic charts are perhaps unique in that they require a specific enrichment. Geographic charts require you to create a geographic hierarchy, as was described in Chapter 4, Section 4.3.2.

5 | Data Visualization

Geo Bubble and Choropleth

Geo bubble and choropleth charts are similar; both render a measure for a given place. The difference is that bubble charts use scaled circles, or bubbles, to highlight their values, whereas choropleth charts use color intensity. Figure 5.25 shows an example of a bubble chart.

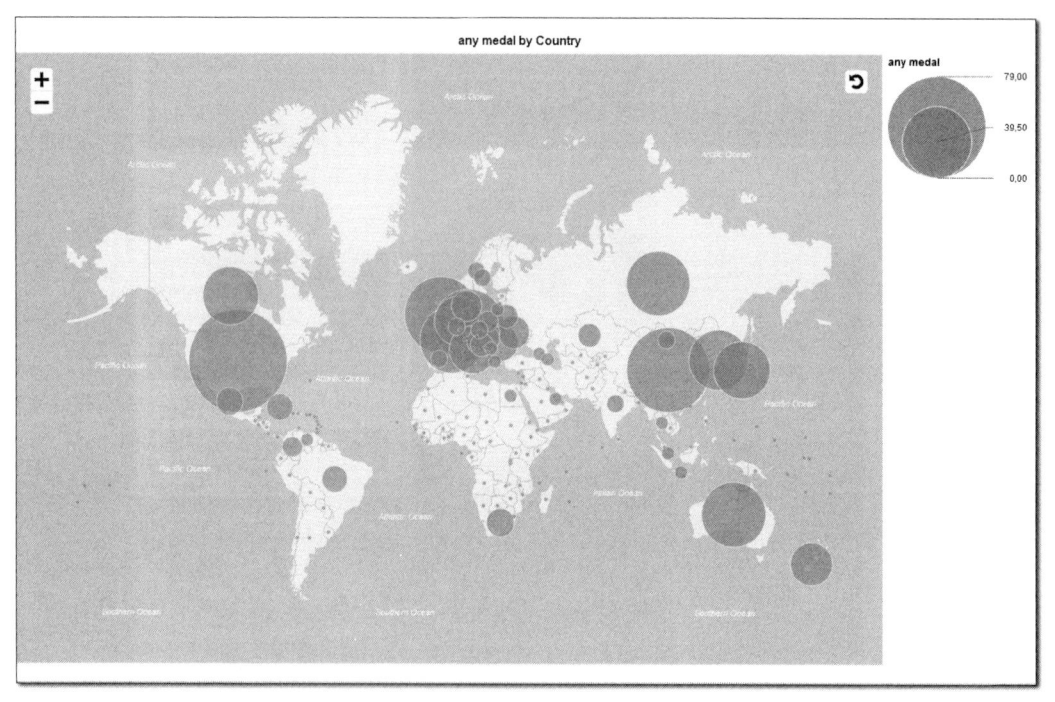

Figure 5.25 Geo Bubble Chart

Each value is marked on a place in the map with a bubble, which has a size relative for the measure. Bubble charts also allow you to choose a second dimension for the color of the bubbles. Choropleth charts use a single color and apply shading to express measure difference by intensity (see Figure 5.26).

Choropleth charts are good at rendering high levels of data, so there is no visual confusion. Choropleth charts also allow you to customize the legend, highlighting color via a menu on the legend (see Figure 5.27).

Charts Types in SAP Lumira | **5.3**

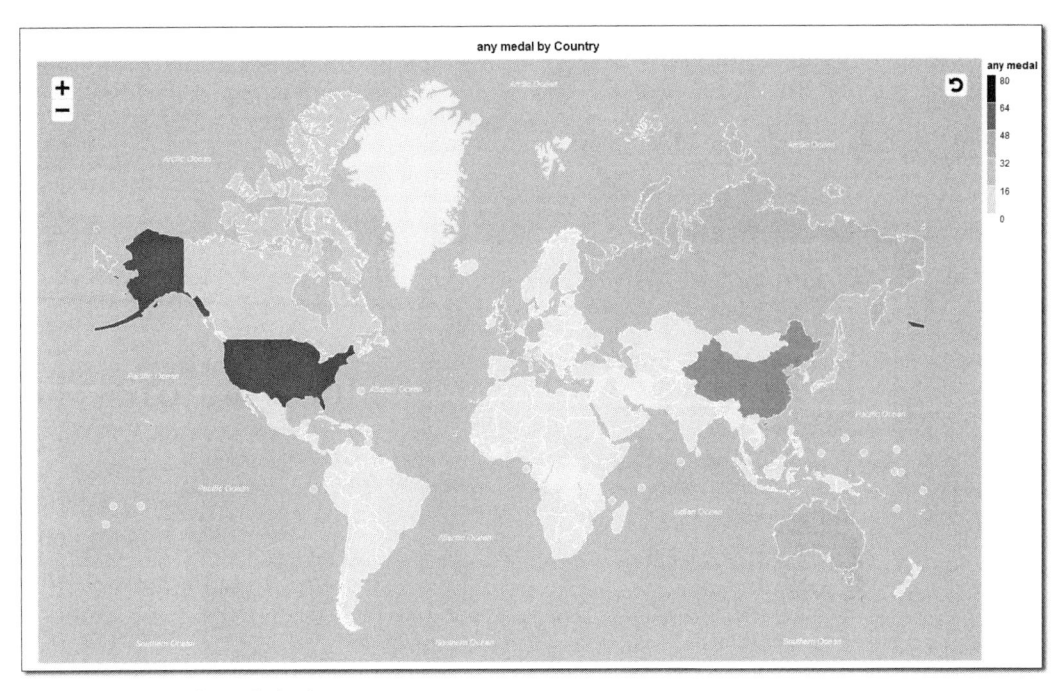

Figure 5.26 Geo Choropleth Chart

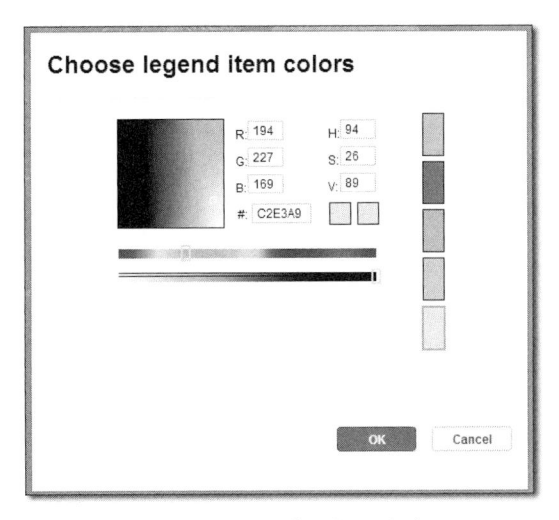

Figure 5.27 Custom Legend for Choropleth

5 | Data Visualization

To do this, right-click on the legend and select CHOOSE LEGEND ITEM COLORS. Select the range you wish to customize, then select the color you want to use. You can use this to create a greater visual distinction—for example, if a limit is reached, then you might highlight a place in a distinctive shade (see Figure 5.28).

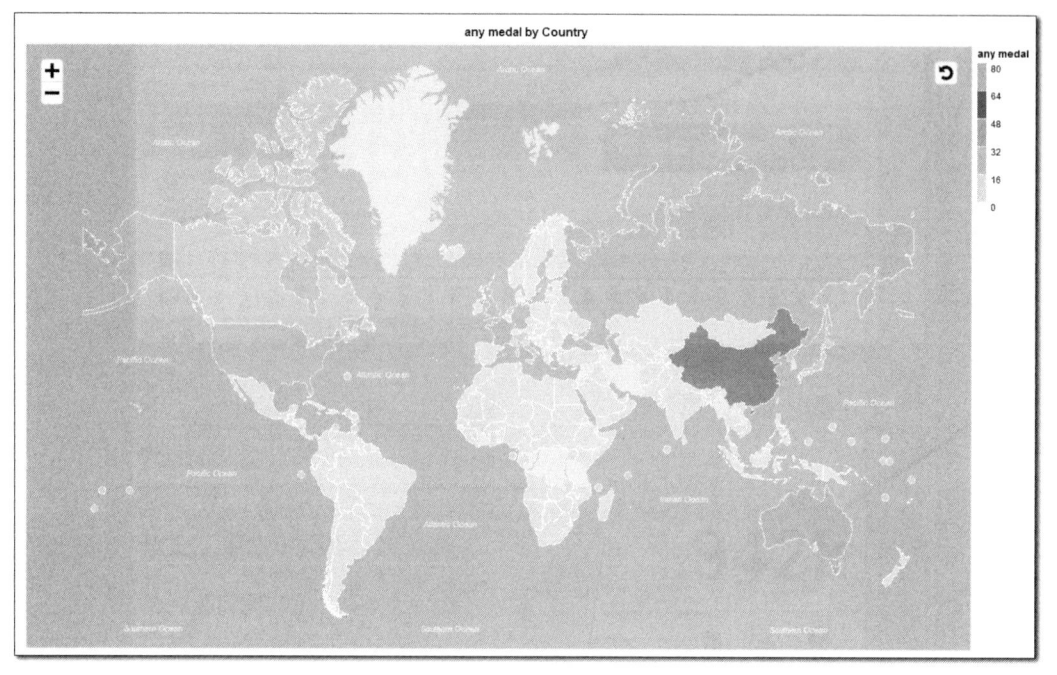

Figure 5.28 Custom Color Legend

Geo Pie

Geo pie charts are similar to bubble charts, but they use an additional dimension (see Figure 5.29). The pie size is determined by the measure and is additionally divided by the extra dimension.

In addition, SAP Lumira has integrated Esri support for building charts. Although this requires an additional account, the perks are substantial.

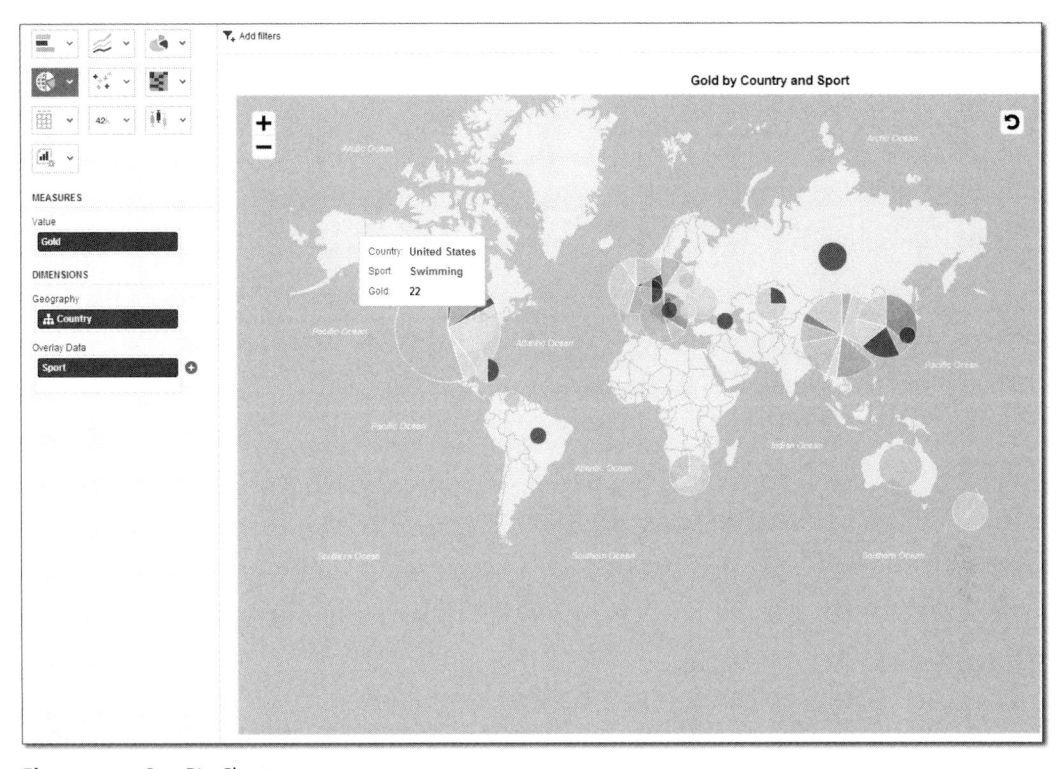

Figure 5.29 Geo Pie Chart

Esri Maps

In addition to the default geo charts provided by SAP Lumira, it is also possible to use maps provided by Esri, an international supplier of GIS (geographic information system) software and geodatabase-management applications. Esri provides maps via an external service, so you need a separate account with Esri in order to use these maps. To set up your account, go to the Esri site at *www.esri.com/software/arcgis/arcgisonline* and choose either a trial or complete account.

To enable Esri in SAP Lumira, go to PREFERENCES and select the GEO MAP SERVICE. In the form, you need to provide your credentials; there is also a link to the required service (see Figure 5.30).

5 | Data Visualization

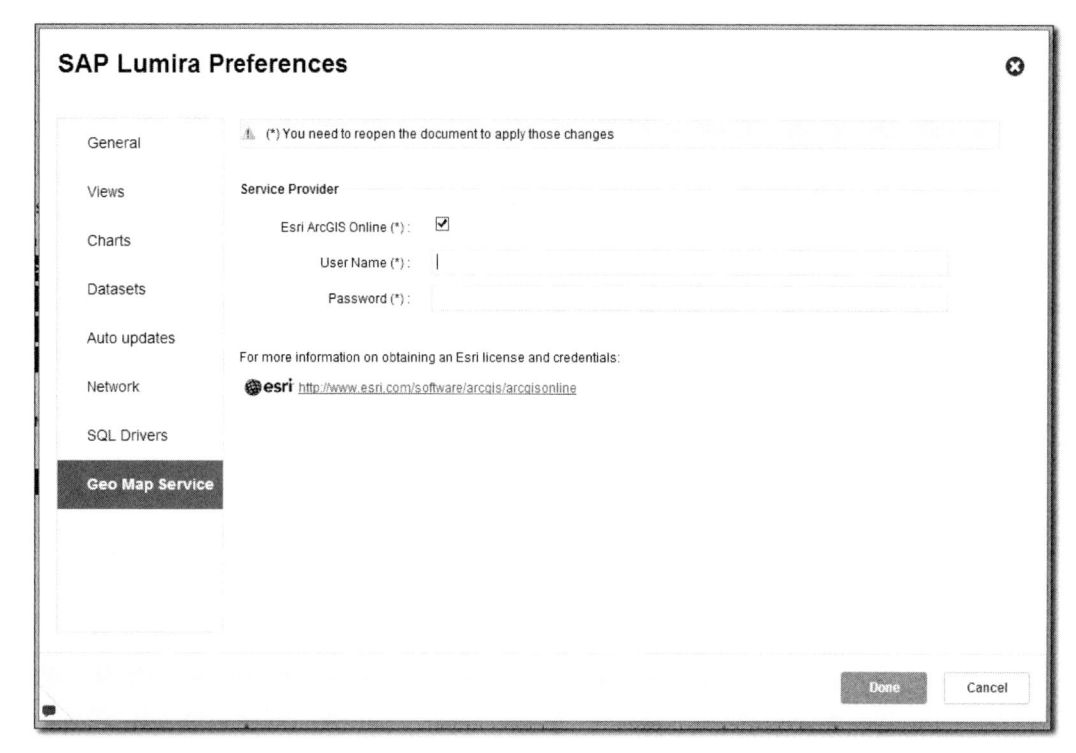

Figure 5.30 Esri Preferences

Esri is then available in the Visualize room under the GEO MAP SERVICE category of charts (see Figure 5.31).

Figure 5.31 Geo Map Menu

Charts Types in SAP Lumira | 5.3

Selecting this option creates a new chart editor; the charts require the same geographically enhanced data as standard geo charts (see Figure 5.32).

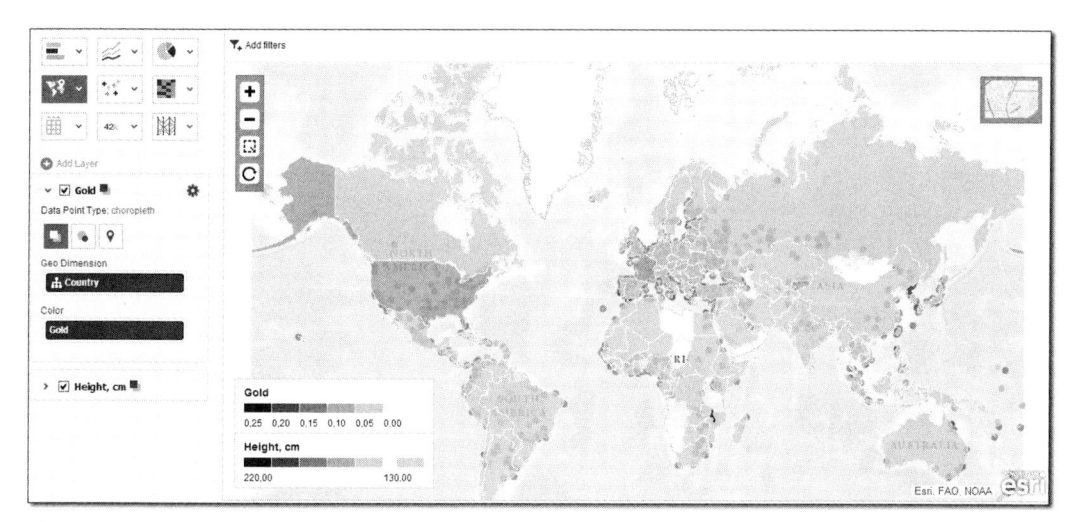

Figure 5.32 Esri Point and Choropleth Chart

Editing or adding values to Esri is different than adding values to other charts, because there is a concept of layers. The FEEDING panel will now offer layers in which you add your geographic entity and measures. These values are seen as an overlay on the map (see Figure 5.33).

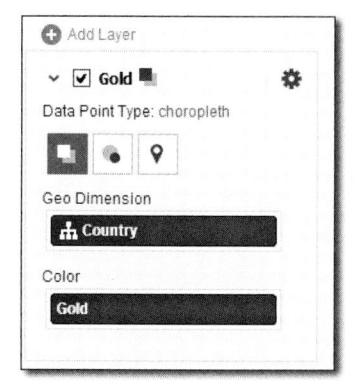

Figure 5.33 Layer Editor

The layer allows you to enter a dimension (the GEO DIMENSION) and a measure. You can specify one of three different types of rendering for the measures:

- Choro
- Bubble
- Point

In addition, you can stack layers so that you can view different facets at the same time. To add a layer, select the Plus icon. After doing so, you can visualize revenue data and also show the locations of the different sites on the same map. Layers can be ordered, toggled on or off, and deleted.

In the top-right corner of the chart, you will also see a menu that lets you change the map type (see Figure 5.34).

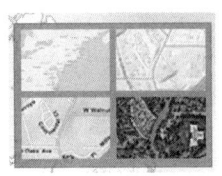

Figure 5.34 Esri Map Type Menu

This changes your map to one of the different rendering types. These different views allow you to change the view that you have of your map. On the left of the map, there is another menu that allows you to interact with the map directly (see Figure 5.35).

Figure 5.35 Map Menu

This menu allows you to perform the following actions:

- Zoom in
- Zoom out
- Select an area to highlight

Charts Types in SAP Lumira | 5.3

- Reset to the original view of the map
- You can, for example, zoom into a map and see individual points at the satellite or street level (see Figure 5.36).

Figure 5.36 Zooming In—Satellite Mode

Esri allows you to see a finer level of detail and provides map interaction (you can use a satellite view to see streets, for example).

We have now covered all of the available charts. It is possible to add your own charts; this will be discussed in Chapter 11. So far, we have seen the types of charts that you can use in SAP Lumira, but there are also a number of other features that enable you to extend your analysis and to visually enhance and customize your visualizations.

5.3.5 Map Charts

Both heat and area charts use space and color to highlight values. Heat charts use color with equal spacing, whereas area or tree charts use space. Values are displayed as tiles in a fixed area.

Tree Map

A tree map is grouped hierarchically, whereas the heat map values are grouped by the legend (see Figure 5.37). Tree maps are considered efficient charts, because they maximize the use of the space and can render a high number of data points without losing too much clarity.

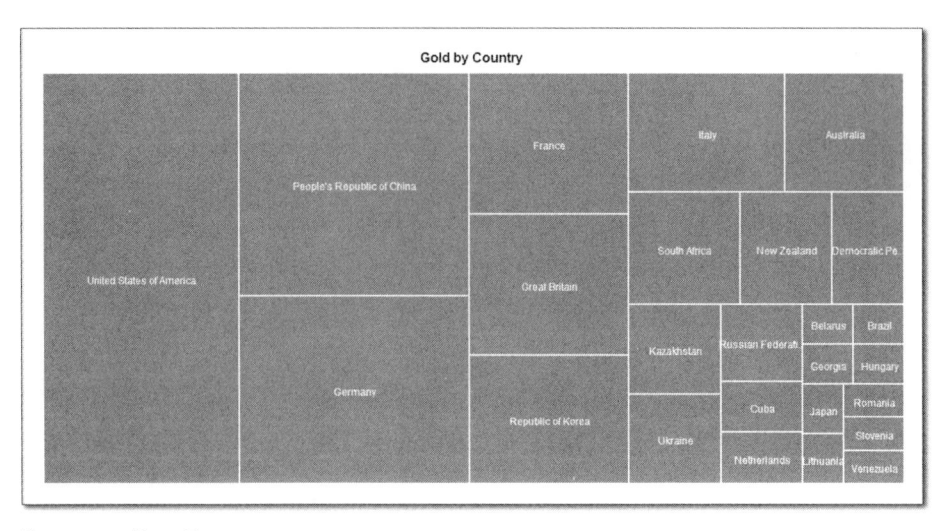

Figure 5.37 Tree Map

It is possible to add a second measure to a tree map (see Figure 5.38).

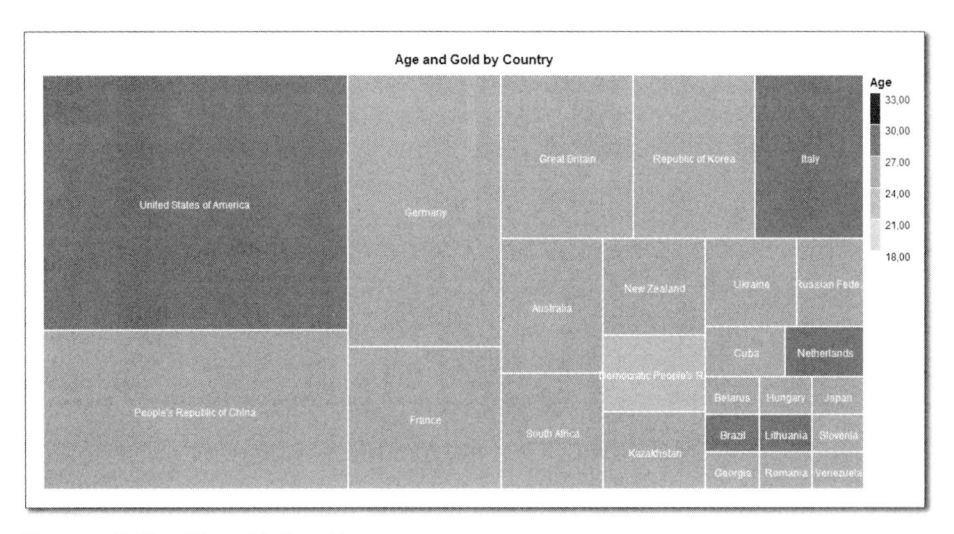

Figure 5.38 Tree Map with Two Measures

The color, like in a heat map, is used to indicate intensity.

Heat Map

Heat maps use color intensity to indicate patterns (see Figure 5.39).

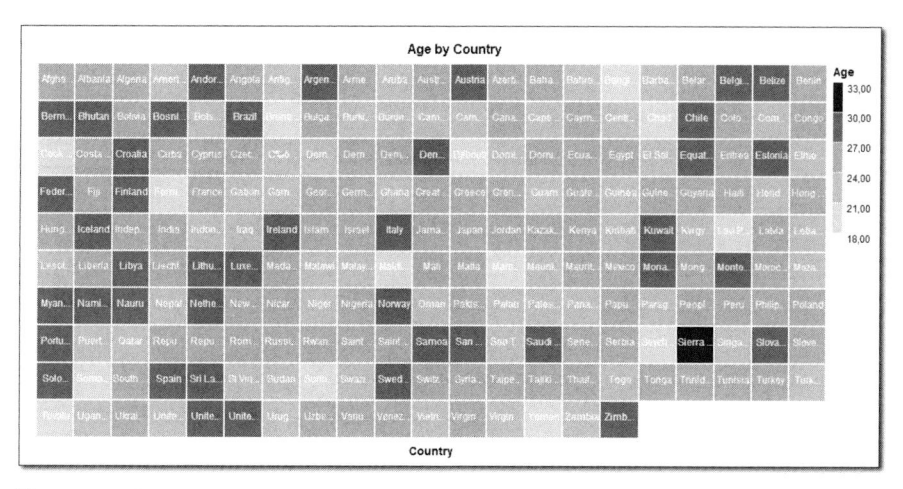

Figure 5.39 Heat Map

Heat maps are like choropleth maps in that it is possible to add a second dimension as well (see Figure 5.40).

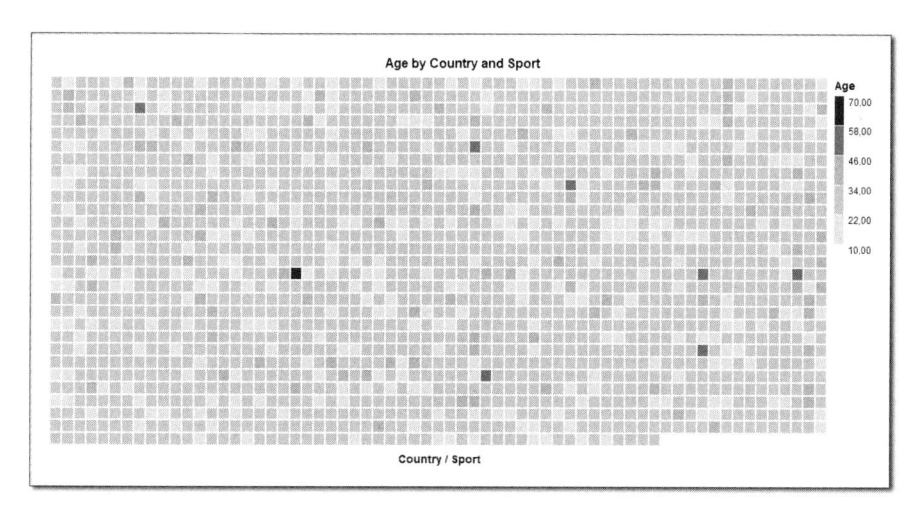

Figure 5.40 Heat Map with Two Dimensions

You can use the legend color to change the highlight colors as with the choropleth map.

5 | Data Visualization

5.3.6 Scatter Charts

Scatter charts typically use multiple measures to plot dimensions as points rather than as values. Scatter plots are very useful for seeing clusters and potential patterns and anomalies. More details of what you can do with scatter charts in SAP Lumira are discussed in the following sections.

Scatter Plots

Scatter plots use two measures to plot points for a given dimension (see Figure 5.41 and Figure 5.42).

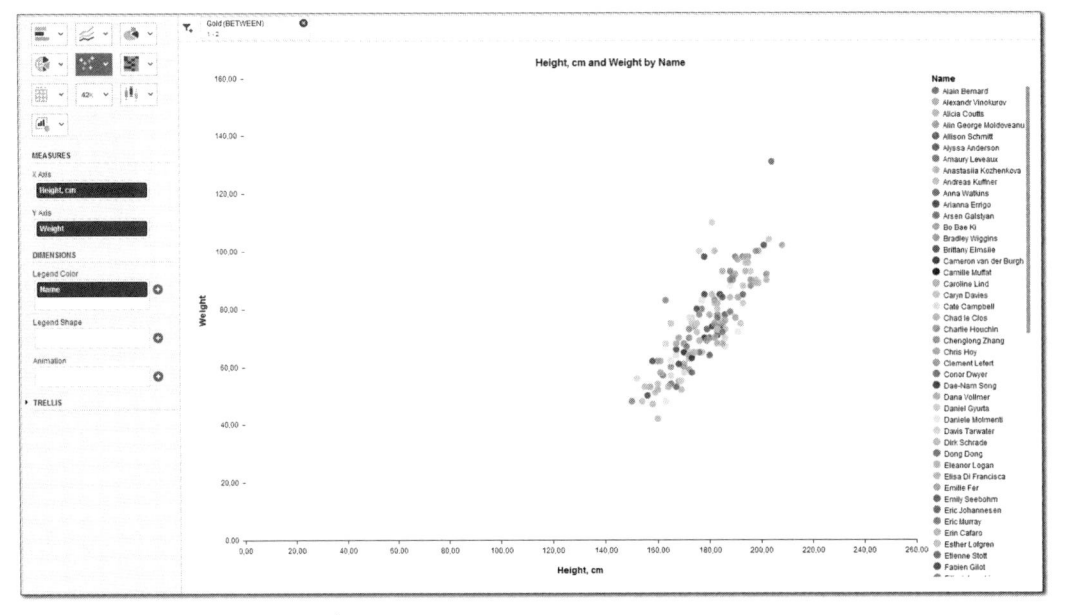

Figure 5.41 Scatter Plot: Names

Here we can see there is relatively clear clustering for height and weight. It is possible to add an additional dimension by dragging and dropping it into a legend, in the legend section as decribed in Section 5.2.2.

Shape will differentiate the data points with shapes so that you can distinguish between different groups. The only difference in Figure 5.42 is that the legend association is by shape, not color.

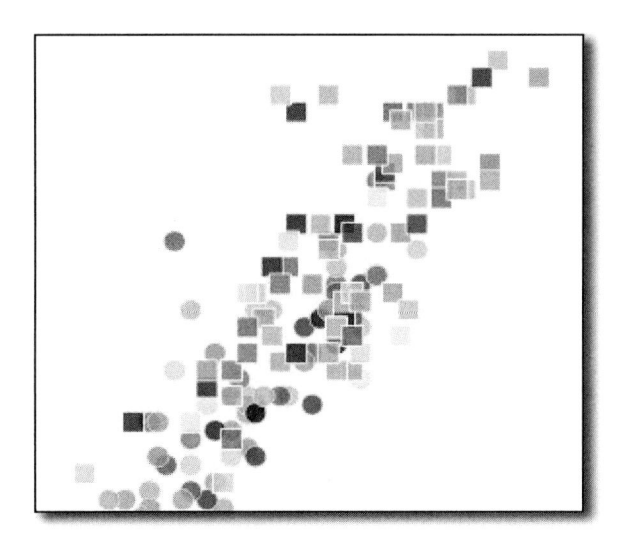

Figure 5.42 Shapes in Scatter Plot: Names (circles) and Sex (squares)

Bubble Charts

Bubble charts are very similar to scatter charts, but you can add up to two more measures. In addition, you can specify the width and height of the bubble to create an oval (see Figure 5.43).

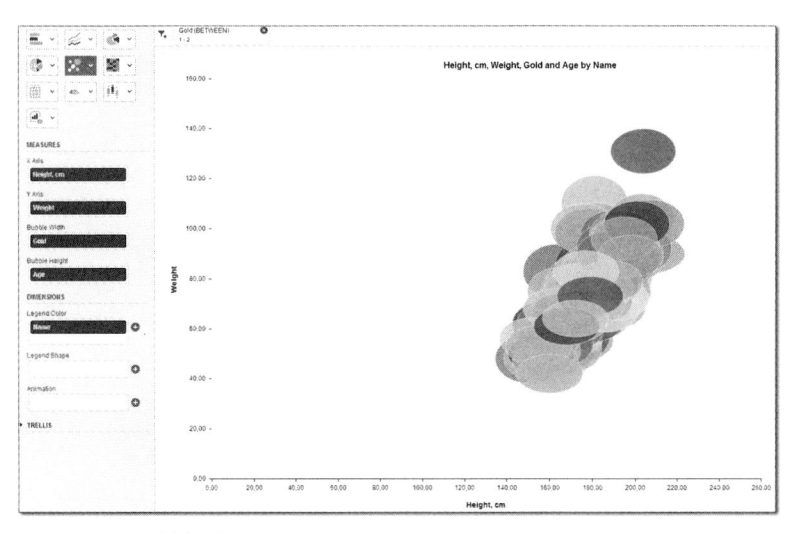

Figure 5.43 Bubble Chart

5 | Data Visualization

Scatter Matrix

A scatter matrix chart creates a matrix of scatter charts, and will create multiple charts that switch the axes of the measures (see Figure 5.44).

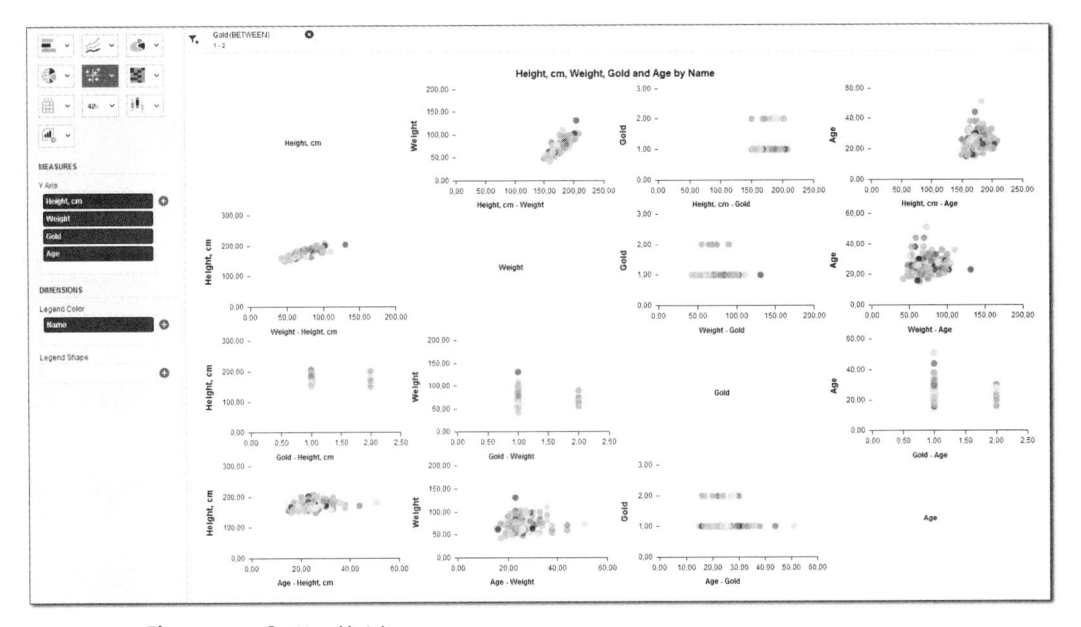

Figure 5.44 Scatter Matrix

There are two charts per pairing—for example, height and weight and then weight and height. Each pair has its inverse, in which the axes are swapped.

5.3.7 Table Charts

Tables are able to display many measures and dimensions, and you can also add subtotals in order to create report-like structures. Tables are very easy to create in SAP Lumira. You can drag in as many measures and dimensions as you would like to see.

As you can see in Figure 5.45, you can also add subtotals to dimensions. This option becomes available in the FEEDING panel when you use a table.

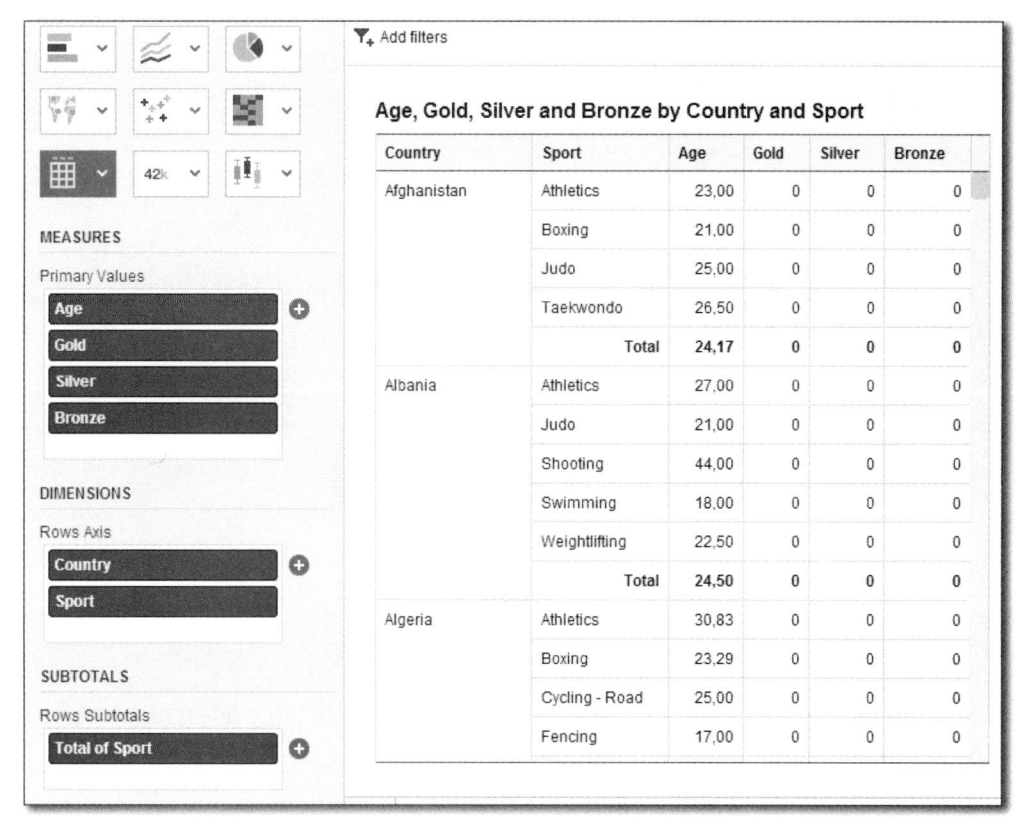

Figure 5.45 Table Chart

One visual aspect to note is that tables do not resize to 100% of the screen as other charts do; you have to scroll in order to see your values.

5.3.8 Point Charts

Point charts are the simplest of charts; they display just one measure. As of this writing, the only point chart available is the numeri point chart. If you want to select a particular value, then you need to create a filter or a custom measure. The value or primary goal of numeri points is for use in infographics; we will discuss infographics further in Chapter 6.

5 | Data Visualization

A numeri point shows the total value of your measure. If you want to customize it, you need to add a filter. For example, to see the total for France you would add France as a filter, as in Figure 5.46.

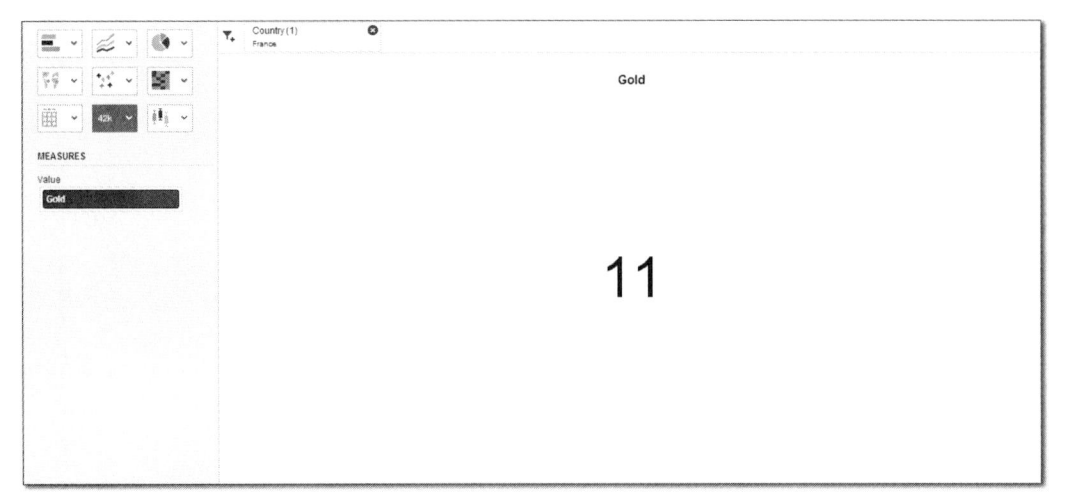

Figure 5.46 Numeri Point

The final charts that we will discuss do not really belong in a specific category, so they should not be considered as a single family of charts.

5.3.9 Special Charts

There is a final category or collection of charts that are somewhat special in that they don't really fit into an existing category. Often they expect a certain type of dataset, so they are less generic than the classic charts we discussed so far.

Box Plot

A box plot depicts numerical data in groups of values based on their relationship to the median. Unlike other charts, box plots aggregate for a given dimension in order to determine the different quartiles of data—that is, the data is split into groups based on the median: the band inside the box is the median, and the bottom and top boxes are respectively the first and third quartiles. In addition, the "whiskers" are the min and max of the data, and outliers are points that do not fit into the data ranges and are plotted separately; there may be several (see Figure 5.47).

5.3 Charts Types in SAP Lumira

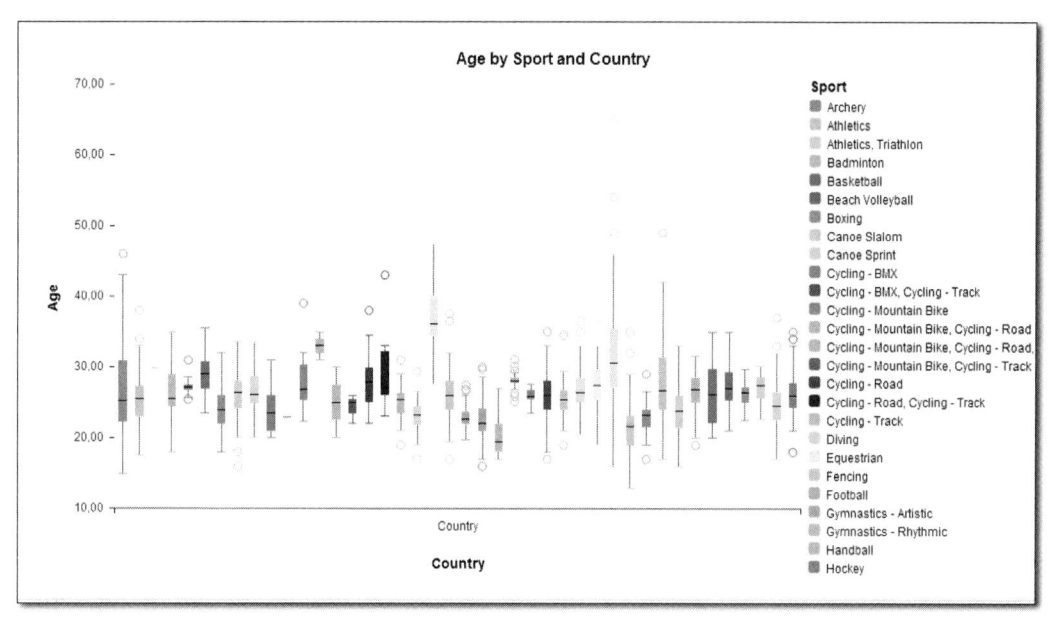

Figure 5.47 Box Plot

To construct the chart, you typically provide a dimension and a single measure, although you can add additional dimensions to the legend. If you add additional dimensions, then you will have a plot per entry. Box plots can be a little complex to understand, so a simpler example will help. In Table 5.1 we see a mixture of semi and totally fictional data that compares peoples' ages with the turtle (long life) and the ant (very short life). This dataset allows us to clearly see how a box plot works.

Name	Age
Peter	43
Calvin	10
Lou	18
Emily	6
Muriel	47
Turtle	110
Ant	0.1

Table 5.1 Sample Data

5 | Data Visualization

Let's plot this data with the box plot to see the different elements in action (see Figure 5.48).

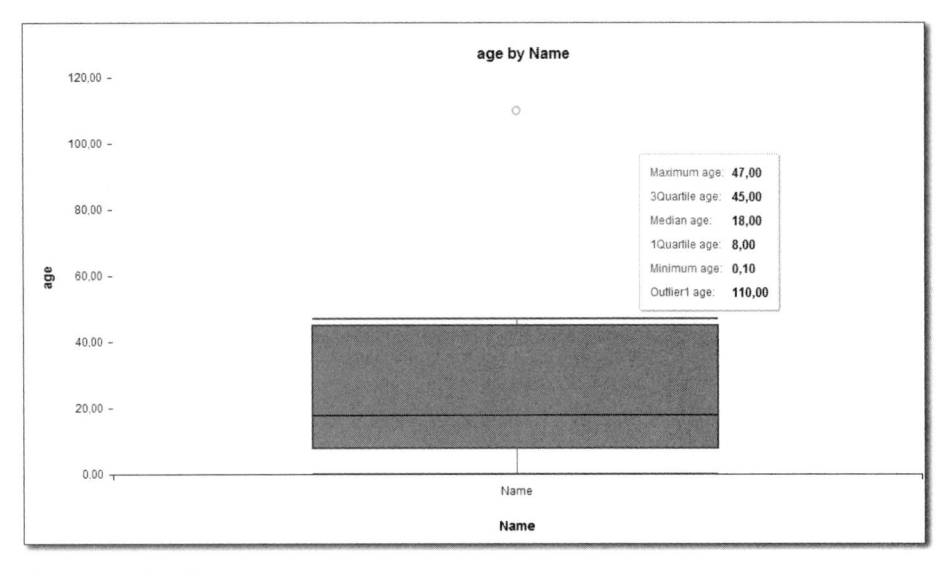

```
                          age by Name
  120,00 -
  100,00 -
                                          Maximum age:    47,00
                                          3Quartile age:  45,00
   80,00 -                                Median age:     18,00
                                          1Quartile age:   8,00
                                          Minimum age:    0,10
   60,00 -                                Outlier1 age:  110,00
   40,00 -
   20,00 -
    0,00
                              Name
                              Name
```

Figure 5.48 Box Plot

The median, middle value is 18. The bottom whisker is 0.1, the min, whereas the max is 47. This means that turtle was seen as an outlier and is drawn above the data. The other quartiles are the division of the values by the median—that is:

(6 + 10) / 2 = 8

(43 + 47) / 2 = 45

Or the average of ages below and above our median.

Tag Clouds

Tag clouds represent values by using the value names and sizing these terms according to their values (see Figure 5.49).

Tag clouds are quite aesthetically pleasing, but they raise some concerns; there is tendency for the eye to be overly drawn to larger values, and the focus is in the center.

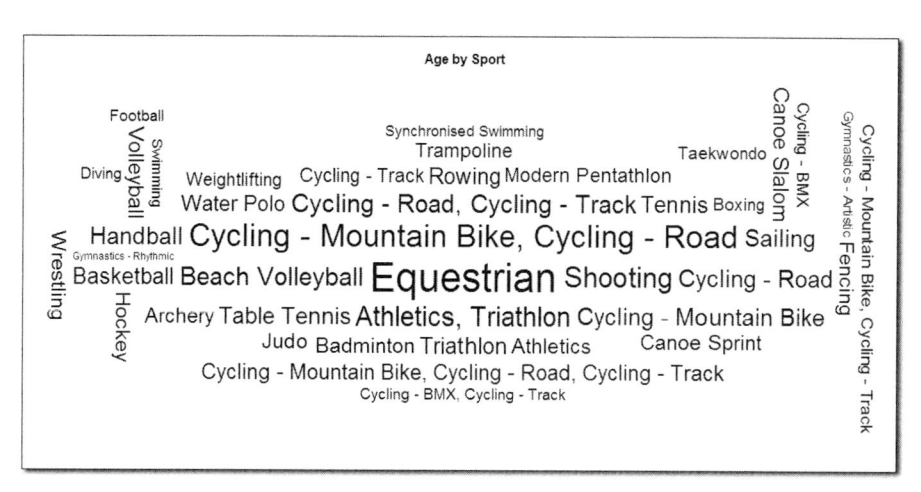

Figure 5.49 Tag Cloud

Radar Charts

Radar charts plot values on a series of axis-like spokes (see Figure 5.50).

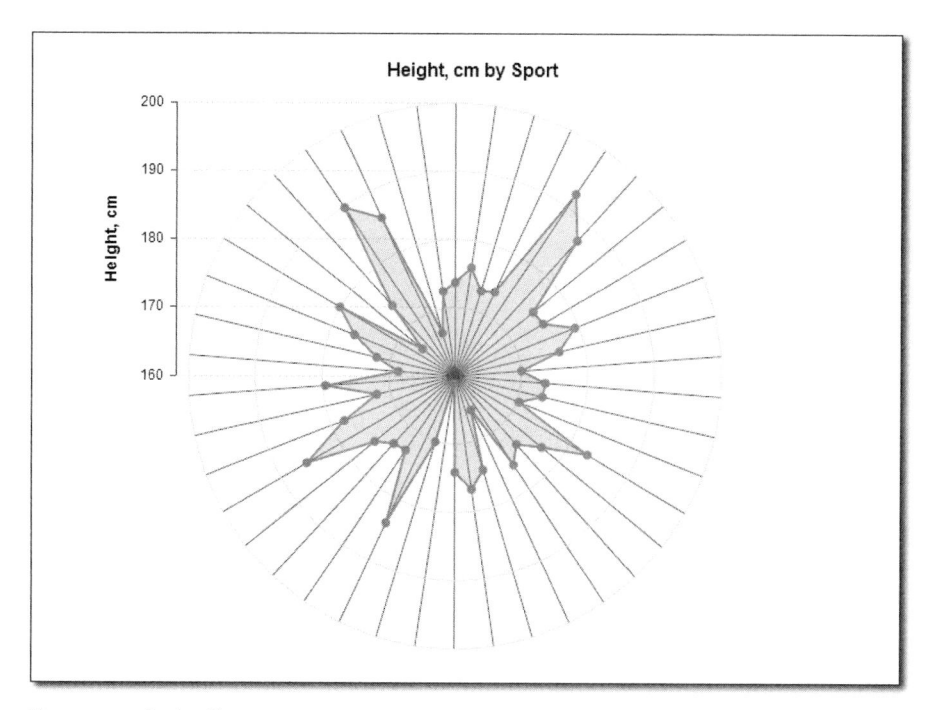

Figure 5.50 Radar Plot

Radar plots are often associated with quality or for comparing common attributes, such as comparing athletes on a range of different characteristics.

Waterfall Charts

Waterfall charts see data as a series of steps in which an initial value is given and subsequent values are drawn in relation to this value. Review the sample data in Table 5.2.

Expense	Amount
Start	45
Bus	12
Food	-34
Ticket	-12

Table 5.2 Sample Data

Plotting this data results in the chart shown in Figure 5.51.

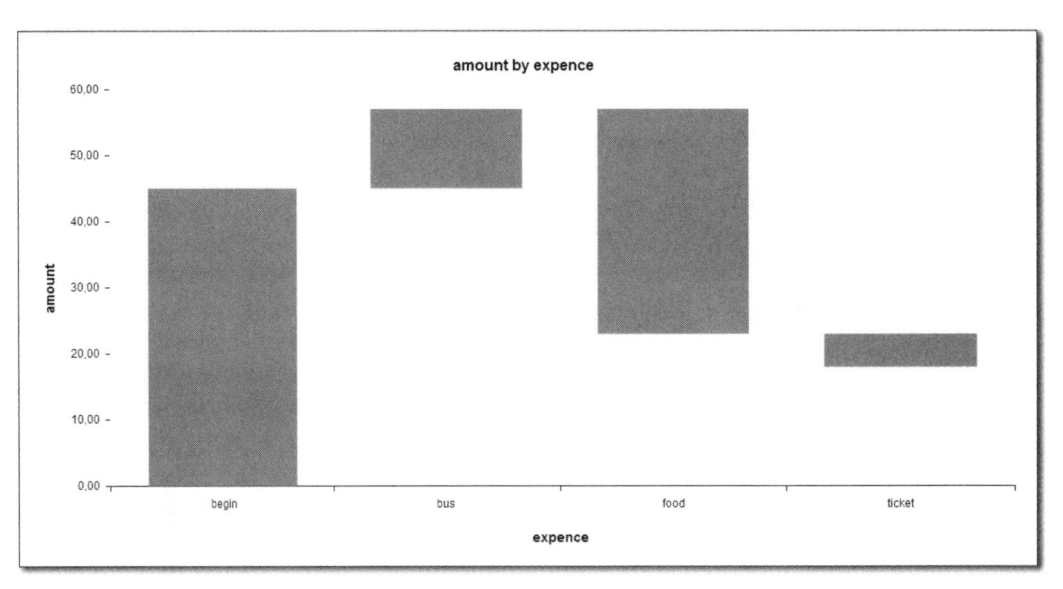

Figure 5.51 A Waterfall Chart

Again, your data may or may not suit the type of chart, because what you have is a running total: the initial value is rendered as a column, but the second value, bus, is drawn from the top of the previous value (begin) If it is a negative value, then the current total is at the bottom, so the subsequent value is drawn from the bottom (the current total).

Network Charts

The network chart draws relationships among entities. Network charts do not require or use a measure (see Figure 5.52).

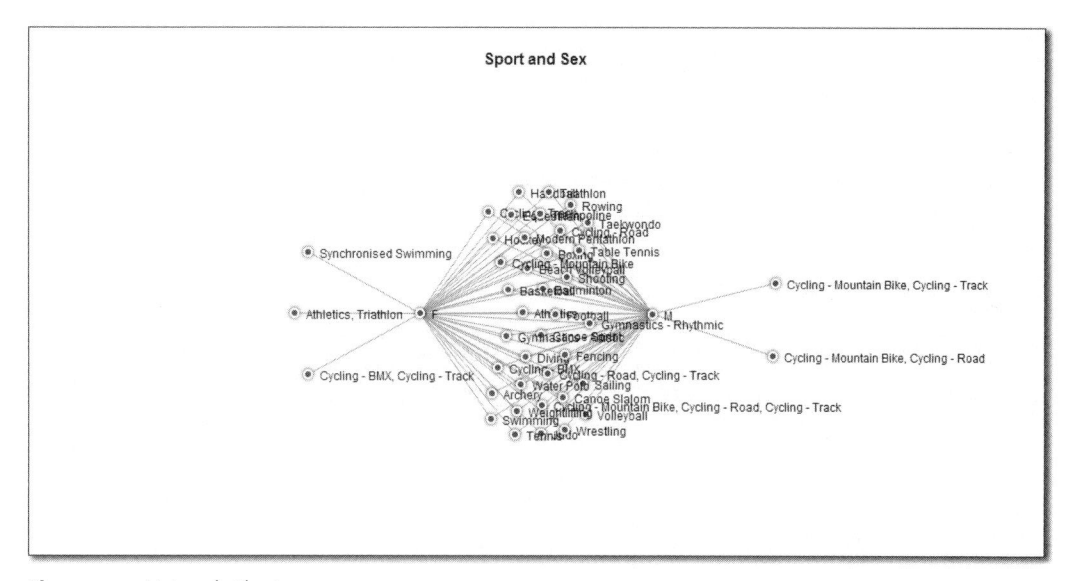

Figure 5.52 Network Chart

The network chart generally is only applicable if you have some kind of graph structure you want to highlight. Here, for example, we can see there are a few exclusively male and female sports, making the chart rather messy.

Tree Charts

The tree chart, like the network chart, describes the relationships among entities. Rather than seeing things as a network, here they are shown as a hierarchy (see Figure 5.53). This is somewhat limited in scope; you can only add two dimensions, and only the first value is used for the "root" node.

5 | Data Visualization

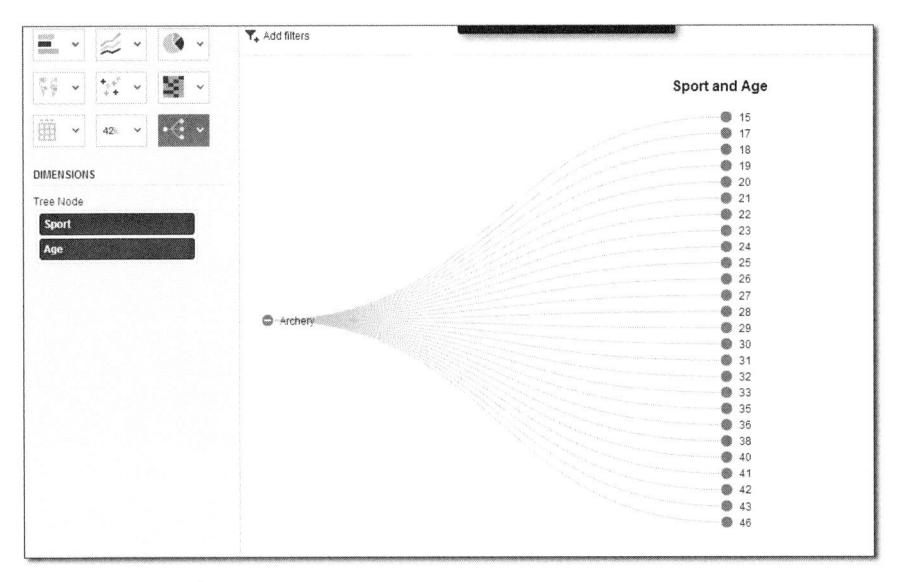

Figure 5.53 Tree Chart

Funnel Charts

A funnel chart is typically used to present stages in a process in which values are presented as a percentage of the total, with diminishing (smaller) values given less space (see Figure 5.54).

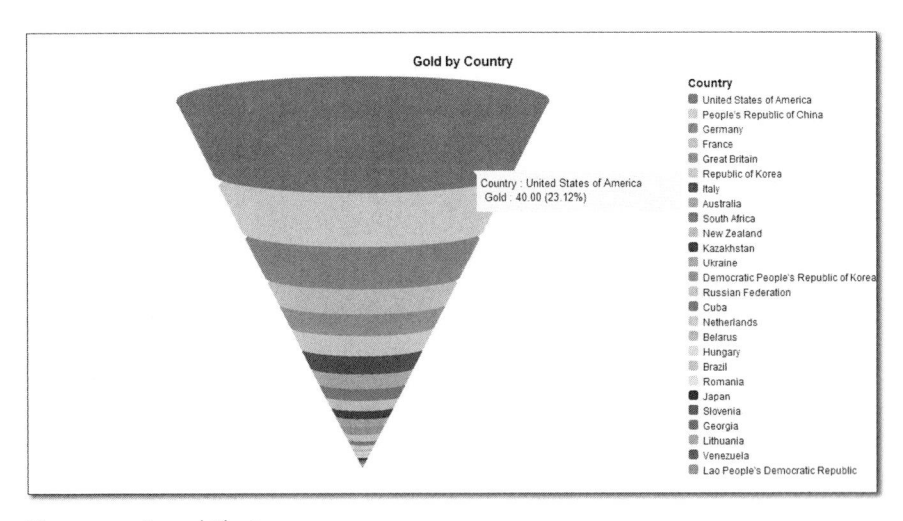

Figure 5.54 Funnel Chart

Values are calculated as a percentage of their total contribution and then rendered from largest to smallest.

Parallel Coordinates Charts

A parallel coordinate chart renders your data as a series of parallel lines between multiple vertices. Each vertex is a different measure, so you can compare a series of values, somewhat like a time series, but in a series of steps (see Figure 5.55).

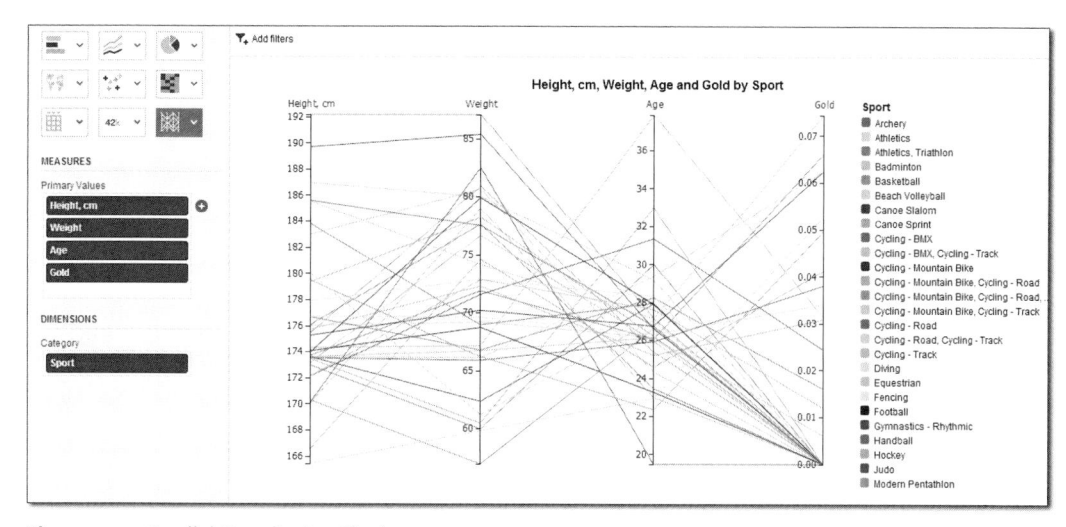

Figure 5.55 Parallel Coordinates Chart

The lines can enable you to view multiple variables and discern patterns.

Now that we have seen all the default chart types installed with SAP Lumira, let's see how these charts display measures.

5.4 Measures in Charts

The Visualize room allows you to add additional calculations and apply ranks and sorts on the measures that you are using in your chart. You can use these measures to perform running calculations, rankings, and some predictions. In this section we will use the sample data BestRunCorp, provided with SAP Lumira.

From a measure that is in the FEEDING panel, select the cog icon to choose from the different options (see Figure 5.56).

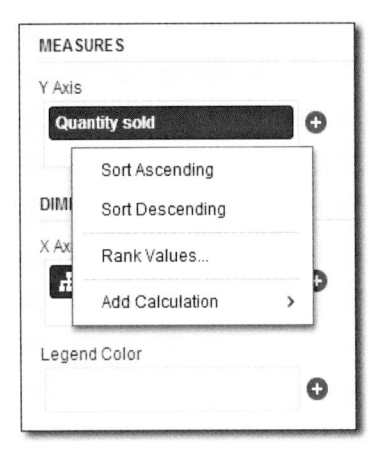

Figure 5.56 The Different Measure Options

In contrast to the object definition, these calculations are local to the chart, so although a change in aggregation will affect all charts, these options are applied locally to only the current chart.

5.4.1 Sorting Charts

Charts can be sorted either ascending or descending and will rank your values according to the direction selected. Note that here you are sorting on the measure and not the dimension that we have been using in the Prepare room. Sorts are independent to the chart type, but the effect might not be visible, because many charts do not have a "visual notion" of ascendance (e.g., a tag cloud or a pie chart). For a column chart, however, the effect is clear (see Figure 5.57).

Initially, values are unsorted or are sorted by the sorting of the dimension (e.g., alphanumerically). Once you have selected the sort, the values are reordered in the direction of the sort (see Figure 5.58).

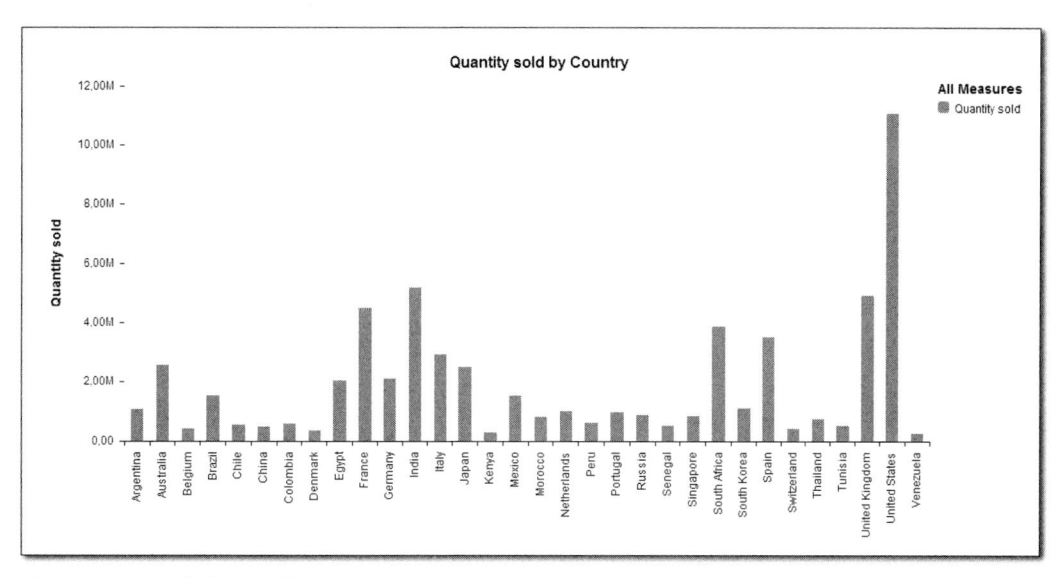

Figure 5.57 Initial Chart without Sort

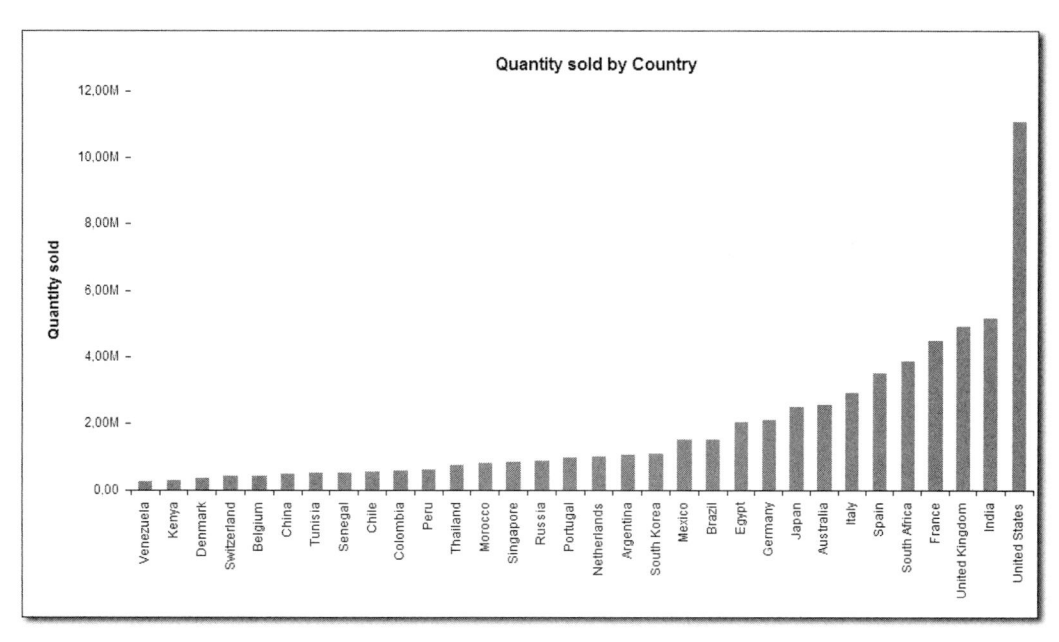

Figure 5.58 Sort Ascending

Ascending will simply render the values from lowest to highest, or, vice versa, descending will rank the values by highest to lowest.

5.4.2 Rank Values

Rank values allow you to create a subset of the TOP *n* or BOTTOM values for a given dimension—for example, the top three countries. First, select RANK VALUES from the menu to get the RANKING dialog box (see Figure 5.59).

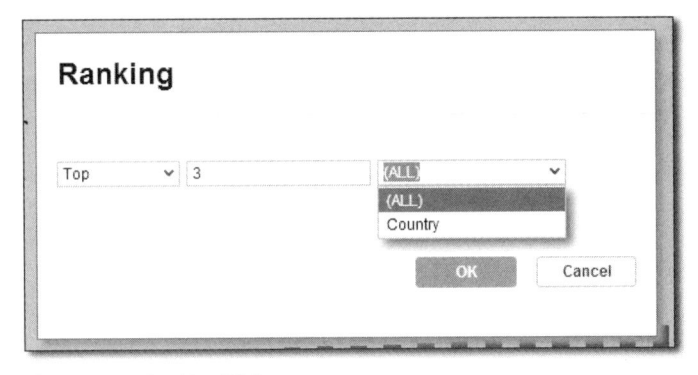

Figure 5.59 Ranking Dialog

The dialog box allows you to select the following:

- Whether the rank is TOP or BOTTOM.
- How many values to see (by default it's 3, but you can enter another value)
- The dimension to use or (ALL).
- The selection of the dimension drives the calculation, because you are determining which values are to be ranked. For example, if you are using COUNTRY and LINES, you can see the top three countries, the top three lines, or the top three countries and their lines. For example, Figure 5.60 displays the top three ALL.

Here, we can see the top three values of both the country and the lines. Alternatively, we can change this to either dimension, and we will see the top three for that given dimension and for all values, as shown in Figure 5.61.

5.4 Measures in Charts

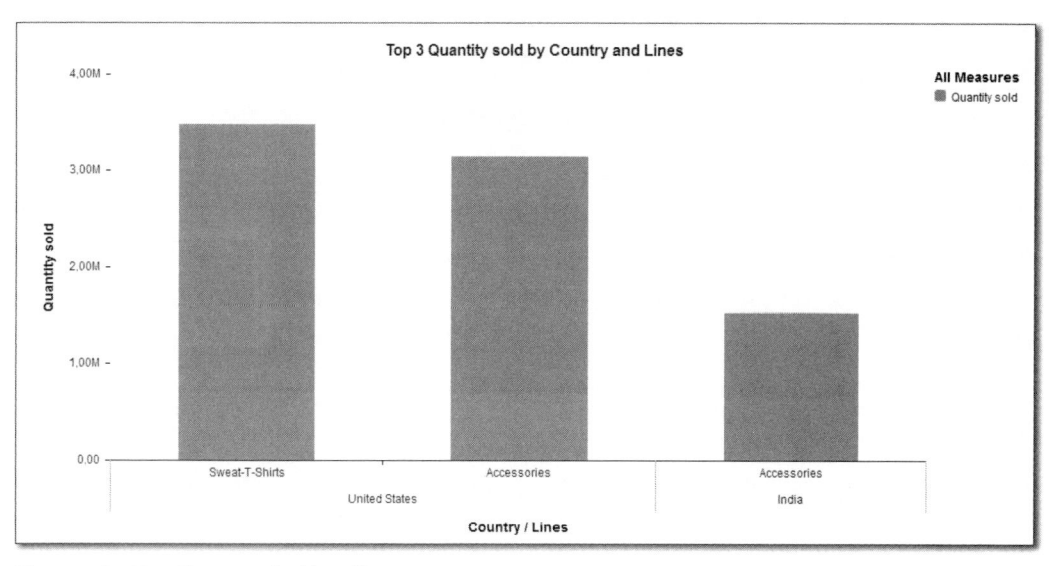

Figure 5.60 Top Three Ranked by All

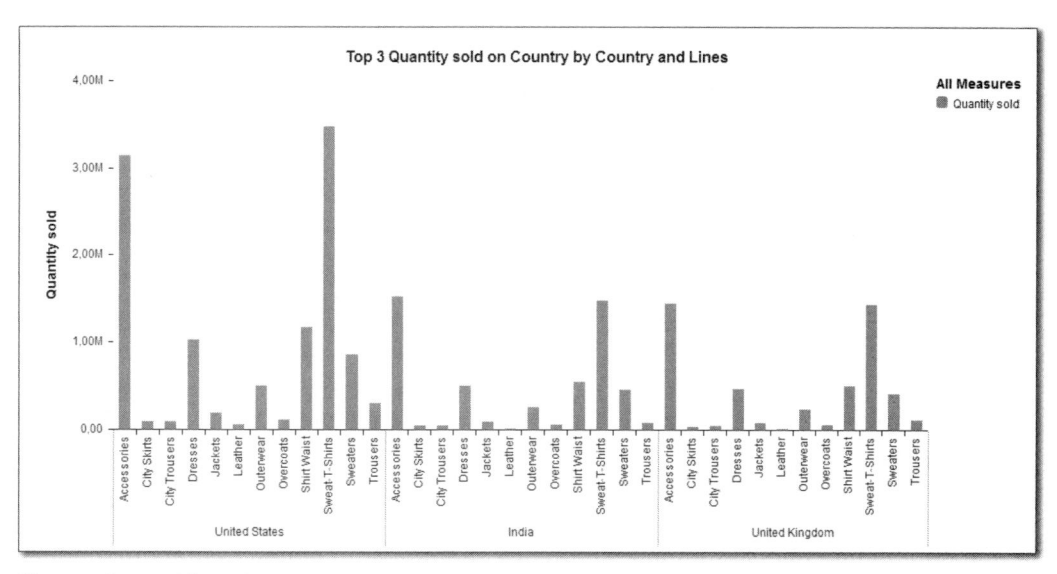

Figure 5.61 Top Three Countries

Here, we get the top three countries and their lines. In contrast, if we select lines, we will see the top three lines and their associated countries (see Figure 5.62).

5 | Data Visualization

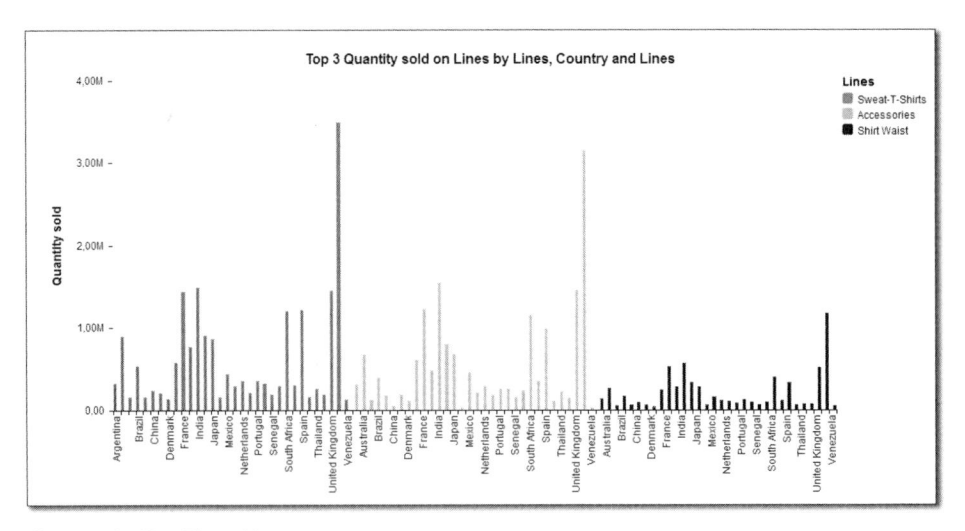

Figure 5.62 Top Three Lines

In summary, ranking allows you to get the top or bottom values for a dataset.

5.4.3 Add Calculations

You can add calculations, such as running counts and sums, to charts. These are available from the ADD CALCULATION menu when clicking on the measure (see Figure 5.63).

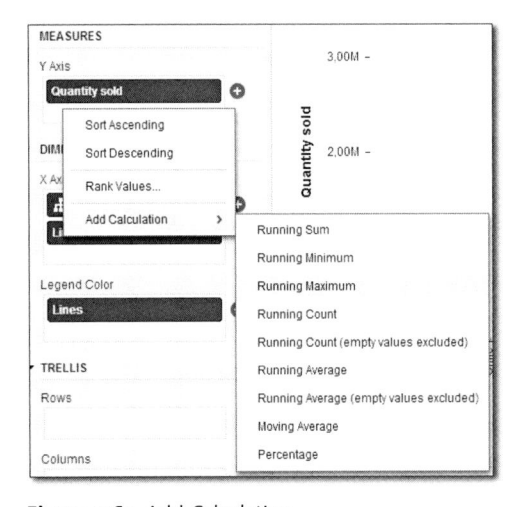

Figure 5.63 Add Calculation

These calculations are based only on the measure as it is used and aggregated in the chart. A RUNNING SUM is a running sum for the dimension that is used in the current chart only. Each calculation is added as a measure to the chart. The different measures are described ahead.

Running Sum

The RUNNING SUM option is calculated from the first value, but for the second column there is an addition of the first value to the second. This addition then continues to the end of the data (see Figure 5.64).

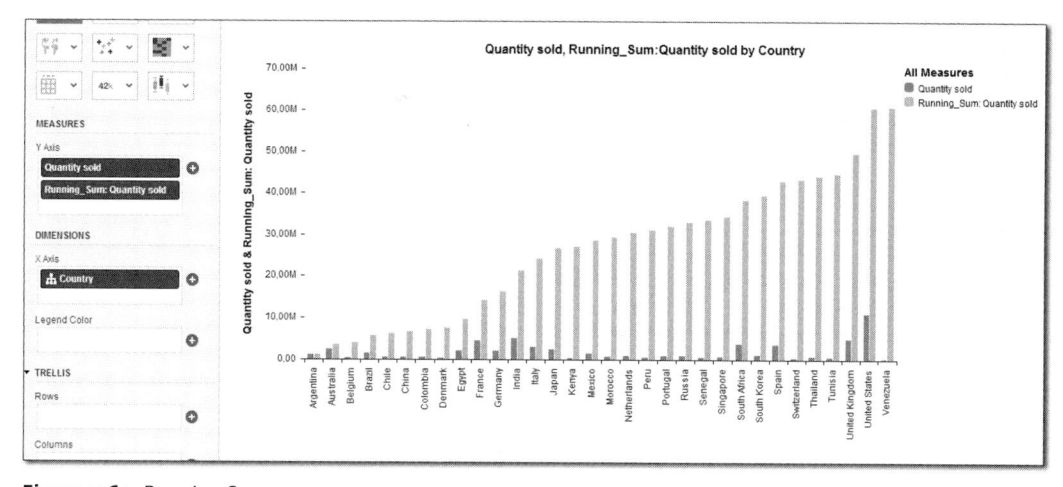

Figure 5.64 Running Sum

The calculation itself is added in the measures section with the prefix RUNNING_ SUM.

Running Minimum

The RUNNING MINIMUM option will, starting from the second value, display the current lowest value. Because the last lowest value will be carried over, you will, in the end, see the lowest value in the dataset (see Figure 5.65).

In Figure 5.65, the lowest value is by coincidence the last value Venezuela, and the running minimum stays constant for most of the chart.

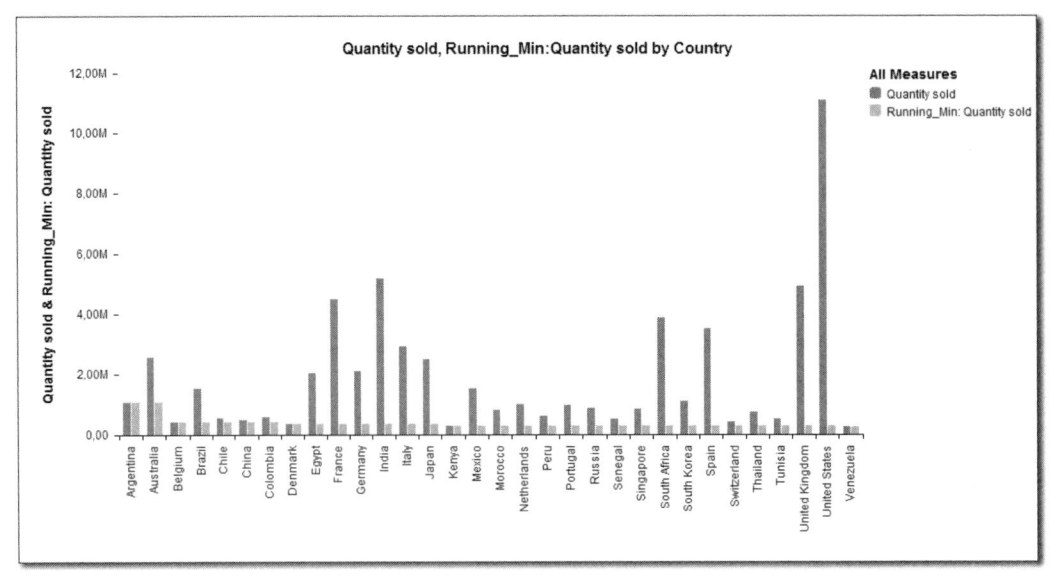

Figure 5.65 Running Minimum

Running Maximum

The RUNNING MAXIMUM option is the opposite of RUNNING MINIMUM; it will display the maximum value. The first value will be the maximum, and each subsequent value will be compared and replaced if it is greater than the current maximum.

Running Count

The RUNNING COUNT option will simply count the position or number of columns. Because this is a simple count, you can quite easily miss the value completely if your measure is aggregating to a higher order. If your y-axis is scaled to 1,000s, or more, with a count which will probably not reach even 100s, then it is unlikely to be visible. One solution to this is to use a dual axis chart (see Figure 5.66).

Using a second axis allows us to see the count more easily.

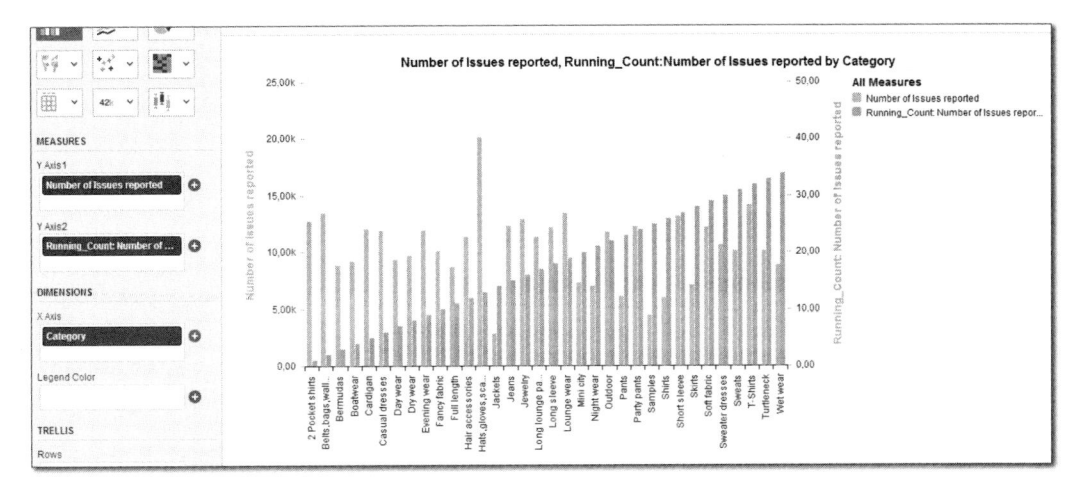

Figure 5.66 Dual Axis Chart with Running Count

Running Count (Empty Values Excluded)
This type of running count will not include empty values in the count.

Running Average

The RUNNING AVERAGE option is the current average (i.e., it's the current running sum divided by the current running count). The value of column 3 will be the average of the first three columns; column 5 will be the average of the first five.

Running Average (Empty Values Excluded)
Excluding the empty values means that the average will be calculated for columns that contain values. This is exactly the same as running average, except that it is a running count with excluded empty values (the running sum will not be affected by a 0 value).

Moving Average

The MOVING AVERAGE option is slightly different; an extra dialog specifies the window to calculate. This allows you to create an average that is less affected by the overall values, because it looks n periods ahead and back (see Figure 5.67).

5 | Data Visualization

Figure 5.67 Moving Average Dialog

You specify the number of values before and after, and you can choose whether to include the current value (see Figure 5.68).

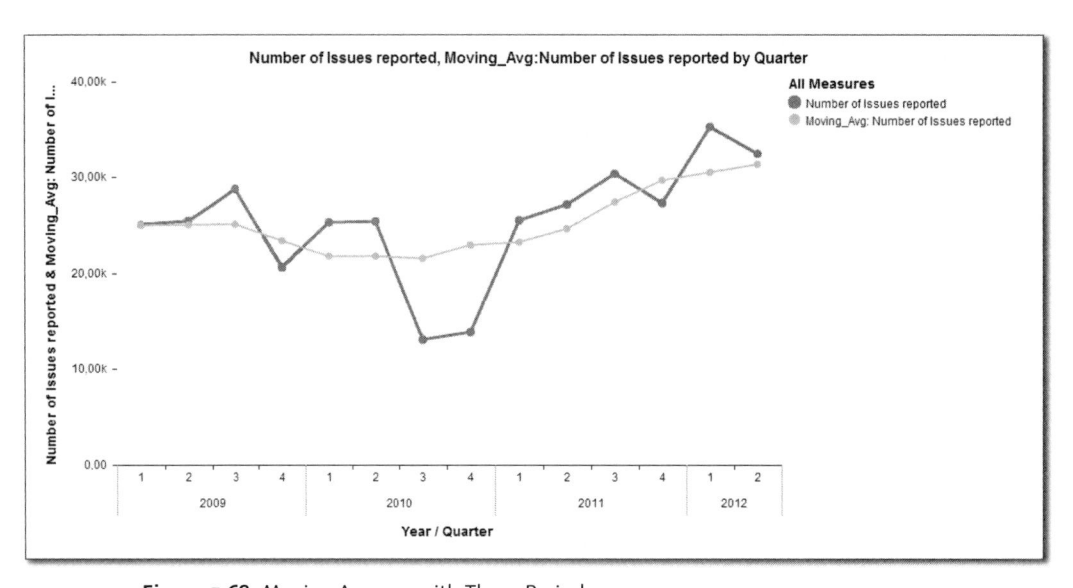

Figure 5.68 Moving Average with Three Periods

We calculate an average for +/- three periods (meaning that the value at each point is the average of the current value with three values before and after). Moving average is used to smooth out possible short term fluctuations in data. For example, in Figure 5.68 we can see that the moving average is closer to a curve as it smoothed out the small highs and lows in the data.

Percentage

Using the PERCENTAGE option will calculate a percentage of each value given the total value. The total of all percentage values should be equal to 100. By default, the axis scale will probably not be 0 to 100, but you can change this to better reflect the relative percent weight (see Figure 5.69).

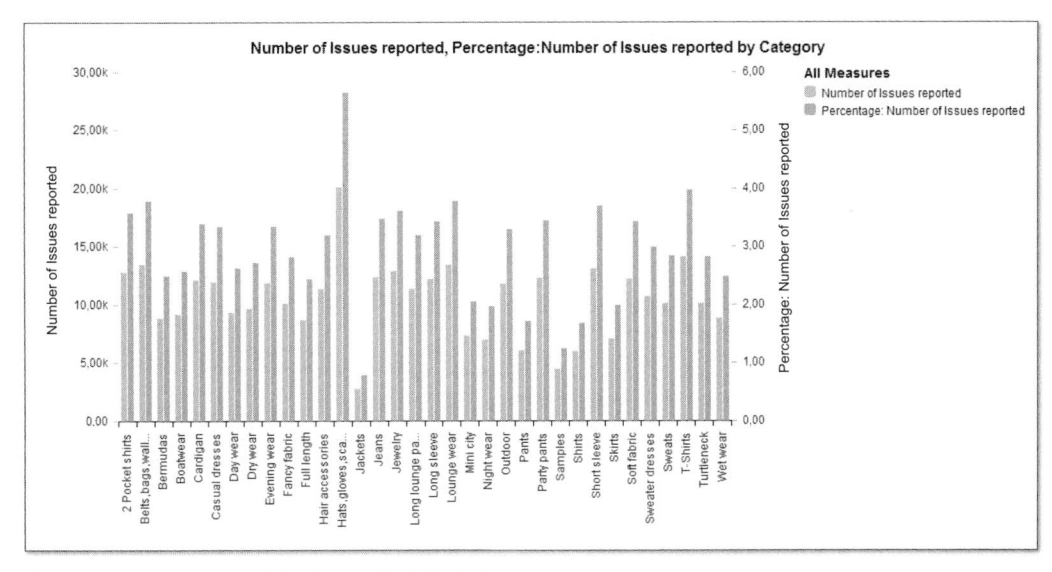

Figure 5.69 Percentage with a 0 to 100 Scale Axis

To change the scale, see Section 5.5.

5.4.4 Predictive Calculations

SAP Lumira Desktop has two additional predictive calculations that can be created in the Visualize room. These calculations are not to be confused with SAP Lumira Predictive, which is another product. The PREDICTIVE CALCULATION menu is only available on a measure that is used in conjunction with a time hierarchy and in a line chart (see Figure 5.70).

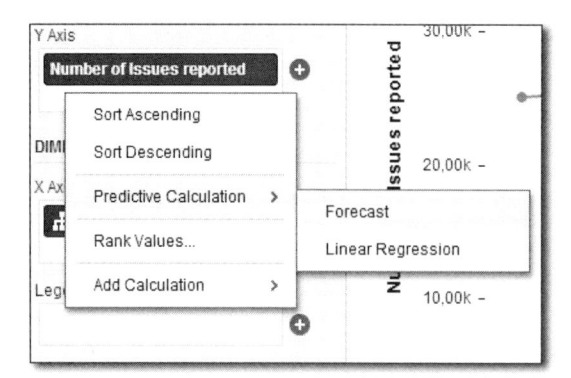

Figure 5.70 Predictive Functions in SAP Lumira

Both the FORECAST and LINEAR REGRESSION options require time data, because they are functions that work over time, either trying to predict what the next values might be or trying to smooth the data to reduce the possible noise. Because both calculations function over time, you need a time hierarchy (not a date) and typically a good series of data that has some cycles or sufficient periods (you need at least two, but more is better).

There are many good resources that explain exponential smoothing, but roughly the goal is to reduce the influence of the past by assigning exponentially reduced weights to past data. The MOVING AVERAGE option, for example, will weight all values equally. Let's look at these two options further:

- FORECAST
  This option will try to predict the possible values for a given number of periods. A forecast will try to generate an actual value given the previous data.

- LINEAR REGRESSION
  This option will try to see the trend in the data, but gives less weight to "noise"—that is, events that are not predictable.

The chart in Figure 5.71 shows the actual values compared to the FORECAST, LINEAR REGRESSION, and MOVING AVERAGE options, allowing for a visual comparison of the different calculations.

The different chart calculations, sorts, and rankings will allow you to extend the scope of analysis available with charts. In addition, you can customize charts in order to optimize them for presentation and legibility.

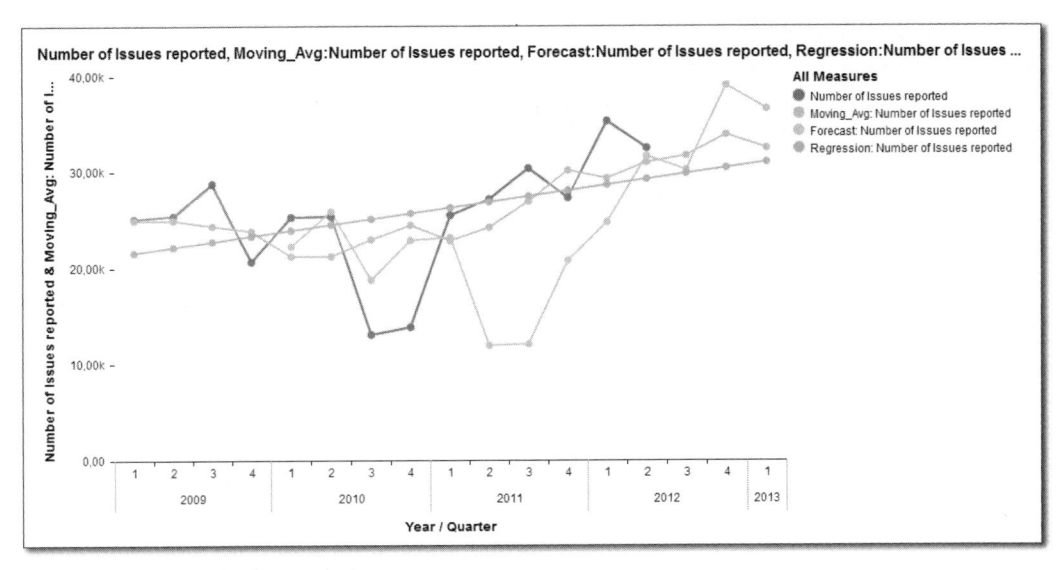

Figure 5.71 Chart with Three Calculations

5.5 Chart Customization

In this section, we will look at chart customization through the cog icons available at the top right of all charts in SAP Lumira. Some charts have fewer or different options, such as pie charts, which have no axis scale (it's always calculated to 100% of the surface area; see Figure 5.72).

Figure 5.72 Chart Customization Options

Customization options include the following:

- SHOW TITLE

  Hides or shows the title of the chart. To change the text of the title itself, you have to double-click the title and edit it directly.

- SHOW LEGEND

  Hides or shows the legend at the side of the chart. By default, the legend is always available.

- SHOW DATA LABELS

  Off by default (hidden). Changing this setting means that each chart's values will be displayed as label on the appropriate chart region.

- USE MEASURES AS A DIMENSION

  Allows you to compare multiple measures in a series of charts. Rather than drawing a single chart with multiple measures, the additional measures are placed in the trellis (see Figure 5.73)

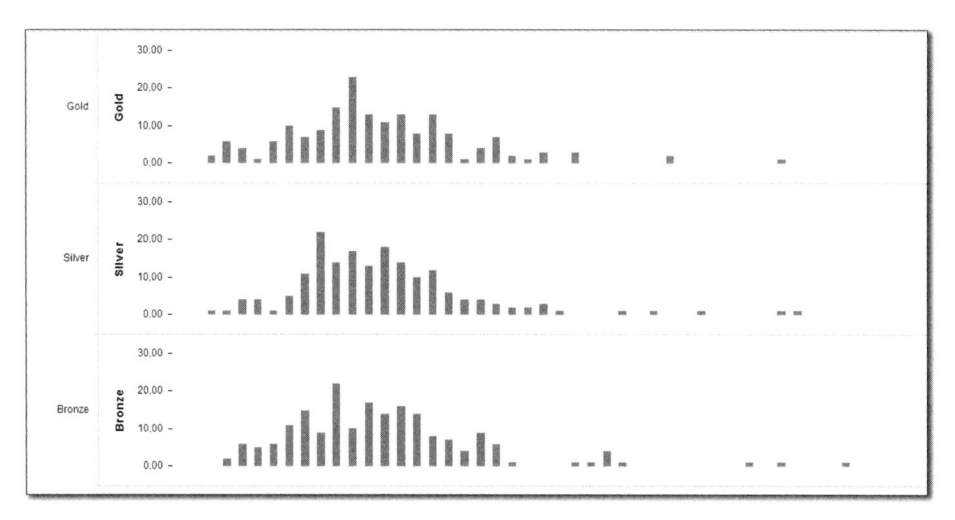

Figure 5.73 Measures as a Dimension

- SET AXIS SCALE

  As mentioned previously, this can be used to change the scale of a chart. For example, using a scale of 0 to 100 for percentage values gives a more accurate impression of the actual value. Selecting this opens a dialog that allows you to set a top and a bottom value.

Now that we know how to customize our charts, let's move on to creating filters for visualizations

5.6 Filters in Charts

You can use filters in charts, and you can create filters for visualization in a number of different ways. Filters that are created in the Prepare room are applied to all other rooms, so all visualization created with a dataset that has a filter will be automatically filtered. The filter will be visible in the filter bar at the top of the Visualize room. Global filters are rendered in a dark grey and are not editable in the Visualize room. You need to go back to the Prepare room in order to edit or delete them.

Local filters can be applied, and are distinguishable from global filters because they are light gray and can be edited or deleted (see Figure 5.74).

Figure 5.74 Local and Global Filter

Note, that the local filter has a DELETE icon and that selecting the crumb will enable you to edit the filter selection. Editing the filters directly works the same way as in Prepare room (you select the values to include or exclude from a list).

Filters can be created from the OBJECT PICKER or from the chart itself (see Figure 5.75).

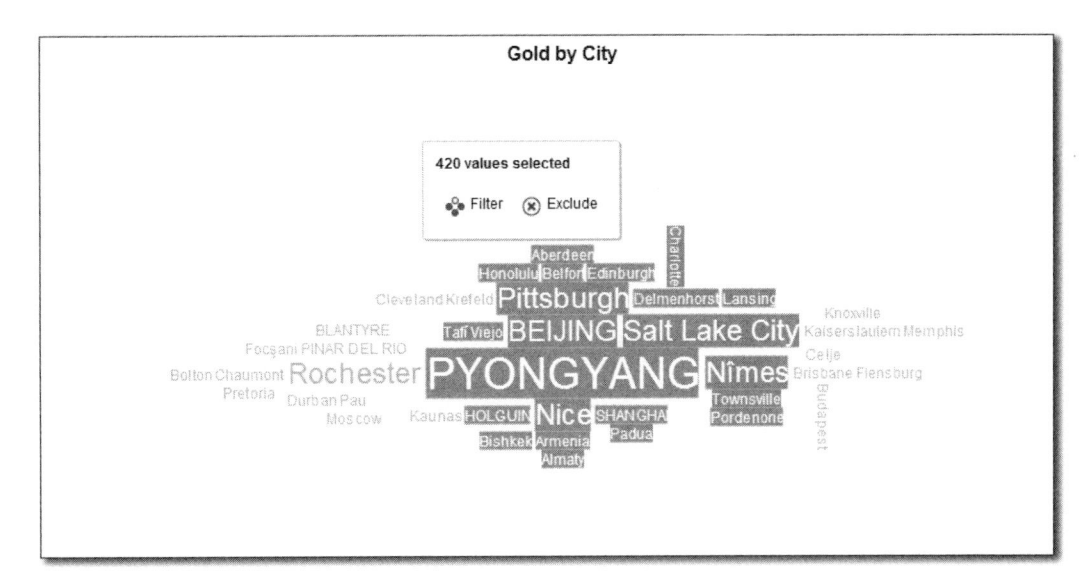

Figure 5.75 Create a Filter with a Lasso

You can select individual elements or use a lasso to select multiple elements. All visual elements of a chart can be used to create a filter:

- Legend
- Axes labels
- The chart elements themselves (a bar, a pie sector, a point, etc.); you can also use the mouse to lasso several elements

On selection of a given element or elements, you will see a pop-up that allows you to choose between a filter or an exclusive filter.

Selecting either of these will immediately create the filter and update the visualization. The difference is that the filter will include only those values selected, whereas the exclusive filter will show all other values.

You can also take advantage of hierarchies to filter data. Hierarchies allow you to filter your data but by using the hierarchical relationship you can navigate through your data.

5.7 Hierarchies and Navigation in Charts

Hierarchies have two main uses in charts: you can use time and geographic hierarchies to create specific types of chart, and hierarchies can also be used to navigate within charts. For example, if you have a simple chart that uses countries from a geographic hierarchy, then an additional menu option appears in the tooltip (see Figure 5.76).

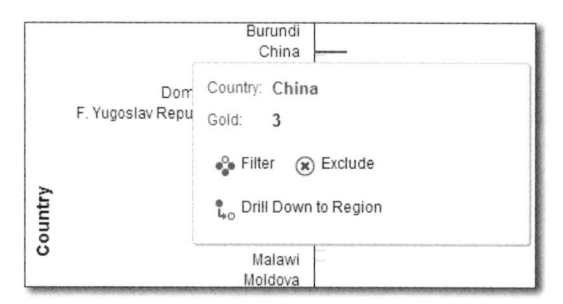

Figure 5.76 Drill Down Menu

Selecting DRILL DOWN TO REGION will essentially create a filter on the element selected (see Figure 5.77).

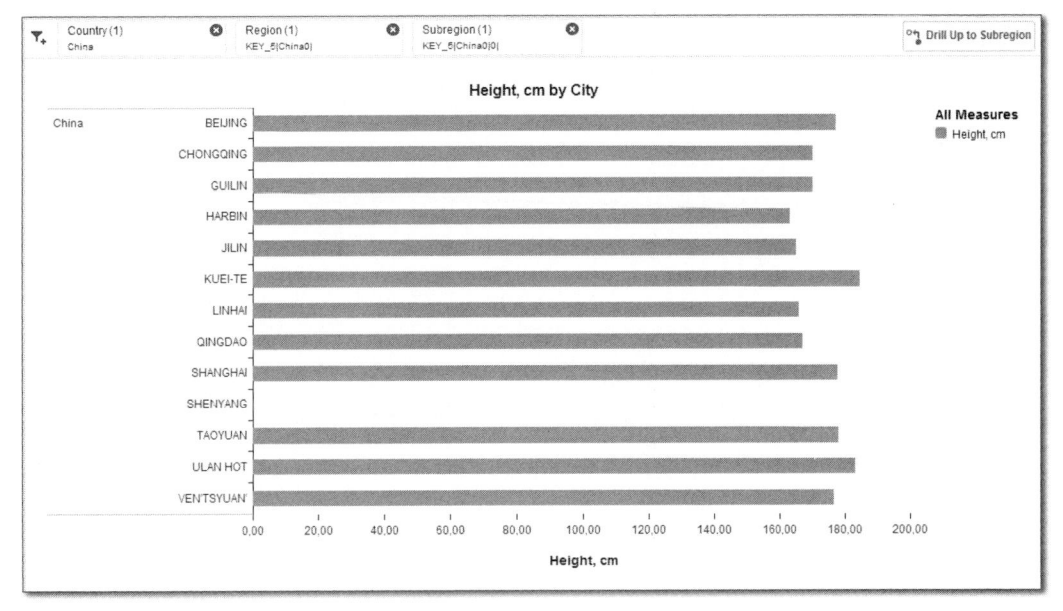

Figure 5.77 Drill Down

You can drill back up by selecting DRILL UP TO COUNTRY in the top-right corner of the chart. Note, that removing the filter is not the same as drilling up. Removing the filter will leave you on the region but without the country context. If you want to drill, you need to use the drill-up/down options only.

Next, we will explore the preference options available for charts in SAP Lumira.

5.8   Chart Preferences

Under SAP LUMIRA PREFERENCES, you will see a CHARTS section that contains a number of settings that can be applied to charts (see Figure 5.78):

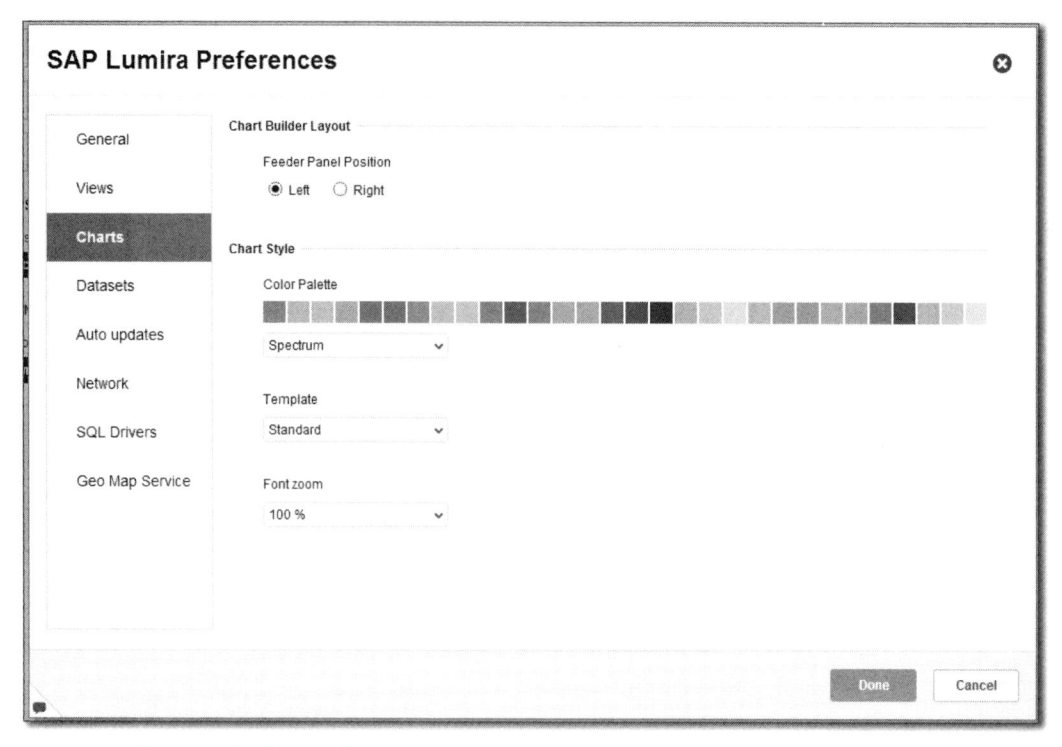

Figure 5.78 Chart Preferences

- The FEEDING PANEL POSITION sets the location of the FEEDING panel, which by default is on the left but can be moved to the right. Note, that on the server the default position is the right.
- The CHART STYLE section contains a number of settings that will change the look of the charts themselves:
    - COLOR PALETTE sets the base colors that are used in your charts. There are several different palettes, such as SPECTRUM, BLACK AND WHITE, and different variations on a base color (see Figure 5.79).
    - The TEMPLATE allows you to choose from STANDARD, FLASHY, and HIGH CONTRAST. These options affect the rendering of the chart. FLASHY tends to add a more dramatic look to the charts, a pseudo-3-D look, whereas HIGH CONTRAST maximizes the contrast—for example, via a black background.
    - FONT ZOOM enlarges the fonts in the charts.

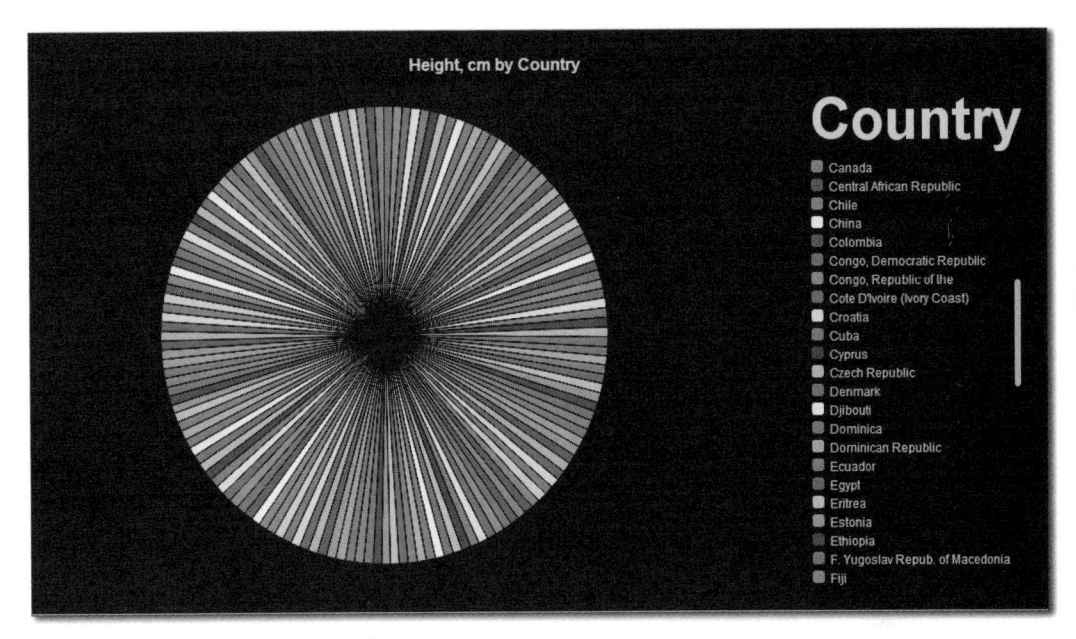

Figure 5.79 Chart Preferences in Action

As can be seen in Figure 5.79, the preferences can have a dramatic effect (hues, high contrast and font zoom).

> **Why You Should Not Use Chart Preferences!**
>
> One problem with chart preferences is that they are local SAP Lumira Desktop settings that are not passed around. This means that these settings affect only the charts that are open while you are in the SAP Lumira Desktop, and they are lost when you publish or share stories. Also, you cannot specify settings on a visualization level or even at a document level.
>
> In Chapter 6, you will create stories, which are essentially groups of visualizations, and you will see how to customize charts with settings that are sharable.

5.9 Visualization Gallery

Underneath the CHART CANVAS is the GALLERY. The GALLERY (see Figure 5.80) is a summary of the different visualizations that you have created and also provides some management actions, such as DELETE.

Figure 5.80 Visualization Gallery

The gallery is a list of all the visualizations that you have created in a document. If you have multiple datasets, then you will notice that the list is contextual: because you can only create visualizations on one dataset at a time, the list is populated with visualizations that were created with the currently selected dataset. Changing the dataset will thus change the list.

The large PLUS icon is used to create a new visualization. Clicking it will create a new, blank visualization at the end of the current list.

Click the cog icon on a visualization thumbnail to open a menu with the following commands (see Figure 5.81):

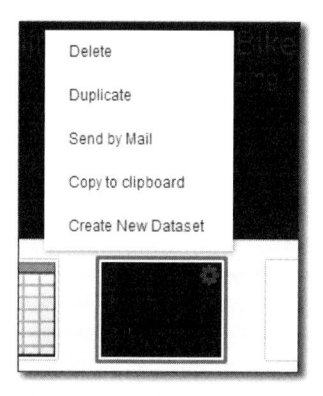

Figure 5.81 Gallery Chart Options

- DELETE
  Deletes the visualization, with a possible warning if the chart is used elsewhere, such as in a story.
- DUPLICATE
  Clones the current visualization in a new copy (like in a copy and paste).
- SEND BY MAIL
  Creates an image of your chart and opens a new message with the chart pasted in. You must select the quality of the image (see Figure 5.82).

Figure 5.82 Export Quality Options

These options determine the size of the image to be created (in pixels):

▶ COPY TO CLIPBOARD
This is similar to the email feature, except that the image is placed in the clipboard. After choosing this option, you can paste the chart directly into another application (CTRL + V to paste into a Microsoft Office application, for example).

▶ CREATE NEW DATASET
This will take the results of the query used to generate the chart and create a new dataset with only these values see Figure 5.83.

Figure 5.83 New Dataset from Visualize Room

The example here is taken from a chart we saw earlier where we created a running minimum by country (see Figure 5.65). Note, that any calculations you used in the visualization are taken into the dataset.

5.10 Related Visualizations

The Visualize room can also suggest visualizations based on dimensions and measures. These suggestions are based on relationships that are found among the attributes (see Figure 5.84).

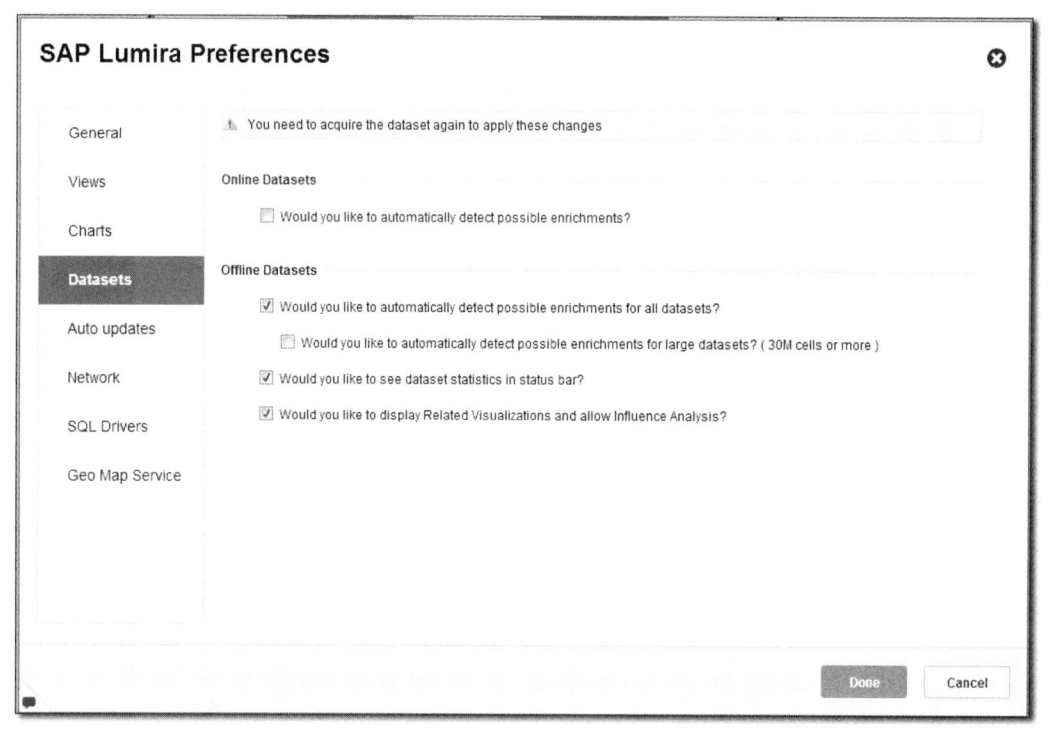

Figure 5.84 Related Visualizations Preferences

To enable or disable this feature, select DATASETS in the PREFERENCES pane, and select the RELATED VISUALIZATIONS checkbox. You will now see a list of related visualizations. These are visualizations that are calculated by looking at measures and finding dimensions that are likely influencers of those measures (see Figure 5.85). Here, we once again use the Titanic survivor data.

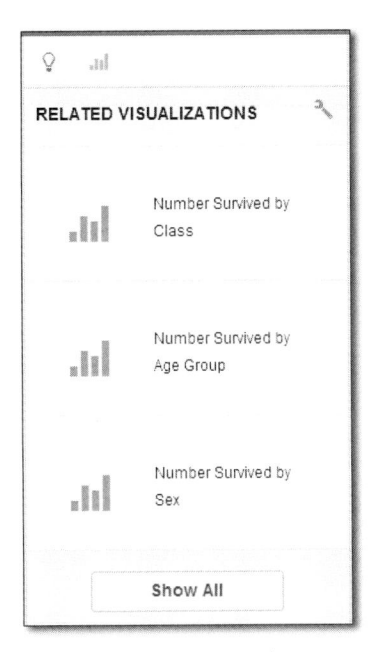

Figure 5.85 Related Visualizations

Selecting any of these will load the chart in the main chart area. You can then use the chart as you would any other.

If you select the WRENCH icon, you will open an editor that allows you to customize the calculation for determining the relevance. You can use this to turn on or off dimensions and measures, thus reducing the number of permutations the influence test will use (see Figure 5.86).

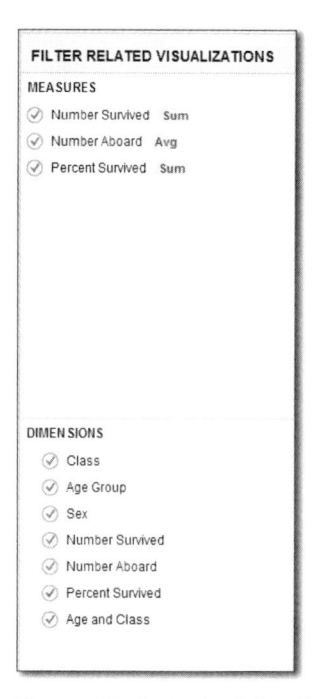

Figure 5.86 Customize Related Visualizations

This removes the selected objects from the detection algorithm, so that you can limit the number of suggestions or focus the selection (see Figure 5.87).

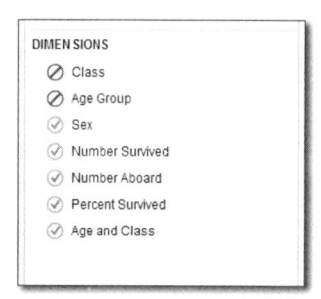

Figure 5.87 Excluded Objects

With the excluded objects set, we can now see in Figure 5.88 that the list has changed compared to the previous list (see Figure 5.85).

We can see that the suggested charts has now changed as our excluded objects are no longer taken into consideration.

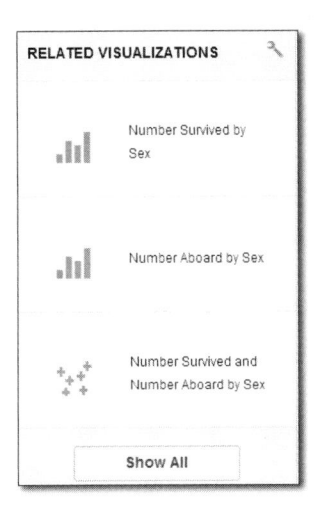

Figure 5.88 Updated Related Visualization List

5.10.1 Influencers

There is a second way of getting visualization suggestions using a technique known as Influence Analysis. In order to use this you should still have the RELATED VISUALIZATIONS tab open and then you just select a measure (see Figure 5.89).

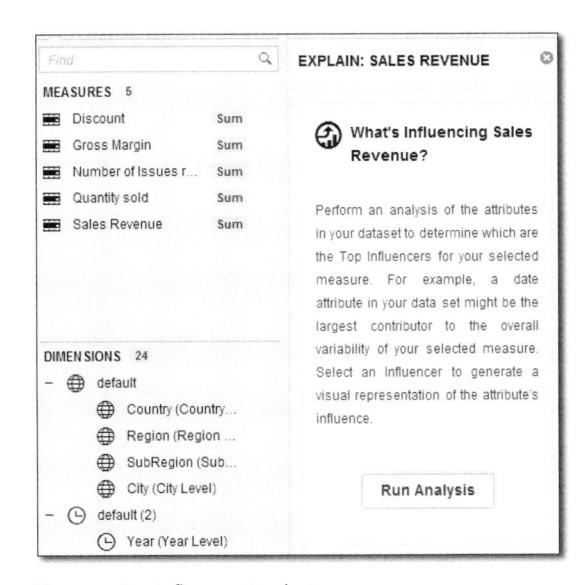

Figure 5.89 Influence Analysis

5 | Data Visualization

The analysis run is a statistical model that tries to determine which are the key measures and/or dimensions that influence this measure. The results are presented as a ranked list. The first item is a fly over chart that ranks the results by perceived influence (see Figure 5.90).

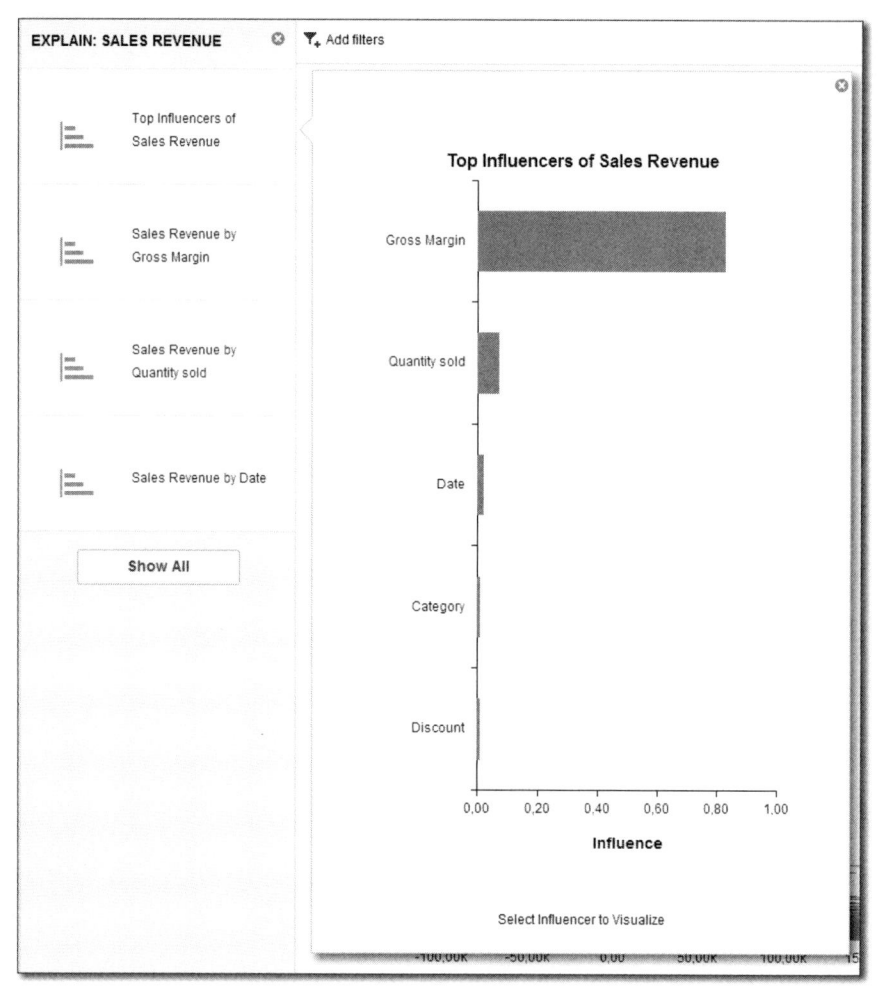

Figure 5.90 Ranked list of Influencers

The other items in the list are charts that will appear in the chart area as per any other chart. To remove the Influence list just click on the blue cross in the top right and this will return you to the related visualizations list.

5.11 Summary

In this chapter, we have seen how to build different types of visualizations using standard and not-so-standard charts. The Visualize room allows you to add additional calculations, such as running sums, to further enhance your analysis.

In the next chapter, we will see how you can share these visualizations with others through stories.

Stories are graphical, navigable narratives used to describe data through the grouping of charts into storyboards. This chapter describes the Compose room, where you will assemble everything in order to prepare your results for presentation and sharing with colleagues. In this chapter, you will take your constructed visualizations and turn them into stories.

6   Story Composition in SAP Lumira

This chapter discusses how to create stories from the data gathered in the acquisition, manipulation, and visualization processes. With charts, text, and images, you can create storyboards that tell a narrative of the gathered data.

To begin, we will take a look at the Compose room and the role it plays in creating our stories in SAP Lumira. Then, we will look at what a story is before going into more detail about the different types of layouts you can use. Finally, we will list the different entities that can be used and how they can be customized.

6.1   Compose Room Overview

The Compose room in SAP Lumira is where the previous hard work of preparing and cleaning data comes to fruition. Here, the construction of visualizations can all be put to use in visuals called *stories*. Stories enable you to present your findings by mixing charts, images, and text together to explain your data. The role of the decision maker is often that of someone who has to be persuasive, and the Compose room provides different types of layouts that can enable you to create persuasive arguments (see Figure 6.1).

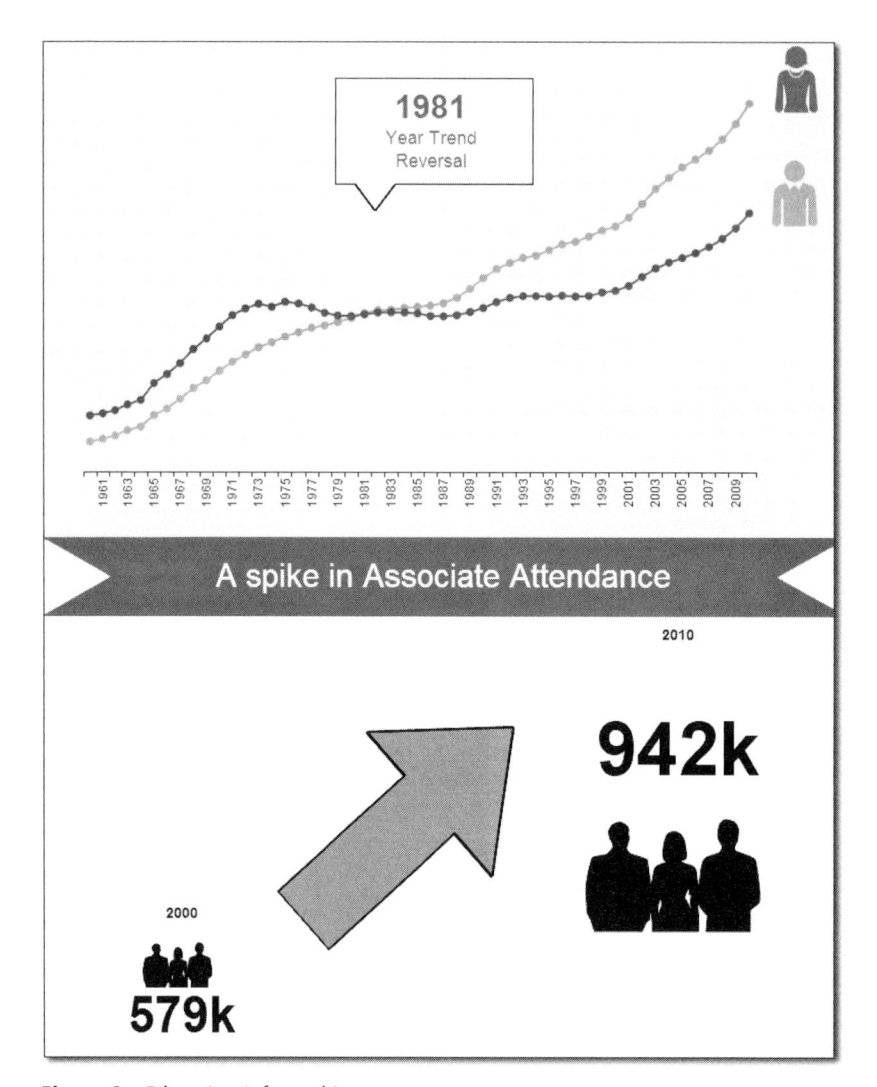

Figure 6.1 Education Infographic

For example, it is possible to create highly visual infographics, like the one shown in Figure 6.1, which in turn use infocharts to place particular emphasis on key data points.

Stories can also contain *interactive boards* and *reports*. These are more classic BI constructions and are closer to the standard dashboards and reports you create with other BI tools (see Figure 6.2).

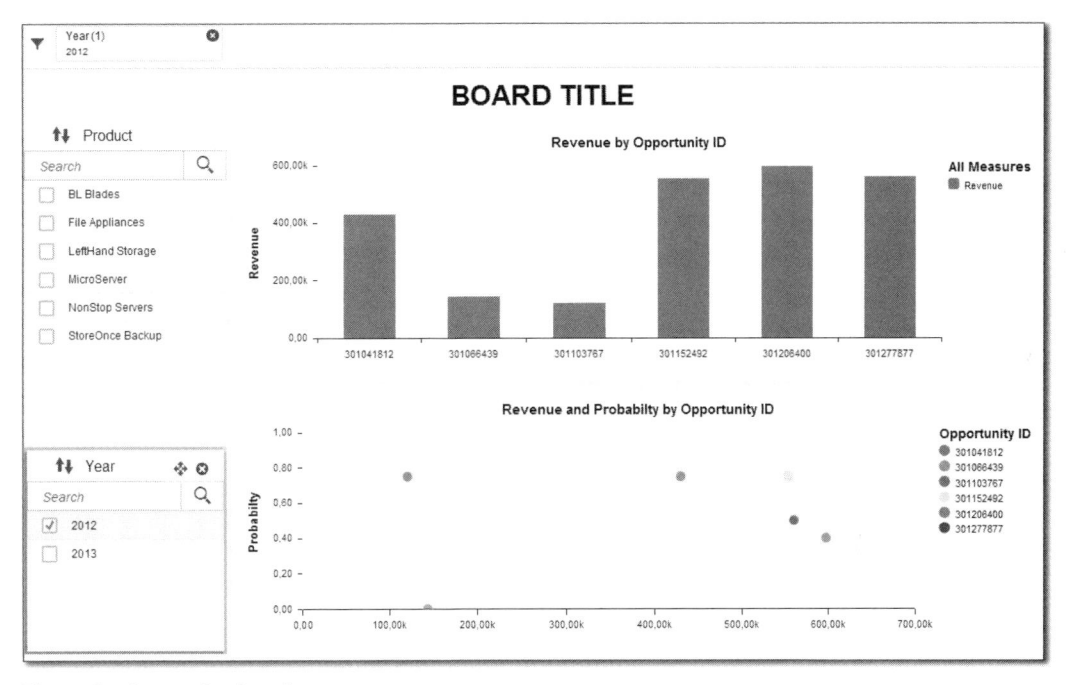

Figure 6.2 Interactive Boards

In reports and interactive boards, you can add controls that allow users to filter the data in order to get a better understanding of the results presented. Finally, once you have completed your story you can publish it.

Let's begin by looking at what makes up on an SAP Lumira story.

6.2 Story Anatomy

Stories are sets of visualizations, which you can think of as pages. Each interactive board can have a different layout, such as infographic or report. There are currently three layouts to choose from:

- **Interactive Boards**
  Interactive boards have a relatively simple layout structure. A board takes up 100% of the space available, and entities in a board take a proportion of the space available in a bow or grid layout. The spacing is always relative, so you

cannot absolutely position and fix an entity. Boards allow for interactivity through controls that users can add, and this then allows you to filter the page.

- **Infographics**
The infographic layout gives much more control to the user, allowing for absolute and overlapping layouts. The downside to this is that they are not interactive. The goal of infographics is to give the user the power to create a very controlled message with charts, infocharts, pictograms, shapes, and text.

- **Reports**
Reports are not as complete as any of the classic reporting tools from SAP, but they allow you to create pages that you can navigate and analyze with through section controls. Reports are dynamic, like interactive boards, so users can interact with and analyze them.

Each page in a story can only have one type of layout, but you can have different layouts over the different pages—for example, the first page could be an infographic, and the second page a report.

Datasets
Interactive boards and reports can only use a single dataset per interactive board, and the data is live (you can use different datasets in the story but not on one single page). By "live," we mean that if you refresh your data or change the structure of a visualization this change is immediately reflected in your interactive board or report.
If you create a new interactive board or report when you have multiple datasets, then the first visualization that you select will restrict your page to that dataset. The dataset selector will change to only display the current dataset and the visualization and control list will be filtered to the chosen dataset.
Infographics can use many datasets per page, because the data is not "live." If you change the dataset through a refresh, then this is not visible in an infographic. You will see how you can update infographics in Section 6.6.

6.3 Creating a Story

You must create a new story to use the Compose room; if you have not created a story, then when you go to the COMPOSE room and you will be prompted to create one, or you can just click the NEW STORY button from the COMPOSE room menu (see Figure 6.3).

Figure 6.3 Compose Room Menu

The dialog box for creating a new story offers you a choice of different layouts to choose from (see Figure 6.4).

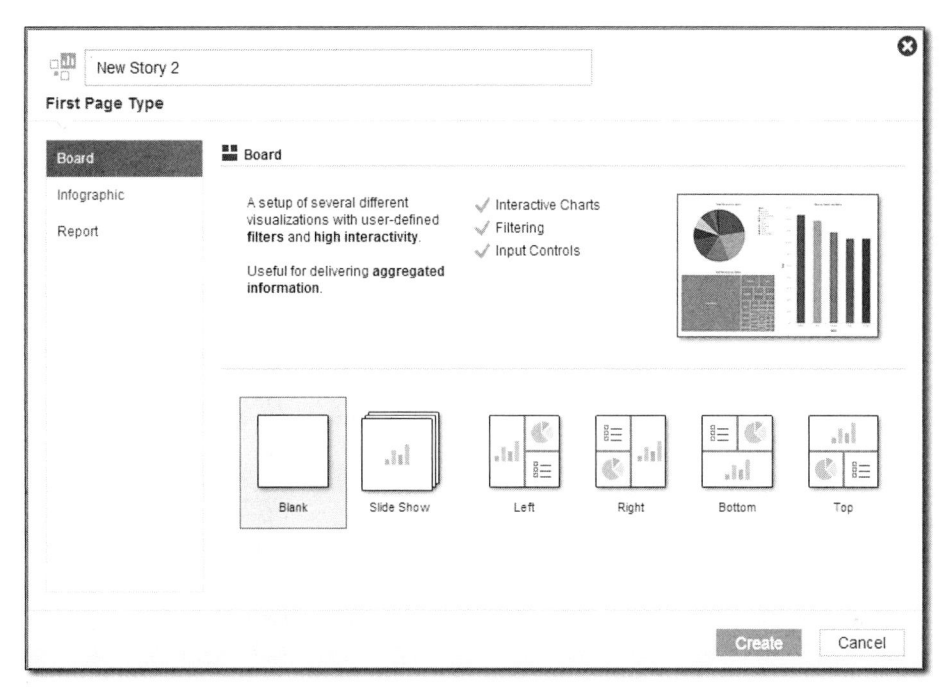

Figure 6.4 New Story Dialog

At the top of the dialog box, you can name your story, and then you can choose one of the different layouts from the left-hand side. For example, in Figure 6.4 we selected BOARD, and we will see a description of the layout along with some templates. Templates are preformatted examples that provide a starting point from which you can build your board.

Note, that the layout uses placeholders to suggest a structure. The type of placeholder does not restrict you; it's simply an image that can be replaced. You can place any type of content onto a placeholder. Infographics have a template called 5W1H that we will look at in Section 6.6.

6.4 Compose Room Organization

Each layout handles entities slightly differently, but the COMPOSE room has a consistent structure (see Figure 6.5).

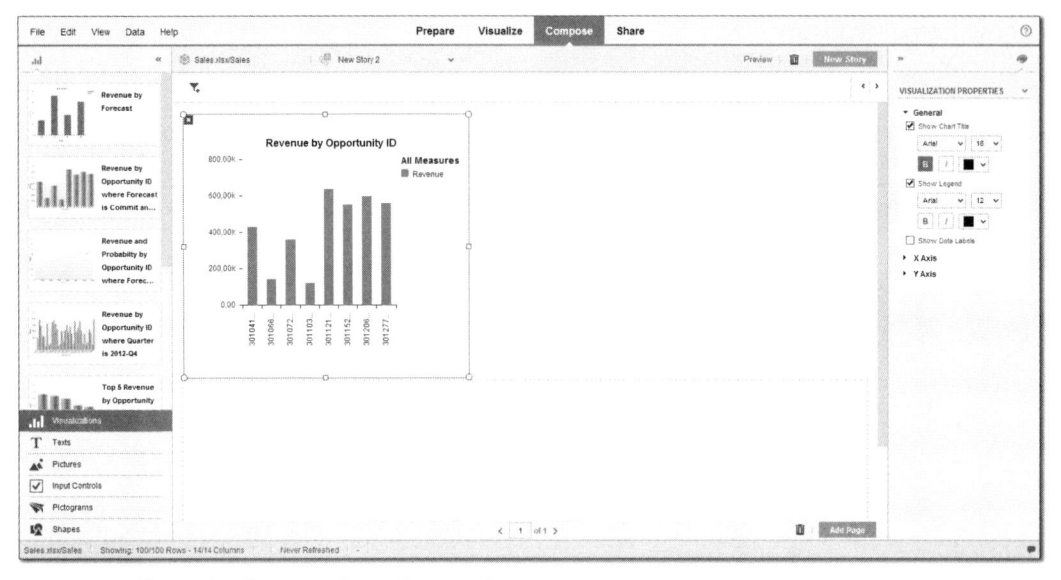

Figure 6.5 Compose Room Organization

The following are entities that can be found in the Compose room:

- ENTITY PICKER
  The left-hand side contains the different entities that you can use. For example, VISUALIZATIONS, TEXTS, and PICTURES. All of these entities are handled in the same way: simply drag and drop each entity onto your layout area. Entities are grouped; choose the group that you need by selecting the name from the section at the bottom. Note that everything that can be dropped onto the canvas will be called an entity.

- CANVAS
  In the center is the content area that will lay out your entities according to the layout style you have chosen. In Figure 6.5, the canvas displays a report.

- PROPERTIES
  On the right-hand side is a PROPERTIES area. This area is contextual, and it allows you to customize selected entities. For example, if you want to change the back-

ground color of an entity, you first select it, as noted earlier, and then edit the properties. Nearly all entities have properties, but the number and type differ from entity to entity and also from layout to layout.

- MENU bar
  At the top is the Compose room-specific menu bar, which contains the following:
  - DATASET SELECTOR: We will look at this in Section 6.8.1; there are some constraints on the use of datasets in stories.
  - STORY SELECTOR: You can switch between different stories here. The combo is also editable, so you can change the name of your story.
  - PREVIEW: Stories are, of course, composed to be shared. We will cover the mechanics of sharing in Chapter 7. However, the PREVIEW action allows you to see what your story will look like to an end user.
  - DELETE: Deletes the current story you are working on.
  - NEW STORY: Creates a new story.
- NAVIGATION and ACTION bar
  At the bottom of the canvas is the NAVIGATION and ACTION bar. There are a few actions here that you can use, such as ADD PAGE, PREVIEW, and CHANGE PAGE. Here you can perform the following actions:
  - Move from page to page by clicking on the arrows or by directly entering the page number.
  - Use the TRASH icon to delete the current page.
  - Add a new page; the dialog box for adding a page is exactly like the NEW STORY dialog box.

Although the Compose room behaves consistently, there is a big difference in functionality among its different layouts. In the following sections, we will take a look at each layout in turn before looking in detail at the different entity types you can use. Let's look first at interactive boards.

6.5 Interactive Boards

To create an interactive board, select one of the templates from the template dialog box (see Figure 6.6).

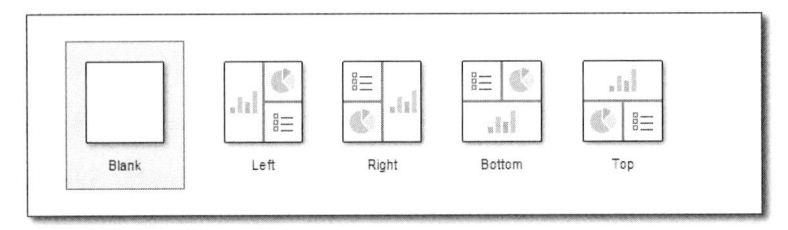

Figure 6.6 Board Template

If you click on the RIGHT template, a new board with that structure will be created (see Figure 6.7).

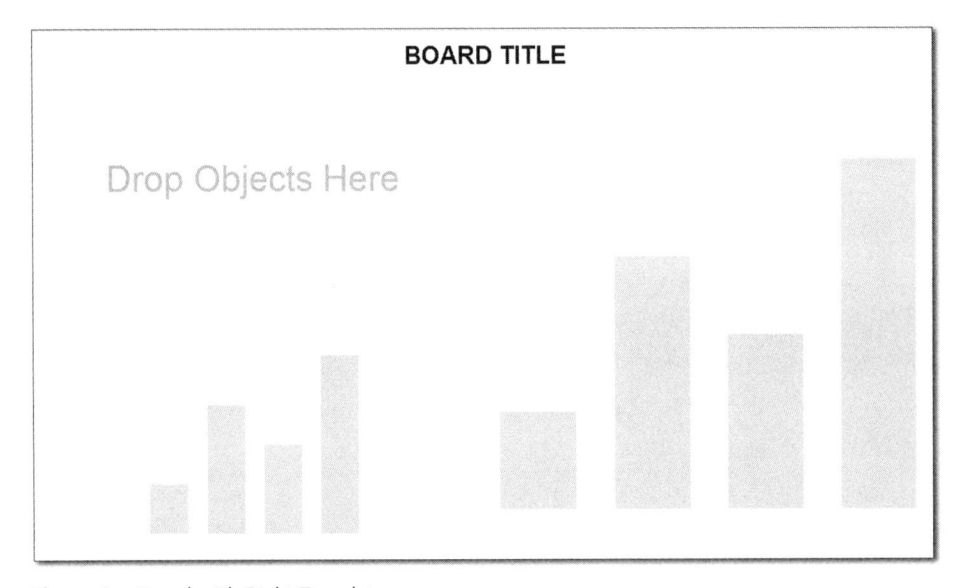

Figure 6.7 Board with Right Template

The layout uses placeholders or ghosts to organize the space, and although placeholders are symbolic (e.g., using chart outlines) you are not actually required to use a chart.

> **Slideshow**
>
> The one exception to this is the slideshow. A slideshow creates one page per visualization, placing one chart per page. It is the only layout that creates multiple pages and can be useful if you really want to create and share your story quickly with minimal effort.

Populating your board is also very simple (see Figure 6.8). To do so, perform the following steps:

1. Choose the type of entity from the left-hand side.
2. Select the entity, and drag it into a region or space on the board.
3. When you see a blue highlighted area, you can drop the entity onto the board.

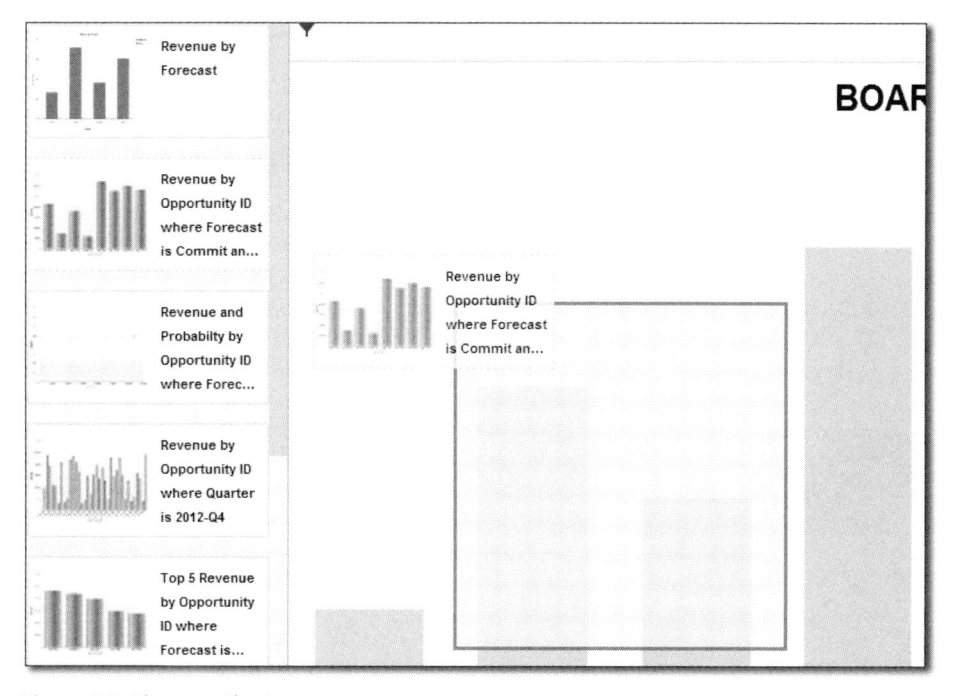

Figure 6.8 Placing a Chart

The blue area will tell you where the entity will be placed. You can place entities onto other entities in order to replace them or in any compass direction (north, south, east, or west) around an existing entity in order to create a new space beside the target entity.

Let's look at how to layout the boards in more detail.

6.5.1 Content Layout

The layout of a board is designed to be consistent across different screen sizes and devices. Each board takes 100% of its width and height and then lays out the proportions of the entities within it. Each entity takes 100% of the space allotted by default, but if you place another entity next to it then the page will create a new section, with the entities sharing the space equally (see Figure 6.9).

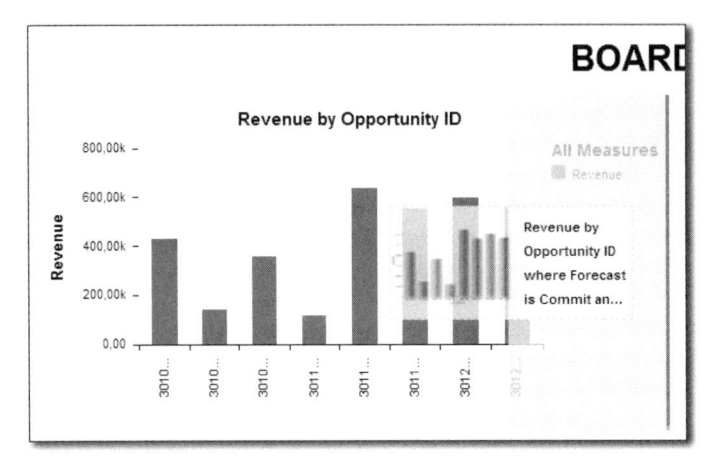

Figure 6.9 Creating a Section

Therefore, if we have an image and add another image next to it, then the result will resemble Figure 6.10.

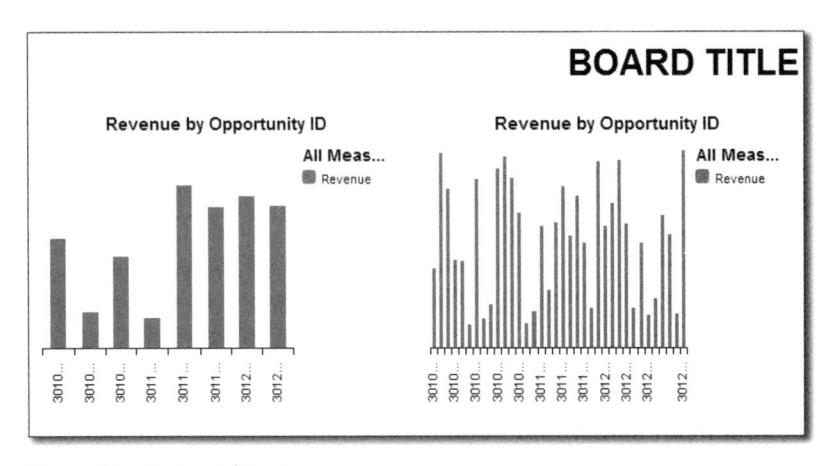

Figure 6.10 Horizontal Section

The new entity will by default take 50% of the previous space, resizing the previous resident in a vertical or horizontal direction depending on the location of the drop: horizontally, as shown in Figure 6.10, or vertically, as shown in Figure 6.11.

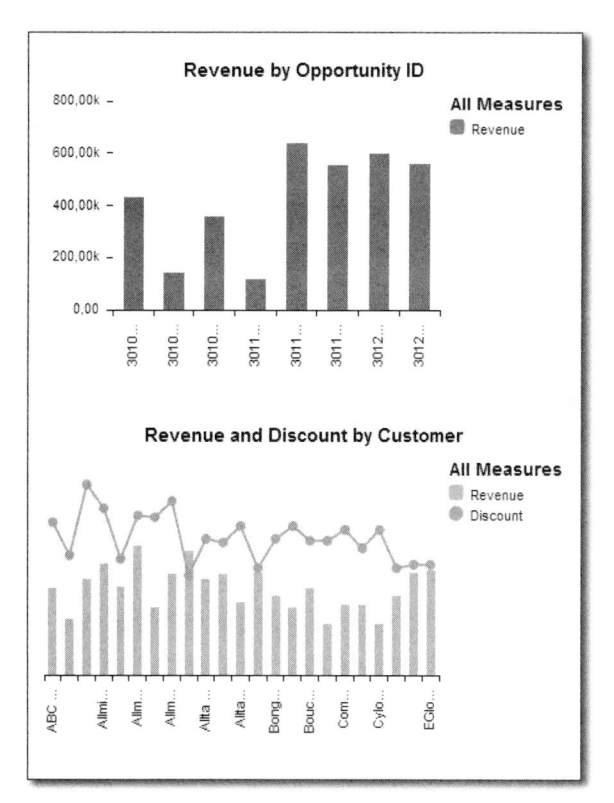

Figure 6.11 Vertical Alignment

Resizing

Entities in the canvas cannot be resized directly; they always take up 100% of their current space. Instead, spaces can be resized by selecting the region between two entities (see Figure 6.12).

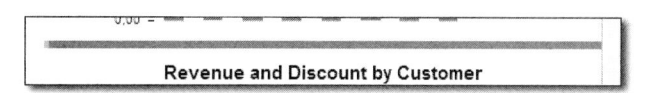

Figure 6.12 Resize Highlight Bar

By moving the separator up or down, you automatically assign more or less space to the entities that are separated. If you have a separation between multiple entities, then the adjustment is made for all of the entities. It can be a little frustrating to get exactly the structure that you want, because spaces are reorganized immediately. If you have a particular structure and delete an entity, then the layout will be reorganized rather than keeping your structure. We recommend that you get the layout right *before* committing to any customization of the entities themselves.

It's possible to move entities by selecting the MOVE icon. You can then place the entity just as you would any other by placing it on or next to another entity. The only real difference is that you will remove the previous entity.

Creating New Sections

As explained previously, we create new sections or areas by simply dropping entities in an area from the desired direction of an existing entity (see Figure 6.13).

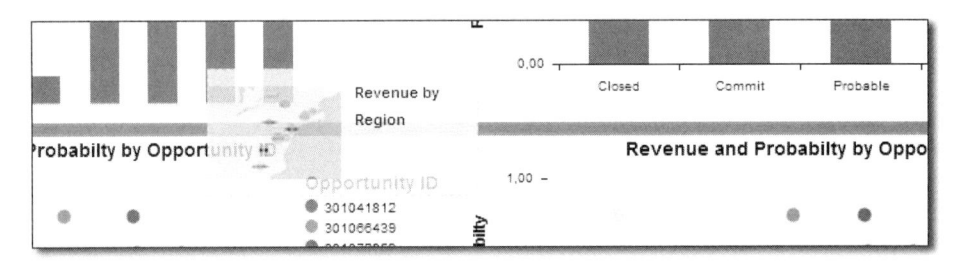

Figure 6.13 Creating a Section

In Figure 6.13, we can see that rather than dropping the entity in an area we are dropping it between two others in order to create a new section. The board layout is meant to be simple, consistent, and dynamic, adjusting as appropriate to the space provided.

6.5.2 Entity Actions

Each entity has some actions in the top-right corner. They can be deleted by selecting the small DELETE icon (an x in a circle; see Figure 6.14). Of the three actions, only DELETE and MOVE are available in the EDIT mode of stories.

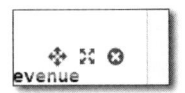

Figure 6.14 Entity Actions

Clicking the DELETE icon will remove the entity and its space, the opposite of a drop, and other entities will gain the associated space. The other icons allow you to move the entity and to zoom. ZOOM expands the selected item out to 100% of the screen (see Figure 6.15).

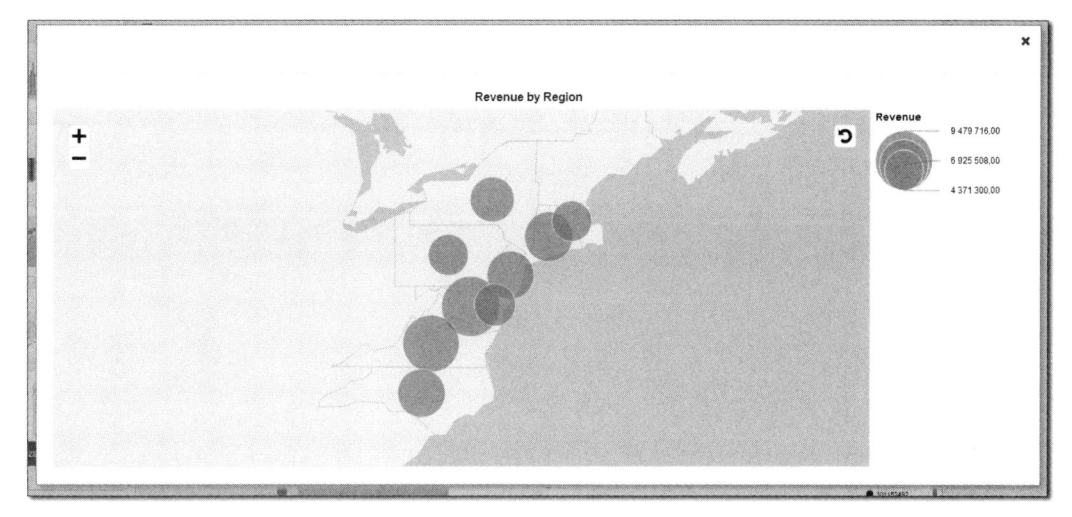

Figure 6.15 Chart in Zoom Mode

This can be useful if your chart is small, because it allows the user to view the chart in more detail. This action in available when viewing boards, not just when editing.

The MOVE icon allows you to move the entity somewhere else (see Figure 6.16).

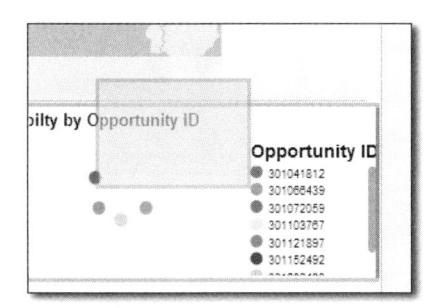

Figure 6.16 Move Mode

MOVE also works the same way as deleting and adding, but it can be more effective, because moving changes the structure of your story.

6.5.3 Page Settings

You can customize the boards via the settings on the right-hand side (see Figure 6.17).

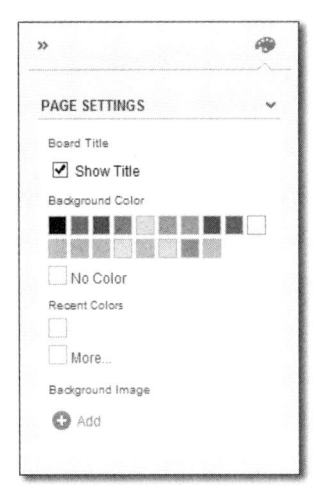

Figure 6.17 Page Settings

In the settings for the page, you can set the following items:

- SHOW TITLE
  Hides or shows the title.

- BACKGROUND COLOR
  Allows you to set the color for the entire page (see Figure 6.18).

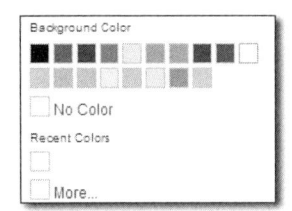

Figure 6.18 Color Settings

In Figure 6.18, we can see that the COLOR PICKER used for choosing colors in stories (each uses the same UI). The available options include the following:

- Choose from a list of basic colors.
- If you want to remove any color, select NO COLOR.

- A list of RECENT COLORS that you have used is available.
- In front of the current color is a MORE... checkbox that allows you to open a COLOR PICKER in which you can specify any color (see Figure 6.19).

Figure 6.19 Color Picker

- You can click on the gradient you want, enter the RGB values, or enter the Hex code directly (#). To close this dialog box and apply the change, click anywhere on screen. The COLOR PICKER is a common component used to select any color setting.
- You can also add a BACKGROUND IMAGE (see Figure 6.20).

Figure 6.20 Add Background Image

You can either load a file from your local disk or import from Fotolia. To use a local image, select IMPORT FROM LOCAL and find the image you want to use via the standard file selector. Fotolia is a third-party image library from which you can buy images for use in SAP Lumira. If you select this option, you will see a search dialog box (see Figure 6.21).

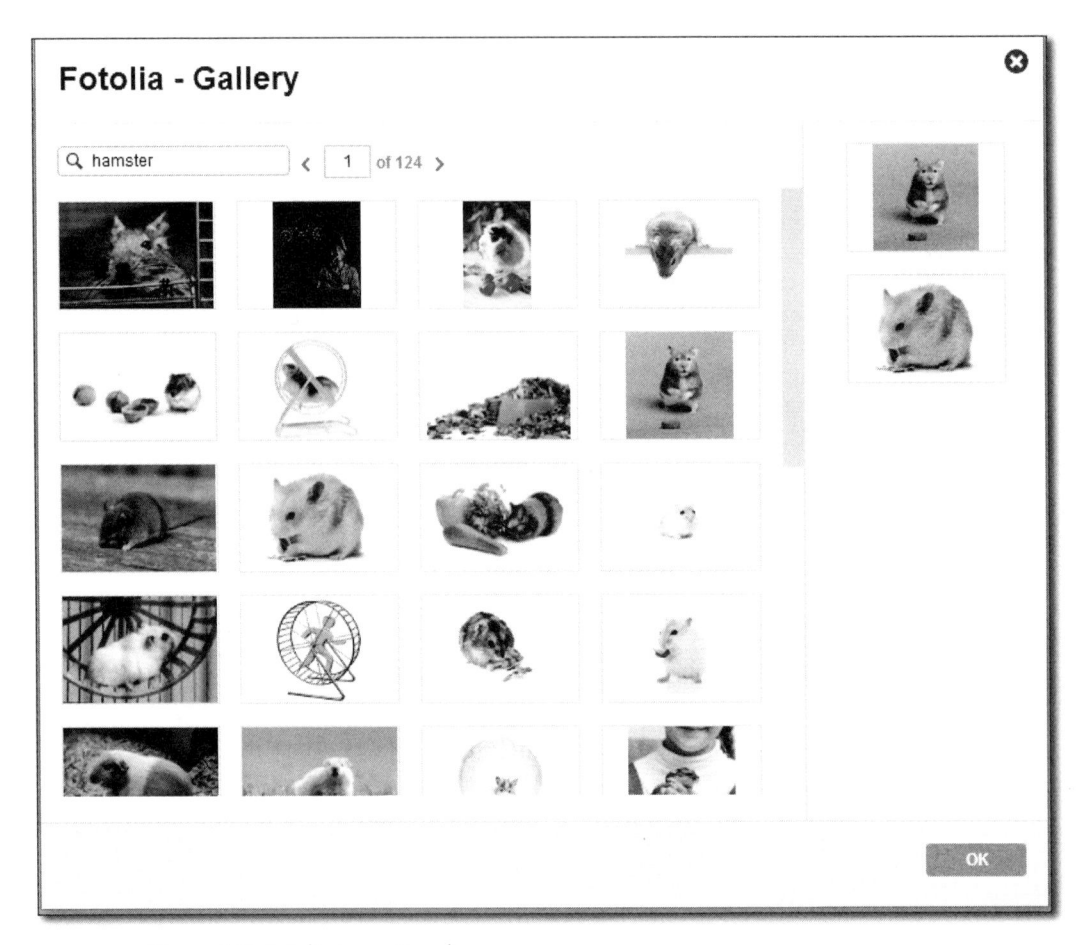

Figure 6.21 Fotolia Image Search

Type a term, and search for the images you want to use. Once you have selected the images you want, you will see them on the right. Click OK, and the image is placed in the background of your board.

Note, that now if you have added an image you can see "through" charts, because they are transparent by default. You will also see a new set of options for this image in the page settings (see OPACITY on the right in Figure 6.22). These settings allow you to remove the image and to adjust the opacity. This can be helpful if the image is quite intense and can increase the legibility of your charts.

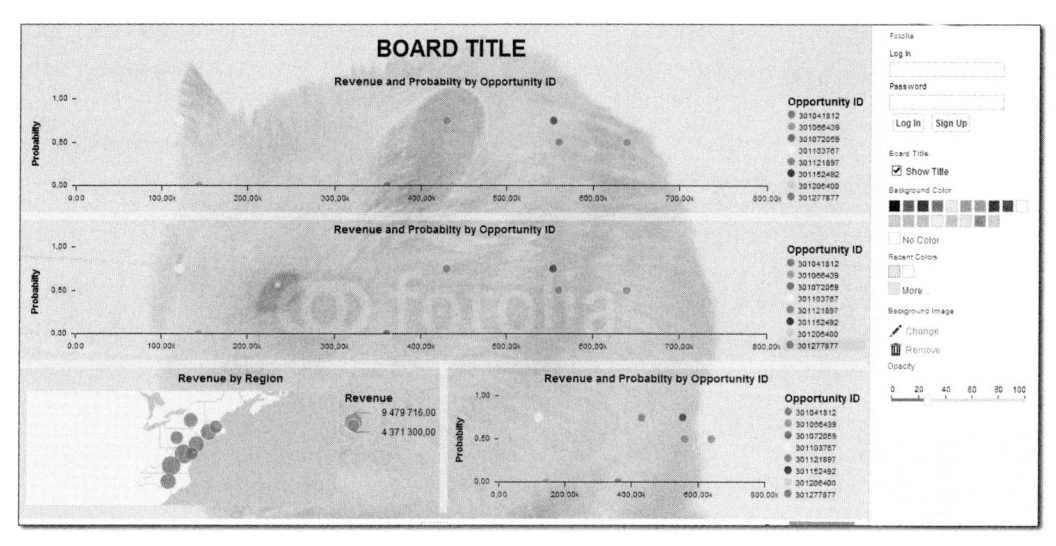

Figure 6.22 Reduced Opacity

Interactive boards provide a quick and simple way to share your results. If you want something more elaborate, then you can try infographics, which allow for a greater level of control in layout and design.

6.6   Infographics

Infographics convey messages with charts, infocharts, pictograms, shapes, and text in SAP Lumira and provide a greater level of control in layout and design.

To create a new infographic, select the second entry in the NEW STORY or PAGE dialog box (see Figure 6.23).

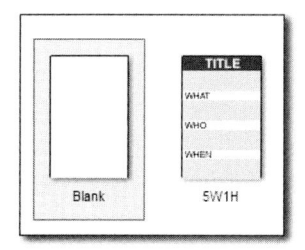

Figure 6.23 Infographic Template

As with interactive boards, the layout is a template that can help you structure your content, but it's a guide and not a strict constraint. The current template provided, 5W1H, is a relatively standard model that is often used in journalism and research.

This template gives you an idea of what infographics are trying to achieve: creating a persuasive argument, not an executive dashboard.

In the sections ahead, we will discuss the infographic layout and how it differs from other layouts in SAP Lumira. Then we will explore the different entity organization, structuring, and actions that can be used. Finally, we will look at our ability to restructure through page settings and section positioning and then use the special refresh data option to prepare our creation for previewing.

6.6.1 Infographic Layout

The infographic layout is very different from the interactive board layout, because it allows you to create pixel-perfect layouts:

- Entities are resizable and do not take 100% of their space. You can resize each entity to any size you like.
- Entities can be layered—that is, placed on top of each other—in contrast to interactive boards that only allow one entity per space.
- Pages can grow and can thus take up more space than is visible on screen. You can and will probably need to scroll to see all of the content.

To place an entity on the canvas, the process is the same: you drag and drop from the ENTITY PICKER onto the canvas. As with interactive boards, you create sections, but with infographics you can create sections with different orientations.

You can create multiple sections by dropping entities next to existing sections, and in this respect it's similar to the creation of sections in interactive boards (see Figure 6.24).

Unlike for interactive boards, you will create another section that is the same size as the other section. If you create multiple sections like this, then the page will grow to accommodate them rather than resizing the existing entities; infographics are not constrained to the screen space and will grow vertically to accommodate new entities.

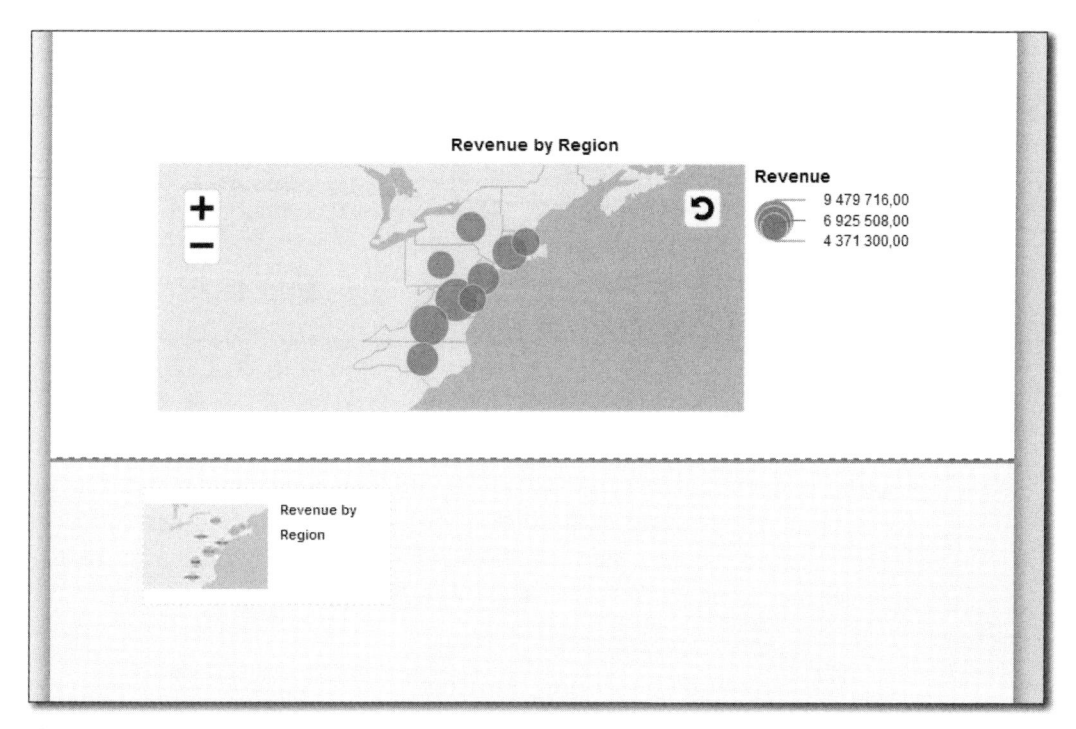

Figure 6.24 Create a Section

The main difference, though, is that you can place and align multiple entities in a single section.

6.6.2 Organizing Entities

It is possible to group entities in a single space; this is unique to the infographic layout. When you drop entities on to others, you do not replace existing entities, as with interactive boards, but you instead stack the entities (see Figure 6.25).

Here we can see some text on top of the chart (for example, in interactive boards this would have required a REPLACE action), and this text can be resized, edited, and moved.

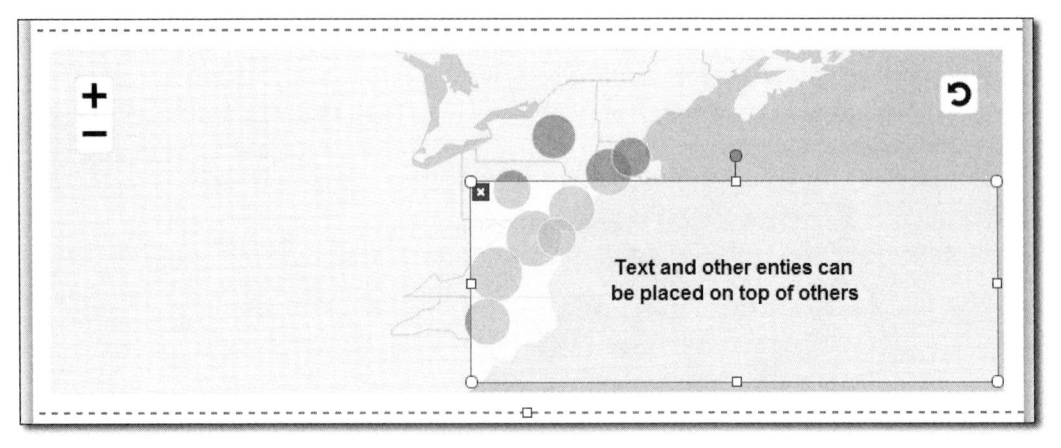

Figure 6.25 Overlapping Entities

These two entities are now part of a single area and can be treated slightly differently. This is an important feature for infographics, because it means that you can place multiple entities over each other in order to annotate and describe your data. For example, you can place additional text over a chart in order to create a custom label.

6.6.3 Resizing and Positioning Entities

Entities can be resized and positioned exactly where you like. Once placed, you will see that there are eight compass points on the box enclosing the entity (see Figure 6.26).

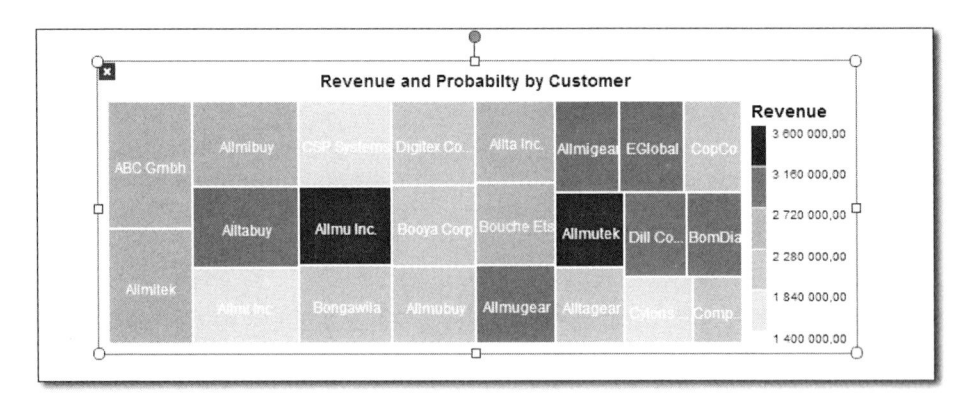

Figure 6.26 Customizing an Entity

Selecting any one of these points and dragging it will automatically resize the entity accordingly. To move or place the entity, first select it and then drag and drop. The "lollipop" on top allows you to rotate the entity. Using these controls allows you to precisely position and organize your layout.

6.6.4 Entity Actions

Although we will look at the customization of entities later in the chapter, here we will show you how to use the ordering of actions to achieve the correct effect. The ACTIONS panel is on the right-hand side of the Compose room and appears whenever you select an entity in an infographic (see Figure 6.27).

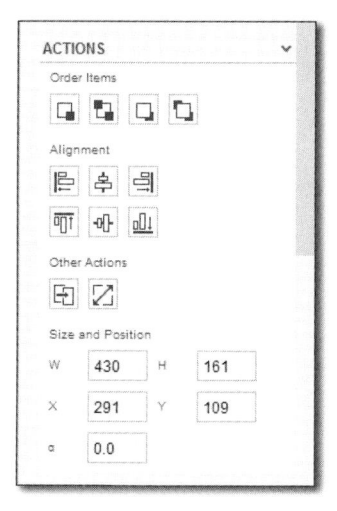

Figure 6.27 Entity Editing Options

The following actions are available for editing entities or a set of entities and are related to size and position:

- ORDER ITEMS
    - SEND BACKWARD: This will send your item to the back. Think of items as being in a stack; each time you add another entity you are adding it to the top of the stack. Visually, items will be viewable in order (see Figure 6.28).
    - SEND TO BACK: This is subtly different; it sends an entity to the very back of the stack.

- **BRING FORWARD**: This is the opposite of send backward; it brings an entity forward one spot in the stack.
- **BRING TO FRONT**: This brings any entity to the top of the visual stack.

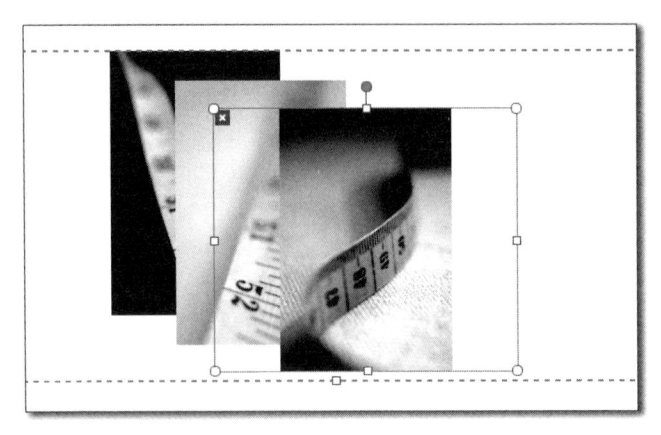

Figure 6.28 Stack Order

In Figure 6.28, the image selected is on top of the stack and if we push it back (send backward) it will appear behind the second image (see Figure 6.29).

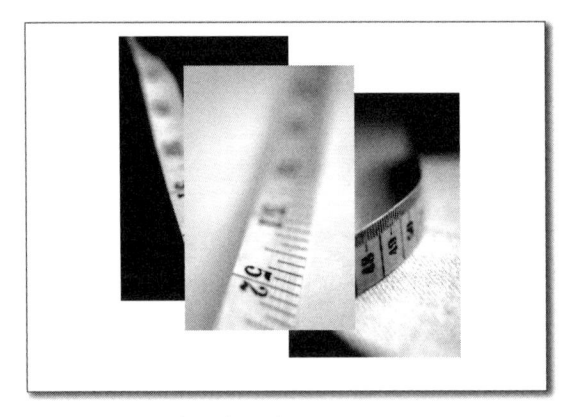

Figure 6.29 Send Backward

- **ALIGNMENT**
  There are five different options for alignment:
  - **LEFT**: This will move to the left of the section and CENTER, RIGHT, TOP, and BOTTOM do the equivalent in their respective directions.

- OTHER ACTIONS
    - DUPLICATE: This option makes an exact copy of the selected entity. The new entity is always on top of the previous one, so you won't see the effect immediately.
    - EXPAND: This useful option lets you force an entity to change size such that it takes up 100% of its current section. This is a lot easier than fiddling with resizing an entity manually.
- SIZE AND POSITION
Because infographics allow you to position your entities exactly as you want, you can also specify the position and size as well as rotation:
    - W: The width in pixels
    - H: The height in pixels
    - X: The x location starting from the top left
    - Y: The y location starting from the top left
    - DEGREE: You can rotate the entity, but it must fit into the space provided, so if the rotation puts a part of the entity outside of the canvas, then the rotation will not be applied (see Figure 6.30).

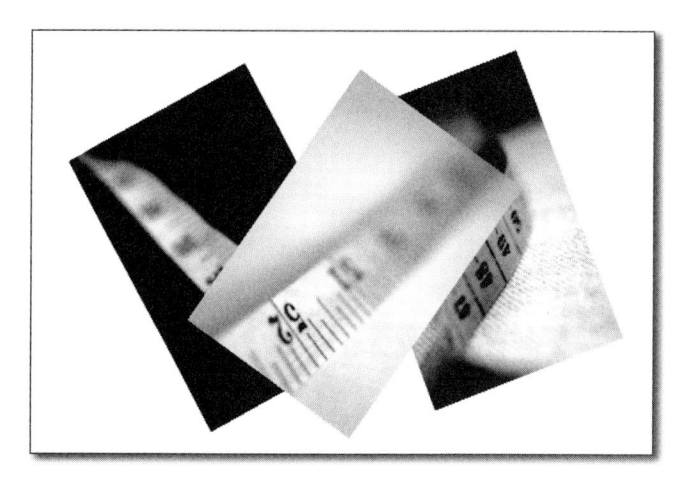

Figure 6.30 Rotating Images

Chart actions allow you a finer level of control over the layout, allowing pixel-perfect positioning and even rotation.

6.6.5 Moving Sections

Sections can be moved and reordered by using the small tab on the left-hand side. You can thus move multiple entities in a single section up or down (this action does not work for vertical sections; see Figure 6.31).

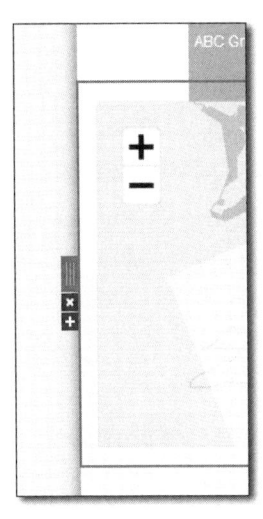

Figure 6.31 Moving Sections in Infographics

The small tab also allows you to delete the entire section and to create a new section below the current one (use the PLUS and DELETE icons respectively).

6.6.6 Page Settings

To see the page properties, you need to select the SLIDE tab (see Figure 6.32).

Figure 6.32 Slide Tab

This tab gives you access to the page settings, although you can only change the color here.

6.6.7 Refresh Data

Infographics have an important feature called REFRESH DATA, which is specific to infographics because the charts are not "live," meaning that once an update to the dataset is set it will not be immediately visible in an infographic (see Figure 6.33).

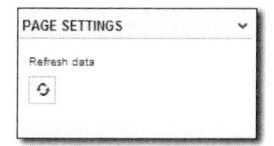

Figure 6.33 Refresh Data Option

Let's look at an example. First, imagine a simple dataset (see Figure 6.34).

Figure 6.34 Simple Dataset

This data can be used to create a bar chart that we can then use in our infographic (see Figure 6.35). Note, that we have added some overlapping text to describe the result.

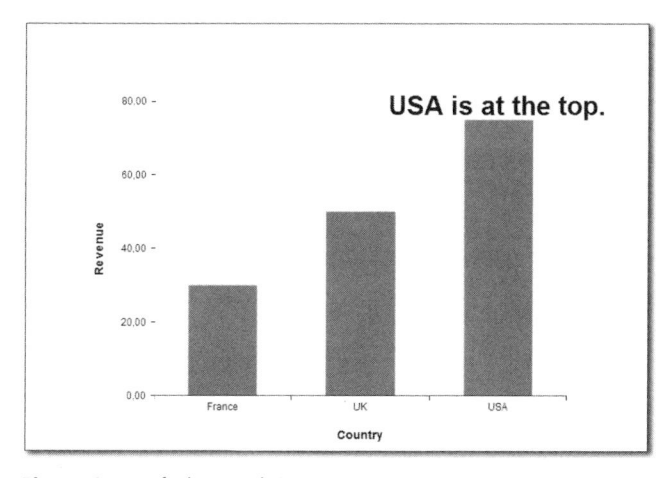

Figure 6.35 Infochart with Text

Note, that the text is not a title but an overlapping text entity that is positioned carefully above the winning column. If our data changes, then our chart will change (see Figure 6.36).

USA	41
China	65
France	89
UK	156

Figure 6.36 Data Changes

We can see that if the chart reflects this change it will "break" the chart. The comment is both wrong and no longer carefully positioned (see Figure 6.37).

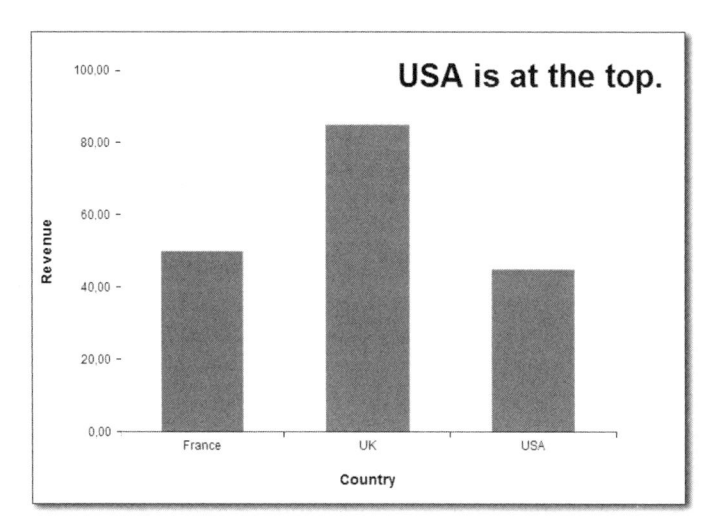

Figure 6.37 Outdated Label

Visualizations are always "live" in that the view is not saved: the query behind the chart is always re-executed each time. Because infographics allow you to create pixel perfect designs, changes in data can change both the physical structure and possibly the sense of your argument. For this reason, the explicit REFRESH DATA action gives the author the ability to verify data changes before updating a story.

6.6.8 Preview

After verifying the data and physical structure of your argument, you will want to preview your creation. Infographics are feature rich in comparison to interactive boards and reports, and because of this there is one additional change in the Compose room. If the page you are previewing is an infographic, then in PREVIEW mode you will see some additional options (see Figure 6.38).

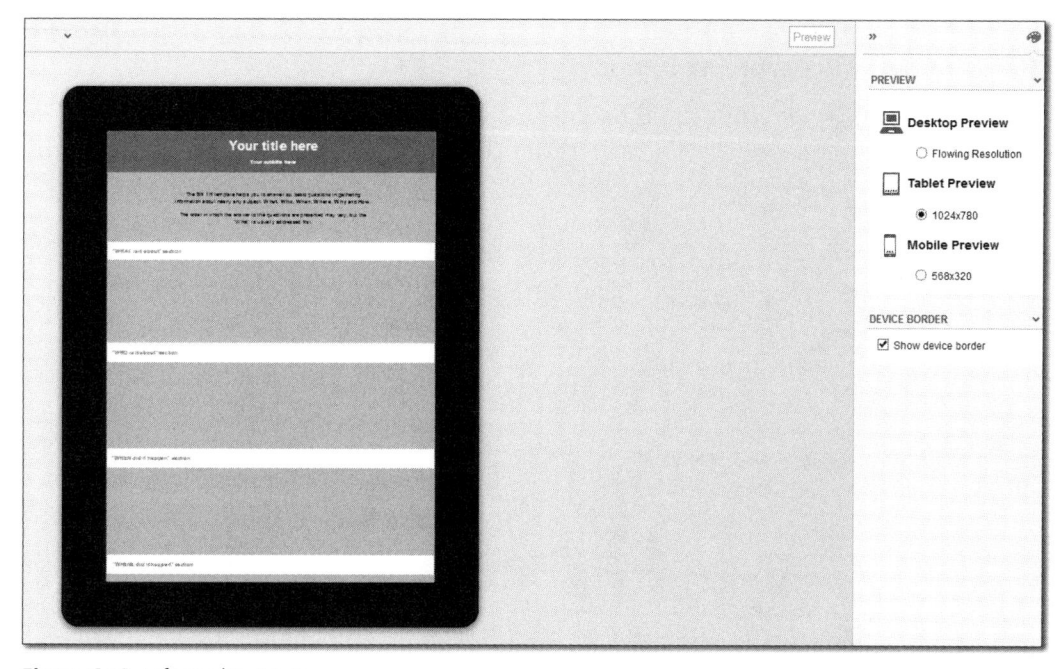

Figure 6.38 Infographic Preview

This PREVIEW mode simulates how infographics will respond to different screen sizes. This is less applicable to interactive boards and reports, because their respective layouts do not change with the screen size, or rather they always adjust to fill 100% of the screen for interactive boards or 100% of the width for reports (you can choose to hide the device border with SHOW DEVICE BORDER).

6.7 Reports

Reports are somewhere between infographics and interactive boards; they allow for interaction with controls as you "grow" the size of the page. However, the differentiating feature is their ability to navigate via sections. Reports are the last option in the NEW STORY/PAGE dialog box. The only template option for report is BLANK. Again, the layout model is different from that of interactive boards or infographics.

Ahead, we will discuss these layout differences and how a report utilizes tables in its design.

6.7.1 Report Flow Layout

Layouts in reporting are different from layouts in other areas in that you place entities on the canvas to create rows. The rows take the size of the largest entity in the row (see Figure 6.39).

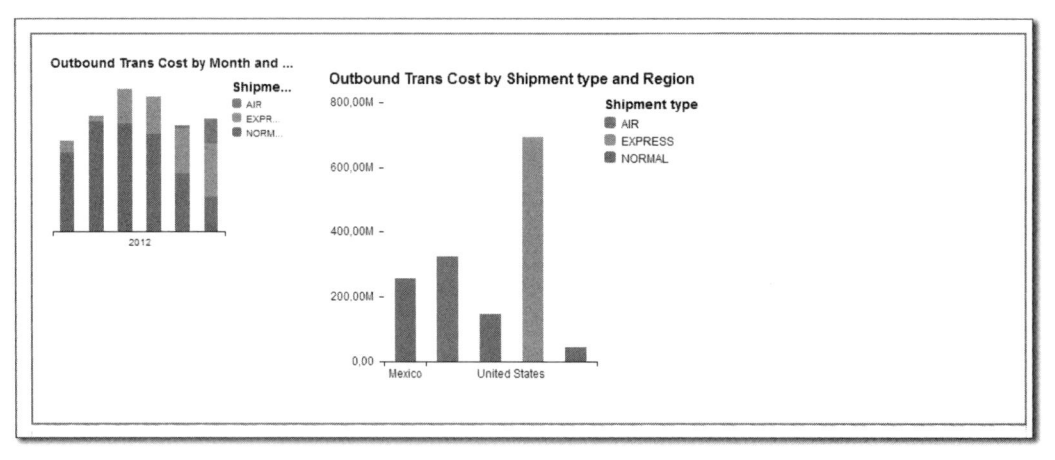

Figure 6.39 A Row in a Report

Our first entity is bigger than the second, and this dictates the height of the row. Entities are auto-arranged: as you add more they are either placed in the row or, if the total width is too large, underneath (see Figure 6.40).

Resizing of entities is possible; as with infographics you click and drag on the corner to resize. Entities will remain in the row, but the row will readjust itself. Note, that you cannot precisely position entities within a row as you can with infographics.

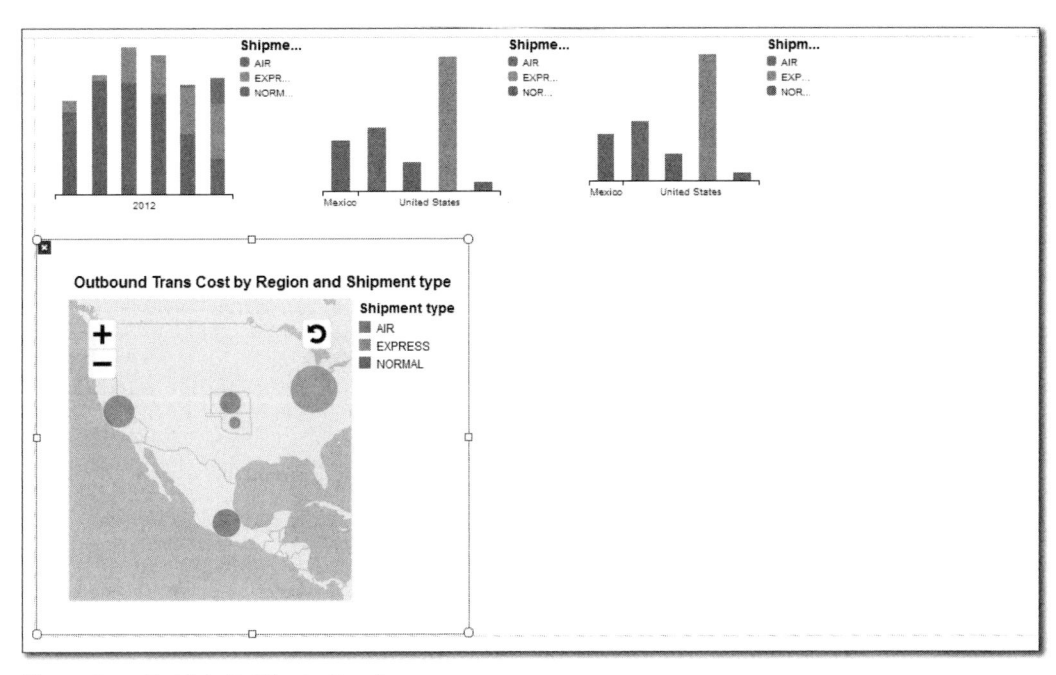

Figure 6.40 Multiple Entities in One Row

To create a new row, you place an entity under an existing row (see Figure 6.41).

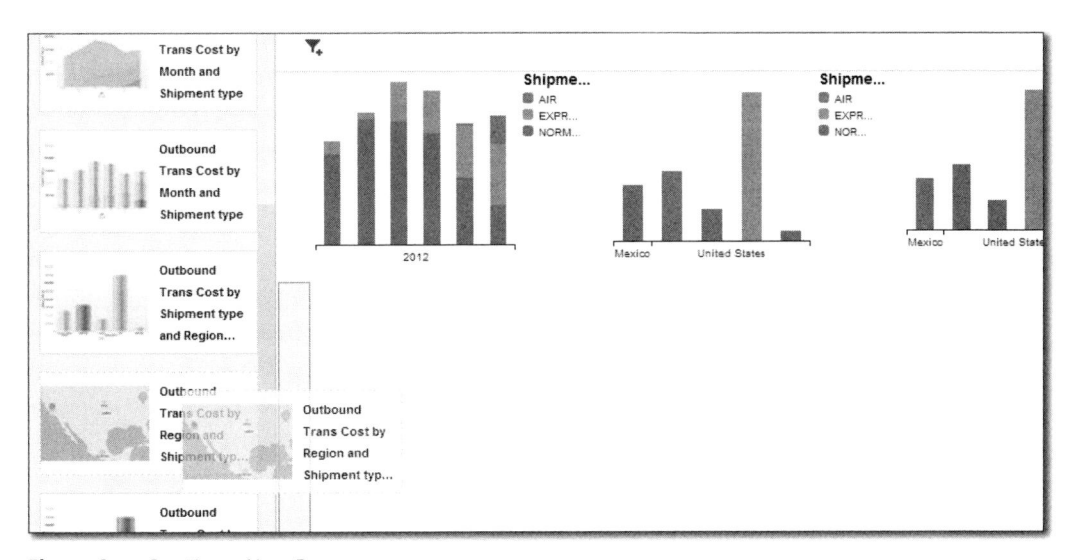

Figure 6.41 Creating a New Row

As with infographics, reports can grow vertically as more sections are added.

6.7.2 Using Tables in Reports

Reports are designed around tables, so the layout treats tables in a quite specific way. Tables are not resized but remain at full size; the report grows vertically to accommodate the table rather than fitting them into a row as in other visualizations (see Figure 6.42).

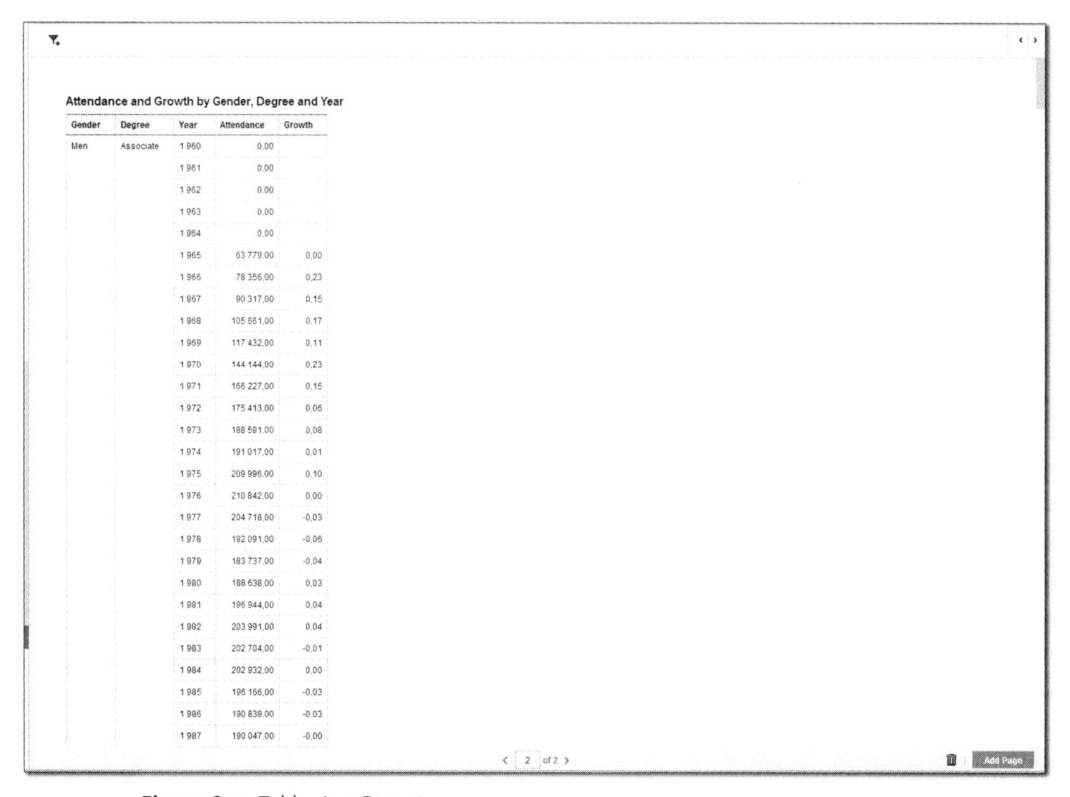

Figure 6.42 Tables in a Report

The idea is that you can then use the controls and section navigation to move through the values. This will filter the table accordingly.

We have looked briefly at the different layouts and how they can be used to position entities. Now we will look at the different entities that are available in the Compose room.

6.8 Customizing Entities

Let's look in detail at the different types of entity that can be used in stories and how they can be customized. Note, that some layouts support different sets of entities:

- **Visualizations:** Supported by all, but pay attention to infocharts (see further discussion ahead)
- **Texts:** Supported by all
- **Pictures:** Supported by all
- **Input controls:** Only boards and reports can use controls, and there are differences in behavior between the two
- **Pictograms:** Only for reports and infographics
- **Shapes:** Only for reports and infographics

Once placed in a story, entities can be customized. Typically, these customizations are contextual—that is, specific to the type of entity used. These settings are covered in detail ahead.

6.8.1 Visualizations

Visualizations are probably, if not certainly, the key entity type, because they represent the link between your story and your data. Once placed on an interactive board, you will see that on selection a new set of properties is available on the right (see Figure 6.43).

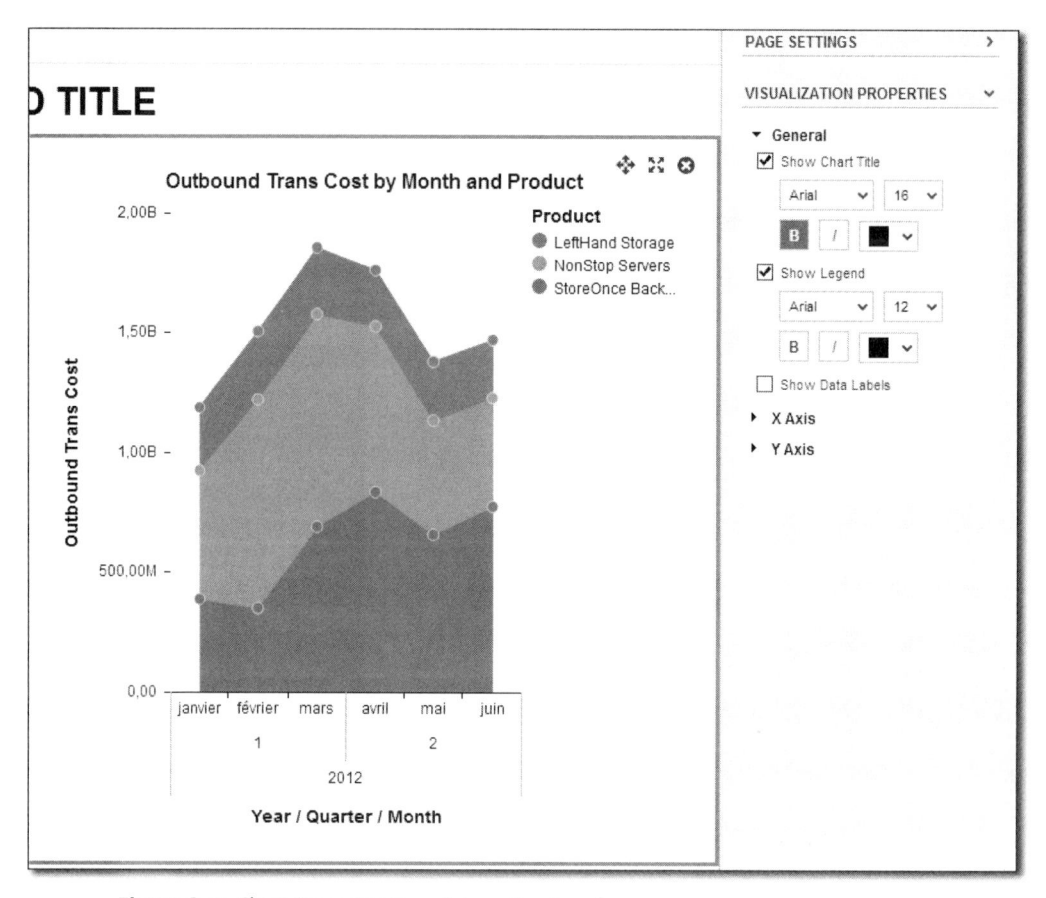

Figure 6.43 Chart Properties in an Interactive Board

You can customize charts by selecting the chart in your interactive board or report and then using the property editor on the right (see Figure 6.44).

Chart properties are quite straightforward; for each visual entity you can show or hide the feature, and you can change the font and style of text:

- SHOW TITLE: Show or hide the chart title
- SHOW LEGEND: Show or hide the legend on the right-hand side of a chart
- SHOW DATA LABELS: Show or hide the data values for each region of a chart

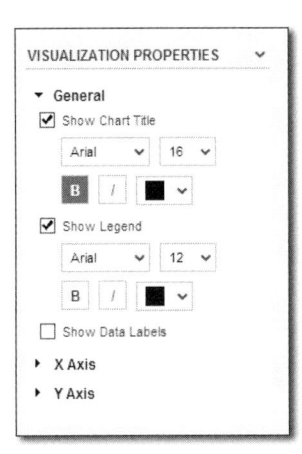

Figure 6.44 Visualization Properties

The axis customizations will depend on the type of chart you are using. For each available axis, you will have the option to hide the axis title and label and/or customize the text (see Figure 6.45).

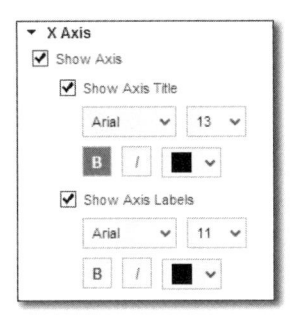

Figure 6.45 Axis Settings

The axis settings are as follows:

- SHOW AXIS: Show or remove the axis
- SHOW AXIS TITLE: Show or hide the title of the axis (the object used)
- SHOW AXIS LABELS: Show or hide the value labels and tick marks

The related font settings are as follows:

- FONT SELECTOR: Pick from the available list of fonts
- FONT SIZE: Pick the font size to use (8 to 28)
- BOLD: Sets the font in bold
- ITALIC: Sets the font in italics
- FONT COLOR: Sets the font color; the COLOR PICKER is the same as in other areas. These settings allow you to alter the visual appearance of your charts, but there is one warning to keep in mind.

> **Chart Customization Warning**
>
> Charts are reference copies, meaning that each time you use a chart in a layout you reference the source chart, but each customization is specific to the layout in which it's used. The customized chart is not shared (see Figure 6.46).
>
> If you delete the source chart, you will also delete all of the references and will lose your customizations.

This is easily demonstrated by creating a simple visualization and placing it twice into a board (see Figure 6.46).

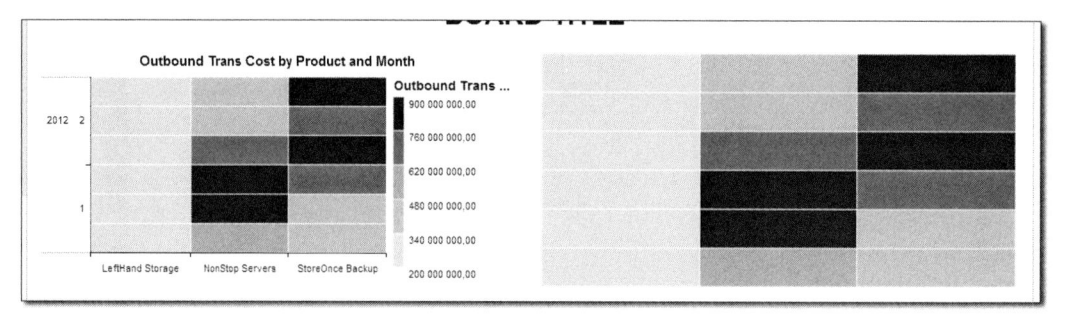

Figure 6.46 Duplicated Chart

Both charts have the same origin, but they look very different. On the right, we removed all details of the chart (legends, title, etc.). As per the warning, deleting the source chart will delete both of the charts.

6.8.2 Infocharts

Infocharts are a special type of visualization that are used only in infographics. To create an infochart, you need to choose one of the following basic chart types:

- Column or bar chart
- Donut
- Line charts
- Numeri points

By dropping one of these onto an infographic, and only an infographic, you will create an infochart. Infocharts have a different type of property editor, which we will see for each infochart, because these properties are specific to each type.

Donut Charts

Donut—but not pie—charts have a number of different customizations. To view these settings, add a donut to an infographic, and use the properties on the right as with any other chart (see Figure 6.47).

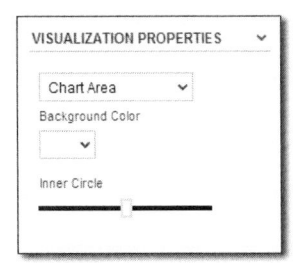

Figure 6.47 Donut Infochart Settings

Each setting available for customization is accessible via the first dropdown (see Figure 6.48).

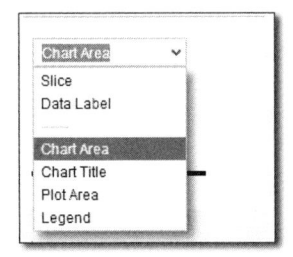

Figure 6.48 Donut Properties

These settings include the following:

- SLICE
  Allows you to highlight a particular section by concatenating the others. Select a slice, and then select the slice menu (see Figure 6.49).

Figure 6.49 Slice Settings

Once selected, you can highlight the slice, which has the effect of graying out the other slices and coloring in the slice. By default, it will also place the slice's value in the center as a label (see Figure 6.50).

You can customize the slice further:

- SHOW NAME: Either shows or hides the slice's name in the center of the donut.
- SHOW PERCENTAGE: Shows or hides the value (note that in this type of infochart the value is always seen as a percentage).

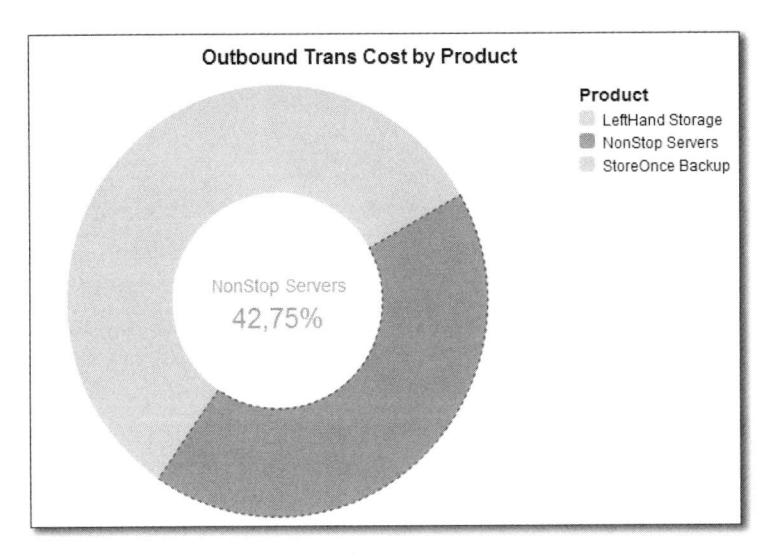

Figure 6.50 Donut with Custom Slice

- DATA LABEL
  Shows or hides the data label. If you are highlighting a slice, then the label is only shown for the slice.

- CHART AREA
  Allows you to set the background color and also to modify the inner circle diameter (see Figure 6.51).

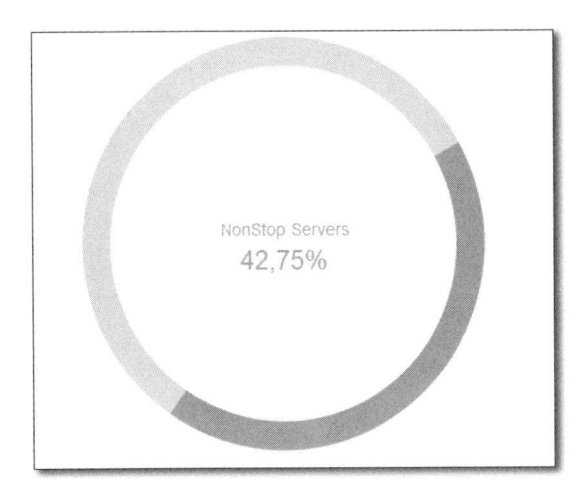

Figure 6.51 Donut with Large Inner Circle

- CHART TITLE
  Allows you to hide and show the title or set the text settings.
- PLOT AREA
  Sets the background color.
- LEGEND
  Shows or hides the legend.

Donut charts are relatively simple, but by changing a few settings you can create an interesting infochart that allows you to focus attention on one clear value.

Bar and Column Charts

Bar charts have a number of customizations, including the ability replace the bars with pictograms. As before, place a bar chart in an infographic to access the menu (see Figure 6.52).

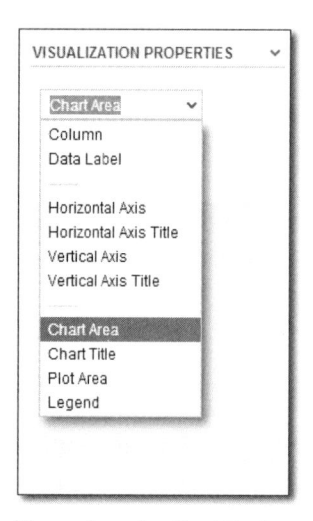

Figure 6.52 Bar Chart Settings

We will go through the settings in turn:

- COLUMN
  You can now put pictograms to use by replacing the default bars with pictograms (see Figure 6.53).

Figure 6.53 Column Pictogram Selector

Your chart will then use the pictogram, scaling and sizing it to represent the value like any other bar (see Figure 6.54).

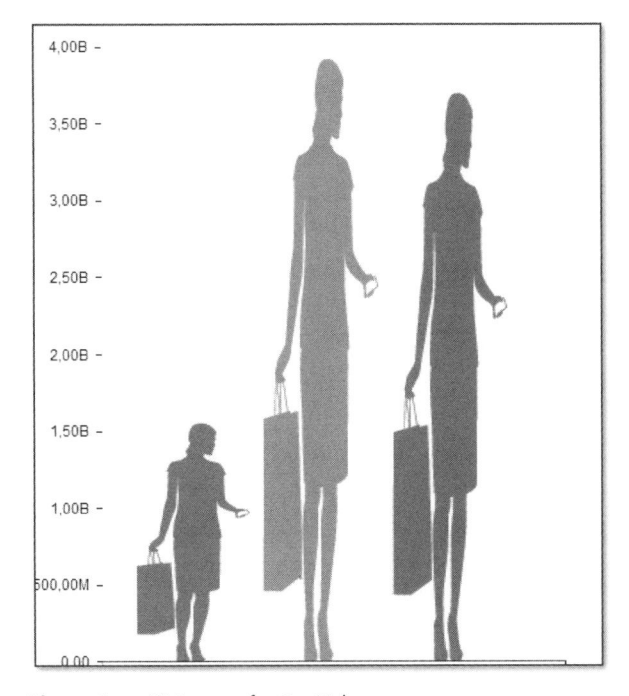

Figure 6.54 Pictogram for Bar Values

- DATA LABEL
  You can show or hide the data label, but you can also replace it with an image.
- HORIZONTAL AXIS
  The additional setting here allows you to use images for the labels as you would data labels.
- HORIZONTAL AXIS TITLE
  As with any other title, you can show or hide and customize the font of this title.
- VERTICAL AXIS
- VERTICAL AXIS TITLE
  See HORIZONTAL AXIS TITLE.
- CHART AREA
  You can set the background color.
- CHART TITLE
  See HORIZONTAL AXIS TITLE.
- PLOT AREA
  You can set the plot area color, but you can also add or remove the gridlines. If you select the gridlines, then you can set the width and the color of those lines.
- LEGEND
  You can show or hide both the legend and the legend title.

By playing with these settings, you can create some interesting effects.

Numeri Points

Numeri points are modifiable for all interactive board types. Because numeri points are a very simple type of chart, the settings to format the value are interesting (see Figure 6.55):

- VALUE: Allows you to set the text settings.
- DECIMAL PLACES: Same as the number formatting.

Customizing Entities | **6.8**

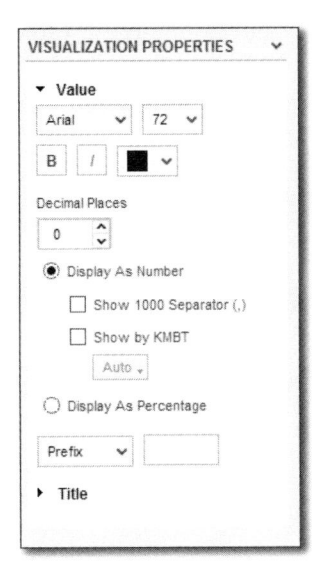

Figure 6.55 Numeri Point Settings

- DISPLAY AS A NUMBER: You can use these settings to convert the raw number into an indicator:

    - The 1000 SEPARATOR acts like a decimal point.

    KMBT allows you to auto-format your number into a value that is rounded to thousands, millions, and so on, using a character to represent the division. Look at Figure 6.56, where you will see the same value in billions (B), millions (M) or thousands (K).

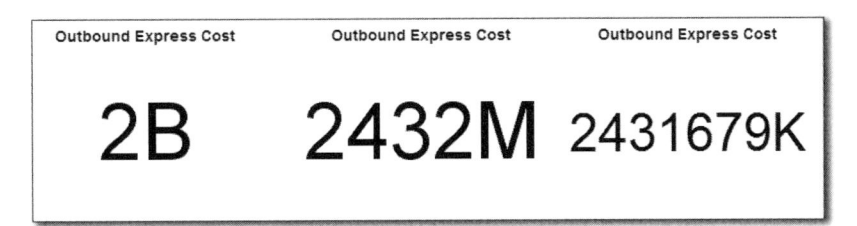

Figure 6.56 Formatted Numeri Points

325

- PREFIX: Allows you to add a three-character prefix to your point. These three characters can also be appended as a suffix. You might use this if you want to describe your value as a quantity (see Figure 6.57)—for example, a power output in kilowatts per hour (kWhk).

2431679400kWh

Figure 6.57 Numieri Point with Suffix

- TITLE: Allows you to customize the font and the location (top or bottom).

Line Charts

The last infochart is the line chart; the settings for a line chart are shown in Figure 6.58 and are as follows:

- MARKER: Allows you to set a pictogram and its color and size for each point. If you want giant orange mugs, for example, it's possible (see Figure 6.59).
- DATA LABEL: Allows you to show or hide the label.
- LINE: You can change the color, the thickness, and the line style (normal or different levels of dots/dashes).
- HORIZONTAL AXIS: You can use images for the labels as you would data labels.
- HORIZONTAL AXIS TITLE: As with any other title, you can show or hide the title and customize the font.
- VERTICAL AXIS: You can choose to hide the line and ticker of the axis as well as the labels.
- VERTICAL AXIS TITLE: See HORIZONTAL AXIS TITLE.
- CHART AREA: Set the background color.
- CHART TITLE: Show or hide the title and determine text settings.
- PLOT AREA: Sets the color and gridline.
- LEGEND: Show or hide both the legend and the legend title.

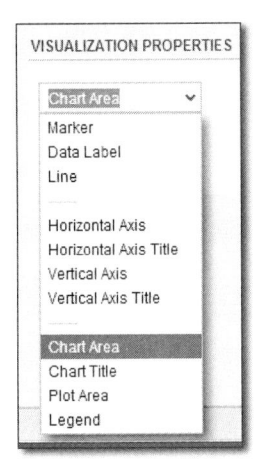

Figure 6.58 Line Chart Settings

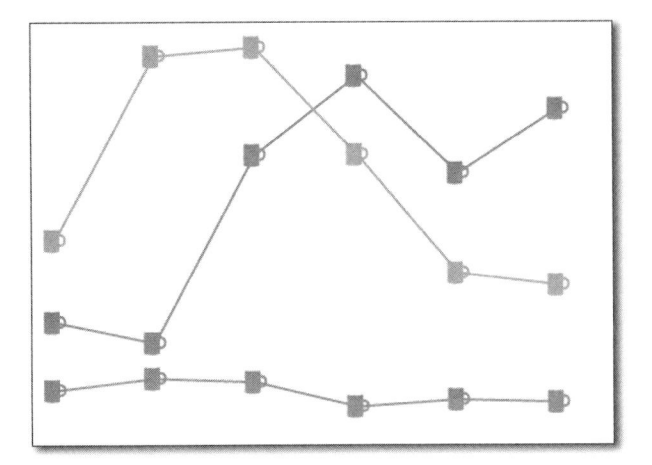

Figure 6.59 Line Chart wih Pictograms

Infocharts are a very different type of chart that allows you to customize your infographics further, so infographics are not treated the same way as interactive boards and reports.

6.8.3 Text

Text is largely the same in all of the layouts. You can add text and then customize the font, style, and color by using the properties editor (see Figure 6.60):

- FONT: Here you will find the standard font settings: size, type and color. In addition, there are extra styles: bold, italic, underline, or strikethrough.
- PARAGRAPH: Sets the orientation of the text:
  - Left, right, center, or justify
  - Top, middle, or bottom
- LISTS: You can use bulleted or numbered lists.
- BACKGROUND COLOR: Works as any other COLOR PICKER and sets the text color.

Text can be used in any of the layouts.

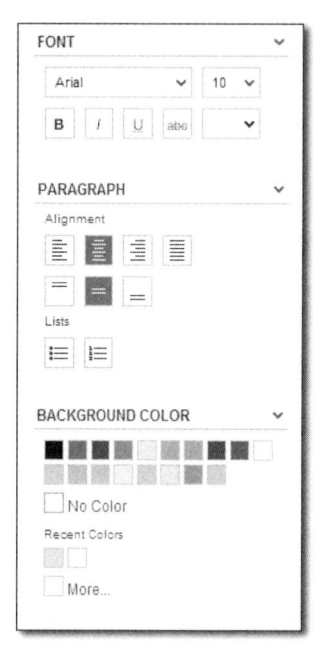

Figure 6.60 Text Settings

6.8.4 Images

As we have seen, you can add background images to interactive boards, but you can also add images as entities to all of the layouts. Select PICTURES from the ENTITY PICKER and then select the PLUS icon (see Figure 6.61).

Figure 6.61 Adding an Image

Adding an image follows the same process as adding background images: upload a local image or select one from Fotolia. Once an image is added, it appears in the gallery as a thumbnail. SAP Lumira retains this reference thumbnail so that you can use these images across different stories and documents. You add an image like any other entity (drag and drop).

Note that an image placed in a story is not a reference but is actually the image itself (a binary representation is persisted in the story). This is to ensure that the story can be published correctly, because a link to a file on your desktop cannot be maintained. This link can be removed by clicking the delete icon in the top-right corner of the thumbnail.

> **Image Size**
>
> Be careful about image size. SAP Lumira can scale images, but it does not try to reduce the quality of the image, so a 3 MB image, even if it's displayed as a tiny company logo, will still be 3 MB in the story.

Image properties relate to their placement within their space. Images may have a specific size, but the area that they are placed in might be quite different. SAP Lumira thus offers several different types of arrangement for your images (see Figure 6.62).

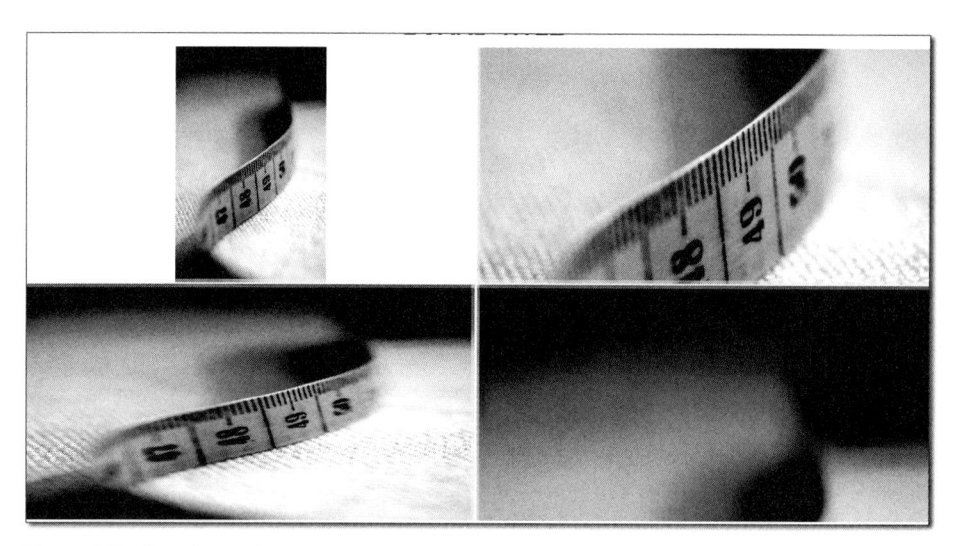

Figure 6.62 Four Image Settings

There are four styles you can apply, and your choice will really depend on the type of image, and the effect you want to achieve:

- CONTAIN
  Ensures that your image retains its original proportions within the space. This might mean that there is free space around the image.
- COVER
  Fixes the horizontal size but adjusts the vertical to keep the correct proportions. This means that there is no spare space, but you might lose some of the image.
- STRETCHED
  Stretches the image to fit 100% of the vertical and horizontal space.
- PAN
  The opposite of cover, this setting keeps the vertical size but adjusts the horizontal.

Finally, you can change your view of the images with the ▪ ▦ ▩ control, which sets the different tile sizes.

6.8.5 Pictograms

Pictograms are distinctive icons that represent a concept or idea. They are made using SVG and have the property of also being reusable in infocharts. You can add new pictograms into your list as you would images, but your pictogram must be an SVG file. There are only two settings for pictograms (see Figure 6.63).

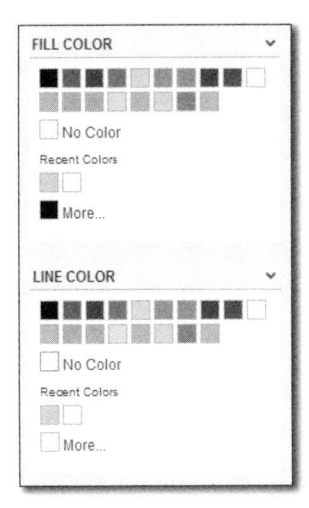

Figure 6.63 Pictogram Settings

The two properties for pictograms allow you to set the FILL COLOR and the LINE COLOR (by default they are black silhouettes). In Figure 6.64 we see how the use of FILL COLOR and LINE COLOR create the pictogram below.

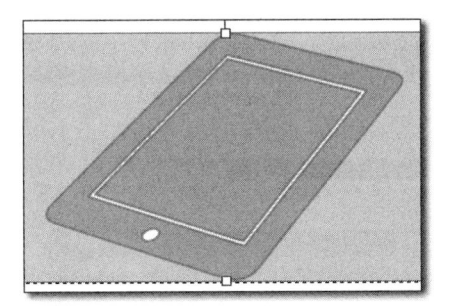

Figure 6.64 Customized Pictogram

The interesting feature of pictograms is that they can be used in infocharts. They can also be placed into infographics and reports, similar to images.

6.8.6 Shapes

Shapes are really just basic geometric pictograms that you can use to connect and annotate your infographics. Like pictograms, they have few settings (see Figure 6.65).

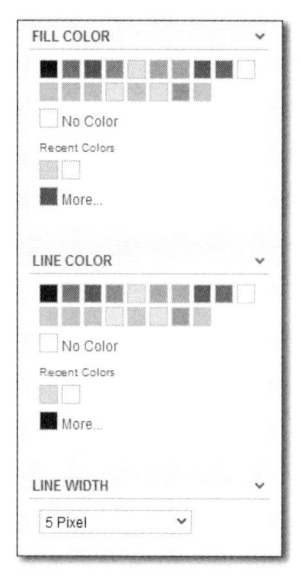

Figure 6.65 Shape Settings

In addition to the fill and line color, you can set the LINE WIDTH. Figure 6.66 depicts a shape created through the SHAPE settings.

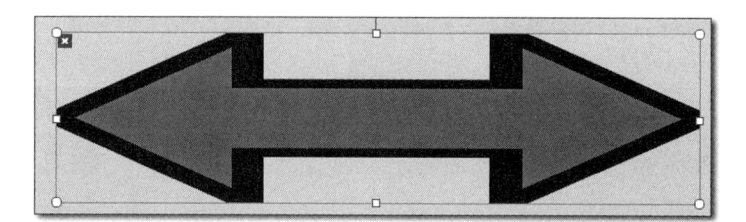

Figure 6.66 Customized Shape

6.8.7 Controls

Controls enable you to add filters to your interactive boards (they are not available in infographics) so that users can interact with the data. Controls are handled differently in interactive boards than they are in reports.

Customizing Entities | **6.8**

Controls in Interactive Boards

Interactive boards allow you to place controls directly into the canvas (see Figure 6.67).

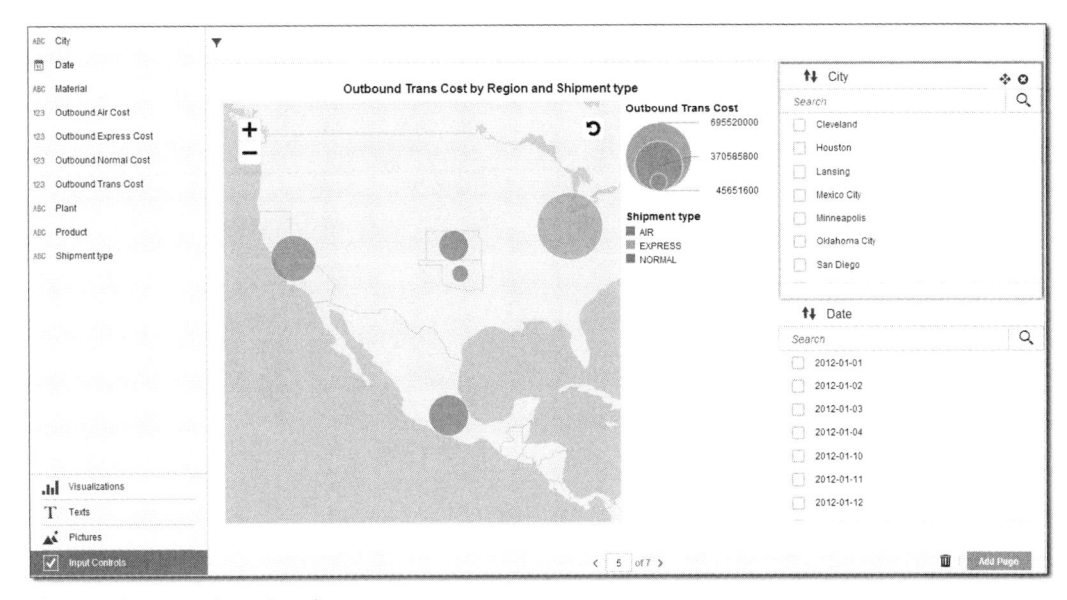

Figure 6.67 Control in a Board

Once you have selected an object, you can place it in the canvas (anywhere), and a list control will appear. You can then interact with that control to make multi- or mono-selections. A selection creates a filter that will appear in the filter bar at the top of the story (see Figure 6.68).

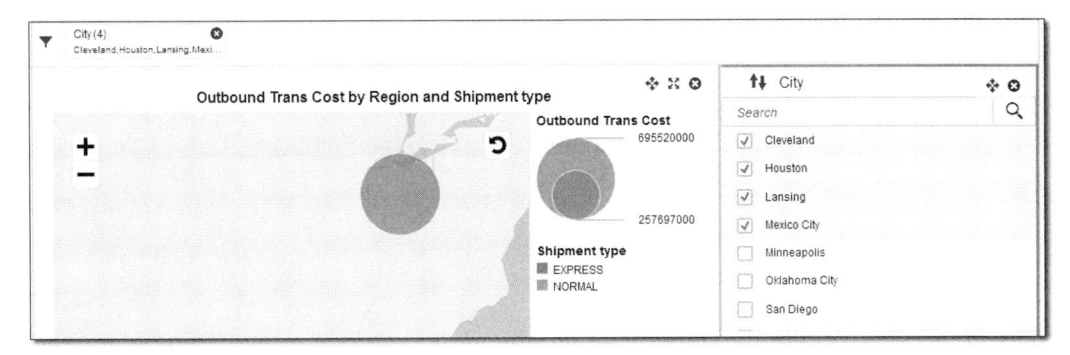

Figure 6.68 Control Selection in Filter Bar

Removing the breadcrumb or unchecking the values in the list will remove the filter.

Controls can be customized to change the selection behavior. You can choose between multi- and mono-selection, and this will change whether the control has a checkbox or a radio button (see Figure 6.69).

Figure 6.69 Board Control Settings

Once the setting is defined and the story has been published for viewing, users cannot change the control behavior.

There is also a SEARCH field for the control. Controls only return a subset of the data available (the first 100 items), but the SEARCH field lets you retrieve other values by entering in a character or phrase (see Figure 6.70).

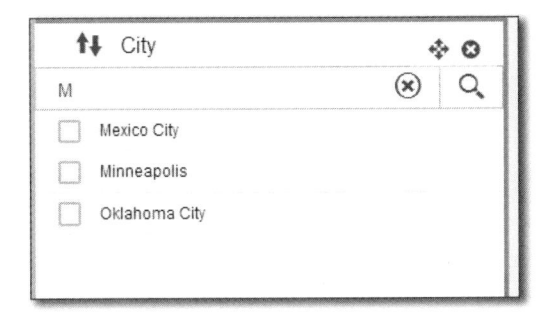

Figure 6.70 Control Search

The returned values will be seen in the list, and you can remove the text in the SEARCH field by clicking the DELETE icon.

Controls in Reports

To create a control in a report, you have to place the object in the filter bar. This creates a default breadcrumb from which you can select a value. If you add multiple breadcrumbs, then the selections will filter the subsequent values in a kind of hierarchy (see Figure 6.71).

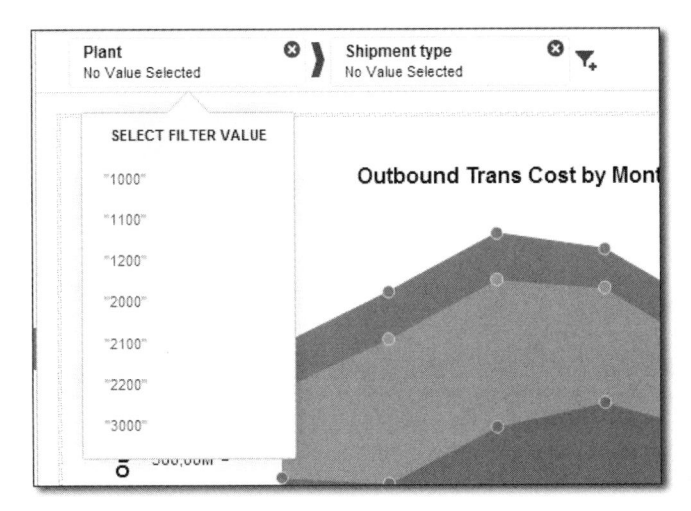

Figure 6.71 Controls in Reports

The ▼ icon allows you to add controls directly into the list. Filters behave as in boards, filtering all the visualizations and other controls in the report. As noted previously, the interesting feature of reports is that you can navigate quickly through filters by using sections.

Controls are different than boards in that they can only be placed in the FILTER BAR. You then choose directly from the crumb to set the values that you want. Multiple filters can be added, with the filters cascading into the subsequent values. Note also that you can navigate via the section control on the right-hand side (see Figure 6.72).

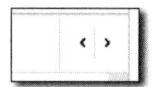

Figure 6.72 Section Control

To use a section control, you have to add the control to the filter bar and select a value. The section control now allows you to step over the values in the control.

Controls only filter the current page and affect all visualizations on that page. As mentioned in previous chapters, filters have different effects depending on where they are created:

- Global filters are seen as dark gray squares in the filter bar. These cannot be changed unless you go back to the Prepare room.
- Filters on visualizations are only seen in the visualization itself and not in the filter bar. To change a filter on a visualization, you need to go back to the Visualize room.
- Filters in stories are dynamic and can be changed. They appear in the filter bar as light gray squares (see Figure 6.73).

Figure 6.73 Global and Local Filter

Controls allow you to add additional dimensions to your reports and interactive boards, allowing users to interact with and analyze your data.

6.9 Summary

In some ways, the Compose room is where you put everything together. You have cleaned your data, added some hierarchies, created some charts and maps, and now you can lay these charts out in a story to present to your friends and colleagues. Through careful use of images, text, and color, you can create compelling visual arguments to persuade and convince. Infographics, with their highly customizable infocharts, allow you to create high-impact displays that you can back up with interactive boards and reports that can be used for analysis and understanding.

The next chapter will discuss how you can share these visualizations and publish them on SAP Lumira and other SAP systems.

Once your document is created, you can email, print, or share it and its dataset to a file system or to other systems, including SAP HANA, SAP Explorer, SAP Lumira Cloud, SAP Lumira Server, SAP BusinessObjects BI 4.1, or SAP StreamWork.

7   Sharing in SAP Lumira

The resources created in SAP Lumira suite are intended to be shared, either to communicate the data they contain or to collaborate with other people on their design.

Sharing can take place via the other deployment modes supported by SAP Lumira suite; if you have other SAP systems, you can share your resources created in SAP Lumira with these systems: SAP HANA, SAP Explorer and SAP StreamWork. You can also share them on SAP BusinessObjects BI 4.1 (Support Pack 3 or higher), if you install its add-on for SAP Lumira and have also an SAP Lumira Server.

In SAP Lumira Desktop, the Share room is used to perform the following exchanges:

- A dataset can be published to SAP Lumira Cloud or SAP Lumira Server. It can also be exported as an information space in SAP Explorer, a view in SAP HANA, or a Microsoft Excel or a text file in SAP StreamWork. Datasets can also be saved as a text or Microsoft Excel file.
- A visualization can be published on SAP StreamWork, sent by email or printed.
- A story can be published on SAP Lumira Cloud, SAP Lumira Server or SAP BusinessObjects BI 4.1.

This chapter first presents an overview of the Share room and then discusses sharing visualizations via printing physical copies or emails before detailing publication to SAP Lumira Server, SAP Lumira Cloud, and the other SAP-supported systems.

It also covers two workflows available for SAP Lumira Cloud:

- Scheduling a publication to SAP Lumira Cloud with up-to-date data through SAP Lumira Agent
- Saving an SAP Lumira document in SAP Lumira Cloud

In the next section an overview of the Share room and the role it plays in collaboration through SAP Lumira will be discussed.

7.1 Share Room Overview

In SAP Lumira Desktop, the SHARE room (see Figure 7.1) is not intended for authoring and design tasks; it is only dedicated to sharing resources created in previous rooms with other people or across an organization.

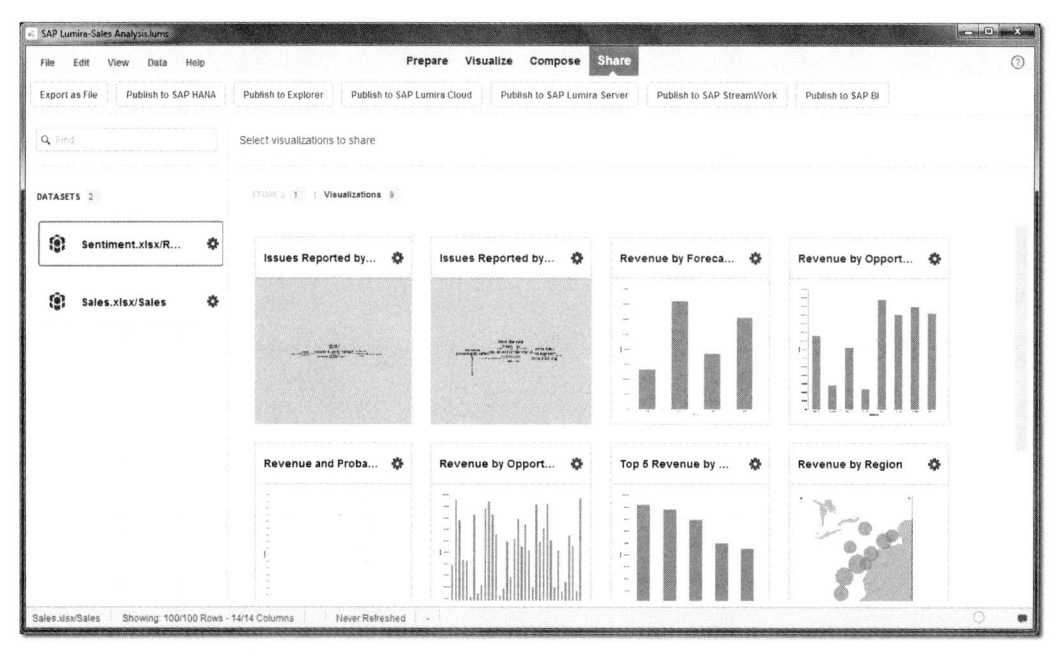

Figure 7.1 Share Room Commands

You enter this room by clicking the SHARE tab. As shown in Figure 7.1, the following elements are found in this room:

- A toolbar on the top of the room contains buttons that correspond to the different exports you can run from this room.
- The left side of the room lists the datasets the document contains. Click the cog icon beside a dataset to open its contextual menu, which contains the following commands:
    - SHOW DETAILS: Open a dialog box containing some statistics about the dataset, as shown in Figure 7.2, including the number of columns, of rows, the columns name and a data sample for these columns.
    - RENAME: Rename the dataset. Type the new name when the focus is on the dataset name.
    - REMOVE: This command is available only if the document contains several datasets. It allows you to delete the dataset from the document. Before the dataset is deleted, you need to confirm, because deleting this dataset also deletes all visualizations based on this dataset.

  A FIND field is displayed on top of the dataset list. Use it to filter the list of dataset names via a string pattern.

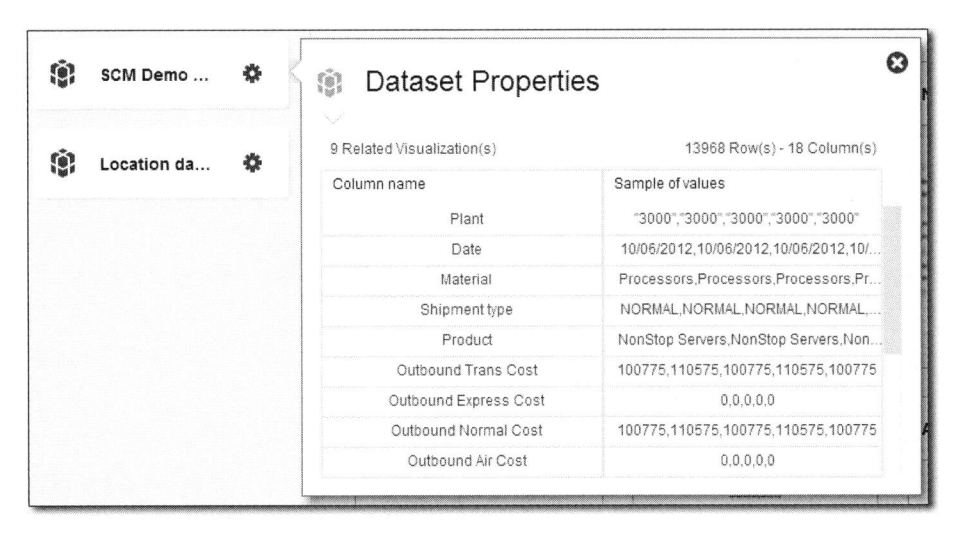

Figure 7.2 Dataset Properties

- The right side of the room lists the stories and visualizations the document contains. Click STORIES to display stories or VISUALIZATIONS to display visualizations. Stories and visualizations are displayed as thumbnails. In the visualization thumbnail, click the cog icon to open the contextual menu, which contains the following commands:

- ENLARGE: Open a dialog box containing a larger version of the visualization. This command is not available for some visualizations, tables for example. Click CLOSE to close this dialog box.
- RENAME: Rename the visualization. Type the new name when the focus is on the visualization name.
- REMOVE: Remove the selected visualization from the document. Before actually removing it, SAP Lumira shows you the list of stories using this visualization. Deleting this visualization removes it from these stories, so you need to confirm this removal first.

Depending on the selected objet (dataset, visualization, or story), the tool bar is updated to display only the actions you can run on this resource, as described in Table 7.1.

	Dataset	Visualization	Story
Printing	N/A	Partly supported	N/A
Emailing	N/A	Supported	N/A
Export as File	Supported	N/A	N/A
SAP HANA	Supported	N/A	N/A
SAP Explorer	Supported	N/A	N/A
SAP StreamWork	Supported	Supported	N/A
SAP Lumira Cloud	Supported	N/A	Supported
SAP Lumira Server	Supported	N/A	Supported
SAP BusinessObjects BI 4.1	Supported	N/A	Supported

Table 7.1 Exports Supported by Other SAP Systems

The sections ahead describe the various methods one can use to publish through SAP Lumira.

7.2 Printing Visualizations

A common way to share your data is to print and physically send them. SAP Lumira supports the printers whose drivers are installed on your machine. This can cover both physical printers and virtual ones, such as print to PDF or fax. Printing is not available for some visualizations, tables for example.

To print a visualization, follow these steps:

1. Open a document and click the SHARE tab to access the SHARE room.
2. Click VISUALIZATIONS. The different visualizations that the document contains are displayed below as thumbnails.
3. Click a thumbnail to select a visualization. You may select several visualizations by pressing the `Ctrl` key when clicking them, as shown in Figure 7.3.

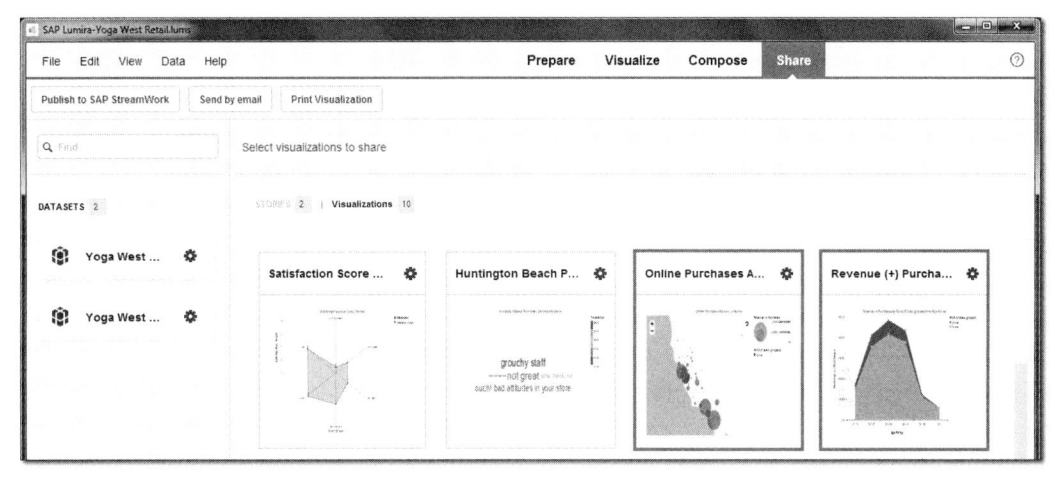

Figure 7.3 Selected Visualizations for Email or Printing

4. In the toolbar, click PRINT VISUALIZATION to open the PRINT VISUALIZATION dialog box, as shown in Figure 7.4. Its left side contains the printing parameters, whereas the right side shows a preview for the printing.

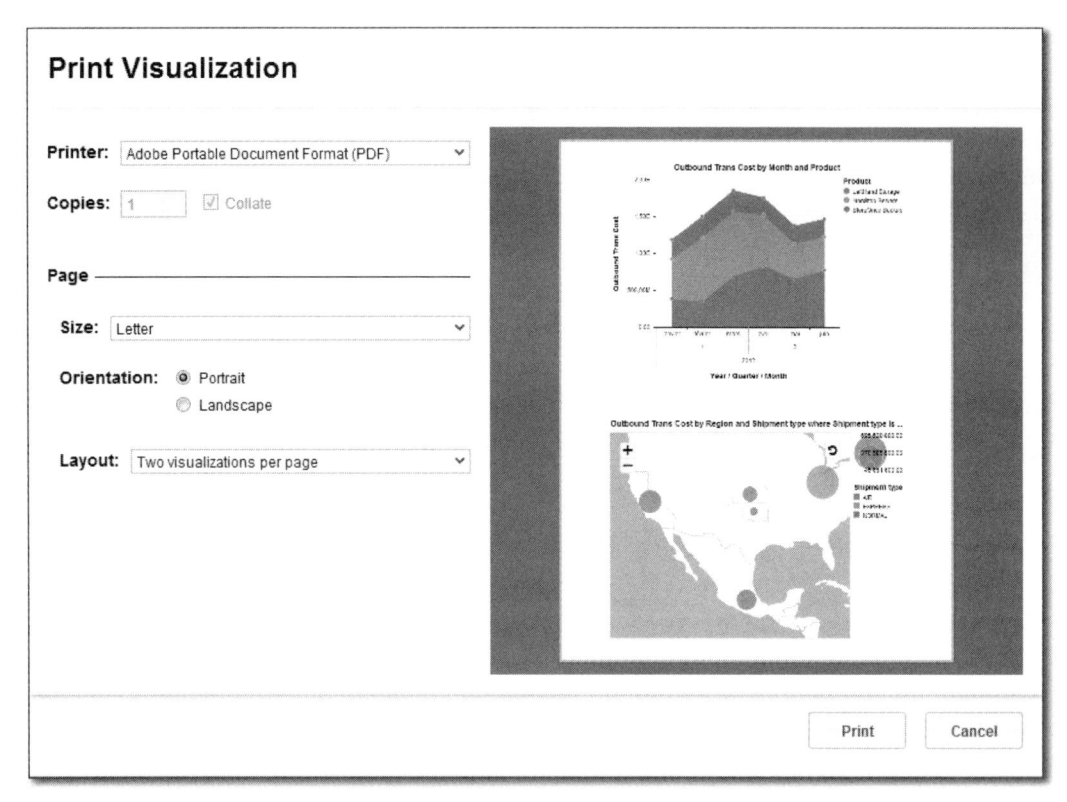

Figure 7.4 Print Visualization Dialog Box

5. In the PRINTER dropdown list, select the printer to use from among the ones registered in your machine: the physical ones or the virtual ones (print to PDF, fax, etc.).

6. In the COPIES field, enter the number of copies to print. If the printer is virtual, then this number is 1. If the number of copies is greater than 1, then the COLLATE checkbox is enabled and you can select it to collate the different copies.

7. In the SIZE dropdown list, select the page dimension for printing.

8. Select the PORTRAIT or LANDSCAPE radio button to select the printing orientation.

9. In the LAYOUT dropdown list, select how to arrange the visualizations in the page to print:
   - ONE VISUALIZATION PER PAGE will print one visualization per page.
   - TWO VISUALIZATIONS PER PAGE will print two visualizations per page.
   - VISUALIZATIONS WITH NOTE will print three visualizations per page and will leave the right side of the sheet blank to add notes.
10. Click PRINT to close the PRINT VISUALIZATION dialog box and send your visualization(s) to your physical or virtual printer.

If printing is not your preference for sharing visualizations, there is also the option to send via email.

7.3   Sending Visualizations by Email

In addition of printing, it is also possible to send visualizations by mail. The visualizations are added in attached objects in a mail to be sent by the mail application configured on your desktop.

To send vizualizations by email, follow these steps:

1. In the Share room, click VISUALIZATION. The different vizualisations the document contains are displayed below as thumbnails.
2. Click a thumbnail to select a vizualisation. You may select several vizualisations by pressing the `Ctrl` key, as shown in Figure 7.3.
3. Click SEND BY EMAIL to open the SEND BY EMAIL dialog box as shown in Figure 7.5.

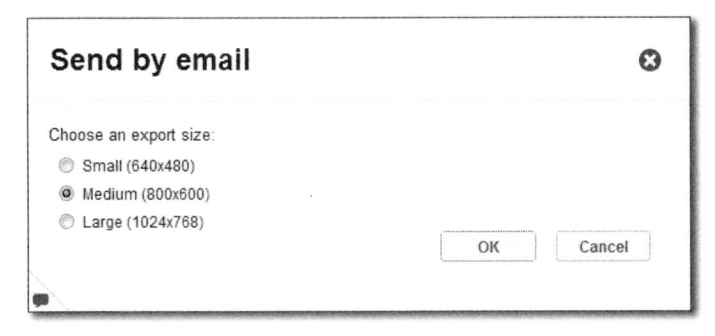

Figure 7.5 Export Visualization Dialog Box

4. Click the radio button to select in what size to generate the picture.

5. Click OK to create a new mail with your default mail application. This email contains generated pictures from vizualizations as attached objects.

6. Complete your mail (destinator, subject, content...) and send it.

> **Visualize Room**
>
> It is also possible to send visualization by email from the Visualize room by selecting the SEND BY MAIL command in a visualization menu.

Now that we know how to share our SAP Lumira visualizations via standard methods such as printing and email, let's look at some of the features available within the suite that allow for further collaboration.

7.4 Publishing a Dataset or a Story to SAP Lumira Cloud

SAP Lumira Cloud is the version of the SAP Lumira suite available on the cloud. It is described in detail in Chapter 8.

As described in Section 7.6, saving a document to SAP Lumira Cloud saves the whole document as a single resource in SAP Lumira Cloud. This save does not allow you to edit this document in SAP Lumira Cloud.

To benefit from SAP Lumira Cloud's edit capabilities (see Chapter 8, Section 8.5), you must publish the stories and datasets contained in the SAP Lumira document. It is not possible to publish a dataset based on a data source accessed in online mode. Once published, you cannot access the published resources from SAP Lumira Desktop, but you still have access to the local document in SAP Lumira Desktop.

When they are published to SAP Lumira Cloud, the stories and datasets are saved under the name given to them in SAP Lumira Desktop. If a resource with the same name exists, then the name is suffixed with a number—for example, My dataset (2)—to differentiate it from the existing one.

To publish a story or a dataset to SAP Lumira Cloud, follow these steps:

1. Open a document and click the SHARE tab to access the SHARE room.
2. In the DATASETS left pane, select a dataset or click STORIES, and when the story thumbnails are displayed select one. You cannot select several datasets or stories at the same time.
3. Click PUBLISH TO SAP LUMIRA CLOUD to open the PUBLISH DATASET TO SAP LUMIRA CLOUD dialog box, if you have selected a dataset, or the PUBLISH STORY TO SAP LUMIRA CLOUD dialog box, if you have selected a story.
4. If you have already connected to SAP Lumira Cloud and have set it to remember your credentials, then you are automatically connected, as seen in Figure 7.6, and you can click NEXT.

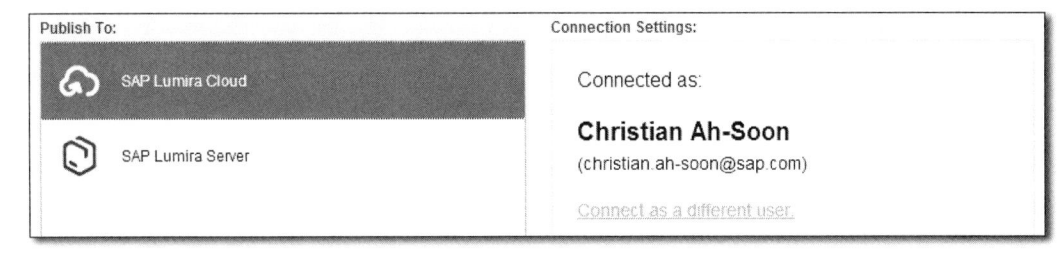

Figure 7.6 Publish to SAP Lumira Cloud Dialog Box—Already Connected

5. Otherwise, if you are yet connected to SAP Lumira Cloud or if you have not saved your parameters from a previous session, then you need to authenticate in the login pane (see Figure 7.7):

   ▶ If you do not have yet an account on SAP Lumira Cloud, then click CREATE A NEW SAP LUMIRA CLOUD ACCOUNT to open the SAP Lumira Cloud registration page in your web browser. From this page, you can register for an account on SAP Lumira Cloud, as described in Chapter 8, Section 8.1.2.

   ▶ Once created, or if you already have an account, enter your credentials in the USERNAME and PASSWORD text fields.

   ▶ Select the REMEMBER ME checkbox to save these credentials, which prevents you needing to type them again to open new sessions later.

   ▶ Click CONNECT to log into SAP Lumira Cloud.

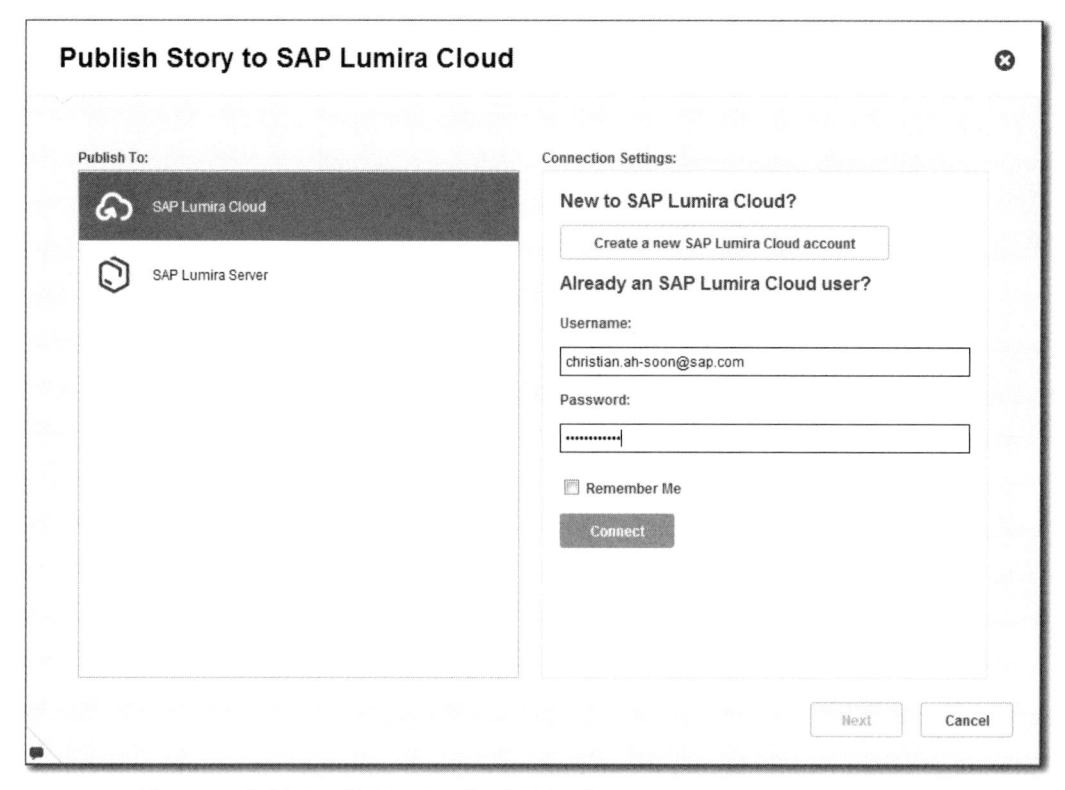

Figure 7.7 Publish to SAP Lumira Cloud Dialog Box

6. The dialog box displays the resources to publish:
    - If you have selected a dataset, then this dataset.
    - If you have selected a story, then this story and all the datasets it relies on.
7. If none of these resources have already been published, as seen in Figure 7.8, then you can click PUBLISH to publish them, and once they are published, as shown in Figure 7.9, click DONE to close the dialog box.

Publishing a Dataset or a Story to SAP Lumira Cloud | **7.4**

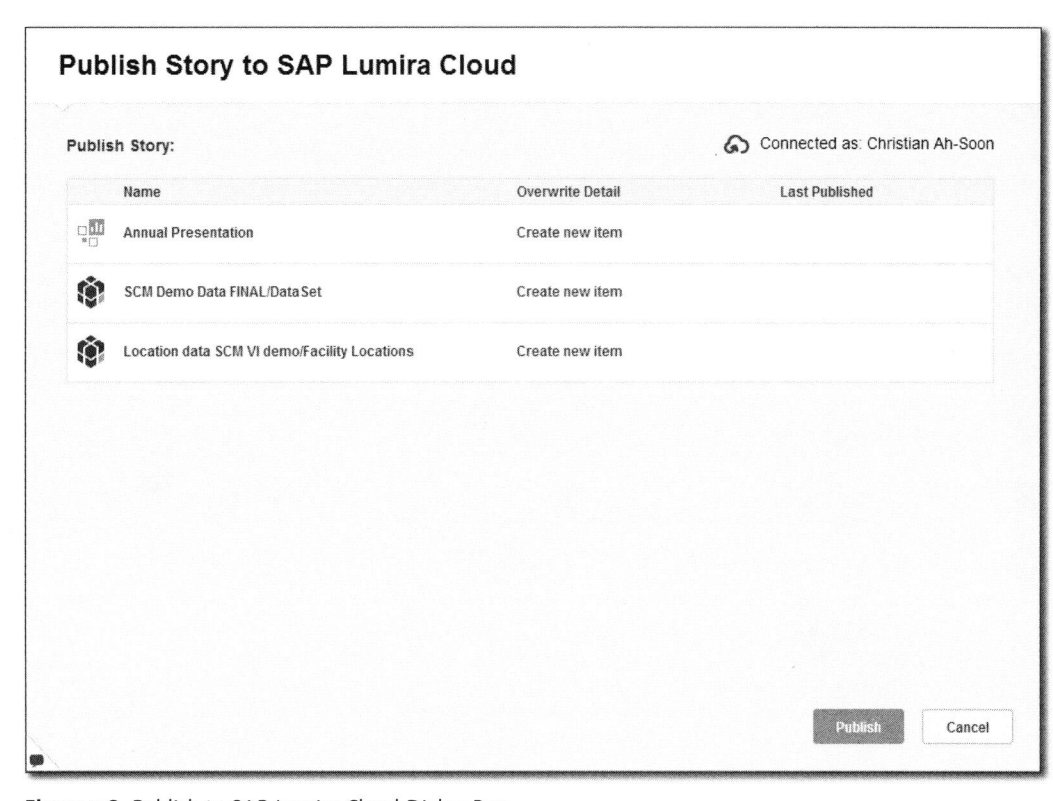

Figure 7.8 Publish to SAP Lumira Cloud Dialog Box

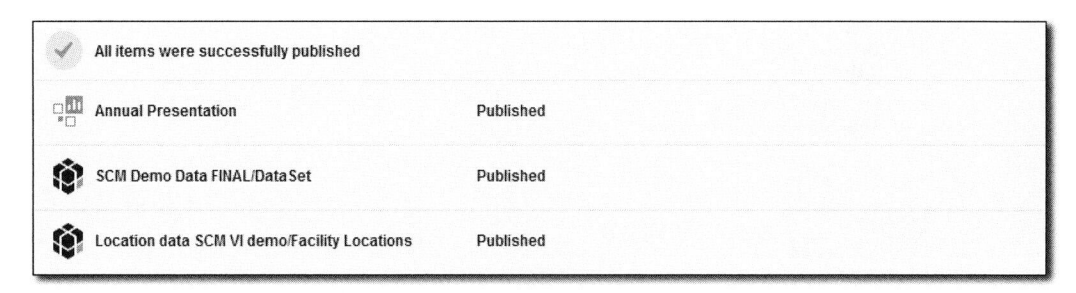

Figure 7.9 Resources Successfully Published to SAP Lumira Cloud

8. If any of these resources has already been published to SAP Lumira Cloud, then, as shown in Figure 7.10, the LAST PUBLISHED column displays when it was last published.

If you are publishing a story, then you can select to not overwrite a dataset by selecting the DO NOT OVERWRITE option in the dropdown list of the OVERWRITE DETAIL column. In this case, the published story uses the dataset already existing in the SAP Lumira Cloud. A story must always be overwritten.

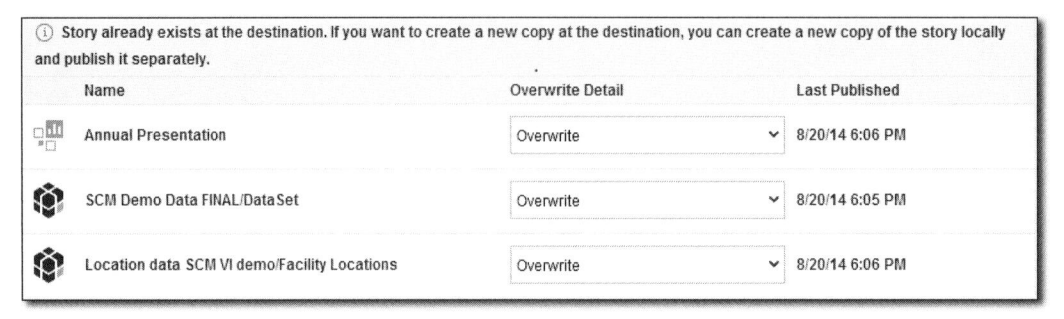

Figure 7.10 Resources Already Published to SAP Lumira Cloud

9. If a dataset is overwritten, then you must click VERIFY to check if its schema has been changed and if it might create inconsistencies with stories based on this dataset and already published in the cloud.

10. Once the verification is complete, as shown in Figure 7.11, click PUBLISH to publish the resources and DONE to close the dialog box after the resources have been published.

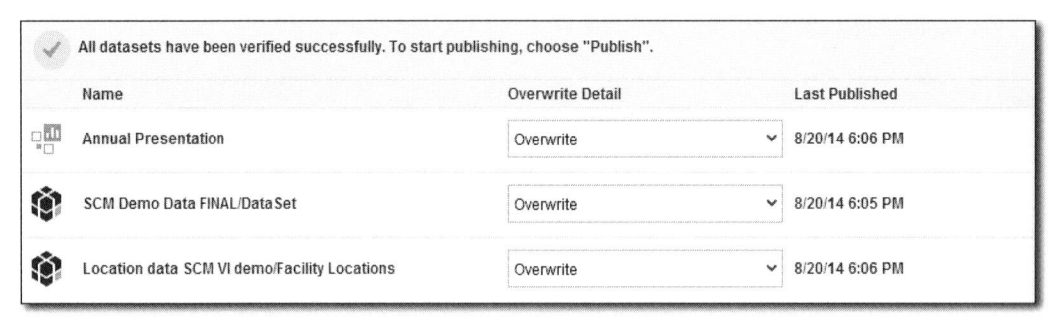

Figure 7.11 Datasets Successfully Verified in SAP Lumira Cloud

The next two sections discuss the two specifications that come with SAP Lumira Cloud for publication: refreshing documents to republish through SAP Lumira Agent, and saving to SAP Lumira Cloud.

7.5 Republishing and Scheduling with SAP Lumira Agent

SAP Lumira Cloud cannot refresh the documents you have published if the data contained in its data source has changed. To have a refreshed version of your stories in SAP Lumira Cloud, you need to manually republish them, or you can use SAP Lumira Agent to automatically republish them.

7.5.1 Scheduling Documents

SAP Lumira Agent (also known as Desktop Synchronization Agent) is an instance of SAP Lumira that runs without a UI. It is initialized when you start SAP Lumira if you set it to do so in the SAP Lumira preferences (see Chapter 2, Section 2.9), but it remains active if you leave SAP Lumira.

SAP Lumira Agent can be used as a scheduler and run in the background to save SAP Lumira documents in SAP Lumira Cloud. It cannot be used to save other resources or to publish to other systems.

You create schedules and edit their parameters in SAP Lumira Desktop. These schedules are identified by their name. These names are local to the machine.

Possible recurrence options include the following:

- DAILY: The schedule is run every day at the same specified hour.
- WEEKLY: The schedule is run different days of the week at the same specified hour.
- MONTHLY: The schedule is run once a month at a specified day and hour.

The hour used for the schedule matches that of the machine on which SAP Lumira Agent is running.

Only one schedule can be assigned to a document.

7 | Sharing in SAP Lumira

When SAP Lumira Agent is started and you click DOCUMENTS in the WELCOME page, a new column, SCHEDULE, is displayed in the lists of all the documents saved in the SAP Lumira Documents folder, as shown in Figure 7.12. This column contains the following:

- The name of the associated schedule. If the document is not scheduled, it displays NONE.
- An icon that gives the schedule status for this document. These icons are described in Table 7.2.

Figure 7.12 Documents List with Schedule Column

Icon	Description
☐	No schedule is assigned to the document.
☐	A schedule is assigned to the document.
☑	The last schedule ran successfully.

Table 7.2 Schedule Icon Description

Icon	Description
(orange)	The refreshed document cannot be published to SAP Lumira Cloud because no session has been opened.
(red)	An error occurred during the schedule that prevented the document refresh.

Table 7.2 Schedule Icon Description (Cont.)

7.5.2 Starting SAP Lumira Agent

To create a new schedule, you first need to start SAP Lumira Agent. To do so, follow these steps:

1. Open the SAP LUMIRA PREFERENCES dialog box, as described in Chapter 2, Section 2.9.
2. In the GENERAL category, select the ENABLE SAP LUMIRA AGENT checkbox.
3. Click DONE to close the SAP LUMIRA PREFERENCES dialog box.
4. Exit, then restart SAP Lumira.

Because you have enabled SAP Lumira Agent, it also starts in the background, and the SAP LUMIRA icon appears in the Windows taskbar to show it is actually started. To explicitly stop SAP Lumira Agent, click this icon to open a menu from which you can call the QUIT APPLICATION command. When you restart SAP Lumira, if the ENABLE SAP LUMIRA AGENT checkbox is still selected, then SAP Lumira Agent is restarted.

To save the documents to SAP Lumira Cloud, SAP Lumira Agent needs to connect to SAP Lumira Cloud. Hence, you need to open a session to SAP Lumira Cloud from SAP Lumira Desktop (see Chapter 8, Section 8.2) and keep it open. Opening this session is not needed to create schedules, but it is mandatory to run them.

7.5.3 Scheduling a Document

To schedule the publication of a document to SAP Lumira Cloud, follow these steps:

1. Start SAP Lumira Agent, as described in Section 7.5.2.
2. In the WELCOME page, click the DOCUMENTS tab to list all of the documents saved in the SAP Lumira Documents folder.

3. Select a document and click the label (NONE or the schedule name) in the SCHEDULE column to open the SCHEDULE DOCUMENT FOR UPDATE dialog box for the selected document:

   ▶ If a schedule has not yet been created for SAP Lumira Agent, then you can only create a new schedule, as seen in Figure 7.13.

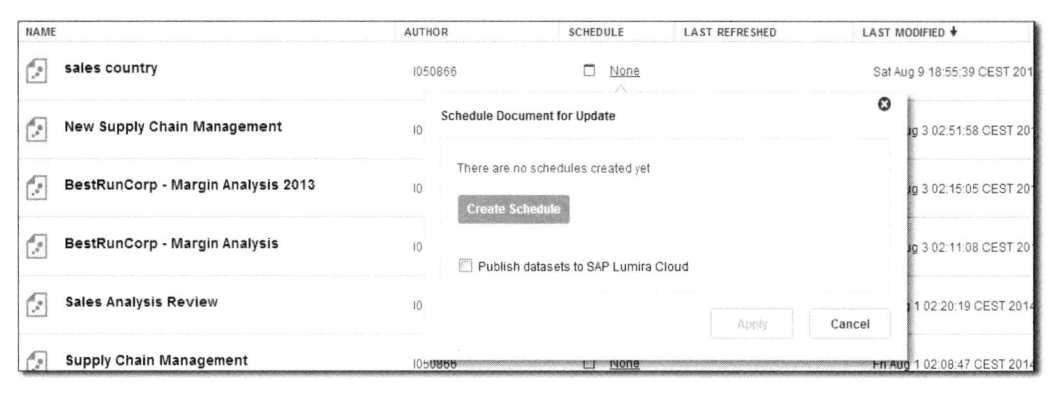

Figure 7.13 Schedule Not Yet Created

   ▶ If some schedules already exist but no one has not been assigned to this document, then the SELECT dropdown list displays NONE, as seen in Figure 7.14. You can choose another schedule in this list or create a new one.

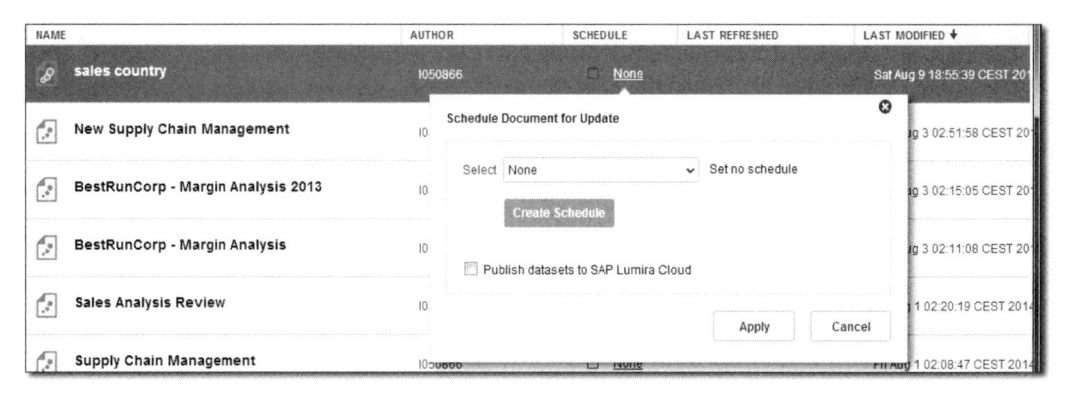

Figure 7.14 No Schedule Assigned to a Document

   ▶ If a schedule has been assigned to the document, then the SELECT dropdown list displays the schedule name, as seen in Figure 7.15.

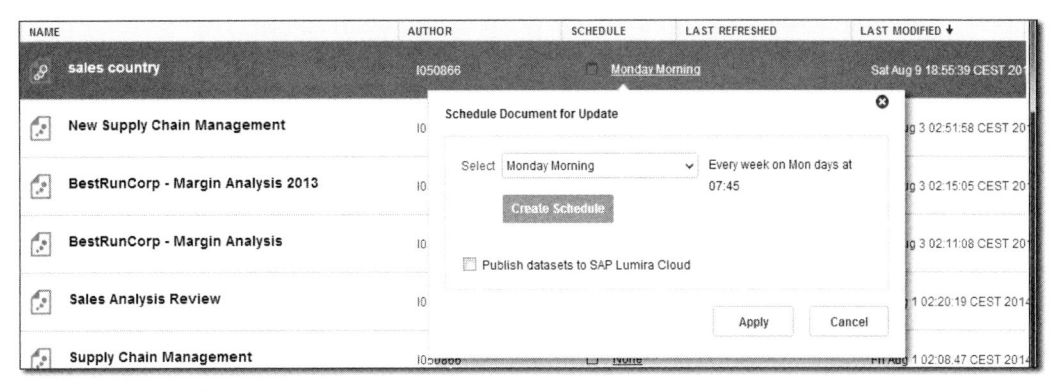

Republishing and Scheduling with SAP Lumira Agent | 7.5

Figure 7.15 Schedule Assigned to a Document

4. The SELECT dropdown list contains the list of created schedules and short descriptions of the schedules, as seen in Figure 7.16. Select an option:

   ▸ NONE to not assign a schedule the document
   ▸ Any existing schedule to assign it to the document

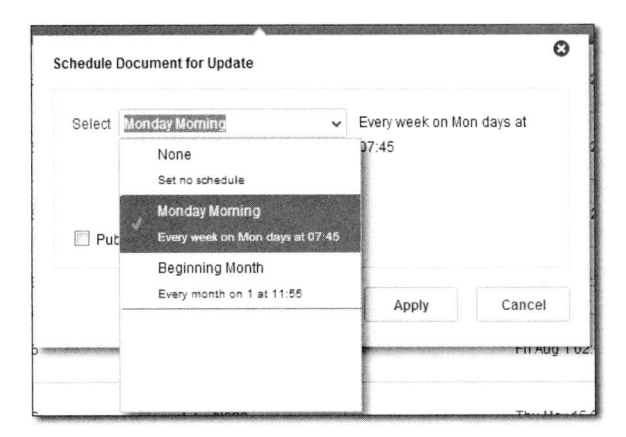

Figure 7.16 Schedule Recurrence Selection

5. If you do not find any existing schedule with the appropriate frequency, then click CREATE SCHEDULE to open the CREATE NEW SCHEDULE window.

6. Enter a name in the NAME text field. This name is used in the SCHEDULE column to identify the schedule parameters.

7. In the FREQUENCY dropdown list, select a frequency option:

355

7 | Sharing in SAP Lumira

- DAILY: Run the schedule every day, as shown in Figure 7.17.
- WEEKLY: Run the schedule on particular days every week. In the ON EVERY line, click the buttons corresponding to the days of the week on which to run the schedule, as shown in Figure 7.18.
- MONTHLY: Run the schedule once a month. In the ON EVERY line, enter the date to run the schedule, as shown in Figure 7.19.

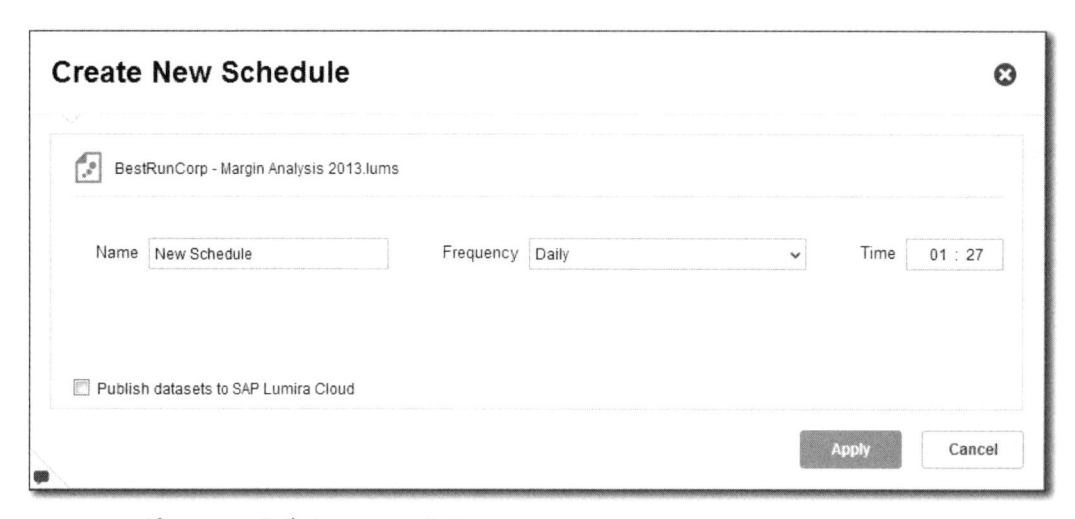

Figure 7.17 Daily Recurrence Option

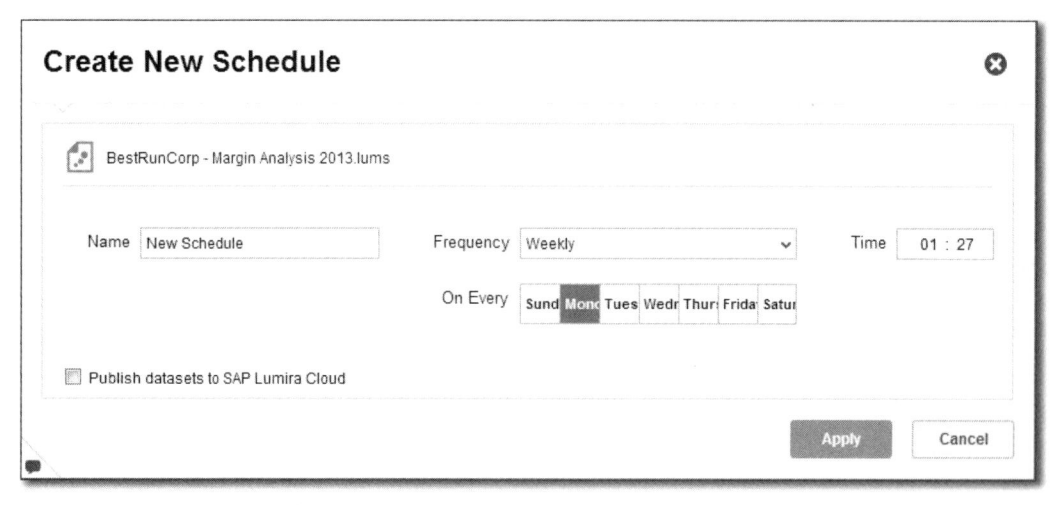

Figure 7.18 Weekly Recurrence Option

Figure 7.19 Monthly Recurrence Option

8. In the TIME text field, enter at what time (in 24-hour format) the document must be published.
9. Select the PUBLISH DATASETS TO SAP LUMIRA CLOUD checkbox to also publish its datasets when the document is published.
10. Click APPLY to close the CREATE NEW SCHEDULE dialog box and schedule the document at the selected frequency.

7.5.4 Managing All Schedules

Instead of editing a schedule attached to each document, you can globally manage all the schedules handled by the SAP Lumira Agent running on your machine.

To do so, SAP Lumira Agent must be enabled and running. If this is the case, then the SAP Lumira WELCOME page contains the ALL SCHEDULES button, as shown in Figure 7.20. Click it to open the ALL SCHEDULES dialog box.

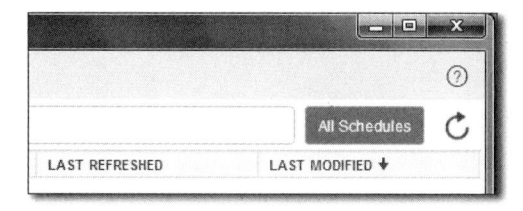

Figure 7.20 All Schedules Button

7 | Sharing in SAP Lumira

As shown in Figure 7.21, in the ALL SCHEDULES dialog box you will see the following elements:

- The left pane contains all the schedules handled by SAP Lumira Agent.
- When you select one of these schedules, its parameters are displayed in the right pane.
- The DOCUMENTS USING SCHEDULES section lists all documents that are published with this schedule.

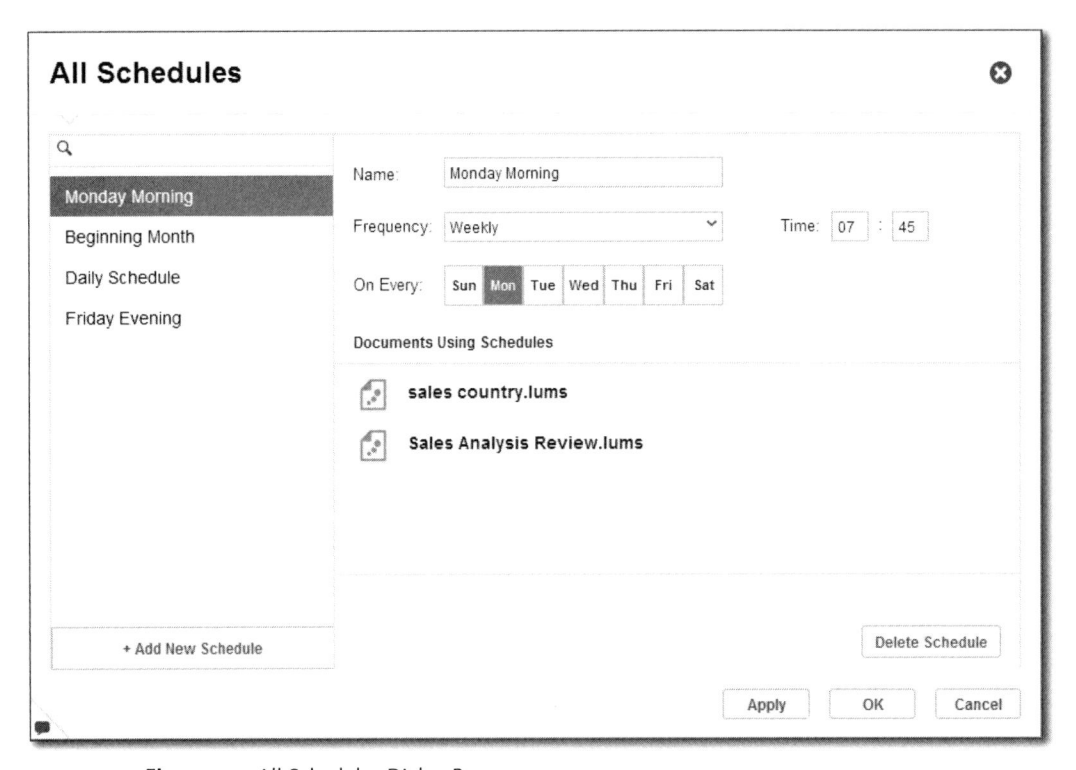

Figure 7.21 All Schedules Dialog Box

To create a new schedule in the ALL SCHEDULES dialog box, perform the following steps:

1. Click ADD NEW SCHEDULE.
2. A new schedule is added to the schedule list.

3. Modify its parameters in the right pane. These parameters are identical to the ones available when creating a new schedule, as described in Section 7.5.3.

4. Click OK to save your changes and close the dialog box.

To edit an existing schedule in the ALL SCHEDULES dialog box, perform the following steps:

1. Select the schedule in the left pane.

2. Modify its parameters in the right pane. These parameters are identical to the ones available when creating a new schedule, as described in Section 7.5.3.

3. Click OK to save your changes and close the dialog box.

To delete an existing schedule, select the schedule in the left pane, then click DELETE SCHEDULE. After clicking through a confirmation window, the schedule is deleted, even if you quit the dialog box by clicking CANCEL.

7.5.5 Running a Schedule

Scheduled documents are processed locally on the machine on which you have scheduled them:

- Schedule parameters are saved locally on this machine.
- The schedules are triggered by the time and day of the machine running SAP Lumira Agent.
- Scheduled documents are refreshed and saved in SAP Lumira Cloud by SAP Lumira Agent running on this machine. Hence, SAP Lumira Agent must be running on the machine.

When a schedule must be processed by SAP Lumira Agent, the document is first refreshed and saved locally. If the refresh is successful, then the document is saved in SAP Lumira Cloud. If the dataset must also be published, then it is also saved in SAP Lumira Cloud. If the document or the dataset has previously been published, then it is replaced by its new, refreshed version.

After the schedule is run, the document list in the WELCOME page is updated to show the result of the schedule for the scheduled document:

- The icon showing the schedule status (see Table 7.2) is updated in the SCHEDULE column.
- The refresh time is updated in the LAST REFRESHED column.

7.6 Saving a Document to SAP Lumira Cloud

You can save a document opened in SAP Lumira Desktop in SAP Lumira Cloud. Because the SAVE command is available from the menu bar, you do not need to be in the Share room to launch it. When you use this command, you can choose to save the document locally on your file system, as described in Chapter 2, Section 2.8.3, or in SAP Lumira Cloud.

> **Note**
>
> Compared to publication to SAP Lumira Cloud described in Section 7.4, the SAVE command allows you to also share the document with other users (see Chapter 8, Section 8.6). However, the document saved in SAP Lumira Cloud cannot be directly viewed or edited in SAP Lumira Cloud. For this, you need to publish the document's stories.

To save and share a document in SAP Lumira Cloud, follow these steps:

1. Open a document in SAP Lumira.
2. Select the FILE • SAVE AS command to open the SAVE OPTIONS dialog box.
3. Click SAP LUMIRA CLOUD to switch to the SAP Lumira Cloud SAVE pane.
4. If you are already connected to SAP Lumira Cloud or if you set it to remember your credentials, then you are automatically connected and do not need to enter your credentials to connect.
5. Otherwise, if you are not yet connected to SAP Lumira Cloud or if you have not saved your parameters from a previous session, then you need to authenticate in the login pane (see Figure 7.22):
    - If you do not have yet an account on SAP Lumira Cloud, then click CREATE A NEW SAP LUMIRA CLOUD ACCOUNT to open the SAP Lumira Cloud registration page in your web browser. From this page, you can register for an account on SAP Lumira Cloud, as described in Chapter 8, Section 8.1.2.

7.6 | Saving a Document to SAP Lumira Cloud

- Once your account is created (or if you already have an account), enter your credentials in the USERNAME and PASSWORD text fields.
- Select the REMEMBER ME checkbox to save these credentials, which prevents you needing to type them again to open new sessions later.

Figure 7.22 SAP Lumira Cloud Login Page

6. Click CONNECT to connect to SAP Lumira Cloud and display the parameters available when saving a document in SAP Lumira Cloud, as shown in Figure 7.23.

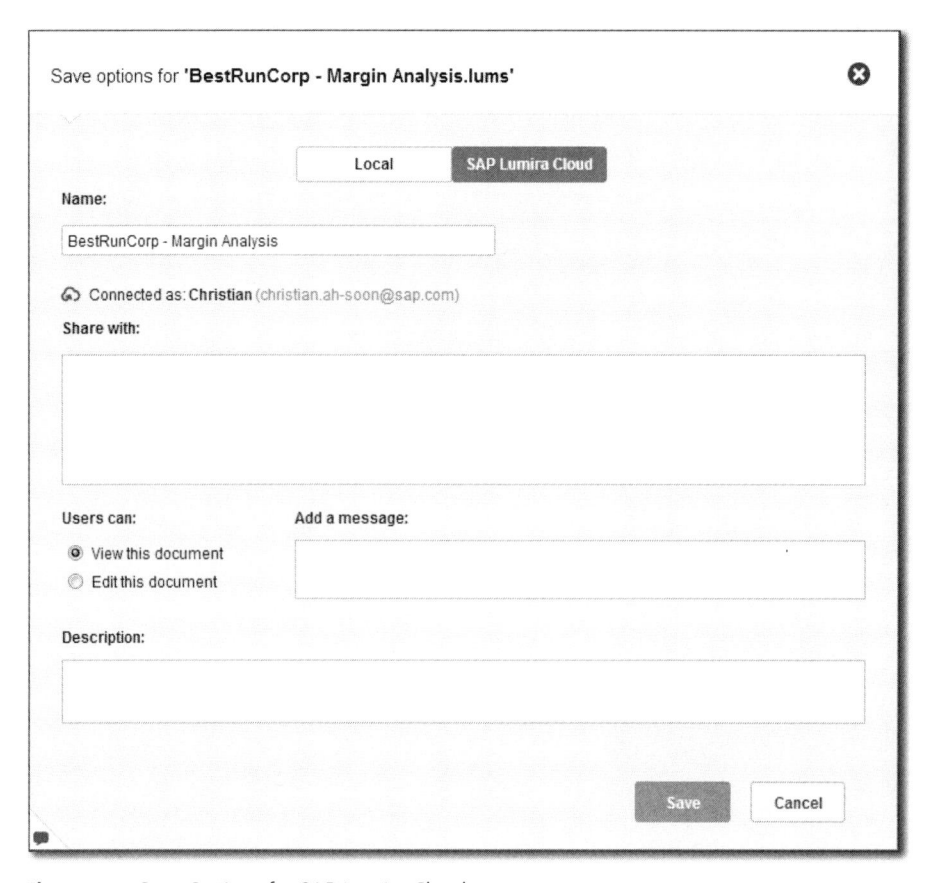

Figure 7.23 Save Options for SAP Lumira Cloud

7. In the NAME text field, enter the name to use to save the document in the cloud.

8. To share the document with other users, enter the following parameters:

   ▸ In the SHARE WITH text field, enter the email addresses of the people you want to invite to share the document.

   ▸ Use the VIEW THIS DOCUMENT or EDIT THIS DOCUMENT radio button to define what actions the recipients can take in the document.

   ▸ In the ADD A MESSAGE text field, type a message to add to the email sent to the recipients.

   ▸ In the DESCRIPTION text field, add a description of the document.

If you have an enterprise license, then you can also select the INVITE MY TEAM checkbox, as shown in Figure 7.24, to share the document with all your team members.

You can find a more detailed description of these parameters in Chapter 8, Section 8.6.

Figure 7.24 Invite My Team Checkbox

9. Click SAVE to save the document in SAP Lumira Cloud, and close the SAVE OPTIONS dialog box.

When the document is saved, it is first saved locally in the local SAP Lumira Documents folder. If a document with the same name exists, then you need to confirm before overwriting it. In SAP Lumira Cloud, if a document with the same name exists, then another document is created with the name suffixed by a number to differentiate it from the existing one.

If you are not on the cloud, and instead are using the server version of SAP Lumira, the next section will discuss the publishing capabilities with this part of the suite.

7.7 Publishing a Dataset or a Story to SAP Lumira Server

SAP Lumira Server is the server for the on-premise deployment of the SAP Lumira suite. Like SAP Lumira Cloud, you can use it to store and share SAP Lumira content. From the SAP Lumira Desktop Share room, you can publish either a dataset or a story to SAP Lumira Server; it is not possible to publish several stories at once.

The URL of the SAP Lumira Server is the one you have defined in the SAP LUMIRA PREFERENCES dialog box in the NETWORK category (see Chapter 2, Section 2.9). You must have an account given to you by your administrator to use SAP Lumira Server.

To publish a story or a dataset to SAP Lumira Server, follow these steps:

1. Open a document and click the SHARE tab to access the SHARE room.
2. In the DATASETS left pane, select a dataset or click STORIES, and when the story thumbnails are displayed select one. You cannot select several datasets or stories at the same time.
3. Click PUBLISH TO SAP LUMIRA SERVER to open the PUBLISH DATASET TO SAP LUMIRA SERVER dialog box, if you have selected a dataset, or the PUBLISH STORY TO SAP LUMIRA SERVER dialog box, if you have selected a story.
4. As shown in Figure 7.25, enter your credentials in the USERNAME and PASSWORD text fields or select the USE SINGLE SIGN-ON (SSO) TO LOG IN INSTEAD checkbox to log in using single sign-on. To configure single sign-on, see Chapter 3, Section 3.1.5.

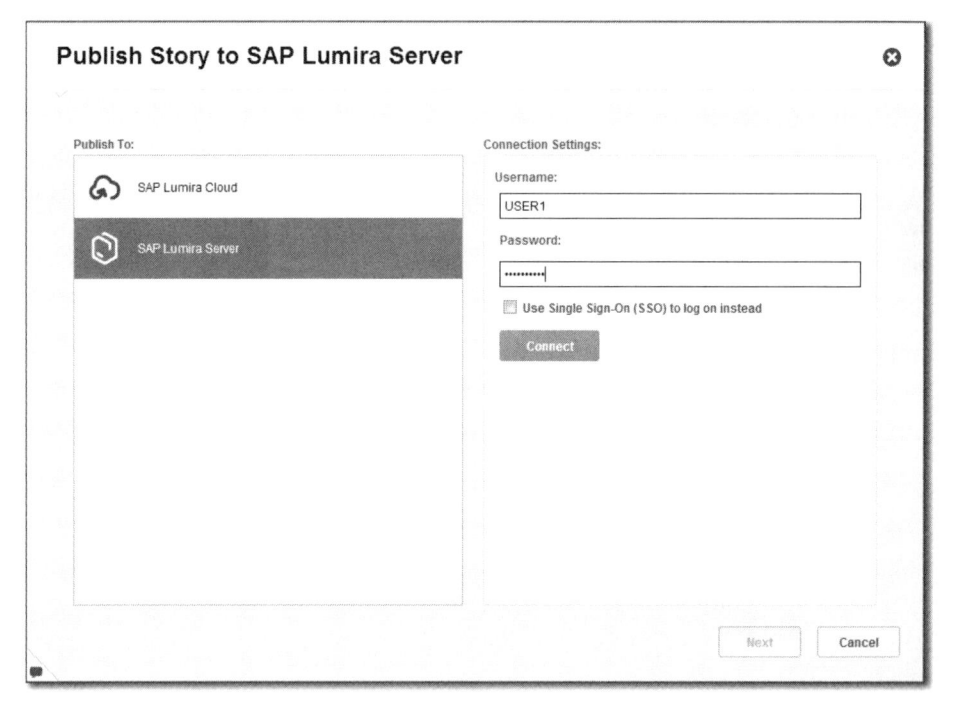

Figure 7.25 Publish to SAP Lumira Server Login Page

5. Click CONNECT to log into SAP Lumira Server.

6. The dialog box displays the resources to publish:
   - If you have selected a dataset, then this dataset.
   - If you have selected a story, then this story and all the datasets it relies on.
7. If none of these resources have already been published, as shown in Figure 7.26, then you can click PUBLISH to publish them. Once they are published, click DONE to close the dialog box.

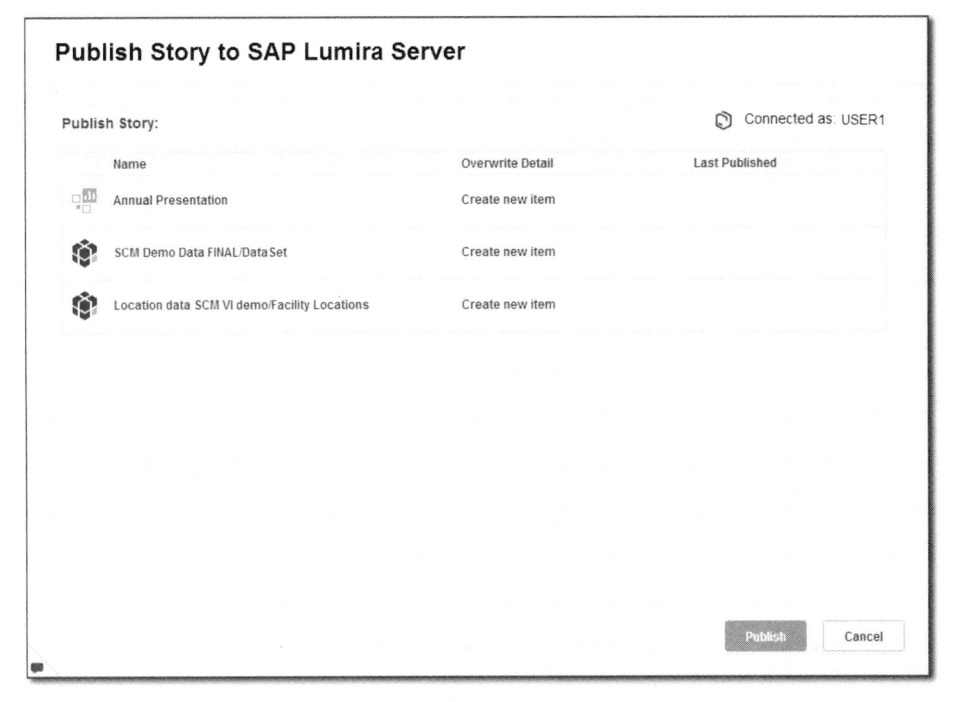

Figure 7.26 Publish to SAP Lumira Server Dialog Box

8. If any of these resources has already been published to SAP Lumira Server, then, as shown in Figure 7.27, the LAST PUBLISHED column displays when it was last published.

   If you are publishing a story, then you can select to not overwrite a dataset by selecting the DO NOT OVERWRITE option in the dropdown list of the OVERWRITE DETAIL column. In this case, the published story uses the dataset that already exists in the SAP Lumira Server. A story must always be overwritten.

7 | Sharing in SAP Lumira

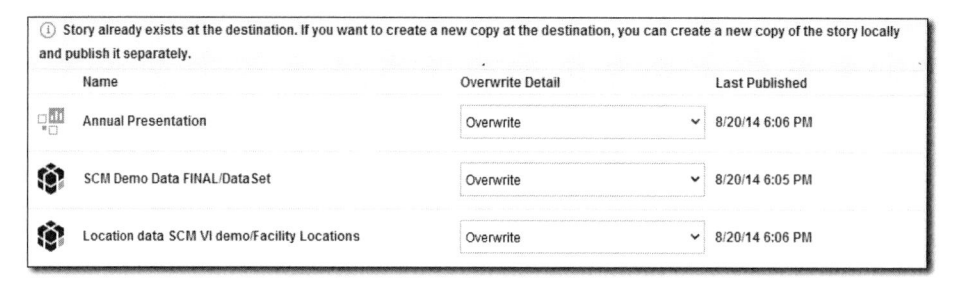

Figure 7.27 Resources Already Published to SAP Lumira Server

9. If a dataset is overwritten, you must click VERIFY to check if its schema has been changed and if it might create inconsistencies with stories based on this dataset and already published in SAP Lumira Server.

10. Once the verification is complete, as shown in Figure 7.28, click PUBLISH to publish the resources and DONE to close the dialog box after the resources have been published.

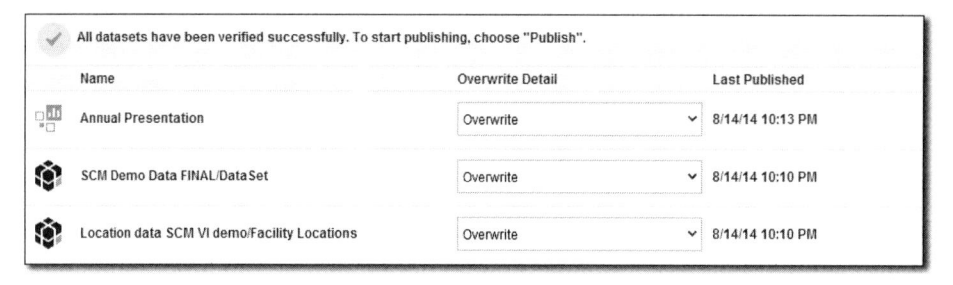

Figure 7.28 Datasets Successfully Verified in SAP Lumira Server

In the next section, we will discuss the ability to export datasets created in SAP Lumira Desktop.

7.8 Publishing Datasets to the File System

Datasets created in SAP Lumira Desktop can be exported into a file on the file system, either as a CSV file (in the generated file, columns are separated with commas) or a Microsoft Excel file (only Microsoft Excel 2013 — .xlsx file extension — is supported). Once generated, you can edit or email these files.

To export the datasets used by your document as a text or Microsoft Excel file, follow these steps:

1. Open a document and click the SHARE tab to access the Share room.
2. Click EXPORT AS FILE to open the EXPORT AS FILE dialog box.
3. In this dialog box, as shown in Figure 7.29, select (or not) the following options by clicking the corresponding checkboxes:
   - EXPORT WITH FILTERS: Select this checkbox to apply filters defined in the Prepare room on the dataset before exporting it.
   - EXPORT THE HIDDEN COLUMNS: Select this checkbox to include the data contained in hidden columns in the export.
   - EXPORT THE APPLICATIVE HIDDEN COLUMNS: Select this checkbox to include the data contained in hidden columns used for intermediary computations in the export.

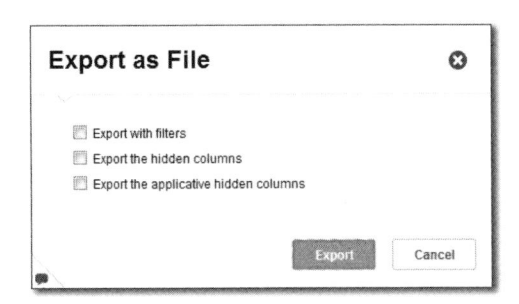

Figure 7.29 Export as File Dialog Box

4. Click EXPORT to open the SAVE AS dialog box.
5. Navigate in the file tree to go to the destination folder for the generated file.
6. In the FILE name field, enter the file name.
7. In the SAVE AS dropdown list, select the format in which to save the file: CSV FILES or EXCEL FILES.
8. Click SAVE to close the SAVE AS dialog box and to generate the file containing the dataset.

The next few sections will discuss the other SAP-supported systems through which SAP Lumira can publish, starting with SAP HANA.

7.9 Publishing a Dataset to SAP HANA

It is possible to export a dataset created in SAP Lumira to SAP HANA. The dataset is created in SAP HANA and exposed as an SAP HANA analytical view. Attribute views can be created if the datasets contain hierarchies. The dataset must have at least one measure aggregated with the `count`, `sum`, `min`, or `max` operator. To export the document dataset to SAP HANA, follow these steps:

1. Open a document and click the SHARE tab to access the SHARE room.
2. In the DATASETS left pane, select the dataset to publish. You can only publish one dataset at a time.
3. Click PUBLISH TO SAP HANA to open the PUBLISH TO SAP HANA dialog box, as shown in Figure 7.30.

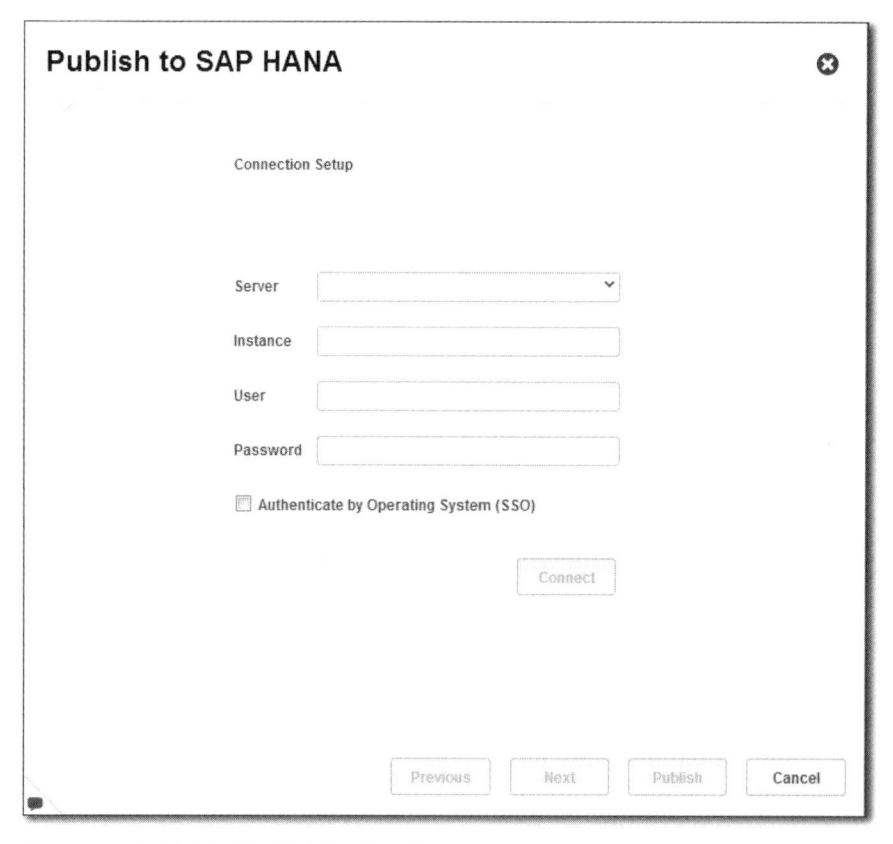

Figure 7.30 Publish to SAP HANA Dialog Box

4. Enter the parameters required to connect to the SAP HANA server:
   - SERVER: SAP HANA server name.
   - INSTANCE: SAP HANA port number.
   - USER and PASSWORD: Credentials to authenticate to the SAP HANA system if you do not use single sign-on.
   - AUTHENTICATE BY OPERATING SYSTEM (SSO): Select this checkbox to authenticate to the SAP HANA server using single sign-on. If you select this option, you do not need to enter USER and PASSWORD to authenticate, but you need to configure single sign-on (see Chapter 3, Section 3.1.5).
5. Click CONNECT to connect to the SAP HANA system. Once connected, the dialog box page displays a tree with the packages and views you have access to in the SAP HANA system, as seen in Figure 7.31.

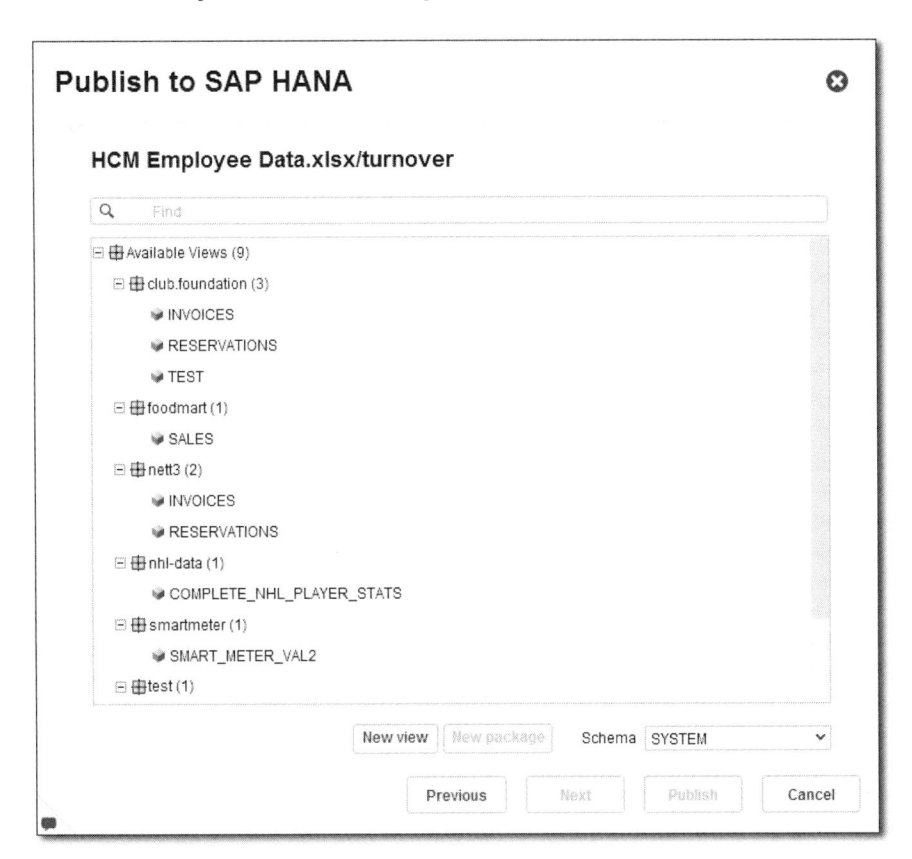

Figure 7.31 SAP HANA View Selection

6. Navigate in this tree to select the view in which the dataset must be saved. Alternately, you may take one of the following actions:

    ▶ Click NEW PACKAGE to create a new package. When the new package is added to the list, the focus is on this package, and you can rename it. Press [Enter] to validate the new name.

    ▶ Select a package and click NEW VIEW to create a new view. When the new view is added to the list, the focus is on this view, and you can rename it. Press [Enter] to validate the new name.

7. In the SCHEMA dropdown list, select in which schema of the SAP HANA database the tables are created.

8. Click PUBLISH to close the PUBLISH TO SAP HANA dialog box and publish the dataset in the selected view in the SAP HANA system, as shown in Figure 7.32.

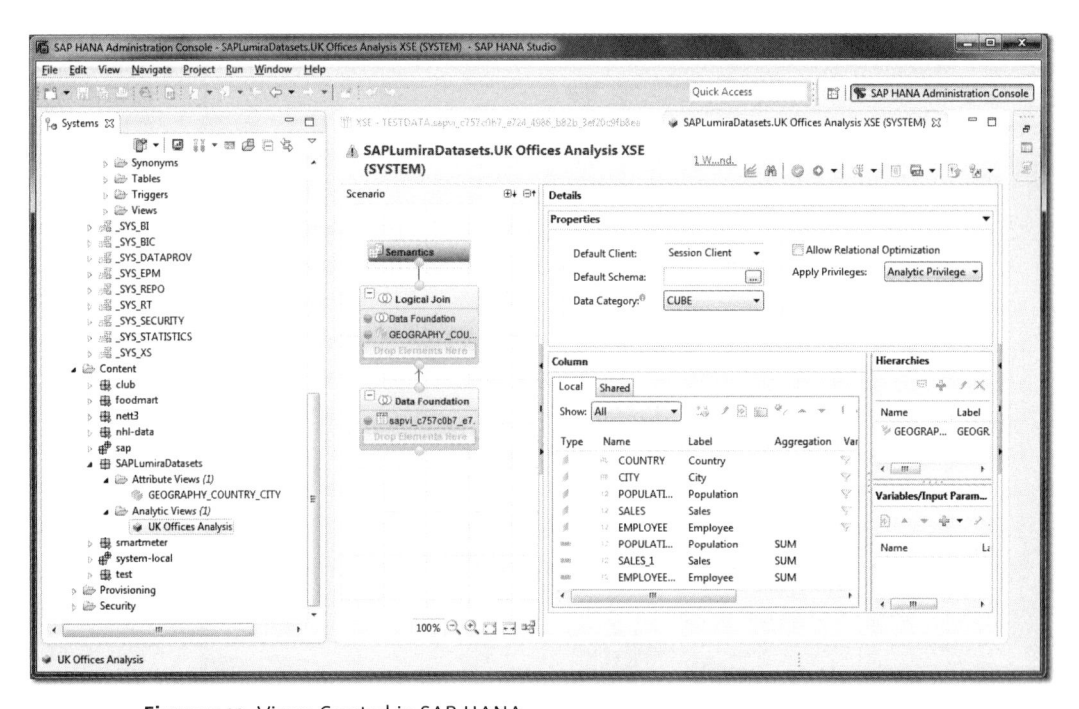

Figure 7.32 Views Created in SAP HANA

7.10 Publishing a Dataset to SAP Explorer

Like SAP HANA, it is also possible to publish a dataset created in SAP Lumira into SAP Explorer 4.0 with Support Pack 4 or higher.

The dataset is saved as a Microsoft Excel file in the CMS repository used by SAP Explorer. The name of this file is the dataset name, prefixed by "Excel-". The publication also creates an information space based on this Excel file, the name of which is the name of the dataset.

To export a dataset to SAP Explorer, you must have the following rights granted in the destination CMS repository:

- SAP Explorer application's MANAGE INFORMATION SPACES: CREATE A NEW INFORMATION SPACE right
- SAP Explorer application's MANAGE INFORMATION SPACES: LAUNCH INDEXING right
- The target folder's ADD OBJECTS TO THE FOLDER right

A dataset cannot be exported if it is an online dataset based on SAP HANA views or SAP BW (only offline datasets can be exported) or if it contains more than 10 million cells.

When exporting a dataset to SAP Explorer, the following points apply:

- Different dimension members with the same caption are considered a single member. For example, the same city with the same name but existing in two different countries generates only one member in the CITY facet, linked to the two countries. In theory, the two cities should be created in the CITY facet, each linked to a different country.
- Only measures using aggregation functions supported by SAP Explorer (none, sum, min, max, and count) are exported. Measures using other functions are not exported.
- Date and number formats are replaced by SAP Explorer date and number formats.

To export the document dataset to SAP Explorer, follow these steps:

1. Open a document and click the SHARE tab to access the SHARE room.
2. In the DATASETS left pane, select the dataset to publish.

3. Click PUBLISH TO EXPLORER to open the PUBLISH TO EXPLORER dialog box, as shown in Figure 7.33.

Figure 7.33 Publish to Explorer Dialog Box

4. Enter the following parameters required to connect to the SAP Explorer server:
    - CMS NAME: The name of the SAP BusinessObjects BI 4.1 server running the SAP server and its port. If you have already connected to this server, then you can also enter its cluster name.
    - AUTHENTICATION TYPE: Use the dropdown list to select one authentication mode to connect to SAP Explorer (ENTERPRISE, LDAP, WINDOWS AD, or SAP). If you use Windows AD authentication, then you need to configure single sign-on (see Chapter 3, Section 3.1.5).
    - USER NAME and PASSWORD: Credentials to authenticate to the CMS repository, using the previously selected authentication mode.

5. Click CONNECT to connect to SAP Explorer and display the list of folders in the CMS repository.
6. Navigate in the CMS repository, and select the folder in which the data source and information space must be created, as shown in Figure 7.34.

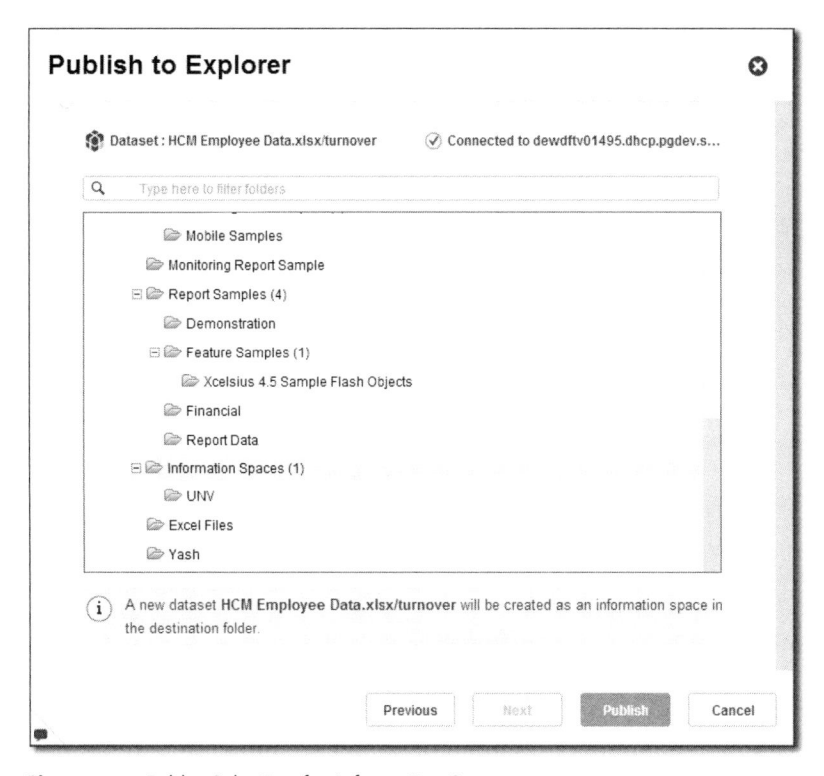

Figure 7.34 Folder Selection for Information Space

7. If the data source has already been published to the same folder, then a dropdown list allows you to choose between the following options (see Figure 7.35):
   - OVERWRITE: The existing files are replaced with the new ones.
   - CREATE NEW COPY: The files are saved, and their names are suffixed by a number—for example, "Excel-My dataset (1)"—to differentiate them from the existing ones.

Figure 7.35 Overwriting Dataset or Creating a New Copy

8. Click PUBLISH to publish the dataset as a Microsoft Excel file, generate the information space in the CMS repository, and close the PUBLISH TO EXPLORER dialog box.

9. Log in to SAP Explorer to check that the information space has been properly created, as seen in Figure 7.36.

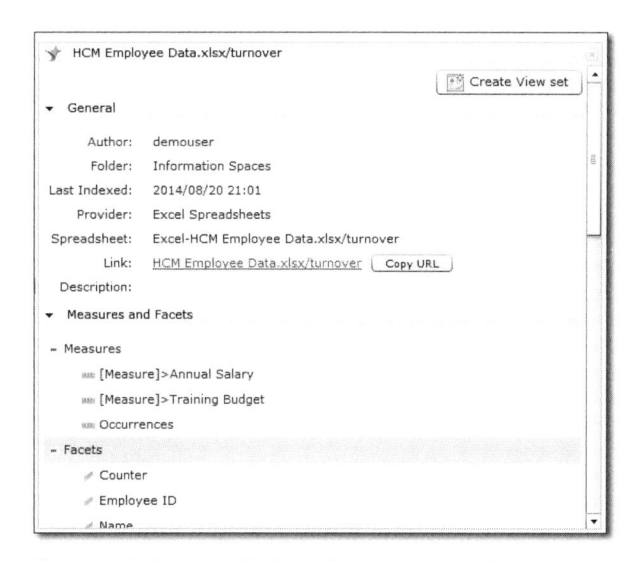

Figure 7.36 Generated Information Space in SAP Explorer

7.11 Publishing Datasets and Visualizations to SAP StreamWork

SAP StreamWork is one of the SAP collaborative tools available on the cloud. Its URL is *https://streamwork.com*. From SAP Lumira Desktop, you can publish a dataset in SAP StreamWork as a CSV or a Microsoft Excel file. You can also publish

7.11 Publishing Datasets and Visualizations to SAP StreamWork

a visualization in SAP StreamWork as a picture. To publish SAP Lumira content in SAP StreamWork, follow these steps:

1. Open a document and click the SHARE tab to access the SHARE room.
2. In the DATASETS left pane, select a dataset or click VISUALIZATIONS, and when the visualization thumbnails are displayed, select one.
3. Click PUBLISH TO SAP STREAMWORK to open the PUBLISH TO SAP STREAMWORK dialog box.
4. In the EMAIL and PASSWORD text fields, enter your credentials to authenticate to SAP StreamWork.
5. Click LOGIN to connect to SAP StreamWork. In the PUBLISH DATASET AS dropdown list, select how to publish the dataset in SAP StreamWork (see Figure 7.37):
    - CSV: Publish it as a CSV file.
    - EXCEL: Publish it as a Microsoft Excel file.
    - NONE: Do not publish the dataset.

Figure 7.37 Publish to SAP StreamWork

6. In the PUBLISH DATASET AS dropdown list, select how to publish the dataset in SAP StreamWork:
   - CSV: Publish it as a CSV file.
   - EXCEL: Publish it as a Microsoft Excel file.
   - NONE: Do not publish the dataset.
7. In the ACTIVITY dropdown list, select the SAP StreamWork activity in which the resources must be saved.
8. If you do not find an appropriate activity in this list, click CREATE ACTIVITY to open a new panel, as shown in Figure 7.38, and create a new activity in SAP StreamWork:
   - Enter a name for the activity in the ACTIVITY NAME field and a description for this activity in ACTIVITY OBJECTIVES.
   - In the PARTICIPANTS text field, enter the email addresses of the users to invite to the activity. Email addresses are analyzed on the fly. Correctly recognized addresses are displayed with a blue background and incorrect ones with a pink background.
   - Click CREATE to create the activity in SAP StreamWork and return to the previous panel.

Figure 7.38 Create Activity

9. Select INCLUDE DOCUMENT to also publish the SAP Lumira document.
10. In the DESCRIPTION text field, enter a description to add to the ABOUT property of all items published to SAP StreamWork.
11. Click PUBLISH to publish the dataset, and close the PUBLISH TO SAP STREAMWORK dialog box. The dataset, and its document if you have selected to publish it as well, are saved in the activity you selected. If you have chosen to create the activity, it is created first.

7.12 Publishing Datasets and Stories to SAP BusinessObjects BI

You can extend SAP BusinessObjects BI platform by installing the SAP BusinessObjects BI for SAP Lumira add-on. This add-on supports SAP BusinessObjects BI 4.1, starting Support Package 3 or higher, but not SAP BusinessObjects BI 4.0. This add-on allows you to use your CMS repository for SAP Lumira content and benefit from the SAP BusinessObjects BI 4.1 platform for your SAP Lumira documents (see Chapter 10). With this add-on in the CMS repository, datasets can be saved in the SAP Lumira Datasets root folder, whereas stories can be saved in the Favorites or Public Folders folders or sub-folders.

More details about this add-on for SAP Lumira can be found in Chapter 10; this section describes only how to publish SAP Lumira dataset and story into an SAP BusinessObjects BI 4.1 system where this add-on has been installed.

The communication with the SAP BusinessObjects BI 4.1 server takes place via a RESTful web service. Ask your SAP BusinessObjects BI administrator the URL for this RESTful web service.

> **RESTful Web Service**
>
> RESTful web service is an exchange protocol based on HTTP web service. SAP BusinessObjects BI 4.1 exposes a public API through a RESTful web service. This API is used by SAP Lumira to connect with SAP BusinessObjects BI 4.1 server. The RESTful web service is hosted on SAP BusinessObjects BI 4.1 by the Web Application Container Server (WACS). By default, its URL is *http://<servername>:6405/biprws*.

To publish a dataset or a story in SAP BusinessObjects BI 4.1, you must have a valid account for the SAP BusinessObjects BI 4.1 platform. You must also have the security right granted "Add objects to the folder" for the destination folder(s).

If you meet these requirements, then follow these steps to publish a dataset or a story in SAP BusinessObjects BI 4.1:

1. Open a document, and click the SHARE tab to access the SHARE room.
2. In the DATASETS pane on the left, select a dataset or click STORIES, and when the story thumbnails are displayed, select one. You cannot select several datasets or stories at the same time.

3. Click Publish to SAP BI to open:
   - The Publish Dataset to SAP BI dialog box if you have selected a dataset.
   - The Publish Story to SAP BI dialog box if you have selected a story, as shown in Figure 7.39.

Figure 7.39 Publish Story to SAP BI Dialog Box

4. Enter the parameters needed to connect to the SAP BusinessObjects BI 4.1 system:
   - REST access URL: The URL to access the RESTful web service
   - Authentication Type: The authentication mode to connect to SAP BusinessObjects BI 4.1
   - User and Password: The credentials to connect to SAP BusinessObjects BI 4.1
5. Click Connect to open a session with the SAP BusinessObjects BI 4.1 system.
6. If you have selected to publish a dataset, you can select the name of the dataset to publish, as shown in Figure 7.40, then click Next.

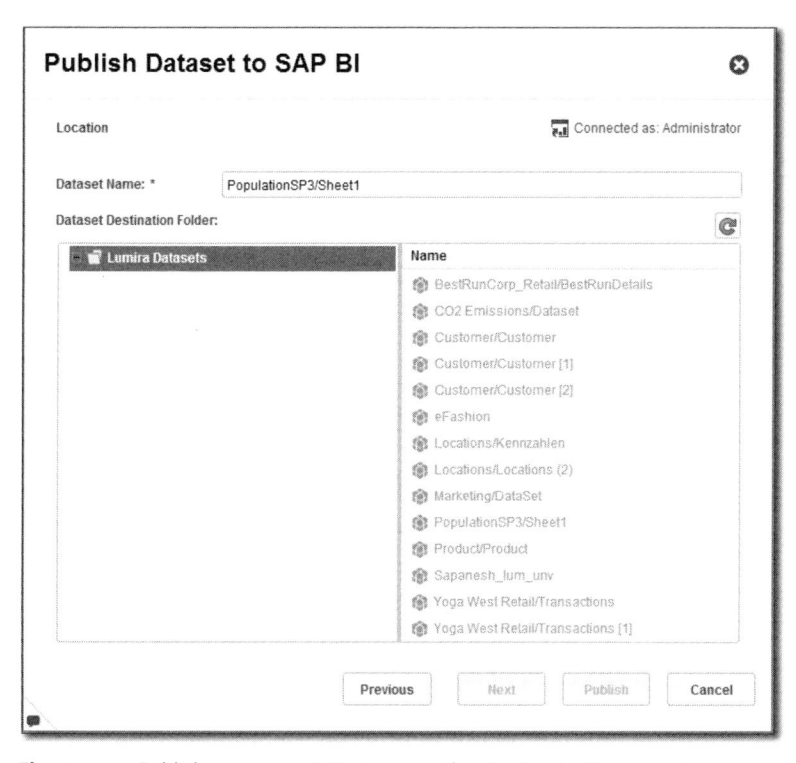

Publishing Datasets and Stories to SAP BusinessObjects BI | **7.12**

Figure 7.40 Publish Dataset in SAP BusinessObjects BI 4.1 CMS Repository

7. If you have selected a story, you can select the target folder under FAVORITES or PUBLIC folders, as shown in Figure 7.41, then click NEXT.

Figure 7.41 Folder Navigation in SAP BusinessObjects BI 4.1 CMS Repository

8. The dialog box displays the resources to publish:
   - If you have selected a dataset, then this dataset.
   - If you have selected a story, then this story and all the dataset(s) it relies on.
9. If none of these resources have already been published, as shown in Figure 7.42, then you can click PUBLISH to publish them, and once they are published, click DONE to close the dialog box.

Figure 7.42 Publish to SAP BI Dialog Box

10. If any of these resources has already been published into SAP BusinessObjects BI 4.1, then, as shown in Figure 7.43, the LAST PUBLISHED column displays when it was last published.

   If you are publishing a story and if one of its dataset has already been published, you can select to not overwrite it, by selecting the DO NOT OVERWRITE option in the dropdown list of the OVERWRITE DETAIL column. In this case, the published story uses the dataset already existing in the SAP BusinessObjects BI 4.1.

Figure 7.43 Resources Already Published into SAP Lumira Server

11. If a dataset is overwritten, you must click VERIFY to check if its schema has been changed because it may create inconsistencies with stories based on this dataset and already published on SAP BusinessObjects BI 4.1.

12. Once the verification has been done, as shown in Figure 7.44, click PUBLISH to publish the resources.

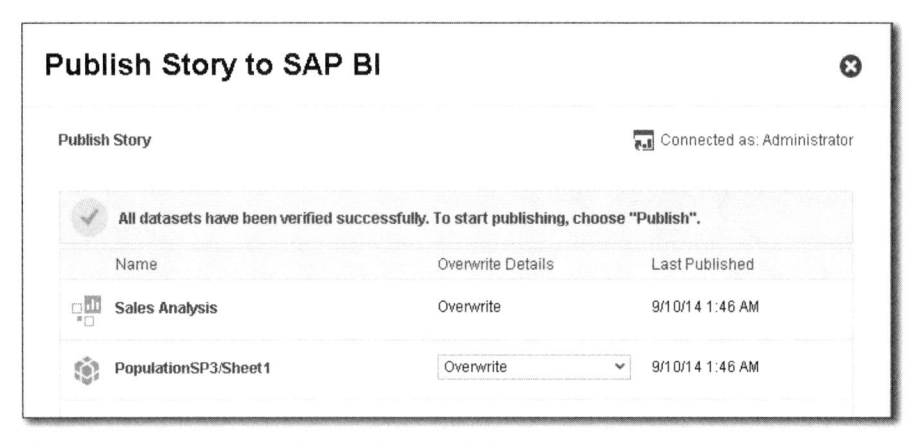

Figure 7.44 Datasets Successfully Verified into SAP BI

13. After the resource(s) have been published, click DONE to close the dialog box.

7.13 Summary

In SAP Lumira Desktop, the Share room can be used to mail or print SAP Lumira visualizations or export an SAP Lumira dataset as a CSV or Microsoft Excel file. This room can also be used to publish SAP Lumira datasets, visualizations, or stories to other SAP systems or other SAP Lumira suite deployments:

- Datasets can be published to SAP HANA, SAP Explorer, SAP StreamWork, SAP Lumira Cloud, SAP Lumira Server, or SAP BusinessObjects BI 4.1 if the add-on for SAP Lumira has been installed.
- Visualizations can be published to SAP StreamWork.
- Stories can be shared to SAP Lumira Cloud, SAP Lumira Server, or SAP BusinessObjects BI 4.1 if the add-on for SAP Lumira has been installed.

SAP Lumira Cloud can also be used to store SAP Lumira documents. Saving these documents to SAP Lumira Cloud can be done manually or automatically through the SAP Lumira Agent, which can be used to refresh the dataset.

In the next chapter, we will discuss the SAP Lumira Cloud at greater length.

The SAP Lumira suite includes SAP Lumira Cloud, where you can share an SAP Lumira document or create it directly from the cloud.

8   SAP Lumira Cloud

In recent years, the cloud model has become increasingly popular for several reasons. Its administration is delegated to the service provider, which reduces the total cost of ownership and allows you to get faster updates without having to manage them. By design, cloud software is scalable and its resources can be adapted on demand. From a user's perspective, the cloud services can be available on any devices from a web browser without having to install any hardware or software. Because the resources are saved on the cloud, they can be used for collaboration.

Due to all of these advantages, it became natural for SAP Lumira suite to propose its own cloud version as an option for users looking for the advantages of the cloud framework. Chapter 7 discussed how SAP Lumira Desktop content can be saved to SAP Lumira Cloud. From within SAP Lumira Cloud, you can access additional capabilities, which will be described throughout the chapter. These capabilities include the following:

- Upload existing SAP Lumira documents or other document types.
- Import data into SAP Lumira Cloud to create datasets and save them in your space.
- Create and edit visualizations and stories, as in SAP Lumira Desktop.
- Share your SAP Lumira documents with colleagues and control who can access them.

However, before taking advantage of these capabilities you will need access to SAP Lumira Cloud.

8.1 SAP Lumira Cloud Access

As most services based on a cloud model, you need to register an account to access SAP Lumira Cloud. Like accessing SAP Lumira Desktop, this whole process is simple in order to ease SAP Lumira Cloud adoption.

8.1.1 License Model

SAP Lumira Cloud supports two licenses: a free license and an enterprise license. The free license is intended to help you become familiar with this cloud service. It is available for one user and provides 1 gigabyte (GB) of free storage in SAP Lumira Cloud.

The enterprise license gives you 5 GB of shared storage for five users. The enterprise license also allows you to manage user access and permissions. This subscription is charged monthly, with a small fee per additional gigabyte of storage (above the first 5 GB) and each additional user per month.

> **License Subscription**
> At the time of writing, the additional subscription fees for SAP Lumira Cloud are $24 per additional user per month and $24 per additional GB per month.

8.1.2 Creating Your Account from SAP Lumira Cloud

To create an account for SAP Lumira Cloud, go to *https://cloud.saplumira.com*. The SAP Lumira Cloud interface is written in HTML5. This means that you can access and use SAP Lumira Cloud from any browser that supports it. The interface adapts itself to the size of the screen, allowing you to use a desktop or mobile device.

> **Secure Socket Layer (SSL)**
> The URL *http://cloud.saplumira.com* is also valid; it redirects you to the URL *https://cloud.saplumira.com*, which supports SSL.

You can register and get your account directly from the SAP Lumira Cloud website. To do so, follow these steps:

1. In a web browser, go to the SAP Lumira Cloud URL: *https://cloud.saplumira.com*.
2. At the login page, as shown in Figure 8.1, click REGISTER NEW ACCOUNT.

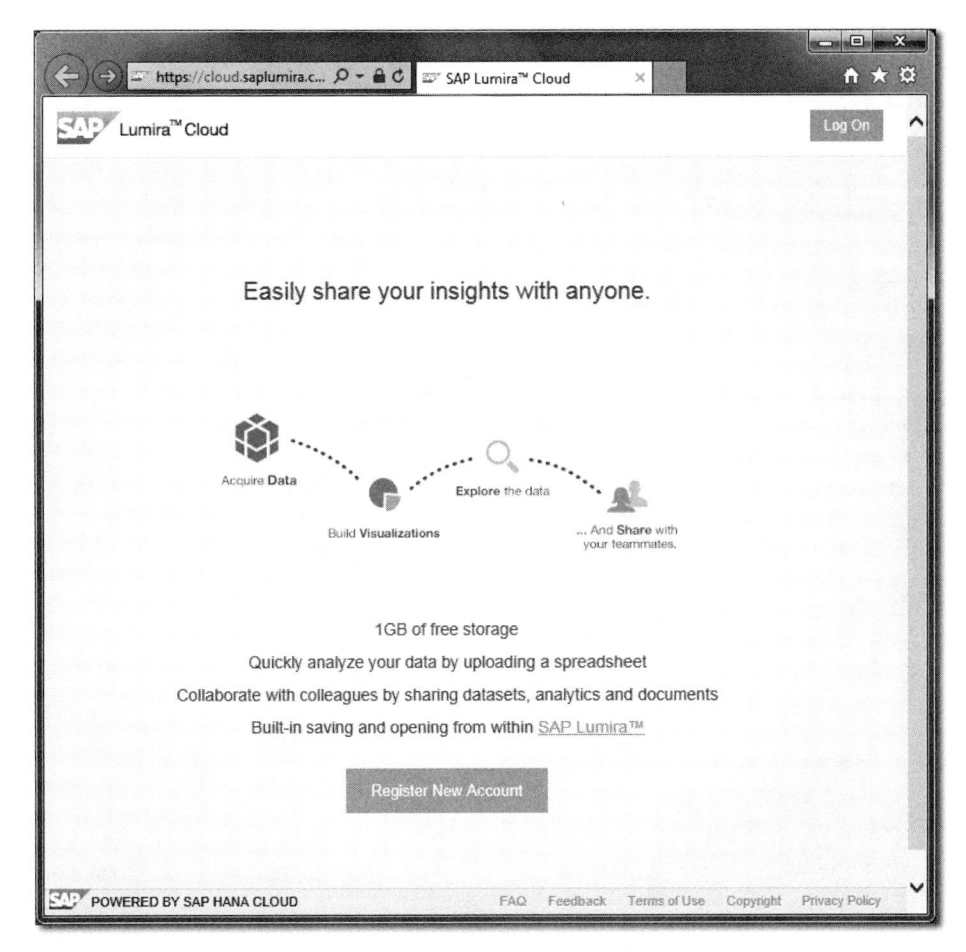

Figure 8.1 SAP Lumira Cloud Login Page

3. The REGISTRATION panel opens, as shown in Figure 8.2. Enter some data to identify you. The email address you enter will be used to send you an email to confirm your registration.

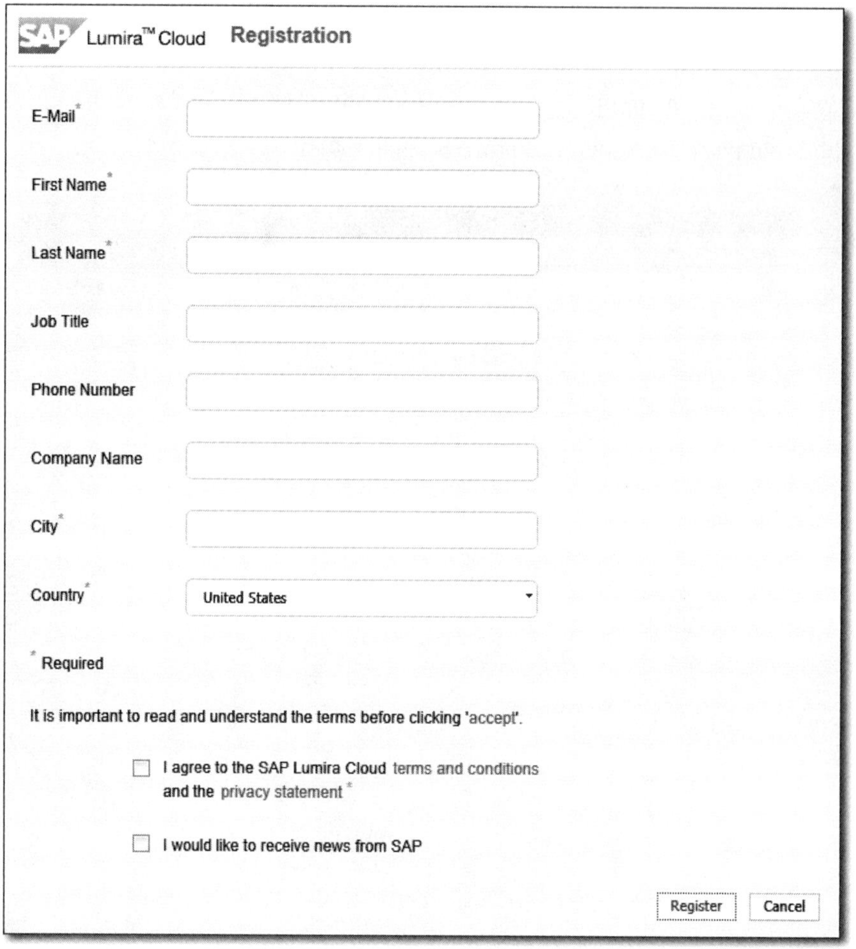

Figure 8.2 Registration Page

4. Click the TERMS AND CONDITIONS and PRIVACY STATEMENT links to read these contractual details. Select the I AGREE TO THE SAP LUMIRA CLOUD TERMS AND CONDITIONS AND THE PRIVACY STATEMENT checkbox to accept them.

5. Click REGISTER to send your data. The THANK YOU message is displayed, as shown in Figure 8.3.

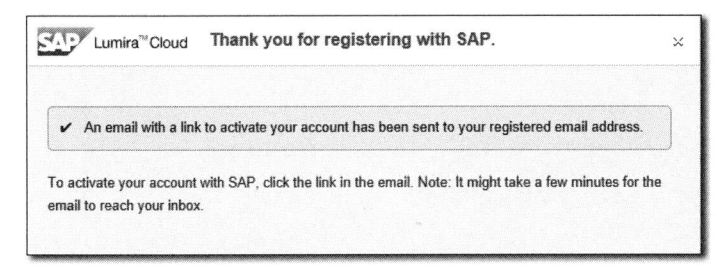

Figure 8.3 Registration Final Message

6. Check the mailbox of the email address you provided when registering your account. You should receive a confirmation email.
7. Once you have received this email, click the link it contains to finalize the activation process. This opens your web browser with the ACCOUNT SUCCESSFULLY ACTIVATED page, as shown in Figure 8.4.

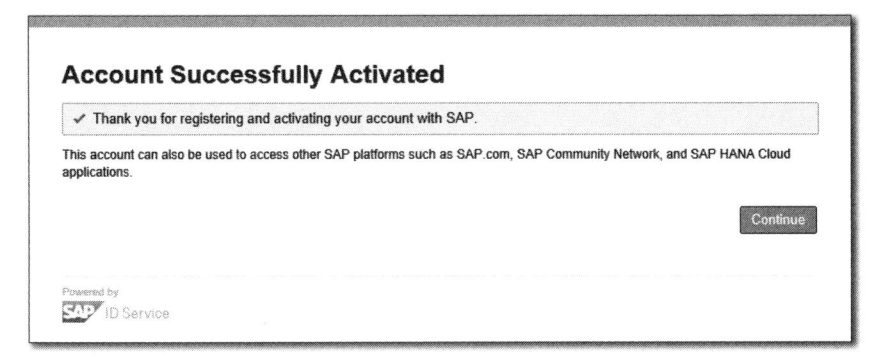

Figure 8.4 Successful Activation Page

8. Click CONTINUE to log into SAP Lumira Cloud and display its home page, as shown in Figure 8.5.

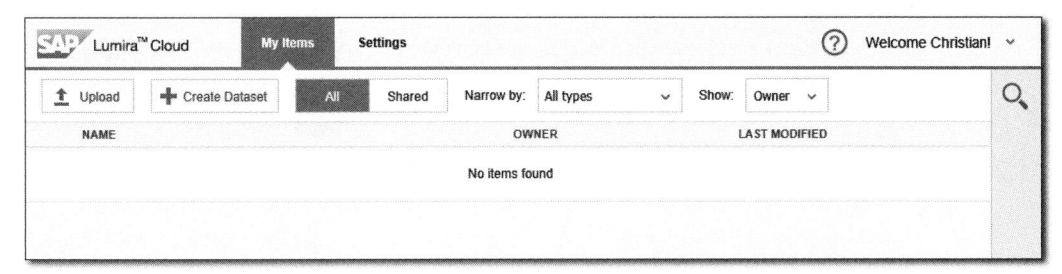

Figure 8.5 SAP Lumira Cloud Home Page

This page and the actions you can perform from it are described starting in Section 8.3.

8.1.3 Creating Your Account from SAP Lumira Desktop

You can also create your SAP Lumira Cloud account directly from SAP Lumira Desktop by following these steps:

1. In SAP Lumira Desktop, go to the WELCOME page (see Chapter 2, Section 2.7.1).
2. In the left pane, click SAP LUMIRA CLOUD to display the SAP Lumira Cloud login fields, as shown in Figure 8.6.
3. Click CREATE A NEW SAP LUMIRA CLOUD ACCOUNT to open a browser to the SAP Lumira Cloud registration page, shown in Figure 8.2.

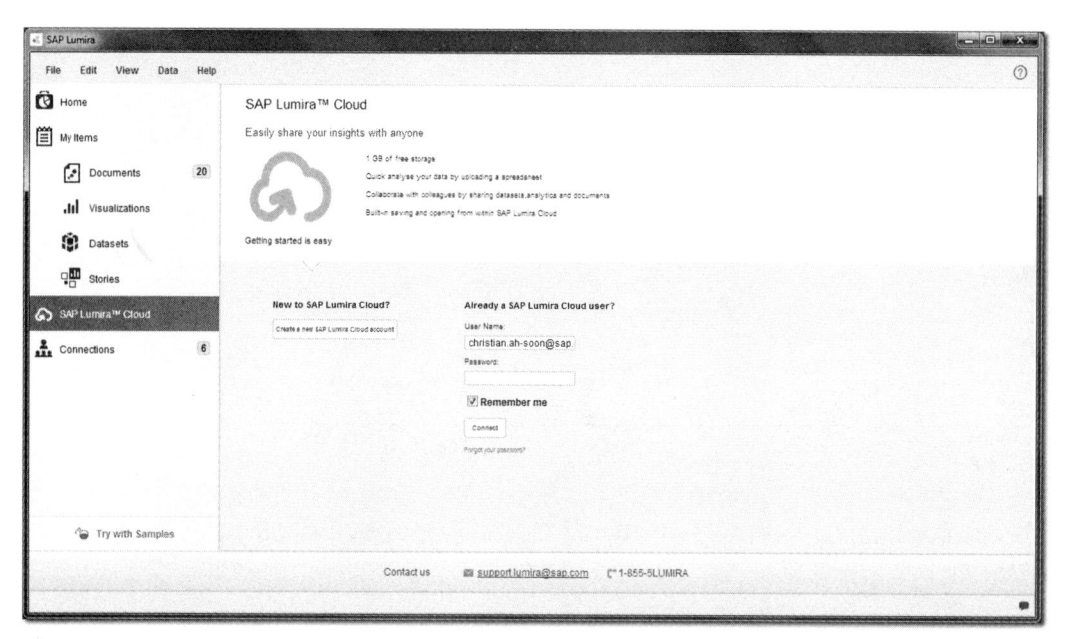

Figure 8.6 Accessing SAP Lumira Cloud from SAP Lumira Desktop

4. As described in Section 8.1.2, on this page you may enter your personal data and continue the process of creating your SAP Lumira Cloud account.
5. Once you have registered, return to SAP Lumira Desktop and enter the information you previously entered in the USER NAME and PASSWORD text fields to connect to SAP Lumira Cloud from the desktop application.

8.1.4 Account Management

The account you create to access SAP Lumira Cloud is managed by the SAP ID service that centralizes accounts for several SAP services or applications (SAP Store, SAP Community Network, etc.).

You cannot modify your password from within SAP Lumira Cloud. You need to modify it from within the SAP ID service available at the URL *https://accounts.sap.com/ui/protected/profilemanagement*. You can access this URL by clicking the GO TO YOUR GLOBAL SAP ID SERVICES PROFILE link in the SETTINGS tab (see Section 8.3.5).

8.1.5 Log In to SAP Lumira Cloud

You can log in to SAP Lumira Cloud by opening its URL (*https://cloud.saplumira.com*) in your web browser. Then click LOG ON and enter your credentials. After validation, you are redirected to the SAP Lumira Cloud user interface (see Section 8.3).

8.1.6 Log Out of SAP Lumira Cloud

If you remain inactive for more than 25 minutes, a message is displayed to warn you that your session is about to expire, as shown in Figure 8.7. Click CANCEL to log out or OK to reset the session timeout. If you do not respond within five minutes, then your session is automatically closed.

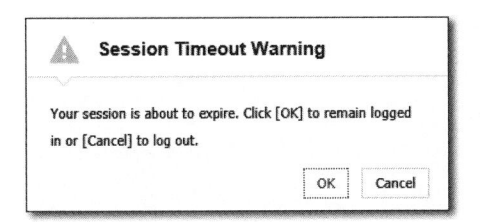

Figure 8.7 Session Timeout Warning

To explicitly log out of SAP Lumira Cloud:

1. Click the down arrow in the top-right corner of the page. A dialog box opens, as seen in Figure 8.8.
2. Click LOG OFF to terminate your session on SAP Lumira Cloud.

Figure 8.8 Log Off Dialog Box

As SAP Lumira Cloud is part of the SAP Lumira suite, we'll discuss next how to connect to SAP Lumira Cloud via SAP Lumira Desktop.

8.2 Connecting from SAP Lumira Desktop

From SAP Lumira Desktop, you can connect to SAP Lumira Cloud and navigate in your space. This allows you to access the SAP Lumira documents that you have saved in the cloud or that have been shared with you by others. You can then retrieve and edit these documents in SAP Lumira Desktop.

Unfortunately, you cannot access the other resource types, such as the stories or datasets that you have published in SAP Lumira Cloud. Once published, you can only access them from SAP Lumira Cloud.

To connect to SAP Lumira Cloud from SAP Lumira Desktop, follow these steps:

1. In SAP Lumira Desktop, go to the WELCOME page (see Chapter 2, Section 2.7.1).

2. In the left pane, click SAP LUMIRA CLOUD to display the SAP Lumira Cloud login page, as shown in Figure 8.6.

3. If you do not have yet an account for SAP Lumira Cloud, you can create it by clicking CREATE A NEW SAP LUMIRA CLOUD ACCOUNT, as described in Section 8.1.3.

    If you already have an SAP Lumira Cloud account, then enter your username and password in the USER NAME and PASSWORD text fields.

4. To save these credentials and avoid needing to retype them in later sessions, select the REMEMBER ME checkbox.

5. Click CONNECT to connect to SAP Lumira Cloud. Once connected, the list of documents you can access in SAP Lumira Cloud are displayed on the right side of the pane, as shown in Figure 8.9.

Figure 8.9 SAP Lumira Cloud Content from SAP Lumira Desktop

Click REFRESH to retrieve the updated list of documents from SAP Lumira Cloud.

6. Click a document to import it locally into your SAP Lumira folder, and open it in SAP Lumira Desktop in your default room (see Chapter 2, Section 2.7.2).

You can edit this document in the Prepare, Visualize, or Compose rooms, as described in Chapter 4, Chapter 5, and Chapter 6. If you save your changes, then they apply only to the copy saved in the SAP Lumira folder on your local disk (see Chapter 2, Section 2.8.1). To save your changes in SAP Lumira Cloud, you need to save the document using the SAVE OPTIONS dialog box, as described in Chapter 7, Section 7.6.

To close your session in SAP Lumira Cloud, follow these steps:

1. On right-top corner of the SAP Lumira Cloud document list, click the ARROW icon to open the LOG OFF dialog box, as shown in Figure 8.10.

2. In this dialog box, click LOG OFF to close your session.

Figure 8.10 SAP Lumira Cloud Log Off Dialog Box

Now that you've gained access and discovered the multiple ways to connect with the cloud, let's discuss its user interface.

8.3 SAP Lumira Cloud User Interface

You access SAP Lumira Cloud from your web browser. Its interface is similar for all supported web browsers and is described in this section.

8.3.1 General Overview

Once you have logged in to SAP Lumira Cloud, its page displays two tabs:

- MY ITEMS
  This tab is your working space; it contains the resources published in SAP Lumira Cloud that you can access. From this tab, you can open these resources and work on them. It is described from Section 8.3.2 to Section 8.3.4.

- SETTINGS
  This tab allows you to administrate your account and the additional accounts if you have an enterprise license. It is described in Section 8.3.5.

In the top-right corner of the page, you can click on the WELCOME link to open the LOG OFF dialog box, as described in Section 8.1.6. You can also click the HELP icon to open SAP Lumira Cloud help. Information about the use of SAP Lumira Cloud can be found at the bottom of the page (terms of use, copyright and privacy policy).

8.3.2 My Items Tab

The MY ITEMS tab is the main space from which to run most of your actions in SAP Lumira Cloud. As seen in Figure 8.11, it displays all resources you have access to as a flat list.

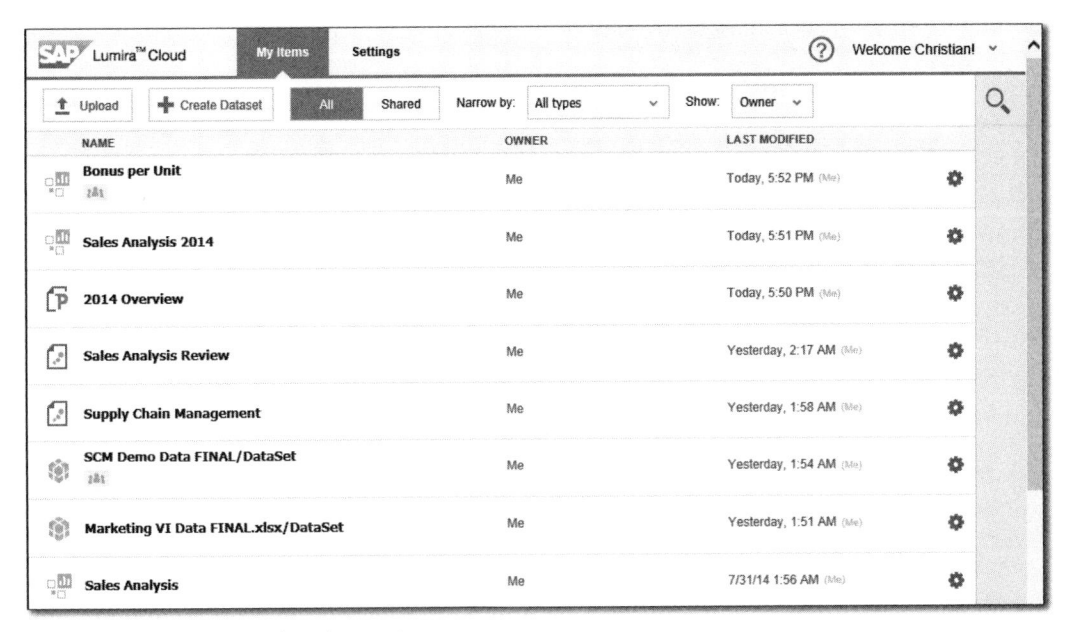

Figure 8.11 Resources Displayed in My Items

The resources are identified by icons depending on their type; these icons are described in Table 8.1.

Icon	Type	Description
	STORY	Stories and visualizations saved in SAP Lumira Cloud.
	STORY	Visualizations supported in previous versions of SAP Lumira Cloud. This visualization format is deprecated (see the "Deprecated Visualizations" note next).
	DATASET	Dataset used by the SAP Lumira stories stored in SAP Lumira Cloud.
	SAP LUMIRA DOCUMENT	SAP Lumira document.
	CSV	CSV file.

Table 8.1 Resource Types in SAP Lumira Cloud

393

Icon	Type	Description
☒	EXCEL SPREADSHEET	Microsoft Excel spreadsheet.
☐	POWERPOINT	Microsoft PowerPoint presentation.
☐	SAP CRYSTAL REPORTS	SAP Crystal Reports report.
☐	DESIGN STUDIO	SAP Design Studio dashboard.

Table 8.1 Resource Types in SAP Lumira Cloud (Cont.)

Deprecated Visualizations

In previous versions of SAP Lumira Cloud, visualizations were supported using a specific format and edited using a dedicated editor. In the current version of SAP Lumira Cloud, it is no longer possible to create such visualizations, but you can still open and view them in their dedicated editor.

You can also convert them into the new story format (see Figure 8.17), which allows you to edit them in the Visualize and Compose rooms (see Section 8.5) for a seamless experience in SAP Lumira Cloud, SAP Lumira Server, and SAP Lumira Desktop.

If the list contains too many items, then you can use any of the following options to filter it:

- Use the ALL and SHARED buttons to display either all resources or only the ones you have shared (see Section 8.6).
- In the NARROW BY dropdown list (see Figure 8.12), you can filter the list of resources to display by type. The possible choices are as follows:
  - ALL TYPES to display all resource types
  - One type from Table 8.1

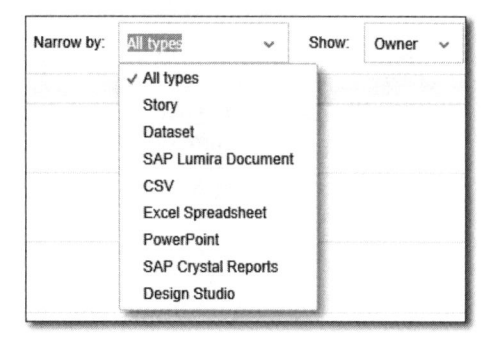

Figure 8.12 Narrow by Dropdown List

- In the SHOW dropdown list (see Figure 8.13), you can select what property to display in the resource list for each resource:
    - OWNER: The account that uploaded or created the resource. If you are this owner, then it displays ME.
    - SIZE: The size of the resource.
    - TYPE: The resource type. Possible values are listed in Table 8.1.

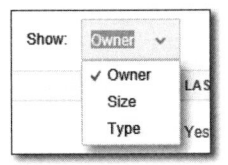

Figure 8.13 Show Dropdown List

In addition to these display options, to find a specific item in the MY ITEMS list, you may use the search tool.

8.3.3 Searching for Items

The right side of the MY ITEM tab displays the SEARCH icon, a magnifying glass. To search items in SAP Lumira Cloud, perform the following steps:

1. Click on the SEARCH icon to open the SEARCH text field, as shown in Figure 8.14.

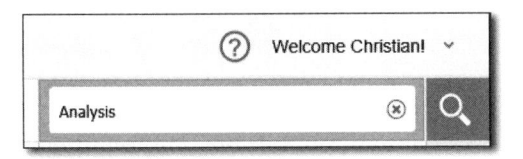

Figure 8.14 Search Text Field

2. In this text field, enter the search pattern, and then press [Enter].
3. The list of resources is filtered with the search pattern you have entered.
4. If you click the SEARCH icon again, then the SEARCH text field collapses, but your search remains displayed, as shown in Figure 8.15, to remind you that the current list of items is filtered.

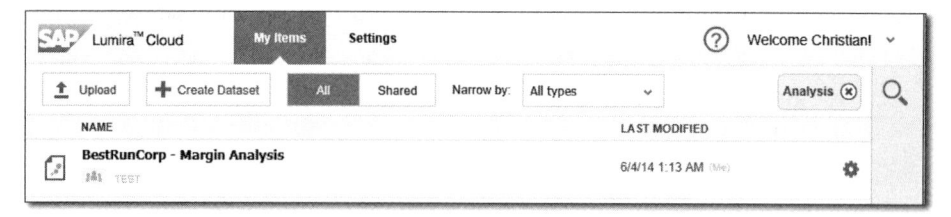

Figure 8.15 Filtered List of Items

5. Click the DELETE icon on the filter to remove it and display the unfiltered list of resources.

8.3.4 Running Actions

Click the cog icon displayed in the same line as the resource. A contextual menu will open up (see Figure 8.16).

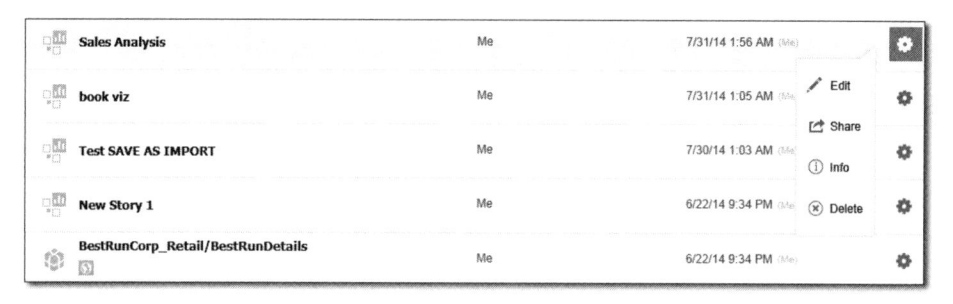

Figure 8.16 Actions Contextual Menu

From this menu, you can select one of the following possible commands:

- EDIT
  This command is available only for stories. It opens the story in the Visualize room for editing.

- EXPLORE
  This command is available only for older, deprecated versions of visualizations (see Section 8.3.2). It opens the visualization into its dedicated viewer. Before this deprecated visualization is opened, SAP Lumira prompts you to convert it into the new story format, as seen in Figure 8.17. If you open the visualization without converting it, you can still convert it later by clicking CONVERT in the top right of the page.

SAP Lumira Cloud User Interface | 8.3

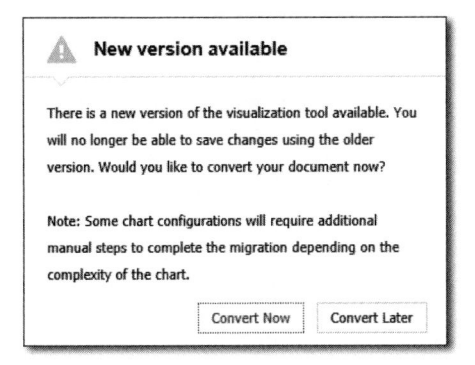

Figure 8.17 Deprecated Story Conversion Message

- DOWNLOAD
  Download the resource locally on your file system.

- SHARE
  Share the selected resource with other users in SAP Lumira Cloud (see Section 8.6).

- INFO
  Open a new window in which you can display and modify the selected resource name and its description, as shown in Figure 8.18. If the resource is a story, then the window displays a link to the story, as shown in Figure 8.19.

- DELETE
  Delete the selected resource. After clicking through a confirmation message, it is deleted from the cloud and removed from the MY ITEMS list.

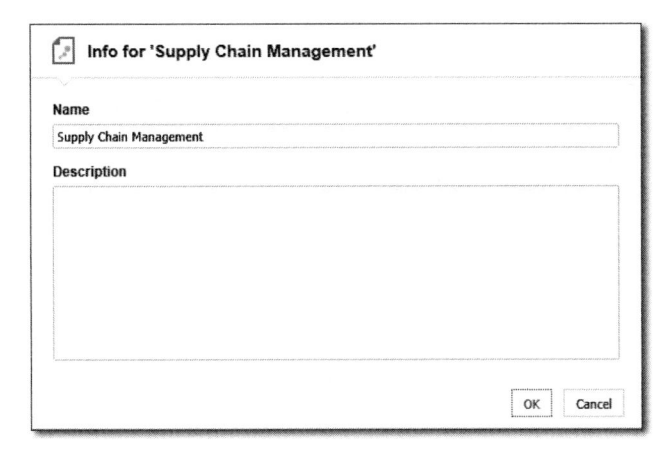

Figure 8.18 Resource Info Dialog Box for an SAP Lumira Document

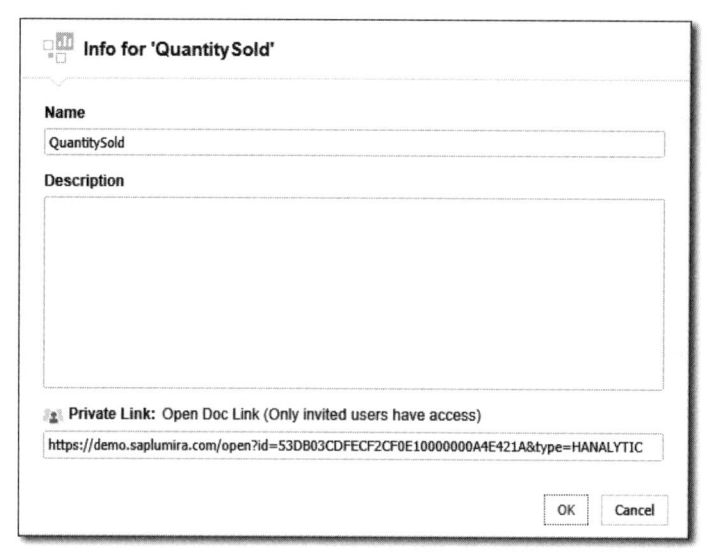

Figure 8.19 Resource Info Dialog Box for a Story

The actions available for each resource type are listed in Table 8.2.

Resource Type	Possible Actions
Dataset	▸ Share ▸ Info ▸ Delete
Story	▸ Edit ▸ Share ▸ Info ▸ Delete
Others (including SAP Lumira Document)	▸ Share ▸ Download ▸ Info ▸ Delete

Table 8.2 Actions Available In Resource Contextual Menus

Resource Type	Possible Actions
Story (deprecated visualization)	▸ Explore ▸ Share ▸ Info ▸ Delete

Table 8.2 Actions Available In Resource Contextual Menus (Cont.)

In addition to these contextual menus, you can click on some resource types in the MY ITEMS list:

- Click a story to open and view it:
  - ▸ To edit it (see Section 8.5), click EDIT in the top-right side of the page, and the document will open in the VISUALIZE room.
  - ▸ To share it (see Section 8.6), click the SHARE icon in the top-right side of the page, and the SHARE WITH OTHERS dialog box will open.
- Click a dataset to open the Visualize room (see Section 8.5), and create a new visualization from this dataset.

8.3.5 Settings Tab

The SETTINGS tab contains details of your profile and—if you have an enterprise license— of your team. To open and modify these parameters on this tab, follow these steps:

1. Click the SETTINGS tab in the main toolbar or click SETTINGS in the LOG OFF dialog box (see Section 8.1.6).
2. As shown in Figure 8.20, the SETTINGS tab contains two subtabs:
   - ▸ PROFILE subtab: Contains the personal information you have provided when you registered.
   - ▸ ACCOUNT INFO subtab: Displays some information about your account in SAP Lumira Cloud. If you have subscribed to an enterprise license, then the TEAM subtab allows you to manage your team members.

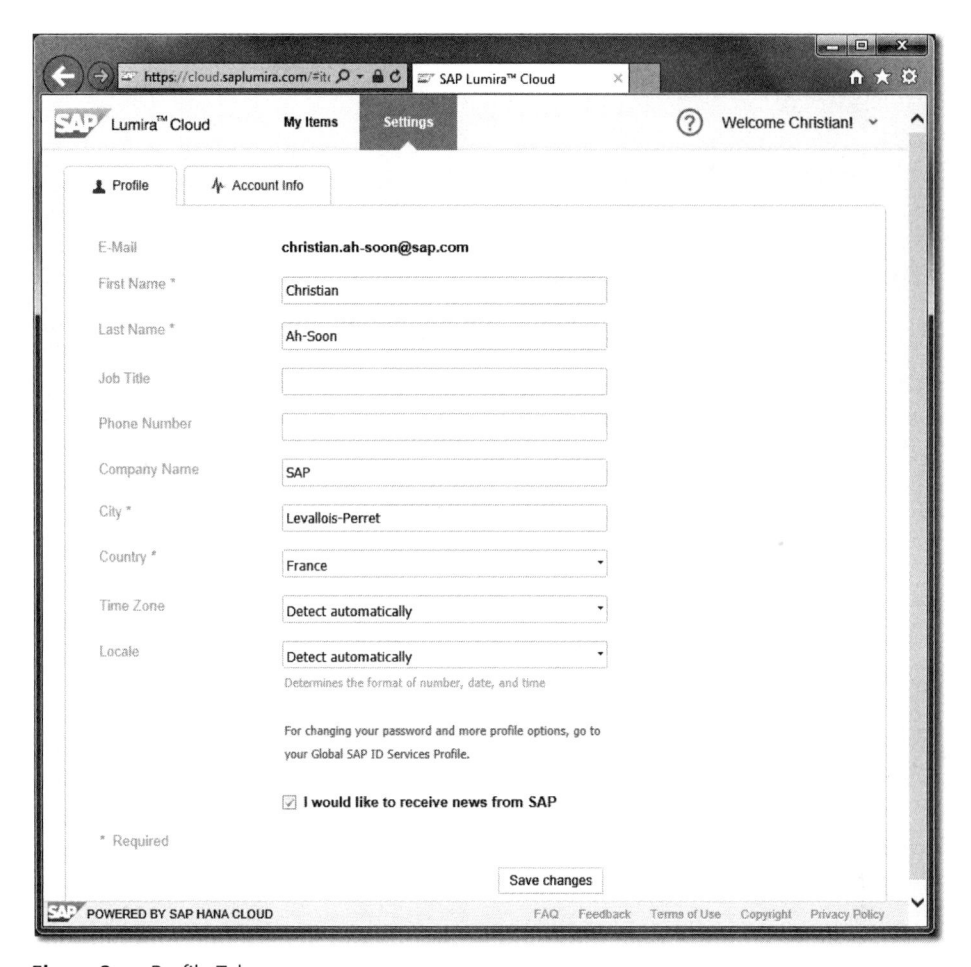

Figure 8.20 Profile Tab

3. You may modify your personal information in the PROFILE subtab:

   ▶ Parameters entered when registering your account: FIRST NAME, LAST NAME, JOB TITLE, PHONE NUMBER, COMPANY NAME, CITY, and COUNTRY. You cannot modify the EMAIL field, because it is used to identify you.

   ▶ TIME ZONE and LOCALE: Use these dropdown lists to modify your time zone and locale. These are used to customize how SAP Lumira Cloud displays your content.

▶ I WOULD LIKE TO RECEIVE NEWS FROM SAP: Select this checkbox to be included in the SAP mailing list and receive emails related to SAP.

4. Click SAVE CHANGES to save your changes in SAP Lumira Cloud.

5. If you have not subscribed to an enterprise license, then click the ACCOUNT INFO subtab to display how you are currently using your 1 GB of free space, as shown in Figure 8.21:

   ▶ The space used by your resources
   ▶ The space used by resources that have been shared to you
   ▶ The remaining free space

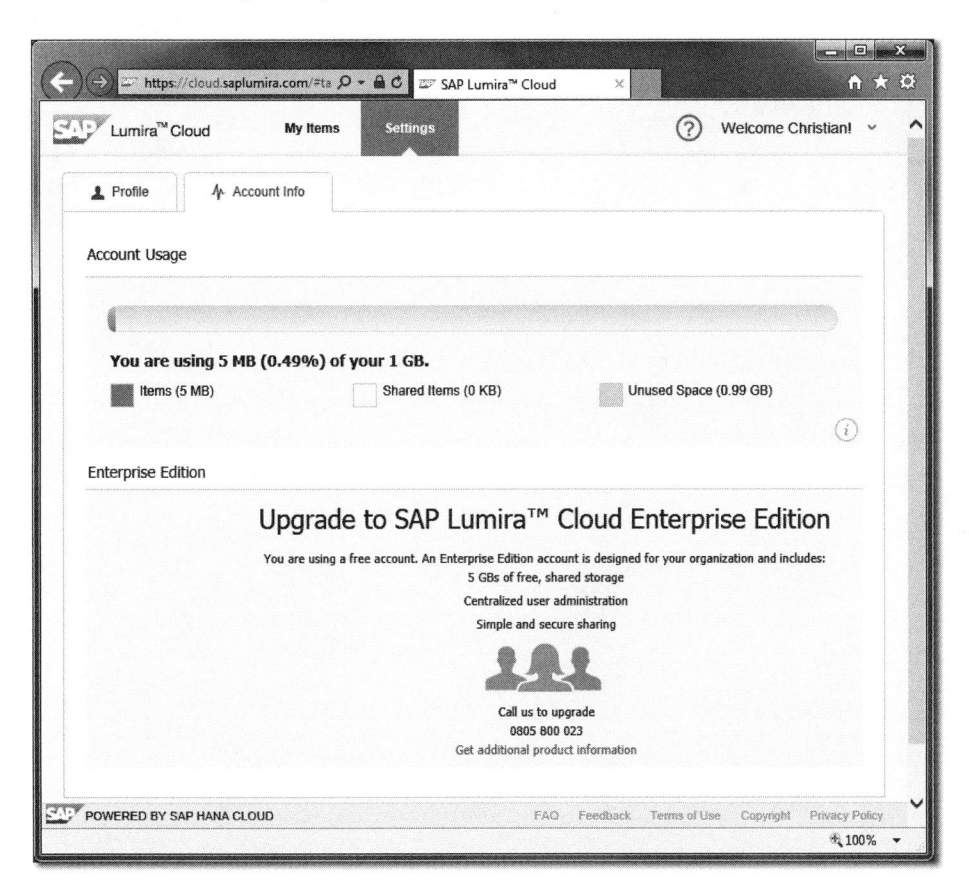

Figure 8.21 Account Info Tab

6. If you have subscribed to an enterprise license, then click the TEAM subtab to manage your team members, as described in Section 8.7.

7. Click MY ITEMS tab to return to the list of resources and work on them.

With a broader understanding of the interface, let's turn our attention to the importing features available in SAP Lumira Cloud.

8.4 Importing to SAP Lumira Cloud

SAP Lumira Cloud offers you a space where you can store your resources. As seen in Chapter 7, Section 7.4 and Chapter 7, Section 7.6, you can publish or save SAP Lumira resources to SAP Lumira Cloud from SAP Lumira Desktop. You can also import content directly from SAP Lumira Cloud.

> **Scheduling Refresh**
>
> In SAP Lumira Cloud, it is not possible to directly schedule content refresh. You must use SAP Lumira Agent (see Chapter 7, Section 7.5).

8.4.1 Uploading Files or SAP Lumira Documents

You can use your available space in SAP Lumira Cloud as a repository for your files. Through this cloud system, you can upload your documents for future access or share. The following are the supported file types you can upload to SAP Lumira Cloud:

- CSV file (.csv file extension)
- Microsoft Excel file (.xls, .xlsx, .xlsb, or .xlsm file extensions)
- SAP Crystal Reports documents (.rpt file extension)
- Microsoft PowerPoint files (.ppt or .pptx file extensions)
- SAP Design Studio documents (.biapp file extension)
- Archive file (.zip extension)

You may also upload an SAP Lumira document (.lums or .svid file extension) to SAP Lumira Cloud by saving it from the SAP Lumira Desktop (see Chapter 7, Section 7.6).

The size of each file you upload cannot exceed 200 MB.

To upload a file to SAP Lumira Cloud, follow these steps:

1. From the SAP Lumira Cloud main page, in the MY ITEMS tab, click UPLOAD to open the SELECT A FILE dialog box, as shown in Figure 8.22.

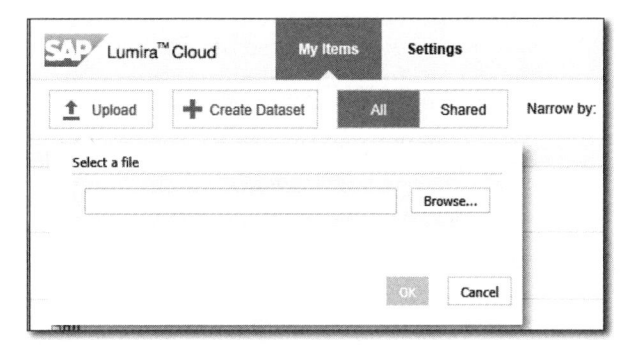

Figure 8.22 Upload File Selection

2. Click the text field or the BROWSE button to open the CHOOSE FILE TO UPLOAD dialog box.
3. Navigate in the file system to select the file to upload.
4. Click OK to close the CHOOSE FILE TO UPLOAD dialog box and display the selected file name in the text field. If the selected file does not have the extension of a supported file type or if its size exceeds 200 MB, then an error message is displayed. In this case, reselect a valid file.
5. Click OK to close the SELECT A FILE dialog box and start the file upload. When the file is uploaded, it appears in the list of items in the MY ITEMS tab.

8.4.2 Importing Data to Create a Dataset

In SAP Lumira Cloud, you may create a dataset to save in the cloud and use it for visualizations or stories. This data acquisition is less advanced than the data acquisition in SAP Lumira Desktop:

- It supports only CSV and Microsoft Excel files (.xlsx file extension) as data sources.
- It supports only data stored in vertical tables.

- It can connect to only one file at a time, whereas SAP Lumira Desktop can use and merge the content of several files to create the dataset.
- It does not propose any formula language to process the data.

When a dataset is created, it is stored in the cloud but does not keep a reference to the data source it comes from.

To create a new dataset in SAP Lumira Cloud, follow these steps:

1. In SAP Lumira Cloud, in the MY ITEMS tab, click CREATE DATASET to open the CREATE DATASET dialog box, as shown in Figure 8.23.

Figure 8.23 Create Dataset

2. Click BROWSE to open the CHOOSE FILE TO UPLOAD dialog box.
3. Navigate in your file system and select the file, and then click OPEN to close the dialog box. If your file does not have the .xlsx or .csv file extension, then an

error message is displayed; otherwise, the file name is displayed in the SELECT FILE text field.

4. Click OK to upload the selected file shown in the dialog box and to preview its content in the table, as shown in Figure 8.24.

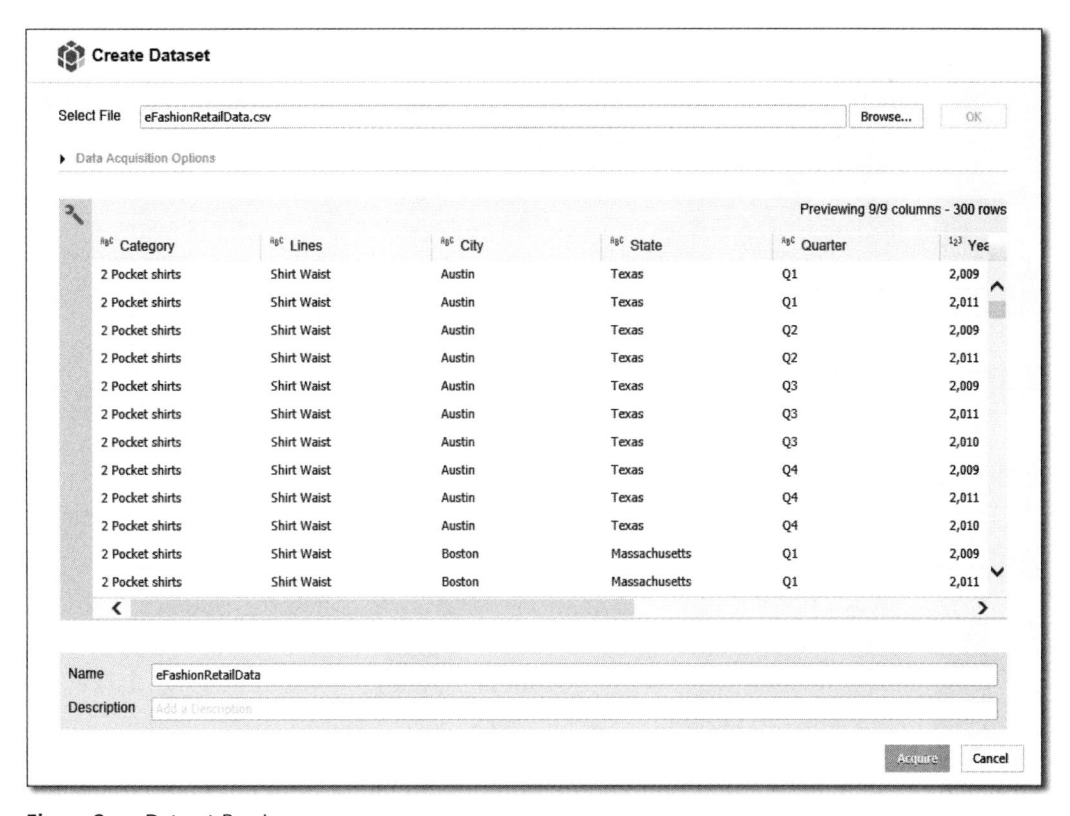

Figure 8.24 Dataset Preview

5. Click the DATA ACQUISITION OPTIONS link to display additional options for the data file acquisition. If the file is a CSV file, then, as shown in Figure 8.25, the possible options are as follows:

   ▸ DELIMITED BY: In this dropdown list, select the character that delimits the columns in the file.

   ▸ SET FIRST ROW AS COLUMN HEADERS: Select this checkbox to use the data in the first line of the file as headers for the columns.

- TRIM VALUES: Select this checkbox to remove possible extra space characters before or after the values retrieved from the text file.
- DEFAULT PREFIX FOR COLUMN NAMING: In this text field, type a prefix to add before the column name.
- NUMBER FORMAT: In this dropdown list, select the format that describes how numbers are saved in the CSV file.
- DATE FORMAT: In this dropdown list, select the format that describes how dates are saved in the CSV file. Table 3.2 in Chapter 3 lists the tokens used in this date format.

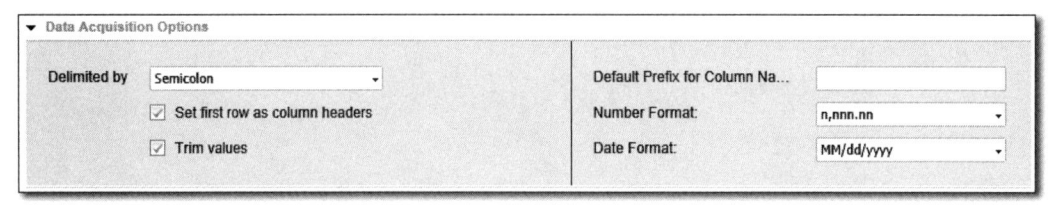

Figure 8.25 CSV Data Acquisition Options

If the data source file is a Microsoft Excel file, then, as shown in Figure 8.26, the possible options are as follows:

- SELECT SHEET: In this dropdown list, select the particular sheet in the file to use as the data source.
- SET FIRST ROW AS COLUMN HEADERS: Select this checkbox to use the data in the first row of the spreadsheet as headers for the columns.

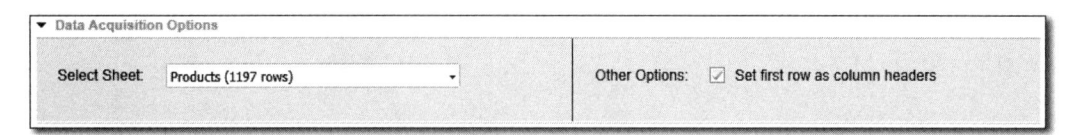

Figure 8.26 Microsoft Excel Data Acquisition Options

Once you have modified your options, you may click the DATA ACQUISITION OPTIONS link to hide them.

6. Click the TOOL icon to modify metadata automatically set when creating the dataset. This opens the ENRICH pane in the left side of the dialog box. As shown

in Figure 8.27, this pane displays all columns found in the data source. They are displayed under the MEASURES section if their data have been analyzed as a measure or under the DIMENSIONS section if recognized as a dimension.

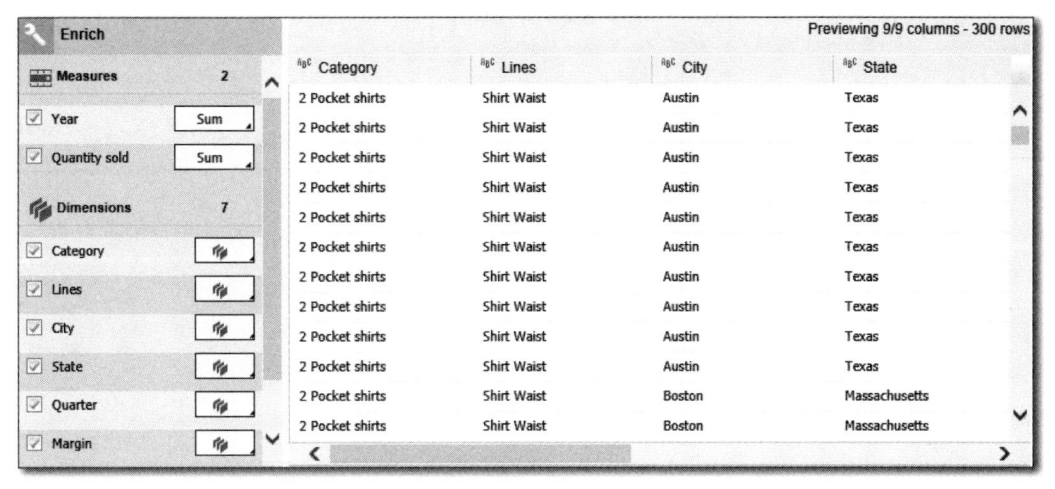

Figure 8.27 Enrich Pane in the Create Dataset Dialog Box

7. Click the button beside a measure. In the contextual menu that opens, as shown in Figure 8.28, you will see the following options:

    ▸ CHANGE TO DIMENSION will turn the measure into a dimension.

    ▸ Choose any aggregation function from among SUM, MIN, MAX, and COUNT to set this aggregation function to this measure.

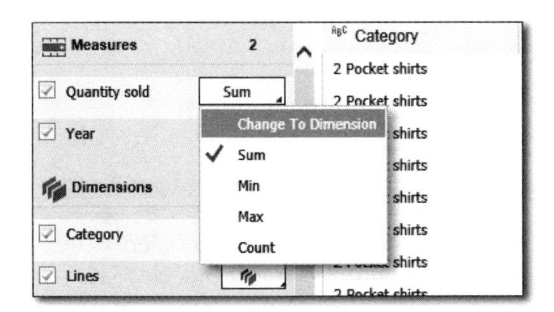

Figure 8.28 Measure Menu

8. Click the button beside a dimension and select the CONVERT TO MEASURE command in the contextual menu that opens, as shown in Figure 8.29, to turn the dimension into a measure.

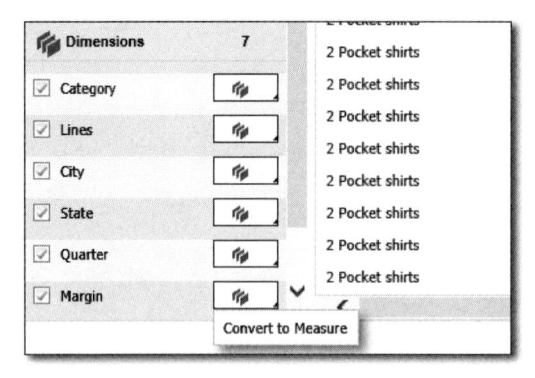

Figure 8.29 Dimension Menu

9. In the NAME and DESCRIPTION text fields, enter a name and a description for this new dataset. By default, the new dataset name is the name of the selected file.

10. Click ACQUIRE to close the CREATE DATASET dialog box and to create the dataset from the selected file. Once created, the new dataset is displayed in the resource list, as shown in Figure 8.30.

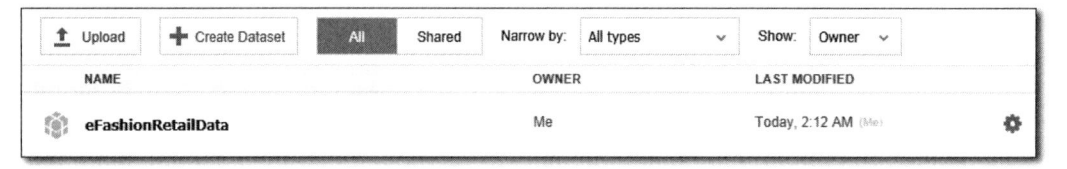

Figure 8.30 New Dataset Displayed

> **Aggregation Functions**
>
> SAP Lumira Cloud supports less aggregation functions than SAP Lumira Desktop. Hence, datasets defined in SAP Lumira Desktop are not supported in SAP Lumira Cloud if they contain measures aggregated with functions not supported by SAP Lumira Cloud.

Now that you've uploaded and imported your data, let's move on to navigating the Visualize and Compose rooms in SAP Lumira Cloud.

8.5 Visualization and Composition Online

Initially limited to document sharing and dataset and visualization creation, SAP Lumira Cloud greatly improved when SAP Lumira 1.17 was released. With the introduction of infographics and reporting, SAP Lumira Cloud has also been extended with online visualization and composition through the integration of the Visualize and Compose rooms.

8.5.1 Accessing Online Rooms

One of SAP Lumira Cloud's objectives is to offer the same seamless experience as SAP Lumira Desktop but on the cloud. To achieve this objective, the same Visualize and Compose rooms located in SAP Lumira Desktop are available in SAP Lumira Cloud by using the same component. As the technology and the code are identical, the user interfaces and workflows are almost the same in the two tools. Any changes and enhancements in these rooms are automatically integrated in both tools.

You can access these two rooms in the following situations:

- When you create new visualizations and stories
- When you edit an existing story that you own
- When you edit an existing story that has been shared with you with the EDIT right (see Section 8.6)

In SAP Lumira Cloud, when you click a dataset in the MY ITEMS tab, the VISUALIZE room opens, so you can create visualizations and a story from this dataset.

When you click a story in the MY ITEMS tab, the story is displayed in viewing mode only. You can only navigate in the story page(s), without modifying them. If you are the story owner or if you are allowed to edit, you can click EDIT in the tool bar to open the story in the VISUALIZE room, as shown in Figure 8.31.

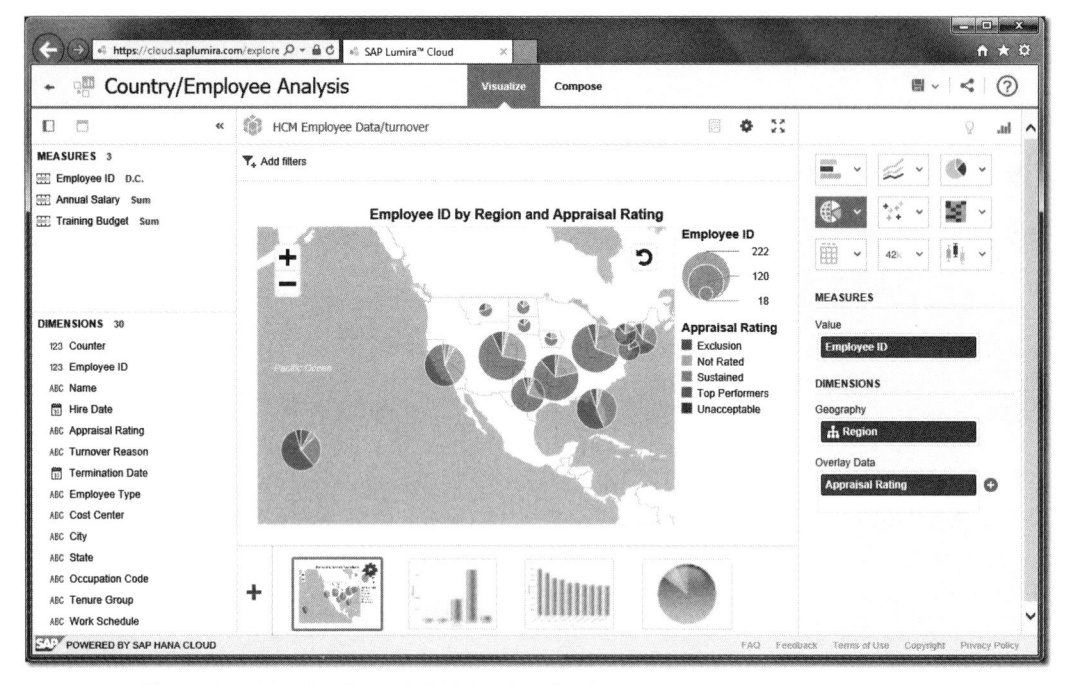

Figure 8.31 Visualize Room in SAP Lumira Cloud

An alternate way to open the story in the Visualize room is to click the cog icon ✿ for the story in the My Items tab. In the contextual menu that opens, select Edit.

To add the boards, infographics or reporting to the story or modify the ones it contains, click the Compose tab on top of the page to open the story in the Compose room.

8.5.2 Working in the Visualize and Compose Rooms

When you are editing a document, by default it opens in the Visualize room (see Figure 8.31).

Once you are in this room, the actions you can perform are exactly the same as in the SAP Lumira Desktop Visualize room; you can create and edit the same visualizations and use the same charts library (for more details on this room's capabilities and its user interface, see Chapter 5). However, the two tools differ in the following respects:

- You cannot use custom visualizations.
- You cannot directly refresh the dataset used by your visualization from the Visualize room. You have to explicitly regenerate your dataset or use SAP Lumira Agent to republish an updated dataset (see Chapter 7, Section 7.5).

After you have saved your story (see Section 8.5.3), you can return to the My Items tab by clicking the left arrow icon at the top-left corner of the interface.

When you are editing a document, by default, it opens in the Visualize room.

To add or modify the boards, infographics, or reports from the Visualize room, click the Compose tab on top of the banner to open the selected item in the Compose room, as shown in Figure 8.32.

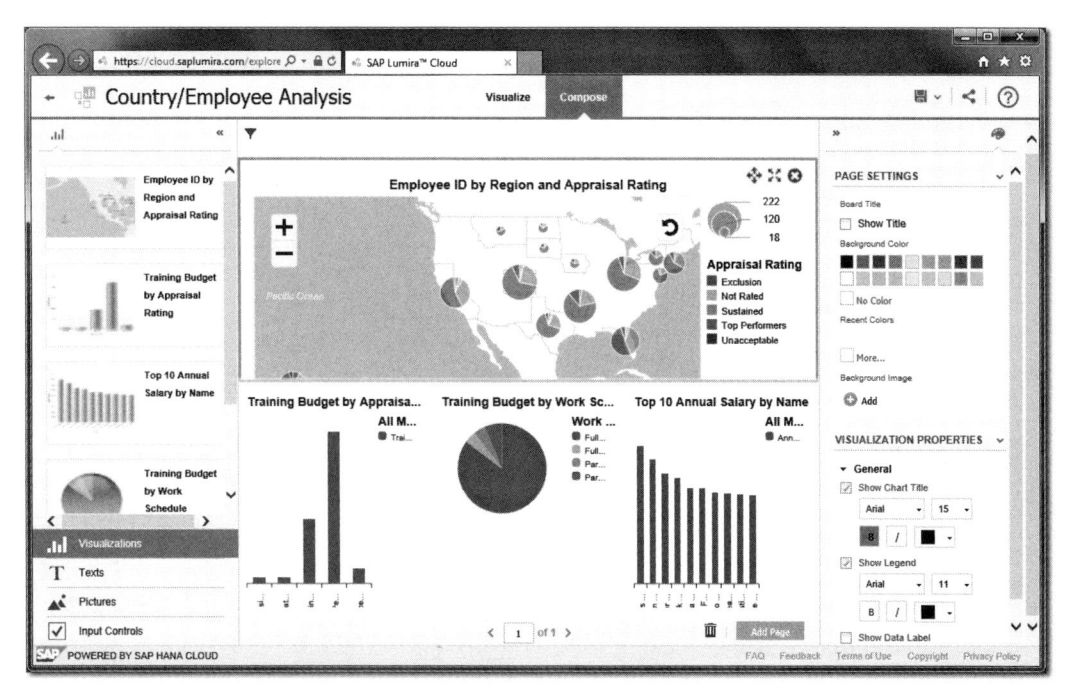

Figure 8.32 Compose Room in SAP Lumira Cloud

As in SAP Lumira Desktop, from this room you can perform the following actions:

- Create and add new stories to the SAP Lumira document or edit existing ones. This covers boards, infographics, or reports.

- Add visualizations to stories.
- Arrange a story's layout.
- Add interactions with filters.
- Preview the final stories and how they display on different devices

The user interface is the same than in SAP Lumira Desktop. So, for more details on these rooms capabilities and their user interfaces, refer to Chapter 5 and Chapter 6.

However, the two tools differ in the following aspects related to the different deployment modes:

- You edit the resource through a web browser and it is saved on the cloud.
- You can add external pictures to your stories, but they are uploaded from your local file system, as seen in Figure 8.33, and saved in a story when the story is saved.

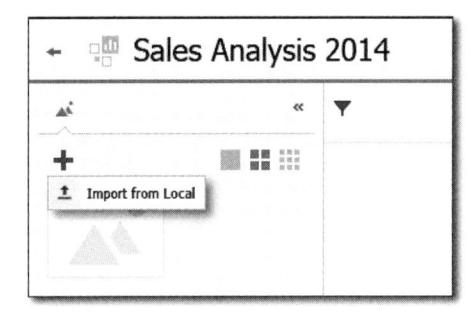

Figure 8.33 Import Picture From Compose Room

- You can only manipulate one story at a time in the Compose room. You cannot add a new story to the current story.
- You cannot directly refresh the dataset used by your story from the Visualize or Compose room. You have to explicitly regenerate your dataset or use SAP Lumira Agent to republish an updated dataset (see Chapter 7, Section 7.5).
- The desktop's preferences are not supported. For example, you cannot choose to position the chart feeder in the left or select a palette or a template for your charts as you can in SAP Lumira Desktop.

After you have saved your story (see Section 8.5.3), you can return to the MY ITEMS tab by clicking the left arrow icon on the top-left corner of the interface.

8.5.3 Saving Your Stories in SAP Lumira Cloud

Once you have finished creating or modifying your story, you may save it in your space, as long as you have enough free space. To save a story, follow these steps:

1. In the tool bar, click the SAVE icon, and in the contextual menu that opens, select the SAVE or SAVE AS commands.
2. If you have selected SAVE AS or if the document is a new document you have just created, the SAVE dialog box will open, as shown in Figure 8.34. Otherwise, the document is saved with its previous name.

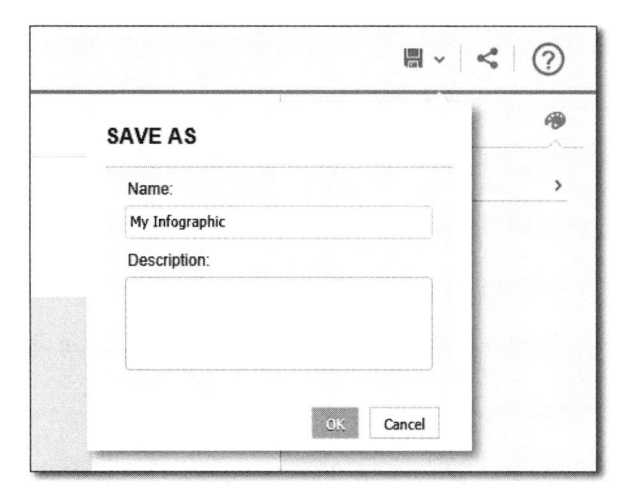

Figure 8.34 Save Dialog Box

3. Enter a name and an optional comment for the story in the NAME and DESCRIPTION text fields.
4. Click OK to close the SAVE dialog box and save the story.
5. When you return to the resource lists, the story is listed in the MY ITEMS list.

Even if you have created only visualizations without organizing them in a story, you can still save a story. This story will contain only your visualizations. If you have not created any visualizations, then you can also save a story; the saved story is considered empty, but it is still a valid story with a name, a description, and a dataset.

You can share these stories through SAP Lumira Cloud, as described next.

8.6 Sharing Resources in SAP Lumira Cloud

SAP Lumira Cloud gives you access to a space in which you can publish your resources. You can share any resource saved in you space in SAP Lumira Cloud with other users, which can be useful for collaborating with others on these resources, or you can simply exchange them with other users.

8.6.1 Sharing Methods

There are two methods to share a resource in SAP Lumira Cloud:

- **Public access**
  This method is available only for a story or dataset. SAP Lumira Cloud generates a URL for the resource to share. Any user can use this link to display the dataset or story, even if he does not have an SAP Lumira Cloud account, because you do not need to authenticate to SAP Lumira Cloud to access a publicly shared resource.

- **Private access**
  This method is available for any resource you share in SAP Lumira Cloud. It is the only option available for resources other than story or dataset. Users with whom you have shared the resource must be registered with SAP Lumira Cloud and authenticate to it to view the resource you have shared.

When you share a story, the datasets it depends are also automatically shared. If the story is publicly shared, then the datasets it relies on are also publicly shared and it is possible to access them through a simple URL.

If you have an enterprise license, then any member of the team can share a resource with the team, which is equivalent to sharing it with all members of the team.

8.6.2 Sharing a Resource

To share a resource in SAP Lumira Cloud, follow these steps:

1. Once connected to SAP Lumira Cloud, in the MY ITEMS list select the resource to share, and click the cog icon to open its contextual menu. Select the SHARE command to open the SHARE WITH OTHERS dialog box.

   If you are editing a story in the Visualize or Compose room, you can also click the SHARE icon in the top-right corner of the page to open this dialog box.

2. Depending on the resource type, this dialog box displays two different interfaces:
    - For stories and datasets, it displays the sharing method (see Section 8.6.1), a link to the resource (for datasets shared publicly and stories), and a list of users to invite, as shown in Figure 8.35.
    - For all other documents, including SAP Lumira documents and deprecated visualizations (see Section 8.3.2), this dialog box displays only the list of users to invite, as shown in Figure 8.36.

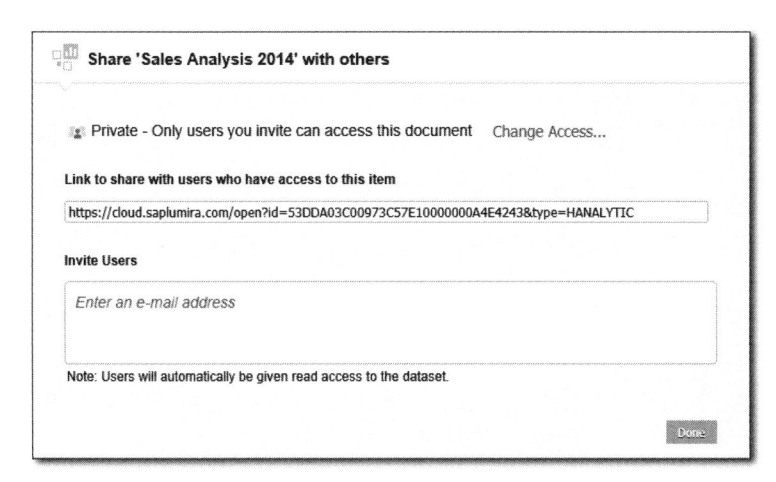

Figure 8.35 Share with Others Dialog Box for a Story or a Dataset

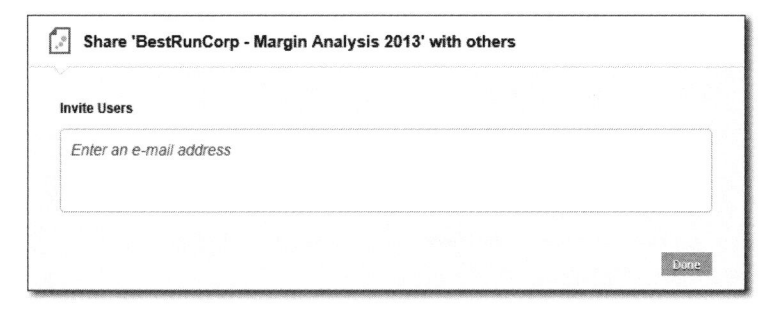

Figure 8.36 Share with Others Dialog Box for Other Item Types

3. If the resource to share is a dataset or a story, click the CHANGE ACCESS link to open the CHANGE DOCUMENT ACCESS dialog box, as shown in Figure 8.37. In this dialog box, select a radio button to choose an access mode for your dataset or story:

▶ PRIVATE: Only users you invite and who have an account in SAP Lumira Cloud can view the dataset or story.

▶ PUBLIC: The document can be accessed from its URL without having to log in to SAP Lumira Cloud.

Figure 8.37 Change Document Access Dialog Box

Click SAVE to save your choice and return to the SHARE WITH OTHERS dialog box.

4. Click the INVITE USERS text field to enter the email addresses of the people with whom you want to share the document. Clicking this text field expands this section with new fields, as shown in Figure 8.38.

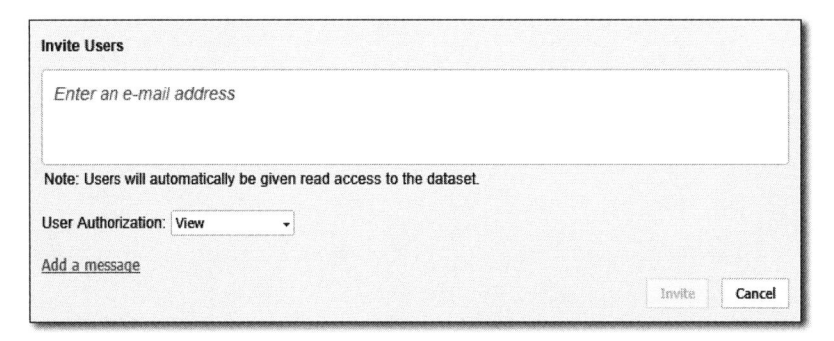

Figure 8.38 Expanded Invite Users Section

5. Use commas to separate several email addresses. Email addresses are analyzed on the fly, but you may click the text field to force this analysis. Correctly recognized addresses are displayed with a blue background (peter.snowdon@sap.com) and incorrect ones with a pink background (bill.sap.com), as shown in Figure 8.39.

Sharing Resources in SAP Lumira Cloud | 8.6

> **Color Images**
> Please note that, though the print book shows the application images in grayscale, full color versions are viewable in the e-book.

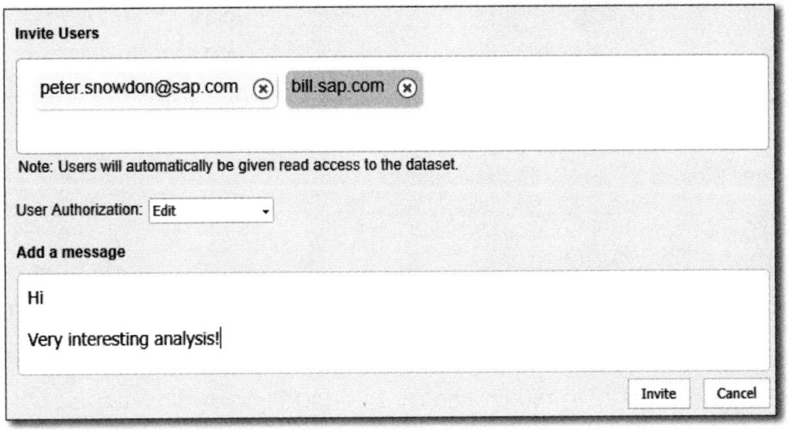

Figure 8.39 Sending the Invitation – Correct Email Address (Left) and Incorrect Email Address (Right)

You can remove email addresses (for example, the incorrect ones) by clicking the DELETE icon ⊗ beside them.

6. In the USER AUTHORIZATION dropdown list, select the authorization level you want to allow for the users you are inviting:

   ▶ VIEW: The default option, which only allows invited users to view the resource.

   ▶ EDIT: This authorization level is not available for datasets. If the resource is a story, then this authorization level allows invited users to edit the story in the Visualize and Compose rooms (see Section 8.5).

7. Click the ADD A MESSAGE link to open the ADD A MESSAGE text field. In this text field, add text to the email sent to invited users.

8. Click INVITE to send your invitations or CANCEL to dismiss your invitations and reset the INVITE USERS section. You must click either INVITE or CANCEL to move to the next step.

9. Click DONE to close the SHARE WITH OTHERS dialog box and share your item.

In the My Items list, an icon below the resource's name indicates if it has been shared and the sharing mode: private—as shown in Figure 8.40 ❶—or public—as shown in Figure 8.40 ❷. If you have shared a story, then you can also see that its datasets have been shared as well.

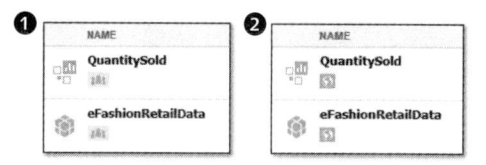

Figure 8.40 Shared Resources—Private ❶ and Public ❷

8.6.3 Changing Sharing Options

After you have shared a document, you can modify its sharing options. To do so, follow these steps:

1. Select the Share command to reopen the Share options dialog box. Because the document has been shared, this dialog box lists the users who can access it, including you as the document's owner, as shown in Figure 8.41.

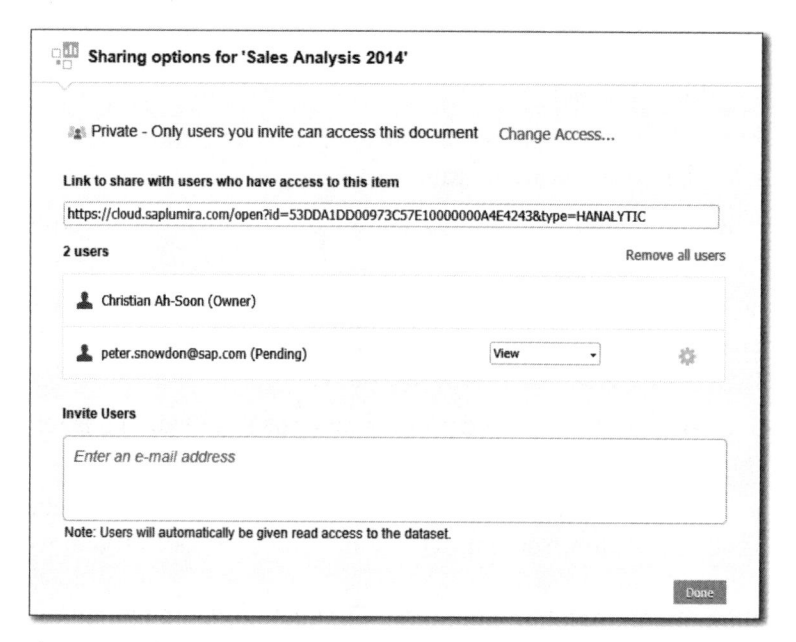

Figure 8.41 Changing Sharing Options

2. From the dialog box, you can modify how the resource is shared and perform the following actions:
    - Change the sharing mode (public or private access) for datasets and stories by clicking the CHANGE ACCESS link, which opens the CHANGE DOCUMENT ACCESS dialog box, as shown in Figure 8.37, and then clicking SAVE.
    - Change the access right for a specific user by selecting EDIT or VIEW in the dropdown list beside the user name and then clicking SAVE.
    - Stop sharing the resource with a specific user by clicking the cog icon beside the user's name, selecting the REMOVE command in the contextual menu that opens, and then clicking SAVE.
    - Stop sharing the resource with all users by clicking the REMOVE ALL USERS link and then clicking OK in the confirmation window that opens.
    - Share it with a new user by adding the user's email address in the INVITE USERS text field and then clicking INVITE.
3. When you have made all of your changes, click DONE to close the SHARING OPTIONS dialog box and save your file.

8.6.4 Accessing a Shared Resource

When a resource is shared with you on SAP Lumira Cloud, you receive a mail with a link to this document. How you access it depends on how it has been shared with you:

- **If it has been shared as a private resource**
  To access it, you must have an SAP Lumira Cloud account and must login to SAP Lumira Cloud with your credentials. The shared resource will appear in the list of resources you can access. Depending on the resource type and the authorization level granted to you, you can open, edit, or download it or create new stories from it.
- **If it has been shared as a public resource**
  You must have received an email with the URL of the resource:
    - If the resource is a story, you can open this link in a web browser to access this story.
    - If the resource is a dataset, this link is an OData data flow for this dataset. You can use OData standard URL to retrieve its data.

You do not need to have an SAP Lumira account to authenticate.

Sharing is all about team work. Next, we will discuss the ability to create and share with members of a team via the enterprise license.

8.7 Creating a Team

When you subscribe to an enterprise license (see Section 8.1.1), this license comes with five accounts by default or more if you pay for additional ones. To ease these accounts management, they are gathered in a team that you can access in the TEAM subtab.

8.7.1 Members Type

All members in the team can create datasets, visualizations, and stories , as well as share content with all members of the team.

However, for to manage users in the team, SAP Lumira Cloud offers a basic security model based on three user types:

- **The team owner**
  There is only one owner in the team. The team owner can invite or remove members and add or remove administrators.
- **The team administrator**
  A team can have one or more team administrators. The team administrators can invite or remove members.
- **Team members**
   These users do not have administrative roles and cannot manage other users.

The team owner and administrators perform their administrative tasks via the TEAM subtab.

8.7.2 Accessing Team Administration

If you have an enterprise license, the ACCOUNT info subtab is replaced by a TEAM subtab. Click this tab to access the team management capabilities.

Creating a Team | **8.7**

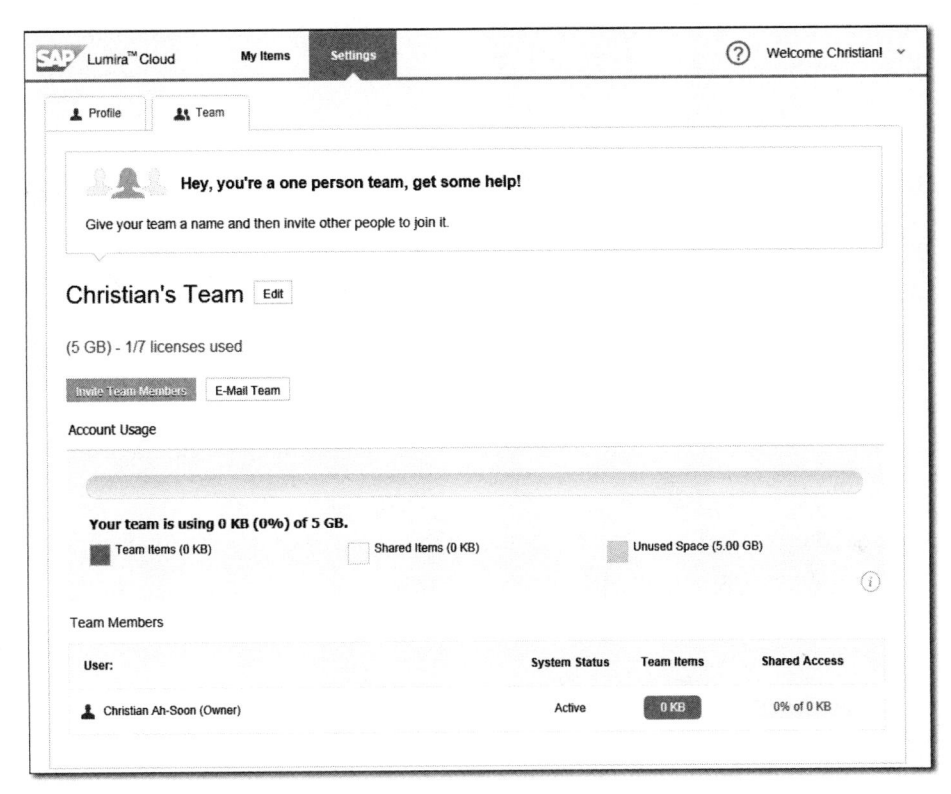

Figure 8.42 Team Subtab for Team Members Management

As seen in Figure 8.42, this page displays the following information:

- The space storage usage, including:
  - Space used by your team members
  - Space used by your team members for resources that have been shared with them
  - Remaining free space
- The list of members in the team

For each member, you can see his type (owner, administrator, or member), and in the SYSTEM STATUS column, you can see if he has yet registered and joined the team (ACTIVE status) or if he has not yet accepted the invitation to join the team (PENDING status).

421

From this page, any team members can see the following beside his name:

- The space he uses for his resources
- The ratio of shared items he can access

If you are an administrator or the team's owner, then you can also see these figures for all members.

From this tab, you can interact with and manage your team members, as described in the next sections.

8.7.3 Inviting and Removing Users

Only the team owner or an administrator can invite new members to the team. To do so, follow these steps:

1. Once connected to SAP Lumira Cloud, go to the SETTINGS tab, and then click the TEAM subtab (see Section 8.7.2).
2. Click INVITE TEAM MEMBERS to open the ADD TEAM MEMBERS dialog box, as seen in Figure 8.43.

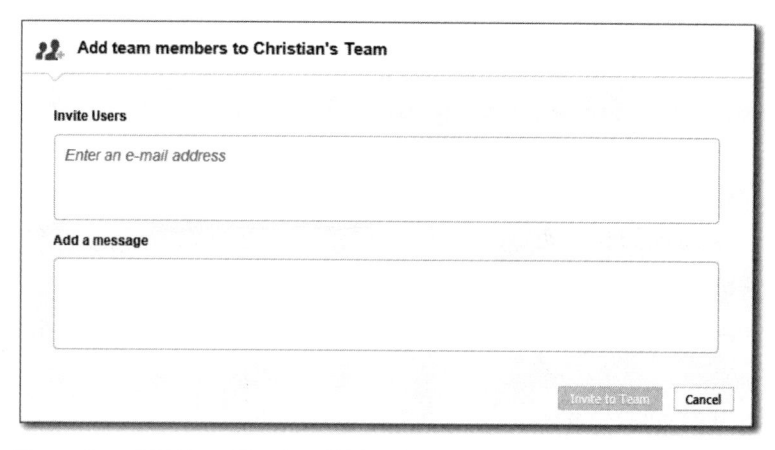

Figure 8.43 Add Team Members Dialog Box

3. In this dialog box, in the INVITE USERS text field enter the email address of the users to invite. Email addresses are analyzed on the fly, but you may click the text field to force this analysis.
4. In the ADD A MESSAGE text field, type a message to add to the invitation mail.

5. Click INVITE TO TEAM to close the ADD TEAM MEMBERS dialog box and send the email to the invited users.
6. In the TEAM subtab, these users are added to the TEAM MEMBERS list with the INVITED status, as seen in Figure 8.44, until they register to join the team. They then appear with the ACTIVE status.

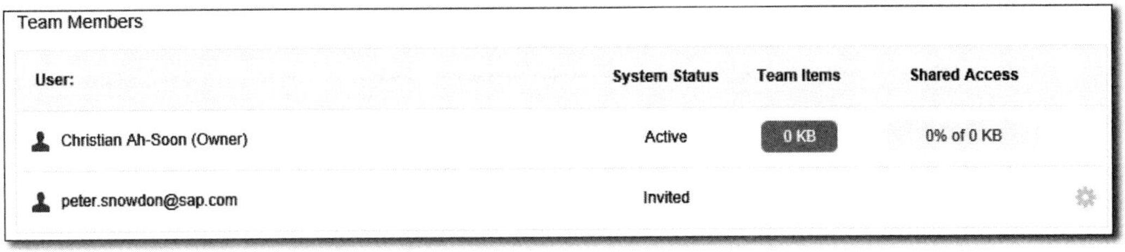

Team Members				
User:		System Status	Team Items	Shared Access
👤 Christian Ah-Soon (Owner)		Active	0 KB	0% of 0 KB
👤 peter.snowdon@sap.com		Invited		⚙

Figure 8.44 Pending Invited User

To remove a user from the team and prevent him from accessing SAP Lumira Cloud with an account from your enterprise license, follow these steps:

1. Once connected to SAP Lumira Cloud, go to the SETTINGS tab, and then click the TEAM subtab (see Section 8.7.2).
2. Click the cog icon beside the name of the user to remove him from the team.
3. In the contextual menu, select the REMOVE command.
4. After clicking through a confirmation, the user is removed from the team. The number of used licenses is decreased, because removing this user has freed one license.

8.7.4 Managing Administrators

Only the team owner can manage the team administrators and promote and demote administrators.

To promote members to administrators, follow these steps:

1. Once connected to SAP Lumira Cloud, go to the SETTINGS tab, and then click the TEAM subtab (see Section 8.7.2).
2. Click the cog icon beside a member name, and in the contextual menu select the MAKE ADMIN command.

3. In the TEAM MEMBERS list, the member is displayed with the ADMIN tag, as shown in Figure 8.45.

User:	System Status	Team Items	Shared Access
Christian Ah-Soon (Owner)	Active	0 KB	0% of 0 KB
peter snowdon (Admin)	Active	0 KB	0% of 0 KB

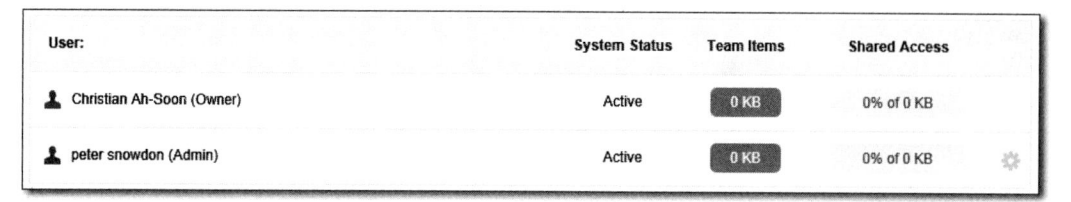

Figure 8.45 New Administrator User

To demote administrators to simple team members, follow these steps:

1. Once connected to SAP Lumira Cloud, go to the SETTINGS tab, then click the TEAM subtab (see Section 8.7.2).
2. Select an administrator, and then click the cog icon beside his name.
3. In the contextual menu, select the REMOVE ADMIN command to set the user as a simple member.

8.7.5 Sending Email

Any member of the team can send an email to any other team members. To do so, follow these steps:

1. Once connected to SAP Lumira Cloud, go to the SETTINGS tab, then click the TEAM subtab (see Section 8.7.2).
2. To send an email to all team members, click E-MAIL TEAM; to send an email to only one member, click the cog icon beside the team member you want to email, and in the contextual menu select the E-MAIL command.
3. In both cases, your email application opens with the addresses of the members you have selected in the recipients field. Type in your email, and send it as you usually do via your email application.

8.7.6 Changing the Team Name

Only the team owner can change the team name. This name can be seen by all members in the SETTINGS page. To change the team name, follow these steps:

1. Once connected to SAP Lumira Cloud, go to the SETTINGS tab, and then click the TEAM subtab (see Section 8.7.2).
2. If you are the team owner, then you should see the EDIT button beside your team's name. Click it.
3. The team name becomes editable, as seen in Figure 8.46.

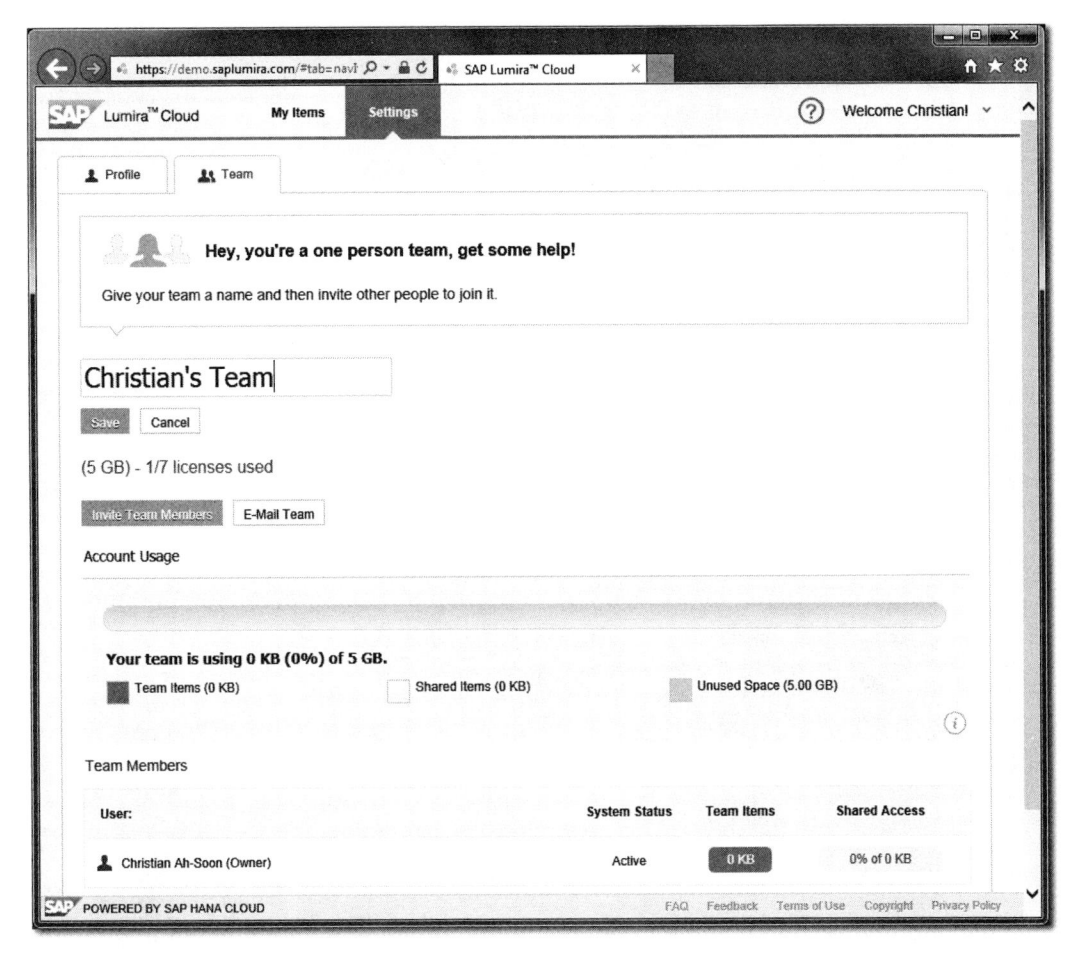

Figure 8.46 Changing the Team Name

4. Change the team name, and then click SAVE.

Next, we'll discuss how to gain mobility with SAP Lumira Cloud.

8.8 Mobile Access

Any mobile device running an HTML5-supported web browser can access SAP Lumira Cloud. SAP Lumira Cloud is also supported by SAP BusinessObjects Mobile on the iPad 3 or higher. You can download its latest version from the Apple App Store.

8.8.1 Setting Up SAP Lumira Cloud Connection in SAP BusinessObjects Mobile

After you have installed SAP BusinessObjects Mobile on your iPad, follow these steps to connect to SAP Lumira Cloud:

1. Start SAP BusinessObjects Mobile.
2. Press the MENU button in the top-right to open the left side pane menu, as shown in Figure 8.47.

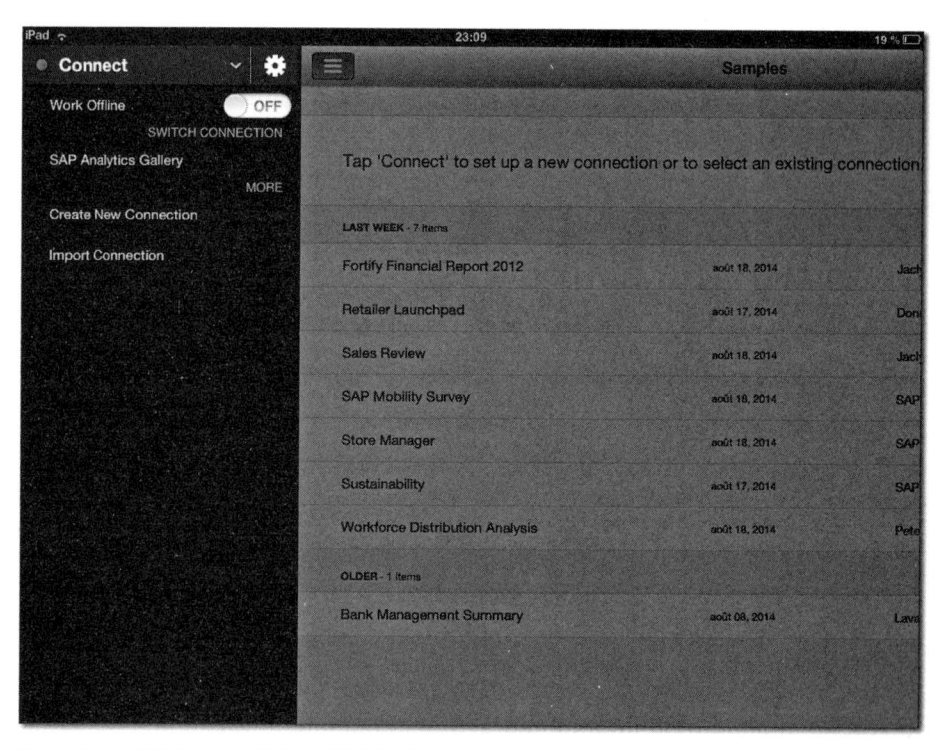

Figure 8.47 SAP BusinessObjects Mobile Menu

3. Select CREATE NEW CONNECTION to open the CREATE NEW CONNECTION dialog box.
4. In the CONNECTION TYPE choice, select SAP LUMIRA CLOUD, as shown in Figure 8.48.

Figure 8.48 Create New Connection in SAP BusinessObjects Mobile

5. In the CONNECTION NAME field, enter a name to identify this connection.
6. In USER NAME and PASSWORD fields, enter your credentials for SAP Lumira Cloud.
7. Set SAVE PASSWORD to ON to save the password and avoid needing to retype it at each connection.
8. Press DONE to create the connection and close the dialog box.
9. When you are asked if you want to connect to your new connection, press YES.
10. SAP BusinessObjects Mobile connects to SAP Lumira Cloud and displays the list of resources you can access in the cloud, as shown in Figure 8.49.

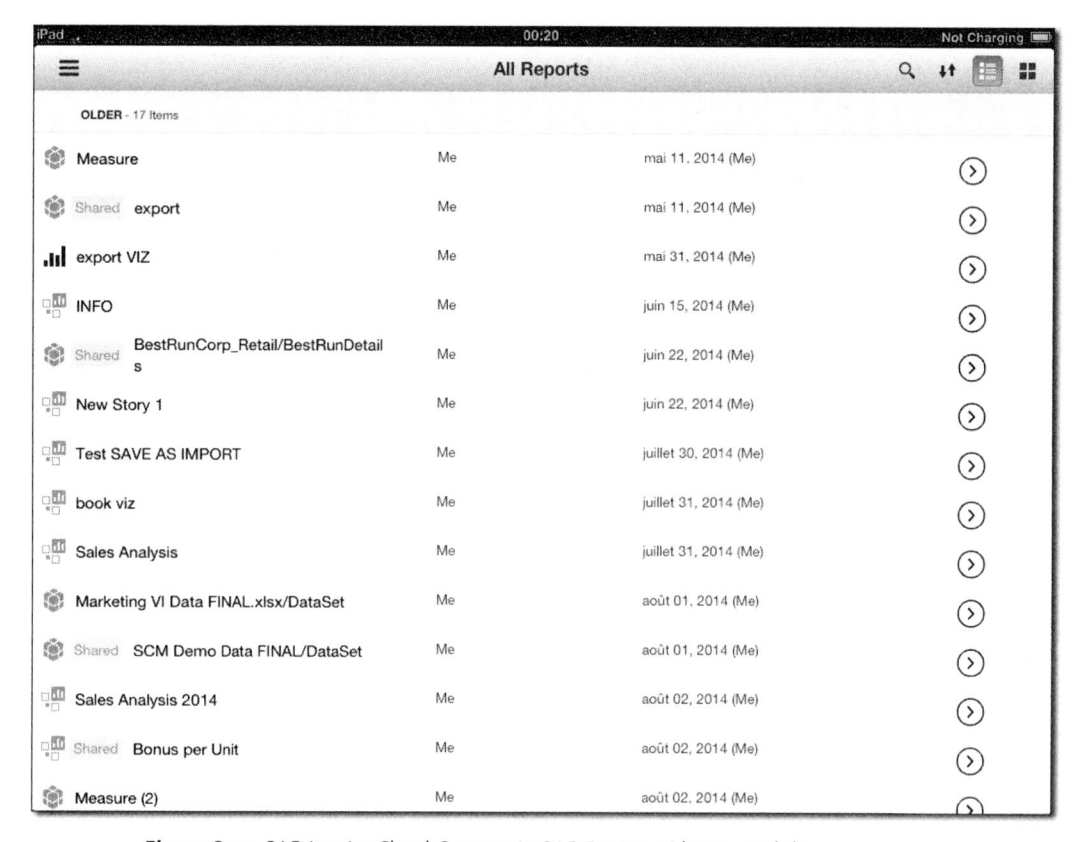

Figure 8.49 SAP Lumira Cloud Content in SAP BusinessObjects Mobile

8.8.2 Working with SAP BusinessObjects Mobile

From the list of resources in your SAP Lumira Cloud space, you can press the right arrow icon › to open the resource contextual menu, as shown in Figure 8.50: ❶ for a dataset or ❷ for a story.

Figure 8.50 Contextual Menu for ❶ a Dataset and ❷ a Story

In the dataset menu, press EXPLORE in order to open the editor in which you can explore and analyze the dataset, as shown in Figure 8.51.

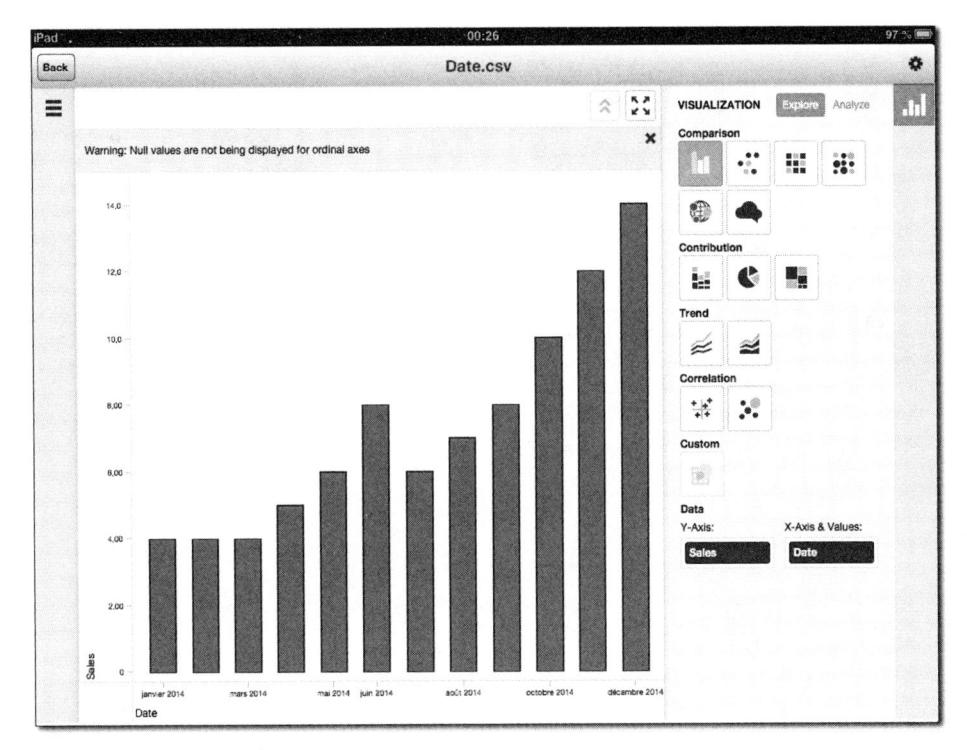

Figure 8.51 Dataset Explore

8 | SAP Lumira Cloud

In the STORY menu, press VIEW in order to open the story in VIEW mode, as shown in Figure 8.52, or press EXPLORE to open it in a room similar to the SAP Lumira Cloud Compose room, as shown in Figure 8.53.

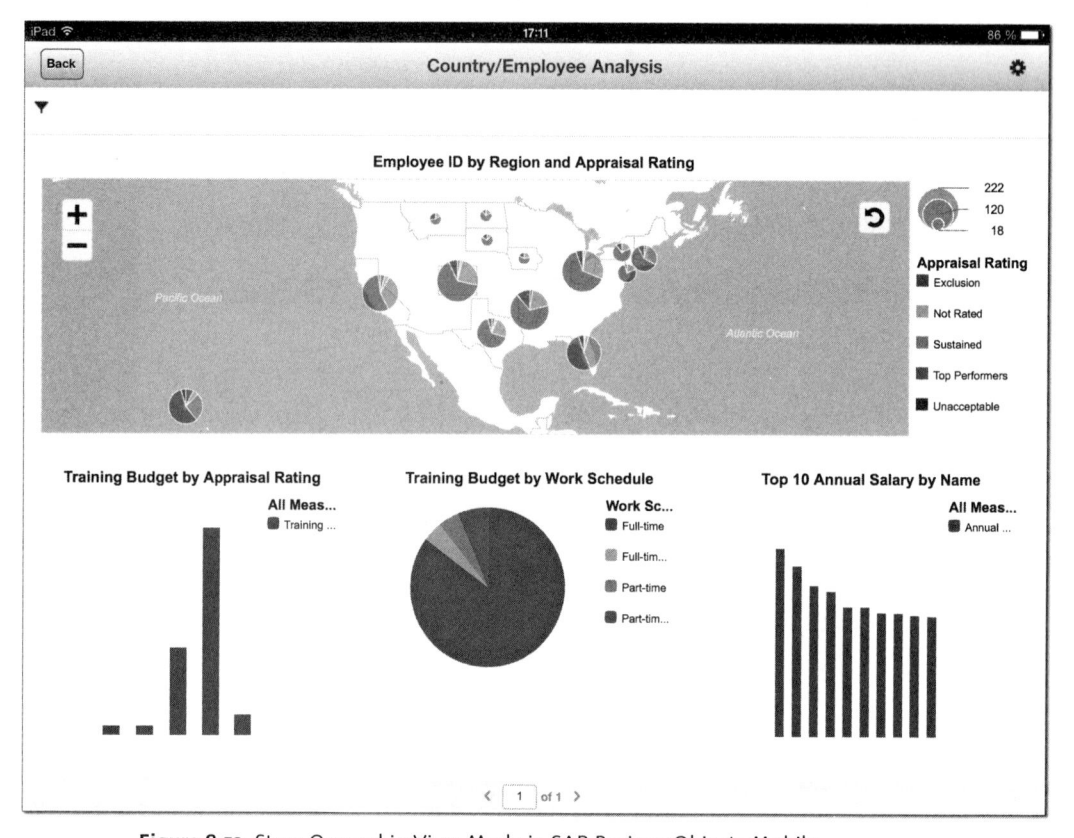

Figure 8.52 Story Opened in View Mode in SAP BusinessObjects Mobile

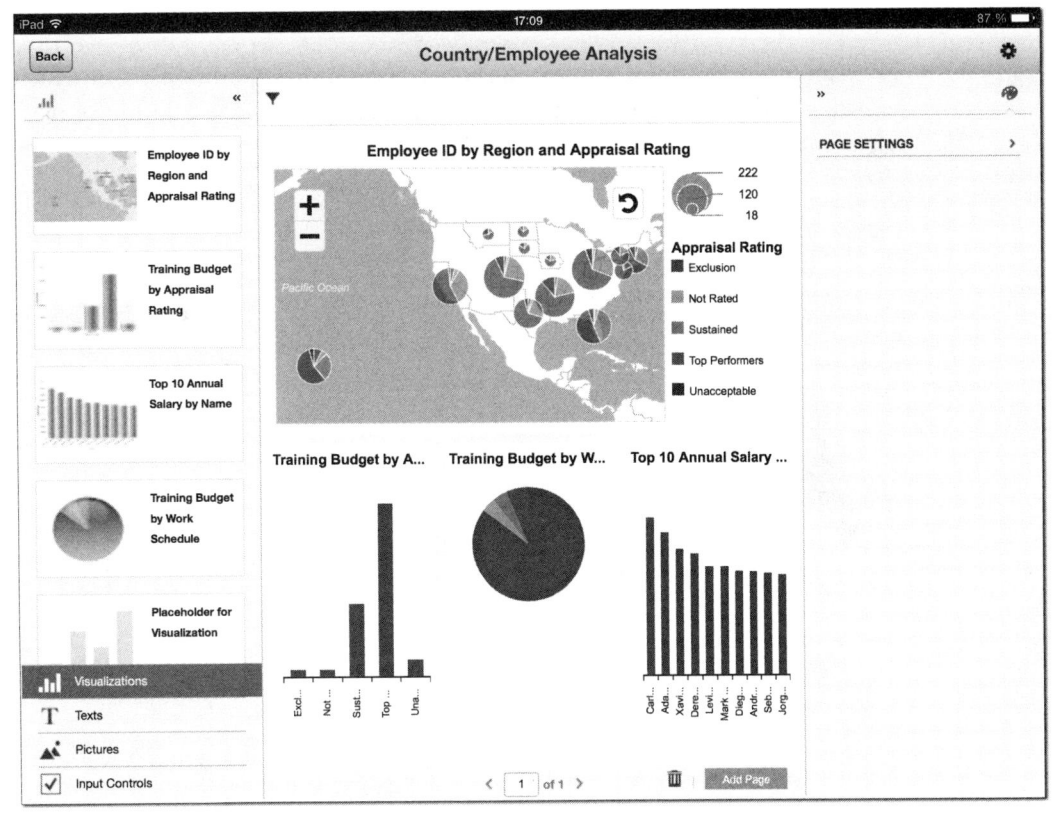

Figure 8.53 Story Opened in SAP BusinessObjects Mobile Compose Room

When you display the story, you can press the cog icon in the top-left corner of the screen to open a menu bar with additional commands to apply to the story, as shown in Figure 8.54.

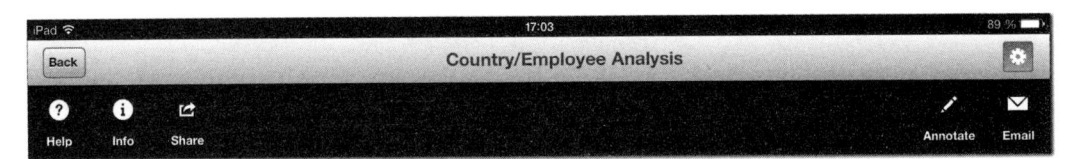

Figure 8.54 Actions Menu for a Story

8 | SAP Lumira Cloud

The possible actions include the following:

- Press SHARE to share the story (see Section 8.6). A dialog box opens in which you can add recipients, their authorization, and a message to add to the message sent to them, as shown in Figure 8.55.

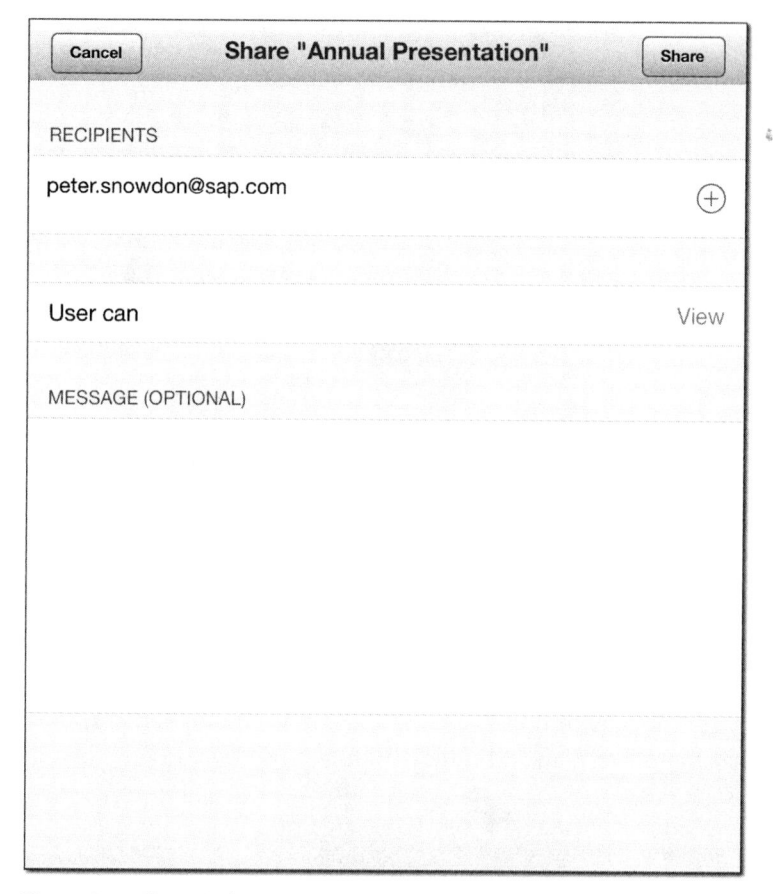

Figure 8.55 Share Dialog Box in SAP BusinessObjects Mobile

- Press EMAIL to open an email that already contains some links to the story, a QR code to access it, and a screenshot of this story. As shown in Figure 8.56, you can add the recipients and modify the email before sending it to the recipients by pressing SEND.

Figure 8.56 Email Dialog Box in SAP BusinessObjects Mobile

8.9 Summary

With a free license, this cloud version allows you to share SAP Lumira content and to create datasets and stories. Because SAP Lumira Cloud embeds the same Visualize and Compose rooms that are in SAP Lumira Desktop, you can enjoy the same experience and ease of use when creating boards, infographics, and reports. Acquiring the enterprise license gives you the right to manage additional accounts in a team and additional space for content storage.

In addition to SAP Lumira Cloud, SAP Lumira suite supports an on-premise deployment that proposes almost the same capabilities. This is SAP Lumira Server, described in the next chapter.

SAP Lumira Server is a server deployment of SAP Lumira Suite. It can be used to create datasets and stories and share them through a web browser. It runs on SAP HANA, benefitting from SAP HANA's framework for security, administration, and lifecycle.

9 SAP Lumira Server

The server deployment in the SAP Lumira suite is handled in the SAP Lumira Server. Although there are advantages offered by SAP Lumira Cloud, your company may not allow you to operate on the cloud for various reasons, such as the following:

- Data is one of your company's main assets and sharing it on a cloud is against the company policies.
- It would be too expensive to purchase licenses for the number of users that need to access SAP Lumira Cloud.

In these cases, you can benefit from SAP Lumira Server's deployment method that also allows you to create, explore, and share datasets and stories while making them available via web browsers or mobile devices. You can deploy this on-premise solution on your own server rather than taking advantage of the cloud.

SAP Lumira Server's functionalities are similar to those of SAP Lumira Cloud; this chapter focuses on its main differences from SAP Lumira Cloud:

- The SAP Lumira Server installation and configuration process and how security is enforced through SAP HANA security
- The use of SAP HANA as the application platform for SAP Lumira Server
- The SAP Lumira Server user interface
- The resources you can import in SAP Lumira Server and how you can work on them in the Visualize and Compose rooms
- Resources sharing in SAP Lumira Server

9 | SAP Lumira Server

Let's first look at downloading SAP Lumira Server.

9.1 Downloading SAP Lumira Server

SAP Lumira Server runs as an application on the SAP HANA platform. Installation is performed using the SAP HANA process. However, you must first download SAP Lumira Server from the SAP Support website.

SAP Lumira Server is provided as an archive SAR file. This archive contains SAP Lumira Server files through the SAPCAR tool, which you also need to download from the SAP Support website. The SAP Lumira Server archive is identical for all supported operating systems.

> **SAP HANA Platforms**
>
> Because SAP Lumira Server runs on SAP HANA, it, like SAP HANA, is only available on the UNIX platform. More details can be found on the SAP Support website at *http://service.sap.com/pam*.

To download SAP Lumira Server and SAPCAR, follow these steps:

1. Use your web browser to go to the SAP Support website: *http://support.sap.com*.
2. Click DOWNLOAD SOFTWARE and then SUPPORT PACKAGES AND PATCHES in the left pane.
3. Click A–Z ALPHABETICAL LIST OF MY PRODUCTS to navigate in the alphabetical list of products and go to the L page.
4. Click SAP LUMIRA SERVER and then SAP LUMIRA SERVER 1 to open the SAP LUMIRA SERVER 1 page.
5. Click COMPRISED SOFTWARE COMPONENT VERSIONS • SAP LUMIRA SERVER 1 • # OS INDEPENDENT • SAP HANA DATABASE, as shown in Figure 9.1. The DOWNLOADS section updates at the bottom of the page, as shown in Figure 9.2.

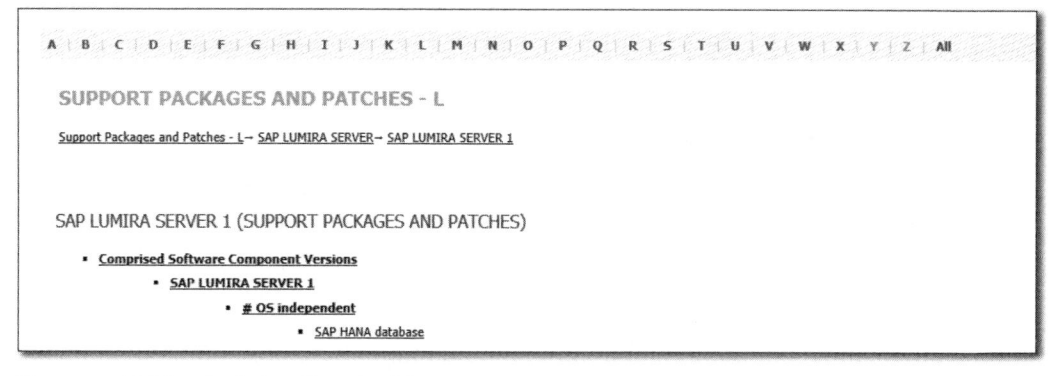

Figure 9.1 SAP Lumira Server Download Page

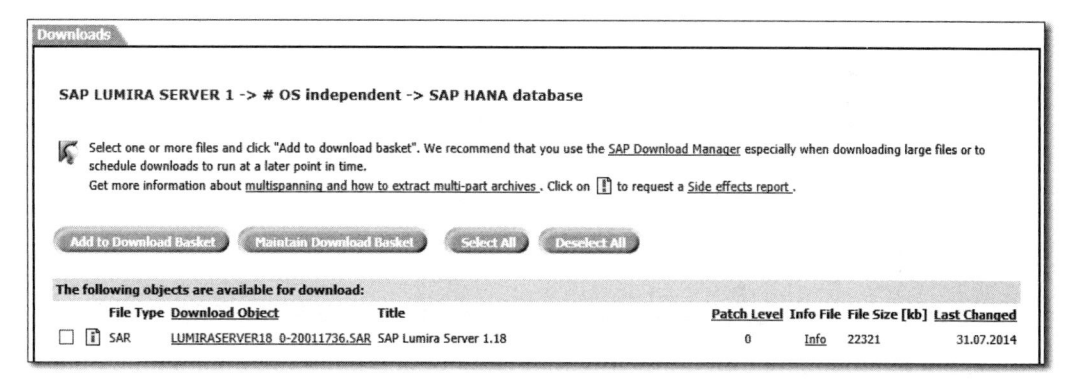

Figure 9.2 Add SAP Lumira Server to Download Basket

6. Click the checkbox before the SAP Lumira Server 1.18 SAR file, and click ADD TO DOWNLOAD BASKET to add it in to list of components to download through SAP Download Manager.

7. In the alphabetical list, go to the S page.

8. Click SAPCAR • SAPCAR 7.20.

9. Select the version for your operating system and click ADD TO DOWNLOAD BASKET to add it to the list of components to download through SAP Download Manager.

10. Start SAP Download Manager, and download both SAP Lumira Server and SAPCAR.

11. Use SAPCAR to extract the SAP Lumira Server delivery unit from the SAR archive. In a command-line window, run the following command:

```
sapcar -xvf SAPLUMIRASERVER18_0-20011736.SAR
```

This extracts the lumiraserver.tgz file.

We will now look at the advantages and requirements of using SAP HANA, then discuss the installation of SAP Lumira Server via SAP HANA Studio. Finally, we will see what security options become available through our HANA-deployment.

9.2 Using SAP HANA for SAP Lumira Server

SAP Lumira Server runs natively on the SAP HANA platform and takes advantage of the application framework it provides, including its in-memory power. Before being able to install and run it properly, you must first check that SAP HANA meets certain requirements to host SAP Lumira Server.

9.2.1 SAP HANA Platform Advantages

SAP Lumira Server is a native SAP HANA XS application hosted on and managed by the SAP HANA platform. As an application platform, SAP HANA provides a global framework for SAP Lumira Server:

- The SAP Lumira Server lifecycle is supported by the SAP HANA framework:
  - SAP Lumira Server installation, upgrade, and uninstall.
  - SAP Lumira Server content and configuration backup and recovery.
- The SAP Lumira Server security model relies on SAP HANA:
  - Users and their credentials are enforced by SAP HANA; authentication can be manual or through single sign-on.
  - Users' authorizations are based on SAP HANA roles.
- Logging and tracing are handled through SAP HANA logs.
- Administration takes place via the SAP HANA Studio application.

Functionally, because SAP Lumira Server is hosted on SAP HANA it has optimized access to the views available on this SAP HANA server. These views are seen as datasets for SAP Lumira Server, which can leverage the power of the SAP HANA platform when accessing them.

9.2.2 SAP HANA Requirements

Your server must have an SAP HANA server installed with the SAP HANA XS Engine. The following components must be installed on it as well:

- SAP HANA Lifecycle Manager (LCM), to deploy SAP Lumira Server on the SAP HANA system
- SAP HANA Application Function Library (AFL) for the self-service analytics component, called the Self-Service Analytics Library (SAL)

Supported versions are listed in Table 9.1.

SAP HANA	SAP AFL	SAP HANA LCM
Support Package 08 Revision 81	Revision 81, Patch Level 2	1.0 Support Package 07 Patch 8 or higher
Support Package 08 Revision 82	Revision 82	

Table 9.1 SAP HANA Revision Requirements

On a client machine, you need to install SAP HANA Studio Support Package 08 in order to connect to the SAP HANA system and administrate it.

9.2.3 Installing SAP Lumira Server with SAP HANA Studio

To deploy SAP Lumira Server on SAP HANA, you can use the SAP HANA Studio graphical user interface; to do so, perform the following steps:

1. Start SAP HANA Studio.
2. Connect to the SAP HANA system with an administration account.
3. In the SYSTEMS panel, right-click SAP HANA, and in the contextual menu select LIFECYCLE MANAGEMENT • PLATFORM LIFECYCLE MANAGEMENT • SAP HANA LIFECYCLE MANAGER to open the LIFECYCLE MANAGEMENT tab, as shown in Figure 9.3.

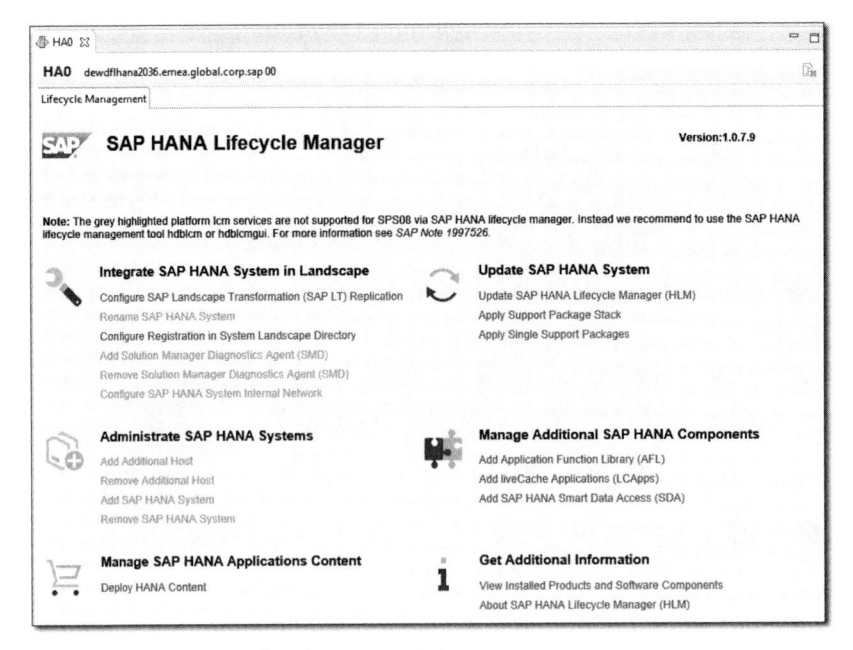

Figure 9.3 SAP HANA Lifecycle Manager Tab

4. In the Manage SAP HANA Applications Content tab, click the Deploy HANA Content link to start the deployment workflow.

5. In the Enter Credentials pane, as shown in Figure 9.4, enter the account password, and then click Next.

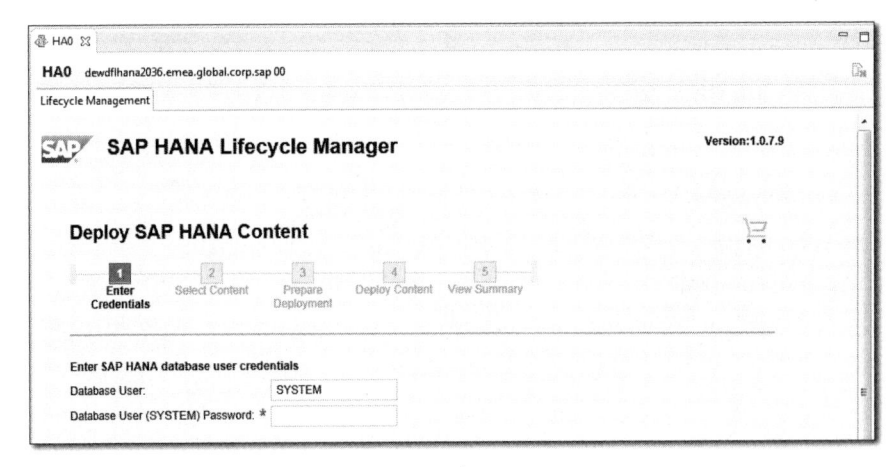

Figure 9.4 SAP HANA Deployment—Password

Using SAP HANA for SAP Lumira Server | 9.2

6. In the SELECT CONTENT pane, as shown in Figure 9.5, select the FROM A PERSONAL COMPUTER checkbox if you have saved the content in the client machine (the lumiraserver.tgz file previously extracted), and then click NEXT.

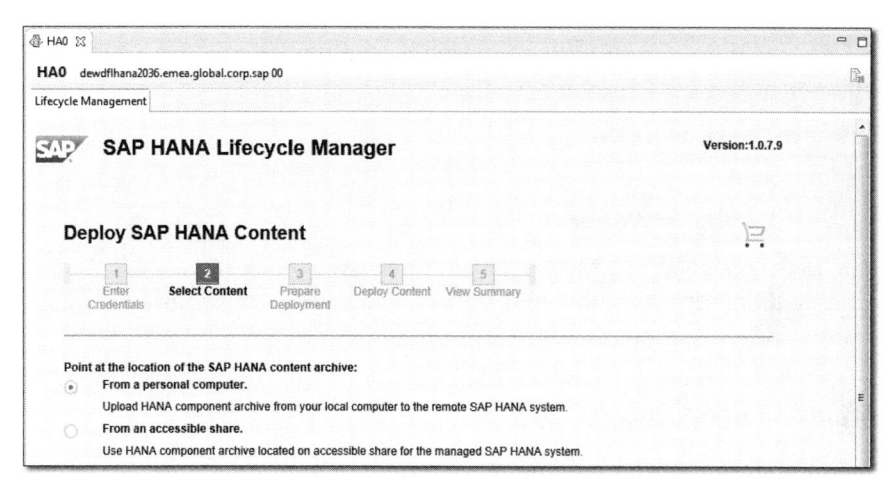

Figure 9.5 SAP HANA Deployment—Archive Location

7. In the LOCATION OF SOFTWARE ARCHIVE FOR UPDATE text field, as shown in Figure 9.6, enter the path in the client machine of the lumiraserver.tgz file previously extracted, and then click NEXT. You may click BROWSE to navigate in the file system to select it.

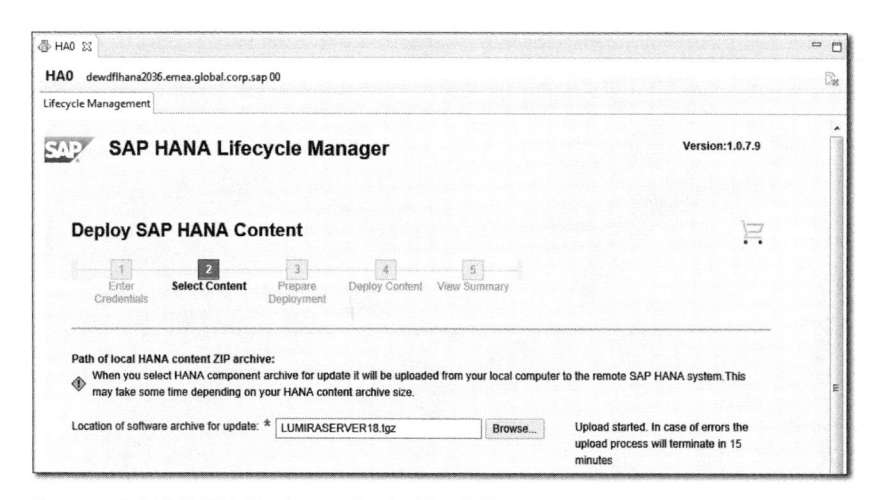

Figure 9.6 SAP HANA Deployment—Archive Path

441

8. The SAP Lumira Server archive is analyzed by SAP HANA, and a summary is displayed in the PREPARE DEPLOYMENT pane. This step may take several minutes, because the TGZ file must be uploaded and analyzed by SAP HANA.
9. Click RUN to start the SAP Lumira Server deployment.
10. The deployment progress is displayed in the DEPLOY CONTENT pane. When the deployment is over, a summary is displayed in the VIEW SUMMARY panel.
11. Click CLOSE to close the tab.

9.2.4 SAP Lumira Server Security

SAP Lumira Server is hosted as an application in SAP HANA and uses its repository for user authentication and authorization. You must use SAP HANA Studio to create users and grant them access to SAP Lumira Server.

Security in SAP HANA Studio

SAP HANA's security model proposes a framework based on users and roles:

- **Users**
  Defined by the account name; authenticated by password or through single sign-on.
- **Roles**
  Granted to users; roles define the actions and the objects users can access, are cumulative, and can be inherited.

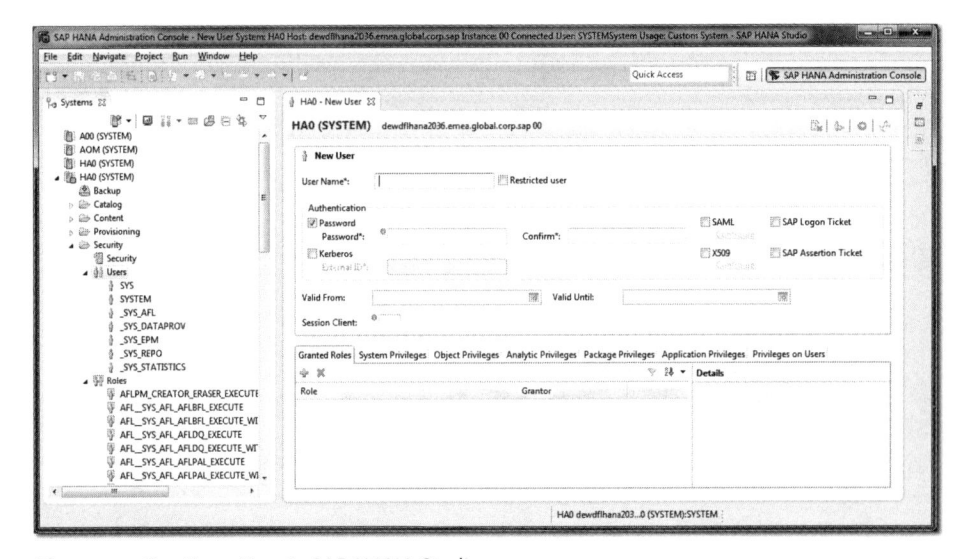

Figure 9.7 Creating a User in SAP HANA Studio

SAP HANA security is stored in the SAP HANA system and is managed in SAP HANA Studio, as shown in Figure 9.7.

SAP Lumira Server Roles

When you deploy SAP Lumira Server in SAP HANA, you also deploy the roles that apply to SAP Lumira Server. These SAP Lumira Server-specific roles are as follows:

- `sap.bi.common::BI_DATA_CONSUMER`
  This role is typically used for passive users that only consume SAP Lumira content published by others. It allows these users to view stories and datasets in SAP Lumira Server.

- `sap.bi.common::BI_DATA_ANALYST`
  This role must be assigned to active or power users who publish or create content in SAP Lumira Server. It allows these users to perform the following actions:
  - View stories in SAP Lumira Server
  - Publish datasets to SAP Lumira Server from SAP Lumira Desktop (see Chapter 7, Section 7.7) or create datasets in SAP Lumira Server (see Section 9.4.2)
  - Publish stories to SAP Lumira Server from SAP Lumira Desktop or create stories in SAP Lumira Server

- `sap.bi.common::BI_TECH_USER`
  This role must only be assigned to technical administrators who manage and maintain the SAP Lumira Server.

- `sap.bi.common::BI_CONFIGURATOR`
  This role must only be assigned to users who set up SAP Lumira Server functionality.

Creating Users and Assigning Roles in SAP HANA Studio

After the SAP Lumira Server deployment on SAP HANA, you must use SAP HANA Studio to create a technical account that is dedicated to SAP Lumira Server administration and used to run the queries to retrieve data from datasets. To create this user, follow these steps:

1. Start SAP HANA Studio.
2. Create a new user called, for example, SYSTEM.

3. Assign the following roles to this user:
   - `sap.bi.common::BI_TECH_USER`
   - `sap.hana.xs.admin.roles::RuntimeConfAdministrator`
   - `sap.hana.xs.admin.roles::SQLCCAdministrator`
4. Use a web browser to log into the SAP HANA XS Administration Tool. This tool is a web-based tool used to configure the environment that runs applications on the SAP HANA platform. Its default URL is *http://<server>:80<instance>/sap/hana/xs/admin*:
   - *<server>* is the server hosting the web application.
   - *<instance>* is the number that identifies the SAP HANA instance hosting SAP Lumira Server.
5. Enter administrative credentials to log into the tool.
6. If you are connecting for the first time using this account, you must change your password.
7. In the left side of the page, use the tree navigator to select SAP • BI • LAUNCHPAD • LOGIC • V2 • REPOCONNECTION.XSSQLC, as shown in Figure 9.8.

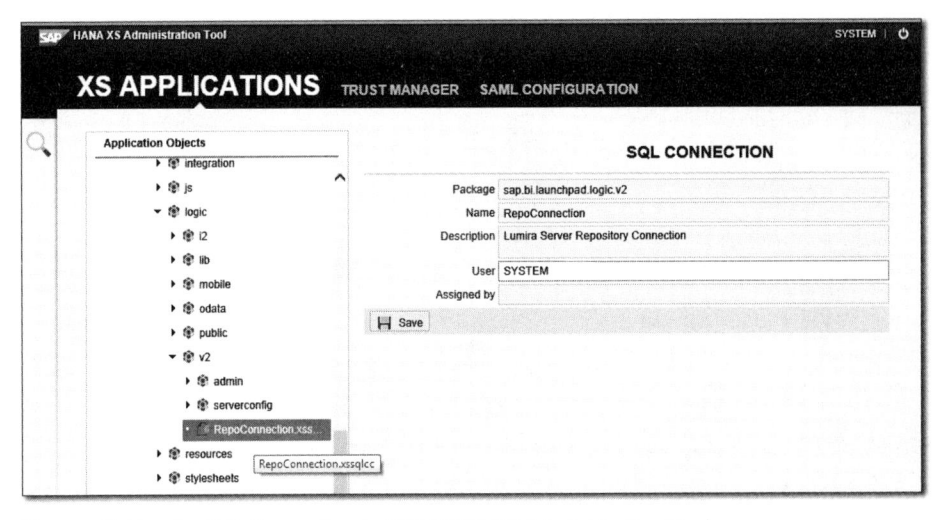

Figure 9.8 User for SQL Connection in SAP HANA XS Administration Tool

8. In the right side of the page, in the USER text field enter the name of the administrative account previously created (SYSTEM, in our example), and then click SAVE.

9. You can now return to SAP HANA Studio to create users and assign them the `sap.bi.common::BI_DATA_CONSUMER` role so that they can view content in SAP Lumira Server. If they are expected to create content, then you can also assign them the `sap.bi.common::BI_DATA_ANALYST` role.

9.3 SAP Lumira Server User Interface

Like SAP Lumira Cloud, you access SAP Lumira Server through a web browser or through SAP BusinessObjects Mobile. As described in the next sections, the UI is also very similar to SAP Lumira Cloud except for the resource types that can be hosted.

9.3.1 Log In to SAP Lumira Server

To connect to SAP Lumira Server, go to its URL in your web browser. Its default URL is *http://<server>:80<instance>/sap/bi/launchpad*:

- *<server>* is the server hosting the web application.
- *<instance>* is the number that identifies the SAP HANA instance hosting SAP Lumira Server (see Figure 9.9).

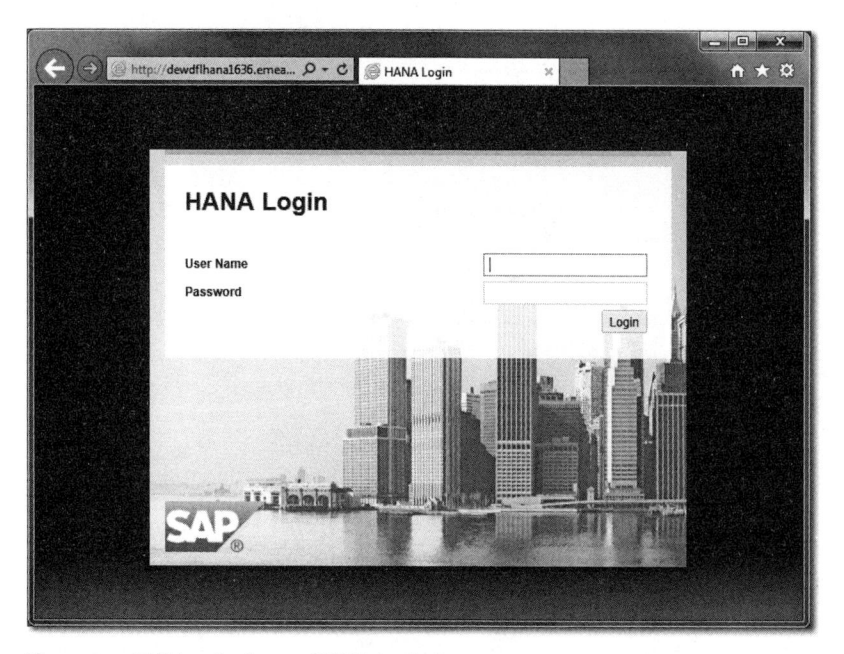

Figure 9.9 SAP Lumira Server HANA Login Page

Enter your credentials in the USER NAME and PASSWORD text fields, and then click LOGIN.

9.3.2 Log Out of SAP Lumira Server

To explicitly log out from SAP Lumira Server, follow these steps:

1. Click the down arrow in the top-right corner of the page. A dialog box opens, as seen in Figure 9.10.

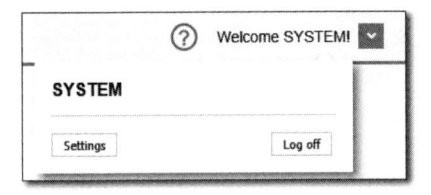

Figure 9.10 Log Off Dialog Box

2. Click LOG OFF to terminate your session on SAP Lumira Server. Your session closes (see Figure 9.11).

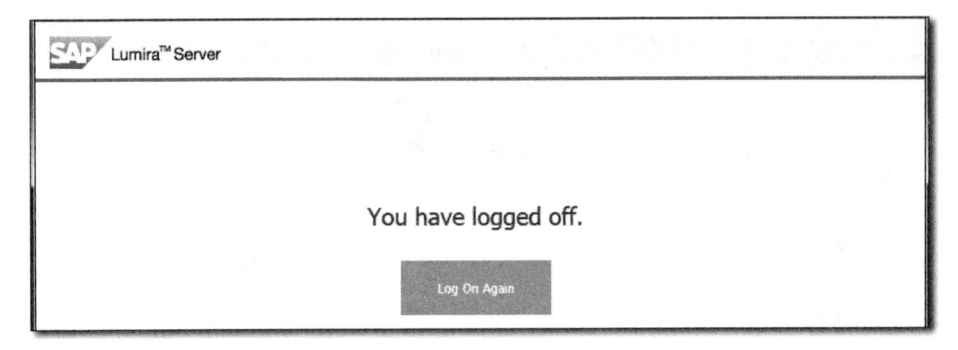

Figure 9.11 Log Off Page

9.3.3 General Overview

The SAP Lumira Server page displays two main tabs:

- MY ITEMS
  This tab is your working space; it displays the list of resources published in SAP Lumira Server. From it, you can open these resources and work on them. It is described from Section 9.3.4 to Section 9.3.6.

SAP Lumira Server User Interface | **9.3**

▶ SETTINGS

This tab allows you to set your locale parameters. It is described in Section 9.3.7.

In the top-right corner of the page, you can click the WELCOME link to open the LOG OFF dialog box, as described in Section 9.3.2. You can also click the HELP icon to open SAP Lumira Server help.

The UI checks the roles that have been assigned to you and only allows access to the capabilities for which your assigned roles authorize you.

9.3.4 My Items Tab

The MY ITEMS tab is the main space in which you run most of your actions in SAP Lumira Server (see Figure 9.12).

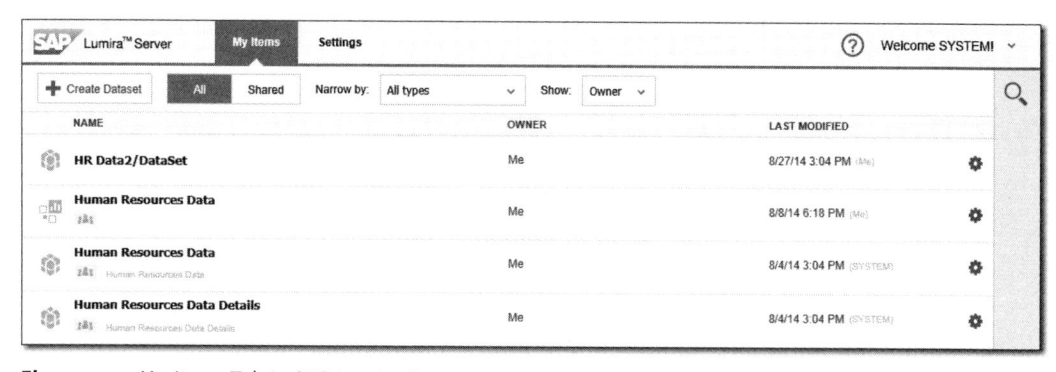

Figure 9.12 My Items Tab in SAP Lumira Server

The MY ITEMS tab displays the list of all resources to which you have access as a flat list. These resources are identified by their names and by icons that depend on their type (see Table 9.2).

Icon	Type	Description
	STORY	Stories and visualizations saved in SAP Lumira Server
	DATASET	Datasets stored in SAP Lumira Server

Table 9.2 Resource Types in SAP Lumira Server

447

If the list contains too many resources, then you can use any of the following options to filter it:

- Use the ALL and SHARED buttons to display either all resources or only the shared ones (see Section 9.6).
- In the NARROW BY dropdown list (see Figure 9.13), you can select to filter the list of resources to display by types. The possible choices are as follows:
  - ALL TYPES: Display both datasets and stories.
  - STORY: Display only stories.
  - DATASET: Display only datasets.

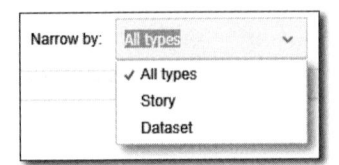

Figure 9.13 Narrow by Dropdown List

- In the SHOW dropdown list (see Figure 9.14), you can select or deselect what properties to display in the resource list for each resource:
  - OWNER: The account that uploaded or created the resource. If you are this owner, then it displays ME.
  - PACKAGE: This property, available only for datasets, displays the SAP HANA package containing the datasets, either the ones created when importing data (see Section 9.4.2) or the ones mapped to SAP HANA views (see Section 9.4.3).
  - TYPE: The resource type. Possible values are listed in Table 9.2.

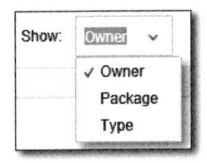

Figure 9.14 Show Dropdown List

In addition to these display options, to find a specific item in the MY ITEMS list you may use the search tool.

9.3.5 Searching for Items

To search for an item in in the MY ITEMS tab, perform the following steps:

1. On the right side of the MY ITEMS tab, click the SEARCH icon to open the SEARCH text field, as shown in Figure 9.15.

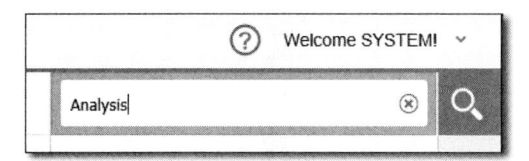

Figure 9.15 Search Text Field

2. In this text field, enter the search pattern, and then press Enter.
3. The list of resources is filtered with the search pattern you have entered.
4. If you click the SEARCH icon again, then the SEARCH text field collapses, but your search remains displayed to remind you that the current list of items is filtered.
5. Click the DELETE icon on the filter to remove it and display the unfiltered list of resources.

9.3.6 Running Actions

Click the cog icon displayed in the same line of the individual resources. In the contextual menu that opens (see Figure 9.16), select one of the possible commands:

- EDIT
  This command is available only for stories. It opens the story in the Visualize room for editing.
- SHARE
  Share the selected resource with other users in SAP Lumira Server (see Section 9.6). Only the resource owner can share it.
- INFO
  Open the INFO dialog box, in which you can display and modify the selected resource name and its description, as shown in Figure 9.17. Click OK to save your changes, if any, and close the INFO dialog box.

▶ DELETE
Delete the selected resource. After clicking through a confirmation message, the resource is deleted from the server and removed from the MY ITEMS list. Only the resource owner can delete it.

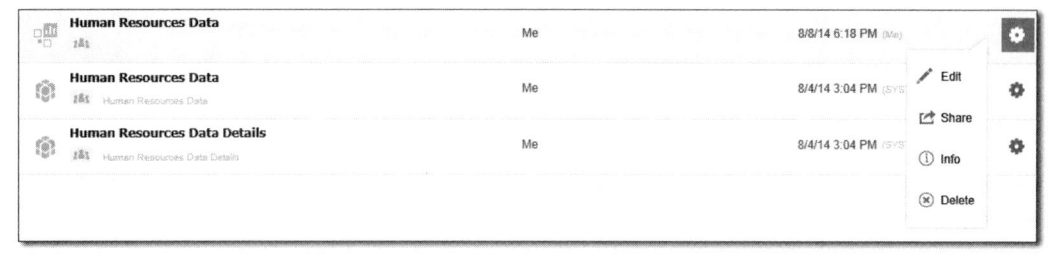

Figure 9.16 Actions Contextual Menu

Figure 9.17 Resource Info Dialog Box

To modify a resource name or description or to edit a story, you must be the resource owner or the resource must have been shared with you in EDIT mode (see Section 9.6).

The actions available for each document type are listed in Table 9.3.

Resource Type	Possible Actions
Dataset	▶ Share ▶ Info ▶ Delete
Story	▶ Edit ▶ Share ▶ Info ▶ Delete

Table 9.3 Actions Available by Resource

In addition to this contextual menu, you can click on the resource in the MY ITEMS list:

- Click a story to open and view it:
  - To edit it (see Section 9.5), click EDIT in the top-right side of the page, and the document will open in the Visualize room.
  - To share it (see Section 9.6), click the SHARE icon in the top-right side of the page, and the SHARE WITH OTHERS dialog box will open.
- Click a dataset to open the Visualize room (see Section 9.5), and create a new visualization from this dataset.

9.3.7 Settings

As shown in Figure 9.18, the SETTINGS tab contains very little information:

- Your login name in the NAME text field.
- The TIME ZONE and LOCALE used to display content in SAP Lumira Server. You may explicitly set a locale using the TIME ZONE and LOCALE dropdown lists or leave this option set to DETECT AUTOMATICALLY to let SAP Lumira Server find your locale automatically.

After making a change, click SAVE CHANGES to save your changes.

Figure 9.18 SAP Lumira Server Settings Tab

9.3.8 Mobile Access

SAP Lumira Server's interface is similar for any supported web browser, because it is also written in HTML5. It can only be accessed through SAP BusinessObjects Mobile, which offers the same capabilities as it does for SAP Lumira Cloud, connecting to both systems similarly. When defining the connection (see Chapter 8, Section 8.8.1), you need to specify SAP Lumira Server as the connection type.

9.4 Importing to SAP Lumira Server

SAP Lumira Server can only contain SAP Lumira resources: stories and datasets. These are not many options compared to SAP Lumira Cloud, but SAP Lumira Server compensates with its privileged access to SAP HANA views.

This section describes how you can upload this content in SAP Lumira Server and take advantage of SAP HANA.

9.4.1 Publishing from SAP Lumira Desktop

It is not possible to save SAP Lumira documents created with SAP Lumira Desktop to SAP Lumira Server, and from SAP Lumira Desktop you can only connect to SAP Lumira Server to publish your resources. As described in Chapter 7, Section 7.7, only stories or datasets can be published from SAP Lumira Desktop to SAP Lumira Server.

To publish in SAP Lumira Server, you must be assigned the role `sap.bi.common::BI_DATA_ANALYST`.

The following differences from SAP Lumira Cloud exist for SAP Lumira Server:

- It is possible to publish a dataset based on an SAP HANA view in online mode. The SAP HANA view must be hosted on the same SAP HANA system that runs SAP Lumira Server. Because SAP Lumira Server runs on the same SAP HANA system, this optimizes the performance to query data from the SAP HANA view.
- It is not possible to access SAP Lumira Server content from SAP Lumira Desktop or to download it locally on your file system.

9.4.2 Importing Data to Create a Dataset

In SAP Lumira Server, you may create a dataset to share in the server for further exploration, with the following restrictions:

- SAP Lumira Server supports only CSV and Microsoft Excel files (.xlsx file extension) as data sources.
- SAP Lumira Server can connect to only one file at a time, whereas SAP Lumira Desktop can merge the content of several files to create the dataset.
- SAP Lumira Server does not propose any formula language to process the data.

From a UI point of view, the process to create a new dataset in SAP Lumira Server is similar to the process described for SAP Lumira Cloud in Chapter 8, Section 8.4.2.

The differences are as follows:

- When a dataset is created, it is stored in the SAP HANA database and exposed through an analytical view. Here again, SAP Lumira Server takes advantage of SAP HANA both as its application platform and for its in-memory database.
- You must be granted the `sap.bi.common::BI_DATA_ANALYST` role to create a dataset.

> **Aggregation Functions**
>
> SAP Lumira Server supports less aggregation functions than SAP Lumira Desktop. Hence, datasets defined in SAP Lumira Desktop are not supported in SAP Lumira Server if they contain measures aggregated with functions not supported not supported by SAP Lumira Server.

9.4.3 Using SAP HANA Dataset

Because SAP Lumira Server relies on SAP HANA, it can benefit from direct access to data saved in SAP HANA. An analytical view saved in SAP HANA is automatically displayed in SAP Lumira Server as a dataset if you have been granted the right to view it.

As for any dataset, if the `sap.bi.common::BI_DATA_ANALYST` or `sap.bi.common::BI_DATA_CONSUMER` role has been assigned to you, then you can use this dataset to create visualizations or stories.

9.5 Visualization and Composition Online

The long-term objective for SAP Lumira Server is to offer the same seamless experience as SAP Lumira Desktop. To achieve this objective, the same Visualize and Compose rooms are used in SAP Lumira Server, SAP Lumira Cloud, and SAP Lumira Desktop. Hence, the user interface is similar in the three applications.

As the Visualize and Compose rooms have already been described in Chapter 5 and Chapter 6 and their integration in SAP Lumira Cloud described in Chapter 8, this section presents only a quick overview of these rooms in SAP Lumira Server.

9.5.1 Accessing Online Rooms

In SAP Lumira Server, when you click a dataset in the MY ITEMS tab, the Visualize room opens with an empty story, where you can create visualizations from the dataset.

When you click a story in the MY ITEMS tab, the story is displayed in viewing mode only. You can only navigate in the story pages and cannot modify them. If you are the story owner or if you are allowed to edit the story, then you can click EDIT in the toolbar to open the story in the Visualize room.

An alternate way to open the story in the Visualize room is to click the cog icon for the story in the MY ITEMS tab. In the contextual menu that opens, select EDIT.

To add boards, infographics, or reports to the story or to modify the elements the story already contains, click the COMPOSE tab on top of the page to open the story in the Compose room.

9.5.2 Working in the Visualize and Compose Rooms

In the Visualize room, as in the SAP Lumira Desktop Visualize room, you can perform the following actions:

- Create the same visualizations as in SAP Lumira Desktop.
- Edit the visualizations that the story contains.
- Use the same charts library as in SAP Lumira Desktop.

In the Compose room, as in the SAP Lumira Desktop Compose room, you can perform the following actions:

- Create and add new stories to the SAP Lumira document or edit existing ones. This covers interactive boards, infographics, and reporting.
- Add visualizations to stories.
- Arrange the story's layout.
- Add interactions with filters.

The user interface is the same as in SAP Lumira Desktop, so for more details on these rooms and their user interfaces refer to Chapter 5 and Chapter 6.

The differences from SAP Lumira Desktop are as follows:

- The resource you edit is saved on the server, and you edit it through a web browser.
- You can only manipulate one story at a time in the Compose room. You cannot add a new story to the current story.

These specificities related to the deployment model introduce some slight differences in the user interface:

- You can add external pictures to a story, but they are uploaded from your local file system and saved in the story.
- You cannot directly refresh the dataset used by your story from the Visualize or Compose room.
- However, if your dataset is an SAP HANA view exposed as a dataset in SAP Lumira Server (see Section 9.4.3) or is created from an SAP HANA view in online mode (see Chapter 3, Section 3.6.2), then the data is directly retrieved from the SAP HANA view. If the SAP HANA view contains variables, then you are prompted to set them before data is retrieved and displayed in visualizations and stories.

In the VISUALIZE or COMPOSE rooms, click GO BACK TO THE PREVIOUS PAGE on the top of the page to return to the MY ITEMS list without saving the current story. Most of the time, you will want to save your changes first, as described in the next section.

9.5.3 Saving Your Story

Once you have finished creating or modifying your story, you may save it to the SAP Lumira Server.

To save the story, follow these steps:

1. In the tool bar, click the SAVE icon, and in the contextual menu that opens, select the SAVE or SAVE AS commands.
2. If you have selected SAVE AS or if the document is a new document you have just created, then the SAVE dialog box opens, as shown in Figure 9.19. Otherwise, the document is saved with its previous name.

Figure 9.19 Save Dialog Box

3. Enter a name and an optional comment for the story in the NAME and DESCRIPTION text fields.
4. Click OK to close the SAVE dialog box and save the story.
5. When you return to the resource lists, the story is listed in the MY ITEMS list.

Even if you have created only visualizations without organizing them in any story, you can still save a story. This story contains only your visualizations. If you have not created any visualizations either, you can also save a story; the saved story is considered empty, but it is still considered a valid story with a name, a description, and a dataset.

Once created, you can also share stories through SAP Lumira Server, as described next.

9.6 Sharing Resources in SAP Lumira Server

Once created, you can also share the following resources saved in SAP Lumira Server with other users in the SAP HANA repository:

- **Datasets:** Other users can create new stories from them.
- **Stories:** Other users can view or edit them.

This sharing capability relies on the SAP HANA security repository model, because you share the resource to a role defined in SAP HANA. For a story, you can also associate an authorization level (VIEW or EDIT). Any user who has been assigned the proper role can access the resource with the rights defined by the authorization level.

By enforcing SAP HANA roles, SAP Lumira Server provides a more elaborate security model than SAP Lumira Cloud.

9.6.1 Sharing Prerequisites

As opposed to SAP Lumira Cloud, SAP Lumira Server does not offer a public access mode for sharing resource. Resources can only be shared with users who can access SAP Lumira Server and are registered in the SAP HANA security repository.

Only a resource's owner can share it, so to share a resource, you must own it and also fulfill other conditions that depend on the resource type:

- You can only share a resource with a role assigned to you.
- To share an online dataset based on an SAP HANA view or an SAP HANA view used as a dataset, you must ensure the users have been granted the SELECT OBJECTS PRIVILEGE for the view and the ANALYTIC PRIVILEGE for the view.
- A story can only be shared with users who have a role that already provides access to all the datasets used by the story.

If these conditions are fulfilled, then you can share a resource in SAP Lumira Server.

9 | SAP Lumira Server

9.6.2 Sharing a Resource

To share a resource in SAP Lumira Server, follow these steps:

1. Once connected to SAP Lumira Server, in the MY ITEMS list select the resource to share, and click the cog icon to open its contextual menu. Select the SHARE command to open the SHARE WITH OTHERS dialog box.

   If you are editing a story in the Visualize or Compose room, then you can also click the SHARE icon in the top-right corner of the page to open this dialog box.

2. Depending on the resource type, this dialog box displays two different interfaces:

   ▸ For a dataset, it displays the list of roles to grant, an authorization level, and a roles selection pane, as shown in Figure 9.20.

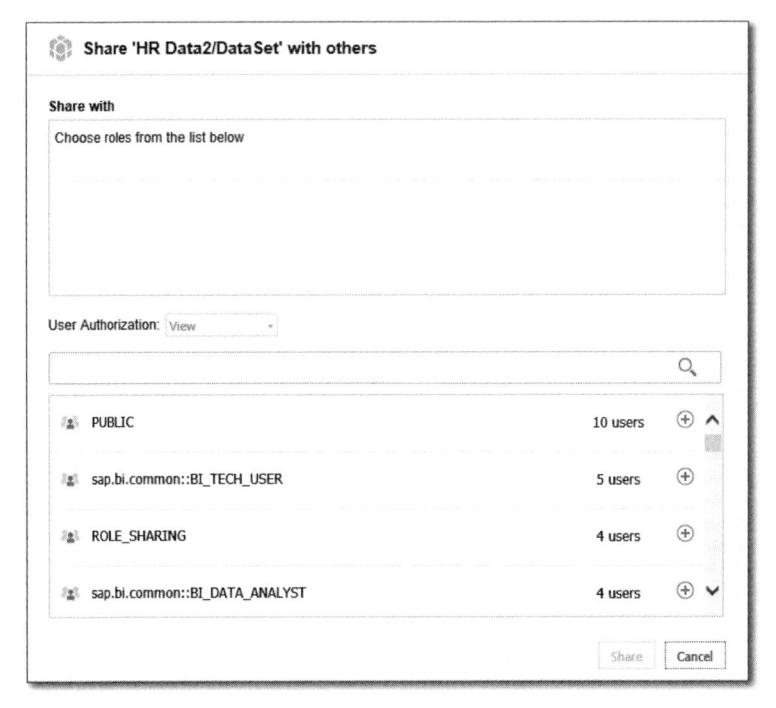

Figure 9.20 Share with Others Dialog Box for a Dataset

▸ For a story, it displays a link to the resource, the list of roles to grant, an authorization level, and a roles selection pane, as shown in Figure 9.21.

Sharing Resources in SAP Lumira Server | **9.6**

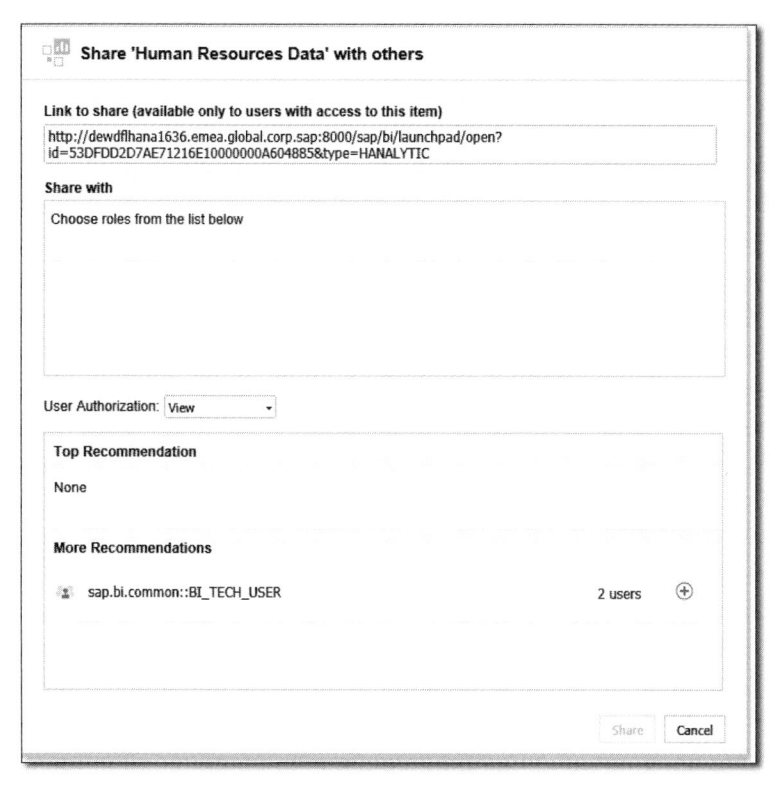

Figure 9.21 Share with Others Dialog Box for a Story

3. To select a role to share the resource with, select this role from the list of roles suggested by SAP Lumira Server in the bottom list. If the resource is a story, this list is split into two sections:

   ▶ TOP RECOMMENDATION: This list contains all roles that have been explicitly shared with all datasets used by the story.

   ▶ MORE RECOMMENDATIONS: This list contains other roles that have been shared with all datasets used by the story but not necessarily explicitly. It can be inherited from other roles.

   To find a specific role, type its name in the text field, and then click on the SEARCH icon.

4. To select a role displayed in the list of proposed roles, click the ADD icon in the same line as the role name. To remove it from the SHARE WITH list, click the DELETE icon in the same line as the role name.

5. If the resource to share is a story, then in the USER AUTHORIZATION dropdown list you can select an authorization level for the role with which you are sharing the story:

   ▶ VIEW: The default option that allows the assigned role to view the resource.
   ▶ EDIT: This option allows the assigned roles to also edit the story in the Visualize and Compose rooms (see Section 9.5) or to modify its name or description in the INFO dialog box (see Section 9.3.6). It does not give the right to share or delete it; only its owner can do so.

6. Click SHARE to close the SHARE WITH OTHERS dialog box and share your resource.

In the MY ITEMS tab, the SHARED icon below the resource's name indicates that it has been shared.

9.6.3 Changing Sharing Options

After you have shared a document, you can modify its sharing option. To do so, follow these steps:

1. Select the SHARE command to reopen the SHARING OPTIONS dialog box. Because the document has been shared, this dialog box lists the roles that can access it, as shown in Figure 9.22.

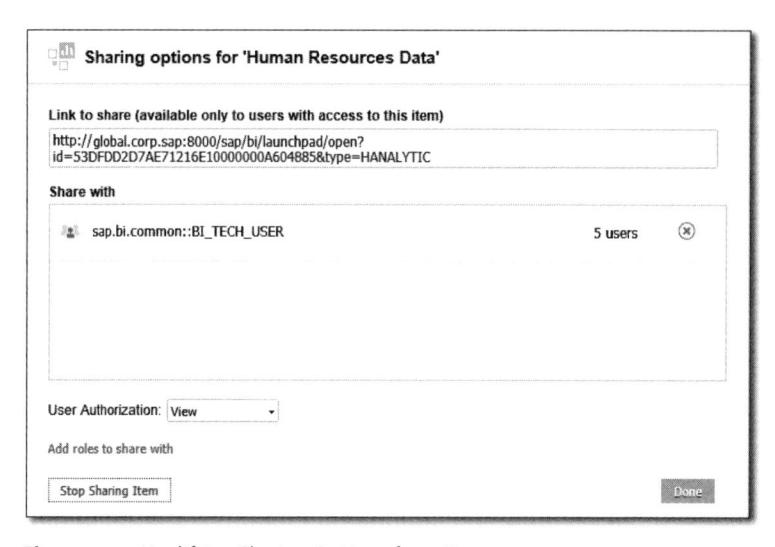

Figure 9.22 Modifying Sharing Options for a Story

2. If you are not the resource owner, then you can only review these details and cannot modify them. Otherwise, if you are the resource owner, you can perform the following actions:

   ▸ To stop sharing the resource with a specific role, click the DELETE icon on the line of the role to remove.

   ▸ To stop sharing the resource with all roles, click STOP SHARING ITEM. Click OK in the confirmation dialog box. The SHARING OPTIONS dialog box closes, and the resource is no longer shared.

   ▸ To add new roles with which to share the resource, click the ADD ROLES TO SHARE WITH link. This link is replaced by the same roles selection pane described in Section 9.6.2, from which you can select the new roles with which to share the resource.

3. Click DONE to apply your changes and close the SHARING OPTIONS dialog box.

9.6.4 Accessing a Shared Resource

To access a resource, you must have an account that can connect to SAP Lumira Server. This account must be assigned to a role with which the resource has been shared. If this is the case, then when you connect to SAP Lumira Server you can see this shared resource in the MY ITEMS list.

The SHARED icon below the resource name shows that the resource has been shared with you. To display only shared resources in the list, you can click the SHARED button in the toolbar.

If the URL of a story has been sent to you, follow these steps to access it:

1. Open this URL address in your web browser.

2. If you are not yet connected, enter your SAP HANA credentials to connect to SAP Lumira Server.

3. If the story has been shared with you through a role you belong to, then the story is directly opened in the web browser, in view mode by default.

4. If the story has been shared with you in EDIT mode, then you can click EDIT to open it in the Visualize or Compose room, modify it, and save it.

9.7 Summary

To benefit from SAP Lumira on the web, SAP Lumira suite contains SAP Lumira Server, an on-premise server deployment mode. SAP Lumira Server is an application running on an SAP HANA platform, and hence it benefits from the SAP HANA framework for installation, administration, security, and so on. Administration tasks are performed in SAP HANA Studio or the SAP HANA XS Administration Tool.

With SAP Lumira Server, you can create or edit datasets, visualizations, and stories and access them through a web browser or SAP BusinessObjects Mobile as you can with SAP Lumira Cloud. Sharing datasets and stories between users is enforced through SAP HANA roles. SAP HANA provides the benefits of in-memory power, on-premise server deployment, and security.

In the next chapter, we will discuss SAP Lumira's integration with SAP BusinessObjects BI 4.1.

The SAP BusinessObjects BI add-on for SAP Lumira allows you to store SAP Lumira datasets and stories in your SAP BusinessObjects BI 4.1 platform and allow them to benefit from the SAP Lumira platform framework.

10   Integrating SAP Lumira with SAP BusinessObjects BI 4.1

As described in the previous chapter, SAP Lumira suite proposes a server deployment through SAP Lumira Server. However, if you already have an SAP BusinessObjects BI 4.1 deployment you can still take advantage of it. This is made possible by the SAP BusinessObjects BI 4.1 add-on for SAP Lumira.

This chapter will describe the smooth integration of your SAP Lumira resources into your existing SAP BusinessObjects BI 4.1 deployment: from installation and configuration to importing your SAP Lumira resources then viewing them in the SAP BusinessObjects BI Launch Pad.

This add-on requires the installation of an SAP Lumira Server on an SAP HANA system that is used in the backend by SAP BusinessObjects BI 4.1.

You'll discover how the add-on allows you to publish datasets and stories in an SAP BusinessObjects BI 4.1 Central Management Server (CMS) repository from SAP Lumira Desktop. Once in the CMS repository, these resources benefit from the SAP BusinessObjects BI 4.1 framework and features, especially access through SAP BusinessObjects BI Launch Pad and administration in the Central Management Console (CMC).

Finally, we will look at the CMC, exploring how to display and manage stories and datasets, then the discover how to refresh and schedule a dataset.

We'll begin with an overview of the SAP BusinessObjects BI 4.1 add-on.

10.1　SAP BusinessObjects BI 4.1 Add-On Overview

As shown in Figure 10.1, this add-on also requires the installation of SAP Lumira Server in order to use its services and to take advantage of the SAP HANA database for storing the SAP Lumira datasets published to SAP BusinessObjects BI 4.1. The add-on for SAP Lumira must be installed on top of SAP BusinessObjects BI 4.1, with a minimal version of Support Package 3. SAP Lumira Server must be version 1.17 or higher.

The add-on installer must be run on any node of the cluster. The installer automatically detects the components to install and activate depending on the services hosted in the node.

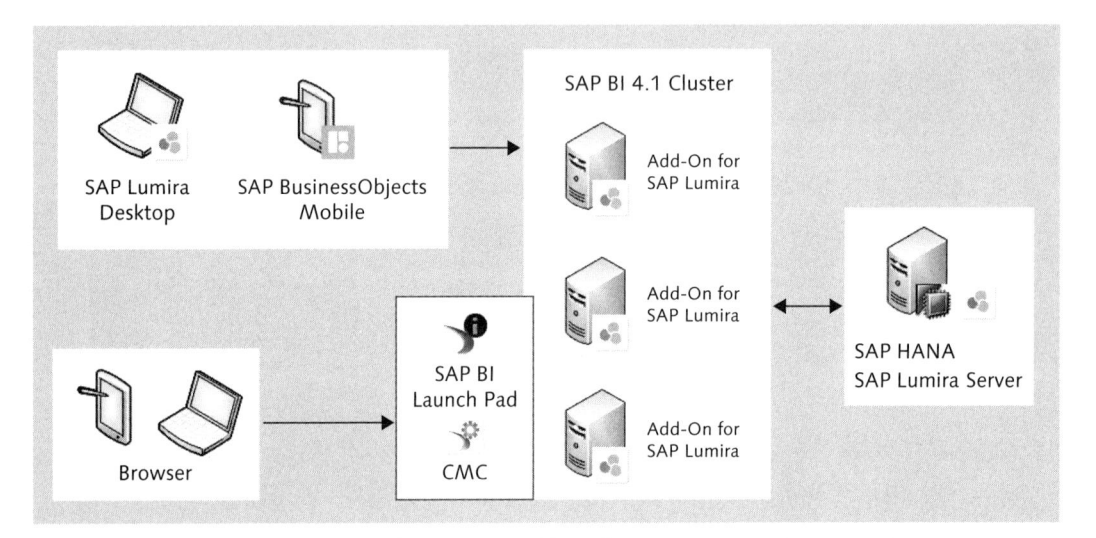

Figure 10.1 SAP BusinessObjects BI 4.1 Add-On for SAP Lumira Deployment Overview

The add-on installs a new service called LumiraService that handles all SAP Lumira requests and manages communication with SAP HANA.

When published in SAP BusinessObjects BI 4.1, SAP Lumira resources benefit from the SAP BusinessObjects BI 4.1 framework capabilities. It can also inherit the configuration you have defined for your other SAP BusinessObjects BI content:

- You can view SAP Lumira stories in SAP BusinessObjects BI Launch Pad or SAP BusinessObjects Mobile.

- Access is secure; users, authentications, and authorizations are defined in the CMS repository and fully enforced by SAP BusinessObjects BI 4.1.
- Stories can be organized in the folder's tree organization or by using categories in the CMS repository.
- Datasets based on universes stored in the same CMS repository can be refreshed and scheduled directly in SAP BusinessObjects BI 4.1 using its scheduling function.
- Datasets and stories can be managed and secured in the CMC.

These features will be discussed later in the chapter; first, we will look at the installation and configuration options of the SAP BusinessObjects BI 4.1 add-on.

10.2 Installing and Configuring SAP BusinessObjects BI 4.1 Add-On in SAP Lumira

Installing the add-on in SAP Lumira requires several steps. It involves not only download and installation but also setting up an SAP Lumira Server. A communication channel must be configured between SAP BusinessObjects BI 4.1 and SAP HANA. To secure this communication, you must use the SAP cryptography library and generate an assertion ticket.

> **Assertion Ticket**
>
> An assertion ticket is created when performing an outbound communication to another system or service provider. It is transmitted in the HTTP header and is intended for one recipient.

The following steps, described in detail in the following sections, must be taken to install the add-on:

1. Download the add-on for SAP Lumira and the cryptography library.
2. Install the add-on for SAP Lumira.
3. Install the cryptography library and generate an assertion ticket.
4. Configure SAP HANA with the assertion ticket.

5. Create a technical user in SAP HANA dedicated to communication with SAP BusinessObjects BI 4.1.
6. Configure the SAP HANA XS HTTP Destination for SAP Lumira Server.
7. Configure SAP BusinessObjects BI 4.1 to communicate with SAP HANA.

10.2.1 Downloading the Add-On for SAP Lumira and the SAP Cryptography Library

Both the SAP BusinessObjects BI add-on for SAP Lumira and the SAP cryptography library can be downloaded from the SAP Support site (*http://service.sap.com/support*) under the SOFTWARE DOWNLOADS tab. To begin the download, perform the following steps:

1. Use your web browser to go to the SAP Support website: *http://support.sap.com*.
2. Click DOWNLOAD SOFTWARE and then SUPPORT PACKAGES AND PATCHES in the left pane.
3. Click A–Z ALPHABETICAL LIST OF MY PRODUCTS to navigate in the alphabetical list of products, and go to the L page.
4. Click SBOP BI, ADD-ON FOR SAP LUMIRA • SBOP BI, ADD-ON FOR SAP LUMIRA • COMPRISED SOFTWARE COMPONENT VERSIONS • SBOP BI, ADD-ON FOR SAP LUMIRA.
5. Click the link of the operating system running your SAP BusinessObjects BI 4.1 server, as seen in Figure 10.2.

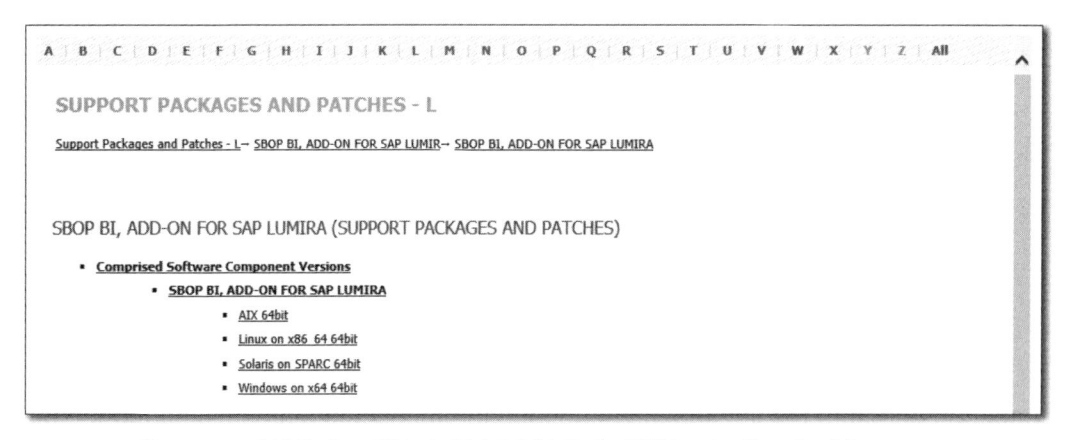

Figure 10.2 SAP BusinessObjects BI 4.1 Add-On for SAP Lumira Download Page

6. Go to the bottom of the page, as seen in Figure 10.3. Click the checkbox next to the SAR archive of the add-on.

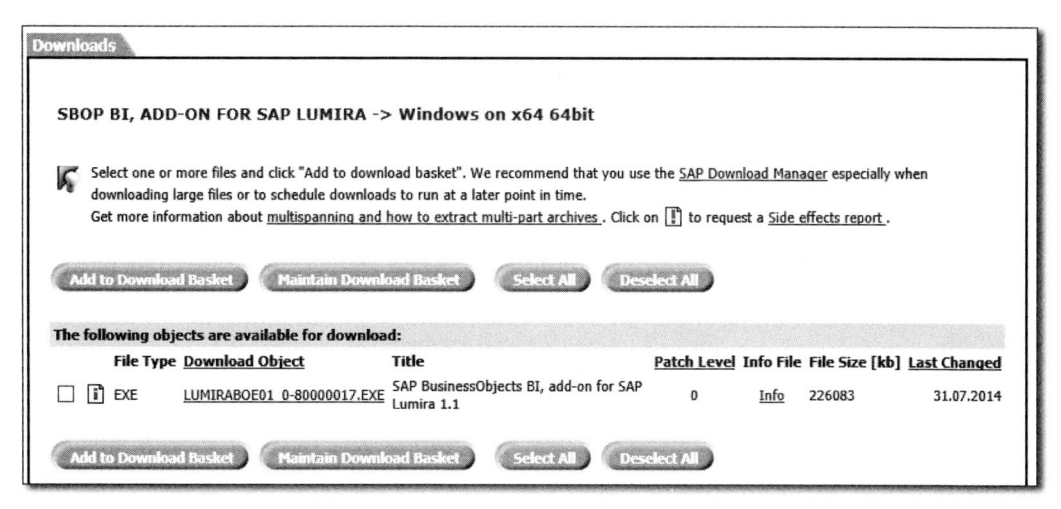

Figure 10.3 Add SAP BusinessObjects BI 4.1 Add-On for SAP Lumira to Download Basket

7. Click ADD TO DOWNLOAD BASKET to select the add-on for download.
8. In the alphabetical list of products, go to the S page.
9. Click SAPCRYPTOLIB • SAPCRYPTOLIB 5.5.5 and select the version of the library for the operating system running SAP HANA.
10. Go to the bottom of the page. Click the checkbox next to the SAR archive of the last patch level of the cryptography library.
11. Click ADD TO DOWNLOAD BASKET to select the add-on for download.
12. Start SAP Download Manager to download the selected packages.
13. When the packages are downloaded, use SARCAR to unzip them (see Chapter 9, Section 9.1).
14. Copy the files of the cryptography library (sapgenpse and libsapcrypto.so) to the server running SAP HANA.
15. Copy the add-on installer to the server running SAP BusinessObjects BI 4.1.

The workflow to run the installer depends on the platform. It is described in Section 10.2.2 for the Windows operating system.

10.2.2 Installing on a Windows Platform

The SAP BusinessObjects BI 4.1 add-on for SAP Lumira must be installed on any node of the cluster hosting SAP BusinessObjects BI 4.1, including the ones hosting the web or application server.

You do not need to stop SAP BusinessObjects BI 4.1. To install the add-on for a Windows platform, perform the following:

1. The add-on installer is a self-extracted file. Run the executable EXE file you retrieved from the SAR archive (see Section 10.2.1).

2. In the SELECT THE SETUP LANGUAGE dropdown list, select the language for the installer.

3. On the CHECK PREREQUISITES pane, the installer performs some system requirement checks. If one of these requirements is not fulfilled, then an error message is displayed in the array.

    If all requirements are fulfilled, as shown in Figure 10.4, then click NEXT.

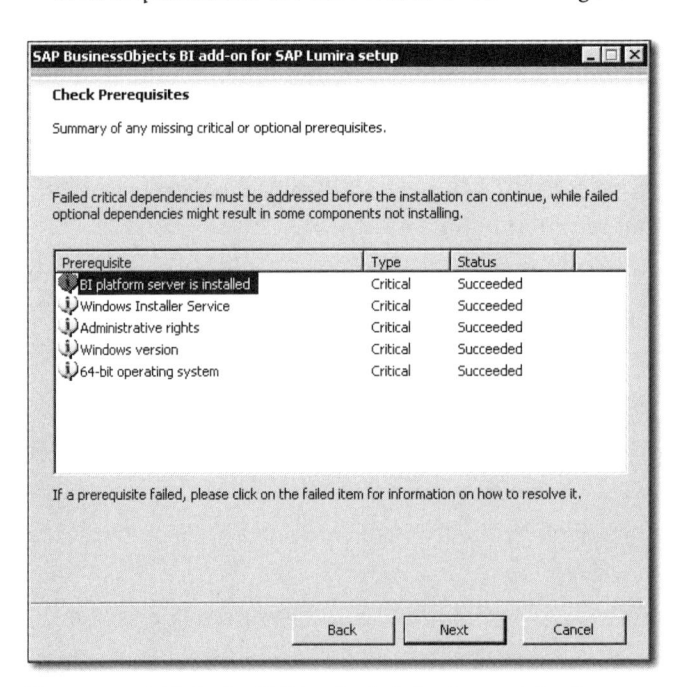

Figure 10.4 Add-On for SAP Lumira Installer Prerequisites Pane

4. In the WELCOME pane, click NEXT.

Installing and Configuring SAP BusinessObjects BI 4.1 Add-On in SAP Lumira | **10.2**

5. In the LICENSE AGREEMENT pane, review the agreement, select the I ACCEPT THE LICENSE AGREEMENT checkbox, and click NEXT.

6. In the SELECT LANGUAGE PACKAGES screen, select the languages to install, and click NEXT.

7. In the EXISTING CMS DEPLOYMENT INFORMATION pane, you need to enter the parameters to connect to the SAP BusinessObjects BI 4.1 system. As seen in Figure 10.5, in the CMS NAME, CMS PORT, and PASSWORD text fields, enter the CMS name, its port, and the password for the administrator account. Click NEXT.

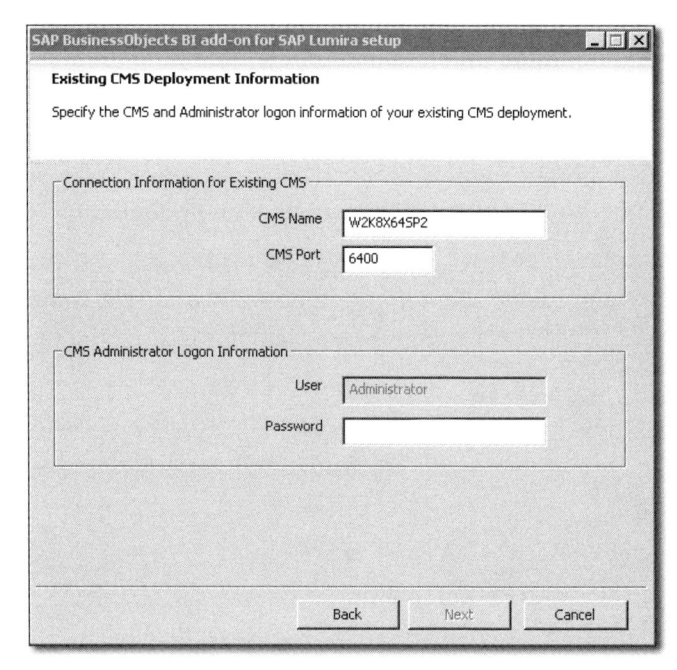

Figure 10.5 Add-On for SAP Lumira Installer CMS Deployment Information Pane

8. In the START INSTALLATION pane, click NEXT to start the installation.

9. A progress bar is displayed while the installation proceeds.

10. When the installation has completed, the post-instruction dialog box reminds you to configure the connection with the SAP HANA server. This step is described from Section 10.2.3 to Section 10.2.7.

11. Click NEXT, and then click FINISH to complete the installation.

469

10.2.3 Installing the Cryptography Library and Generating the Assertion Ticket

The next step requires you to access the machine running SAP HANA in order to install the cryptography library and to generate the assertion ticket. In the next sections, `<SID>` refers to the SAP HANA System ID—for example, IHS.

Follow these steps:

1. Log into the SAP HANA machine as the `root` user.

2. Copy the sapgenpse and libsapcrypto.so files (see Section 10.2.1) into the */usr/sap/<SID>/SYS/global/security/lib/* directory.

3. Go to this directory, and set execute permissions for these files:
    ```
    cd /usr/sap/IHS/SYS/global/security/lib
    chmod 755 ./sapgenpse ./libsapcrypto.so
    ```

4. Add this directory into the library environment variable (`LD_LIBRARY_PATH` or `LIBPATH`). For example, for `LD_LIBRARY_PATH`, enter the following command:
    ```
    export LD_LIBRARY_PATH=/usr/sap/IHS/SYS/global/security/lib
    ```

5. Use the `su` command to change the current user to the administrative account for the SAP HANA system. This user is `<SID>adm` (for example `IHSadm`), and the command to type is `su IHSadm`.

6. Create the sec directory under the directory */usr/sap/<SID>/HDB<Instance>/<server>*:
    ```
    mkdir /usr/sap/IHS/HDB00/<servername>/sec
    ```

7. Go to the directory that contains the cryptography files:
    ```
    cd /usr/sap/IHS/SYS/global/security/lib/
    ```

8. Use the following command lines to generate the sapsrv.pse, saplogonSign.pse, and sapcli.pse files (these are personal security environment files in which public key information is stored):
    ```
    ./sapgenpse gen_pse -p /usr/sap/<SID>/HDB<instance>/<server>/sec/sapsrv.pse -x "" "<dn>"
    ./sapgenpse gen_pse -p /usr/sap/<SID>/HDB<instance>/<server>/sec/sapcli.pse -x "" "<dn>"
    ./sapgenpse gen_pse -a DSA -p /usr/sap/<SID>/HDB<instance>/<server>/sec/saplogonSign.pse -x "" "<dn>"
    ```

Where:

- `<instance>` is the SAP HANA instance.
- `<server>` is the name of the server hosting SAP HANA.
- `<dn>` defines a distinguished name with the attributes listed in Table 10.1.

For example:

```
./sapgenpse gen_pse -p /usr/sap/IHS/HDB00/dewdflhana2036/sec/
sapsrv.pse -x "" "CN=dewdflhana2036,C=CA,S=BC,O=SAP-AG,OU=HR"
./sapgenpse gen_pse -p /usr/sap/IHS/HDB00/dewdflhana2036/sec/
sapcli.pse -x "" "CN=dewdflhana2036,C=CA,S=BC,O=SAP-AG,OU=HR"
./sapgenpse gen_pse -a DSA -p /usr/sap/IHS/HDB00/dewdflhana2036/sec/
saplogonSign.pse -x "" "CN=dewdflhana2036,C=CA,S=BC,O=SAP-AG,OU=HR"
```

Attribute Abbreviation	Name
CN	Server name
C	Country
S	State
O	Company
OU	Department

Table 10.1 Attributes List

10.2.4 Configuring SAP HANA with an Assertion Ticket

Once an assertion ticket has been generated, you need to configure SAP HANA to use it:

1. Open SAP HANA Studio.
2. In the SYSTEMS panel, right-click the system name, and in the contextual menu select the CONFIGURATION AND MONITORING • OPEN ADMINISTRATION command to open the ADMINISTRATION CONSOLE.
3. Click the CONFIGURATION tab.
4. In the NAME column, look for INDEXSERVER.INI, and click this line to expand it.
5. In the tree, go to AUTHENTICATION, as shown in Figure 10.6.
6. Right-click the SAPLOGONTICKETTRUSTSTORE variable, and in the contextual menu select CHANGE to open the CHANGE CONFIGURATION VALUE dialog box, as seen in Figure 10.7.

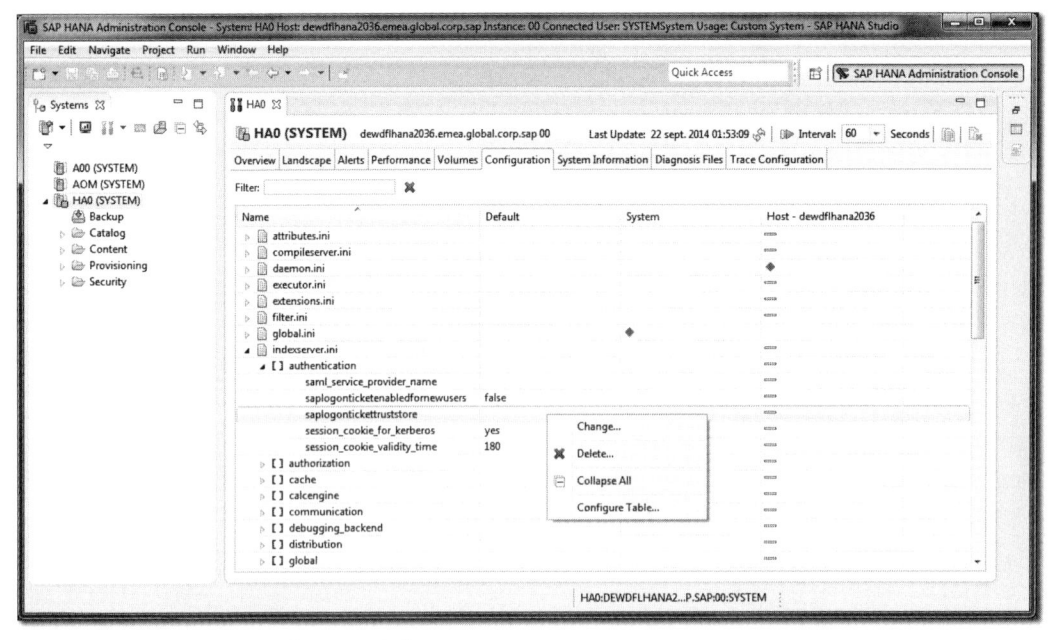

Figure 10.6 Configuration Tab

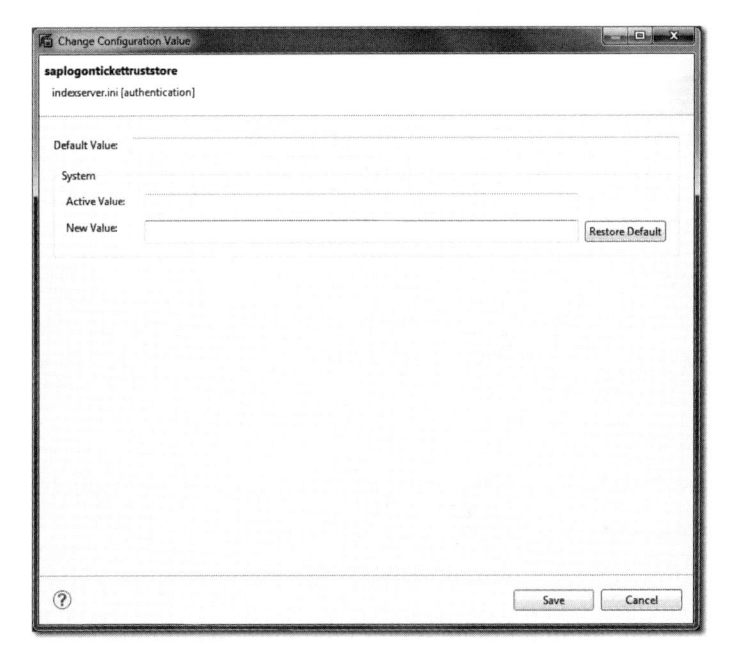

Figure 10.7 Change Configuration Value Dialog Box

7. In the NEW VALUE text field, enter the path of the saplogonSign.pse file (see Section 10.2.3). Click SAVE to save your changes and close the dialog box.

8. Repeat these steps to open the XSENGINE.INI file, and set the path of the saplogonSign.pse file (see Section 10.2.3) in the AUTHENTICATION • SAPLOGONTICK-ETTRUSTSTORE variable, as seen in Figure 10.8.

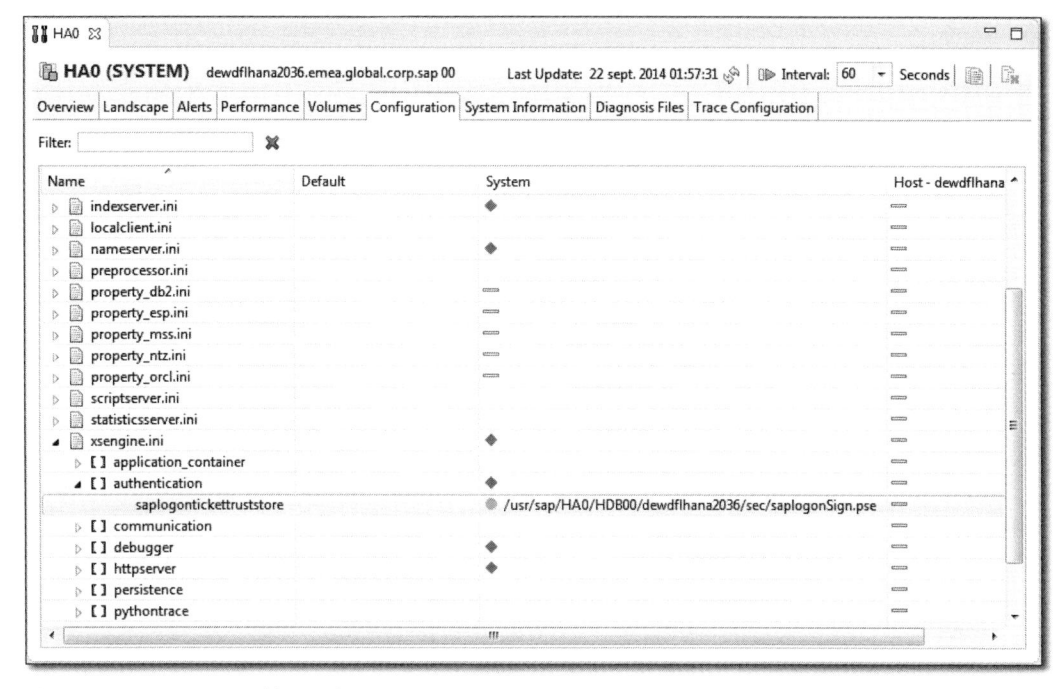

Figure 10.8 Setting Variables in the xsengine.ini File

9. Click SAVE in the tool bar to save your changes.

10. To take these changes into consideration, restart the SAP HANA server by right-clicking the system name and selecting the CONFIGURATION AND MONITORING • RESTART SYSTEM command from the contextual menu.

10.2.5 Creating a User in SAP HANA Dedicated to SAP BusinessObjects BI 4.1

You need to create a technical user for SAP BusinessObjects BI 4.1 to communicate with SAP HANA.

1. In SAP HANA Studio, create a new user. Keep note of this user's credentials.
2. In the tab containing this user's properties, select the SAP ASSERTION TICKET checkbox.
3. Add the following roles for this user:
    - `sap.bi.services.datasetmanager.db.roles::SAP_BI_DATASETMANAGER_ADMIN`
    - `sap.bi.common::BI_DATA_ANALYST`
4. Save this new user in SAP HANA.

10.2.6 Configuring SAP Lumira Server HTTP

Because communications between SAP HANA and SAP BusinessObjects BI 4.1 are performed via HTTP, you need to configure how SAP Lumira Server is exposed through HTTP:

1. Use a web browser to log into the SAP HANA XS Administration Tool using the account dedicated to SAP BusinessObjects BI 4.1 you previously created (see Section 10.2.5).

    By default, the SAP HANA XS Administration Tool URL is *http://<server>:80<instance>/sap/hana/xs/admin*:
    - *<server>* is the server hosting the web application.
    - *<instance>* is the SAP HANA instance hosting SAP Lumira Server.

2. Because this is the first time you are logging in for this user, you must change the user's password.

3. In the left side of the page, use the tree navigator to select SAP • BI • SERVICES • DATASETLOADFRESH • LOGIC • BI • WACSHTTPCONFIG.XSHTTPDEST, as shown in Figure 10.9.

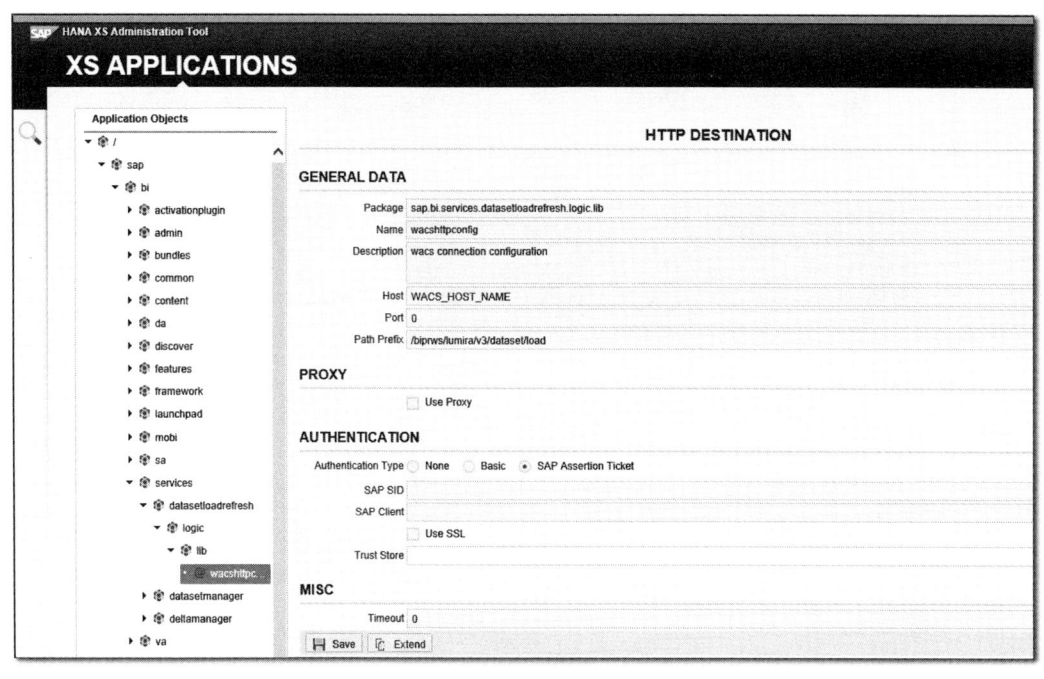

Figure 10.9 SAP HANA XS Administration Tool

4. Click EXTEND to open the EXTEND DESTINATION dialog box, as shown in Figure 10.10.

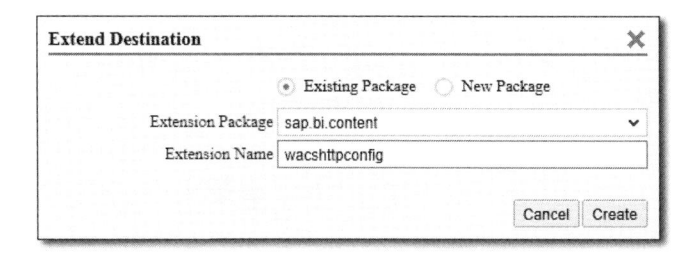

Figure 10.10 SAP HANA XS Administration Tool—Extend Destination

5. Click CREATE to create the file and close the EXTEND DESTINATION dialog box.
6. In the left side of the page, use the tree navigator to select SAP • BI • CONTENT • WACSHTTPCONFIG.XSHTTPDEST, and edit the parameters of this file you have deployed.

7. In the right side of the page, as shown in Figure 10.11, modify the following parameters under the GENERAL DATA section:

   ▸ HOST: Enter the host name of the SAP BusinessObjects BI 4.1 server.
   ▸ PORT: Enter the port number of the WACS (see Chapter 7, Section 7.12).

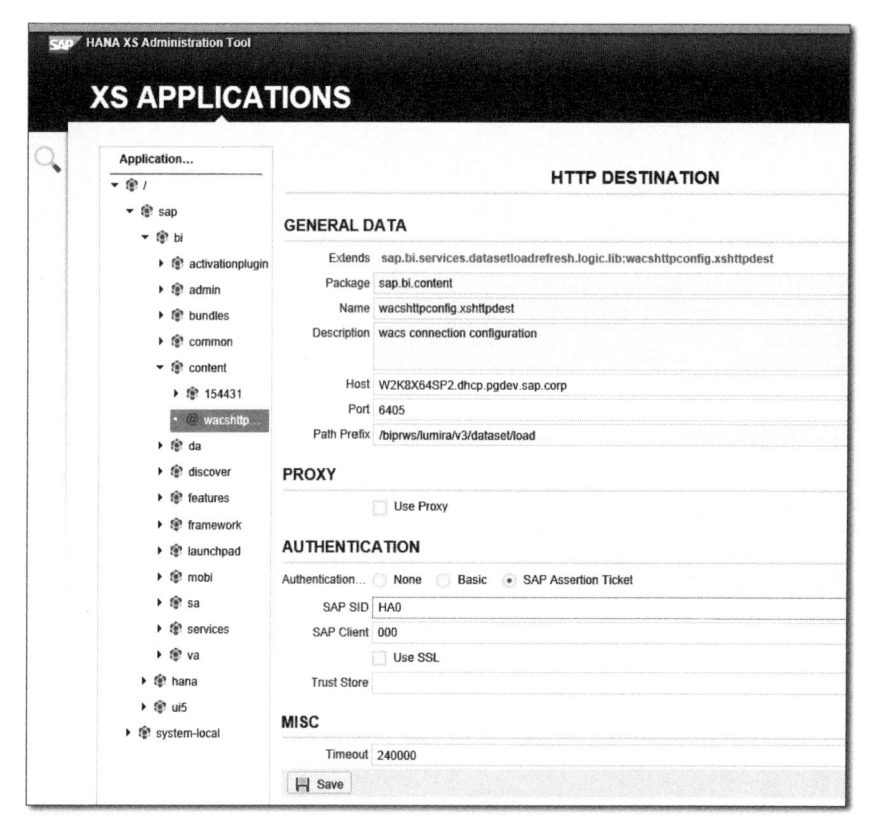

Figure 10.11 SAP HANA XS Administration Tool—Edit File Parameters

Under the AUTHENTICATION section, enter the following parameters:

▸ AUTHENTICATION TYPE: Select the SAP ASSERTION TICKET radio-button.
▸ SAP SID: Enter the SAP HANA System ID.
▸ SAP CLIENT: Enter 000 for the SAP client number.

Under the MISC section, enter a timeout value in milliseconds for the TIMEOUT parameter.

10.2.7 Configuring SAP BusinessObjects BI 4.1 to Communicate with SAP HANA

The final steps to configure this add-on must be performed in the CMC by defining how the SAP BusinessObjects BI 4.1 system uses the ticket and user previously created to exchange information with SAP HANA.

Follow these steps:

1. In a web browser, log into the CMC using an administrator account. By default, the CMS's URL is *http://<hostname>:<port>/BOE/CMC*:

    ▶ <hostname> is the hostname for SAP BusinessObjects BI 4.1.

    ▶ <port> is the port number for SAP BusinessObjects BI 4.1.

2. In the CMC home page, click the SERVERS link or the SERVERS tab to open the SERVERS page.

3. In the left pane, click the SERVERS LIST to display the list of servers in the right pane.

4. Look for the server running SAP Lumira services. Its name must end with LUMIRA, as seen in Figure 10.12. Because the SERVERS LIST covers several pages, you may need to search additional pages. Double-click the server to open the PROPERTIES dialog box, as shown in Figure 10.13.

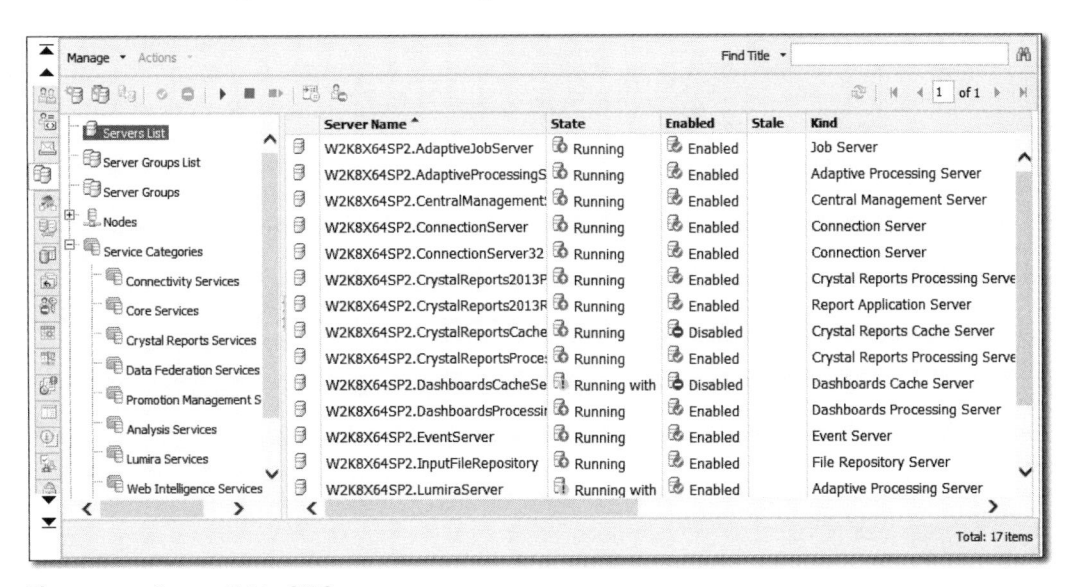

Figure 10.12 Servers List in CMC

5. In the right side of this dialog box, enter the following parameters under the LUMIRA PROXY SERVICE section, as seen in Figure 10.13:

   ▶ HANA HOSTNAME: Enter the server hosting the SAP HANA server.

   ▶ HANA INSTANCE NUMBER: Enter the instance number of the SAP HANA server.

   ▶ USE SSL TO TALK TO HANA: If you have configured SAP HANA to communicate using SSL, then select this checkbox to use SSL for exchanges between SAP BusinessObjects BI 4.1 and SAP HANA.

   ▶ HANA DATABASE USER and HANA DATABASE PASSWORD: Enter the credentials of the user you have previously created for SAP HANA and SAP BusinessObjects BI 4.1 communication (see Section 10.2.5).

   ▶ OS USER and OS PASSWORD: Enter the credentials of the administrative account for the SAP HANA system. This user is <SID>adm (for example, IHSadm).

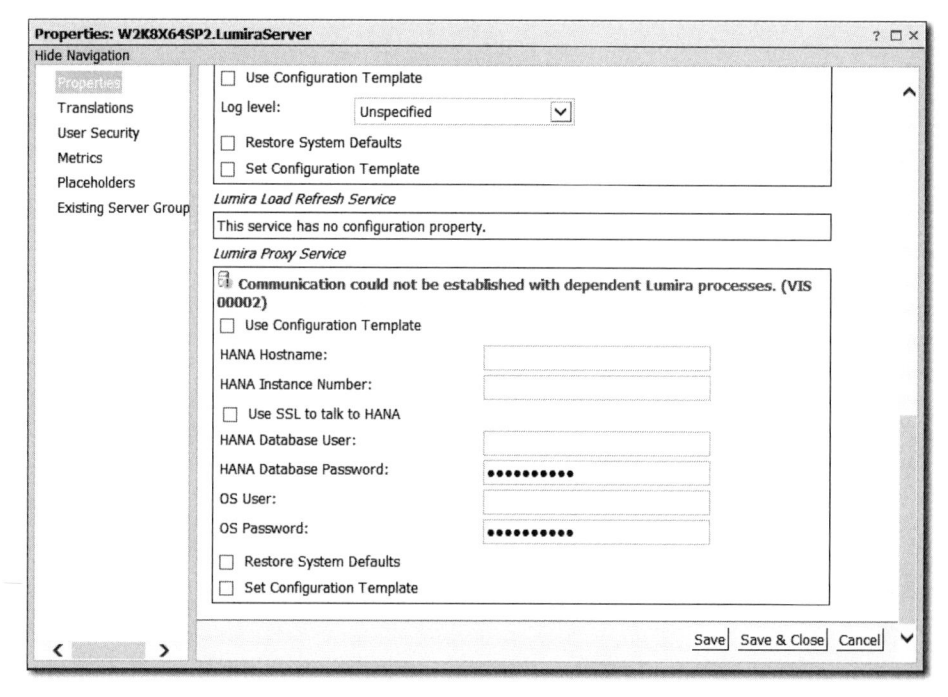

Figure 10.13 LumiraServer Properties Dialog Box

6. Click SAVE to save your changes and close the PROPERTIES dialog box.

7. In the SERVERS tab in the SERVERS LIST, select the LUMIRASERVER server, and click the RESTART icon ■▶ in the toolbar to restart it.

8. When the server has been properly restarted, you may leave the CMC.

The add-on installation and configuration of the SAP Lumira add-on are now completed.

To test that the add-on is working properly, the next two sections will discuss the importing SAP Lumira datasets and stories to SAP BusinessObjects BI 4.1 and then displaying them in the SAP BusinessObjects BI Launch Pad.

10.3 Importing SAP Lumira Resources into SAP BusinessObjects BI 4.1

Once you have installed the add-on for SAP Lumira on SAP BusinessObjects BI 4.1, you can upload SAP Lumira resources to the SAP BI 4.1 CMS repository, including datasets retrieved from a data source in offline mode and stories based on such datasets.

As described in Chapter 7, Section 7.12, the only way to upload these resources into SAP BusinessObjects BI 4.1 is to use SAP Lumira Desktop, through the Share room.

10.3.1 Dataset InfoObject

In the CMS repository, a new LUMIRA DATASET InfoObject has been created to support datasets. These objects are stored in the SAP Lumira Datasets root folder as a flat list. They contain dataset descriptions and where their data is stored, because the datasets' actual data is not stored in the CMS repository but in the SAP HANA system hosting SAP Lumira Server.

When datasets are published from SAP Lumira Desktop to SAP BusinessObjects BI 4.1, their data are stored in the SAP HANA database.

No data is stored in the SAP BusinessObjects BI platform, so when you view the dataset the data is fetched from the SAP HANA database in real time.

These datasets data are stored separately from the datasets created or published in the SAP Lumira Server:

- It is not possible to access these datasets from SAP Lumira Server.
- It is not possible to access SAP Lumira Server datasets from SAP BusinessObjects BI 4.1.

The datasets published in SAP BusinessObjects BI 4.1 are static unless they are based on universes stored in the same CMS repository (see Section 10.6). It is not possible to publish datasets created in online mode (see Chapter 3, Section 3.1.3).

10.3.2 Story InfoObject

In the CMS repository, a new LUMIRA STORY InfoObject has been created to support stories. As with other reports, stories can be saved in your MY FAVORITES folder and PUBLIC FOLDERS or subfolders.

10.4 Viewing SAP Lumira Content in SAP BusinessObjects BI Launch Pad

The stories published in the CMS repository can be viewed through an SAP BusinessObjects BI Launch Pad. Its default URL is *http://<hostname>:<port>/BOE/BI*:

- *<hostname>* is the hostname for SAP BusinessObjects BI 4.1.
- *<port>* is the port for SAP BusinessObjects BI 4.1.

To log in to the SAP BusinessObjects BI Launch Pad, you need an account defined in the CMS repository.

In SAP BusinessObjects BI Launch pad, when you navigate in the CMS repository folders, both in your MY FAVORITES folder and PUBLIC FOLDERS or subfolders, SAP Lumira stories are displayed as any other objects. As seen in Figure 10.14, they can be identified by the SAP Lumira story icon and their type: LUMIRA STORY.

Figure 10.14 SAP Lumira Story in SAP BusinessObjects BI Launch Pad

In the SAP BusinessObjects BI Launch Pad, SAP Lumira stories benefit from the capabilities provided by the framework. Commands are available through the right-click contextual menu, as shown in Figure 10.15, or through the menu bar to display stories' properties, copy, move, or delete them, or add them to categories.

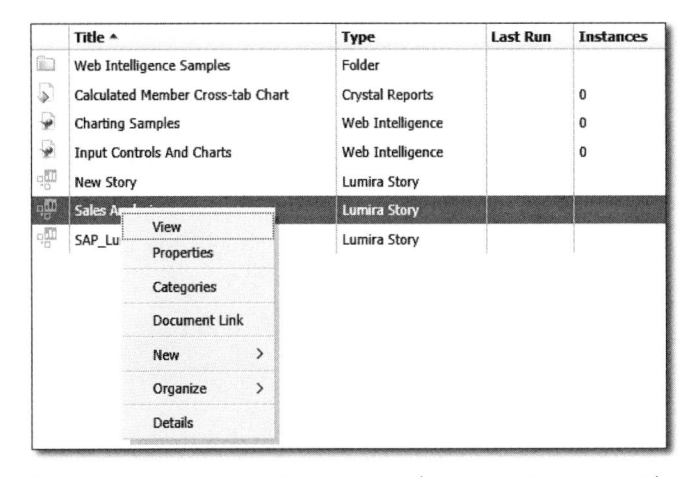

Figure 10.15 SAP Lumira Story Contextual Menu in SAP BusinessObjects BI Launch Pad

You can open a story by double-clicking it or clicking the VIEW command in the right-click contextual menu or menu bar. This opens the story in a new tab, as shown in Figure 10.16. SAP BusinessObjects BI Launch Pad integrates an SAP Lumira viewer that displays the stories as they would display in SAP Lumira Desktop.

481

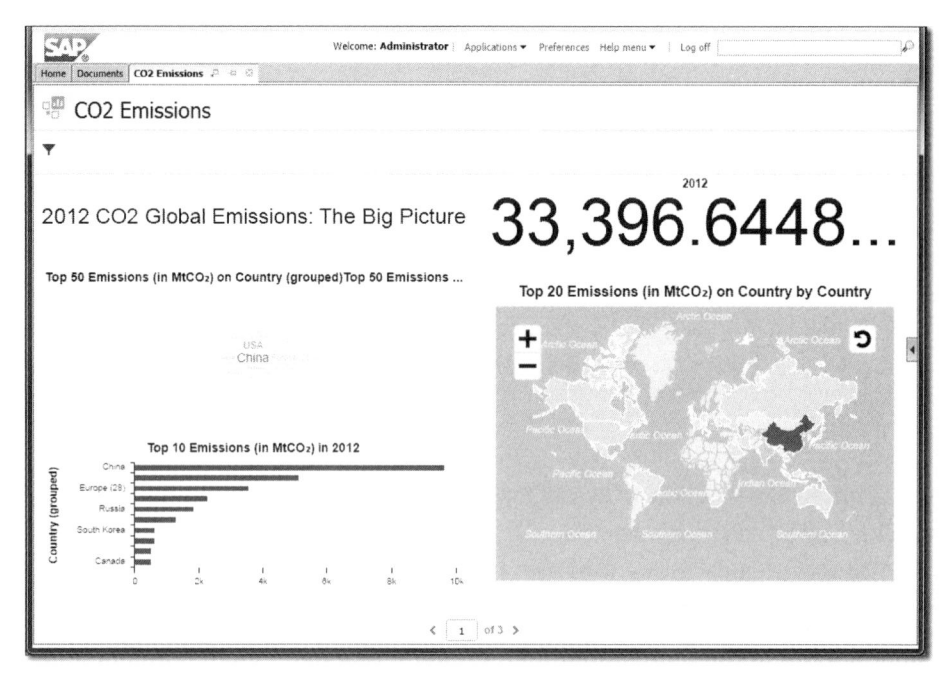

Figure 10.16 SAP Lumira Story Displayed in SAP BusinessObjects BI Launch Pad

However, this SAP Lumira viewer does not allow you to modify the stories. The Visualize and Compose rooms are not integrated in SAP BusinessObjects BI Launch Pad as they are in SAP Lumira Cloud or SAP Lumira Server. Hence, you cannot create a dataset and create and edit visualizations and stories as you can with SAP Lumira Cloud or SAP Lumira Server.

However, a major benefit of the SAP BusinessObjects BI add-on integration is the ability to save stories and datasets in the CMC, which will be discussed in the next section.

10.5 Central Management Console

One of the main advantages that the add-on brings is that stories and datasets are saved in the SAP BusinessObjects BI 4.1 CMS repository and hence can be administered using the CMC. As with any object in the CMS repository, stories and datasets are stored as InfoObjects.

Additional Reference

This section does not detail how to set rights in the CMC. To learn more about this subject, refer to *SAP BusinessObjects BI Security* (SAP PRESS, 2013).

10.5.1 Displaying Stories and Dataset

When you connect to the CMC, a new section, LUMIRA DATASETS, is available in the CMC home page, at the bottom of the ORGANIZE section, as seen in Figure 10.17.

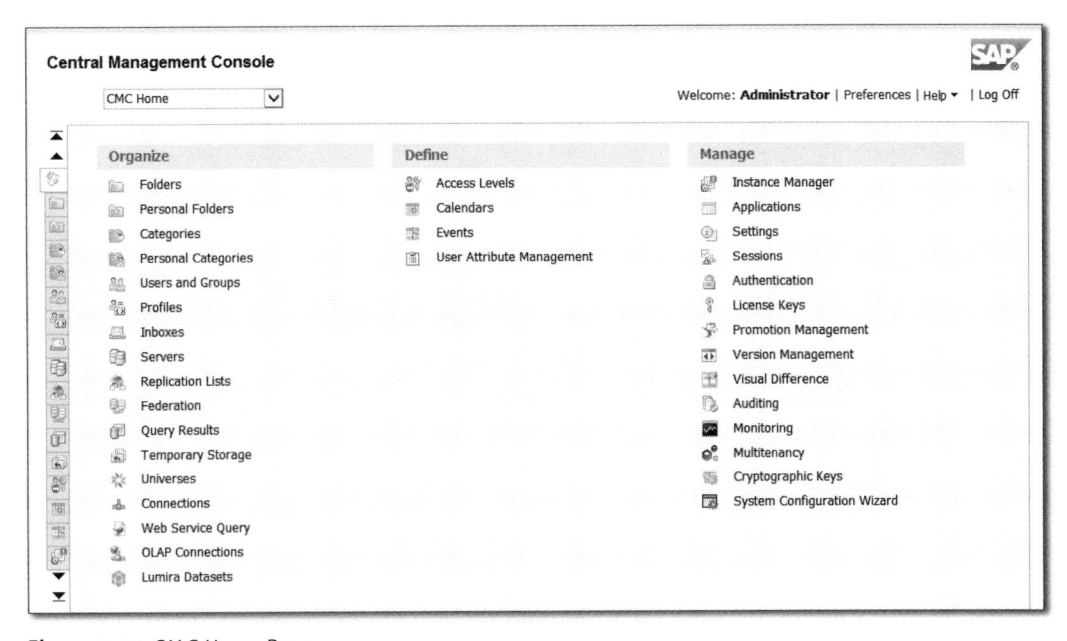

Figure 10.17 CMC Home Page

10.5.2 Managing Datasets in the CMC

In the CMC, in the LUMIRA DATASETS tab, right-click a dataset. The commands available in the contextual menu that opens depend on the dataset type:

▶ If the dataset is not created from a universe stored in the same CMS repository, then it does not contain the commands for scheduling, as shown in Figure 10.18 ❶.

▶ If the dataset is created from a universe stored in the same CMS repository, then it contains the commands for scheduling, as shown in Figure 10.18 ❷.

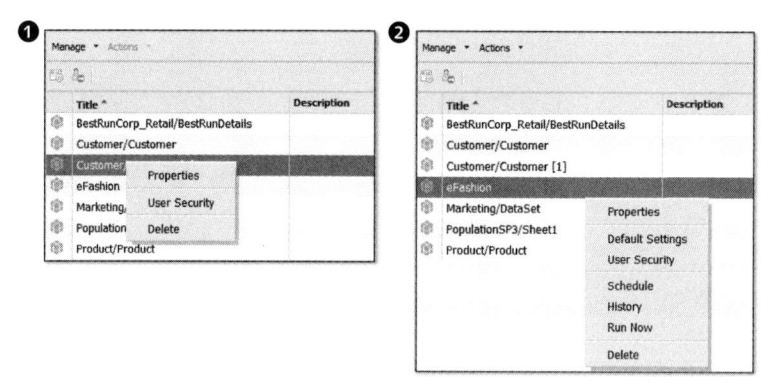

Figure 10.18 Dataset Contextual Menus in CMC

These commands are described in Table 10.2.

Commands	Datasets	Description
PROPERTIES	All	Open the PROPERTIES dialog box containing the dataset InfoObject properties.
DEFAULT SETTINGS	Universe only	Open the DEFAULT SETTINGS dialog box for the dataset InfoObject.
USER SECURITY	All	Open the USER SECURITY dialog box for the dataset; from this dialog box, you can assign security rights to the dataset (see Section 10.5.4).
SCHEDULE	Universe only	Open the SCHEDULE dialog box (see Section 10.6).
HISTORY	Universe only	Open the HISTORY dialog box that displays the scheduling history for this dataset (see Section 10.6).
RUN NOW	Universe only	Refresh the dataset (see Section 10.6).
DELETE	All	Delete the dataset after a confirmation message.

Table 10.2 Commands Available from the Dataset Contextual Menu in the CMC

10.5.3 Managing Stories in the CMC

In the CMC, you may go to the FOLDERS or PERSONAL FOLDERS tab to access the stories that these areas contain. Select a story, and right-click it to open the contextual menu containing the commands you can call for story management, as shown in Figure 10.19.

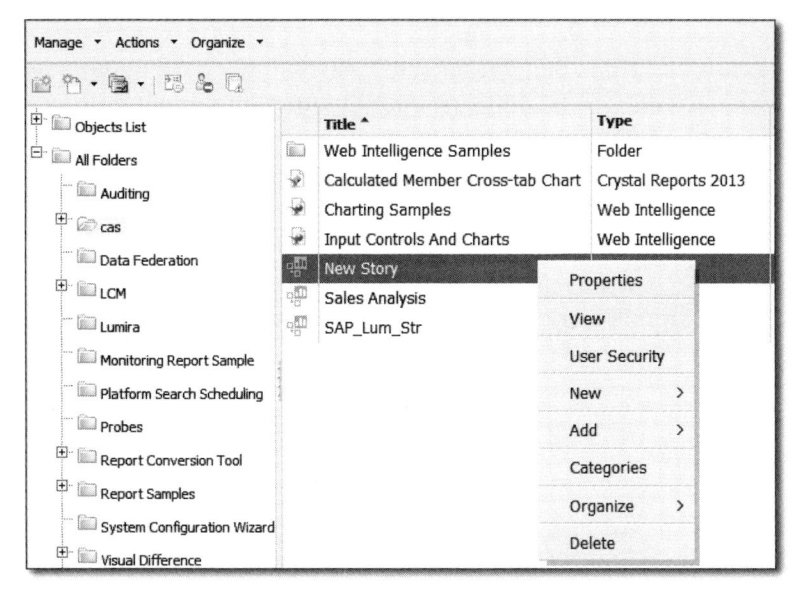

Figure 10.19 Story Contextual Menu In CMC

These commands are described in Table 10.3.

Commands	Description
PROPERTIES	Open the PROPERTIES dialog box containing the story InfoObject properties.
VIEW	To open a window that displays the story.
USER SECURITY	Open the USER SECURITY dialog box for the story; from this dialog box, you can assign security rights to the story (see Section 10.5.4).
NEW	The commands in this submenu are not applicable to a story.
ADD	The commands in this submenu are not applicable to a story.
CATEGORIES	Open the CATEGORIES dialog box, in which you can add the selected story to categories.
ORGANIZE	Open a submenu containing commands to copy or move the story or to create a shortcut to the story.
DELETE	Delete the story after clicking through a confirmation message.

Table 10.3 Commands Available from the Story Contextual Menu in the CMC

10.5.4 Dataset and Story User Security

There are no specific custom rights created for datasets and stories. Security is managed using the general rights enforced by SAP BusinessObjects BI 4.1.

Now that we have looked at the benefits and advantages of the CMC in our add-on, the next section will discuss the semantic layer of SAP BusinessObjects BI 4.1, and how it enables us to refresh and schedule datasets.

10.6 Universe Refresh and Scheduling

If you publish an SAP Lumira story in a CMS repository that queries its data from a universe published in the same CMS repository, then you can benefit from the semantic layer services running on the SAP BusinessObjects BI 4.1 platform to refresh the document by retrieving updated data from the universe and its underlying data sources.

10.6.1 Refreshing or Scheduling a Dataset

In SAP BusinessObjects BI 4.1, you can only refresh a dataset created from a universe (see Chapter 3, Section 3.7). The universe must be published in the same CMS repository as the dataset.

At refresh time, the security defined for the universe and assigned to the user running the query applies:

- Universe overloads for universes created with the universe design tool (.unv)
- Data security profiles and business security profiles for universes created with the information design tool (.unx)

Updated data retrieved by the refresh through the universe are also updated in the dataset saved in the SAP HANA database, which stores the dataset data.

You can use the SAP BusinessObjects BI 4.1 schedule capabilities to schedule this dataset refresh. Scheduling can be performed via all schedule options available in the SAP BusinessObjects BI 4.1 framework: recurrence options (as shown in Figure 10.20) and the scheduling server.

Refreshing a dataset, either scheduled or not, does not support a universe's parameters and contexts.

To schedule a dataset refresh, follow these steps:

1. In the CMC, go to the DATASETS tab.
2. Select the dataset to schedule, and right-click it.
3. If the dataset is created from a universe, then the contextual menu that opens contains commands to manage the dataset scheduling, as shown in Figure 10.18 ❶.
4. Select the RUN NOW command to refresh the dataset immediately.
5. Select the SCHEDULE command to open the SCHEDULE dialog box (see Figure 10.20) and schedule the refresh. In this dialog box, you can schedule the refresh as you would for any other document type. The same scheduling options are available.
6. Click SCHEDULE to save the schedule options and close the SCHEDULE dialog box.

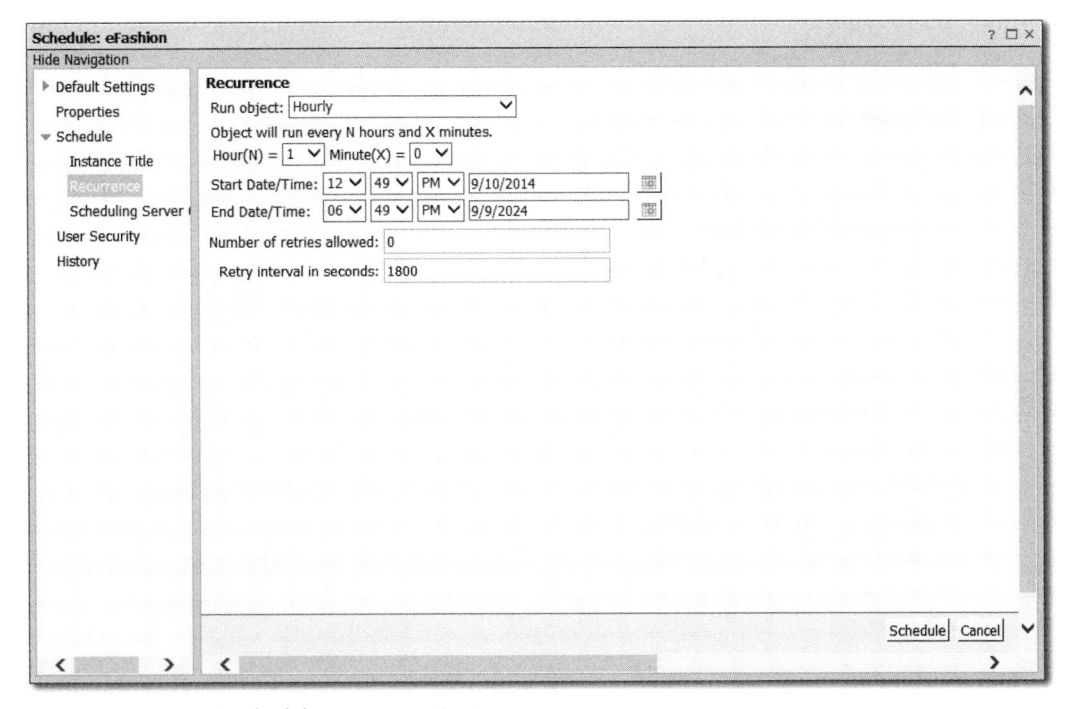

Figure 10.20 Dataset Schedule Recurrence Option

The history of all scheduled instances for this dataset can be displayed in the HISTORY panel, as shown in Figure 10.21. Data is stored in SAP HANA only for the most recently refreshed dataset. Data for other instances of the dataset are not kept.

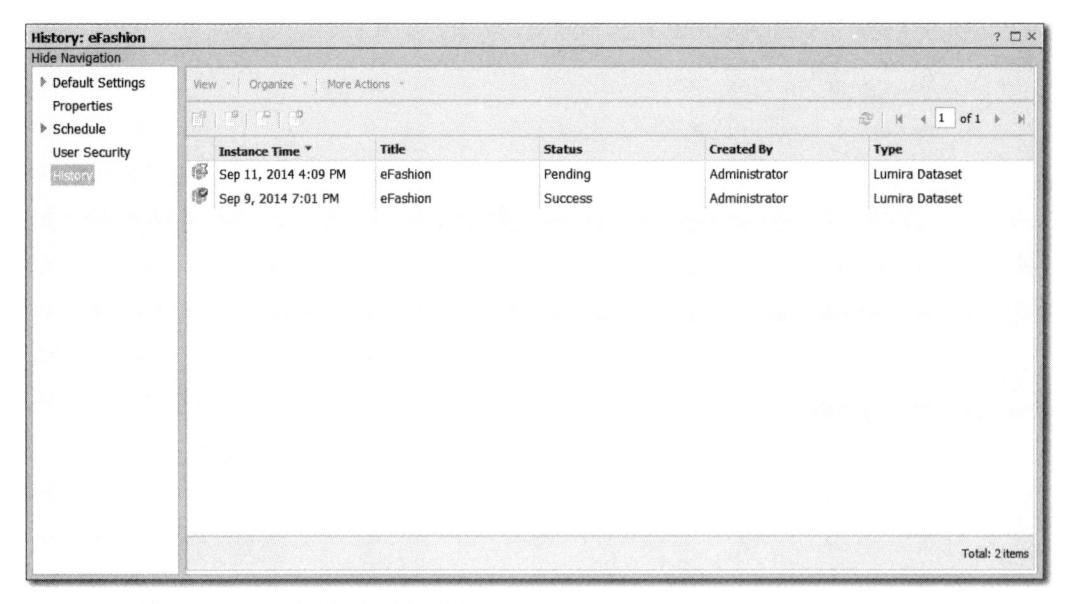

Figure 10.21 Dataset Schedule History

10.7 Summary

The SAP BusinessObjects BI 4.1 add-on for SAP Lumira allows you to benefit from the SAP BusinessObjects BI 4.1 framework to host, manage, and secure SAP Lumira datasets and stories. Its installation requires installing an SAP Lumira Server and configuring secure communication between SAP BusinessObjects BI 4.1 and SAP HANA.

With this add-on, you can publish your stories and offline datasets to the SAP BusinessObjects BI 4.1 CMS repository. You can access and display your story from the SAP BusinessObjects BI Launch Pad. Datasets and stories cannot be refreshed unless they have been created on top of universes. This refresh can be scheduled using the SAP BusinessObjects BI 4.1 scheduler.

In the next chapter, we will discuss software development kits (SDK) available for SAP Lumira.

SAP Lumira exposes extension points, enabling you to customize SAP Lumira by adding your own content. In this chapter, we will discuss how you can extend SAP Lumira to support your own charts and data sources.

11   SAP Lumira Software Development Kits

This chapter will introduce the two software development kits, also known as SDKs, available in SAP Lumira:

- **VizExtensions:** Allows you to add third-party charts
- **Data Source:** Enables access to any type of data for acquisition

In addition, you'll learn the basics of adding your own charts via standard web technologies. These charts will appear in the Visualize room, which will allow you to render your charts using data provided by SAP Lumira.

Using the Data Source SDK, you will be able to access sources of data that are not available through the acquisition phase. For example, you might have a log file or REST API to which you want to enable access. Charting has undergone a mini revolution in recent years, with technologies like d3.js simplifying chart creation and thus creating a demand for more visually appealing, innovative charts. Hand-in-hand with this revolution in charting, we see that the data landscape has changed, with more and more public and semipublic sources (sources that are available publicly but require secure access) and also different types of data structures. The NoSQL database market has become an accepted alternative to classic SQL databases. Hadoop and MongoDB are just two of the more popular examples, but there are many others as well as REST APIs for accessing public data.

Given that these changes are occurring at an accelerated rate, SAP Lumira exposes two extension points you can use to add your own charts or data sources. These extension points allow you to enable access to new types of public or private data sources or take advantage of the latest visualizations.

> **Geek Alert!**
>
> Both of these extension points require coding, and thus involve various levels of skill. Therefore, this chapter may be beyond what you are looking for. However, it is possible to deploy the sample custom charts without any programming knowledge, so we recommend looking at Section 11.1 as you will see how to deploy custom charts even if you do not develop them.
>
> Chart extensions are JavaScript and HTML intensive, so you should have an understanding of HTML5, JavaScript, and ideally SVG and d3.js. Data source extensions are not restricted to any programming language but do require you to be able to provide an executable application, which could be problematic. Neither extension point has any relationship to the other, so learning one will not help you with the other. This also means that you can read either section without being obligated to look at the other.

The difference between the two SDKs is such that it is unlikely you would choose one over the other. However, the choice as to whether you should use either SDK really boils down to your needs.

The next sections discuss these two SDKs and their available extensions. The first SDK we will examine is VizExtensions.

11.1 The VizExtensions Software Development Kit

The VizExtensions SDK is designed to add d3.js-type charts to SAP Lumira. It is possible to change to use another technology than d3 but it would still have to be embeddable within the HTML structure of SAP Lumira. There are also data modeling issues to consider. SAP Lumira is essentially an aggregation engine and typically expects dimensions and measures, so typically charts that aggregate data are easier to integrate than other, less analytical charts—for example, org or Gantt charts. To keep things simple we will use a d3.js example in this section.

11.1.1 VizExtensions Samples

It is possible to add your own charts to SAP Lumira so that you can benefit from its data preparation tools and user interface with your own personalized or corporate visualizations. The caveat is that chart development assumes that you understand or are prepared to learn JavaScript programming and typically under-

The VizExtensions Software Development Kit | 11.1

stand HTML5 and SVG. It is not in the scope of this book to teach you all of these technologies, but we will introduce you to the basics of using the SDK.

SAP Lumira provides some example extensions for you to try, and these can be deployed without and coding experience. The samples include a bullet chart, which can be deployed as follows:

1. These samples are available under your desktop installation. Go to your install directory (by default, for SAP Lumira this will be PROGRAM FILES):

    ▸ *<installation folder>\SAP Lumira\Desktop*

2. You will see the following three folders (see Figure 11.1):

    ▸ The EXTENSIONS folder is where we will place our code for our chart extensions.

    ▸ The SAMPLES folder contains the example charts you can deploy immediately to test the extension feature. We will deploy the samples from here to the EXTENSIONS folder.

    ▸ The third folder, UTILITIES, contains an HTML5 application called VizPacker. This application helps you create and bundle your extension correctly and prepare it for delivery. We will not need this application to deploy the samples.

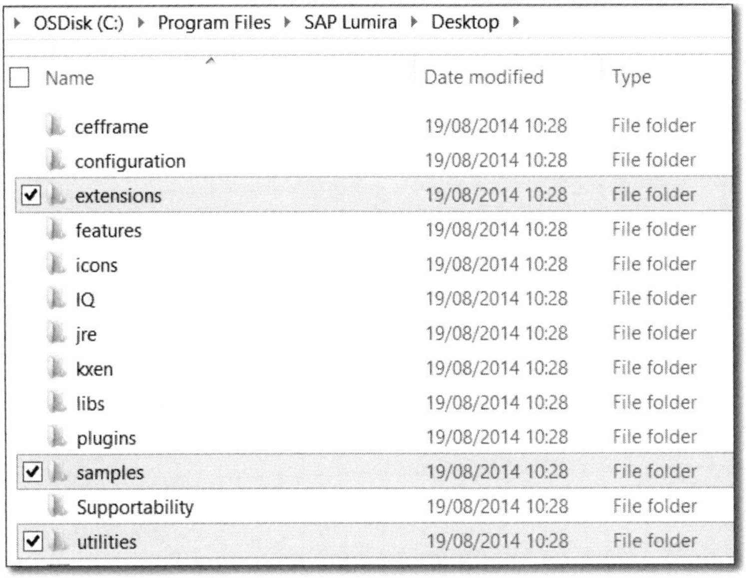

Figure 11.1 Three Folders Required for Creating Extensions

3. The samples provided with SAP Lumira are bundled as ZIP archives with all the resources required to deploy a chart:

    ▸ *<installation folder>\SAP Lumira\Desktop\samples\extensions\charts*

4. Typically, you will see three ZIP files and a readme (see Figure 11.2). In order to deploy a sample, you have to do the following:

    ▸ Unzip the contents of a given sample—for example, sap.viz.ext.bullet.zip—to the EXTENSIONS directory (you may need to run this operation as an administrator, because it will create folders in your PROGRAM FILES directory).

    ▸ The contents should be unzipped "as is" and might need to be merged with any existing files and folders. The files and folder paths should be respected—for example:

    – *<installation folder>\Desktop\extensions***features***sap\viz\ext\bullet*
    – *<installation folder>\Desktop\extensions***bundles***sap\viz\ext\bullet*

5. The features and the bundles folders should already exist, so you should unzip to these folders. The name of the extension is a fully qualified name in order to ensure uniqueness. Thus, sap.viz.ext.bullet should have resources in an equivalent folder structure: *\sap\viz\ext\bullet*.

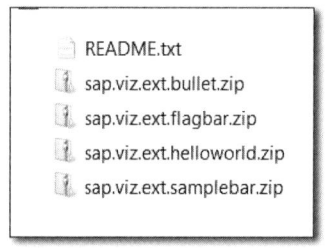

Figure 11.2 Chart Samples Folder

> **Note**
> Your own extensions will need to respect these naming and folder conventions.

6. You should have resources in two locations:

    ▸ The FEATURES folder contains a definition file that describes the visualization.

    ▸ The BUNDLES folder contains the resources of your visualization.

Once you have completed these steps, you can test to see if the chart is working. For the charts to be registered, you need to restart SAP Lumira. After restarting, the bullet chart should appear in the Visualize room under a new menu in the chart gallery (see Figure 11.3).

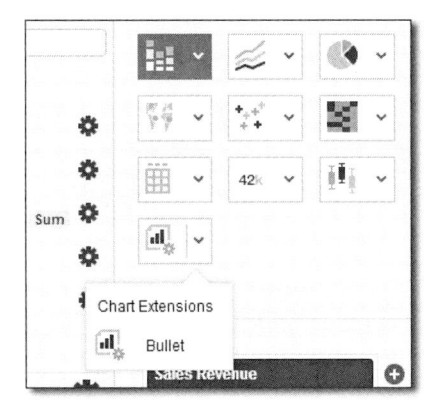

Figure 11.3 Extension Chart Menu

Here we should see our sample, and selecting it is like selecting any other chart: the FEEDING panel will reflect the required objects, and we construct our chart in exactly the same way (see Figure 11.4).

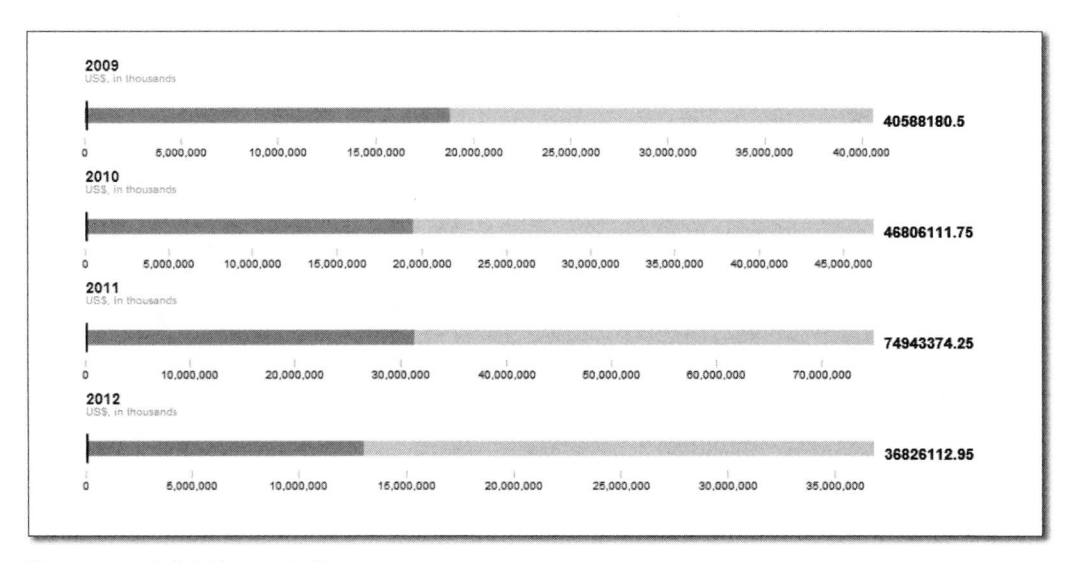

Figure 11.4 Bullet Chart in Action

493

Note that all extensions will be under this menu. You can try any of the samples. At SCN there are also many examples created by others that you can access for free, or at SAP Marketplace you can buy extensions produced by third parties (*http://marketplace.saphana.com*).

Now that we have looked at deploying an existing chart, let's turn our attention to the harder part: creating our own charts.

11.1.2 VizExtensions Custom Charts

The VizExtensions SDK allows you to create your own charts in SAP Lumira. To do so, there are three principles to understand:

- You need to correctly deploy and package your code so that SAP Lumira knows to load the extension. The easiest way to do this is with the VizPacker tool, which we will look at in the next section.
- You need to control how SAP Lumira will expose and interact with your chart. This includes the FEEDING panel and the different customization and display options.
- Finally, you have to provide the code that renders your chart, and this code must be capable of interpreting the data that SAP Lumira will provide.

This last step is the critical part: turning data into a visualization is our goal, and the SAP Lumira tools try to simplify the other steps, allowing you to focus on the last part. First, we will look at the VizPacker tool before moving onto the code.

11.1.3 VizPacker

VizPacker is a tool that helps you easily design, create, and preview charts, packaging fundamental code and files based on the modules and design schemas chosen. To run VizPacker, go to the UTILITIES folder. There you will find the VizPacker directory, which contains an HTML file called VizPacker.html. You have to open this file in the Google Chrome browser (note that Chrome is the *only* supported browser), and you will see the editor shown in Figure 11.5.

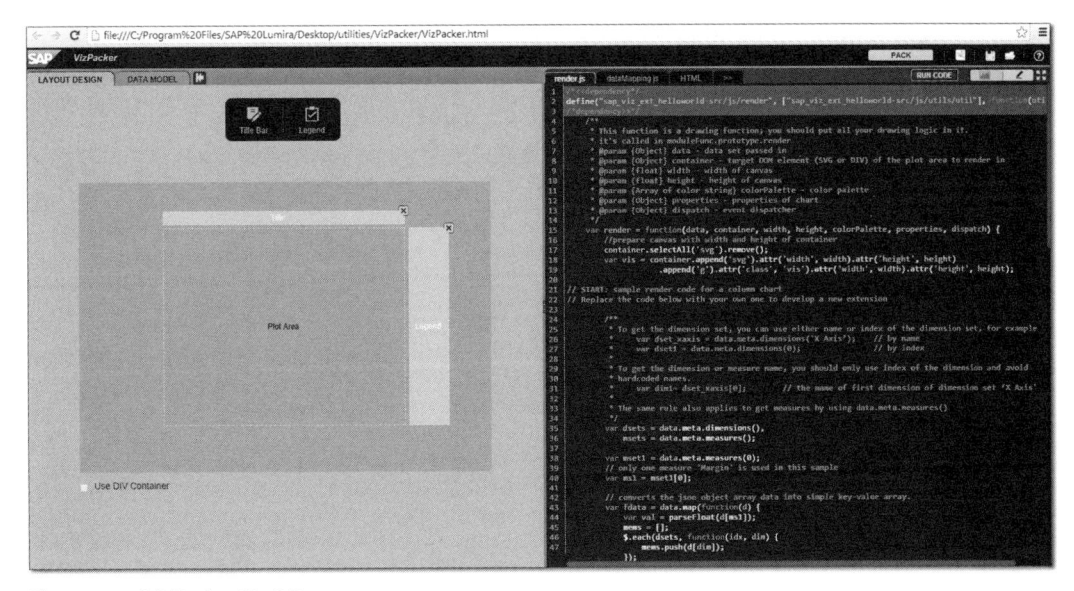

Figure 11.5 VizPacker Start Page

By default, you will see two pages side-by-side: the left-hand side contains two tabs that enable you define the overall visual container and type of data model that you want to use, and the right-hand side contains all of the code that you are using and that you need to create your chart.

To help you get started, the utility has an example bar chart built in. Selecting the small chart button on the top-right-hand side will display this example chart or your own chart (see Figure 11.6).

Figure 11.6 Show Chart Button (Grayed-Out Bar Chart)

Selecting this button will show or hide the chart (see Figure 11.7).

11 | SAP Lumira Software Development Kits

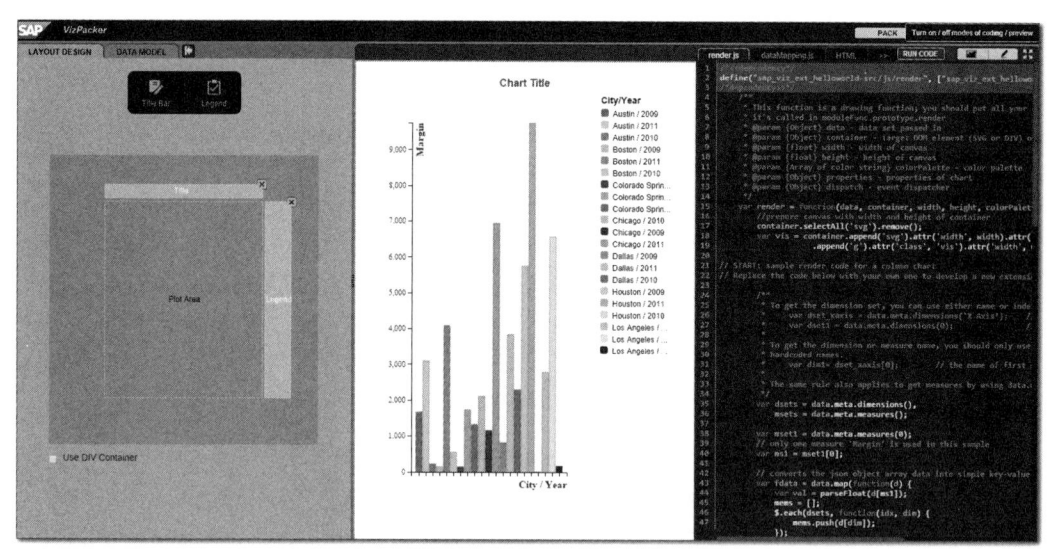

Figure 11.7 VizPacker with all Panels Open

From left to right, you will see the following elements:

- A layout/data model area on the left lets you configure the overall chart settings, such as whether you want a title or what kind of data you expect.
- The center is the chart area, in which you can preview what your chart looks like.
- On the right, the code itself is displayed.

> **Saving VizPacker Files**
>
> You can save the state of your chart editor at any point.
>
> The saved file is called a profile, and it's treated as a download. This means that by default in Chrome your profile will save to your DOWNLOADS folder. Conversely, the open dialog in Chrome will open in your DOCUMENTS folder, so you need to find the profile or move the profile.

Next, we will look at the layout design available with VizPacker.

Layout Design

The LAYOUT DESIGN tab enables you to customize the general appearance of the chart. To change any setting, simply select and click the area of interest, and it will open the appropriate dialog box. Clicking anywhere else on the screen will close and apply the changes. Note that these settings are specific to the SDK framework, and you do not need to understand this functionality initially. However, it's important to look at the LAYOUT DESIGN tab, as seen in Figure 11.8.

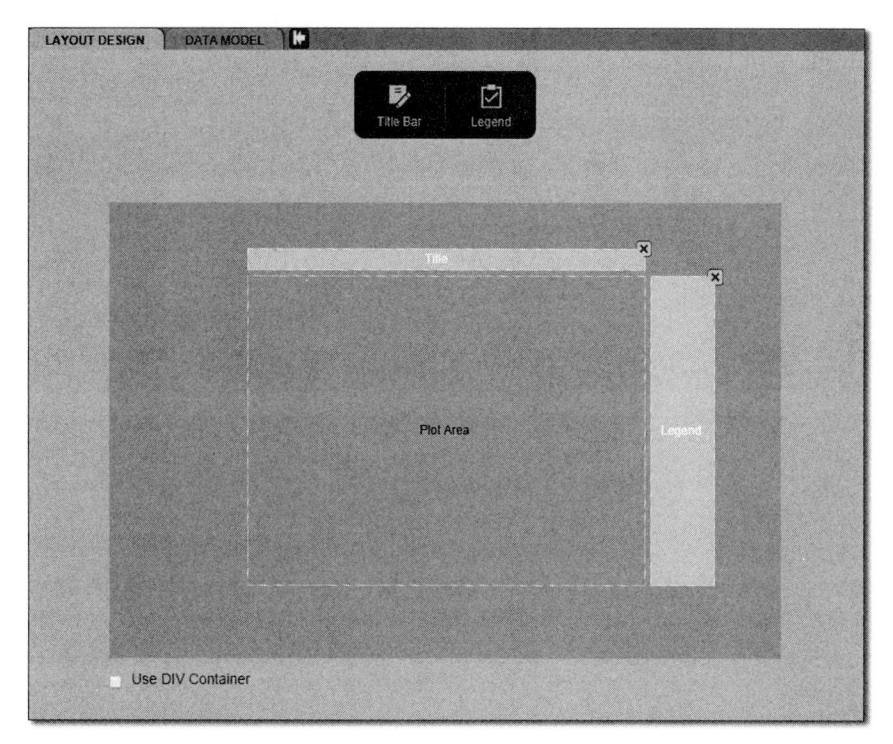

Figure 11.8 The Layout Design Tab

The LAYOUT DESIGN tab allows you to do the following:

- The title and legend allow you to customize or remove these elements. Selecting any of these shows the settings that can be modified, and selecting the DELETE icon removes it from your chart. Note, these areas will be rendered by SAP Lumira and not by your chart. If you prefer to manage these yourself, then you should remove them and render them independently (we will not cover that in this book).
- The plot area defines the module name of the chart. The module name must be unique: typically, you would use something like ext.path.MyModule. This qualified name forms the unique name. Each visual element—plot area, title,

legend, and so on—is seen as a module. These modules are named with a unique identifier and label. The SDK uses these to register what visual elements are required and will be used (see the Data Model section ahead).

▶ The chart setting allows you to name the extension and the deployment structure, which is also the unique identifier of your extension (see Figure 11.9).

Figure 11.9 Chart Export Settings

It's important to understand these settings:

▶ The ID must be unique, and it also represents the folder path or deployment path. Each period (.) will be translated into a folder, and it's not recommended to use the root or a single folder. An example might be mycompany.test.charts.examplechart which will become *mycompany/test/charts/examplechart*.

▶ The name is just the visual name of your chart and can be anything but will typically follow the naming you used previously—for example, Example Chart.

> **Note**
> The ID must be in lowercase *not* uppercase or camel case. You must respect this rule, or your chart will not appear in SAP Lumira.

The checkbox underneath USE DIV CONTAINER specifies whether you want an SVG or an HTML (DIV) element as the container for your chart (see Figure 11.10).

Figure 11.10 Use DIV Container

We will point out where the difference occurs in the code in the next section. If you select DIV, then the HTML element passed into your code will be a DIV. If left unchecked, then it will be an SVG element.

It can be a little confusing at first to understand these elements, and it's easier to use the defaults initially and change them once you have a better understanding of the SDK.

Data Model

The tab next to LAYOUT DESIGN is the DATA MODEL and it is basically a "mock" or static dataset that enables you to test your chart. VizPacker is not connected to SAP Lumira, so it provides an independent data model to test your development. You can use either the provided sample data or upload your own CSV file (see Figure 11.11). The options for formatting the data are limited, because this is intended as a test tool not an acquisition framework.

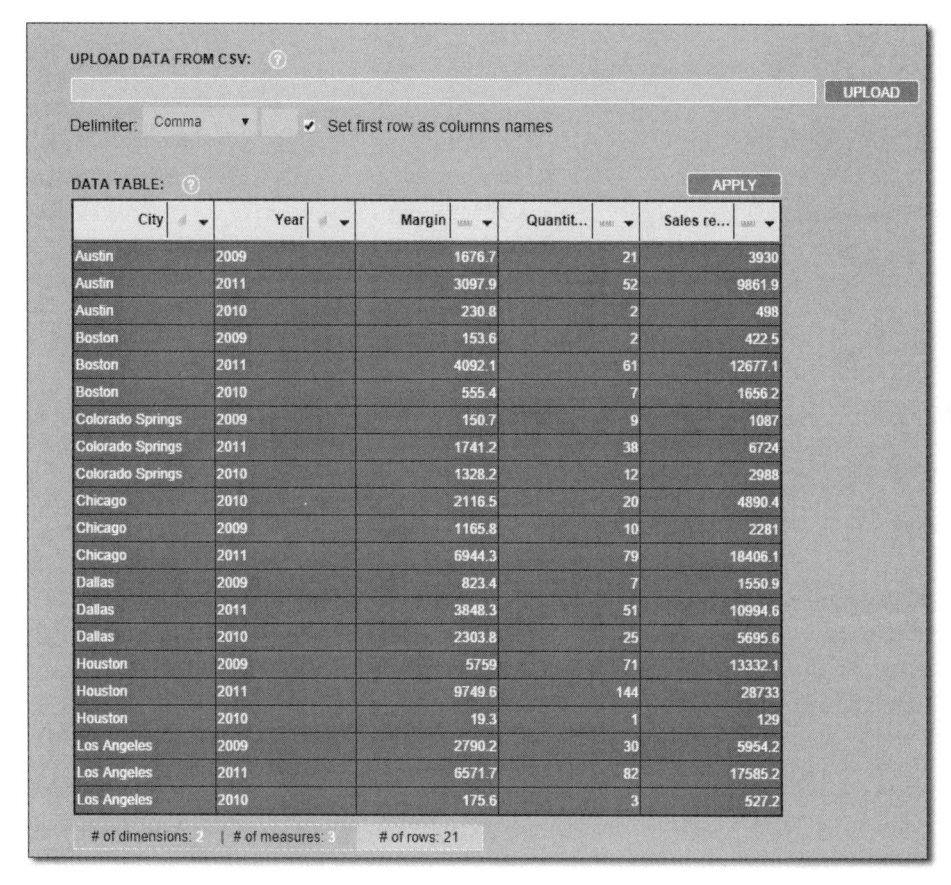

Figure 11.11 Default Sample Data Model in VizPacker

11 | SAP Lumira Software Development Kits

The model is rendered as a table, but the metadata of the columns is important; this is the metadata you will use to parse the data and thus structure your chart. For example, if we delete all but one measure and one dimension, then our chart will be updated (see Figure 11.12).

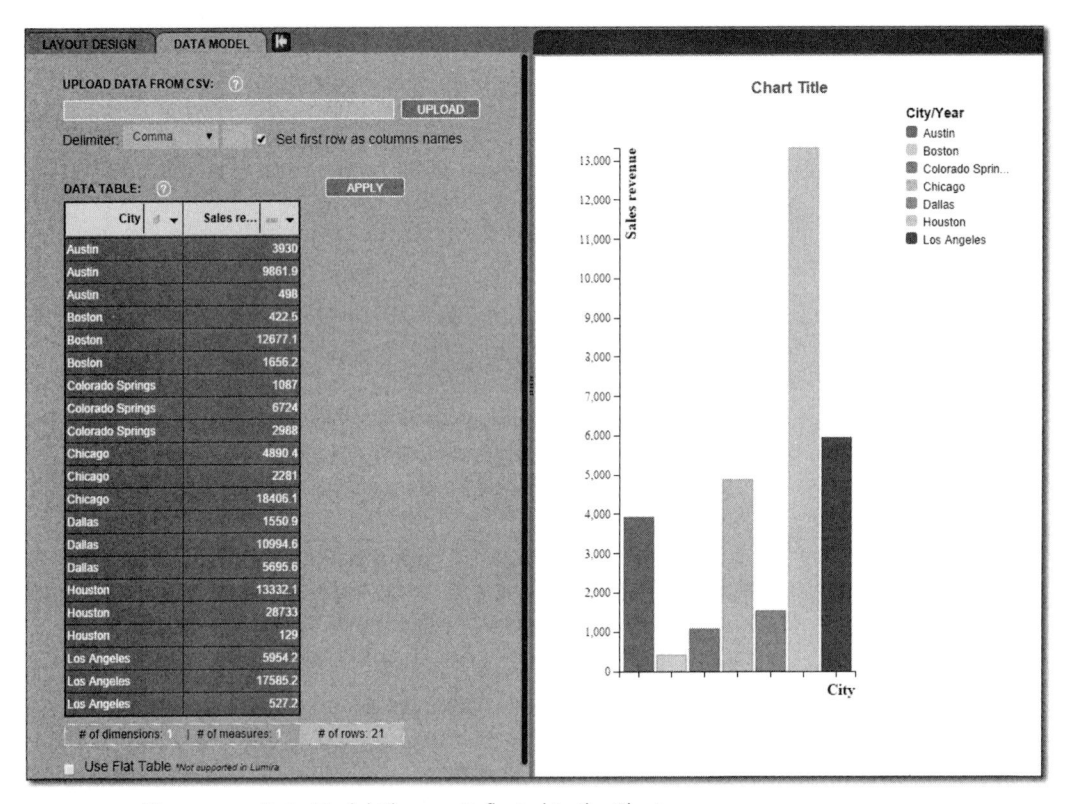

Figure 11.12 Data Model Changes Reflected in the Chart

All the changes that you make in either the data model or the layout design are translated into code changes in flow.js. This file is used to describe your application, and in theory you can modify it manually, but VizPacker simplifies this and reduces the chance of error.

> **Warning**
> Modifying flow.js manually will *not* update the editor state, so your code will be out of sync.

Flow.js

The snippet below the tabs shows the flow.js file. The flow API is used by SAP Lumira to register the different elements used in your chart (see Listing 11.1).

```
var element  = sap.viz.extapi.Flow.createElement({
    id : 'sap.viz.ext.module.ChartModuleName',
    name : 'My Chart Module',
    });
element.implement('sap.viz.elements.common.BaseGraphic', moduleFunc);
```
Listing 11.1 Flow Element Declaration

This is part of the SDK, and you should not really do anything with it except respect the naming conventions. We are simply declaring an element that will implement the `BaseGraphic` class of the SDK. If you look in more detail at flow.js, you will see that we are also adding the feed objects (the dimensions and measures) that will be used to create the UI in SAP Lumira (see Listing 11.2).

```
    var ds1 = {
        "id": "sap.viz.ext.module.ChartModuleName.DS1",
        "name": "X Axis",
        "type": "Dimension",
        "min": 1,
        "max": 2,
        "aaIndex": 1,
        "minStackedDims": 1,
        "maxStackedDims": Infinity
    };
    //ms1: Margin
    var ms1 = {
        "id": "sap.viz.ext.module.ChartModuleName.MS1",
        "name": "Y Axis",
        "type": "Measure",
        "min": 1,
        "max": Infinity,
        "mgIndex": 1
    };
    element.addFeed(ds1);
    element.addFeed(ms1);
    flow.addElement({
        'element':element,
        'propertyCategory' : 'My Chart Module'
    });
```
Listing 11.2 Feeding Declaration

11.1.4 Chart Deployment

Before we actually write our own chart, let's deploy the chart we have created (see Figure 11.13). This is the same as deploying a sample:

- We named our project sap.lumira.press.helloworld.
- We removed the title.
- We expect one dimension and one measure.

Figure 11.13 Deployment Menu

The SAP LUMIRA icon only opens a help dialog. To deploy, select PACK, which will open a new dialog box and also create a ZIP file. You will see the window shown in Figure 11.14 if successful.

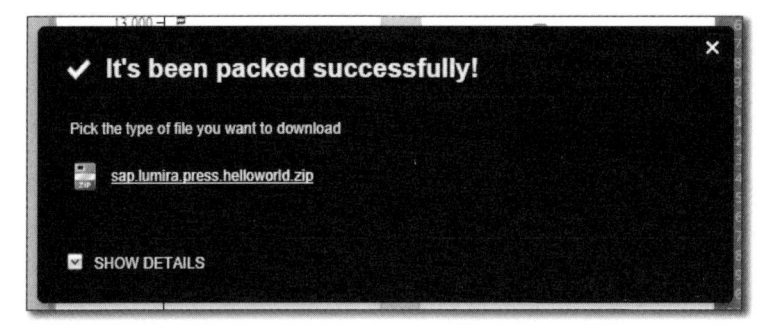

Figure 11.14 Successful Packaging

In order to deploy, you need to follow exactly the same steps as you followed for the sample:

1. Select the link for sap.lumira.press.helloworld.zip, or go to your browser's DOWNLOADS folder and find the file.
2. Extract all the folders to the VizExtensions folder in SAP Lumira, exactly as you did to deploy the sample. In Figure 11.15, we can see the deployed chart.

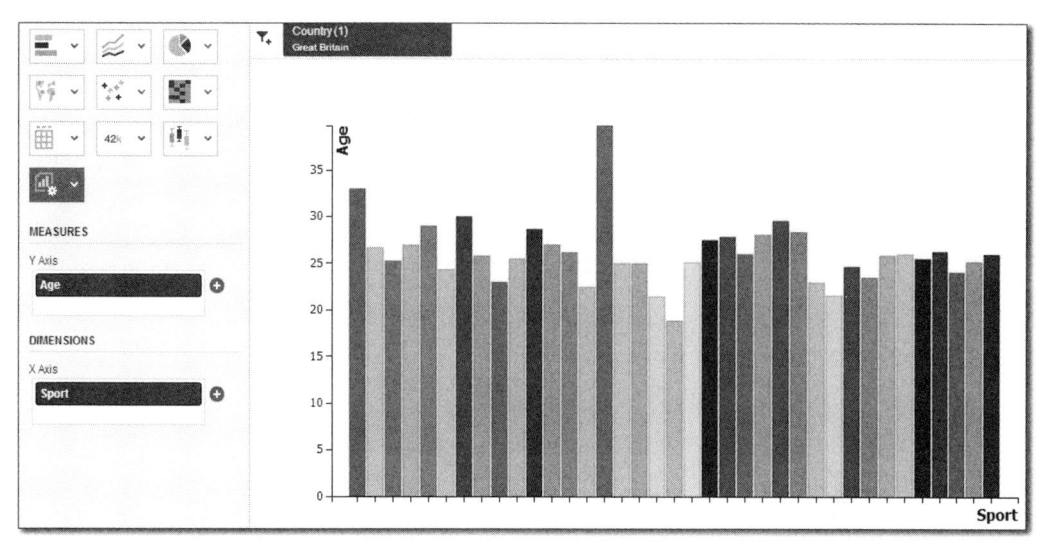

Figure 11.15 Deployed Custom Chart

You may have noticed that an additional folder called EXAMPLES was also created. There is no risk in extracting this folder as well. Alternately, you can ignore this folder.

Writing Code in render.js

Now you can start to write some code. All of the code used will be put into render.js (see Figure 11.16).

Figure 11.16 render.js

This function is called at rendering time, and it is here that you place the code that draws your chart. The sample code for rendering the bar chart should be there by default.

The `render` function should not be renamed. The parameters passed into render are as follows:

- `Data`
  The actual data model, a JSON model that you will need to parse; there are some utilities that can flatten this into a simpler CSV format.

- `container`
  As mentioned previously, the container is the HTML element that wraps your chart. This will be where you append your content, and it will be either a DIV or a SVG element.

- `width` and `height`
  The width and height are the dimensions of your chart area.

- `colorPalette`
  The color range that the chart library uses and which can be seen in use in Listing 11.4. The palette is a color range that is provided by SAP Lumira, which you can use as a base set of colors. You are not obligated to respect these settings.

- `Properties`
  Properties of the chart are passed in and are related to the settings in the layout design. These are not strictly required, and the default property passed in is only the `borderColor`. You can use this to define a border and apply the same color if you wish.

- `Dispatch`
  A callback that can be used for interaction and events. We will not cover this parameter in this chapter, but there is an example of how to use `dispatch` in line 109 in the sample code provided with the VizPacker tool when its first opened.

That was a long preamble, but now we can finally write some code.

Hello World

Let's try to create a standard Hello World example in which we will replace the existing code with a very simple snippet that writes HELLOWORLD. Make sure that you have render.js open in VizPacker (see Figure 11.17).

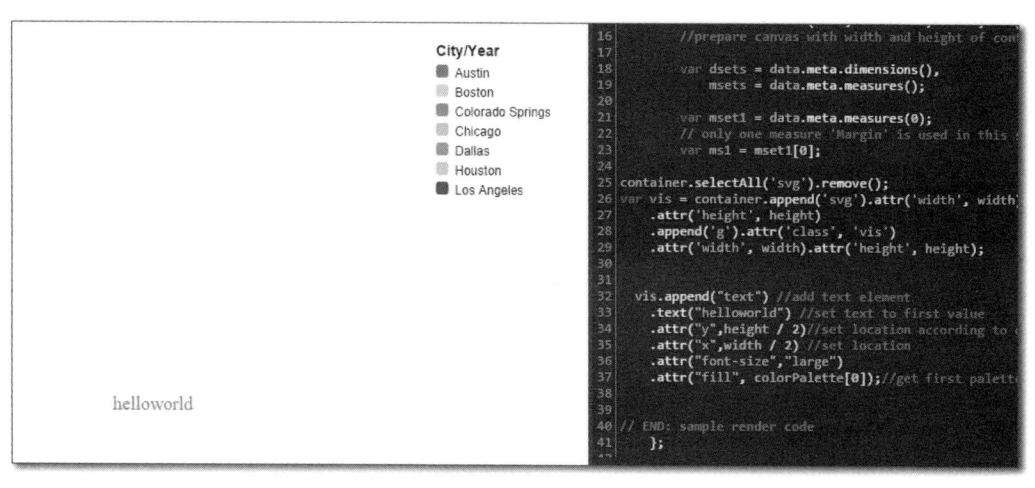

Figure 11.17 Hello World

The code required to render this example can be seen in Listing 11.3 and Listing 11.4.

```
//prepare canvas with width and height of container
container.selectAll('svg').remove();
var vis = container.append('svg').attr('width', width)
      .attr('height', height)
      .append('g').attr('class', 'vis')
      .attr('width', width).attr('height', height);
```
Listing 11.3 Initialize Background SVG Element

These lines create the required SVG element and set it to the width and height passed in the code. Next we create the text element that will say HelloWorld using some of the parameters passed into the render function (// indicates a code comment, and each comment explains the code; see Listing 11.4):

```
vis.append("text") //add text element
   .text("helloworld") //set text to first value
   .attr("y",height / 2)//set location according to defined width/height
   .attr("x",width / 2) //set location
   .attr("font-size","large")
   .attr("fill", colorPalette[0]);//get first palette color
```
Listing 11.4 Append Text SVG

You will have noticed that the legend is still visible; we did not remove it using the LAYOUT DESIGN. The next step in our example is to use the data, so let's quickly change `helloworld` to a value in the dataset (see Figure 11.18).

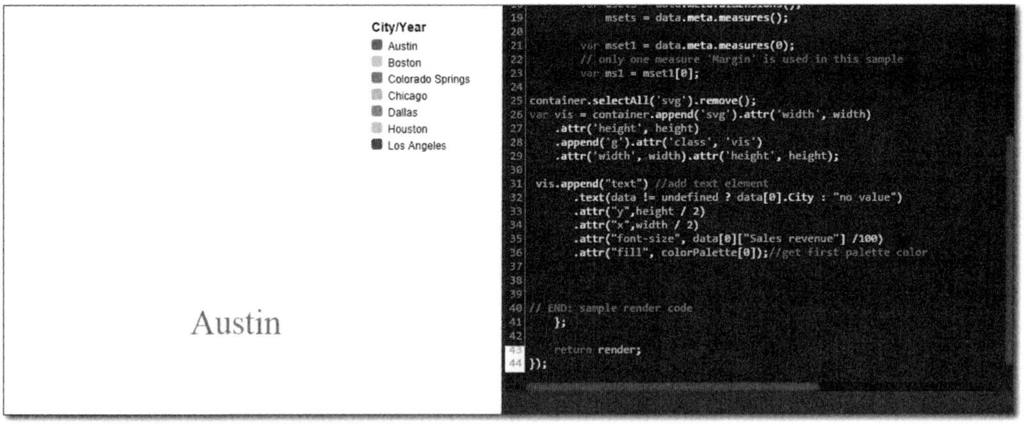

Figure 11.18 Mono Value Chart

Listing 11.5 causes AUSTIN to be displayed with a size relative to quantity sold.

```
vis.append("text") //add text element
    .text(data != undefined ? data[0].City : "no value")
    .attr("y",height / 2)
    .attr("x",width / 2)
    .attr("font-size", data[0]["Quantity sold"] + "px")
    .attr("fill", colorPalette[0]);//get first palette color
```

Listing 11.5 Text Element Using Parameters

Note that we used the data model (`data`) to derive Austin and the quantity sold. We are beginning to use the parameters of the charts, but clearly here we are using our knowledge of the data (`City` and `Quantity sold` are used directly), which will not work for other datasets.

Deployment Example

In the Hello World example, we saw where we can write the code for rendering the chart and how to use the parameters and access the data model.

Let's now look at a more complex example in which we render a series of bubbles or circles using a dimension for the elements and the measure values for the relative size. The following example is based on a d3 sample using a bubble chart (see Figure 11.19).

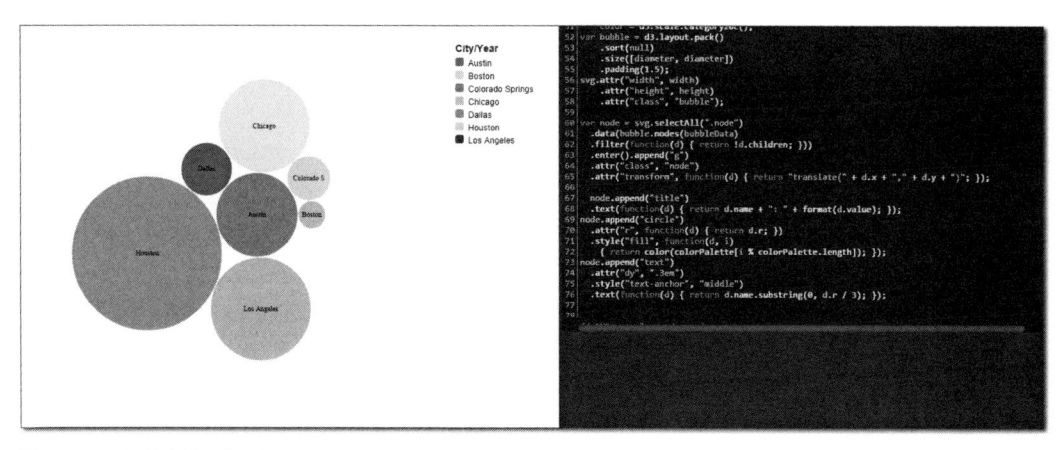

Figure 11.19 Bubble Chart

Although this example is quite simple, it covers most of the basic features of extension charts with d3. Let's look at the code step-by-step (see Listing 11.6).

```
        container.selectAll('svg').remove();
        var svg = container.append('svg')
.attr('width', width)
.attr('height', height)
.append('g')
.attr('class', 'vis')
.attr('width', width)
.attr('height', height);
```
Listing 11.6 SVG Initialization

The first lines in Listing 11.6 are no different than before except that we have changed our top element name to SVG. The next lines uses the data's metadata to retrieve the dimension and measures names (see Listing 11.7). The goal here is to make a chart that works for different sources so we use the metadata to retrieve the objects names.

```
var dsets = data.meta.dimensions();
var msets = data.meta.measures(0);
```
Listing 11.7 Getting the Metadata

In this example, we only want to use the first measure and dimension. If there are more we ignore them. It is possible to use a provided utility that will convert your data to a d3-acceptable CSV format; see dataMapping.js in the CODE tab of Viz-Packer however the bubble example does not use CSV so we will have to convert the data programmatically (see Listing 11.8).

```
var ds1 = dsets[0];
var ms1 = msets[0];
```

Listing 11.8 Getting the First Dimension and Measure

The next lines initialize our bubble data model—that is, they convert the SAP Lumira data model into the chart data model (see Listing 11.9).

```
var bubbleData = {};
bubbleData.children = [];
for(var index = 0; index < data.length; index++){
    bubbleData.children[index] = {};
    bubbleData.children[index].name = data[index][ds1];
    bubbleData.children[index].value = data[index][ms1];
}
```

Listing 11.9 Setting Bubble Chart Data

We create an array inside a parent node, `bubbleData`, which contains the values. Each value takes the first dimension and first measure data and sets it into a child node. This is the data model expected by our d3 chart. The data at the end will look like the example shown in Figure 11.20 (note that the screenshots are from the Chrome debugger).

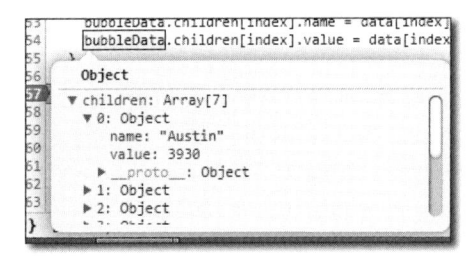

Figure 11.20 Expected Data Model of Bubble Chart

What you will initially receive is the data model passed as in Figure 11.21.

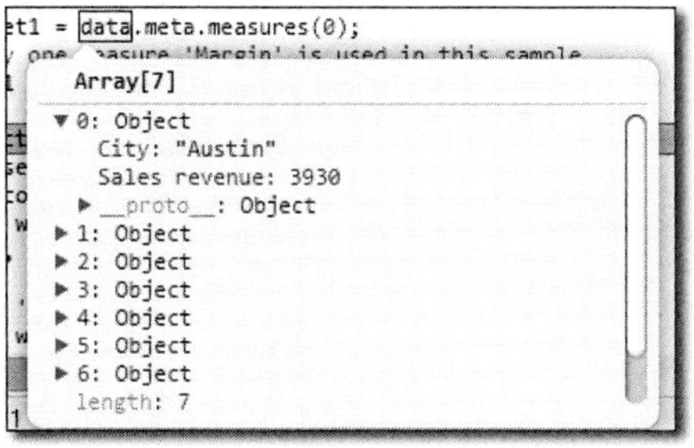

The VizExtensions Software Development Kit | 11.1

Figure 11.21 Source Data Model

We are simply converting the data into our model using the metadata. Note, that because we are using the model in a flat way (ignoring the other dimensions) we will see the values for `Year` and `City` but we only use the `City` label. We would add the year to the label to make this clearer.

Listing 11.10 shows the lines that set the drawing area.

```
var diameter = 450,
    format = d3.format(",d"),
    color = d3.scale.category20c();
var bubble = d3.layout.pack()
    .sort(null)
    .size([diameter, diameter])
    .padding(1.5);
svg.attr("width", width)
    .attr("height", height)
    .attr("class", "bubble");
```
Listing 11.10 Initializing the Chart

Finally, we can render the chart (see Listing 11.11).

```
var node = svg.selectAll(".node")
  .data(bubble.nodes(bubbleData)
  .filter(function(d) { return !d.children; }))
  .enter().append("g")
  .attr("class", "node")
  .attr("transform", function(d) { return "translate(" + d.x + "," +
    d.y + ")"; });
```
Listing 11.11 Rendering the Chart

The result looks like the screenshot in Figure 11.22.

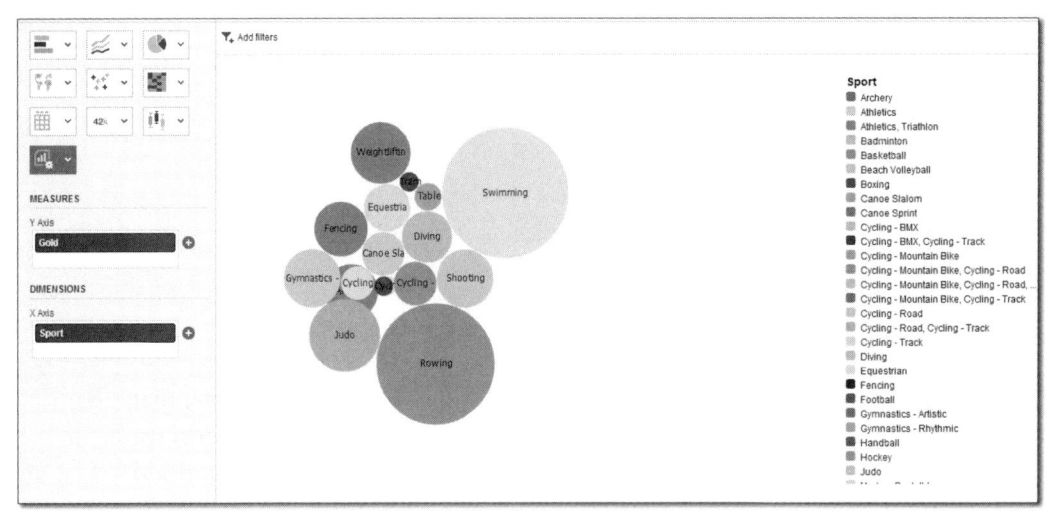

Figure 11.22 The Final Bubble Chart

The code to rendering the chart is shown in Listing 11.12. This is the core part of the code, and in order to understand it we have to refer to the d3 documentation referenced previously. For a given dataset, we are using the d3 Pack layout, and we then iterate through the data and render them in turn. The rest of the code adds text and uses the palette to assign a color.

```
node.append("title")
   .text(function(d) { return d.name + ": " + format(d.value); });
node.append("circle")
   .attr("r", function(d) { return d.r; })
   .style("fill", function(d, i)
       { return color(colorPalette[i % colorPalette.length]); });
node.append("text")
   .attr("dy", ".3em")
   .style("text-anchor", "middle")
   .text(function(d) { return d.name.substring(0, d.r / 3); });
```
Listing 11.12 Bubble Rendering Code

Now that we have created our chart, we can deploy exactly as we have for the previous examples. You use VizPacker to package the code, and then extract to the EXTENSIONS folder in SAP Lumira.

We can see that it is quite easy to add some simple charts with a relatively small amount of code. There are many improvements that could be made to our example, but before we finish our look at charting we need to know how to deal with any problems we might encounter.

11.1.5 Debugging

Programming rarely works well the first time, so you need to know how to debug your extension. A JavaScript debugger is included in SAP Lumira.

To configure this debugger, open the SAPLumira.ini file:

<installation folder>\SAP Lumira\Desktop\SAPLumira.ini

In order to enable the debugger, you need to add the following line to the file:

`Dhilo.cef.frame.debug=true`

Optionally, to disable the cache when debugging you can change the following setting:

`Dhilo.cef.cache.enabled=true`

so that it becomes:

`Dhilo.cef.cache.enabled=false`

Then, click SAVE to save the file, and restart SAP Lumira to apply the changes. These settings allow you to debug and also to optionally remove the cache of the pages.

After making this change, you can access the debugger via a new right-click menu. Simply right-click anywhere on the application window, and select SHOW DEV-TOOLS (see Figure 11.23).

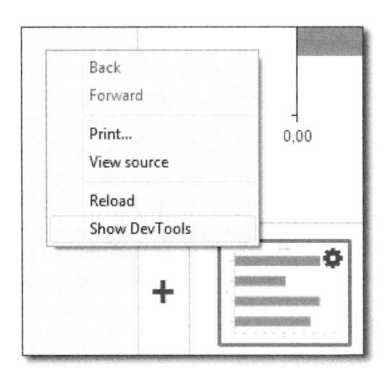

Figure 11.23 Debug Enabled in SAP Lumira

From there, you will have access to what is essentially the Chrome debugger. You will typically need to find your source file—for example, under sources press ⌃ + ⓞ, and search for your chart name. Because the files are packaged under the directory you have created, you should see your render.js (see Figure 11.24).

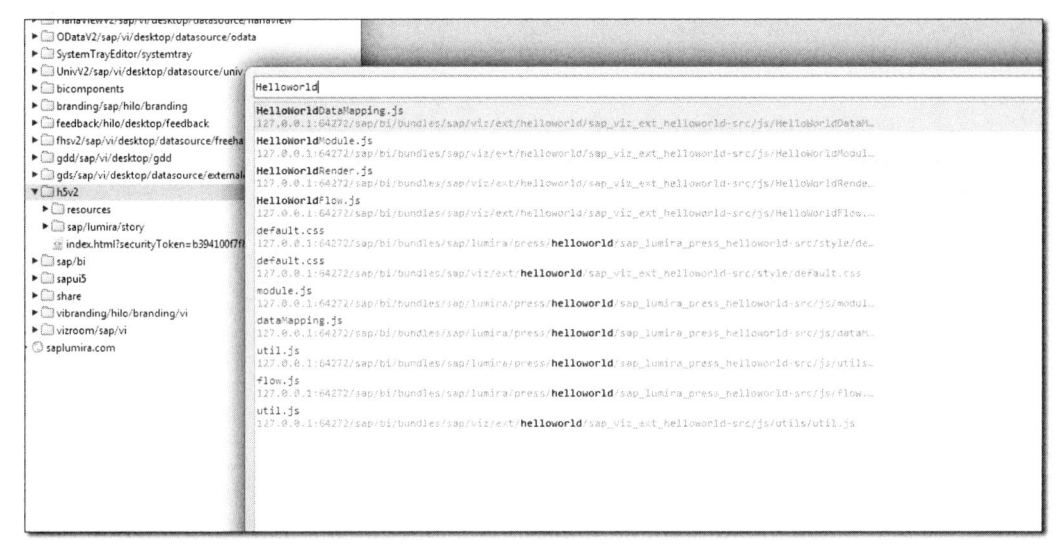

Figure 11.24 Finding Your Code

You can then enter a breakpoint to debug, or check in the console to see what errors have occurred in case of a problem.

If you want to edit your code, then you must edit the deployed version (under the EXTENSIONS folder and not the VizPacker), and you need to refresh the application (right-click again, and select RELOAD).

Debugging Outside of SAP Lumira

Debugging in SAP Lumira or VizPacker can be quite difficult. VizPacker can export an EXAMPLES folder with an HTML example file for running your project independently. For example, here it would be called example-sap.lumira.press.helloworld.html (the name of course will depend on your deployment definition). This file is useful: it enables you to run your charts with the absolute minimum of overhead. One slight issue is that the normal deployment location of the HTML file is *<installation folder>\SAP Lumira\Desktop\extensions\examples*, but the HTML file references some third-party extensions that are delivered to *<installation folder>\SAP Lumira\Desktop\libs*, so you should either move the HTML file up one additional folder (e.g., examples/examples) or modify the lines that import the external libraries:

```
<script type="text/javascript" src="../../../libs/require.js">
```

to the following location, where the relative path is one folder lower:

```
<script type="text/javascript" src="../../libs/require.js">
```

Note, if you deploy your example somewhere else, then you will need to refer to or include the third-party JavaScript libraries referenced here.

11.1.6 Summary

This was a quite short introduction to the VizExtension SDK, but there is no better alternative than trying it for yourself. There are many other examples and tutorials on the web for those that need further information.

11.2 The Data Source Software Development Kit

The Data Source SDK lets you bring data into SAP Lumira from any source that you can transform into a CSV file (in fact, the SDK treats all extensions as a type of CSV provider). Perhaps you have a file or REST source that you would like to use without any external manipulation (meaning that you might be able to convert a JSON to CSV and then import it) or without an external third-party driver (meaning that you could use MongoDB with a SQL driver and use JDBC).

The Data Source SDK allows you to add your own custom connection for data acquisition. The term SDK used here is not really appropriate; it's more of an extension mechanism in which you have to obey certain protocol rules. There are no actual APIs to implement. As the SDK is very open, there are no technological restrictions: you do not need to implement a protocol or standard, such as JDBC or OData, and you don't have to use JavaScript or another specific language.

The extension works by basically talking to an external process that reads and writes to standard output. If you can create an executable file and can format your data into a tabular format, then you can probably use the Data Source SDK.

> **Windows Only EXE**
>
> The strong caveat to this is that you must provide a Windows 64-bit executable file. BAT files, scripts, and executable JAR files are insufficient: it has to be an EXE.

The problem with being technology independent is that there is no API or interface to compile against. If you want to check your code, then you have to test it. There is a test application provided with SAP Lumira, but you cannot truly debug via this application, because it executes your standalone process not your code.

The basic steps to writing an extension are as follows:

- Write some code according to the requirements of the SDK. This boils down to returning values in the correct format.
- Test and validate that your code works with the test application.
- Deploy as an executable in SAP Lumira.

11.2.1 Prerequisites

By default, the extension point is not activated, so you need to edit the SAPLumira.ini file again and add the following lines:

- `Dactivate.externaldatasource.ds=true`
- `Dhilo.externalds.folder=<installation folder>\SAP Lumira\Desktop\daextensions`
- `activate.externaldatasource.ds`
  This tells SAP Lumira that you want to use the feature.
- `hilo.externalds.folder`
  This is the location to which the extensions will be deployed. It needs to be the complete path to the folder not the EXE.

You must also create the folder specified with the same name and path—for example:

<installation folder>\SAP Lumira\Desktop\daextensions

You will add your extensions here. To test the activation of the feature, you have to start or restart SAP Lumira, and then under NEW DATASET dialog box you will see a new entry EXTERNAL DATASOURCE (see Figure 11.25).

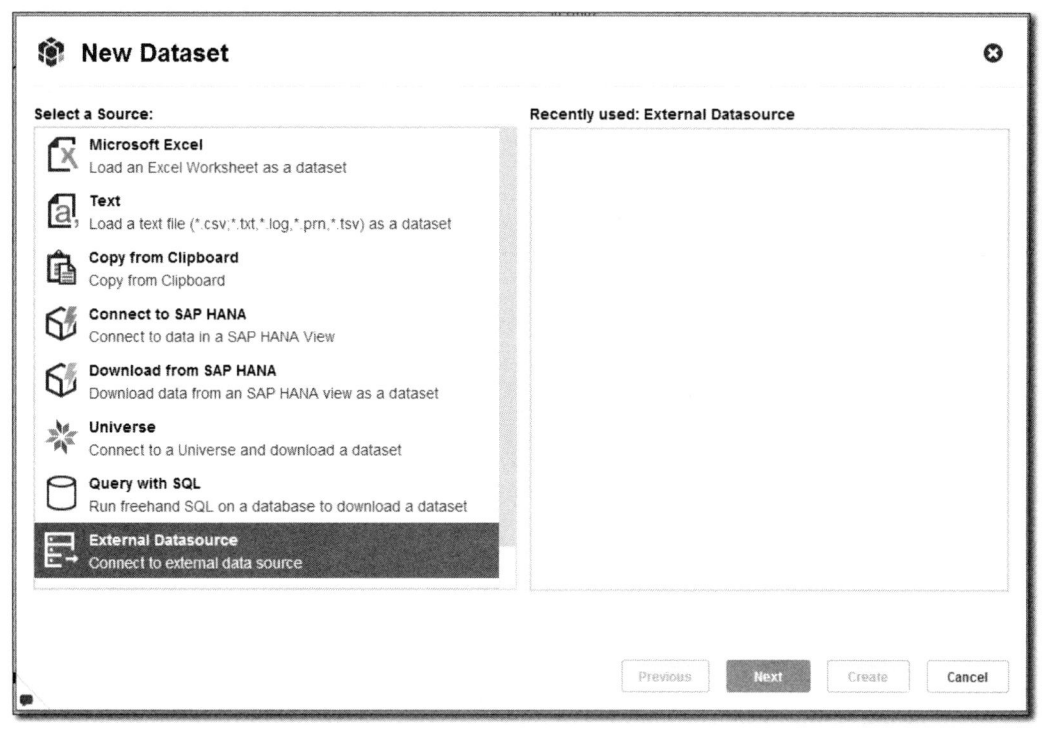

Figure 11.25 New Dataset Dialog Box

If this option appears, then the feature has been correctly enabled. We now need to build and deploy our extension.

> **Example Warning**
>
> As noted, the extension needs to be an executable, and not all programming languages have direct support. The example that we will present here is written in Java and uses an open source engine that can turn a JAR into an executable.
>
> Some people prefer code to comments, so the example provided contains all the code needed to talk to SAP Lumira.
>
> We used Eclipse for development and launch4j to create the executable.

11.2.2 Talking to SAP Lumira

The Data Source SDK extension will communicate with SAP Lumira via a simple protocol: SAP Lumira will launch your application and pass in a command argument that you need to parse in your application. This argument will pass in which step of the acquisition process you are in (preview, refresh, or error) and any arguments you might require as well as standard arguments that you can reuse.

You will then respond, and really there is only one response: write the data to standard output, which SAP Lumira reads as a CSV file and parses to create the dataset.

11.2.3 SAP Lumira Arguments

Because it's an executable application, your application will be launched with a set of arguments that you need to parse and use to determine where you are in the workflow. There are four possible results:

- PREVIEW: This is where you see the data in the acquisition phase.
- EDIT: This comes into play when a user wants to change a connection.
- REFRESH: This comes into play when the user refreshes the data.
- ERROR: If there is a problem, then SAP Lumira will return an error status.

Your application will communicate with SAP Lumira via a standard IO. You should not write to a file or particular stream but just the default output—for example, `System.out.println()` in Java or `print` in many other languages, such as Python.

The arguments that can be passed in are given in Table 11.1.

Argument	Value
-mode	The state of the workflow, which can be: - `preview` - `edit` - `refresh` - `error` These strings are literals, so you should check for `preview`, not `PREVIEW`, or use a case-insensitive test.
-size	The number of rows to return—for example, in preview mode you might limit your return result to avoid performance issues (typically to 300). You are not obligated to respect this parameter.
-locale	The user locale is passed. You might typically have a UI element that can be localized, for example.

Table 11.1 Data Source Arguments

Argument	Value
-params	A string containing all other required arguments. These arguments are concatenated into a single name=value block—for example: myParameter=myValue; Each parameter is on a single line with the name, the value, and a separator.

Table 11.1 Data Source Arguments (Cont.)

11.2.4 Task Manager Extension

We will now create an extension that enables you to view the task manager results in SAP Lumira in order to see who is consuming the most memory.

In this book, we have used Java, which is quite well-known and accessible but does have the drawback of not producing EXE files. To get around this, it is possible to use a third-party framework. Here, we will be using launch4j. We will not go into the details of how to use this framework, but it can be easily found and reused.

The main function is where the program starts its function. We will begin here, and then move onto how to return the data and test it locally.

Main Function

This code is a single class that is executed via its `main` method. The `main` method will be called and will receive the arguments via the standard input arguments (see Listing 11.13).

```
public static void main(String[] args) throws IOException {
        ...//code would be here
}
```
Listing 11.13 Main Code

`Args` represents the command-line arguments that we have seen previously; we need to parse them in order to know where we are and to get any parameters that we might need.

First, check for the mode (see Listing 11.14).

```
if (args[i].equalsIgnoreCase("-mode")
```
Listing 11.14 Mode-Checking Code

The value after this argument will be the actual mode to check and to set the mode type (see Listing 11.15).

```
if(args[i + 1].equalsIgnoreCase("preview")) {
      mode = Mode.PREVIEW;
} else if (args[i + 1].equalsIgnoreCase("edit")) {
      mode = Mode.EDIT;
} else if (args[i + 1].equalsIgnoreCase("refresh")) {
      mode = Mode.REFRESH;
}
```
Listing 11.15 Retrieving Mode Type

Of course, your code should check for errors—for example, it should check that there is a value at i + 1. You can now check for and retrieve the other parameters. In this example, you do not need any parameters, but the logic is roughly as shown in Listing 11.16.

```
} else if (args[i].equalsIgnoreCase("-size")
&& i + 1 < args.length) {
      size = Integer.parseInt(args[i + 1]);
} else if (args[i].equalsIgnoreCase("-params")
            && i + 1 < args.length) {
      params = args[i + 1];
}
```
Listing 11.16 Retrieving Other Parameters

Retrieve the type and set the appropriate value. Here, params represents the arguments that are passed in as a name–value pair block.

Returning Data

The goal is to send the data to SAP Lumira, so once we have the mode we can format it and return it. This example will make no distinction between the different modes (there is no connection to alter and the data size is always small, so we will not make any restrictions; Listing 11.17).

```
sendDSInfoBlock();
writeTaskList(System.out, "beginData", "endData");
System.out.close();
```
Listing 11.17 beginData Header

Let's look at each of these lines in turn:

- `sendDSInfoBlock()`
  You must write your parameters back to SAP Lumira including any additional arguments if required. Note, that the format for sending parameters is not the same as the return format (see discussion ahead).

- `writeTaskList`
  Next, call your method that writes out the data. The arguments are as follows:
  - The output stream (here it must be `System.out`)
  - `"beginData"` is a literal that must come before the data.
  - `"endData"` is another literal that must come after the data.

Be sure to close the stream to ensure that the application can be closed correctly.

Let us first see the `sendDSInfoBlock()` code (see Listing 11.18).

```
void sendDSInfoBlock() {
System.out.println("beginDSInfo");
System.out.println("csv_separator;,;true");
System.out.println("csv_date_format;M/d/yyyy;true");
System.out.println("csv_number_grouping;,;true");
System.out.println("csv_number_decimal;.;true");
System.out.println(
"csv_first_row_has_column_names;true;true");
System.out.println("endDSInfo");
}
```

Listing 11.18 Writing the DSInfo Properties

The parameters here are used by SAP Lumira to parse your data, and you should not try to reuse these labels for another purpose. Again, if you want to add your own arguments, then use the same syntax:

```
System.out.println("my_required_parameter;/value/path;true");
```

You must start the blocks with `beginDSInfo` and `endDSInfo` on separate lines.

> **Important: println, Not Print**
>
> Note, we are using `println` that writes a line with return not `print`. You could add your own carriage return—for example, `print("beingDSInfo\n")`—if you want to build one large string.

Next, return the data. The complete code is provided here for your interest (see Listing 11.19).

```
public void writeTaskList(PrintStream out,
String header,
String footer) throws IOException{
out.println(header);
Process p = Runtime.getRuntime().exec (System.getenv("windir")
+"\\system32\\"+"tasklist.exe /v /FO CSV");
BufferedReader input = new BufferedReader(new InputStreamReader
    (p.getInputStream()));
String line = null;
while ((line = input.readLine()) != null) {
      out.println(line); // <-- Parse data here.
}
out.println(footer);
}
```

Listing 11.19 Writing Your Data

This code will first print the header on one line. The following code retrieves the data. The details are left as an exercise for the reader, but the general thrust is as follows:

1. Start the process with some arguments, and type `tasklist.exe /?` in a DOS command line to see the options that are available. We want the verbose option and CSV format.

2. Capture the output and pass it directly to SAP Lumira: `out.println(line);` (line-by-line).

3. At the end, print the footer.

That is it for the code. We now have to test, build, and deploy it.

Testing Locally

To get an idea of whether it's working, it is quite easy to execute your code. You just have to fake the arguments required (see Listing 11.20).

```
if(args == null || args.length == 0){//for testing
    args = new String[]{ "-mode", "preview" };
}
```

Listing 11.20 Forcing Preview Mode for Debugging

Or pass them in directly to your application's command line:

`java classToRun.class -mode preview`

Each argument is a pair, so you can pass in any argument(s) in the following form:

`argument_name value -other_argument value2`

Testing in SAP Lumira is also possible, but you must first create your executable.

11.2.5 Creating an EXE

Here we used launch4j, which is an open source project that can turn your JAR file into an executable JAR. The steps can be found on the site (*launch4j.sourceforge.net/*), but from Eclipse you need to export your JAR as an executable JAR in order to specify the main class—that is, the executable class—in your manifest (see Figure 11.26).

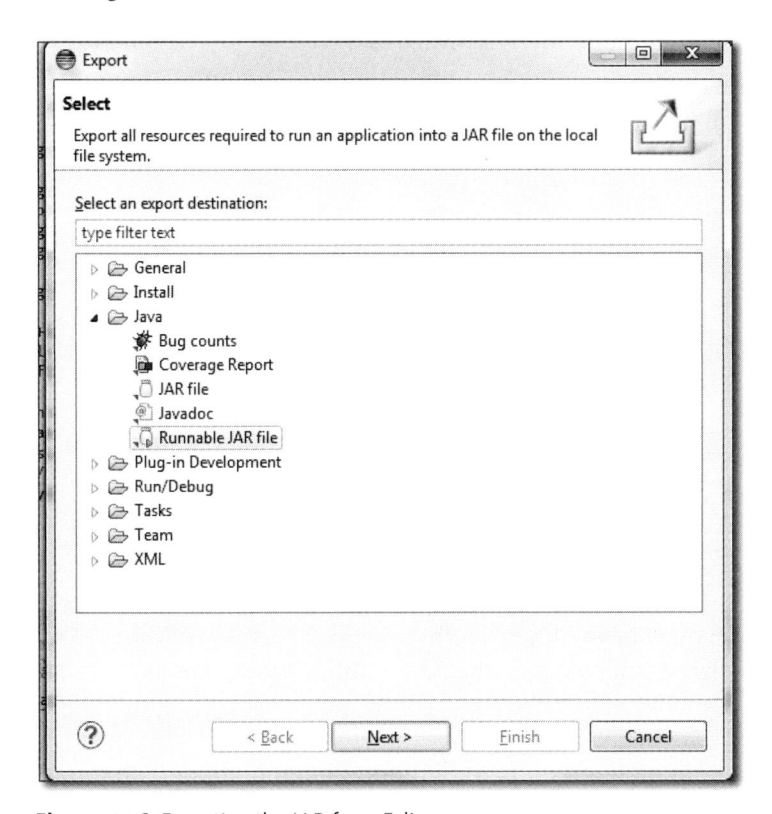

Figure 11.26 Exporting the JAR from Eclipse

Export your project, as a RUNNABLE JAR FILE. The options to set are shown in Figure 11.27, but the key is that we need to specify the main class that we want to be used as the entry point for the jar file.

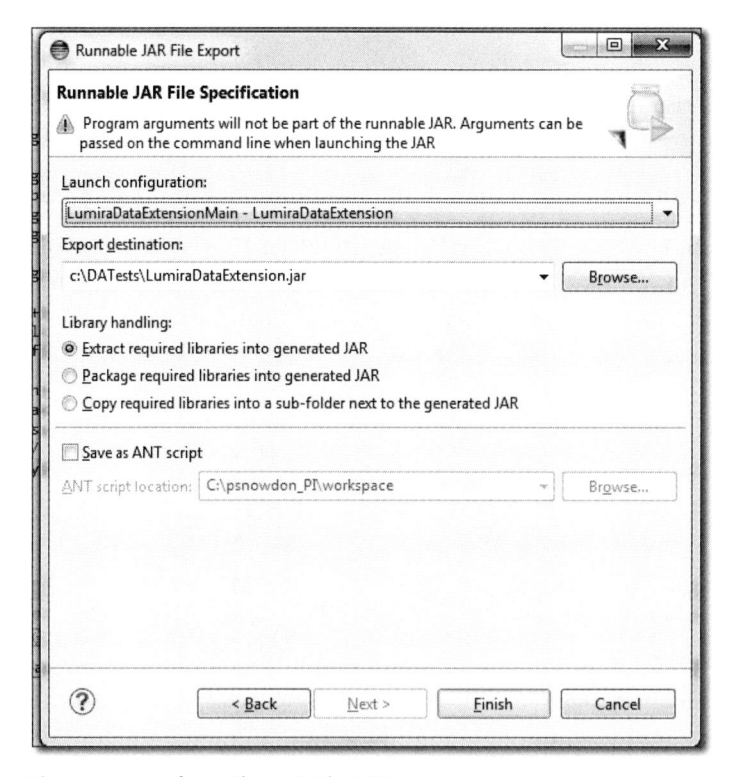

Figure 11.27 Defining the JAR File Settings

In this example, the JAR is sent to *C:\DATests*.

Once you have installed launch4J, assuming that you installed to C:\Launch4j, you can now execute the command `launch4j.exe LumiraDataExtension.xml`.

The XML file is a config file that is required by launch4j. It's the file that tells you how to configure the executable—for example, what is the target JAR file, where should the EXE be placed, and what are the Java runtime requirements.

Testing the EXE

You can test your code by using the test EXE functionality in your SAP Lumira install—for example:

<install-folder>SAPLumira\Desktop\utilities\DAExtensions\DAExtensionsTest.exe

<your path>\LumiraDataExtension.exe

<your path>\DATests\

The arguments are the executable file and the location of a folder for the results.

If all goes well, you should see a screen like that shown in Figure 11.28 (when things do not work, you will only see the log file).

Name	Date modified	Type	Size
DAExtensionTest.log	26/06/2014 10:49	Text Document	1 KB
LumiraDataExtension.exe	26/06/2014 10:49	Application	27 KB
LumiraDataExtension.jar	26/06/2014 10:48	Executable Jar File	4 KB
TestEdit.csv	26/06/2014 10:49	Microsoft Excel C...	12 KB
TestPreview.csv	26/06/2014 10:49	Microsoft Excel C...	12 KB
TestRefresh.csv	26/06/2014 10:49	Microsoft Excel C...	12 KB

Figure 11.28 Output of Test Application

You can open these files to see if everything is OK. Each CSV represents the stage of the application that was tested and a log file that describes the stages and parameters passed. If there are errors, you can also look in the log file.

11.2.6 Deployment

Once you are satisfied that everything is working, you should close SAP Lumira and copy your EXE file to the folder specified in the SAPLumira.ini file (the DATA EXTENSIONS folder). Once the EXE file is in place, you can restart SAP Lumira, and the EXTERNAL DATASOURCE option should now be available.

On selection, this option will now present all the extensions as a list (see Figure 11.29).

Figure 11.29 Data Source Extension List

Currently, we have only added one extension, and on selection, because there is no UI, you will see your CPU data directly in the preview panel (see Figure 11.30).

If you require a UI, then the UI would normally appear now. Now your extension acts like any other source. CREATE will create a new SAP Lumira document, in which we can quickly do some manipulation and create a measure on MEMORY in order to chart the memory consumption of your machine (see Figure 11.31).

The Data Source Software Development Kit | **11.2**

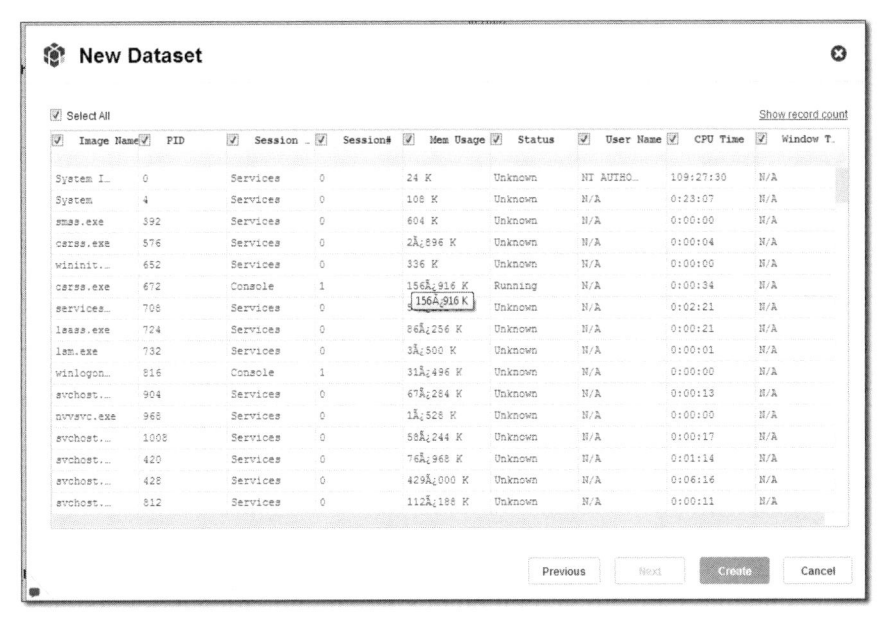

Figure 11.30 Task Manager Results in Preview Mode

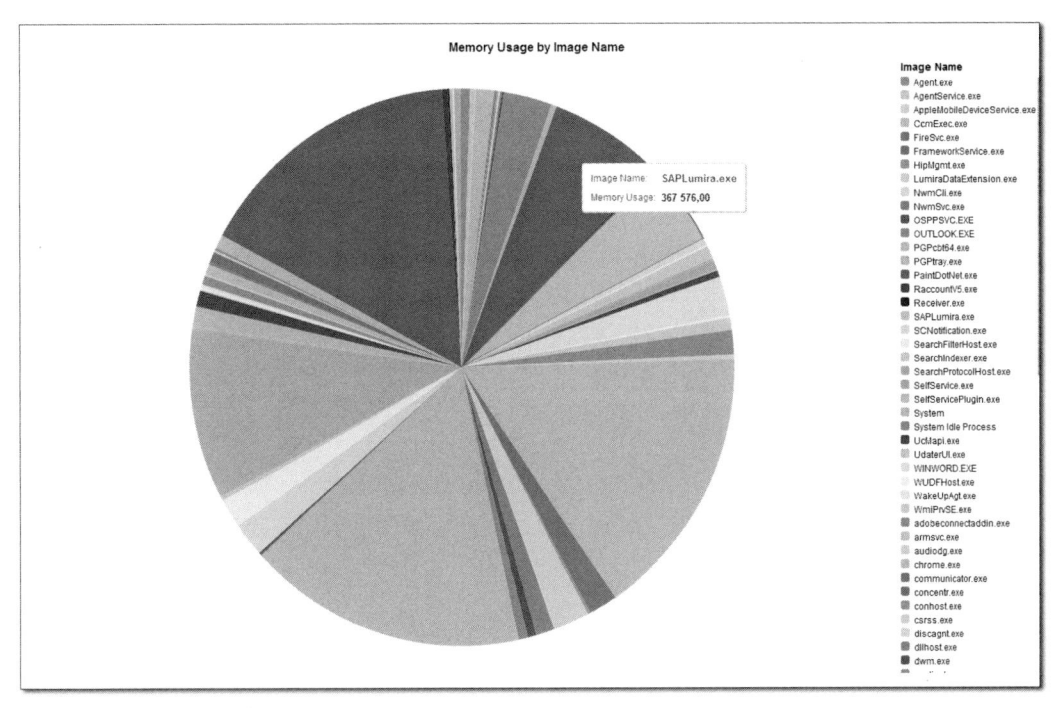

Figure 11.31 Pie Chart of Memory Usage

525

In the chart, we see a summary of the different applications and their memory consumption.

11.3 Summary

SAP Lumira has two interesting SDKs that allow you to extend SAP Lumira to new sources and new visualizations. The VizExtensions SDK allows you to add your own charts to SAP Lumira. These charts might be some of the many d3 examples, as we have seen here with the bubble chart, or your own personalized charts specific to distinct types of data sets. The Data Source SDK allows you to add connections to any type of data that you can format into a simple tabular format. These SDKs help ensure the utility of SAP Lumira, because you can add in additional features to your specific deployments.

To conclude our journey through the SAP Lumira suite, an overview of what has been discussed, along with what we can expect for the future of SAP Lumira, will be provided in the next chapter.

12 Conclusion

As displayed on its Welcome page, SAP Lumira is a breeze to learn!

The objective of this book was to show you the different capabilities offered by SAP Lumira Desktop and the SAP Lumira suite, and how easy it was to utilize this advanced new visualization tool. As shown, SAP Lumira offers powerful capabilities to retrieve data from data sources, and manipulate and process datasets before turning them into beautiful visualizations, such as boards, infographics, and reports.

In addition, SAP Lumira's integration with other SAP platforms such as SAP HANA, SAP BusinessObjects BW, SAP Explorer, SAP BusinessObjects BI 4.1 and SAP StreamWork, provides further convenience.

Given that SAP Lumira releases run on a short cycle, you may expect to see new capabilities in a short and mid-term period to answer new requirements such as:

- **New data sources and platforms**
  New drivers should be added in order to support new data sources, especially for big data.
- **Better integration with SAP BusinessObjects BI 4.1 and SAP BW**
  Connecting to SAP universes or SAP BW to retrieve data should be enhanced in order to take full advantage of data sources capabilities such as prompt and filter support.
- **Improved data processing**
  New formula and functions should be added to transform, analyze, filter, merge, and search data retrieved from data sources.
- **Enhanced and new visualizations**
  Visualizations shoud be optimized for better interactivity, additional support of Esri maps, and big data. New visualizations should be added as well.
- **Simplified deployment for SAP Lumira Server**
  Deploying SAP Lumira Server requires many manual steps. These deployments should be simplified for a better TCO.

- **Closer integration with SAP BusinessObjects BI 4.1**
  Through its add-on for SAP Lumira, SAP BusinessObjects BI 4.1 should propose a smoother integration with SAP Lumira:
  - Its deployment should be simplified by removing its dependencies to SAP Lumira Server or SAP HANA.
  - SAP BusinessObjects BI Launch Pad should propose the same authoring experience than in SAP Lumira Cloud or Desktop.
  - Security framework should be better enforced.
- **Extended Software Development Kits**
  SAP can rely on an active partner's network to create an ecosystem around SAP products. They can embed them in their own applications, extend them by adding new capabilities, or write administration tools to facilitate administration tasks. In order to help these partners, new SAP Lumira SDKs should be also released, in addition to the ones already available.
- **Integration into SAP landscape**
  As SAP portfolio contains other useful products for data artisan, SAP Lumira will continue to integrate with them to take advantage of their capabilities: SAP InfiniteInsight or SAP Data Services for example.

SAP Lumira's current and future features are something anyone working in data visualization wants in their toolkit. With this book you can now confidently go forth and utilize its innovative interface.

The Authors

Christian Ah-Soon has worked for SAP BusinessObjects for 15 years as a program manager on transversal areas like administration, security, internationalization, installation, semantic layers, and SDKs. He is co-author of *SAP BusinessObjects BI Security* (SAP PRESS, 2013) and *Universe Design with SAP BusinessObjects BI: The Comprehensive Guide* (SAP PRESS, 2014). Christian holds a Ph.D. in computer science and graduated from TELECOM Nancy.

Peter Snowdon has worked for SAP BusinessObjects for many years in different roles starting as a developer and moving into product management and currently is an engineering manager. Peter has, in a previous life, tried a number of different topics including Building, Architecture, Accident Analysis, and has an MA in English Literature and Economics as well as an M.Sc. in IT.

Index

.lums, 46, 66
@prompt, 131
30-day trial, 37
32-bit, 39, 41, 83, 98
3-D column charts, 230
64-bit, 39, 41, 83, 98

A

Action panel, 151
Actions, 449
   column actions, 199
   common actions, 191
   Concatenate, 181
   convert to text, 189
   create calculated dimension, 190
   data actions, 191
   date actions, 199
   named group, 180, 196
   numeric actions, 196
   string actions, 192
   value actions, 199
activate.externaldatasource.ds, 514
active, 76
Active Directory, 83
Activity
   create, 376
Add objects to the folder, 371
Add-on, 464
Advanced parameters, 102
Aggregation, 222, 453
   types, 158
   visualization, 159
alert, 76
Amazon Web Services, 36
Analytic privilege, 457
Analytical views, 110
Android, 31
API, 501
Apple App Store, 426
Archive location, 441

Area charts, 232
Arguments, 516
Assertion ticket, 465, 471
Associated values, 156
Attribute
   abbreviations, 471
   views, 110
Authentication, 476
Authorization level, 457
Auto Update Provider, 58
Auto-configuration
   rules, 215
Auto-enrichment, 212
Automatic detection, 84
Automatic updates, 58
Axes, 272
   dual axes, 229
   settings, 317
   two axes, 233

B

Background image, 299
Bar charts, 228, 322
BaseGraphic, 501
Better integration, 527
BEx query, 135
BI
   future trends, 23
BI Launch Pad, 464, 479, 480
   SAP Lumira stories, 481
Big data, 22, 24
BI-LUM-DSK, 72
BI-LUM-OD, 72
BI-LUM-SRV, 72
BO_trace.ini, 75
Boolean, 157
Box plots, 250
Bubble charts, 247, 508
   geo bubble charts, 236
Bundles folder, 492

C

Calculated
  dimension, 27, 175
  measures, 176
  objects, 174
Calculation, 152
  views, 110
Canvas, 290
Cascading list of values, 131
Central Management Console, see CMC
Central Management Server, see CMS
Charts, 27, 70, 318
  anomalies, 246
  building, 220
  customization, 269
  feeder, 70
  filters, 271
  hierarchies and navigation, 272
  measures, 257
  preferences, 273, 275
  sorting, 258
  types, 227
  zoom, 297
Choropleth charts
  custom legend, 237
  geo choropleth charts, 236
Class, 225
Closer integration, 528
Cloud, 23, 31
CMC, 465, 477, 482
  commands, 484, 485
  home page, 483
  manage datasets, 483
  servers list, 477
  stories, 484
CMS, 477
  deployment, 469
  repository, 122, 371, 465, 479
  rights, 371
Coding, 490
Color palette, 70, 274
Color picker, 299
Color settings, 298
colorPalette, 504
Column actions, 199
  apply to all cells, 199
  insert at caret position, 200

Column charts, 227, 322
  line charts, 231
Column types, 153
Commands, 484
Common actions, 191
Complex filters, 128
Compose room, 63, 285, 409, 411, 454, 455
  entities, 290
  menu, 288
  organization, 290
Configuration, 465, 472
Connection lists, 143
Connection Server, 96, 123
Connections, 62, 390
Container, 504
Contexts, 130
Controls, 332
  interactive boards, 333
  reports, 335
Convert Case, 192
Convert to Measure, 408
Convert to Text, 196
count, 160
Cross table, 94
Cryptography library, 466
  installation, 470
CSV, 513
  file, 86, 366, 393, 406
Custom hierarchies, 173
  edit, 174

D

Data, 487
Data acquisition, 79
Data actions, 191
Data artisan, 24
Data Federator Query Server, 123
Data grid display, 151
Data manipulation, 149
Data menu, 64
Data Model tab, 499
Data Source
  communication with Lumira, 515
  deployment, 523
Data sources, 80
  editing, 142
  licenses, 80

Data sources (Cont.)
  new, 527
  prerequisites, 514
Data types, 157
Data visualization, 217
Dataset Selector, 151
Datasets, 24, 192, 212, 288, 368, 371, 403, 447
  adding, 206
  appending, 210
  clipboards, 144
  creating, 81
  display, 483
  InfoObject, 479
  merging, 207
  multiple, 206
  properties, 341
  publishing, 366
  text files, 86
Date, 157
  actions, 199
  formatting, 188
Debugging, 511, 512
Delete, 450
Delimited By, 87, 405
Desktop Synchronization Agent, 351
Dimensions, 113, 156
  calculated dimension, 175
  numeric, 115
DIV
  container, 498
Documents, 66
  saving, 67
Donut charts, 234, 319
Downloading, 39
Drill down, 273
Duplicate, 276

E

Edit menu, 64
Enhanced visualization, 527
Enriched metadata, 66
Enrichment files, 212, 214
  format, 213
Enrichment syntax, 213

Enterprise license, 414
Entities, 290
  customizing, 315
  visualizations, 315
Entity Picker, 290
Errors, 74
  messages, 74
Esri, 239
  choropleth chart, 241
  map type, 242
  preferences, 240
exe
  creating, 521
  testing, 523
Expectations, 22
Export as File, 367
Extension chart, 493
Extensions folder, 491
Extract data, 26

F

Facets, 154
Facets view, 153
Features folder, 492
Feedback, 72
Feeding panel, 219, 220
File
  conversion, 67
  extensions, 65
  format, 65
  menu, 64
  syntax, 214
  system, 366
Fill, 193
Filters, 115, 128, 201, 203, 271
  combining, 203
  crumb, 203
  display in other rooms, 204
  global filters, 202, 271
  predefined filter, 128
Fixed Width, 88
Flow.js, 501
Forecast, 268
Formulas
  examples, 178

533

Formulas (Cont.)
   syntax, 177
   table, 180
Fotolia, 299
Free, 25
Functions, 181
   AddMonthToDate, 178, 181
   AddWeekToDate, 181
Funnel charts, 256

G

Gallery, 219, 275
   chart options, 276
Geo dimensions, 167
Geo map, 23, 24
   service, 71
Geographic charts, 235
Geographic information systems
   GIS, 239
Geographic likeliness, 166
Geographical hierarchies, 153, 165, 235
   By Longitude/Latitude, 171
   by names, 166
   editing names, 170
Global filters, 204, 271
Grid view, 153
Group by Range, 197

H

Hadoop, 106
   advanced parameters, 107
   databases, 80
Heat charts, 243
Heat maps, 245
HelloWorld, 504
Help menu, 65
Hierarchical list of values, 131
Hierarchies, 27, 161, 272
   custom, 173
   geographic hierarchies, 165
   level-based, 161
   time hierarchy, 162
hilo.externalds.folder, 514
HiveQL, 106
Home, 60
HTML5, 31, 384
HTTP, 474

I

IHS, 470
Images, 328
   size, 329
Importing, 402, 452, 453
Improved data processing, 527
Info, 449
Infocharts, 309, 318
Infographics, 30, 286, 288, 301
   entity actions, 305
   infocharts, 318
   layouts, 302
   moving sections, 308
   organizing entities, 303
   page settings, 308
   preview, 311
   refresh data, 309
   resizing and positioning entities, 304
InfoObject, 482
   datasets, 479
   stories, 480
InfoProviders, 135
Information Design Tool, 122
Information space, 373
Information spaces
   launch indexing, 371
In-memory database, 110
Input parameter, 117
Installation, 35, 41, 465
Installation Manager, 48
Integration, 463
Interactive boards, 28, 287
   entity actions, 296
   layouts, 291
   page settings, 298
   resizing, 295
   sections, 294
Interactive control, 28
Interoperability, 32
Interval expression, 120
iOS, 31
iPad, 426

J

JAR, 99, 521
JavaScript
  libraries, 513
JDBC, 96
  driver properties, 102
Join, 208
  inner join, 210
  left outer join, 209
  types, 208

K

keep, 76
Kerberos, 83
Keycode, 37, 52
  file, 39

L

Launch4j, 521
Layout Design tab, 496, 499
Legends, 224, 272
  custom, 237
  custom color, 238
  legend feed, 224
libsapcrypto.so, 467
Licenses, 36, 37, 384
  Enterprise license, 384
  Free license, 384
  personal edition, 37
  price, 36
  standard edition, 37
Line charts, 230, 326
  column charts, 231
Linear regression, 268
List of prompts, 133
List of values, 131
Local filters, 271
Locale, 400
log_dir, 76
log_ext, 76
Lumira Story, 480
LumiraService, 464

M

Mail, 345
Mailing list, 401
Main, 517
Map charts, 243
  heat maps, 245
  tree maps, 244
Max retrieval time, 126
Max rows retrieved, 126
Measures, 113, 154, 157, 221, 257
  calculations, 262
  creating, 160
  sorting, 258
Microsoft Excel, 26, 91, 366, 394, 403, 453
  datasets, 93
Microsoft PowerPoint, 394
Middleware, 26, 98
Mobile, 23
  access, 452
MongoDB, 513
Moving average, 265
Multicolumn list of values, 131
Multiple expressions, 121
My Items, 61, 461

N

Navigation, 272
Network, 71
Network charts, 255
New requirements, 527
Node, 464
Nokia, 27
Number formatting, 188
Numeri points, 250, 324
  formatted, 326
Numeric, 157
  actions, 196
Numerical data, 250

O

Object Picker, 150, 156, 188, 218
Objects, 156
  actions, 188
  calculated objects, 174

Objects (Cont.)
 excluded objects, 280
 measures, 157
 Privilege, 457
 semantic objects, 157
OData, 26, 96, 98, 108
 connection parameters, 109
Offline mode, 26, 80
Offline parameter, 85
OLAP engine, 110
Online help, 72
Online mode, 26, 66, 81
Online parameter, 85
On-premise, 23
Opacity, 301

P

Page settings, 298
Parallel coordinates charts, 257
Parameters, 76
 BO_trace.ini, 76
 connection parameters, 142
Percentage, 267
Personal Edition license, 37
Pictograms, 323, 331
 properties, 331
Pie charts, 233
 3-D pie chart, 235
 geo pie charts, 238
Point charts, 249
 numeri points, 250
Port, 476
Predict room, 63
Predictive, 23
 calculations, 267
 functions, 268
 menu, 267
Preferences, 55, 69
Prepare room, 63, 150, 191
 menu bar, 151
Prerequisites, 42, 457
Preview, 311
Printing, 343
println, 519
Product Availability Matrix, 39
Prompts, 137

Proxy
 configuration, 54
 HTTP, 71
 service, 478
Public
 access, 457
 data, 222
Publish dataset as, 375, 376
Publishing, 368
 SAP Lumira Server, 453

R

Radar charts, 217, 253
Range
 expression, 121
Ranking, 128
 rank values, 260
Rapid acquisition, 26
Recurrence
 options, 351
Refresh, 146, 486
Refresh data, 309
Register, 51
Related visualizations, 278
Relational database, 26, 95, 110
render.js, 503
 parameters, 504
Reports, 28, 288, 311
 flow layout, 312
 tables, 314
Requirements, 22
Resources
 private, 419
 public, 419
 sharing, 414, 458, 461
RESTful web service, 377
Retrieve data, 24
Retrieve duplicate rows, 126
Returning data, 518
Right
 Add objects to the folder, 371, 377
 Create and edit query on this universe, 123
 Data access, 123
 Manage information spaces: Create a new information space, 371

Right (Cont.)
  Manage information spaces: Launch indexing right, 371
  View objects, 123
Right-click, 59
Roles, 442
Rooms, 63
  access, 454
  tab, 63
Running average, 265
  empty values excluded, 265
Running count, 264
  empty values excluded, 265
Running maximum, 264
Running minimum, 263
Running sum, 263

S

Sample, 62
Samples folder, 491
SAP BusinessObjects BI 4.1, 32, 463
  add-on, 464
  filters, 128
  importing resources, 479
  installation, 465
  publishing, 377
  Universes, 121
SAP BusinessObjects BW, 26, 134
  range selection, 140
  retrieving data, 134
  variables, 137
SAP BusinessObjects Mobile, 426, 445, 452, 464
SAP BusinessObjects Web Intelligence, 22
SAP Client, 476
SAP Crystal Reports, 22, 394
SAP Dashboard, 22
SAP Design Studio, 394
SAP Download Manager, 437
SAP Explorer, 22, 33, 374
  publishing, 371, 372
SAP HANA, 31, 97, 98, 110, 149, 436, 465, 470, 471
  advantages, 438
  Application Function Library, 439

SAP HANA (Cont.)
  communication, 477
  data, 487
  database, 479
  dedicated user, 474
  deployment, 440
  offline mode, 111
  online mode, 116
  publishing, 368
  requirements, 439
  SAP Lumira Server, 438
  security, 442
  security repository, 457
  server, 469
  system ID, 470
  users and roles, 443
  variables and parameters, 117
  views, 370
  XS HTTP, 466
SAP HANA Lifecycle Manager, 439, 440
SAP HANA One, 36
SAP HANA Self-Service Analytics Library, 439
SAP HANA Studio, 439, 471
SAP HANA XS Administration Tool, 444, 475
SAP Java Connector, 98
SAP landscape, 528
SAP Lumira
  documents, 402
  download page, 466
  installer, 468
  registration, 51
  resources, 479
  viewer, 481
  website, 40
SAP Lumira Agent, 48, 351, 402, 411
  document, 353
  getting started, 353
  scheduling, 351, 357
SAP Lumira Cloud, 25, 31, 340, 351, 383
  account, 52
  account management, 389
  actions, 396
  Compose room, 411
  free, 25
  importing, 402
  login, 389
  login page, 361

Index

SAP HANA (Cont.)
  logout, 389
  mobile access, 426
  My Items, 393
  publishing, 346
  registration, 384, 386
  SAP BusinessObjects Mobile, 428
  SAP Lumira Desktop, 390
  saving, 360
  settings, 399
  sharing, 414
  stories, 346, 413
  user interface, 392
  Visualize room, 410
SAP Lumira Desktop, 21, 35, 339, 390
  download, 39
  file formats, 26
  predictive calculations, 267
  SAP Lumira Cloud account, 388
  search, 395
  uninstall, 47
  updating, 54, 57
SAP Lumira Server, 31, 363, 435
  actions, 449
  configuration, 474
  datasets, 453
  download, 437
  importing, 452
  installation, 436, 439
  lifecycle, 438
  login page, 364
  mobile access, 452
  My Items, 447
  preferences, 363
  publishing, 363, 452
  resource types, 447
  roles, 443
  SAP HANA dataset, 454
  saving, 456
  security, 442
  settings, 451
  shared access, 461
  sharing, 457, 458
  stories, 363, 451
  user interface, 435, 445
SAP Marketplace, 27
SAP Predictive Analysis, 63

SAP StreamWork, 25, 33
  publish dataset, 375, 376
  publishing, 374
SAP Support, 58, 466
SAP Visual Intelligence, 66
sap.bi.common, 443
SAPCAR, 436
SAPCRYPTOLIB, 467
saplogontickettruststore, 473
Saving, 68, 456
Scatter charts, 246
  scatter matrix, 248
Scatter matrix, 248
Scatter plots, 246
Scheduling, 359, 486
Screenshot, 73
  editor, 74
SDK, 27, 489, 513, 528
  Data Source, 513
  VizExtensions, 489
Search, 449
Section navigation, 28
Secure Socket Layer (SSL), 384
Security, 465
Self-service BI, 22, 24
Semantic layer, 486
Semantic objects, 149
Severity, 76
Shapes, 332
  settings, 332
Share icon, 458
Share room, 63, 339, 340
Sharing, 339, 457, 461
  access, 419
  invite, 416
  options, 418
  Private access, 414
  Public access, 414
Simplified deployment, 527
Single sign-on, 83
Single-value expression, 120
size, 76
Slice, 320
Slideshow, 292
Sorting, 201, 205
Special charts, 250
Split, 192

Spreadsheets, 92
SQL, 26, 95
　datasets, 100
　driver, 71, 513
　install/uninstall drivers, 98
　standard drivers, 96
　supported drivers, 96
Stack charts, 228
Stacking, 306
Standalone desktop application, 21
Stories, 24, 285, 451, 465
　anatomy, 287
　composition, 285
　creating, 288
　display, 483
　icon, 480
　InfoObjects, 480
　management, 484
　saving, 456
　selector, 291
　sharing options, 460
　types, 28
String, 157
　actions, 192
Supply Chain Management, 208
Support, 71

T

Table charts, 248
Tables, 314
Tag clouds, 252
Targeted dimension, 171
Task Manager extension, 517, 525
Teams, 363, 420
　administration, 420, 423
　e-mail, 424
　members type, 420
　team name, 424
　Team tab, 421
　user management, 422
　user types, 420
Templates, 274, 289
Testing
　locally, 520
Text, 327
　files, 26, 86

Thumbnail, 345
Time hierarchy, 153, 162
　dimensions, 163
　table, 165
Time zone, 400
Token, 89
Tool bar, 64
Tracing, 75
Tree charts, 255
Tree maps, 244
　two measures, 244
Trellis, 225, 233
　on class, 226
Trim values, 406
Trimming, 90, 194

U

Uninstall, 47
Universe Design Tool, 122
Universe only, 484
Universes, 26, 121, 486
　dataset refresh, 487
　dataset scheduling, 487
　multidimensional universe, 122
　query panel, 126
　refresh, 147
　retrieving data, 123
　support, 122
Unzip, 492
Updates, 54
　new, 57
　notification, 59
Uploading, 402
URL, 363, 377
User interface, 59, 392, 445
Users, 442
Utilities folder, 491

V

Value actions, 199
　apply to all cells, 199
　insert at caret position, 200
Variables, 118
Vertical table, 94

View, 110
 menu, 64
Views, 70
Visualizations, 24, 315, 344
 create, 27
 create custom, 27
 gallery, 275
 map to dataset metadata, 27
 properties, 317
 use in story, 28
Visualize room, 63, 217, 278, 409, 410, 454, 455
VizExtensions, 489, 490
 chart deployment, 502
 custom charts, 494
 debugging, 511
 deployment, 506
 folder, 502
 HelloWorld, 504
 Visualize room, 493

VizPacker, 491, 494, 512
 data model, 499
 flow.js, 501
 layout design, 496
 page, 495
 sharing files, 496

W

WACS, 476
Waterfall charts, 254
Web Application Container Server, 377
Welcome page, 60, 388, 390
Windows, 468, 514
 clipboard, 89
 Control Panel, 48
Workflow, 25

- Your one-stop reference for all things WebI

- From report creation to publication, and everything in between

- Updated for release 4.1, SAP HANA, and more

Jim Brogden, Heather Sinkwitz, Dallas Marks, Gabriel Orthous

SAP BusinessObjects Web Intelligence
The Comprehensive Guide

Report creation. Data display via charts. Report sharing. Get both the basic concepts and the actionable details to advance your work with SAP BusinessObjects Web Intelligence! Updated for WebI 4.1, this third edition includes UI and functionality changes and coverage of new topics like SAP HANA and mobility. Work smarter in WebI!

691 pp., 3. edition 2014, 79,95 Euro / US$ 79.95
ISBN 978-1-4932-1057-2

www.sap-press.com

- Introduce yourself: installation and configuration, the IDE, usage scenarios

- Acquaint yourself: the design process, components and properties, scripting

- Advance yourself: design principles, visualization methods, full application examples

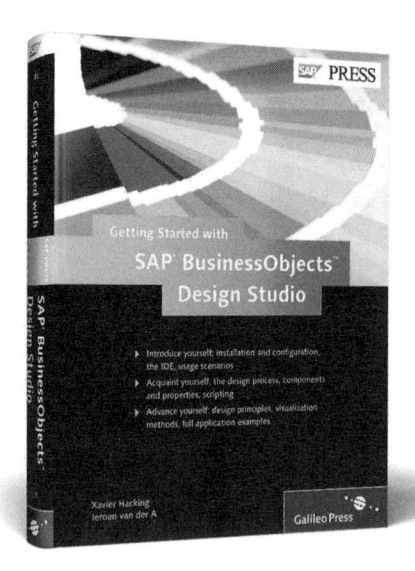

Xavier Hacking, Jeroen van der A

Getting Started with SAP BusinessObjects Design Studio

There's a new dashboard design kid on the block, and it's time you introduced yourself. How is Design Studio different from BEx WAD and Dashboards, and what can it do? This book will answer these questions, and will teach you how to use the tool to start building effective, interactive dashboards. What are you waiting for?

468 pp., 2014, 69,95 Euro / US$ 69.95
ISBN 978-1-59229-895-2

www.sap-press.com

More information: www.sap-press.com

- Everything you need to know about the new Information Design Tool and UNX universes

- Explore step-by-step universe design, from connecting to different data sources, to creating data foundations, to building business layers

Christian Ah-Soon, Didier Mazoué, Pierpaolo Vezzosi

Universe Design with SAP BusinessObjects BI
The Comprehensive Guide

Are you the master of your UNX universes? This comprehensive resource spans universe creation to universe publication. You'll learn to build single- and multisource data foundations and business layers and to convert UNV to UNX using the new Information Design Tool. Up to date for SAP BusinessObjects 4.1, this book offers the step-by-step instructions and screenshots you need design universes for the world.

729 pp., 2014, 79,95 Euro / US$ 79.95
ISBN 978-1-59229-901-0

www.sap-press.com

Galileo Press

- Get your system up: sizing, installation, configuration

- Get your system running: security, monitoring, mobility

- Get your system current: Upgrade Management Tool, Promotion Management, new features

Greg Myers, Eric Vallo

SAP BusinessObjects BI System Administration

Users keeping you on your toes? Stay one step ahead with this guide to BOBJ administration. From sizing to troubleshooting, get the background you need to administer a system that does what it's supposed to do. Revised for release 4.1, this book will help you keep your system up to snuff.

approx. 503 pp., 2. edition, 69,95 Euro / US$ 69.95
ISBN 978-1-4932-1000-8, Nov 2014

www.sap-press.com

Interested in reading more?

Please visit our website for all new
book and e-book releases from SAP PRESS.

www.sap-press.com

SAP PRESS